# TRIBES IN ANCIENT INDIA

Bhandarkar Oriental Series No. 4

# TRIBES IN ANCIENT INDIA

BY

BIMALA CHURN LAW,
M.A., B.L., Ph.D , D.Litt

ISBN: 978-93-5128-899-2(HB)

First Published in 1943
Indian Reprint in 2017

*Published by*

Kalpaz Publications
C-30, Satyawati Nagar,
Delhi – 110052
E-mail: kalpaz@hotmail.com
Website: kalpazpublications.com
Ph.: +91-9212142040

# PREFACE

The present book is the outcome of my continued study of the history of tribes of Ancient India. In past years I wrote some books on tribes which have been well received by scholars and the present treatise is an improvement of them and I have added many new tribes to it. The object of the volume is to present a comprehensive and systematic account of some tribes inhabiting different parts of India, viz. north, south, east, west and central, who played an important part in the early history of India.

In preparing the volume, I have utilised original works in Sanskrit, Pali, Prakrit, Tibetan and Chinese and I have also derived help from other sources, such as epigraphy, archaeology, numismatics, and the itineraries of the Chinese pilgrims. In a work of this kind, legends cannot altogether be ignored as they very often contain a substratum of truth. In my treatment I have spared no pains to make full use of the materials that may be gathered from our ancient literature. Modern literature on the subject, too, has been duly utilised. I have tried as far as possible to separate legends from authentic history. But the task is fraught with difficulties and it is not always easy to draw the dividing line. It must, however, be admitted that the history of India is not complete without a thorough knowledge of the history of tribes. Hence an attempt has been made here to present an exhaustive and careful study of the ancient Indian tribes without *parti pris* and in a spirit of scientific research. I believe that this work will remove a long-felt want and will prove to be of some use to scholars interested in the history of ancient India.

I am grateful to the Bhandarkar Oriental Research Institute, Poona, for having kindly included it in their series.

43 Kailas Bose Street,
*Calcutta*, *September*, 1943.

BIMALA CHURN LAW

# CONTENTS

# BIBLIOGRAPHY


Abhidhānacintāmaṇi (Hemacandra)
Abhidhānaratnamālā
Abhidharmakoṣa (Vasubandhu)
Adhyātma Rāmāyaṇa (Kālī Śaṅkar Vidyāratna ed.)
Ain-i-Akbari
Aitareya Āraṇyaka (Anecdota Oxoniensia)
Aitareya Brāhmaṇa
Alexander's Invasion (McCrindle)
Altindisches Leben (Zimmer)
Amarakoṣa
Ancient and Hindu India (V. A. Smith)
Ancient Geography of India by Cunningham (Ed. S. N. Majumdar)
Ancient India (E. J. Rapson)
Ancient India (S. K. Aiyangar)
Ancient India as described by Ptolemy (Ed. S. N. Majumdar)
Ancient India: its invasion by Alexander the Great (McCrindle)
Ancient Indian Historical Tradition (F. E. Pargiter)
Aṅguttara Nikāya (P.T.S.)
Annals of the Bhandarkar Oriental Research Institute
Antiquities of Kathiawar and Kacch (Burgess)
Apadāna (P.T.S.)
Archaeological Survey of India (Annual Reports)
Archaeological Survey of South India (Reports)
Arthaśāstra, Bārhaspatya (F. W. Thomas)
Arthaśāstra, Kauṭilya (R. Shama Śāstrī Ed. and Tr.)
Asiatic Researches
Aśoka (V. A. Smith)
Aśoka (Woolner)
Aśokāvadāna
Aṣṭādhyāyī, Pāṇini
Atharva-Saṃhitā (Whitney & Lanman—Harvard Oriental Series)
Atharvaveda
Atharvaveda-Saṃhitā (Roth & Whitney—Harvard Oriental Series)
Atthasālinī (P.T.S.)
Avadāna Śataka
Avadānakalpalatā (Bibliotheca Indica Series)
Āpastamba Śrauta Sūtra

Bālabhārata or Pracaṇḍapāṇḍava of Rājaśekhara (Nirṇayasāgar Press ed.
Barāhasaṃhitā
Barhut (Barua)
Barhut Inscriptions (Barua & Sinha)
Baudhāyana Śrauta Sūtra
Bhagavadgītā
Bhagavatī Sūtra (Dhanpat Singh ed.)
Bhaṭṭikāvyam
Bombay Gazetteer
Book of the Kindred Sayings, The (P.T.S.)

Inscriptions of Bengal (Varendra Research Society)
Inscriptions of the Early Gupta Kings (J. F. Fleet)

Jaiminīya Upaniṣad Brāhmaṇa
Jaina Sūtras I & II (Jacobi, S.B.E. Vols. XXII & XLV)
Jātaka (Cowell and Fausböll)—All the volumes
Journal of the Asiatic Society of Bengal (J.A.S.B.)
Journal of the Buddhist Text Society
Journal of the Department of Letters, Calcutta University
Journal of the Royal Asiatic Society of Great Britain and Ireland (J.R.A.S.)
Journal of the U.P. Historical Society

Kalpasūtra and Nirayāvalī sūtra
Kāmasūtra, Vātsāyana (Punjab ed.)
Karatoyāmāhātmya
Karmaśataka (M. L. Feer)
Karpūramañjarī (Sten Konow)
Kāṭhaka-Saṃhitā
Kathāsaritsāgara (Durgaprasad and Kaśīnāth)
Kathāvatthu (P.T.S.)
Kauśāmbī in Ancient Literature, M.A.S.I. No. 60 (B. C. Law)
Kauśītakī Upaniṣad
Kāvyamīmāṃsā (Rājaśekhara) (Gaekwad's Oriental Series)
Khuddakapāṭha Commentary (P.T.S.)

Lalitavistara (Lefmann)
Lalitavistara (R. L. Mitra—Bibliotheca Indica Series)
L'art Graeco Bouddhique der Gāndhāra (J. Foucher)
Lāṭṭāyana Śrauta Sūtra
Laws of Manu, S.B.E. (Bühler)
Lé Mahāvastu (Senart)
Lé Nepal (S. Lévi)
Life and Work of Buddhaghosa, The (B. C. Law)
Life of Hiuen Tsang (Beal)
Life of the Buddha, The (Rockhill)
List of Southern Inscriptions (Keilhorn)

Mahābhārata (Vaṅgavāsī ed.)
Mahābhārata (M. N. Dutta tr.)
Mahābhārata, Vanaparva (Mahārājā Burdwan's ed.)
Mahābhāṣya (Patañjali)
Mahābodhivaṃsa (P.T.S.)
Mahāvaṃsa, P.T.S. (Geiger)
Mahāvaṃsa Ṭīkā (Sinhalese ed.)
Mahāvīra: His Life and Teachings (B. C. Law)
Majjhima Nikāya (P.T.S.)
Mānasī
Mānava Dharmaśāstra (J. Jolly)
Maṇimēkhalai
Mañjuśrīmūlakalpa (Ganapati Śāstrī ed.)
Manorathapurāṇī (P.T.S. and Sinhalese eds.)
Manual of Buddhism (Spence Hardy)
Manual of Indian Buddhism (Kern)

Manusaṃhitā
Mārkaṇḍeya Purāṇa (Pargiter)
Memoirs of Central India (Malcolm)
Milindapaño (Trenckner)
Minor Anthologies of the Pāli Canon, The (B. C. Law—S.B.B., P.T.S. publication)
Modern Review
Mudrārākṣasa (Viśākhadatta)
Mysore and Coorg from Inscriptions (Rice)

Natural History (Pliny)
Nepāl Vaṃśāvalī
Niddesa (P.T.S.)
Nirukta (Yāṣka)
Numismatic Chronicle

Old Brāhmī Inscriptions in the Udayagiri and Khaṇḍagiri Caves (B. M. Barua)
On Yuan Chwang's Travels in India (T. Watters)
Origin and Development of the Bengali Language, The (S. K. Chatterjee)
Origin of the Bengali Script, The (R. D. Banerjee)

Pāli Grammar by Kaccāyana (Ed. S. C. Vidyābhūṣana)
Pañchālas and their capital Ahichchhatra, M.A.S.I. No. 67 (B. C. Law)
Pāṇini (Goldstücker)
Papañcasūdanī (P.T.S.)
Paramatthadīpanī on the Petavatthu (P.T.S.)
Paramatthadīpanī on the Theragāthā (P.T.S.)
Pariśiṣṭaparvan (Jacobi)
Pāṭaliputra (Manoranjan Ghosh)
Periplus of the Erythraean Sea, The (Schoff)
Political History of Ancient India, 4th Ed. (H. C. Ray Chaudhuri)
Prabodhacandrodaya
Prācīna Mudrā (R. D. Banerjee)
Pratijñāyaugandharāyaṇa (Bhāsa)
Psalms of the Brethren (P.T.S.)
Psalms of the Sisters (P.T.S.)
Public Administration in Ancient India (P. N. Banerjee)
Pūjāvalīya (Sinhalese ed.)
Purāṇas—all.

Questions of King Milinda (S.B.E.).

Raghuvaṃśa
Rājataraṅgiṇī (Stein)
Rājagṛha in Ancient Literature, M.A.S.I. No. 58 (B. C. Law)
Rājgīr and its neighbourhood (D. N. Sen)
Rāmacarita
Rāmāyaṇa (Bombay and Vaṅgavāsī eds.)
Rāmāyaṇa (Griffith's tr.)
Ratnāvalī and Priyadarśikā (Harṣa)
Records of the Buddhist Religion (I-tsing)
Ṛgveda (Wilson's tr.)
Ṛgveda Brāhmaṇa (Keith)
Romantic Legend of Śākya Buddha, The (Beal).

Samantapāsādikā (P.T.S.)
Saṃhitopaniṣad Brāhmaṇa
Saṃyutta Nikāya (P.T.S.)
Sāṅkhāyana Āraṇyaka (Keith)
Sanskrit-English Dictionary (Monier-Williams)
Sanskrit Texts (Muir)
Sāratthapakāsinī (P.T.S.)
Sāsanavaṃsa (P.T.S.)
Śatapatha Brāhmaṇa (Eggeling, S.B.E.)
Saundarananda-Kāvya (B. C. Law's tr.)
Selections from the Mahābhārata (Johnson)
Shan-hsien-lü
Śirīkalpasūtram (Bhavnagar ed.)
Social Organisation in North-East India in Buddha's time (Fick)
Some Kṣatriya Tribes of Ancient India (B. C. Law)
South Indian Epigraphy, Annual Reports of
South Indian Inscriptions (Hültzsch)
Śrāvastī in Indian Literature, M.A.S.I., No. 50 (B. C. Law)
Sthavīrāvalī-charita (Hemchandra)
Studies in Indian Antiquities (H. C. Ray Chaudhuri)
Study of the Mahāvastu, A (B. C. Law)
Successors of the Sātavāhanas (D. C. Sircar)
Sumaṅgalavilāsinī (P.T.S.)
Suttanipāta (P.T.S.)
Suttanipāta Commentary (P.T.S.)
Svapnavāsavadattā (Bhāsa) (Sukhthankar's tr.)

Taittirīya Brāhmaṇa
Taittirīya Samhitā
Thera-Therīgāthā (P.T.S.)
Therīgāthā Commentary (P.T.S.)
Thūpavaṃsa (P.T.S.)
Travels of Fā-Hien (Legge)
Travels of Fā-Hien and Sung-Yun (S. Beal)

Udāna (P.T.S.)
Udāna Commentary (P.T.S.)
Udāna-vaṇṇanā (Siamese ed.)
University of Nālandā, The (H. D. Sankalia)
Upaniṣads—all
Uttarādhyayana Sūtra (J. Charpentier)
Uvāsagadasāo (Hoernle)

Vaijayantī (G. Oppert)
Vaiṣṇavism, Śaivism and Minor Religious Systems (R. G. Bhandarkar)
Vājasaneyī-Saṃhitā
Vaṃsatthapakāsinī (P.T.S.)
Vāṅgālār Itihāsa (R. D. Banerjee)
Veda of the Black Yajus' School (Keith)
Vedic Index (Macdonell and Keith)
Vedic Mythology (Macdonell)
Vimānavatthu Commentary (P.T.S.)
Vinaya Piṭaka (Oldenberg)

Vinaya Texts, I-III (S.B.E.)
Viṣṇudharmottara Mahāpurāṇa
Viṣṇupurāṇa (Wilson's ed.)
Vividha-tīrtha-kalpa (Singhee Jaina Granthamālā Series)

Zur Litteratur und Geschichte des Weda (Roth)

CHAPTER I

# THE KĀMBOJAS

The Kāmbojas appear to have been one of the early Vedic tribes. The earliest mention of them occurs in a list of ancient Vedic teachers given in the *Vaṃśa Brāhmaṇa* of the *Sāmaveda*, where we find one of the teachers to be Kāmboja Aupamanyava, i.e., Kāmboja, the son of Upamanyu (*Vaṃśa Brāhmaṇa*, edited by Pundit Satyavṛata Sāmaśramī). We are told that the sage Ānandaja received the Vedic learning from Śāmba, son of Śarkarākṣa, and also from Kāmboja, son of Upamanyu. It is interesting to note that he received this instruction from two teachers, whereas one teacher only was the usual rule. From the order in which the names are given, Śāmba appears to have been his first teacher, and the Kāmboja teacher must have been approached later, perhaps because he was distinguished for special pre-eminence in Vedic learning. We lay stress on this fact because it shows that the Kāmbojas, in early Vedic times, must have been a Vedic Indian people, and not Iranian, as has been supposed by several scholars. From the list of teachers we also find that both the teachers of Ānandaja had received their education in Vedic lore from the same sage, viz., Madragāra Śauṅgāyani, whose name shows that he belonged to the Madra people.[1] This connection between the Madras and the Kāmbojas is natural, as they were close neighbours in the N.W. of India.

The Kāmbojas are not mentioned in the *Ṛgveda* itself, but indirect evidence may help to justify the assumption that they were included among the Vedic Aryans in the Ṛgvedic era. A sage Upamanyu is mentioned at *Ṛgveda*, I, 102, 9, and it is not unreasonable to conjecture that he may have been the father of the Kāmboja teacher of the *Vaṃśa Brāhmaṇa* list. Such a possibility is suggested by Zimmer.[2]

The next important mention of the Kāmbojas is in a passage of Yāska's *Nirukta* (II, 8), which shows that they spoke a dialect of the Vedic tongue differing in some respects from the standard language, which in Yāska's time was apparently in language of the Madhyadeśa, the region around the Ganges-Jumna Doab. The Kāmbojas appear from Yāska's remarks to have been a Vedic people who had retained

---

[1] *Vedic Index*, I, p. 138.

[2] *Altindisches Leben*, p. 102.

the original sense of an ancient verb (*śavati*) while it was lost among other sections of the same people, who were separated from them by geographical barriers. Sir George Grierson, however, deduces from Yāska's remarks that, as *śavati* is an Iranian, not a Sanskrit, word, the Kāmbojas cannot have been Indo-Aryans. He holds that they either spoke Sanskrit with an infusion of Iranian words to which they gave Indian inflexions, or else spoke a language partly Indo-Aryan and partly Iranian.[1]

Yāska also attempts a (pseudo-) philological explanation of the name Kāmboja, by connecting it with Kambala, 'blanket', and further with the root *Kam*, to love, enjoy. He suggests that the Kāmbojas may have been so called because they were Kamanīya-bhojas or 'enjoyers of pleasant things', and adds that a Kambala is a pleasant thing. Though we cannot take this etymology seriously, there can be no doubt that the warm blanket, Kambala, was a pleasant thing to a people living in the rigorous climate of the N.W. highlands.

The Kambalas or blankets manufactured by the Kāmbojas are referred to in the *Mahābhārata*, which tells us that at the great Rājasūya sacrifice, the Kāmboja king presented to Yudhiṣṭhira 'many of the best kinds of skins, woollen blankets, blankets made of the fur of animals living in burrows in the earth, and also of cats—all inlaid with threads of gold' (*Sabhāparvan*, Chap. 51, 3); and again, 'The king of Kāmboja sent to him hundreds and thousands of black, dark and red skins of the deer called Kadali, and also blankets (*Kambala*) of excellent texture' (*Sabhāparvan*, Chap. 48, 19).

The next mention of the Kāmbojas is made by Pāṇini. His Sūtra (IV, 1, 175) lays down the rule that the word Kāmboja denotes not only the Kāmboja country or tribe, but also the Kāmboja king.

With regard to the location of Kāmboja, Rhys Davids says that it was a country in the extreme N.W. of India, with Dvārakā as its capital.[2] Dr. S. K. Aiyangar places it in the territory answering to the modern Sindh and Gujarat [3] and Dr. P. N. Banerjee too in his *Public Administration in Ancient India* (p. 56) assigns Kāmboja to a country near modern Sindh. Both these writers agree with Prof. Rhys Davids in locating the capital at Dvārakā. Kāmboja is mentioned in *Petavatthu* (II, 9, 1), but from the commentary on that passage (*PvA*, 111) it appears that Dvārakā is *not* its capital.[4] V. A. Smith seems to place the Kāmbojas among the mountains either of Tibet or of the Hindu Kush. He further says that they

---

[1] *J.R.A.S.*, 1911, pp. 801-2.

[2] Rhys Davids, *Buddhist India*, p. 28.

[3] *Ancient India*, p. 7.

[4] See also B. C. Law, '*Buddhist Conception of Spirits* (2nd Ed.), p. 102.

are supposed to have spoken an Iranian tongue (*Early History of India*, 4th Ed., p. 193 and f.n. 1). According to McCrindle, Kamboja was Afghanisthan, the Kaofu (Kambu) of Hsüan Tsang (McCrindle, *Alexander's Invasion*, p. 38). In the *Vedic Index*, it is stated that the Kāmbojas were settled to the N.W. of the Indus and were the Kambujiya of the old Persian inscriptions (see also D. R. Bhandarkar, *Carmichael Lectures*, 1918, pp. 54-5). According to Sir Charles Eliot (*Hinduism and Buddhism*, Vol. I, p. 268), the Kāmbojas were probably Tibetans; in another volume of the same work,[1] he calls them an ambiguous race who were perhaps the inhabitants of Tibet or its border lands. M. Foucher in his *Iconographie Bauddhique* (p. 134) points out that the Nepalese tradition applies the name Kambojadeśa to Tibet. Doubtful would be the attempt to connect Cambyses (O.P. Ka(m)bujiya) with the frontier people of Kāmboja.[2] Dr. H. C. Ray Chaudhuri [3] points out that from a passage of the *Mahābhārata* we learn that a place called Rājapura was the home of the Kāmbojas (*Mbh.*, VII, 4-5, '*Karṇa Rājapuraṃ gatvā Kambojā nirjitāstyayā*'). The association of the Kāmbojas with the Gāndhāras enables us to identify this Rājapura with Rājapura of Hsüan Tsang (Watters, *On Yuan Chwang*, Vol. I, p. 284), which lay to the S. or S.E. of Punach.[4]

Pāṇini belonged to the north-west quarter of India and hence had an accurate knowledge of the customs and dress of the Kāmbojas. The *Mayūravyaṃśakādigaṇa* of Pāṇini speaks of the Kāmbojas as *muṇḍa* or shaven-headed. Apparently the Kāmbojas were in the habit of completely shaving their heads, as would also appear from a passage quoted by Raghunandana from the *Harivaṃśa* and pointed out by Max Müller [5]: 'The Sakas (Scythians) have half their head shorn, the Yavanas (Greeks?) and Kāmbojas the whole, the Pāradas (inhabitants of Paradene) wear their hair free, and the Pahlavas (Persians) wear beards'.

Coming to the Pāli Buddhist literature we find the Kāmboja country spoken of several times in the canonical texts as one of the sixteen great States (*Mahājanapadas*) that were most prominent in India about the time of the Buddha (see, e.g. *Aṅguttara Nikāya*, Vol. I, p. 213; Vol. IV, p. 252–6).

---

[1] Vol. III, p. 6.

[2] *Cambridge History of India*, Ancient India, p. 334, f.n.

[3] *Political History of India from the accession of Parikshit to the coronation of Bimbisāra*, p. 77.

[4] R. D. Banerjee refers to a Kāmboja or Cambodia on the east side of Samataṭa (Bengal), which must be identical with Sir Charles Eliot's Camboja, as distinct from Kamboja.

[5] *History of Ancient Sanskrit Literature*, p. 28.

In the *Harivaṃśa*, we find that the people of Kāmboja were formerly Kṣatriyas. It was Sagara who caused them to give up their own religion (*Harivaṃśa*, 14). From verses 43 and 44 of Chap. X of the *Manusaṃhitā*, we find that the Kāmbojas, Śakas, Yavanas, and other Kṣatriya tribes were gradually degraded to the condition of Śūdras on account of their omission of the sacred rites, and of their not consulting the Brahmins. Kauṭilya's *Arthaśāstra* states that the corporations of warriors (*kṣatriya-śreṇī*) of Kāmboja and other countries lived by agriculture, trade and profession of arms (*Vārtāśastropajīvin*).[1]

The horses of Kāmboja were famous throughout all periods of Indian history. In the *Sumaṅgalavilāsinī*, Kāmboja is spoken of as the home of horses (*Kāmbojo assānaṃ āyatanaṃ*).[2] The *Mahābhārata* is full of references to the excellent horses of Kāmboja. In the *Sabhāparvan* (51, 4), we read that the king of Kāmboja presented to Yudhiṣṭhira three hundred horses of variegated colours, speckled like the partridge and having fine noses like the *śuka* bird. In the great battle of Kurukṣetra, the fast and powerful horses of Kāmboja were of the utmost service.[3]

The Jaina *Uttarādhyayana Sūtra*[4] tells us that a trained Kambojan horse excels all other horses in speed, and no noise can frighten it. In the *Campeyya Jātaka*[5] we read that a king of Kāśī, being requested by a Nāga king to visit his abode, ordered well-trained Kambojan horses to be yoked to his chariot.[6] Viṣṇuvardhana, who later became ruler of Mysore, owned Kambojan horses, which were evidently much coveted for their speed.[7] The *Aṭṭhakathā* on the *Kunāla Jātaka* furnishes us with the interesting piece of information that the Kāmbojas were in the habit of capturing horses in the forest by tempting them into an enclosed space by means of aquatic plants which they smeared with honey.[8]

In the *Raghuvaṃśa*, Kālidāsa makes Raghu meet the Kāmbojas after defeating the Hūṇas on the bank of the Vaṅkṣū or the Oxus. The Kāmbojas, being unable to meet the prowess of Raghu, bowed low before him, just as their walnut trees were bent down on account of Raghu's elephants being tied to them. An immense treasure including excellent horses was offered as tribute to Raghu by the Kāmbojas.[9]

1 *Arthaśāstra*, trsl. by Shāma Shāstrī, p. 455.

2 I, 124.

3 See, e.g. *Mbh.*, *Bhīṣmaparvan*, 71, 13; 90, 3; *Droṇaparvan*, 22, 7; 22, 22-3; 22, 42; *Karṇaparvan*, 38, 13; *Sauptikaparvan*, 13, 12.

4 *Jaina Sūtras*, S.B.E., pt. II, p. 47.

5 *Jātaka* (Fausböll), Vol. IV, p. 464.

6 See also *Mahāvastu*, II, p. 185.

7 S. K. Aiyangar, *Ancient India*, p. 236.

8 *Jātaka*, V, 446.

9 *Raghuvaṃśa*, IV, 69-70.

The Kāmbojas occupy a prominent place among the Kṣatriya tribes of the *Mahābhārata*. In the geographical enumeration of the peoples of India, the Kāmbojas are located in the north.[1] They were the allies of Duryodhana, and by their bravery, and especially through the prowess of their king Sudakṣiṇa, they rendered great service to the Kuru side in the Kurukṣetra war. Sudakṣiṇa was one of the few Mahārathas or great heroes in the field.

Drupada advised Yudhiṣṭhira to ask the Kāmbojas and other tribes on the western frontiers for their assistance,[2] but the Pāṇḍavas were not able to obtain their alliance. Duryodhana was more successful, perhaps through his kinship with the neighbouring Gāndhāras, and later boasted to the Pāṇḍavas of his alliance with the Kāmbojas and other northern peoples.[3] He gives an important place to the Kāmbojas by mentioning them together with the greatest heroes on his side (see *Mbh.*, Chap. 160, 40). Bhīṣma too extols the prowess of the Kāmboja king, Sudakṣiṇa, of whom he says, 'In my opinion Sudakṣiṇa of Kāmboja is equal to one Ratha. The best of the chariot-warriors under him are strikers with fierce force. The Kāmbojas, O great king, will cover the land like a swarm of locusts' (*Mbh.*, *Udyogaparvan*, Chap. 165, 1–3).

When the Kaurava army took up their position on the field, the Kāmbojas occupied the van of Duryodhana's army, along with the home forces of the Pauravas themselves. We are told: 'The Pauravas, the Kaliṅgas and the Kāmbojas with their king Sudakṣiṇa and Kṣemadhanvā and Śalya took up their positions in front of Duryodhana' (*Mbh.*, *Bhīṣmaparvan*, Chap. 17, 26-7).

The Kāmbojas appear to have been consistently in the thickest of the fight.[4] Their king Sudakṣiṇa was eventually killed in a duel with Arjuna. The verses which describe him as he lay slain on the battle-field are worth quoting for their poetic imagery: 'Like a charming Karṇikara tree,—which in the spring grows gracefully on the top of a hill, with beautiful branches,—lying in the grove when uprooted by the tempest, the prince of the Kāmbojas, accustomed to sleep on the most precious bed, lay lifeless on the bare ground. Adorned with precious ornaments, graceful, possessing eyes of coppery hue, wearing around his head a tiara of gold radiant like the flames of fire, the mighty armed Sudakṣiṇa, prince of the Kāmbojas, felled by Pārtha with his arrows, and lying dead on the ground, appeared beautiful like a charming hill with a flat summit'.[5]

---

[1] *Mbh.*, *Bhīṣmaparvan*, Chap. 9. [2] *Mbh.*, *Udyogaparvan*, 18.

[3] '*Udīcya Kāmbojaśakaiḥ Khaśaiśca*' (*Mbh.*, *Udyogaparvan*, Chap. 160).

[4] See *Bhīṣmaparvan*, Chap. 45, 66–8; Chap. 56, 7; Chap. 75, 17; Chap. 87, 10; also *Droṇaparvan*, Chap. 7, 14; 19, 7.

[5] *Mbh.*, *Droṇaparvan*, Chap. 92, 61–75.

In the fierce battle that ensued, when Sātyaki, urged on by Yudhiṣṭhira, was following in the track of Arjuna, the Kāmbojas arrested his progress. Then, we are told, Sātyaki slew thousands of the Kāmbojas, worked havoc among them, and pressed onward.[1]

Again, when Karṇa assumed the leadership of the Kuru army, the Kāmbojas were there taking an active part by his side[2]; and even after Sudakṣiṇa's younger brother had laid down his life for the cause,[3] we still hear of the Kāmbojas delivering an attack on Arjuna.[4]

We thus find the Kāmbojas leading a large army to the field of Kurukṣetra and laying down their lives like the valiant Kṣatriyas. Afterwards it appears from the later sections of the *Mahābhārata*, viz. the *Śānti* and *Ānuśāsanika parvans*, that their country had been overrun by barbarous hordes, so that the ancient Kṣatriya population was overwhelmed, and we find the Kāmbojas ranked with the Yavanas and looked down upon as one of the barbarous peoples. Thus a verse of the *Śāntiparvan* enumerates the Kāmbojas along with many peoples not included in what we may call 'Indo-Aryan society',[5] and in another chapter they are placed among the barbarous peoples of the Uttarāpatha (northern regions).[6] The *Ānuśāsanika-parvan* (33, 21) speaks of the Kāmbojas as having been degraded to the rank of Śudras for want of Brāhmaṇas in their country. These passages go to show that at the time when these *parvans* were added to the Epic, the Kāmbojas were losing touch with Brahmanical society, probably owing to admixture with uncivilised invaders from the North.

Turning to the other great epic, we read in the *Ādi Kāṇḍa* of the *Rāmāyaṇa* that the Kāmbojas were created by the divine cow Sabalā, at the request of Vashiṣṭha (20–24). The *Kiṣkindhyā Kāṇḍa* (Chap. 43) tells us that Sugrīva sent a monkey named Sugrīva to North India in search of Kāmboja and other countries (11-12).

The *Vāyupurāṇa* informs us that after killing the Haihayas, King Sagara was engaged in annihilating the Kāmbojas, Śakas, Yavanas, Pahlavas and others. All these tribes, however, secured the aid of Vashiṣṭha, Sagara's spiritual preceptor. Listening to the words of Vashiṣṭha, Sagara set the Kāmbojas free after having completely shaven their heads (Vaṅgavāsī Edition, Chap. 88). It is stated in the *Harivaṃśa* that the Ikṣvāku King Vāhu was dethroned by Kāmbojas and others (Chaps. 13, 14).

---

1 *Mbh.*, Chap. III, 59-60; *Droṇaparvan*, 119, 51; 118, 9.
2 *Ibid.*, *Karṇaparvan*, Chap. 46, 15.
3 *Ibid.*, *Karṇaparvan*, Chap. 56.
4 *Ibid.*, Chap. 88. See also *Śālyaparvan*, Chap. I, 26; Chap. 8, 25.
5 *Ibid.*, *Śāntiparvan*, Chap. 65, 14.
6 *Ibid.*, 207, 43-4.

In the *Jātakas* we read that the Kāmbojas were a N.W. tribe who were supposed to have lost their original Aryan customs and to have become barbarous.[1] In the *Bhuridatta Jātaka* we find that many Kāmbojas who were not Ariyas falsely held that peoples were purified by killing insects, snakes, frogs, etc.[2] It is stated in the *Sāsanavaṃsa* [3] that in the 235th year of the Buddha's Parinibbāna, the Thera Mahārakkhita went to the Yonaka province and established the Buddha's doctrine in Kāmboja and other places. In other passage of the *Sāsanavaṃsa*, we find the son of the king of Kāmboja referred to as a Buddhist monk, Tāmalinda, who sailed from Ceylon to India with the Thera Uttarājīva.[4] Also in the *Sāsanavaṃsa*, we read of Sirīhaṃsya, who came from Kāmboja and conquered the city of Ratanapura. Fearing the increasing power and influence of the Buddhist monks, which might become a danger if they turned their minds to secular objects, he determined on a wholesale slaughter. He invited all the great theras of Jeyyapura, Vijayapura and Ratanapura together with their disciples, to meet him in the forest Toṅ-bhī-luḥ; and there he caused them, to the number of 3,000, to be surrounded and slain by his army. Many shrines were demolished and books burnt at the same time.[5]

The Emperor Aśoka sent missionaries to the nations on the borders of his empire, viz. the Kāmbojas, Yavanas, etc., with the object of converting them to Buddhism. He celebrates their conversion to the true Dhamma in Rock Edict XIII (see V. A. Smith, *Aśoka*, p. 168); while Rock Edict V tells us that Censors were created by Aśoka for the establishment of the law of piety, for the increase of the law, and for the welfare and happiness of the Kāmbojas, Gāndhāras and others living on the W. frontier of his dominions.

In the ninth century A.D. the Kāmbojas are said to have been defeated by Devapāla, the great king of the Pāla dynasty of Bengal.[6] But during the latter part of the 10th century the tables were turned, and the rule of the Pāla kings of Bengal was interrupted by the Kāmbojas, who set up one of their chiefs as king.[7] In a place called Vānagarh in Dinājpur, Bengal, mention is made of a certain king of Gauḍa, born in the Kāmboja family. It is probable that the Kāmbojas first attempted to conquer Gauḍa during the reign of Devapāla, but were defeated at that time.[8] R. P. Chanda surmises

---

1 *Jātaka* (Fausböll), VI, p. 208; *Ibid.* (Cowell), VI, p. 110, f.n. 2.
2 *Ibid.* (Fausböll), Vol. VI, pp. 208, 210.
3 *Sāsanavaṃsa*, P.T.S. Ed., 49.
4 p. 40, P.T.S. edition.
5 *Ibid.* (P.T.S.), p. 100.
6 R. D. Banerjee, *Vāṅgālār Itihāsa*, p. 182.
7 V. A. Smith, *Early History of India*, 4th Ed., p. 414.
8 Banerjee, *Vāṅgālār Itihāsa*, p. 184.

that in the middle of the tenth century A.D., the Kāmbojas again attacked North Bengal, and that its present inhabitants (of Koch, Mech, and Paliā) are descended from them.[1] The Kāmboja rulers were expelled by Mahīpāla I, the ninth king of the Pāla line, who is known to have been reigning in A.D. 1026, and may be assumed to have regained his ancestral throne about A.D. 978 or 980.[2]

---

[1] Banerjee, *Vāṅgālār Itihāsa*, p. 205.
[2] V. A. Smith, *Early History of India*, 4th Ed., pp. 414-15.

## CHAPTER II

# THE GANDHĀRAS

Gandhāra formed an integral part of India from the earliest epoch of Indo-Aryan civilisation, and is unique among the countries of India, in that its history may be traced in unbroken continuity from Rigvedic times down to the present day [1] (Rapson, *Ancient India*, p. 81). The Gandhāris [2] or people of Gandhāra are mentioned in the hymns of the *Ṛgveda*, while the name Gandhāra occurs in the other Vedas, and in the Epics and Purāṇas as well as the Buddhist books.

Gandhāra was on the N.W. frontiers of India in the neighbourhood of the Kāmbojas, Madras and similar other tribes, but there are differences of opinion among scholars with regard to its exact boundaries. It is generally accepted that Gandhāra denotes the region comprising the modern districts of Peshawar in the N.W. Frontier Province and Rawalpindi in the Punjab; but in the Old Persian inscriptions it seems to include also the district of Kābul in Afghānistān (see Rapson, *Ancient India*, p. 81). Rhys Davids (*Buddhist India*, p. 28) says that Gandhāra (modern Kandahar) [3] was the district of E. Afghānistān, probably including the N.W. Punjab. Vincent Smith apparently concurs with this view, saying that Gandhāra was equivalent to the N.W. Punjab and the adjoining regions.[4] Dr. S. K. Aiyangar holds that Gandhāra was equivalent to E. Afghānistān, extending from the Afghan mountains to the district somewhat to the East of the Indus (*Ancient India*, p. 7). According to Dr. D. R. Bhandarkar, Gandhāra included the western Punjab and E. Afghānistān. Its capital was Takshaśīlā where ruins are spread near Sarāīkālā in the Rawalpindi District of the Punjab.[5] In the *Ain-i-Akbari*, Gandhāra forms the district of Pukely lying between Kashmir and Attock. Gandhāra, says N. L. Dey, comprised the modern districts of Peshawar and Hoti Murdan or what is called the Eusofzai

[1] Rapson, *Ancient India*, 81.

[2] Gandhāri is the Vedic form, later supplanted by Gandhāra.

[3] There is no proved etymological connection between the names Kandahar and Gandhāra. See McCrindle, *Ptolemy*, p. 116.

[4] V. A. Smith, *Aśoka*, 170.

[5] *Carmichael Lectures*, 1918, p. 54.

country.[1] Cunningham, relying on the narratives of the Chinese pilgrims, Fā Hien and Hsüan Tsang, gives the following boundaries to Gandhāra (Chinese *Kien-to-lo*): Laghmān and Jalālābād on the west, the hills of Swāt and Bunir on the N., the Indus on the E., and the hills of Kālabāgh on the South (*Ancient Geography*, p. 48; and see McCrindle, *Ancient India as described by Ptolemy*, p. 116). According to Strabo, the country of the Gandarai, which he calls Gandaritis, lay between the Khoaspes (Kunar) and the Indus, and along the river Kophes (Kabul). The name is not mentioned by any of the historians of Alexander, but it must have been known to the Greeks as early as the time of Hekataios, who calls Kaspapyros a 'Gandaric city'. Herodotus mentions the Gandarioi.[2] Rennell placed them to the west of Baktria in the province afterwards called Margiana, while Wilson took them to be the people south of the Hindu Kush, from about the modern Kandahar to the Indus, and extending into the Punjab and to Kashmir (*Ancient India as described by Ptolemy*—McCrindle, pp. 115-6). In some books, the name 'Cave country' was applied to Gandhāra (Watters, *On Yuan Chwang*, Vol. I, p. 200).

From the above observations, and also from the various references to Gandhāra in Indian literature, it appears that the boundaries of the country varied at different periods in its history. At one time it appears to have included the Afghan District round Kandahar, but afterwards it receded to the mountains on the Indian frontier.

In the *Ṛgveda* the long wool of the sheep reared by the Gandhāris is referred to by Lomaśā, the queen of King Bhāvya or Bhavayavya, who ruled on the banks of the Sindhu (Indus); she says to her husband, 'I am covered with down like a ewe of the Gandhārins' (*Ṛgveda*, I, pp. 126, 7; Wilson's Trans., II, p. 78). From the facts that the verse is brought in very abruptly and that it is in a metre different from the rest of the hymn, Wilson observes that it is 'probably a fragment of some old popular song' (Trsl., p. 19). This would, therefore, attribute a knowledge of the Gandhāris to the Vedic Aryans in very ancient times.

A hymn in the *Atharvaveda* consigns Takman or fever to the Gandhāris along with other people like the Mūjavants, the Aṅgas and the Magadhas. The authors of the *Vedic Index* explain this mention of two northern peoples (the Gandhāris and Mūjavants)

[1] Discoveries have been made in this district of Buddhist architecture and sculpture of the time of Kanishka (first century A.D.). See N. L. Dey, *Geographical Dictionary*, p. 23.

[2] Book III, c. xci. He describes them as being clad in cotton garments, and bearing bows of reed, and arrows tipped with iron. See Rapson, *Ancient India*, p. 87; and McCrindle, p. 116.

with two eastern tribes (Aṅgas and Magadhas), by noting that 'the latter two tribes are apparently the Eastern limit of the poet's knowledge; the two former the Northern'.[1]

In the Brāhmaṇa literature also we find mention of the Gandhāris (e.g. *Chāndogya Upaniṣad*, 6, 14—the familiar example of the man who is led blind-folded from the land of the Gandhāras, and has to find his way back by asking directions from village to village).

The *Aitareya Brāhmaṇa* (VII, 34) mentions Nagnajit, a king of Gandhāra, among the Vedic teachers who propagated the Soma-cult, —so it is evident that Gandhāra was not excluded from Vedic 'Aryandom'. In the *Śatapatha Brāhmaṇa* (VIII, 1, 4, 10) also we find King Svarjit Nāgnajita or Nagnajit of Gandhāra referred to,—though in this case his opinion on a point of ritual is treated with scant respect as he was merely a *Rājanya-bandhu*, i.e. belonging to the princely order, and not a Ṛṣi. But this King Nagnajit is mentioned with great regard and respect in later literature from the great Epic onwards,[2] and in a technical book on painting he is quoted as the originator of that art.[3]

Coming to the next period of Vedic literature, viz. the period of the Sūtras, we find the people of Gandhāra mentioned in the Śrauta-Sūtras of Baudhāyana, Āpastamba and Hiraṇyakeśī, along with other Aryan peoples of the east and the west.[4]

The *Mahābhārata* contains many legends about Gandhāra. In the *Ādiparvan* we find that Dhṛtarāṣṭra, king of the Kurus, married the daughter of Suvala,[5] King of Gandhāra, and 100 sons were born to them (Chap. 10, p. 118; Chap. 63, p. 72). A princess of Gandhāra was one of the wives of Ajamīḍha who was the originator of the Kuru family. Gandhāra, it is said, was named after this Gāndhārī (*Ādiparvan*, Chap. 95, p. 105). In the *Udyogaparvan* we find that King Yayāti sent his son Yadu into exile in Gandhāra, because he began to disregard his Kṣatriya superiors, becoming vain on account of his strength (Chap. 149, p. 771). In the *Droṇaparvan* it is said that Karṇa brought Gandhāra under the sway of Duryodhana (Chap. 4, p. 997); while in the *Aśvamedhaparvan* we read that Arjuna went to the Punjab (*Pañcanada*), where he had a hard fight with the son of Śakuni, King of Gandhāra. The Gandhāran army

---

1 *Vedic Index*, I, p. 219.

2 In the *Kumbhakāra Jātaka*, for example, it is said that he ruled over Gandhāra and Kashmir, and later became a monk.

3 *Dokumente der Indischen Kunst, Erstes Heft, Malerei, des Citra Lakṣaṇa*, edited by Berthold Laufer.

4 *Baudhayāna Śrauta Sūtra*, XXI, 13; *Āpastamba Śrauta Sūtra*, XXII, 6, 18; *Hiraṇyakeśī Śrauta Sūtra*, XVII, 6.

5 Suvala is also mentioned in the *Sabhāparvan* (Chap. 34, p. 245).

was put to flight, but Arjuna spared the life of Śakuni's son (Chaps. 83-4, pp. 2093-4).

It would be wearisome to recount in detail all the references from the *Mahābhārata* to the actions of the Gandhāras in the long-drawn-out battle of Kurukṣetra. We may note, however, that the Gandhāras, led by their King Śakuni, made up a powerful division of the Kuru army. When at the commencement of the battle Duryodhana came out in procession at the head of his vast army, Śakuni's contingent of hill troops (*pārvatīya*) surrounded him on all sides.[1] This would seem to indicate that the warriors from the hills of Gandhāra were the most trusty of Duryodhana's soldiers, for they were chosen to form his bodyguard. After various adventures (*Bhīṣmaparvan*, Chap. 46, p. 76; Chap. 51, p. 14; Chap. 58, pp. 7–10), the Gandhāras on the 5th day of the battle, together with the Kāmbojas, Madras and other peoples of the N.W. frontier made an onset against Arjuna, under the lead of Śakuni (*Bhīṣmaparvan*, Chap. 71, pp. 13–17). The Gandhāras and their princes further distinguished themselves throughout the battle (see *Bhīṣmaparvan*, Chap. 90; *Droṇaparvan*, Chap. 20; Chap. 29, pp. 2–27; Chap. 48, p. 7; Chap. 85, pp. 16-17; *Śalyaparvan*, Chap. 8, p. 26). Evidently great reliance was placed on their prowess, and perhaps especially on their fast horses; for it appears that, like their neighbours, the Kāmbojas, the Gandhāras reared a large number of horses in their country, and their troops fought for the most part on horseback. References which do not give them credit are, e.g. *Karṇaparvan*, Chap. 44, p. 46 and Chap. 45, p. 8, where Karṇa says that the Gandhāras along with the other races on the N.W. frontier are men of disgusting practices and customs; and *ibid.*, Chap. 95, p. 6, where it is said that Śakuni cravenly fled from the field, surrounded by thousands of the Gandhāras (Cf. also *Droṇaparvan*, Chap. 29, pp. 2–27).

Gandhāra is also mentioned in the *Purāṇas*. According to the *Matsya, Vāyu* and *Viṣṇu Purāṇas*,[2] a certain Gāndhāra was born in the family of Druhyu, one of the sons of Yayāti, and the kingdom of Gandhāra was named after him. According to the *Bhāgavata* and *Brahma Purāṇas*,[3] Gāndhāra was fourth in the line of descent from Druhyu. Gāndhāra had four children, namely, Dharma, Dhṛti, Durgam and Pracetā.[4] Pracetā had 100 sons who, being the kings of the Mleccha country, conquered the north (*Viṣṇupurāṇa*, 4th

[1] *Bhīṣmaparvan*, 20, 8; see also *ibid.*, Chap. 16, p. 28.

[2] *Matsyapurāṇa*, 48; *Vāyupurāṇa*, 99; *Viṣṇupurāṇa*, 4th Aṅka, Chap. 17.

[3] 9th Skandha, Chap. 23 (*Bhāgavata*); Chap. 13 (*Brahma*).

[4] According to the *Matsyapurāṇa*, three children: Dharma, Vidusa and Pracetā.

Aṅka, Chap. 17). Mention is also made of the Gandhāra people in Varāhamihira's *Bṛhatsaṃhitā* (Kern's Edition, p. 92).

Turning from legend or semi-legend to fact, we note that in the days of Aśoka and some of his immediate successors, Gandhāra was one of the most flourishing seats of Buddhism. We learn from Rock Edict V that Aśoka appointed *Dharma-mahāmātras* (high officers in the department of dharma or religious conduct) to further the welfare and happiness of the Gandhāras.[1] Fā-Hien, the Chinese pilgrim, who visited India at the beginning of the fifth century A.D., relates that Gandhāra was the place where Dharmavivardhana, son of Aśoka, ruled. Here the Buddha, when a Bodhisattva, was supposed to have given his eyes for another man.[2] Buddhist scholastic philosophy reached its culmination in the fifth century A.D., at the time when two famous Gandhārans, Asaṅga and Vasubandhu, flourished. Asaṅga, at first an adherent of the semi-orthodox Mahīsāsakas, later became a great teacher of Yogācāra. Vasubandhu likewise became a convert to Mahāyānism; he was celebrated as the author of the *Abhidharmakoṣa.* Other notable Buddhist scholars who made Gandhāra, and particularly its capital Takṣaśīlā (Taxila) famous throughout India were Dhammapāla,[3] Yasadatta,[4] and Aṅgulimāla.[5] For legendary accounts of Gandhāra as associated with Buddhism, see, e.g. *Gandhāra Jātaka, Sāsanavaṃsa* (P.T.S., p. 12), *Divyāvadāna* (Cowell and Neil, pp. 60-1).

Hsüan Tsang, who visited India in the seventh century A.D., has left an interesting account of Gandhāra. He records the ruined state of monasteries and shrines which two centuries before showed no traces of decay. The kingdom of Gandhāra, according to him, was about 1,000 li [6] from north to south. On the east it bordered on the river Sin (= Sindhu). The capital was called Po-lu-sha-pu-lo, i.e. Puruṣapura, and was about 40 li in circuit. The royal family was extinct, and the kingdom was governed by deputies from Kapiśa. The towns and villages were deserted; but the country was rich in cereals, producing a variety of flowers and fruits, and abounding in sugarcane. The Chinese pilgrim goes on to say: 'The climate is warm and moist. The disposition of the people is timid and soft; they love literature, and while most of them belong to heretical schools, a few believe in the true law (i.e. Buddhism)'. In the town of P'i-lo-tu-lo (i.e. Salātula), he observes, Pāṇini was born (see *Buddhist Records of the Western World* (Beal), Vol. I, pp. 97-8; p. 114).

---

[1] Cf. Chapter on Kāmbojas.

[2] Legge, *Travels of Fa-Hien*, pp. 31-2.

[3] *Psalms of the Brethren*, p. 149.

[4] *Ibid.*, p. 201.

[5] *Ibid.*, pp. 319 *et seq.*

[6] One li = approx. 576 metres.

The early capital cities of Gandhāra (each being the centre of its own kingdom) were Puṣkalāvatī or Puṣkarāvatī, and Takṣaśilā (Taxila), —the former being situated to the west and the latter to the east of the Indus. It would appear that in early times the Gandhāra territory lay on both sides of the Indus, but was later confined to the western side (McCrindle, p. 115). As we have just seen, Hsüan Tsang knew Puruṣapura (= Peshawar) as the capital; and yet another city, namely, Kāpiśa, was a Gandhāran capital during the days of Greek rule.[1]

According to Cunningham, the most ancient capital of Gandhāra was Puṣkarāvatī, which is said to have been founded by Puṣkara, son of Bharata and nephew of Rāma.[2] Puṣkalāvatī's antiquity is undoubted, as it was the capital of an Indian Prince named Hasti (Greek Astes) at the time of Alexander's expedition (326 B.C.). It is called Peukelaotis by Arrian and Peukalei by Dionysius Periegetes. Together with Takṣaśilā, Puṣkalāvatī came under the Śaka rule during the reign of Maues[3] (c. 75 B.C.). Tārānātha mentions the town as a royal residence of Kaniṣka's son (Vincent Smith, *Early History of India*, 4th Ed., p. 277, f.n. 1).

Shi-shi-ch'eng, the Chinese name for Takṣaśilā, the Eastern capital of Gandhāra, means 'severed head'. The legend goes that when the Buddha was a Bodhisattva in this city, he gave his head away in charity, and the city took its name from this circumstance.[4] The city as described by Arrian was great, wealthy and populous. Strabo and Hsüan Tsang praise the fertility of its soil. Pliny calls it a famous city, and states that it was situated on a level where the hills sank down into the plains. About 80 years after Takṣaśilā's submission to Alexander, it was taken by Aśoka; while by the early part of the second century B.C. it had become a province of the Graeco-Baktrian monarchy,—only to be conquered in 126 B.C.[5] by the Indo-Skythian Sus or Abars, who retained it until it was taken from them by a different tribe of the same nationality, under Kaniṣka (c. 78 B.C.). About the middle of the first century A.D. it is said to have been visited by Apollonius of Tyana and his companion Damis, who described it as being about the size of Nineveh, walled like a Greek city, with narrow but well-arranged streets. Takṣaśilā must have been destroyed long before the Muhammadan

[1] Rapson, *Ancient India*, pp. 133, 141-2.

[2] *Viṣṇupurāṇa*, Wilson's Edition, Vol. IV, Ch. 4.

[3] *Cambridge History of India*, Vol. I, p. 560; see also Brown, *Coins of India*, 24.

[4] Legge, *Fā-Hien*, p. 32.

[5] But note discrepancy in dates of conquest.

invasion, for it is not mentioned by any Muhammadan author who has written upon India.[1]

Cunningham says that the site of Takṣaśilā is found near Shah-Dheri just one mile to the N.E. of Kāla-ka-sarāi, in the extensive ruins of a fortified city around which he was able to trace no less than 55 stūpas (of which two are as large as the great Mānikyāla tope), 28 monasteries and 9 temples. Now the distance from Shah-Dheri to Ohind is 36 miles, and from Ohind to Hashtnagar another 38, making 74 miles in all,—which is 19 in excess of the distance between Taxila and Peukelaotis (Puṣkalāvatī) as recorded by Pliny. To reconcile the discrepancy, Cunningham suggests that Pliny's 60 miles or LX should be read as 80 miles or LXXX, which is equivalent to 73½ English miles or within half a mile of the actual distance between the two places (Cunningham, *Ancient Geography*, p. 105). Dr. Bhandarkar says[2] that in Aśoka's time Takṣaśilā does not appear to have been the capital of Gandhāra, for from his Rock Edict XIII it seems that Gandhāra was not in his dominions proper, but was feudatory to him; while from the Kaliṅga Edict I, we learn that Takṣaśilā was directly under him, as one of his sons was stationed there. The deduction that Takṣaśilā was not the capital of Gandhāra at that time is confirmed by Ptolemy's statement that the Gandarai (Gandhāra) country was situated to the west of the Indus with its city Proklais, i.e. Puṣkarāvatī.[3]

Takṣaśilā was visited by Hsüan Tsang in the seventh century A.D. (when it was a dependency of Kashmir).[4]

Takṣaśilā figures prominently in Buddhist and Jain stories. It was associated with Mahāvīra, the founder of Jainism[5] (see *Heart of Jainism* by Mrs. Sinclair Stevenson, p. 80, f.n.), and with traditions regarding the Buddha. It is stated in the *Dīpavaṃsa* that a Kṣatriya prince named Dīpaṃkara, and his sons and grandsons governed their great kingdom in Takṣaśilā[6] (Pāli Takkhasilā). In the *Dutiyapalāyi Jātaka* we find that King Gāndhāra (= the Gandhāran) of Takṣaśilā attacked and surrounded Benares with his four-fold army, and boasted that nobody would be able to defeat him. But the King of Benares said to him: 'I shall destroy your army like mad elephants destroying a *nalavana* (bamboo grove)'. King Gāndhāra forthwith

---

[1] See McCrindle, *Ancient India as described by Ptolemy*, pp. 119 *et seq.*

[2] *Carmichael Lectures*, 1918, p. 54, f.n.

[3] See also *Fā-Hien's Travels* (Legge's Ed.), pp. 31-2 where the traveller distinguishes Takkhasīlā from Gandhāra.

[4] V. A. Smith, *Early History of India*, 4th edition, p. 368. Watters, *On Yuan Chwang*, Vol. I, p. 240.

[5] S. Stevenson, *Heart of Jainism*, p. 80, f.n.

[6] *Dīpavaṃsa*, ed. Oldenberg, III, 31.

fled, terrified, to his own kingdom.[1] But we find the situation reversed in the *Palāyi Jātaka*: Brahmadatta, King of Benares, leads an army to Takṣaśilā, but is so struck by the splendour of the city gate, which he mistakes for a palace, that he does not dare to make an attack on so mighty a king (the king being pictured as the Bodhisattva), and returns baffled to his own country.[2]

Takṣaśilā was a great seat of learning in Ancient India. Various arts and sciences were taught there, and pupils from different parts of India would flock to the city for instruction.[3] Here also magic charms [4] and spells for understanding the cries of animals [5] were taught. According to *Jātaka* (IV, 391), only Brahmans and Kṣatriyas were admitted to the university. The details of Taxila's importance as a seat of learning have been given by me elsewhere,[6] and a brief notice is all that is necessary here.

As regards the authentic political history of Gandhāra itself, as distinct from that of its capitals, we find that in the Buddha's time Pukkusāti, King of Gandhāra, is said to have sent an embassy and a letter to King Bimbisāra (Skt. Bindusāra) of Magadha.[7] Prof. Rapson states [8] that Gandhāra was in all probability conquered by Cyrus (558–530 B.C.), and remained a Persian province for about two centuries. After the downfall of the Persian empire in 331 B.C., it came under the sway of Alexander the Great, together with the Persian province of 'India' or 'the country of the Indus'. Through Gandhāra and the 'Indian' province was exercised the Persian influence which so greatly modified the civilisation of N.W. India. Later, as we have seen, Gandhāra was feudatory to Aśoka, but it declared its independence shortly after his death,—only to fall very soon under the sway of the Greek kings.[9] According to Whitehead,[10] it was Euthydemos (circa. 230–195 B.C.) who conquered Gandhāra. R. D. Banerjee, however, presumes [11] that the conqueror was Diyadāta (Diodotos) II, as some gold coins of his reign have been discovered by Sir John Marshall in the ruins of Taxila. Whitehead's supposition is the more probable, if we are to assume that Gandhāra was subject to the Maurya Empire until

1 *Jātaka* (Fausböll), Vol. II, pp. 219–21.
2 *Ibid.*, pp. 217-8.
3 See, e.g. *Psalms of the Brethren*, p. 136.
4 *Jātaka*, II, No. 185, p. 100.
5 *Ibid.*, III, No. 416, p. 415.
6 See B. C. Law, *Historical Gleanings*, Chap. I, pp. 1–8.
7 Rhys Davids, *Buddhist India*, p. 28.
8 Rapson, *Ancient India*, pp. 81-82.
9 R. D. Banerjee, *Vāṅgālār Itihāsa*, pp. 31-2.
10 *Catalogue of Coins in the Punjab Museum*, Lahore, Vol. I, p. 4.
11 *Prācīna Mudrā*, p. 27.

Aśoka's death in 227 B.C., for the house of Diodotos was supplanted by Euthydemos in 230 B.C.

A rival Greek prince, Eucratides (circa. 175–155 B.C.) wrested Gandhāra, with other territories, from Demetrios, the 4th Bactrian king.[1] The family of Eucratides was supplanted in its turn by Śaka satraps in Kāpiśa and Taxila, but continued to hold the Kabul Valley until finally overpowered by the Kushāṇas.[2] At the end of the fifth century A.D., Gandhāra was occupied by the Hūṇas.[3] After this, information is scanty until we come to the late 9th century, when Lalliya founded the Hindu Shāhiya dynasty, with its capital at Ohind, on the Indus.[4] In the 11th century (1021 A.D., according to Vincent Smith) Trilocanapāla, the last king of the Shāhiya dynasty, was defeated on the banks of the river Toṣi by Sultan Mahmud of Ghazni, and after his reign no account is available of the Hindu rule in Gandhāra, apart from the fact that his son Bhīmapāla regained his independence for five years.[5]

We may close this chapter by making one or two remarks on the trade relations of Gandhāra, and by giving some references for the further study of the celebrated school of art which takes its name from this country. The Jātakas testify to the existence of trade relations between the Kashmir-Gandhāra kingdom and the north-eastern kingdom of Videha (see, e.g. *Gandhāra Jātaka* and Fick, *The Social Organisation in N.E. India in Buddha's Time*, p. 272). Horse-dealers figure prominently amongst the Gandhāran traders, and we learn from the *Vāyupurāṇa* that the Gandhāran horses were considered the best of all (Chap. 99). We find references to the production of valuable blankets or woollen shawls (*kambala*) in the *Vessantara Jātaka* (Fausböll, *Jātaka*, Vol. VI, pp. 500-1), and also in the *Suttanipāta* Commentary (II, 487). In later times (9th and 10th centuries) it was in Gandhāra that the finest 'double-die' coins were struck.[6]

The story of Gandhāra art is a complete study in itself, and all we can do here is to give some references to authorities on the subject, for example, Vincent Smith's *History of Fine Art in India and Ceylon*; James Fergusson's *History of Indian and Eastern Architecture* (2nd Edition, London, 1910); A. Foucher, *L'Art gréco-bouddhique du Gandhāra*; Sir John Marshall, *A Guide to Taxila*; and contributions to A.S.I. (Annual Reports) by J. Ph. Vogel, D. B. Spooner, Sir John Marshall and A. Cunningham.

---

1 See Rapson, *Ancient India*, p. 133; Brown, *Coins of India*, pp. 23-4.
2 *Ibid.*, pp. 133 and 142.
3 V. A. Smith, *Early History of India*, 4th Ed., p. 328.
4 *Ibid.*, 4th Ed., p. 388.
5 R. D. Banerjee, *Prācīna Mudrā*, p. 198.
6 See Brown, *Coins of India*, p. 53.

# CHAPTER III

## THE KURUS

The Kurus form one of the most ancient and prominent of the Indo-Aryan Kṣatriya tribes. In one of the verses of a Rigvedic hymn (X, 33, 4) occurs the word, *Kuruśravaṇa*, which is interpreted by some scholars either as 'the glory of the Kurus', or as 'the hearer of the praises of the Kurus'; but is more generally taken to be the name of a particular king, a ruler of the Kuru tribe. In the hymn which follows this one, the charities of the prince Kuruśravaṇa are praised, and there can be no doubt that '*Kuruśravaṇa*' is here the name of a particular sovereign, especially as some of his ancestors are also mentioned (see *Ṛgveda*, X, 33, 1 and 4–9; Wilson, *Ṛgveda*, Vol. VI, pp. 89-90). The seer mourns the death of his generous donor, and, in the last four verses, it seems that he consoles Upamaśravas, the son of Kuruśravaṇa, and mentions Mitrātithi, grandfather of Upamaśravas. But the Bṛhaddevatā (supported by Kātyāyana's *Sarvānukramaṇī*) states that it was for the death of his grandfather Mitrātithi that Upamaśravas is being consoled in these verses.

In the same hymn, Kuruśravaṇa is also called Trāsadasyava or 'descendant of Trasadasyu'. Trasadasyu is well known in the Ṛgveda (IV, 38, 1; VII, 19, 3, etc.) as a king of the Pūrus. Trasadasyu's people, the Pūrus, were settled on the Sarasvatī (see *Vedic Index*, I, 327), a locality which accords well with the later union of Pūrus and Kurus. According to the *Vedic Index*, 'it is likely that the Tṛtsu-Bharatas who appear in the *Ṛgveda* as enemies of the Pūrus, later coalesced with them to form the Kuru people',[1] for there is evidence that the Bharatas, like the Pūrus, occupied the territory in which the Kurus were later found. Two of them are spoken of in a hymn of the *Ṛgveda* (III, 23) as having kindled fire on the Dṛsadvatī, the Āpayā and the Sarasvatī—that is to say, in the sacred places of the later Kurukṣetra.[2]

Professor Keith also urges this view of the incorporation of the Bharatas with the Kurus in his chapter contributed to the Cambridge History of India (p. 118, *Cam. Hist.*), while Prof. Rapson concurs with him, observing that the Bharatas who were settled in the

[1] *Vedic Index*, I, 167.

[2] For further evidence of the merging of the Bharatas in the Kurus, see *Vedic Index*, I, 167-8.

country of the Sarasvatī in Rigvedic times were later merged in the Kurus; and that their whole territory, the new together with the old, became famous in history under the name 'Kurukṣetra'—'the field of the Kurus'. This was the scene of the great war of the descendants of Bharata, and the centre from which Indo-Aryan culture spread, first throughout Hindusthan, and eventually throughout the whole sub-continent.[1].

Another king, whose glories as a generous donor are sung in a hymn of the *Ṛgveda* (VIII, 23), namely Pākasthāman, is given the designation Kaurayāṇa,—most probably a patronymic; while in the *Atharvaveda* (XX, 127, 8) a man called Kauravya is described as having enjoyed prosperity under the rule of King Parīkṣit. Evidently, therefore, the name Kuru was already applied in the early Vedic age to a prominent tribe of Indo-Aryan Kṣatriyas.

It is, however, in the Brāhmaṇa literature that the Kurus acquire the greatest prominence among the Kṣatriya tribes of ancient India. In the Brāhmaṇa literature, the Kurus are often connected with the Pañcālas and from the way in which the Kuru-Pañcālas are mentioned, there is no room for doubt that it was in the country inhabited by them that some of the most famous Brāhmaṇa works were composed. Thus the *Aitareya Brāhmaṇa* in its chapter on the *Mahābhiṣeka* of Indra states: 'Then in this firm middle established quarter the Sādhyas and the Āptyas, the gods, anointed him (i.e. Indra) . . . for kingship. Therefore in this firm middle established quarter, whatever kings there are of the Kuru-Pañcālas with the Vaśas and Uśīnaras, they are anointed for kingship' (*Aitareya Brāhmaṇa*, VIII, 14, Tr. Keith, *Ṛgveda Brāhmaṇas*, p. 331). From the way in which mention is made of the country of the Kuru-Pañcālas, it is evident that the author of the *Aitareya Brāhmaṇa* was a native of that region. The authors of the *Vedic Index*[2] are of the opinion that the great *Brāhmaṇas* were composed in the Kuru-Pañcāla country, though Weber[3] would suggest a different locality for the *Tāṇḍya Mahābrāhmaṇa* of the *Sāmaveda*, and the *Śatapatha Brāhmaṇa* of the White *Yajurveda*.

Eliot points out that at the time when the Brāhmaṇas and earlier Upaniṣads were composed (circa 800–600 B.C.), the principal political units were the kingdoms of the Pañcālas and Kurus in the region of Delhi.[4] The Kurus are comparatively seldom mentioned alone, their name usually being coupled with that of the Pañcālas; and the Kuru-Pañcālas are often expressly referred to as a united

[1] *Cambridge History of India*, I, 47.

[2] I, 165.

[3] *History of Indian Literature*, pp. 68 and 132.

[4] *Hinduism and Buddhism*, Vol. I, p. 20.

nation. Speech is said to have its particular home in the Kuru-Pañcāla land; and the mode of sacrifice of the Kuru-Pañcālas is proclaimed to be the best. The Kuru-Pañcāla Brahmins are famous in the Upaniṣads: for example, in the last kāṇḍa of the *Śatapatha Brāhmaṇa* we find mention of the Brahmins of the Kuru-Pañcāla country being invited and given huge largesses by Janaka, king of Videha (cf. *Bṛhadāraṇyaka Up.*, III, 1, 1, foll.).

The *Śatapatha Brāhmaṇa* (XII, 9, 3, 3) speaks of a Kauravya King Balhika Prātipīya (Kauravya and Kaurava being interchangeable variants); while Yāska's *Nirukta* [1] also asserts that Devāpi Ārṣṭiṣeṇa and Śāntanu were Kauravyas. The Kuru kings are mentioned by the name Koravya in the Pāli Buddhist literature, as we shall show below.

The *Chāndogya Upaniṣad*, which is the remnant of an ancient *Brāhmaṇa* work belonging to the *Sāmaveda*, contains an account of the destruction of crops in the Kuru country by locusts or by a hailstorm, and it further recounts the story of how a famished Ṛṣi (Uṣasti Cākrāyaṇa) of the Kuru land was forced to partake of food that was unclean, and how in spite of this temporary impurity under the stress of famine, the Ṛṣi was successful in winning for himself the highest functions at the subsequent sacrifice performed by the king at Ibhyagrāma (*Chāndogya Upaniṣad*, I, 10, 1–7; *Sacred Books of the East*, Vol. I, pp. 18-19).

We have seen that the *Aitareya Brāhmaṇa* speaks of the country of the Kuru-Pañcālas as belonging to the 'dhruvā madhyamā dik', i.e., to what is known in later literature as the Madhyadeśa or middle country. Prof. Rapson points out that the territories occupied by the Kurus extended to the East far beyond the limits of Kurukṣetra. The Kurus must have occupied the northern portion of the Doab, or the region between the Jumna and the Ganges, having as their neighbours on the east the North Pañcālas, and on the south, the South Pañcālas, who held the rest of the Doab as far as the land of the Vatsas, the corner where the two rivers meet at Prayāga (Allahabad).[2]

The great law-giver Manu speaks of the country of the Kurus and other allied peoples (Matsyas, Pañcālas and Śūrasenakas) as forming the sacred land of the Brahmarṣis (Brahmanical sages), ranking immediately after Brahmāvarta (*Manu*, II, 17–19). He indirectly praises the prowess of these peoples by saying that they should be placed in the van of any battle-array (*Manu*, VII, 193).

In the first verse of the *Bhagavadgītā*, the only book in India which is reverenced by people of all kinds of religious belief, the land

[1] II, 10.

[2] Rapson, *Ancient India*, p. 165.

of Kurus is called Dharmakṣetra, or the holy land. In other parts of the *Mahābhārata*, too, Kurukṣetra is mentioned as a land which was especially holy. Thus the *Vanaparvan* (Chap. 129, pp. 394-5) tells us that Kurukṣetra was the holy spot of the righteous Kurus. It was here that Nahuṣa's son, Yayāti, performed many religious ceremonies, that divine and royal sages performed the Sārasvata Yajña, and that Prajāpati performed his Yajña. In the Brāhmaṇa texts also, Kurukṣetra is regarded as a particularly sacred country, for within its boundaries flowed the sacred streams Dṛṣadvatī and Sarasvatī, as well as the Āpayā.[1]

The 'field of the Kurus', or the region of Delhi, was the scene of the war between the Kurus and Pāṇḍus, in which all the nations of India were ranged on one side or the other, according to the Epic in its present form. It has been the great battle-field of India ever since, as it forms a narrow strip of habitable country lying between the Himalayas and the Indian Desert through which every invading army from the Punjab must force its way. Because of this strategical importance, Delhi became the capital of India under the Mughal emperors who came into India by land from the N.W. (Rapson, *Ancient India*, p. 173).

Besides the Kurus of the Madhyadeśa, we find references to another Kuru people, viz. the Uttara-Kurus. The *Aitareya Brāhmaṇa* mentions the country of the Uttara-Kurus in its chapter on the *mahābhiṣeka* of Indra (*Ait. Br.*, VIII, 14; Tr. Keith's *Ṛgveda Brāhmaṇas*, pp. 330-1). The authors of the *Vedic Index* are of the opinion that the Uttara-Kurus were a historical people at the time when this passage of the *Aitareya Brāhmaṇa* was written. They observe: 'The Uttara-Kurus, who play a mythical part in the Epic and later literature, are still a historical people in the *Aitareya Brāhmaṇa*, where they are located beyond the Himalaya (*pareṇa Himavantaṃ*). In another passage, however, the country of the Uttara-Kurus is stated by Vāsiṣṭha Sātyahavya to be a land of the gods (*deva-kṣetra*), but Jānaṃtapi Atyarāti was anxious to conquer it, so that it is still not wholly mythical. It is reasonable to accept Zimmer's view that the northern Kurus were settled in Kaśmīr, especially as Kurukṣetra is the region where tribes advancing from Kaśmīr might naturally be found.[2]

In Buddhist literature, Uttara-Kuru is very often mentioned as a mythic region, but there are some passages which go to show that there was a faint memory of a country that once had a historical existence [see, e.g. the reference to 'Kurudīpa', *Dīpavaṃsa*, p. 16; and the statement in the *Sāsanavaṃsa* (p. 12) that the place of the

---

[1] *Vedic Index*, I, p. 169.

[2] *Ibid.*, I, p. 84.

inhabitants of Uttaradvīpa is called the kingdom of Kurus (*Kururaṭṭhaṃ*)].

The Southern Kurus are mentioned in the *Papañcasūdanī* (P.T.S. edition, p. 225), while the *Aṅguttara Nikāya* tells us that Kuru was one of the sixteen *mahājanapadas* or prominent countries of Jambudīpa (= India), having abundant food and wealth, and the 'seven kinds of gems'.[1] In Buddhist literature, as in the Brāhmaṇa literature, the Kurus are comparatively seldom mentioned alone, their name being usually coupled with that of the Pañcālas. We read in the *Papañcasūdanī* that there was no *vihāra* for the Buddha's habitation in the Kuru kingdom, but that there was a beautiful forest outside the town of Kammāsadhamma where he used to dwell. We are told further that the inhabitants of the Kuru kingdom enjoyed good health, and their mind was always ready to receive instruction in profound religious truths, because the climate was bracing at all seasons, and the food was good. The Buddha delivered some profound and learned discourses to the Kurus, e.g. the Mahānidāna and Mahāsatipaṭṭhāna Suttantas of the *Dīgha Nikāya*. (For fanciful stories of the Kurus' meditation on Satipaṭṭhāna, see further *Papañcasūdanī*, P.T.S., pp. 227–9.)

The Buddhist literature is full of stories in which the land of Kuru and its princes and people play a leading part. For instance, the Thera Raṭṭhapāla, who contributed some verses to the Theragāthā, was born in the town of Thullakoṭṭhika in the country of the Kurus, and we are told that he converted the King 'Koravya' to Buddhism.[2] The Dhammapada Commentary relates the story of Aggidatta, the chaplain of the king of Kosala (Mahākosala, predecessor of Pasenadi). After his retirement, Aggidatta dwelt on the borders of the Kuru country and Aṅga-Magadha, together with his 10,000 disciples; and the inhabitants of these countries used to supply the whole company with food and drink. Eventually Aggidatta and all his followers were converted by the Buddha.[3]

In the Therīgāthā commentary (p. 87) we read that a therī named Nanduttarā was reborn in a Brahmin family in the city of Kammāsadamma (or Kammāsadhamma) in the kingdom of the Kurus. She first became a Jain, but was later converted by Mahākaccāyana, accepted ordination from him, and attained arahantship. In the *Paramatthadīpanī* (pp. 201–4) we have an account of the miseries suffered after death by a certain Serinī, a heretical woman of the Kuru capital.

---

[1] *Aṅguttara Nikāya*, Vol. I, p. 213; Vol. IV, pp. 252, 256 and 260; *Dīgha Nikāya*, II, pp. 200, 201 and 203.

[2] *Psalms of the Brethren*, pp. 302–7; *Majjhima Nikāya*, II, pp. 65 *et seq.*

[3] See *Dhammapada Comm.*, Vol. III, pp. 241-2; 246-7.

Returning to the history of the tribe itself, we find that the authors of the *Vedic Index* consider that the Kurus represent a comparatively late wave of Aryan immigration into India. 'The geographical position of the Kuru-Pañcālas', they say, 'renders it probable that they were later immigrants into India than the Kosala-Videhas or the Kāśīs who must have been pushed into their more eastward territories by a new wave of Aryan settlers from the west'.[1]

In the *Papañcasūdanī*, there is a fanciful story of the origin of the Kurus. Mahāmandhātā, king of Jambudīpa, was a cakravartin, and therefore subject to no restrictions of place. He conquered Pubbavideha, Aparagoyāna and Uttara-Kuru, besides the Devalokas. When he was returning from Uttara-Kuru, a large number of the inhabitants of that country followed Mahāmandhātā to Jambudīpa, and the place where they settled became known as Kururaṭṭham.[2]

The ancient capital of the Kurus was Hastināpura which was situated on the Ganges in what is now the Meerut district of the United Provinces. Indraprastha, the modern Indrapat near Delhi, was the second capital. According to the Epic story, the blind king Dhṛtarāṣṭra continued to rule at the old capital Hastināpura on the Ganges, while he assigned to his nephews, the five Pāṇḍus, a district on the Jumna where they founded Indraprastha.[3] While the ancient capital of the Kurus sank into insignificance, the new city erected by the Pāṇḍavas has not only come down to our time, but has acquired a fresh lease of life as the seat of the central government of the British Indian Empire. Another city of the Kuru country, according to the Prākrit legend given in the commentary on the *Uttarādhyayana Sūtra*, was Ishukāra (Prākrit Usuyāra or Isuyāra), 'a wealthy and famous town, beautiful like heaven'.[4] We have already referred to the town of Kammāsadhamma, which must have been well known in the Buddha's time It is also called Kammāsadamma,—derived by popular etymology from Kammāsa (a prince) and *damma* (from *dam*, to tame), because Kammāsa was brought under control by the Bodhisattva when he was born as a son of King Jayaddisa of Pañcāla (*Papañcasūdanī*, pp. 226-7). The story of Kammāsa is narrated in full in the Jayaddisa Jātaka, in which we find that the Bodhisattva was born as the son of King Jayaddisa of Pañcāla. One of the King's other sons was carried away by a Yakkhinī (ogress) who brought him up, and taught him cannibalistic habits. After many attempts to capture him had failed, he was at last brought under control by the Bodhisattva. He was

---

[1] *Vedic Index*, I, pp. 168-9.
[2] *Papañcasūdanī*, pp. 225-6.
[3] Rapson, *Ancient India*, p. 173.
[4] *Jaina Sūtras*, II, p. 62n.

called Kammāsa ('spotted, blemished') because of a boil which appeared on his leg.[1] It is apparent that this story is simply a variation of the Purānic story of Kalmāṣapāda.

The Epic and Purānic tradition regarding the origin of the Kurus is as follows: Pūru,[2] the son of Yayāti by Vṛṣaparva's daughter Śarmiṣṭhā, and grandson of Nahuṣa, was fifth in descent from Pururavā, son of Ilā, daughter of Manu, the father of mankind (Mānava-vaṃśa); and the dynasty which sprang from this Pūru was celebrated as the Paurava dynasty. Tenth in descent from Pūru was Saṃvaraṇa. When his kingdom was conquered by the king of the Pañcālas, Saṃvaraṇa fled in fear, together with his wives, children and ministers, and took shelter in a forest on the banks of the Sindhu (Indus). He eventually regained his kingdom, with the help of his priest, the sage Vaśiṣṭha; and a son named Kuru was born to him, by Tapatī, daughter of Sūrya. The people were charmed by the manifold good qualities of Kuru, and anointed him king. After the name of this king, the plain became famous as Kurukṣetra or the field of Kuru.[3]

In the Epic period, the Kurus became the most powerful Kṣatriya tribe in northern India, after the downfall of the Magadha empire of Rājagṛha when Bhīmasena, who belonged to the younger branch of the Kauravas, killed the Samrāṭ (Emperor) Jarāsandha. Bhīmasena's grandson, Pratīpa, had three sons, Devāpi, Vāhlika and Śāntanu. The eldest son, Devāpi, was a leper, and for this reason King Pratīpa was prevented by his subjects and by the advice of wise men from placing him on the throne. Devāpi became an ascetic, while Vāhlika went to rule over his maternal uncle's land, and, after Pratīpa's death, granted permission to his brother Śāntanu to reign over the Kuru country.[4]

After Śāntanu came his sons Citrāṅgada and Vicitravīrya, both of whom died childless. However, in a semi-miraculous manner, two sons (Dhṛtarāṣṭra and Pāṇḍu) were born posthumously to Vicitravīrya's wives. Dhṛtarāṣṭra married Gāndhārī, daughter of Suvala, king of the Gandhāras, and had by her one hundred sons, known as the Kurus or Kauravas, of whom the eldest was Duryodhana who could work miracles by the power of mantras.[5]

[1] *Jātaka* (Fausböll), V, pp. 21 *et seq.*

[2] *Mahābhārata*, *Droṇaparvan*, Chap. 61, p. 1035.

[3] *Ādiparvan*, Vaṅgavāsī Ed., Chap. 75, pp. 86–8; Chap. 85, p. 96; Chap. 94, p. 104.

[4] *Udyogaparvan*, Chap. 149, p. 771.

[5] *Ibid.*, Chap. 61, p. 707 (Vaṅgavāsī Ed.); and *Śāntiparvan*, Chap. 4, p. 1378, for further details about Duryodhana. For detailed (largely legendary) genealogies of the descendants of Kuru, see *Viṣṇupurāṇa*, IV, Chap. 20; and *Bhāgavata Purāṇa*, Skandha 9, Chap. 22.

As Dhṛtarāṣṭra was blind from birth, Pāṇḍu, though younger, was placed on the throne left vacant by the death of Vicitravīrya. Matters grew complex when sons were born to both the brothers, and the difficulty was not lessened when Dhṛtarāṣṭra took over the government on the premature death of Pāṇḍu, had his five nephews brought up with his own sons, and finally appointed his eldest nephew, Yudhiṣṭhira, to be heir-apparent. Dhṛtarāṣṭra's own sons, consumed with jealousy, set various plots on foot against their cousins, and eventually the old king decided on a compromise, giving Hastināpura to his sons, and to his nephews a district where they built the city of Indraprastha. Here the Pāṇḍavas, in the words of Prof. Macdonell, 'ruled wisely and prospered greatly. Duryodhana's jealousy being aroused, he resolved to ruin his cousins, with the aid of his uncle Śakuni, a skilful gamester'.[1] Yudhiṣṭhira was thereupon challenged to a game of dice with Śakuni, a challenge which he could not refuse, as this was a matter of honour among Indian Kṣatriyas in those days. Owing to dishonest tricks on Śakuni's part, Yudhiṣṭhira was defeated, and lost everything, his kingdom, wealth, army, brothers, and finally Draupadī, the joint wife of the five Pāṇḍavas. In the end it was arranged that the Pāṇḍavas should go into banishment for twelve years, and to remain *incognito* for a thirteenth, after which they might return and regain their kingdom. They passed their period of banishment in the forest, and remained *incognito* for the thirteenth year at the court of King Virāṭa of the Matsyas.

The Matsya king and his people honoured Yudhiṣṭhira and his brothers, and were grateful to them for preventing the predatory excursions of the Trigarttas and Kurus against their cattle. The bond with the Matsyas was further cemented by the marriage of Virāṭa's daughter with Abhimanyu, the son of Arjuna. The Pāṇḍavas were further related through Draupadī with the powerful king of Pañcāla; and they had a firm friend in Kṛṣṇa, the hero of the Yādavas. It was felt, accordingly, that a successful attempt might be made to recover the dominions out of which they had been cheated. The King of Pañcāla suggested that they should resort to war, and kings of other neighbouring countries were invited to help the Pāṇḍavas. But before the war began the brothers made a last unsuccessful attempt to negotiate peace, sending Kṛṣṇa Vāsudeva as their emissary to the Kuru court.[2]

After the failure of negotiations, allies were invited from far and near; even the kings of the south contributed their quota, for by that

[1] *Sanskrit Literature*, p. 292.

[2] *Mbh., Udyogaparvan*, Vaṅgavāsī Ed., Chap. 127.

time the Kṣatriyas had spread over the whole of India, and, according to the Epic account, all of them were ranged on one side or the other. Dhṛṣṭadyumna was made generalissimo of the Pāṇḍava forces, Arjuna being the greatest hero on their side, with Kṛṣṇa Vāsudeva as his chief, so to speak. Being prevented by a vow from taking up arms in the battle, Kṛṣṇa took upon himself the duty of driving his friend's chariot.

The Indian army in those days, as in later times, consisted of four divisions, viz. foot-soldiers, elephants, chariots, and horses. Arriving at Kurukṣetra, the Pāṇḍavas encamped with their troops on the western part of the field, facing the numerically much stronger force of Duryodhana and his allies (*Mbh., Udyogaparvan*, Chap. 198; Chap. 151, Chap. 154). Of the 18 *akṣauhiṇīs* or regiments that assembled on the battle-field, 11 were on Duryodhana's side, and 7 on that of his cousins. In individual heroes also Duryodhana's army was apparently much stronger. But the Kurus, in spite of their preponderant strength, felt misgivings on the eve of the battle, while the Pāṇḍavas were buoyed up with the righteousness of their cause. The commander of Duryodhana's army was the old warrior Bhīṣma, and the allies of the Kurus included the peoples of Kośala, Videha, Aṅga, Vaṅga, Gandhāra, Sindhu, and many other States. Duryodhana caused his camps to be made to look like a second Hastināpura, and into these camps he made soldiers with their horses enter in groups of a hundred each, arranging names and emblems for all of them so that they might be recognised in the battle.

When the two powers were thus ready to fight, the Kurus and the Pāṇḍavas were bound to follow the traditional rules of a fair fight among the Kṣatriyas of India. Only men equally situated or matched could fairly fight one another. Combatants armed with the same kind of weapons should be ranged against one another. Those that left the battle-field should never be killed, a fleeing enemy was not to be pursued, and one devoid of arms should never be struck. A chariot-warrior should fight only with another chariot-warrior, and, similarly, with horse and foot-soldiers, and those riding on elephants. One engaged in a personal combat with another, one seeking refuge, one retreating, one whose weapon was broken, and one clad in armour should never be struck; neither should non-combatants on the field of battle, such as charioteers, attendants engaged in carrying weapons, players on drums and blowers of conches, be smitten.[1]

[1] *Mbh., Bhīṣmaparvan*, Chap. I.

This was the tacit understanding between the two armies, and the rules were generally not violated except under very special circumstances.

The Kuru army with Bhīṣma at its head advanced first, then the Pāṇḍava army led by Bhīmasena. The soldiers of both sides rushed upon one another with loud yells and a simultaneous blowing of conches. The fight raged furiously for ten days, at the end of which Bhīṣma fell, and both forces were withdrawn for a lull.

On Bhīṣma's death, Droṇa was made commander of the Kaurava troops, and the fight raged for a further eight days, until finally Abhimanyu, Droṇa, Karṇa, and Śalya were all slain, and a great disorder prevailed, especially in the Kuru army, now consisting only of a few scattered soldiers. Sahadeva, one of the Pāṇḍu princes, killed the gamester Śakuni, and Duryodhana himself was killed by Bhīmasena after making a last desperate rush at the enemy. With Duryodhana's death, the victory in the Kurukṣetra war fell to the Pāṇḍavas; but only a handful of their followers came out of the fray alive.

With the death of the hundred sons of Dhṛtarāṣṭra, the Kuru line through him became extinct, and the Pāṇḍavas now became lords of the Kuru kingdom, Yudhiṣṭhira being acclaimed king. The Pāṇḍus were reconciled to the aged Dhṛtarāṣṭra who retired to the forest after remaining at Hastināpura for fifteen years, and he and his queens finally perished in a forest conflagration. Yudhiṣṭhira himself did not reign long. When he heard of Kṛṣṇa's accidental death, and of the destruction of the Vṛṣṇis, he determined to leave the world, and he and his brothers retired to the forest, leaving the young prince Parīkṣit,[1] grandson of Arjuna, to rule over Hastināpura.

Parīkṣit was learned in the science of the duties of kings, and is credited with having possessed all noble qualities. He is described as a highly intelligent ruler, and a great hero, who wielded a powerful bow, and never missed his aim. One day he was lost in the forest, having been led astray by a deer whom he had struck but failed to kill. While roaming about, he met a sage and asked him whether he had seen a deer running that way. The sage was observing a vow of silence, and did not reply. Angered at this, the king took up a dead snake with the end of his bow, placed it around the sage's neck, and went away. The son of the sage, hearing of this, cursed the king, saying that within a week he would be reduced to ashes by the bite of Takṣaka, king of the snakes. Hearing of the curse, the

[1] So called because he was begotten at the time of the decrease (parikṣīṇa) of the Kuru race.

sage was sorry, and warned the king; but in spite of elaborate precautions, the curse was fulfilled, and Parīkṣit died of snake-bite.

Parīkṣit's son, Janamejaya, now ascended the throne, and resolved to avenge his father's death by holding a snake sacrifice. Ṛsis by the force of their *mantras* caused the snakes in their thousands to fall into the sacrificial fire. However, Takṣaka's nephew, Āstīka, son of a snake princess and the ṛsi Jaratkāru, won the king's favour, caused him to suspend the sacrifice, and saved the snakes from total destruction.

Here the kernel of the Epic account ends. It will be readily seen that it is a mixture of history and legend; but the historicity of the battle itself, and of the Kuru kings who ruled shortly afterwards, need not be doubted.

Turning once more to the Buddhist literature, we find numerous stories of kings of the Kuru land. For instance the Bodhisattva is described in the Dhammapada commentary as having once been born to the chief queen of the Kuru king (Dhanañjaya, according to the *Kurudhamma Jātaka*, Fausböll, Vol. II, pp. 366 foll.), in the capital city, Indapatta (Indraprastha). He went to Taxila to complete his education, and was then appointed a viceroy by his father. When he came to the throne, he, together with his family and his chief officials, used to obey the 'Kuru-dhamma'. This Kuru-dhamma consisted in the observance of the five 'sīlas' or rules of moral conduct, and it possessed the mystic virtue of bringing prosperity to the country. At this time the king of Kaliṅga was troubled by a dearth of rain in his kingdom. The Bodhisattva, king of the Kurus, had a royal elephant named Añjanavasabha, which was brought to the kingdom of Kaliṅga in the belief that its mere presence would bring rain. This device not having the expected result, it was concluded that rain did not fall in Kaliṅga because the Kuru-dhamma was not observed there; and Brahmins were sent to the kingdom of Kuru to make themselves acquainted with the Kuru-dhamma, and write it out for the king of Kaliṅga. Thereupon, King Kāliṅga observed the Kurudhamma faithfully, and forthwith the longed-for rain poured down in showers in his kingdom, and his crops were saved.[1] The *Kurudhamma Jātaka*, cited above, also narrates this story, and there are further references to King 'Dhanañjaya Koravya' in other *Jātakas* (Cowell, Vol. IV, pp. 227–231; Vol. V, pp. 31–7; and *ibid.*, p. 246). In the latter passage we are told that the kingdom of Kuru extended over three hundred leagues. The king's chief minister is called Sucīrata in one story,[2]

[1] *Dhammapada Commentary*, IV, pp. 88-9.
[2] *Jātaka* (Fausböll), V, p. 57.

and Vidhūra in another.[1] In each case the king is said to have been very righteous and charitable. In yet another Jātaka version of the story, we are told, as usual, that there reigned in the city of Indapattana, in the kingdom of the Kurus, a king named Dhanañjaya, of the race of Yudhiṭṭhila (Yudhiṣṭhira). The Bodhisattva was born in the house of his family priest (not in the king's own family in this case). After learning all the arts at Taxila, he returned to Indapattana and after his father's death he became family priest and adviser to the king. He was called Vidhūrapaṇḍita.[2]

The story of King Dhanañjaya-korabba and his wise minister appears to have been very popular in Jātaka times, for its events find repeated mention in the tales. The Jātaka contains an account of further incidents concerning Dhanañjaya and Vidhūra, notably the defeat of Dhanañjaya at dice, and the meditation of Vidhūrapaṇḍita in a friendly rivalry between the king and Sakka (Indra).[3]

Though the Buddha principally confined his ministering activity to N.E. India, the Buddhist Pali texts show that he travelled widely over regions in Northern India; and the Kuru country too appears to have been favoured by his discourses (see, e.g. *Aṅguttara Nikāya*, Vol. V, pp. 29–32; *Saṃyutta Nikāya*, Vol. II, pp. 92-3; *Ibid.*, pp. 107–9; *Majjhima Nikāya*, Vol. I, pp. 55 *et seq.*; *Ibid.*, pp. 501 *et seq.*; Vol. II, pp. 261 *et seq.*; pp. 54 *et seq.*; Dhammapada Commentary, Vol. I, pp. 199–203 and *cf. Ibid.*, Vol. III, pp. 193 *et seq.*; *Dīgha Nikāya*, Vol. II, pp. 55 *et seq.*; *Ibid.*, pp. 290 *et seq.*). It is in nearly every case that the town of Kammāsadhamma is mentioned as the scene of the Buddha's discourses.

Some time before the fourth century B.C., the monarchical constitution of the Kurus gave place to a republic, for we are told by Kauṭilya[4] that the Kurus were '*rāja-śabda-upajīvinaḥ*', or 'enjoying the status of *rājās*',—i.e. all citizens had equal rank and rights.

The Kurus appear to have played some part in Indian politics as late as the ninth century A.D., for when Dharmapāla installed Cakrāyudha on the throne of Kanauj, he did so with the consent of the neighbouring powers, amongst whom the Kurus are specifically mentioned.[5]

[1] *Jātaka* (Fausböll), IV, p. 361.

[2] *Ibid.*, VI, pp. 255 foll.

[3] *Ibid.*, Vol. VI, pp. 255 foll.

[4] See Shāma Shāstrī's translation of the *Arthaśāstra*, p. 455. Shāma Shāstrī renders '*rāja-śabda-upajīvinaḥ*' by 'lived by the title of a rājā', but this is too vague to convey the meaning. For a fuller discussion on the subject, see Chapter on the Licchavis.

[5] Smith, *Early History of India*, 4th Ed., p. 413.

# CHAPTER IV

## THE PAÑCĀLAS

The Pañcālas, like the Kurus, are most intimately connected with the Vedic civilization of the Brāhmaṇa period. The *Śatapatha Brāhmaṇa* [1] tells us that they were called Krivis in ancient times. In an enumeration of the ancient monarchs who had performed the Aśvamedha sacrifice, a king Kraivya Pañcāla is mentioned, and it is definitely stated that Krivi was the ancient name of the Pañcāla tribe. Krivi appears as a tribal name in the *Ṛgveda*.[2] Zimmer is of the opinion that the Krivis resided in the region near the Sindhu and the Asiknī in the Punjab, and the authors of the *Vedic Index* express the same view.[3] But the only piece of evidence in favour of this hypothesis is that Krivi is mentioned in a verse of a Ṛgvedic hymn, in which the names of those rivers occur in a subsequent verse (VIII, 20, 25). The *Ṛgveda* does not clearly testify to any connection between the rivers and the people.

Zimmer [4] hazards another (more far-fetched) conjecture, viz. that the Pañcālas with the Kurus made up the Vaikarṇa people; and the *Vedic Index* [5] lends its support to this theory. But the only evidence in support of this view is that the word Vaikarṇa appears in the dual in a verse of the *Ṛgveda*,[6] and the Kuru-Pañcālas appear combined as a dual people in the Brāhmaṇa literature. We are hardly justified in assuming any connection between these two facts, and moreover, it is doubtful whether 'Vaikarṇayoḥ' in the *Ṛgveda* passage referred to, is a tribal name at all. Wilson following Sāyaṇa translates 'Vaikarṇayoḥ' by 'on the two banks (of the Paruṣṇī)'.[7] This meaning agrees very well with the context, as the subject-matter of the hymn is the crossing of the Paruṣṇī by King Sudās.

In the later Vedic Saṃhitās and the Brāhmaṇa literature, the Pañcālas are frequently referred to, and often combined with the Kurus. The *Kāṭhaka Saṃhitā* (XXX, 2) speaks of the Pañcālas as being the Vaṃśa or people of Keśin Dālbhya, and says that, as a result of certain rites performed by him, they were divided into

---

[1] XIII, 5, 4, 7.

[2] *Yābhirdaśasyathā Kriviṃ, Ṛgveda*, VIII, 20, 24; *Yābhiḥ Kriviṃ vāvṛdhuḥ, Ṛgveda*, VIII, 22, 12.

[3] *Vedic Index*, I, 198.

[4] *Altindisches Leben*, 103.

[5] *Vedic Index*, I, 198.

[6] *Vaikarṇayoḥ, Ṛgveda*, VII, 18, 11.

[7] Wilson, *Ṛgveda*, Vol. IV, p. 59.

three parts. The same Saṃhitā (X, 6) refers to the celebration of the Naimiśīya sacrifice in the country of the Kuru-Pañcālas. Here a discussion between Vaka-Dālbhya and Dhṛtarāṣṭra Vaicitravīrya is narrated, but there is nothing to justify Weber's conjecture of a quarrel between the Pañcālas and the Kurus. In the *Aitareya Brāhmaṇa*, the Pañcālas are mentioned along with the Kurus as one of the peoples in the *Madhyamā dik* or midland. Similarly, the Kuru-Pañcālas are mentioned in the Kāṇva recension of the *Vājasaneyi Saṃhitā* (XI, 3, 3,). In the *Jaiminīya Upaniṣad Brāhmaṇa*, the Kuru-Pañcālas are mentioned many times, and in the *Gopatha Brāhmaṇa* (I, 2, 9), they are referred to as a dual group beside other similar groups, such as the Aṅga-Magadhas, Kāśī-Kośalas, Śālva-Matsyas, etc. The *Śatapatha Brāhmaṇa* assures us that 'speech sounds higher here among the Kuru-Pañcālas',[1] and also informs us that the kings of the Kuru-Pañcālas performed the *rājasūya* or royal sacrifice. The *Taittirīya Brāhmaṇa* (I, 8, 4, 1, 2) says that the kings of the Kuru-Pañcālas marched forth on raids in the dewy season and returned in the hot season.[2] The *Kauṣītakī Upaniṣad* (IV, 1) also speaks of the Kuru-Pañcālas, and in the *Bṛhadāraṇyaka Upaniṣad* they are repeatedly mentioned,—as, for instance, when we read[3] that the Brāhmaṇas of the Kurus and the Pañcālas flocked to the court of Janaka, king of Videha. A Vedic teacher, Pañcāla-Caṇḍa by name, is mentioned in the *Aitareya* and the *Sāṅkhāyana Āraṇyakas*,[4] and most probably this sage belonged to the Pañcāla country, as his name suggests.

The *Bṛhadāraṇyaka* (VI, 1, 1) and *Chāndogya Upaniṣad* (V, 3, 1) tell how Śvetaketu Āruṇeya went to the assembly (*pariṣad*) of the Pañcālas where the Kṣatriya, Pravāhaṇa Jaivali, put to him several questions which neither Śvetaketu nor his father was able to answer. Śvetaketu's father, though a Brāhmaṇa, was glad to learn the answers to these questions from Pravāhaṇa Jaivali, although the latter was a Rājanya or Kṣatriya.[5]

Several of the Pañcāla kings are mentioned in the Vedic literature. For instance, Durmukha was a great and powerful king of the Pañcālas, who, according to the *Aitareya Brāhmaṇa* (VIII, 23) made extensive conquests in every direction. Another powerful Pañcāla king who performed the horse sacrifice was Śona Sātrāsāha, about whom several gāthās are quoted in the *Śatapatha Brāhmaṇa*.[6]

The name Pañcāla has given rise to much speculation, it being supposed that the first part, Pañca ('five'), has something to do with

1 *S.B.E.*, Vol. XXVI, p. 50.
2 *Vedic Index*, I, 165.
3 *Bṛh. Up.*, III, 1, 1.
4 *Vedic Index*, I, p. 469.
5 See also *Chāndogya Up.*, I, 8, 1-2, for another mention of Pravāhaṇa Jaivali.
6 *S.B.E.*, Vol. XLIV, p. 400.

five tribes that were merged together into a united nation. The evidence in favour of this hypothesis is not very clear. It has been suggested that the five peoples are the five tribes of the *Ṛgveda*, but, as the *Vedic Index* (I, 469) points out, the suggestion is not very probable. The problem of the origin of the name Pañcāla and its probable connection with Pañca, five, struck the authors of the Purāṇas. Many of them traced the name to five princes, whose names vary slightly in different works. In the *Bhāgavatapurāṇa*, 9th Skandha, Chap. 21, we learn that King Bharmāśva, born in the family of Duṣmanta, had five sons, Mudgala, Yavīnara, Vṛhadviśa, Kāmpilya, and Sañjaya. As these five sons were capable of guarding the five countries, they were named Pañcāla (alam = sufficient for, capable of). Then in the *Viṣṇupurāṇa*, Chap. 19, Aṅka 4, we are told that Haryaśva, born in the family of Kuru, had five sons, Mudgala, Sriñjaya, Vṛhadisu, Pravīra and Kāmpīlya. He was under the impression that his five sons were competent to protect five provinces, and they became famous as Pañcālas. The *Vāyupurāṇa* (Chap. 99) tells us that Ṛkṣa, born in the family of Dvimīḍha, had five sons, Mudgala, Sriñjaya, Vṛhadisu, Yavīyāna and Kāmpīlya. The provinces of these five afterwards became famous as Pañcāla. Similarly, in the *Agnipurāṇa* (Chap. 278) we read that Vāhyāśva, born in the family of Kuru,[1] had five sons, Mukula, Sriñjaya, Vṛhadiṣu, Yavīnara and Krimila, who were known as Pañcālas. In the *Saṃhitopaniṣad Brāhmaṇa*, there is a reference to the Prācya Pañcālas.[2]

In the Epic, the Pañcāla country is divided into a northern and a southern part, so that evidently the Pañcālas had spread and added to their country by conquest since the Vedic period. There is a Jātaka story about the foundation of Uttara-Pañcāla, which seems to show that a Cedi prince went to the north and formed the Uttara-Pañcāla kingdom with colonists from the Pañcāla and Cedi countries. The *Cetiya Jātaka* tells us that the king of Ceti (Cedi) had five sons. Kapila, the family priest, said to the fourth prince: 'You leave by the north gate and go straight on till you see a wheel-frame all made of jewels: that will be a sign that you are to lay out a city there and dwell in it, and it shall be called Uttara-Pañcāla'.[3]

The *Mahābhārata* gives a different story of the division of the Pañcāla country. There, in the *Ādiparvan*, we read that the Brahmin Droṇa and Prince Drupada had been friends in their boyhood. But their friendship changed to enmity in their manhood when Drupada, on being raised to the throne, treated the poor

[1] Pargiter, *The North Pañchāla Dynasty*, *J.R.A.S.*, 1918, pp. 229 foll.
[2] *Vedic Index*, I, p. 469.
[3] *Jātaka* (Fausböll), III, pp. 460-1.

Brahmin's son with contempt. Droṇa, bent upon taking revenge, taught the science of war to the youths of the rival clan of the Kurus and, when their education was completed, he one day called all his pupils together and bade them seize Drupada, King of Pañcāla, in battle, and bring him captive. That, said Droṇa, would be the most acceptable teacher's fee (*dakṣiṇā*) for him. A great battle ensued, in which the Pañcālas were defeated and their capital attacked. Drupada was seized and offered to Droṇa by his disciples. Droṇa asked Drupada whether he would desire to revive old friendship, and told him that he would grant him half his kingdom as a boon. Drupada accepted the offer. Droṇa then took the northern half of the kingdom which came to be known as Uttara-Pañcāla: while Drupada ruled over the other half, known as Southern Pañcāla. That is to say, the country extending from the river Bhāgīrathī to the river Carmanvatī in the south, with its capital at Kāmpilya, fell to Drupada's share, and the northern half with its capital at Ahicchatra was taken over by Droṇa.[1]

The plain of the Kurus, the (country of the) Matsyas, Pañcālas and Śūrasenakas—these, according to Manu, formed the land of the Brahmarṣis, ranking immediately after Brahmāvarta.[2]

One of the earliest cities of Pañcāla was Parivakrā or Paricakrā, where King Kraivya Pañcāla performed his horse sacrifice.[3] Another city, Kāmpīla, appears to have been mentioned in the *Yajurveda Saṃhitā*, where 'the epithet Kāmpīla-vāsinī is applied to a woman, perhaps the *mahiṣī* or chief wife of the king, whose duty it was to sleep beside the slaughtered animal of the horse sacrifice (Aśvamedha). The exact interpretation of the passage is very uncertain, but both Weber and Zimmer agree in regarding Kāmpīla as the name of the town known as Kāmpīlya in the later literature, and the capital of Pañcāla in Madhyadeśa'.[4] The *Viṣṇupurāṇa* (Chap. II) and the *Bhāgavatapurāṇa* (Chap. 22) say that Kāmpīlya, son of King Haryaśva, was celebrated as Pañcāla. Among the hundred sons of Nīpa of the Ajamīḍa dynasty, Samara is mentioned as the king of Kāmpīlya.[5] We have seen that Kāmpīlya became the capital of King Drupada when he was invested with the sovereignty of the

---

[1] *Mbh.*, *Ādiparvan*, Chap. 140. Rapson (*Ancient India*, p. 167) says: 'In history, they (i.e. the Pañcālas) are sometimes divided into two kingdoms—South Pañchāla, the country between the Jumna and Ganges to the east and south-east of the Kurus and Sūrasenas, and North Pañchāla, districts of the United Provinces lying east of the Ganges and north-west of the Province of Oudh . . . ' Cunningham (*Ancient Geography*, p. 360) says: 'The great kingdom of Pañcāla extended from the Himalaya mountains to the Chambal river'.

[2] *Manusaṃhitā*, II, 19.

[3] *Vide ante.*

[4] *Vedic Index*, Vol. I, 149.

[5] *Viṣṇupurāṇa*, IV, 19.

southern Pañcāla country. In the *Ādikāṇḍa* of the *Rāmāyaṇa* (Sarga 33) we are told that King Brahmadatta used to live in the city of Kāmpīlya. Cunningham identifies Kāmpīlya with Kampil, on the old Ganges between Budaon and Farokhabad.[1] According to N. L. Dey,[2] it was situated at a distance of 28 miles north-east of Fatgarh in the Farokhabad district. It was the scene of the *svayamvara* of Drupada's daughter, Kṛṣṇā or Draupadī, who became the wife of the five sons of Pāṇḍu. Drupada's palace is pointed out as the most easterly of the isolated mounds on the bank of the Bur-Gaṅgā.[3]

Ahicchatra, where Droṇa established his capital, as we have seen, was another notable town of the Pañcālas. When the Kuru army was marshalled on the field, it is stated that their rear extended as far as the city of Ahicchatra[4]; so that northern Pañcāla was contiguous with the Kuru land, and not very far from the Kurukṣetra battle-field. According to Cunningham, the history of Ahicchatra goes back to 1430 B.C. The name is written Ahikṣetra, as well as Ahi-cchatra, but the local legend of the Ādi-Rājā and the Nāga suggests that Ahi-cchatra is the correct form, for Ahicchatra means 'Serpent Umbrella'. This grand old fort is said to have been built by Rājā Ādi, an Ahir, whose future elevation to sovereignty was foretold by Droṇa, when he found him sleeping under the guardianship of a serpent with expanded hood. The fort is also called Ādikot, but the more common name is Ahicchatra.[5] The form of the name in Ptolemy by a slight alteration becomes Adisadra, which has been satisfactorily identified with Ahicchatra.[6] According to V. A. Smith, Ahicchatra City is the modern Rāmnagar in the Bareilly district. It was still a considerable town when visited by Hsüan Tsang in the seventh century.[7] The name of the city, it appears, was extended to the whole of the country of Uttara-Pañcāla, for we find the Chinese pilgrim giving a description of the 'country' of Ahicchatra. He observes that it was about 3,000 li in circuit and the capital about 17 or 18 li. It was naturally strong, being flanked by mountain crags. It produced wheat, and there were many woods and fountains. The climate was agreeable and the people sincere and truthful. They loved religion, and applied themselves to learn-

[1] Cunningham, *Ancient Geography*, p. 360; *Uvāsagadasāo*, Vol. II, p. 106.
[2] *Geographical Dictionary*, p. 33.
[3] N. L. Dey, *op. cit.*, p. 33. See also *Mahābhārata, Ādiparvan*, Chap. 94, pp. 181-2.
[4] *Mahābhārata*, V, Chap. 19.
[5] Cunningham, *Ancient Geography*, p. 360.
[6] McCrindle, *Ancient India as described by Ptolemy*, p. 133.
[7] Smith, *Early History of India*, 4th Ed., pp. 391-392.

ing. There were about 10 *saṅghārāmas* and some 1,000 priests who studied the Hīnayāna; and also some 9 deva temples with 300 sectaries. They sacrificed to Īśvara and belonged to the company of 'ashes-sprinklers' (Pāśupatas). Outside the chief town was a Nāga tank by the side of which was a stūpa built by King Aśoka. It was here that the Tathāgata (Buddha) preached the law for the sake of a Nāga-rāja for seven days. By the side of it were four little stūpas.[1]

In modern times, Ahicchatra was first visited by Capt. Hodgson, who describes it as the ruins of an ancient fortress several miles in circumference, which appears to have had 34 bastions, and is known in the neighbourhood by the name of the Pāṇḍu's fort.[2]

In the kingdom of Pañcāla there also existed the city of Kānyakubja.[3] R. D. Banerjee, on the authority of a copper plate discovered at Khalimpura, points out that the kings of the Bhojas, Matsyas, Kurus, Yadus and Yavanas were forced to acknowledge Cakrāyudha as the king of Kānyakubja.[4]

Many are the stories told about the Pañcālas and their dealings with the Kurus. In the *Ādiparvan*[5] we read that there was a king named Saṃbaraṇa, father of Kuru, of the Puru dynasty, who was the ruler of the world. At one time his kingdom was much afflicted, his subjects died, and disorder prevailed everywhere. The kingdom was afterwards conquered by the King of Pañcāla, and Sambaraṇa fled with his wife and children to a forest on the banks of the river Sindhu.

In connection with the expedition resulting in the victory of Bhīmasena, we note that Bhīmasena went to the east, attacked the Pañcāla country and brought it under his sway.[6] At the outset of his expedition, Karṇa also attacked Pañcāla, defeated Drupada, and exacted tribute from him and his subordinate kings.[7]

During the Kurukṣetra war, Drupada, king of the Pañcālas, helped the Pāṇḍavas with his son, Dhṛṣṭadyumna, and an *akṣauhiṇī* of troops[8]; and Dhṛṣṭadyumna was made the commander-in-chief of the entire Pāṇḍava force. Various kinds of horses are described as having been used by the famous heroes of Pañcāla during the war.[9] In the *Udyogaparvan* we read that Yudhāmanyu and

[1] Beal, *Buddhist Records of the Western World*, Vol. I, pp. 200-201.

[2] McCrindle, *Ancient India as described by Ptolemy*, p. 134.

[3] *Epigraphia Indica*, Vol. IV, p. 246.

[4] *Vāṅgālār Itihāsa*, Pt. I, pp. 167-8.

[5] Chap. 94, p. 104.

[6] *Sabhāparvan*, Chap. 29, p. 241.

[7] *Mahābhārata*, Vaṅgavāsī Edn., *Vanaparvan*, Chap. 253, p. 513.

[8] *Udyogaparvan*, Chaps. 156-7, pp. 777-8.

[9] See *Droṇaparvan*, Chap. 22, pp. 1012-13.

Uttamañjā, two other princes of Pañcāla, went to the battle-field.[1] They were killed by Dhṛtarāṣṭra's army. Mitravarmā and Kṣatradharmā, the Pañcāla heroes, were killed by Droṇa; and Kṣatradeva, son of Śikhaṇḍī, was killed by Lakṣmaṇa, son of Duryodhana.[2]

Pañcāla continued to be one of the great and powerful countries of Northern India, down to the time when the Buddha lived. The *Aṅguttara Nikāya* mentions it as one of the sixteen *mahājanapadas* of 'Jambudīpa', having an abundance of the seven kinds of gems, etc.[3] Pañcāla had a large army consisting of foot-soldiers, men skilful in fight and in the use of steel weapons.[4]

We read in the *Kumbhakāra Jātaka*[5] that in the kingdom of Uttara-Pañcāla, in the city of Kampilla, there was a king named Dummukha, who became a Pacceka-buddha. We have seen before that Durmukha was the name of one of the powerful Pañcāla sovereigns in the Vedic period. A Pañcāla monarch of the same name is also mentioned in the Jaina works.

In the *Gaṇḍatindu Jātaka* we read that during the reign of Pañcāla, king of Kampilla, the people were so much oppressed by taxation that they took their wives and families and wandered in the forest like wild beasts. By day they were plundered by the king's men and by night by robbers.[6]

The *Saṃyutta Nikāya* narrates that once while the Buddha was staying at Vaiśālī, Visākha of the Pañcālas was in the meeting hall where he distinguished himself by his pious discourse.[7] Visākha was the son of the daughter of the king of the Pañcālas, and afterwards became known as the Pañcālī's son. After the death of his father, he succeeded to his title, but when the Buddha came to his neighbourhood, he went to hear him, believed, and left the world.[8]

Pañcāla and its princes also figure in the Jaina literature. It is stated in the *Uttarādhyayana Sūtra* that the king of the Pañcālas did no fearful actions.[9] The Jain writers also refer to Brahmadatta, king of the Pañcālas,[10] and to Dvimukha of Pañcāla, who was a Pratyekabuddha.[11]

[1] *Udyogaparvan*, Chap. 198, pp. 807-8. See also *Bhīṣmaparvan*, Chap. 19, p. 830.
[2] *Karṇaparvan*, Chap. 6, p. 1169.
[3] Vol. I (P.T.S.), 213; IV, 252, 256, 260.
[4] *Jātaka* (Fausböll), VI, p. 396.
[5] *Ibid.*, III, p. 379.
[6] *Ibid.*, Vol. V, p. 99.
[7] *The Book of the Kindred Sayings*, II, p. 190.
[8] *Psalms of the Brethren*, pp. 152-3; *vide* also *Thera-therīgāthā*, P.T.S., p. 27.
[9] *S.B.E.*, Vol. XLV, *Jaina Sūtras*, Pt. II, p. 60.
[10] *Ibid.*, p. 61.
[11] *Ibid.*, p. 87.

In the post-Aśokan period Pañcāla was invaded by the Greeks, as we infer from the *Gārgī Saṃhitā*, which is dated about the second or third century A.D.[1]

In the sixth and fifth centuries B.C., the Pañcālas were a monarchical clan, but became a saṅgha (probably an oligarchy) in the fourth century, when Kauṭilya lived. In Kauṭilya's *Arthaśāstra* we read that the corporation of Pañcāla 'lived by the title of rājā'.[2] The change was very probably brought about in the following way. Members of the royal family were often given a share in the administration of a country, and in proportion as this share became less and less formal, the state organization would lose the form of absolute monarchy and approach that of an oligarchy.[3]

Sir Charles Eliot notes that the kingdom of Pañcāla passed through troublous times after the death of Harṣavardhana, but from about 840-910 A.D. under Bhoja and his son, it became the principal power in Northern India, extending from Bihar to Sind. In the twelfth century, it again became important under the Gaharwar dynasty.[4]

In the district of Bareilly in the United Provinces, many old copper coins have been discovered amongst the ruins of ancient Ahicchatra. The word 'mitra'[5] occurs at the end of the names of the kings engraved on the coins. In many places of the United Provinces, coins of this kind are discovered every year. There are three symbols above the names of the kings. Carlyle of the Archaeological Dept. explains the symbols as Bodhi tree, Śivaliṅgaṃ surrounded by snakes, and stūpa covered by fungus. Such coins are found in large numbers at Ahicchatra, so Cunningham calls them Pañcāla-mudrā. They generally weigh 250 grs., the smaller ones weighing not less than 16 grs.[6] According to the *Cambridge History*,[7] several Pañcāla coins have on the obverse Agni, with head of flames, standing between posts on railing, on the reverse, in incuse, Agimitasa; above, three symbols. Whether Agnimitra whose coins are found in North Pañcāla and who was, therefore, presumably king of Ahicchatra, can be identified with the Śuṅga king of that name, is uncertain.[8]

---

1 See Max Müller, *India, What can it teach us?* 1883, p. 298.

2 '*Rājaśabdopajīvinaḥ*'—*Arthaśāstra*, Shāma Śāstrī's Translation, p. 455.

3 *Carmichael Lectures*, 1918, p. 165.

4 *Hinduism and Buddhism*, Vol. I, p. 27.

5 For a detailed discussion, see B. C. Law, *Pañchālas and their Capital Ahichchhatra*, *M.A.S.I.*, No. 67, pp. 12 foll.

6 R. D. Banerjee, *Prācīna Mudrā*, pp. 106-7.

7 *Cambridge History of India*, Vol. I, p. 538.

8 *Ibid.*, p. 520.

The method of striking the early coins was peculiar, in that the die was impressed on the metal when hot, so that a deep square incuse, which coins the device, appears on the coin. A similar incuse appears on the later double-die coins of Pañcāla, Kauśāmbī, and on some coins of Mathurā. This method of striking may have been introduced from Persia, and was perhaps a derivative from the art of seal-engraving.[1] Brown says that there is little foreign influence traceable in the die-struck coins, all closely connected in point of style, which issued during the first and second centuries B.C. from Pañcāla, Ayodhyā, Kauśāmbī and Mathurā. A number of these bear Brāhmī inscriptions and the names of ten kings, which some would identify with the old Śuṅga dynasty, have been recovered from the copper and brass coins of Pañcāla, found in abundance at Rāmnagar in Rohilkhand, the site of the ancient city, Ahicchatra.[2]

[1] Brown, *Coins of India*, p. 19.
[2] *Ibid.*, p. 20.

## CHAPTER V

# THE ŚŪRASENAS

The Śūrasenas are not mentioned in the Vedic literature, but in the *Mānavadharma-śāstra* they are spoken of in high terms as belonging to the Brahmarṣi-deśa, or the country of the great Brahmanical seers, whose conduct was an example to all Aryans.[1] Accordingly at the time of Manu's Code (between the second century B.C. and the second century A.D.), the Śūrasenas were among the tribes who occupied a rank in Indo-Aryan society second only to that of the small population of the narrow strip of Brahmāvarta. Therefore they must have belonged to the Vedic people, though probably they had not acquired sufficient political importance in very early times to find a mention in the *Ṛgveda* or the subsequent Vedic literature. They claimed descent from Yadu, a hero whose people are repeatedly referred to in the *Ṛgveda* [2]; and it is probable that the Śūrasenas were included among the Ṛgvedic Yadus.

Manu also pays a high tribute to the martial qualities of the Śūrasenas, inasmuch as he advises a king when arranging his troops on the battle-field, to place the Śūrasenas in the very front line.[3]

In an enumeration in the *Mahābhārata* [4] of the various peoples of Bhāratavarṣa, the Śūrasenas are mentioned along with the Śālvas, Kuru-Pañcālas and other neighbouring tribes; and we read in the *Virāṭaparvan* (Chaps. I and V) that the Pāṇḍavas passed through the Śūrasena country on their way to Virāṭanagara, from the Dvaitavana forest, where they had sojourned during their exile. It is easy to locate the Śūrasenas, inasmuch as their capital, Mathurā, has been a great city from the early times of Indo-Aryan history down to the present day. They must have occupied 'the Muttra district and possibly some of the territory still farther south',[5] according to the Cambridge History of India. Prof. Rhys Davids says [6]: 'The Śūrasenas, whose capital was Madhurā, were immediately south-west of the Macchas, and west of the Jumna'.

In the *Rāmāyaṇa*,[7] we read that Sugrīva, when sending out his monkey generals in search of Sītā, told those who were going towards

[1] *Manusaṃhitā*, II, 19; and see Matsya chapter.
[2] *Vedic Index*, II, 185.
[3] *Manusaṃhitā*, VII, 193.
[4] *Mbh.*, *Bhīṣmaparvan*, Chap. 9, p. 822.
[5] *Cambridge History of India*, Vol. I, p. 316.
[6] *Buddhist India*, p. 27.
[7] *Kiṣkindhyā Kāṇḍa*, 11-12, 43rd sarga.

the north to search the country of the Śūrasenas. In the Bhagavadgītā section of the *Mahābhārata*, the Śūrasenas are mentioned as forming part of the army of Duryodhana in the Kurukṣetra war. They guarded Bhīṣma, and took a prominent part in the battle, to the point of having their army destroyed.[1] Elsewhere in the *Mahābhārata*,[2] we read that Sahadeva, while proceeding southwards in the course of his conquests before the Rājasūya sacrifice, conquered the country of Śūrasenas.

In the Pāli Buddhist *Tripiṭaka*, Śūrasena is mentioned as one of the sixteen '*mahājanapadas*' which were prosperous and had an abundance of wealth.[3] One of the Jātaka stories narrates how the Śūrasenas, along with the Pañcālas, Matsyas and Madras, witnessed a game of dice between Dhanañjaya Korabba and Puṇṇaka Yakkha.[4]

The capital of the Śūrasenas, as we have seen, was Mathurā on the Jumna, at present included in the Agra division of the United Provinces. It lay on the upper Jumna, about 270 miles in a straight line north-west of Kauśāmbī. In the Pāli Buddhist literature, the name is Madhurā; Rhys Davids in his *Buddhist India* (p. 36) says that it is tempting to identify it with the site of the modern Mathurā, in spite of the difference in spelling. In the *Lalitavistara*,[5] the city of Mathurā is mentioned as having been suggested as a possible locality for the birth of the Bodhisattva, when various places were being discussed by the gods in the Tuṣita heaven. From this it is evident that at the time that the *Lalitavistara* was composed, that is, in the early centuries of the Christian era, Mathurā was one of the most prominent cities of India.

The Greek historians make mention of Mathurā. It was noticed by Arrian, on the authority of Megasthenes, as the capital of the Śūrasenas; and Ptolemy also mentions it.[6] The town was surrounded by numbers of high mounds, one of which has since yielded numbers of statues and inscribed pillars, which prove that it represented the remains of at least two large Buddhist monasteries dating from the beginning of the Christian era.[7]

In the fifth century A.D., Mathurā was visited by the Chinese pilgrim Fā-Hien, who passed through a succession of monasteries

---

1 *Bhīṣmaparvan*, Chap. 106, p. 974; *Ibid.*, Chaps. 107–121, pp. 906–993; *Droṇaparvan*, Chap. 6, pp. 998-9; *Ibid.*, Chap. 19, p. 1009; *Karṇaparvan*, Chap. 5, pp. 1167-8.

2 *Sabhāparvan*, Chap. 31, pp. 242-3.

3 *Aṅguttara Nikāya*, I, p. 213; *Ibid.*, IV, pp. 252, 256 and 260.

4 Fausböll, *Jātaka*, Vol. VI, p. 280.

5 Ed. Lefmann, pp. 21-2.

6 Cunningham, *Ancient Geography*, (Majumder's Ed.), p. 429. The Greek writers also make mention of another city of the Śūrasena country, named Cleisobora (= *Kṛṣṇapur* = *Bṛndāban*).

7 Cunningham, *Ancient Geography*, p. 374.

filled with a number of monks.[1] It was also visited later by Hsüan Tsang who described the country as being above 5,000 li in circuit, the capital being above twenty li in circuit. The soil, according to him, was very fertile, and agriculture was the chief industry: mango trees were grown there in orchards. The country also produced a fine striped cotton cloth, and gold. Its climate was hot, the manners and customs of the inhabitants were good. There were Buddhist monasteries, and deva-temples, and the professed adherents of the different non-Buddhist sects lived pell-mell.[2]

Buddhism was predominant in Mathurā for several centuries.[3] The king of Mathurā in the Buddha's time bore the title of Avantiputto, and was therefore related to the royal family of Ujjayinī in Avanti. In the *Majjhima Nikāya* (II, pp. 83ff.) we read that king Avantiputto went to Mahākaccāna, one of the Buddha's most influential disciples, and discussed with him the pride of the Brāhmaṇas, and their view that they were vastly superior to all other castes. Mathurā was the residence of Mahākaccāna, 'to whom tradition attributes the first grammatical treatment of the Pāli language, and after whom the oldest Pāli grammar is accordingly named'.[4] In Kaccāyana's Pāli Grammar we read that the distance from Mathurā to Saṅkassa was 4 yojanas.[5] A famous stūpa was built at Mathurā in honour of Moggaliputta Tissa (*Cambridge History of India*, Vol. I, p. 506).

Mathurā was visited by the Buddha,[6] but we do not find many references to the city in his time; whereas it is mentioned in the *Milindapañho* as one of the most famous places in India; so that the time of its greatest growth must have been between these dates.[7]

Besides Buddhism, the Jaina cult was also practised at Mathurā which was one of the few centres of the cult in the centuries immediately before and after the Christian era.[8] The Jains seem to have been firmly established in the city from the middle of the second century B.C.; while many dedicatory inscriptions prove that they were a flourishing community at Mathurā in the reigns of Kaniṣka, Huviṣka and Vāsudeva.[9]

[1] Legge, *Travels of Fā-Hien*, p. 42.
[2] Watters, *On Yuan Chwang*, Vol. I, p. 301.
[3] Eliot, *Hinduism and Buddhism*, Vol. II, p. 159.
[4] Rhys Davids, *Buddhist India*, p. 36.
[5] Book III, Chap. I, p. 157, S. C. Vidyābhūṣaṇa's edition.
[6] *Aṅguttara Nikāya*, II, 57; *Vimānavatthu Comm.*, pp. 118-9.
[7] Rhys Davids, *Buddhist India*, p. 37.
[8] Smith, *Early History of India*, 4th Ed., p. 18; and Rapson, *Ancient India*, p. 174.
[9] Eliot, *Hinduism and Buddhism*, Vol. I, p. 113.

Mathurā was also known in the time of Megasthenes (300 B.C.) as the centre of Kṛṣṇa worship [1]; it was well known as the birthplace of the hero Kṛṣṇa.[2] Cunningham points out [3] that Śūrasena was the grandfather of Kṛṣṇa, and after him Kṛṣṇa and his descendants, who held Mathurā after the death of Kaṃsa, were called the Śūrasenas.

Another cult which arose in Mathurā was the Bhāgavata religion, the parent of modern Vaiṣṇavism [4]; but in the Śaka-Kushan period, the city had ceased to be a stronghold of Bhagavatism.[5] The paucity of Bhāgavata inscriptions at Mathurā probably indicates that Bhagavatism did not find much favour at the royal court, because from the first century B.C. to the third century A.D., the people were usually Buddhists.[6]

Mathurā, then, was a city in which many divergent religious sects flourished side by side. To the Hindus its sanctity was, and still is, very great. As the birthplace of Kṛṣṇa, it was and is one of the seven holy places of Hinduism.[7]

In the semi-legendary accounts of the Purāṇas, we find some details regarding Mathurā. In the *Viṣṇupurāṇa* for instance, we read that Lavana, son of the monster Madhu, was killed by Śatrughna who founded the city of Mathurā.[8] The demons attacked Mathurā, the home of the Vṛṣṇis and Andhakas;[9] and the Vṛṣṇis and Andhakas, being afraid of the demons, left Mathurā and established their capital at Dvārāvatī.[10] Mathurā was also besieged by Jarāsandha, king of Magadha, with a huge army of 23 *akṣauhiṇīs*.[11] At the time of his 'great departure' (*mahāprasthāna*), Yudhiṣṭhira installed Vajranābha on the throne of the city.[12]

The earlier rulers of Mathurā find a place in the Purāṇas,[13] but only in the general summary of those dynasties which were contemporary with the Purus. On the eve of the rise of the Gupta power, says the *Vāyupurāṇa* (Chap. 99), seven nāga kings reigned in Mathurā. They were followed by Magadha kings.[14]

[1] *Cambridge History of India*, Vol. I, p. 167.
[2] See, e.g. Hopkins, *The Great Epic of India*, p. 395, n. 1.
[3] *Ancient Geography*, p. 374.
[4] *Cambridge History of India*, Vol. I, p. 526.
[5] H. C. Ray Chaudhuri, *Early History of the Vaiṣṇava Sect*, p. 99.
[6] *Ibid.*, p. 100.
[7] *Cambridge History of India*, Vol. I, p. 316.
[8] 4th Aṃśa, Chap. 4.
[9] *Brahmapurāna*, Chap. 14, śloka 54.
[10] *Harivaṃśa*, Chap. 37.
[11] *Ibid.*, Chap. 195, śloka, 3.
[12] *Skandapurāṇa, Viṣṇukhaṇḍa*; *Bhāgavata Māhātmya*, Chap. I.
[13] *Cambridge History of India*, Vol. I, p. 526.
[14] *Viṣṇupurāṇa*, 4th Aṃśa, Chap. 23.

As regards Buddhist semi-historical records, we read in the *Lalitavistara* [1] of a king of the Śūrasenas named Suvāhu, who had his capital at Mathurā. He is said to have been a heretic, but a great king of Jambudīpa (India).[2] Mathurā is also mentioned in the earliest chronicle of Ceylon, the *Dīpavaṃsa*,[3] where we are told that sons and grandsons of Prince Sādhina reigned 'over the great kingdom of Madhurā, the best of towns'.

In the *Ghata Jātaka* we read that in Upper Madhurā there reigned a king named Mahāsāgara, who had two sons, Sāgara and Upasāgara. On his death the elder son became king and the younger Viceroy (= heir-apparent?). Upasāgara quarrelled with Sāgara and went to Uttarāpatha in the Kaṃsa district, to the city of Asitañjana which was ruled over by King Mahākaṃsa, who had two sons, Kaṃsa and Upakaṃsa, and one daughter, Devagabbhā. It was foretold that this daughter would bear a son who would kill his maternal uncles. Believing this prediction, on the death of King Mahākaṃsa the two brothers kept their sister in a separate round tower specially built for her, so that she should remain unmarried. But despite their precautions, Devagabbhā and Upasāgara saw each other, fell in love, and contrived to meet. When her brothers discovered the intrigue, they gave Devagabbhā in marriage to Upasāgara, and a daughter was born soon afterwards. The two brothers were pleased, and allotted to their sister and brother-in-law a village named Govaḍḍhamāna. In course of time, Devagabbhā gave birth to ten sons, and her serving woman Nandagopā to ten daughters. Devagabbhā, however, secretly exchanged her ten sons for the ten daughters of her maid. When the boys grew up, they became plunderers and their fosterfather, Andhaka-Veṇhu, was often rebuked by King Kaṃsa. At last Andhaka-Veṇhu told the king the secret of the birth of the ten sons. An arena was prepared for a wrestling match in the city. When the ten sons entered the ring and were about to be caught, the eldest of the ten, Vāsudeva, threw a wheel which cut off the heads of Kaṃsa and Upakaṃsa, and himself assumed the sovereignty of the city of Asitañjana.[4] The Jātaka story ends with the accession of Vāsudeva to the throne of Mathurā. The *Petavatthu* Commentary gives a different story of the adventure of the ten sons who were born to the king of Uttara-Madhurā.[5]

[1] Ed. Lefmann, pp. 21-2.
[2] *Romantic Legend of Sākya Buddha*, p. 29.
[3] Oldenberg, *Dīpavaṃsa*, p. 27.
[4] *Jātaka* (Fausböll), Vol. IV, pp. 79 foll.
[5] *Petavatthu Comm.*, 111 ff.; see also B. C. Law, *Buddhist Conception of Spirits*, 2nd Ed., p. 99.

A king of Mathurā named Brahmamitra was probably contemporary with king Indramitra of Ahicchatra, for both names are found in the dedicatory inscriptions of queens on pillars of the railing at Buddhagayā, which is generally assigned to the earlier part of the first century B.C.[1] Rapson points out [2] that in the second century B.C. Mathurā was governed by native princes whose names are known from their coins; and it passed from them into the possession of one of the families of Śaka satraps, *c.* 100 B.C. Menander (Milinda), king of Kabul and the Punjab, presumably occupied Mathurā,[3] and many of his coins have been discovered there.[4] Numismatic evidence seems to prove [5] that the Hindu kings of Mathurā were finally replaced by Hagāna, Hagāmāsha, Rājuvula, and other Śaka Satraps who probably flourished in or about the first century A.D. In the second century A.D. Mathurā was under the sway of Huvishka, the Kushān king. This is evidenced by a splendid Buddhist monastery which bears his names.[6]

The epigraphic evidence that in the first century B.C. the region of Mathurā had passed from native Indian to foreign (Śaka) rule is confirmed and amplified by the evidence of coins. A Muttra (i.e. Mathurā) inscription, according to R. Chanda, records the erection of a *toraṇa, vedikā* and *catuḥśāla* at the Mahāsthāna of Vāsudeva, in the reign of the Mahākṣatrapa Soḍāsa.[7] The Mathurā nāga statuette inscription is evidence of serpent worship in Mathurā, which is important in view of the story of Kāliya nāga and his suppression by Kṛṣṇa, recorded in the Purāṇas compiled during the Gupta period.[8]

Brown [9] says that cast coins were issued at the close of the third century by the kingdoms of Mathurā, Ayodhyā and Kauśāmbī, some of which bear the names of local kings in the Brāhmī script. In the ruins of Mathurā, many ancient copper coins along with many coins of the Greek and Śaka rulers were discovered.[10] Among the coins discovered in this region, those of the Arjunāyanas are of special interest.[11]

The Pre-Kushan sculptures of Muttra are the most instructive, because they all emanate from the same school. These sculptures may be divided into three main classes, the earliest belonging approxi-

---

[1] *Cambridge History of India*, Vol. I, p. 526. [2] *Ancient India*, p. 174.
[3] Smith, *Early History of India*, p. 199.
[4] R. D. Banerjee, *Prācīna Mudrā*, p. 50. [5] Smith, *op. cit.*, p. 227.
[6] *Ibid.*, p. 271.
[7] *Early History of the Vaiṣṇava Sect*, pp. 98-9. [8] *Ibid.*, p. 100.
[9] *Coins of India*, p. 19. [10] *Prācīna Mudrā*, pp. 105, 106.
[11] Cunningham, *Coins of India*, pp. 89-90; see also R. D. Banerjee's *Prācīna Mudrā*, p. 109.

mately to the middle of the second century B.C., the second to the following century, and the last being associated with the rule of the local Satraps. The sculptures of the third class are more exceptional. Their style is that of the early school in a late and decadent phase, when its cut was becoming conventionalised and lifeless. A little before the beginning of the Christian era, Muttra had become the capital of a satrapy either subordinate to, or closely connected with, the Scytho-Parthian kingdom of Taxila. As a result, there was an influx there of the semi-Hellenistic Art, too weak in its environment to maintain its own individuality, yet still strong enough to interrupt and enervate the older traditions of Hindusthan . . . As an illustration of the close relations that existed between Muttra and the north-west, the votive tables of Loṇa-śobhikā is particularly significant, the stūpa depicted on it being identical in form with the stūpas of the Scytho-Parthian epoch at Taxila, but unlike any monument of the class in Hindusthan.[1] Sir Charles Eliot points out[2] that we need not feel surprise if we find in the religious thought of Muttra elements traceable to Greece, Persia or Central Asia, because we know that the sculptural remains found at Mathurā indicate the presence of Graeco-Bactrian influence.

Smith remarks[3] that Mathurā was probably the original site of the celebrated iron pillar at Delhi, on which the eulogy of a powerful king named Chandra is incised. As Rapson says, we possess a most valuable monument of the Śaka Satraps of Mathurā, which was discovered by Bhagavānlāl Indrajī, who bequeathed it to the British Museum. 'It is in the form of a large lion carved in red sandstone and intended to be the capital of a pillar. The workmanship shows undoubted Persian influence. The surface is completely covered with inscriptions in Kharoṣṭhī characters which give the genealogy of the Satrapal family ruling at Muttra. These inscriptions show that the Satraps of Muttra were Buddhists'.[4]

---

1 *Cambridge History of India*, Vol. I, p. 633.
2 *Hinduism and Buddhism*, Vol. II, p. 158.
3 *Early History of India*, p. 386.
4 Rapson, *Ancient India*, pp. 142-3, 158.

## CHAPTER VI

# THE CEDIS

The Cedis formed one of the most ancient tribes among the Kṣatriyas in early Vedic times. As early as the period of the Ṛgveda, the Cedi kings had acquired great renown by their munificent gifts at sacrifices, and also by their great prowess in battle. Ṛṣi Brahmātithi of the family of Kāṇva sings the praises of King Kaśu, the Caidya, in a hymn addressed to the Aśvins (*Ṛgveda*, VIII, 5, 37–9). From this account, even making allowances for some exaggeration, which is inevitable in these Dānastutis or laudatory verses for munificence and charity, one may conclude that the Cedi king was very powerful, for he is described as making a gift of ten Rājās or kings as slaves to a priest who officiated at one of his sacrifices.

The Cedis are not expressly mentioned in the later Vedic literature, but it would be wrong to suppose that they had become extinct, for they appear in the *Mahābhārata* as one of the leading powers of Northern India. It is probable that they were not so prominent in their sacrificial rites, or their political power, in the Brāhmaṇa age as they had been in the earlier era of the Ṛgvedic hymns; but there were ups and downs in the history of every great Kṣatriya power in India.

Another well-known Cedi monarch of ancient times, Vasu, who acquired the designation of Uparicara, is glorified in the *Mahābhārata*, and traditions about him and his successors are also recorded in the Jātakas. This Cedi king appears to have been characterised by great religious merit. Himself a Paurava, he is recorded to have been, through his daughter Satyavatī, the progenitor of the Kauravas and the Pāṇḍavas.

In the *Ādiparvan* of the *Mahābhārata*,[1] we read that Vasu, the Paurava, conquered the beautiful and excellent kingdom of the Cedis on the advice of the god Indra, whose friendship he had acquired by his austerities, and who, pleased with his asceticism, presented him with a great crystal car.[2] Because of his riding on it and moving through the upper regions like a celestial being, he came to be known as Uparicara.[3] King Uparicara Vasu had one son and one daughter by an apsarā named Adrikā. The daughter,

[1] M. N. Dutt, *Mahābhārata*, p. 83.
[2] *Ibid.*, p. 84.
[3] *Ibid.*, p. 85.

who was named Satyavatī, became the mother of Kṛṣṇadvaipāyana and others, and was the queen of King Śāntanu. The son afterwards became a virtuous and powerful monarch named Matsya. We further read that Uparicara Vasu Ċaidya had a few other sons, namely, Bṛhadratha, Pratyagraha, Kuśāmba and others, who founded kingdoms and cities which were named after them.[1] The *Vāyupurāṇa* (Chap. 99) also confirms the story of the conquest of the Cedi country by Vasu the Paurava. We read there that Yayāti had a chariot which used to move according to his desire. This chariot came into the hands of Vasu, king of the Cedis. According to another account, Vasu, a descendant of Kuru, conquered the Yādava kingdom of Cedi, and established himself there, whence he was known as Caidya-Uparicara. His capital was Śuktimatī on the river of the same name. He extended his conquests eastwards as far as Magadha and apparently also north-west over Matsya. He divided his territories of Magadha, Cedi, Kauśāmbi, Karūṣa and apparently Matsya among his five sons. His eldest son Bṛhadratha took Magadha with Girivraja as his capital, and founded the famous Bārhadratha dynasty there.[2]

Another section of the *Mahābhārata*[3] also speaks of the greatness of the Cedi monarch, Uparicara Vasu, and describes an Aśvamedha sacrifice which he performed.

In the Cetiya Jātaka,[4] we find a dynastic list of the ancestors of Upacara or Apacara, who was the ruler of Sotthivatinagara[5] in the kingdom of Ceti. King Upacara had five sons one of whom went to the east, and founded Hatthipura; while the second son went to the south, and founded Assapura; the third to the west, and founded Sīhapura; the fourth to the north, and founded Uttarapañcāla; and the last son went to the north-west, and founded Daddarapura.

The next Cedi monarch who appears to have acquired considerable power in the Epic period is Śiśupāla who is called Damaghoṣasuta (*Mbh.*, I, 7029) or Damaghoṣātmaja (II, 1594; III, 516). He allied himself with the great Jarāsandha and on account of his heroism was appointed generalissimo of the Magadhan emperor.[6] His conduct appears to have roused the displeasure of many of the Kṣatriya tribes of his time, but he was looked upon with such fear that he was considered as an incarnation of the great Daitya Hiraṇya-Kaśipu,[7] and the Epic tells us that he bore a charmed

1 M. N. Dutt, *Mbh.*, p. 84; *Mbh. Ādiparvan*, Chap. 63, pp. 69–71.
2 Pargiter, *Ancient Indian Historical Tradition*, p. 282.
3 *Mbh.*, *Śāntiparvan*, Chaps. 136 and 137, pp. 1802–4.
4 *Jātaka* (Fausböll), Vol. III, pp. 454–461. See also Pañcāla chapter.
5 Evidently identical with Śuktimatī.
6 *Mbh.*, II, 14, 10-11.
7 *Ādiparvan*, 67, 5.

life unassailable by any ordinary mortal.[1] He was related on his mother's side to the Satvats or Yādavas, but he allied himself with Kaṃsa and Jarāsandha, enemies of the Yādavas, destroyed their city, Dvārakā, and molested them in other ways.

The Yādava hero, Kṛṣṇa, had been awaiting a suitable opportunity to remove this great enemy of his family. Such an opportunity was afforded him at the Rājasūya sacrifice of Yudhiṣṭhira who, by his conquests, had acquired the position of a suzerain among the Kṣatriya monarchs of Northern India. Yudhiṣṭhira, finding it incumbent upon him, according to the procedure of the sacrifice, to make an *arghya* (offering) to the most honoured and worthy individual present in the assemblage gathered at his court on this occasion, was advised by Bhīṣma to offer the arghya to Kṛṣṇa. This aroused the ire of Śiśupāla who strongly protested against this decision, and succeeded in securing the support of a large number of other kings. Śiśupāla challenged Kṛṣṇa, being desirous to slay him with all the Pāṇḍavas. Kṛṣṇa related all of Śiśupāla's misdeeds, and then thought of his magic discus which came into his hand; therewith he instantly cut off the head of Śiśupāla; the kings beheld a fiery energy issuing out of the body of Śiśupāla and entering Kṛṣṇa's body; the sky, though cloudless, poured showers of rain. Yudhiṣṭhira caused his brothers to perform the funeral rites of Śiśupāla, the son of Damaghoṣa; then he, with all the kings, installed the son of Śiśupāla in the sovereignty of the Cedis.

The Purāṇas corroborate the Epic story of Śiśupāla. We read in the *Agnipurāṇa* (4, 14) that Damaghoṣa, king of the Cedis, married Śrutaśravā, sister of Vasudeva; and Śiśupāla was their son.[2] Further details from the *Mahābhārata* may be summarised as follows. Damaghoṣa's son, Śiśupāla, king of the Cedis, attended the Svayaṃvara of Draupadī.[3] Bhīmasena went to the kingdom of Cedi and easily subdued Śiśupāla.[4] Karṇa conquered the son of Śiśupāla, and other neighbouring kings.[5] Dhṛṣṭaketu who, after the death of his father, had been placed upon the throne of the Cedis by Yudhiṣṭhira, became a friend of the Pāṇḍavas, and when the great war broke out, he was appointed leader of the Cedi army which marched to the battle-field to help the Pāṇḍavas.[6] The Cedis must have been very powerful at the time, for we are told that Dhṛṣṭaketu led one complete *akṣauhiṇī* to the field.[7] Dhṛṣṭaketu went to the battle-field on a Kambojian horse which had variegated

---

[1] II, Chaps. 42 and 43.

[2] *Vāyu P.*, Chap. 96; *Brahma P.*, Chap. 14.

[3] *Mbh.*, *Ādiparvan*, Chap. 87, p. 177.

[4] *Ibid.*, *Sabhāparvan*, Chap. 29, p. 241.

[5] *Ibid.*, Chap. 253, pp. 513-4.

[6] *Ibid.*, *Udyogaparvan*, Chap. 156, p. 777; Chap. 198, pp. 807-8.

[7] V, 19.

colours like a deer.[1] The Cedi king along with Bhīma and others was placed in the front of the Pāṇḍava army.[2] He and his brother Suketu were killed in the Kurukṣetra war.[3] Bhīma mentioned eighteen kings who by their great strength ruined their friends and relations, and among them was Sahaja of the Cedi dynasty.[4] From the Aśvamedhaparvan of the *Mahābhārata*,[5] we learn that Arjuna fought and defeated Sarabha, the son of Śiśupāla, at the city of Śukti in the kingdom of Cedi.

The *Viṣṇupurāṇa* (4–12) and the *Agnipurāṇa* (275) tell us that the descendants of Cedi, son of Kauśika, were known as Caidyas. The *Mārkaṇḍeya Purāṇa* (Chaps. 129–31) refers to a Cedi princess, Suśobhanā by name, who was one of the many queens of King Maru. It is recorded in the *Viṣṇupurāṇa* (4, 12) that Vidarbha, son of Jyāmagha, had three sons of whom Kauśika was one. Cedi was a son of Kauśika, and the descendants of this Cedi were known as Caidyarājās.[6] In the *Matsyapurāṇa* (Chap. 44), Cedi is written as Cidi.[7] The *Kūrmapurāṇa* (Chap. 24) tells a similar story of the origin of the name of Cedi. King Vidarbha, it says, had a son named Cidi, and after him, his descendants came to be known as Caidyas. Dyutimān was the eldest of his sons, the others being Vapusmān, Bṛhatmedhā, Śrīdeva and Vītaratha. Pargiter observes[8] that Cedi and other kingdoms, e.g. Vatsa, did not come under the rule of the Pauravas; but we may note that the famous king Vasu Uparicara was a Paurava by birth. Pargiter suggests that Pratyagraha may have taken Cedi.[9]

In the *Mahābhārata*, we find the Cedis allied in a group with such western tribes as the Pañcālas, Matsyas and Karūṣas, and also with peoples who lived in the east, such as the Kāśīs and Kośalas. We read of the Cedi-Kārūṣakāḥ bhūmipālāḥ, or rulers of the Cedis and Kārūṣakas, who espoused the cause of the Pāṇḍavas.[10] Elsewhere the Cedi-Pañcāla-Kaikeyas are grouped together.[11] Again, we are told that Dhṛṣṭaketu was the leader of the Cedi-Kāśī-Karūṣa peoples[12]; and we find the group Cedi-Kāśī-Karūṣa fighting together.[13] Sometimes the Cedis are grouped together with the Kārūṣas and the

[1] *Droṇaparvan*, Chap. 22, pp. 1012-3.
[2] *Bhīṣmaparvan*, Chap. 19, p. 830. See also Chap. 59, p. 935.
[3] *Mbh.*, *Karṇaparvan*, Chap. 6, p. 1169.
[4] *Ibid.*, *Udyogaparvan*, Chap. 74, p. 717. Cf. *Ibid.*, Chap. 72, p. 714.
[5] Chapters 83-4, pp. 2093-4.
[6] *Vāyupurāṇa*, Chap. 95.
[7] *Agnipurāṇa*, Chap. 275.
[8] *Ancient Indian Historical Tradition*, p. 293.
[9] *Ibid.*, p. 118.
[10] V, 22.
[11] V, 144.
[12] V, 196.
[13] VI, 47; VI, 106; VI, 115; VI, 116.

Matsyas [1]; or with the Kārūṣas, Matsyas, and Pañcālas [2]; or with the Kārūṣas and Kośalas.[3] These examples could be further multiplied; but we can gather from those already quoted that the Cedis are found combined with the Matsyas in the majority of cases, and it seems that the Matsyas were their immediate neighbours on the west, and the Kāśīs on the east.

The capital of the Cedi king, Dhṛṣṭaketu, is called Śuktimatī,[4] and is described as named after Śukti or oyster.[5] This city appears to have stood on the river Śuktimatī which, we are told,[6] flowed near the capital of the Cedi king, Vasu Uparicara, and which is also described in the geographical chapter of the Bhīṣmaparvan (VI, 9) as one of the rivers in Bhāratavarṣa.

The *Viṣṇudharmottara Mahāpurāṇa* (Chap. 9) mentions Cedi as a *janapada* or country, and so does the *Padmapurāṇa* (3rd chapter). Cedi (Ceti) is also mentioned in the Jaina and Buddhist literatures as one of the sixteen *mahājanapadas*.[7] The Cetis, says Rhys Davids, were probably the same tribe as that called Cedi in older documents, and had two distinct settlements. One, probably the older, was in the mountains in what is now called Nepal. The other, probably a later colony, was near Kauśāmbī to the east, and has been confused with the land of the Vaṃsa (Vatsa).[8] S. Krishnaswami Aiyangar in his *Ancient India* [9] agrees with Rhys Davids that one branch of the Cedis had their local habitat in Bundelkhand, the other being located somewhere in Nepal. D. R. Bhandarkar says that Ceta or Cetiya corresponds roughly to the modern Bundelkhand [10]; while Rapson says that in the post-Vedic period the Cedis occupied the northern portion of the Central Provinces.[11] In the *Cambridge History of India* (p. 84), we read that the Cedis dwelt in Bundelkhand to the north of the Vindhyas; while Pargiter says [12] that Cedi lay along the south of the Jumna. The following is a summary given by N. L. Dey in his *Geographical Dictionary* (p. 14): According to Tod, Chanderi, a town in Malwa, was the capital of Śiśupāla who was killed by Kṛṣṇa. According to Dr. Führer, Dahala Maṇḍala was the ancient Cedi. Some are of opinion that Cedi comprised the southern portion of Bundelkhand and northern portion of Jabbalpur. Kālañjara was the capital of Cedi under the Gupta kings. Cedi was also called Tripuri.

[1] VI, 54; VIII, 30. [2] VI, 59. [3] VII, 21.
[4] *Mbh.*, III, 22. [5] *Mbh.*, XIV, 83. [6] *Mbh.*, I, 63.
[7] *Aṅguttara Nikāya*, Vol. IV, pp. 252, 256 and 260; Cf. *Bhagavatī Sūtra*.
[8] *Buddhist India*, p. 26. [9] p. 8.
[10] *Carmichael Lectures*, 1918, p. 52. [11] *Ancient India*, p. 162.
[12] *Ancient Indian Historical Tradition*, p. 272.

Cunningham remarks that in the inscriptions of the Kalachuri or Haihaya dynasty of Cedi, the Rājās assumed the titles of 'Lords of Kālañjarapura and of Tri-Kaliṅga'. Kālañjar is the well-known hill-fort in Bundelkhand; and Tri-Kaliṅga or the 'three Kaliṅgas' must be the three kingdoms of Dhanaka or Amarāvatī on the Kistnā, Andhra or Warangal, and Kaliṅga or Rājāmahendri.[1]

It is stated in the *Vessantara Jātaka* that Cetaraṭṭha (i.e. Cedi-rāṣṭra, kingdom of the Cedis) was 30 yojanas distant from Jetuttara-nagara, the birthplace of King Vessantara. It was inhabited by 60,000 Khattiyas (Kṣatriyas) who are also described as Cetiya-rājās. Vessantara with his wife and children started from Jetuttara at breakfast-time and reached the capital of Cetaraṭṭha in the evening. The Cedis' hospitality to strangers is illustrated by this story; for we read that the Cedis offered food and hospitality to Vessantara who had been banished from the kingdom of his father Śivi; and when the prince proceeded to Vaṅkapabbata, the '60,000 Khattiyas' followed him to a certain distance as a kind of bodyguard.[2]

In the *Ādiparvan* of the *Mahābhārata*, we read that the kingdom of Cedi was full of riches, gems and precious stones, and contained much mineral wealth. The cities in the kingdom were full of honest, virtuous, and contented people. Here sons were mindful of their parents' welfare; here lean kine were never yoked to the plough or to the cart engaged in carrying merchandise,—they were all well-fed and fat. In Cedi, the four castes were engaged in doing their respective duties.[3]

In the *Vedabbha Jātaka*, we read that in a village in Benares there was a brahmin who was acquainted with a charm called Vedabbha. He went to the Cetiya country with the Bodhisattva, who was his pupil. Five hundred robbers caught them in a forest on the way, took the brahmin prisoner, and told the Bodhisattva to fetch a ransom for him. By repeating his charm, the brahmin caused money to shower from the sky; whereupon the robbers took the money and released him. But the first band of robbers was attacked by another band of the same number; and eventually the brahmin and all the robbers were destroyed, so that when the Bodhisattva returned with the ransom money, he found none there.[4] This account shows that the way from Benares to Cedi was frequented by robbers and was unsafe for travellers.

[1] *Ancient Geography*, p. 518.
[2] *Jātaka* (Fausböll), Vol. VI, pp. 514-5.
[3] M. N. Dutt, *Mahābhārata*, Ādiparvan, p. 84.
[4] *Jātaka* (Fausböll), Vol. I, pp. 253 foll.

In the *Aṅguttara Nikāya*,[1] we read that on several occasions Mahācunda, an eminent disciple of the Buddha, dwelt in the town of Sahajāti among the Cedis. The same Nikāya [2] further tells us that Anuruddha (first cousin and disciple of the Buddha) dwelt among the Cedis in the Deer-Park of Pācīnavaṃsa. In the *Dīgha Nikāya*,[3] we read that the Buddha went to the Cedis and other tribes while out preaching; while the *Saṃyutta Nikāya* [4] informs us that many theras were dwelling among the Cedis in the Sahañcanika.

The Cedis of the Vedic period, like other tribes, e.g. the Purus, were a group of families, says Dr. V. A. Smith, and in each family the father was master. The whole tribe was governed by a Rājā whose power was checked to an undefined extent by a tribal council. The details recorded suggest that the life of the people was not unlike that of many tribes of Afghanistan in modern times, before the introduction of fire-arms.[5]

The later kings of Cedi used an era according to which the year 1 was equivalent to A.D. 248-9. This era, also called the Traikūṭaka, originated in Western India, where its use can be traced back to the fifth century. The reason for its adoption by the kings of Cedi is not apparent.[6] Rapson remarks that each of certain eras, e.g. the Traikūṭaka, Cedi, or Kalacuri era of 249 A.D., the Gupta era of 319 A.D., and the era of King Harṣavardhana of 606 A.D., marks the establishment of a great power in some region of India, and originally denoted the regnal years of its founder.[7]

Kokalladeva I of the Cedi dynasty helped Bhojadeva II (c. 907–910 A.D.) to ascend the throne of Kanouj; and it is evident from the stone inscription of the kings of the Cedi dynasty discovered at Vishari that Kokalladeva I erected two wonderful monuments.[8] During the reign of Mahīpāladeva of Bengal (c. 978–1030), Gāṅgeyadeva of the Cedi dynasty attacked Gauḍa and occupied Mithilā.[9] Towards the close of the eleventh century, Kānyakubja (Kanouj) came under the sway of Karṇadeva (c. 1040–1070), son of Gāṅgeyadeva.[10]

Numismatists suppose that Gāṅgeyadeva issued a new coinage in Uttarāpatha.[11] Only coins of this monarch of the Cedi dynasty of

---

1 Vol. III (P.T.S.), pp. 355-6; Vol. V, pp. 41 ff.; 157–161.
2 P.T.S., Vol. IV, pp. 228 ff.
3 Vol. II, pp. 200, 201, 203, *Janavasabha Suttanta*.
4 Vol. V, pp. 436-7.
5 *Ancient and Hindu India*, p. 22.
6 V. A. Smith, *Early History of India*, 4th Ed., p. 409.
7 *Ancient India*, p. 22.
8 R. D. Banerjee, *Vāṅgālār Itihāsa*, p. 202.
9 *Ibid.*, p. 224.
10 *Prācīna Mudrā*, p. 215.
11 *Ibid.*, p. 211.

Dāhala have been discovered, and no coins of the kings prior or posterior to him in the dynasty are known to us.[1] Gold, silver and copper coins of Gāṅgeyadeva have been discovered. On one side is the name of the king in two lines, and on the other a figure of a four-armed goddess.[2]

Coins of one king of the Cedi or Kalacuri dynasty of Kalyāṇapura have also been discovered. On one side of the coins is engraved the figure of the boar-incarnation, and on the other is written 'Murāri' in Nāgarī characters. Murāri, as R. D. Banerjee says, is perhaps another name of Someśvaradeva, the second king of the above-mentioned Cedi dynasty.[3]

---

1 *Prācīna Mudrā*, p. 212.
2 *Ibid.*, p. 212
3 *Ibid.*, p. 184.

## CHAPTER VII

# THE MADRAS

The Madras[1] were an ancient Kṣatriya tribe of Vedic times. They are not mentioned in the early Vedic Saṃhitās, but the Vaṃśa Brāhmaṇa of the *Sāmaveda* mentions an ancient Vedic teacher, Madragāra Śauṅgāyani, from whom Aupamanyava, the Kāmbojan, received the Vedic lore (cf. chapter on Kāmbojas). From the name Madragāra, scholars infer that Śauṅgāyani belonged to the Madra tribe,[2] and the fact that Vedic learning had spread so much among the Madras as to give one of them a prominent place in a list of ancient teachers would seem to show that the Madras belonged to the Vedic Aryandom before the age of the *Brāhmaṇas*. Their Vedic learning in *Brāhmaṇa* times is testified to by the *Śatapatha Brāhmaṇa* where we find that sages of N. India, most probably of the Kuru-Pañcāla district, repaired to the Madra country to receive their education in Vedic learning. In the *Bṛhadāraṇyaka Upaniṣad* (III, 7, 1), Uddālaka Āruṇi tells Yājñavalkya: 'We dwelt among the Madras in the houses of Patañcala Kāpya, studying the sacrifice'. And again, Bhujyu Lāhāyani says, 'We wandered about as students, and came to the house of Patañcala Kāpya' (*Bṛh. Up.*, III, 3, 1).

In the *Aitareya Brāhmaṇa* (VIII, 14, 3), we find the mention of a section of the Madra people, the Uttara or N. Madras who lived beyond the Himālayas (*pareṇa Himavantam*) in the N. regions close to the Uttara-Kurus. Uttara-Madra is supposed by scholars to have been located in Kashmir.[3]

In the *Rāmāyaṇa*, we read that Sugrīva sent monkeys to the Madrakas and other tribes in quest of Sītā.[4] In the *Viṣṇupurāṇa* (2, 3, 17), mention is made of Madra together with Ārāma, Pārasīka, etc. and in the *Matsyapurāṇa* (114, 41) together with Gāndhāra, Yavana, etc. In the same *Purāṇa* (208, 5), King Aśvapati of Śākala in the kingdom of the Madras is referred to. Madra (Pāli *Madda*) is not mentioned in the list of sixteen *Mahājanapadas* in Buddhist literature. It has been supposed by some that Madra is to be identified with Vāhlika[5] (see Chapter on Vāhlikas). The Madras

---

[1] Mr. H. C. Ray has contributed a paper to the *J.A.S.B.* (New Series, Vol. XVIII, 1922, No. 4) on the same subject.

[2] *Vedic Index*, II, p. 123.

[3] Zimmer, *Altindisches Leben*, p. 102.

[4] *Rāmāyaṇa* (Griffith's translation), Additional Notes, p. 43.

[5] N. L. Dey, *Geographical Dictionary*, p. 49.

held the central portions of the Punjab;[1] they appear in the Epic period to have occupied the district of Sialkot, between the rivers Chenab and Ravi,[2] or, according to some, between the Jhelum and the Ravi.[3] The Madra tribe or kingdom is mentioned in the *Bhīṣmaparvan* of the *Mahābhārata* (Chap. IX), in Varāhamihira's *Bṛhatsaṃhitā*,[4] and in Pāṇini's grammar (II, 3, 73; IV, 4, 67). It is evident from the Allahabad Pillar Inscription that the Madra territory was contiguous with that of the Yaudheyas.[5]

The capital of the Madras was Sāgala (Pāli) or Śākala[6] (Sanskrit), which has been identified by General Cunningham with Sanglawala-Tiba, to the west of the Ravi (*Ancient Geography of India*, p. 180). According to Cunningham, Śākala is still known as Madradeśa or the district of the Madras. It lay about 32 N. by 74 E.[7]

It appears from *Hwui-lih* that the pilgrim Hsüan Tsang visited Śākala. The old town of Śākala (*She-ki-lo*), according to the great pilgrim, was about 20 li in circuit. Although its walls had been thrown down, the foundation was still firm and strong, and in the midst of it a town of 6 or 7 li in circuit had been built. There was in Śākala a Saṅghārāma (monastery) with about 100 priests of the Hīnayāna school, and N.W. of the Saṅghārāma was a stūpa about 200 feet high, built by Aśoka; while a stone stūpa of about the same height, also built by Aśoka, stood about 10 li to the N.E. of the new capital.[8]

The *Milinda Pañho* gives a splendid description of the Madra capital: 'There is a great centre of trade called Sāgala the famous city of yore in the country of the Yonakas. Sāgala is situated in a delightful country, well-watered and hilly, abounding in parks and gardens, groves, lakes and tanks, a paradise of rivers and mountains and woods. Wise architects have laid it out. Brave is its defence, with many strong towers and ramparts, with superb gates and entrance archways, and with the royal citadel in its midst, white-walled and deeply moated. Well laid out are its streets, squares, cross-roads and market places. Its shops are filled with various costly merchandise. It is richly adorned with hundreds of alms-halls of various kinds and splendid with hundreds of thousands of magnificent

[1] V. A. Smith, *Early History of India* (4th Ed.), p. 302.

[2] *Cambridge History of India, Ancient India*, pp. 549-550.

[3] Cunningham, *Ancient Geography*, p. 185; and see also *ibid.*, pp. 5-6.

[4] Kern, *Bṛhatsaṃhitā*, p. 92.

[5] R. C. Majumdar, *Corporate Life in Ancient India*, p. 272.

[6] *Mbh.*, II, 1196; VIII, 2033.

[7] Cunningham, *Ancient Geography of India*, p. 185; Rhys Davids, *Buddhist India*, p. 39.

[8] Beal, *Records of the Western World*, Vol. I, pp. 166 *et seq.*

mansions . . .' The passage goes on to describe the traffic of elephants, horses, carriages and pedestrians; the welcome given to teachers of all creeds, and the rich produce, precious metals, and delicacies which are to be found in the city. It is described as rivalling Uttara-Kuru in wealth and Āḷakamandā, the city of the Gods, in glory (*Milinda Pañho*, pp. 1 and 2, and Trsl. *S.B.E.*, Vol. 35, pt. I, pp. 1–3).

According to the evidence of the Sanskrit Epics and Pāli Jātakas, the Madras were Kṣatriyas, and they entered into matrimonial alliance with the Kṣatriya dynasties of the Gangetic kingdoms (see the account of the marriage of Pāṇḍu, the Kuru king, and a Madra princess; cf. also *Mbh.*, *Ādiparvan*, Chap. 95 (marriage of Parīkṣit and Mādravatī).

The Jātakas bear ample testimony to the fact that the Madra princesses were sought in marriage by the great Kṣatriya houses of N. India. Thus we read in the Kusa-Jātaka that a certain king of Madra had seven daughters of great beauty. The eldest of them, Pabhāvatī, was given in marriage to Kusa (or Kuśa), son of King Okkāka, and the kingdoms of Madra and Kusāvatī were thus united by matrimonial alliance.[1]

The same story of the union of Prince Kuśa of the great Ikṣvāku family with a Madra princess is told in the *Mahāvastu-Avadāna*, with some variations. At Benares, we are told, there was a king named Kuśa belonging to the Ikṣvāku family. His ministers, in quest of a beautiful bride for the king, reached the city of Kānyakubja in the kingdom of Śūrasena where the Madra king Mahendra ruled. Seeing his beautiful daughter, they approached the king who readily consented to give her in marriage to King Kuśa of Benares. But King Kuśa's appearance was repulsive, and his wife Sudarśanā, discovering the defects in him, left Benares and returned to Kānyakubja. When he discovered his wife's absence, Kuśa immediately set out in pursuit. Arriving at his father-in-law's palace, he tried by various means to regain his wife's favour, but in vain. Finally he disguised himself as a cook and prepared some delicious soup through which he won the king's favour. In the meantime, seven Kṣatriya kings from neighbouring countries came to win Sudarśanā, but they were refused. Then Kuśa, practically single-handed, drove all the seven kings away, and having saved his father-in-law's kingdom, returned with his wife to his own country. The Madra king, Mahendra, on the advice of his son-in-law, gave his remaining seven daughters in marriage to the seven

[1] *Jātaka* (Fausböll), Vol. V, pp. 284 foll.

kings who had come to attack him, and thereby strengthened his position.[1]

From the *Kāliṅga-Bodhi Jātaka* we observe that even a prince of the royal house of Kāliṅga in the far east sought the hand of a princess of the Madra country. A daughter was born to the king of Madra in the city of Sāgala. It was foretold that the girl should live as an ascetic but that her son would be universal monarch. The kings of India heard of this prediction and surrounded the city with the object of seeking the princess's hand. The king of Madra could not give his daughter in marriage to any one of them without incurring the wrath of the others. So he fled to a forest with his wife and daughter. The prince of Kaliṅga, who was also in the forest, happened to meet the Madra princess, and fell in love with her. Learning that she was a Kṣatriya like himself, he obtained her parents' consent to their marriage, and a matrimonial alliance was thus established between the royal houses of Madra and Kaliṅga.[2] In the *Chaddanta Jātaka*, we find that the royal houses of Benares and Madra were allied with each other through matrimony[3] (see also *Jātaka*, Vol. VI, p. 1). The great Ceylonese chronicle (*Mahāvaṁsa*, 8, 7) records an alliance between a Madra princess and a prince of Eastern India.

The Madras, according to the *Arthaśāstra* of Kauṭilya (p. 455), were a corporation of warriors, and enjoyed the status of *rājās* (*rājaśabdopajīvinaḥ*). The *Mahābhārata*[4] tells us that it was a family custom of the Madras to receive a fee from the bridegroom when they gave their daughters in marriage. The marriage proposal was first made by the bridegroom's party to the bride's party. When Pāṇḍu, the Kuru prince, won the hand of Kuntī, the daughter of a Bhoja king, in a Svayaṁvara (the ceremony of a woman's choosing her husband), Bhīṣma wished him to take a second wife as well. Bhīṣma accordingly set out with a retinue and coming to the city of the Madra king named Śalya of the Vāhlika dynasty, asked the king to give his sister in marriage to Pāṇḍu. Śalya told him of the custom of receiving a fee; Bhīṣma consented and having given the Madra king much wealth as fee for the bride, he brought her to Hastināpura, where the marriage ceremony was performed.[5]

In the Great Epic, we have further details of Śalya, king of the Madras. On the eve of the Kurukṣetra war, Yudhiṣṭhira sent messengers asking Śalya for his assistance. The king set out with his brave sons and a huge army. When on the march, this army

[1] *Mahāvastu*, II, p. 440 *et seq.*
[2] *Jātaka* (Fausböll), Vol. IV, pp. 228 foll.
[3] *Ibid.*, Vol. V, pp. 37 foll.
[4] *Ādiparvan*, Chap. 113.
[5] *Ibid.*, see also Chap. 95.

occupied the space of half a yojana. Hearing of the Madra king's might, Duryodhana decided to seek his alliance, and received him on the way, giving him a great ovation. Śalya was highly pleased with his reception, and offered Duryodhana a boon. Thereupon Duryodhana solicited his help in the ensuing Kurukṣetra war; and King Śalya consented, subsequently asking Yudhiṣṭhira to release him (on certain conditions) from his previous promise. After severe fighting, and many vicissitudes, the Madra soldiers were killed by Arjuna.[1]

The legend of Sāvitrī and Satyavān, so popular all over India, is connected with the Madra country, for Sāvitrī was the daughter of Aśvapati, king of Madra. This story is too well-known to require repetition here.[2]

As far as authentic history is concerned, we learn that the Madra dominions, including the capital, Śākala, came under the sway of Alexander the Great (326 B.C.) who placed them under the Satrap of the adjacent territory between the Jhelum and the Chenab.[3]

In the course of the centuries following the death of the Buddha, the Buddhist religion spread from the N.E. districts of India to the extreme West, no doubt largely owing to the powerful proselytising zeal of the great Maurya Emperor Aśoka. About 78 A.D., we find Menander (Milinda), a powerful Greek king, ruling at Śākala, and the Pāli '*Milinda Pañho*' gives a full account of this king's conversion to Buddhism.[4] During Menander's reign, the people knew of no oppression, since all their enemies had been conquered. Even before Menander's time, Śākala seems to have come under Buddhist influence (see, e.g. Mrs. Rhys Davids' *Psalms of the Sisters*, p. 48; *Psalms of the Brethren*, p. 359).

In the fourth century A.D., the Madras are recorded as having paid taxes to Samudragupta.[5]

At a later date, in the early part of the sixth century A.D., Śākala became the capital of the Hūṇa conqueror, Mihirakula.[6] From the records of the travels of Hsüan Tsang, the Chinese pilgrim, we read that some centuries before his time there was in the town of

[1] *Mbh.*, *Udyogaparvan*, Chaps. 8 and 19; *Droṇaparvan*, Chap. 103; *Bhīṣmaparvan*, Chaps. 51; 105-6; *Karṇaparvan*, Chaps. 5-6.

[2] *Mbh.*, *Vanaparvan*, Chaps. 291–8, pp. 509–523, Mahārājā of Burdwan's Edition.

[3] *Cambridge History of India, Ancient India*, Vol. I, pp. 549-550.

[4] *Questions of King Milinda* (*S.B.E.*), Pt. I, p. 6; Rapson, *Ancient India*, pp. 128–131.

[5] *Corpus Inscriptionum Indicarum*, Vol. III, p. 14; *Gupta Inscriptions, Text and Translations.*

[6] *Cambridge History of India*, Vol. I, pp. 549-550.

Śākala a king named *Mo-hi-lo-kiu-lo* (Mahirakula), who established his authority in that town, and subdued all the neighbouring provinces. This king was of a cruel nature, and, becoming enraged by the conduct of certain Buddhist priests, ordered his men to destroy all the priests 'through the five Indies', to overthrow the law of the Buddha and to leave nothing remaining.

Bālāditya, king of Magadha, heard of Mahirakula's cruel persecutions, and, after strongly guarding the frontiers of his kingdom, refused to pay tribute to him. Hearing that Mahirakula was marching against him, Bālāditya fled, followed by his soldiers, to the islands of the sea. Mahirakula forthwith left his army in the charge of his younger brother, and himself put out to sea to attack Bālāditya, but was captured by the latter's soldiers. Bālāditya, however, took pity on the captured sovereign and released him. Finding that his kingdom had meanwhile been usurped by his brother, Mahirakula went to Kashmir, where he was received with honour by the king, and given some territory over which to rule. After some years he betrayed his trust, killed the king, and placed himself on the throne. He then plotted against the kingdom of Gāndhāra, killed all the members of the royal family, and the chief minister, destroyed all Buddhist topes and temples, and appropriated the wealth of the country. However, retribution soon followed, for he was dead before the year was out.[1]

It appears that the kingdom of Madra was still intact in the ninth century A.D., when we find the Madras as the allies of Dharmapāla, the monarch of Bengal, who with the help of the Madras and other northern powers dethroned Indrarāja, king of Pañcāla.[2]

[1] Beal, *Records of the Western World*, Vol. I, pp. 165–172; Watters, *On Yuan Chwang*, I, p. 289

[2] V. A. Smith, *Early History of India*, 4th Ed., p. 413.

## CHAPTER VIII

# THE MĀLAVAS

The Mālava tribe played an important rôle in the history of Ancient India. First settled in the Punjab, they gradually spread themselves over considerable portions of N. India and established their settlements in Rajputana, Central India, in different localities of the modern United Provinces, in the country known in ancient days as Lāṭa-deśa (comprising Broach, Cutch, Vadnagar and Ahmedabad), and finally in modern Malwa. They successfully maintained their tribal organisation from the time of Pāṇini till at least as late as the time of Samudragupta (fourth century A.D.).

The earliest definite mention of the Mālavas is made in the writings of Alexander's historians who refer to them as Malloi, Malli or Mallai, associated with the Oxydrakai, Sudracae, Hydrakai or Sydracae. These two tribes have long been identified with the Mālavas and Kṣudrakas of Sanskrit literature.[1] Pāṇini does not actually mention them by name, but his sūtra V, 3, 117, speaks of certain tribes as '*āyudhajīvī saṃghas*', or tribes living by the profession of arms, and the ***Kāśika*** says that amongst these Saṃghas were the Mālavas and Kṣudrakas. The Mālava tribe is actually mentioned in the *Mahābhāṣya* of Patañjali (IV, 1, 68).[2]

In the time of Alexander (and probably also earlier), the Mālavas were settled in the Punjab, but it is difficult to locate exactly the territory they occupied. Smith thinks that they (the Malloi) occupied the country below the confluence of the Hydaspes (Jhelum) and Akesines (Chenab), that is, the country comprising the Jhang district and a portion of the Montgomery district.[3] According to McCrindle, they occupied a greater extent of territory, comprising the modern doab of the Akesines and Hydraotes (= Chenab and Rāvī)

---

[1] *Ind. Ant.*, Vol. I, p. 23.

[2] According to the Jain *Bhagavatī Sūtra*, Mālava is included in the list of the sixteen *Mahājanapadas* along with Malaya. The Mālava country of the *Bhagavatī* is probably identical with Avanti of the *Aṅguttara Nikāya* (P.H.A.I., p. 82, 4th Edn.). According to Weber, Āpiśali (according to Jayaswal, Kātyāyana) speaks of the formation of the compound—'*Kṣaudraka-Mālavāḥ*'. Smith points out that the *Mahābhārata* couples the tribes in question as forming part of the Kaurava host in the Kurukṣetra war. Curtius tells us that the Sudracae and the Malli had an army consisting of 90,000 foot-soldiers, 10,000 cavalry, and 900 war-chariots (*ibid.*, pp. 156-7).

[3] *J.R.A.S.*, 1903, p. 631.

and extending to the confluence of the Indus and Akesines—identical with the modern Multan district and portions of Montgomery.[1] Ray Chaudhuri locates them in the valley of the lower Hydraotes (Rāvī) on both banks of the river.[2]

While sailing along the Hydaspes, Alexander heard that the Malloi and the Oxydrakai had combined together and prepared themselves 'to give him hostile reception'. But it is difficult to ascertain from the mass of contradictory information of the Greek authorities whether the two tribes were able to give the conqueror a united opposition. While Curtius tells us that their combined army was led by a Kṣudraka hero, Diodorous says that the Syrakusoi (Kṣudrakas) and Malloi could not agree as to the choice of a leader, and consequently did not take the field together. According to Arrian as well, the Malloi had agreed to combine with the Oxydrakai against Alexander, but the conqueror had advanced so suddenly that their design was thwarted, and the two tribes could hardly have had the opportunity to unite against the common enemy.[3] The Malloi were certainly taken by surprise by Alexander's army, and suffered a defeat which was, however, not final. More than once the brave tribe offered determined opposition from their fortified cities which fell one by one to the sword of Alexander and his general Perdikas. The men deserted their cities, and preferred to make the desert and jungle their home rather than submit to the conquering hordes. Alexander then sent two of his generals, Peithon and Demetrius, against the largest city of the Malloi. But the Malloi had already abandoned that city, and crossed the Hydraotes, where they stood to offer further opposition. Eventually, however, when they saw that they were in danger of being surrounded by the Greek cavalry, they repaired to their capital city nearby, and made a last effort to resist the foreign invader. But they could not achieve any success. Their city-walls were razed to the ground and the citadel captured; but in the course of the heavy fighting Alexander himself was seriously wounded. He took revenge on the enemy by ordering all the inhabitants of the city, including women and children, to be put to the sword. This city has wrongly been assigned by Diodorous and Curtius to the Oxydrakai;[4] but both Arrian and Plutarch definitely state that the city belonged to the Malloi and not to the Oxydrakai. Even after this defeat and massacre, the Malloi do not seem to have been completely annihilated;

---

[1] *Invasion of India*, App. Note, p. 357.
[2] *P.H.A.I.*, 4th Ed., p. 202.
[3] McCrindle, *Invasion of India*, p. 236, f.n. 1; p. 150.
[4] *Ibid.*, App. Note Q., p. 351.

for Arrian tells us that the leading men from the Malloi and Oxydrakai came to Alexander to discuss the terms of a treaty which was eventually concluded.

Indeed, the Mālavas seem to have occupied their territory in the Punjab for some time afterwards. We have already referred to the reference to the tribe in the *Mahābhāṣya*; and it is not improbable that the *Mahābhārata* locates the tribe in the same place when it couples them with the Trigarttas,[1] as well as with the Śivis and Ambaṣṭhas.[2] But before long they seem to have migrated southwards and settled somewhere in Rajputana, where the tribes seem to have held their ground at the time of Samudragupta. A large number of coins found at Nagar, about 45 miles north of Koṭa, have on them the legend '*Mālavānām Jayaḥ*' ('victory of the Mālavas') in characters ranging in General Cunningham's opinion from perhaps B.C. 250 to 250 A.D. 'These coins', he says, 'show that the Mālavas existed as a recognised and important clan, long before the time when their tribal constitution which led to the establishment of their era, took place'.[3] Some of these coins, which are very small, have on them a legend that has been read as *Magaya*, *Magojaya*, *Majupa*, *Mayojapa*, *Mapaya* and so forth. 'Some scholars have taken these legends as denoting so many names, but the probability is that these letters constitute not names so much as abbreviations. In fact it was suggested to me long ago by Prof. D. R. Bhandarkar that the three letters *Ma ga ja* which occur, e.g. on coins 82–4 of Smith's *Catalogue of Coins in the Indian Museum*, Vol. I, and which had been taken to be the name of a king, look like an abbreviation of the legend: '*Mālava-gaṇasya jayaḥ*', which occurs for instance on coins Nos. 58–61 . . . What looks like the letter *pa* in Mapaya may be *la*; and Mapaya might thus stand for Mālaya, equal to Mālava. Mr. Douglas[4] has pointed out that the tribal name is sometimes written Mālaya instead of Mālava. Similarly *Ma pa ja* may be explained as equivalent to Mālajayaḥ, equal to Mālava-jayaḥ. Again, *Ma go ya sa* may be equivalent to '*Mālavagaṇasya yaśaḥ*'.[5] That the Mālavas had migrated to the Jaipur region of Rajputana from the Punjab is supported by the fact that the legend on some of the Mālava coins found in Rajputana has to be read from right to left as in Kharoṣṭhi, which was the prevalent script in the Punjab and the north-west from very early times.

---

[1] *Droṇaparvan*, Chap. 10, p. 17. [2] *Sabhāparvan*, Chap. 32, p. 7.

[3] *C.A.S.R.*, Vol. VI, 1871–3, pp. 72ff.

[4] R. O. Douglas in his paper '*On some Mālava Coins*', *J.P.A.S.B.*, Vol. XIX, N.S., pp. 42ff.

[5] A. C. Banerjee, '*The Mālavas*', *A.B.O.R.I.*, Vol. XIII, Pts. III–IV, 1931-2, pp. 218ff.

The Mālava occupation of the Nāgar area near Jaipur in Rajputana is also upheld by the Nasik Cave Inscription of Uṣavadāta, the Śaka, son-in-law of the Kṣatrapa Nahapāna. The power of Nahapāna and his allies seems to have been threatened by the Malayas (= Mālavas) who had already besieged the Uttamabhadras, allies of the Śaka king. Nahapāna sent Uṣavadāta, and the Malayas fled at the very sound of his approach, and were taken prisoner by the Uttamabhadras. Uṣavadāta afterwards went to Puṣkara, six miles west of Ajmere.[1] The Scythic invasions and conquests could not, however, destroy the tribal organisation of the tribe, for in the Allahabad Pillar inscription of Samudragupta they are included in the list of tribal states of the western and south-western fringe of Āryāvarta. Among them the most important were the Mālavas, Ārjunāyanas, Yaudheyas, and Ābhīras, all of whom were settled in Rajputana at this time. The Bijayagadh Inscription (*J.R.A.S.*, 1897, p. 30) definitely locates the Yaudheyas at this time in the Bharatpur State of Rajputana. The Ābhīras also occupied some region in Western Rajputana, the place called Abiria in the Periplus of the Erythrean Sea.

According to the Purāṇas, the Mālavas are associated with the Saurāṣṭras, Avantis, Ābhīras, Śūras, and Arbudas,[2] and are described as dwelling along the Pāriyātra mountains. Thus it seems that they occupied other territories besides the Punjab or Rajputana. After Samudragupta's time when, as we have seen, the tribe was settled in Rajputana, the Mālavas seem to have migrated to the Mandasor region in the north-west part of Central India, where most of the records connected with the successors of Samudragupta have been found. This region is certainly to be identified with the ancient Mahājanapada of Avanti (mentioned in the *Aṅguttara Nikāya*), as well as Avanti of the Junāgaḍh Rock inscription of Rudradāman, and Malaya (= Mālava) of the Jain *Bhagavatī Sūtra* referred to above whose capital was Ujjayinī. This tract of country along with the region round Bhilsa comprises what is now known as Malwa (Mālava). It is well-known that the years of the Vikrama Era in the Gupta epoch were known as Kṛta; and the Mālavas were associated with them (cf. Mandasor Inscr. of Naravarman, C.I.I., Vol. III); and wherever the Kṛta years are specified in the inscriptions of the Gupta period, the name of the Mālavas almost invariably occurs. We find the princes of Mandasor using the Era

[1] *Ep. Ind.*, Vol. VIII, p. 44.

[2] *Bhag.*, XII, I, 36; Viṣṇu, Bk. II, Chap. III; Brahma, Chap. XIX, śloka 17. The *Rāmāyaṇa* (*Kiṣk. Kāṇḍa*, Canto XLII) locates the tribe in the east; but the Bengal recension does not know of them.

(commencing 58 B.C.) traditionally handed down by the 'Mālava-gaṇa'. And it is not only in the Mandasor region that inscriptions have been found associating the Mālavas with the Kṛta Era; they have also been found among other places at Kāṃsuvāṃ in the Kotah State and Nāgarī in Udaipur State.

In the period following that of Skandagupta and his successors (i.e. after about 550 A.D.), the Mālavas seem to have migrated further to the east so as to cover the region from Bhilsa (Eastern Malwa) to Prayāg. In the *Harṣacarita* of Bāṇa, Kumāragupta and Mādhava-gupta, two sons of King Mahāsenagupta (of the line of Kṛṣṇa-gupta), who were appointed by Prabhākaravardhana to wait upon his sons, Rājyavardhana, and Harṣavardhana respectively, are referred to as 'Mālavarājaputrau'. It follows that Mahāsenagupta was a king of Mālava. He was most probably succeeded by a king named Devagupta, who is referred to in the Madhuvan and Banskhera inscriptions of Harṣavardhana, and who must be identical with the 'wicked Mālava King' who cut off Grahavarman Maukhari in battle, but was himself defeated by Rājyavardhana.[1] It is difficult to identify the Mālava Kingdom of Mahāsenagupta and Devagupta, but it was most probably identical with Pūrva-Mālava which lay between Prayāga and Bhilsa. It could not be the Mo-la-po (= Mālava) of Hsüan Tsang, for Mo-la-po was then under the Maitrakas of Valabhi; nor could it be the Mālava country whose capital was Ujjayinī, for Ujjayinī was at that time ruled by a brahmin dynasty, and the Guptas were not brahmins. Moreover, according to Vātsyāyana, Ujjayinīdeśa was called Apara-Mālava or Western Mālava; where only Mālava, without any prefix, is referred to, it should be taken to mean Eastern (Pūrva) Mālava.[2]

Just about this time, the celebrated Chinese pilgrim Hsüan Tsang in the course of his Indian travels visited the kingdom of 'Mo-la-po'; its capital was on the south-east of the river Moha (= Mahi). Mo-la-po was a country where learning was much prized.[3] This Mo-la-po must now be identified with Mālavaka or Mālavaka-āhāra, referred to in a number of Valabhi grants as included in the kingdom of the Maitrakas of Valabhi. The Mālavaka-āhāra lay between Bhṛgukaccha or Broach, Cutch, Valabhi, and Vadnagar (Smith), and corresponds roughly to the modern districts of Kaira and Ahmedabad, together with parts of the Baroda State and some adjoining territories.[4] That the Mo-la-po of Hsüan Tsang cannot be

---

[1] *P.H.A.I.*, 4th Ed., pp. 514 foll.

[2] *Ujjayinideśabhavastu evāpara-Mālavya-Mālavya iti Pūrva-Mālava bhava,*— N. Ray, *The Maukharis of Kanoj*, *Cal. Review*, 1928, Feb., p. 210 f.n.

[3] Watters, *On Yuan Chwang*, II, p. 242.

[4] *Ibid.*, II, p. 341.

identified with Mālava (i.e. Western Mālava) whose capital was Ujjayinī is also proved by the fact that the pilgrim describes the former as being included within the territory of Valabhi. 'The diminutive suffix *Ka* also indicates that it was then known as Lesser Mālava to distinguish it from Mālava proper' (C.A.G.I., Mazumdar's Notes, p. 728). The Mālavaka country is also referred to in the *Gurvāvalī Sūtra* of Dharmasāgaragaṇi, where Śrī Devendrasundarī is represented as having gone from Mālavaka to Gurjaratrā or Gujrat; [1] and it is also mentioned in the Tewar Stone Inscription of the region of Jayasiṃhadeva of the Cedi year 928.[2] The Mālavas and their country,—evidently meaning the region around Ujjayinī and Bhilsa, i.e. modern Malwa, are mentioned in a number of later epigraphic records, e.g. in the Sagartal inscription of the Gurjara Pratihāras, the Paithāna Plates of Rāṣṭrakūṭa Govinda III, and a host of others.

We have seen that the Mālavas migrated eastwards as far as Prayāga, probably in the second half of the sixth century A.D. During the rule of the Pālas of Bengal and Bihar they seem to have migrated still further east; for in the copper-plates of the Pāla kings (excepting Dharmapāla), reference is made not only to the Kulikas, the Khasas and Hūṇas, but also to the Mālavas who seem to have migrated to Bengal as mercenary troops.

The name of the tribe survives to this day not only in the modern province of Malwa (which is a transformation of the word Mālava), but also in those of two Brāhmaṇa castes called 'Mālavis' or 'Mālavikas'. They are the Brāhmaṇas of Mālava proper and the adjoining country, but are not only found in their special habitat, but also in Gujrat on the one hand, and Central and United Provinces on the other.[3]

[1] Weber, *Die Sk. Pr. Handschriften der Berliner Bibliothek*, II, 290.

[2] *Ep. Ind.*, Vol. II, pp. 18-9.

[3] See *Ann. B.O.R.I.*, Vol. XIII, parts III–IV, 1931-2, p. 229.—'In *Ep. Ind.*, V, 229, the Daṇḍanāyaka Anantapāla, a feudatory of Vikramāditya VI, is said to have subdued the Sapta Mālava countries up to the Himālaya mountains. This proves that there were as many as seven countries called Mālava. These were probably (1) *Mo-la-po* (Mālavaka-āhāra of Valabhi grants) on the Mahi, governed by the Maitrakas, (2) *Avanti* ruled by a Brāhmaṇa family in the time of Hsüan Tsang, (3) *Pūrva Mālava* (round Bhilsa), (4) District round *Prayāga*, (5) Fatehpur District, in U.P., (6) Cis-Sutlej districts of the Punjab, (7) Some Himalayan territory' (*P.H.A.I.*, 4th Ed., p. 492, f.n. 4).

## CHAPTER IX

# THE ŚĀLVAS

The Śālvas were an important people of Ancient India, and are referred to in Pāṇini's *Aṣṭādhyāyī*, in the Epics, and in the Purāṇas. But they do not seem to have been able to maintain their integrity until the beginning of the historical period, for they are scarcely referred to in inscriptions or in later Sanskrit or Pāli literature.

Perhaps the earliest mention of the Śālvas as a tribe is found in the *Gopatha Brāhmaṇa* (1, 2, 9), where they appear in connection with the Matsyas. The Matsyas were inhabitants of the region identical with the kingdom of King Virāṭa of the *Mahābhārata*, and the Matsya capital has been identified with Virāṭ in the Jaipur State; and the Śālvas probably occupied the territory now occupied by the native state of Alwar.[1] According to the *Mahābhārata*,[2] the Śālva country was situated near Kurukṣetra and was the kingdom of the father of Satyavān, husband of Sāvitrī.[3] The capital of the Śālvas seems to have been Śālvapura,[4] which is also called Saubhaganagara. King Śālva's kingdom or territory was also known as Mārttikāvata or Mṛttikāvatī.[5] Śālva is said to have attacked Dvārāvatī, but to have been killed by Kṛṣṇa.[6]

In the great Kurukṣetra war the Śālvas along with the Matsyas, Kekayas, Ambaṣṭhas, Trigarttas, and others, lent their support to the army of Duryodhana against the Pāṇḍavas, and, along with the Ambaṣṭhas and Trigarttas, formed a unit of the army led by Bhīṣma.[7] In the *Udyogaparvan* (54, 18) they are associated with the Pañcālas, Kekayas, and Śūrasenas; and (56, 18) with the Mālavas. In the *Bhīṣmaparvan*,[8] the Śālvas, Matsyas, Ambaṣṭhas, Trigarttas, Kekayas, Sauvīras, and six other tribal states are said to have arrayed themselves by the side of Bhīṣma. The mighty Śālva king is said to have been laid low on the battle-field by Bhīmasena

[1] Cunningham, *An. R.A.S.I.*, XX, p. 120; *Matsyapurāṇa*, Chap. 113.

[2] *Virāṭaparvan*, Chap. I.

[3] *Vanaparvan*, Chap. 282.

[4] *Mbh.*, *Vanaparvan*, Chap. 14.

[5] Pargiter, *A.I.H.T.*, p. 279. 'Mārttikāvata must be distinguished from Mṛttikāvatī. Mārttikāvata existed before, e.g. according to the story of Rāma Jāmadagnya' (*Mbh.*, III, 116, 11076; VII, 70, 2436)—*Ibid.*, f.n. 7.

[6] *Vanaparvan*, Chap. 14.

[7] *Bhīṣmaparvan*, Chap. 20, 10, 12, 15.

[8] Chap. 18, 13-4.

(*Karṇaparvan*, Chap. 5, 42).[1] The Śālvas are several times referred to in the *Mahābhārata*[2] as Dānavas and Daityas, i.e. demons,—probably because of their fabled enmity to Viṣṇu who is termed 'Śalvāri', foe of Śālva.

The *Vāyu* and *Matsyapurāṇas* locate the Śālvas amongst the central peoples (i.e. Madhyadeśa); but the *Viṣṇupurāṇa*[3] places them in the extreme west, along with the Sauvīras, Saindhavas, Hūṇas, Śākalas, Madras, etc.; and the *Brahmapurāṇa* (Chap. 19, 16–18) also locates them in the Aparānta or western country. In the Bengali recension of the *Rāmāyaṇa* (*Kiṣk. Kāṇḍa*, XLIII, 23) also they are classed among the western nations.

Commenting on *Śālvāvayava* in the śloka '*Śālvāvayava pratyagrathakalakūtāśmakādiñ*' (4, 1, 173), the *Kāśika* on Pāṇini's *Aṣṭādhyāyī* names Udumbara, Tilakhala, Madrakāra, Yugandhara, Bhuliṅga, and Saradatta as the six *avayavas* or parts of the Śālvajanapada. Bhuliṅga here is probably the same as 'Bolingai' of Ptolemy.[4] In the śloka '*na prācya Bhargādi Yaudheyādibhyaḥ*' (4, 1, 178), the *Kāśika* includes the Karūṣas, Kaśmīras, and Śālvas. The *Kāśika* on another sūtra (4, 2, 76) refers to a city of the Śālvas named Vaidhumāgni, built by Vidhumāgni; and elsewhere the *Kāśika* includes the Śālvas among the Kacchādi-gaṇa, along with the Kaśmīras (4, 2, 133; 4, 1, 169).

1 According to *Mbh.*, XII, 234, 8607 and XIII, 137, 6267, Dyutimant was a certain king of the Śālvas who gave his kingdom to Ṛcīka.

2 III, 14, 633-4; 17, 695, 710; 885-6.

3 II, Chap. III, śloka 16–8.

4 McCrindle's *Ptolemy*, p. 163.

## CHAPTER X

# THE UŚĪNARAS

The Uśīnaras were an ancient, petty tribe dwelling to the north of the Kuru country.[1] The *Gopatha Brāhmaṇa* (II, 9) tells us that the Uśīnaras and Vasas (Vatsas) were regarded as northerners. In the *Ṛgveda* (X, 59, 10) the tribe is alluded to in a passage which refers to their queen Uśīnarāṇī. Pāṇini, the grammarian, also refers to the Uśīnara country.[2] The *Aitareya Brāhmaṇa* contains a geographical passage (VIII, 14) which assigns the Kurus and Pañcālas, together with the Vasas and Uśīnaras, to the Middle Country, the later Madhyadeśa. In the *Kauśītakī Upaniṣad* (IV, 1) too, the Uśīnaras are associated with the Kuru-Pañcālas and the Vasas.

Zimmer thinks that the Uśīnaras earlier lived farther to the north-west. This theory is based on the fact that the Anukramaṇī of the *Ṛgveda* ascribes one hymn (X, 179) to Śivi Auśīnara; and that the Śivis were known to Alexander the Great's followers as the Siboi, living between the Indus and Akesines (Chenab). The authors of the *Vedic Index*[3] do not accept Zimmer's view, and observe: 'This is in no way conclusive, as the Sibis, at any rate in Epic times, occupied the land to the north of Kurukṣetra, and there is no reason whatever to show that in the Vedic period, the Uśīnaras were farther west than the Middle Country'. Pargiter,[4] however, holds that Uśīnara and his descendants occupied the Punjab. Uśīnara established separate kingdoms on the eastern border of the Punjab, viz. those of the Yaudheyas, Ambaṣṭhas, etc., and his famous son Śivi Auśīnara originated the Śivis in Śivapura and, extending his conquests westwards, founded, through his four sons, the kingdoms of the Vṛṣadarbhas, Madras, Kekayas and Suvīras, thus occupying the whole of the Punjab except the north-west corner.[5] According to tradition, King Uśīnara was descended from the Ānavas.[6] He had five wives, Mṛgā, Kṛmi, Navā, Darvā and Dṛṣadvatī, who respectively had five sons, Mṛga, Kṛmi, Nava, Suvrata and Śivi. The city of Mṛga was Yaudheya; and the *Harivaṃśa* connects the Yaudheyas with Uśīnara.[7]

[1] *Cambridge History of India*, Vol. I, p. 84.
[2] *Sūtras*, II, 4, 20; IV, 2, 118.
[3] Vol. I, p. 103.
[4] *Ancient Indian Historical Tradition*, p. 109.
[5] *Ibid.*, p. 264.
[6] *Ibid.*, p. 88.
[7] Pargiter, *Mārkaṇḍeya Purāṇa*, p. 380.

The story of Uśīnara's offering to sacrifice himself for a pigeon, and his subsequently being granted a boon by Indra, is one of the favourites of Indian mythology, and is too well-known to repeat here.[1] In the *Śāntiparvan* of the *Mahābhārata*,[2] we read that Nārada said to Sañjaya: 'Uśīnara Śivi was dead. He encircled the whole world like a skin'. Elsewhere in the same *parvan* [3] it is stated that Uśīnara became the sole emperor of the world, a patent exaggeration.

In the *Śrīmadbhāgavatam* we read that a famous king of Uśīnara named Suyajña was killed in battle.[4]

The Buddhist Jātakas refer more than once to King Uśīnara.[5] For instance, in one Jātaka we read that there once reigned a king named Uśīnara. His people were wicked and followed unrighteousness. During his reign, the religion of the Buddha began to disappear. Sakka (Sakra) observed the miserable plight of the people, due to the decadence of the religion of the Buddha. He turned the god Mātali, his charioteer, into the shape of a huge black hound and entered the city with him. The people were terrified by the loud barking of the hound. Sakka said that it was hungry; but even when all the food in the city was given to the hound, it did not stop barking. The king said that it must be a goblin, not a hound. Sakka then explained that he had come with the hound to revive the religion of the Buddha, and thus to establish the people in the virtues of liberality.[6]

A mountain named Usīragiri or Usīraddhaja is referred to in the *Divyāvadāna* (p. 22) and elsewhere; and Dr. H. C. Ray Chaudhuri points out that this may be identical with the Uśīnaragiri mentioned in the *Kathāsaritsāgara* (Ed. Durgāprasād and Kāśīnāth, 3rd Edn., p. 5). Uśīnaragiri is placed near Kanakhala,[7] and Usīraddhaja is mentioned in the *Vinaya Piṭaka* [8] as forming the northern boundary of the Middle Country; accordingly, it is possible that the two are identical and associated with the Uśīnara country.

[1] *Mbh.*, *Vanaparvan*, Chaps. 130, 131.
[2] Chap. 29, 39.
[3] *Ibid.*, 40; and see 41–3.
[4] Chap. II, śloka 28, 7th Skandha, p. 393.
[5] See, e.g. *Nimi Jātaka* (Fausböll), VI, p. 99; and *Mahānāradakassapa Jātaka*, *ibid.*, Vol. VI, p. 251.
[6] *Jātaka*, (Fausböll), Vol. IV, pp. 181 foll.
[7] *Political History of Ancient India*, 4th Ed., p. 55.
[8] *Vinaya*, I, p. 197 (Oldenberg).

CHAPTER XI

# THE VĀHLĪKAS

Vāhlīka, Vālhīka and Valhīka are variant names of a people who lived in the northern division of India from very early times. A king of the tribe, Bālhīka Prātīpya, is referred to in the *Śatapatha Brāhmaṇa* (XII, 9, 3, 1–3 and 13), and is represented as having opposed the restoration of Duṣṭarītu, king of the Sṛñjayas (*Vedic Index*, II, pp. 470-1). Bālhīka (or Vāhlīka) Prātipeya (or Prātipīya), son (or descendant) of this Pratīpa, as Pargiter points out (*A.I.H.T.*, p. 166, f.n. 2), is mentioned in the *Mahābhārata* (*Ādiparvan*, Chap 95, verse 44; *Udyogaparvan*, Chap. 47, verse 6). In the *Sabhāparvan* (Chap. 27, verse 22), mention is made of Vālheka, which is evidently another name for Vālhīka.

According to the *Vāyupurāṇa* as well as the *Kāvya Mīmāṃsā* of Rājasekhara, the Vālhīka country [1] is placed in the northern division. In the Bengal recension of the *Rāmāyaṇa* (see, e.g. *Kiṣkindhyā Kāṇḍa*, 44, verse 13) the Vālhīkas are associated with the people of the north, and sometimes (e.g. *ibid.*, 43, verse 5) with those of the west. We may conclude, then, that the Vālhīka country should be identified with some region beyond the Punjab. A reference in the *Udyogaparvan* to its having been famous for its horses seems to connect the Vāhlīka country with Kāmboja; this, together with the difficulty of approach to the country which is referred to in the account of Arjuna's *digvijaya* [2] may perhaps justify us in assuming that the tribe had its habitat somewhere in the neighbourhood of Gandhāra and Kāmboja. That the Vāhlīkas were settled beyond the Indus is definitely proved by the Meharauli Iron Pillar Inscription of Chandra, where the mighty King Chandra [3] is described as 'one . . . by whom having crossed in warfare the seven mouths of the Indus the Vāhlīkas were conquered'. Accordingly, the country of the Vālhīkas may perhaps be identified with the region now known as Balkh; in other words, the Vāhlīkas should be identified

[1] Also mentioned in *Śiva Purāṇa*, VII, 60, 20.

[2] *Sabhāparvan*.

[3] Chandra has been identified by some with Candravarman of the *Allahabad Pillar Inscription* of Samudragupta, as also with the king of the same name mentioned in the *Susunia Rock Inscription*.

with the 'Baktrioi' occupying the country near Arachosia in the time of the geographer Ptolemy.[1]

The *Uttarakāṇḍa* of the *Rāmāyaṇa* (Chap. 100, verse 3) refers to a dynasty of kings who are said to have descended from one Kārdama or Kardameya. They were related to the Aila race, and were associated with Vālhi or Vālhika over which they seem to have held sway. In another chapter of the *Uttarakāṇḍa* (103, verse 21) the Vāhli or Vahlika country is said to have been situated outside the Madhyadeśa, which must have extended as far as the Sarasvatī in the west. A Kārdamaka Vaṃśa or dynasty is referred to in the Kanheri Inscription of the minister (amātya) Śateraka. In his *Political History of Ancient India* (4th Edn., p. 423), Dr. H. C. Ray Chaudhuri makes the illuminating suggestion that this Kārdamaka Vaṃśa probably derived its name from the river Kārdama in Pārasīka or Persia.[2] In that case Vāhlika, the home of the Kārdama or Kārdamaka kings, should be sought for somewhere in Persia; and we have a further justification for identifying the country of the Vāhlīkas with Balkh in Iran.[3]

The Vāhlīkas or Vālhīkas should *not* be identified with the Vāhīkas, who seem to have lived between the Sutlej and the Indus. A passage in the *Karṇaparvan* (Chap. 44) seems to describe their position:

> '*Śākalaṃ nāma nagaramāpagā nāma nimnagā*
> *Jarttikā nāma Vāhīkāsteṣāṃ Vṛttaṃ sunindilam*' (verse 10).
> '*Śatadrukāṃ nadīṃ tīrttvā tāñca ramyāṃ Irāvatīm*' (verse 17).

This passage states that the Vāhīkas were also known as Jarttikas (= Jāt?) and Āraṭṭas,[4] and that their capital was at Śākala,[5] modern Sialkot, west of the Rāvi. Another portion of the same passage suggests that in the Āraṭṭa countries religion was in dis-repute; it was thus an impure region, and the Aryans of Mid-India were forbidden to go there. This is also reflected in the Vārttikas of Pāṇini by Kātyāyana who derives the word Vāhīka from 'vahi' or 'bahi', meaning 'outside', -suggesting those who were outside the pale of Aryandom. According to Pāṇini and his scholiast Patañjali, Vāhīka was another name for the Punjab (IV, 2, 117; V, 3, 114;

[1] Dr. H. C. Ray Chaudhuri, *P.H A.I.*, 4th Edn., p. 449, f.n.; and *Ind. Ant.*, 1884, p. 408.

[2] Comm. on *Arthaśāstra*, II, 11: *Pārasīkeṣu Karddama nāma nadī.*

[3] For fuller details of the Kārdamaka kings and their association with Vāhlika, see Ray Chaudhuri's paper on '*The Kārddamaka kings*' in *I.H.Q.*, Vol. IX, No. 1, pp. 37–9.

[4] The Āraṭṭas were the Arattai of the Periplus of the Erythrean Sea, p. 41.

[5] It will be remembered that Śākala was King Milinda's capital.

*Ind. Ant.*, I, 122). That the Vāhīkas were held in disrepute is also proved by verse 41 of the *Karṇaparvan*, which says:

> '*Vahiśca nāma Hīkaśca Vipāśāyāṃ Piśācakau*
> *Tayorapatyaṃ Vāhīkā naiṣā sṛṣṭiḥ prajāpateḥ.*'

According to this verse, Vahi and Hīka were names of two Piśācas (demons) of the Vipāśā river (Beas). Their descendants, the Vāhīkas, were not (worthy of being called) 'a creation of Prajāpati' (the Creator).

## CHAPTER XII

# THE TRIGARTTAS

The earliest mention of the Trigarttas to which a fairly definite date can be assigned is made in the *Aṣṭādhyāyī* of Pāṇini, the celebrated grammarian, who flourished in the middle of the sixth century B.C. at the latest. Besides a direct reference to the tribe or country of the Trigarttas in a certain Sūtra,[1] there are indirect references to the tribe in at least two other Sūtras, according to the scholiast on Pāṇini. In '*na prācya Bhargādi Yaudheyādibhyaḥ*' (Sūtra IV, 1, 178) *Bhargādi* is said to stand for the regions (*janapada*) of the Bhargas, Karūṣas, Kaśmīras, and Śālvas, whereas *Yaudheyādi* is taken to include the country or tribe of the Trigarttas as well as of the Yaudheyas (see chap. on Yaudheyas). The other reference to '*Yaudheyādi*' is in Sūtra, V, 3, 117, which mentions the Yaudheyas (and Trigarttas implicitly) as forming an '*Āyudha-jīvī Saṃgha*'. We may infer, then, that the Trigarttas, like the Yaudheyas, were a Kṣatriya tribal republic depending mainly on arms. This close association of Trigarttas and Yaudheyas probably means that their territories were contiguous.

In the *Mahābhārata*, also, these two tribes are often associated, both having rallied on the side of Duryodhana.[2] Two Trigartta heroes famous as Saṃsaptakas (bound by an oath to kill others) seem to have played an important part in the Kurukṣetra war.[3] The Trigarttas along with the Śālvas, Ambaṣṭhas, and other tribes were included in the army of Bhīṣma.[4] In the course of the war the Trigarttas seem to have had a hard fight with Nakula, the fourth Pāṇḍava,[5] while on another occasion their King Suśarmā fought a stiff battle with Arjuna.[6] As a result of the war, the Trigarttas along with the Kaśmīras, Mālavas, Śivis, Yaudheyas, Ambaṣṭhas, and other tribes were totally defeated, and they all paid homage to Yudhisṭhira.[7]

[1] V, 3, 116: Dāmanyādi *Trigarttaṣaṣṭhāchaḥ*.

[2] *Sabhāparvan*, Canto 52, 14-15; *Droṇaparvan*, Canto 18, 16.

[3] *Udyogaparvan*, Canto 57, 18. Before the actual war, five Trigartta brothers acted as agents of Duryodhana in harassing the Pāṇḍavas while they were living *incognito* in the Virāṭa country (*Udyogaparvan*, Canto 165, 9).

[4] *Bhīṣmaparvan*, Canto 20, 10, 12, 15; Canto 81, 3; Canto 82, 13.

[5] *Ibid.*, Canto, 72, 7.

[6] *Ibid.*, 96, 17; 102, 22; 104, 8.

[7] *Sabhāparvan*, 34, 7-12; 52, 14-15.

The Trigarttas, as described in the *Mahābhārata*, seem to have been a Punjab tribe. This is borne out not only by Hemachandra's *Abhidhānacintāmani*,[1] which speaks of Trigartta and Jālandhara (modern Jullundur) as synonymous, but also by a reference in the *Rājataraṅginī* (V, 144), which implies that the tribe inhabited a region not far from Kashmir. Epigraphic evidence[2] as well points to the fact that modern Jullundur was the ancient Trigartta country. In the Purāṇas,[3] the Trigarttas are reckoned among the mountain tribes. Cunningham identifies the Trigartta country with Kangra, which is situated in Jullundur between the mountains of Chamba and the upper course of the Beas.[4] 'Trigartta' is interpreted to be the land watered by the three rivers,—the Ravi, the Beas, and the Sutlej.[5] It is also explained as the country of the three strongholds, and is identified by some scholars with the modern hill-state of Kotoch, which is still called 'Trigartaka Mulk', or the region of the Trigarttas (Prof. Johnson's *Selections from the Mahābhārata*, p. 64, f.n. 8).[6]

The Trigartta tribe or country (*janapada*) is also mentioned in the *Daśakumāracaritam* in connection with Mitragupta's travels.[7]

Not very much is known of the authentic political history of Trigartta, but it seems certain that from about 700 to 1150 A.D., the country was practically a dependency of one or other of the Kashmir dynasties. From the *Rājataraṅginī* (V, 130–50), for instance, we learn that Kārkoṭa Sankaravarman, King of Kashmir (c. 883–902 A.D.), set out on a series of expeditions to recover the lost possessions of his father Avantivarman. Then Pṛthvicandra, King of Trigartta, who had previously given his son Bhavacandra as a hostage, came towards Sankaravarman to do homage; but fearing capture, fled far away. Kalhaṇa's description does not show that Trigartta was actually conquered, and Stein is probably right in assuming that no material success was achieved by Sankaravarman in the hills, east of the Ravi. The Trigartta country is said to have acknowledged the supremacy of the King of Kashmir during the reign (in Kashmir) of Ananta of the line of Abhinava (1028–63 A.D.).

---

1 IV, 24—'*Jālandharās-trigarttāḥ syuḥ*'. 2 *Ep. Ind.*, Vol. I, pp. 102, 116.

3 *Mārkaṇḍeya P.*, 57, 57; *Matsya P.*, 114, 56. The *Brahmapurāṇa* (14, 46) refers to a daughter, Jijñāsā by name, of a certain Trigartta king, who was married to Śiśirāyaṇī.

4 Cunningham, *A.S.R.*, V, p. 148; cf. *Bṛhatsaṃhitā*, Chap. 14; also Stein's *Rājataraṅginī*, Vol. I, p. 81.

5 Cunningham, *A.S.R.*, V, p. 148.

6 According to Nundolal Dey, North Canara was also called Trigartta in ancient times (*Gokarṇa-Bhāgavata*, X, Chap. 79).

7 *B.S.S.*, p. 108.

## CHAPTER XIII

# THE YAUDHEYAS

The Yaudheyas were a republican tribe of the Punjab known as early as the time of Pāṇini, the celebrated grammarian (*c.* sixth century B.C.), whose Sūtras contain what are probably the earliest reference to this people. In '*na prācya Bhargādi Yaudheyādibhyaḥ*' (IV, 1, 178) the term *Yaudheya-ādi* includes the two tribes, Yaudheyas and Trigarttas (according to Scholiast). Elsewhere in the Sūtras (V, 3, 117) the Yaudheyas (counting the Trigarttas with them) are referred to as forming an '*Āyudha-jīvī Saṃgha*', or a tribal republican organisation depending mainly on arms (cf. the name 'Yaudheya' = warrior).

The historical tradition of the tribe, however, goes back still farther than Pāṇini's time. The Purāṇas [1] refer to the Yaudheyas as having been descended from Uśīnara, while the *Harivaṃśa* too connects the Yaudheyas with the Uśīnaras.[2] According to Pargiter, King Uśīnara established the Yaudheyas, Ambaṣṭhas, Navarāṣṭra, and the city of Kṛmila, all on the Eastern border of the Punjab; while his famous son Śivi Auśīnara originated the Śivis or Śibis in Śivapura.[3] In the *Mahābhārata*,[4] the Yaudheyas are described as having been defeated by Arjuna, along with the Mālavas and Trigarttas; while in the *Sabhāparvan* (Chap. 52, 14-5), the Yaudheyas, together with the Śibis, the Trigarttas, and the Ambaṣṭhas, are represented as having paid homage to Yudhiṣṭhira. Elsewhere in the Great Epic (*Droṇaparvan*, Chap. 159, 5) the tribe is mentioned along with the Madrakas and Mālavas.[5]

The *Bṛhatsaṃhitā* places the Yaudheyas along with the Ārjunāyanas in the N. division of India. According to Ray Chaudhuri, they may have been connected with the Pandoouoi or Pāṇḍava tribe mentioned by Ptolemy as settled in the Punjab [6];

---

[1] *Brahmāṇḍa Purāṇa*, III, Chap. 74; *Vāyu P.*, Chap. 99; *Brahma P.*, Chap. 13; *Matsya P.*, Chap. 48; *Viṣṇu P.*, Chap. 17, etc.

[2] *Harivaṃśa*, Chap. 32; cf. also Pargiter, *Mārk. P.*, p. 380.

[3] *A.I.H.T.*, p. 264.

[4] *Droṇaparvan*, Chap. 18, 16; *Karṇaparvan*, Chap. 5, 48.

[5] '*Yaudheyānadrijān rājan Madrakān Mālavānapi*'. Here '*Adrijān*' has been interpreted by some as signifying a tribe, the '*Adrijas*' (possibly = the Adraistai of the Greeks); but it seems more likely that it is simply an epithet qualifying the Yaudheyas ('mountain-born'). There is no mention in Sorensen's *Index to the names in the Mahābhārata* of '*adrija*' used as the name of a tribe.

[6] *Ind. Ant.*, XIII, 331, 349.

for Yaudheya appears in the *Mahābhārata* (*Ādiparvan*, Chap. 95, 76) as the name of a son of Yudhiṣṭhira.[1]

Cunningham identifies the Yaudheyas with the Johiya Rajputs, and the country of the Yaudheyas with Johiyabar (= Yaudheya-vāra), the district around Multan. The Johiyas, he points out, are divided into three tribes; and he finds a strong confirmation of his identification in the fact that in the coins of the Yaudheya clan there can be traced the existence of three different tribes. These coins are of three classes, of which the first bears the simple inscription: 'jaya-Yaudheya-gaṇasya', i.e. '(money) of the victorious Yaudheya tribe'. The second class has 'dvi' at the end of the legend, and the third has 'tri', which are taken by Rapson to be contractions for 'dvitiyasya' and 'tritiyasya', or second and third, as the money of the second and third tribes of the Yaudheyas. As the coins are found to the West of the Sutlej, it is almost certain that they belong to the Johiyas who now occupy the line of the Sutlej.[2]

The Yaudheyas are known from the Bijayagadh (Bijegarh?) Stone Inscription[3] (C.I.I., Vol. III, pp. 250-1) to have occupied the Bijayagadh region of the Bharatpur State, and we may assume that they had extended their rule quite far to the South by about 150 A.D., the date of the Junāgarh (Kathiawar) Inscription of Rudradāman,[4] which contains that monarch's boast of having 'rooted out the Yaudheyas'. The tribe was not entirely extinguished, however, for in the Allahabad Pillar Inscription of Samudragupta (fourth century A.D.) the Yaudheyas are included in the list of tribal states who paid him homage (Mālavas, Ārjunāyanas, Yaudheyas, Madrakas, Ābhīras, Prārjunakas, Kākas, and Kharaparikas).[5]

[1] Ray Chaudhuri, *P.H.A.I.*, 4th Edn., p. 457.

[2] Cunningham, *Ancient Geography*, p. 245; pp. 281-2. Rapson, *Indian Coins*, p. 14.

[3] Paleographically the inscription is of an early date, the characters being of the so-called Indo-Scythic form. The leader of the Yaudheya tribe who is referred to in the inscription is styled Mahārāja and Mahāsenāpati.

[4] *Ep. Ind.*, Vol. VIII, pp. 36ff.

[5] Ray Chaudhuri, *P.H.A.I.*, 4th Edn., p. 457.

# CHAPTER XIV

## THE KEKAYAS

The Kekayas were a well-known tribe of Ancient India, and played an important part not only in the events recorded in the *Rāmāyaṇa*, but also in the great Kurukṣetra war of the *Mahābhārata*. They were known as early as the *Śatapatha Brāhmaṇa* and the *Chāndogya Upaniṣad*, and continued for some considerable time to be one of the important tribes of the Punjab. The territory of the Kekayas, according to the *Rāmāyaṇa*,[1] lay beyond the river Vipāśā (Beas) and extended up to the borders of the ancient Gandhāra kingdom. According to the Puranic tradition,[2] the Kekayas were descended from the (non-Aryan) Anu tribe or the family known as the Anavas, who appear from the Rigveda (8, 74) to have dwelt in the same territory of the Punjab as that later occupied by the Kekayas (according to the *Rāmāyaṇa*). Rājaśekhara in his *Kāvyamīmāṃsā* places the Kekaya country in the northern division (Uttarāpatha) of India, along with the Śakas, Hūnas, Kāmbojas, Vāhlikas, etc. In the *Mahābhārata* they are associated with the Vāhlikas, while in the Purāṇas more emphasis seems to be laid on their association with the Madras.

The earliest known king of the Kekayas was Aśvapati.[3] He was a theologian who is said to have instructed a number of Brāhmaṇas. The name of a Kekaya king several times referred to in the *Rāmāyaṇa* [4] was also Aśvapati; but it is difficult to say whether the two were identical. King Aśvapati of the *Rāmāyaṇa* was the father of Kaikeyī, second queen of Daśaratha, and maternal grandfather of Bharata (*Ayodhyākāṇḍa*, Chap. 70). The capital city of King Aśvapati, according to the *Rāmāyaṇa*, was Rājagṛha or Girivraja,[5] identified by Cunningham with Jālālpur on the Jhelum (= Giryak: Cunningham's *Arch. Sur. Rep.*, II). We learn from

[1] II, 68, 19–22; VII, Chaps. 113-4.

[2] *Brahmāṇḍa P.*, III, 74; *Vāyu P.*, Chap. 99; *Brahma P.*, Chap. 13; *Harivaṃśa* (Chap. 31); *Matsya P.*, Chap. 48; *Viṣṇu P.*, IV, Chap. 18; *Garuḍa P.*, I, Chap. 139; and *Bhāgavata P.*, IX, Chap. 23.

[3] *Śatapatha Brāhmaṇa*, X, 6, 1, 2; *Chāndogya Up.*, V, 11, 4 *et seq.*

[4] *Ādikāṇḍa*, Cantos XII, LXXIV, LXXXVII; *Ayodhyākāṇḍa*, Cantos II, XXXV, XXXVII, etc.

[5] *Rām.*, II, 67, 7; II, 68, 22. This Girivraja or Rājagṛha is not to be confused with the Girivraja or Rājagṛha of Magadha (*S.B.E.*, XIII, p. 150).

Jaina sources that one-half of the Kekaya kingdom was Aryan, and the Kekaya city was known as Seyaviya.[1]

The Kekayas fought on Duryodhana's side in the Kurukṣetra war. They seem from the Purāṇas [2] to have been intimately related to the Uśīnaras and the Śivis, for they were traditionally descended from one of the four sons of Śivi Uśīnara. The latter is said to have originated the Śivis in Śivapura and extending his conquests westwards, to have founded through his four sons the kingdoms of the Vṛṣadarbhas, Madras, Kekayas or Kaikeyas, and Suvīras or Sauvīras.[3] In the *Viṣṇupurāṇa* mention is made of a king of Kekaya or Kaikeya named Dhṛṣṭaketu (Bk., IV, Chap. XIV).

A branch of the Kekayas seems in later times to have migrated as far south as the Mysore country, where they established a settlement. They were probably an ancient ruling family of Mysore, and were connected by marriage with the Ikṣvākus, a famous royal dynasty, known from inscriptions discovered from the ruins of the Jagayyapeta stūpa in the Kṛṣṇā district,[4] as well as from Nāgārjunikoṇḍa.[5]

[1] *Ind. Ant.*, 1891, 375.

[2] *Vāyu P.*, Chap. 99; *Matsya P.*, Chap. 48; *Viṣṇu P.*, IV, Chap. 18; *Agni P.*, Chap. 276, etc.

[3] Pargiter, *A.I.H.T.*, p. 264. See also Chap. on *Yaudheyas*, for further information about Śivi and his father Uśīnara.

[4] Dubreuil, *A.H.D.*, pp. 88, 101; see also *Archaeological Survey of South India*, Vol. I, pp. 110-111.

[5] Ed. Vogel, *Ep. Indica*, Vols. XX, XXI; *Annual Report of South Indian Epigraphy*, 1926, p. 92; 1927, pp. 71–74.

## CHAPTER XV

# THE ĀBHĪRAS

The Ābhīras as a tribe are well-known in the history of ancient India. Probably coming into prominence for the first time during the age roughly covered by the Epics, at a later period they came to occupy an independent kingdom, and establish more centres than one in the country. The tribe can still be traced in the present Āhīrs (Āhīr being the Prakrit form of the Sanskrit word Ābhīra) who, in tribal groups, abound largely in the United Provinces, Bihar, Nepal and some portions of Rajputana. They are a band of simple, sturdy people, mostly cowherds and agriculturists.

According to the *Mahābhārata* (*Sabhāparvan*, Chap. 51), the Ābhīras were located in the western division of India (Aparāntaka). The Epic evidence is supported by that of the author of the *Periplus of the Erythrean Sea*, a Greek record of commercial geography of the first century B.C., as well as by Ptolemy, the Greek geographer who flourished in the middle of the second century A.D. Later epigraphic evidence also definitely places the Ābhīras in the west, but the Purāṇas seem to locate them in the northern division or Uttarāpatha. 'The fact seems to be', says Wilson, 'that the people along the Indus, from Surat to the Himalayas, are often regarded as either western or northern nations, according to the topographical position of the writer'.[1] A more definite location of the tribe is provided by a śloka in the *Mahābhārata*, which places them in West Rajputana, 'where the Sarasvatī disappears'.[2]

The *Mahābhāṣya* of Patañjali (second century B.C.) is perhaps the earliest authority that introduces the Ābhīras into Indian history. At 1, 2, 3 of that work, the Ābhīras are associated with the Śūdras, who are most likely identical with the Sodrai or Sogdoi of Greek historians of Alexander's time. The tradition of their association with the Śūdras[3] is upheld not only by the above-mentioned śloka of the *Mahābhārata* (IX, 37, 1), but also by the Purāṇas. The *Viṣṇupurāṇa*[4] places them in the extreme west along with the Surāṣṭras, Śūdras, Arbudas, Kārūṣas, and Mālavas, dwelling along the Pāripātra mountains. The *Mārkaṇḍeya Purāṇa* (Chap. 57, verses 35, 36) groups the Ābhīras with the Vāhlikas, Vāṭadhānas, Śūdras,

---

[1] Wilson, *Viṣṇu Purāṇa*, II, 168, f.n. 4.

[2] *Mbh.*, IX, 37, 1.

[3] Some scholars read Śūra for Śūdra.

[4] *Viṣṇu P.*, Ed. Wilson, Bk. II, Chap. III, pp. 132–5.

Madrakas, Surāṣṭras, and Sindhu-Sauvīras, all of whom are said to have occupied tracts of country that are included in the Aparāntaka or western country. According to Pargiter, the Ābhīras who are referred to in the *Mahābhārata* had something to do with the events following the great Kurukṣetra war: 'Some years after the battle, the Yādavas of Gujarat were ruined by fratricidal strife, and Kṛṣṇa died. Under Arjuna's leadership they abandoned Dvārakā (on which the sea encroached) and Gujarat and retreated northwards, but were attacked and broken up by the rude Ābhīras of Rajputana'.[1]

Both Ptolemy and the *Periplus* stress the close association of the Ābhīras and the Surāṣṭras. The *Periplus* mentions the country of Aberia (doubtless identical with Ābhīra) and its seaboard Syrastrene (= Surāṣṭra); while Ptolemy speaks of Abiria (= Aberia = Ābhīra) as having been included in Indo-Scythia, by which was meant practically the whole of the country along the lower course of the Indus. Indo-Scythia in Ptolemy's time was divided into three parts, viz. Syrastrēnē (Surāṣṭra), Patalene (= Skt. Pātāla), and Abiria (Skt. Ābhīra),—Abiria being identified with the region east of the Indus, above the insular portion formed by its bifurcation.[2]

By the middle of the second century B.C. the Ābhīras and their country must have been overpowered by the Bactrian Greeks who, not long after the expedition of Antiochus the Great (Antiochus III of Syria, 223—187 B.C.), had planned to extend their kingdom to the south of the Hindu Kush. It seems that these Bactrian Greeks occupied the whole of the country which Ptolemy designates as Indo-Scythia, and which included Aberia or Abiria. In Ptolemy's time, however, the Abiria or Ābhīra country was ruled over by the Śaka rulers or Kṣatrapas of W. India, who seem to have held sway over the entire realm of Indo-Scythia (cf. the Junāgaḍh Inscription of the Śaka ruler Rudradāman who flourished in the second century A.D.; *Ep. Ind.*, Vol. VIII, pp. 36ff.). The Guṇḍa Inscription of the Śaka king Rudra Siṃha (A.D. 181), who was third in succession from Rudradāman, refers to an Ābhīra general named Rudrabhūti who excavated a tank in his realm. Shortly afterwards[3] we find a certain Īśvaradatta, who was probably a native of Ābhīra, holding the office of Mahākṣatrapa. It is likely that Īśvaradatta was the same person as Īśvarasena,[4] an Ābhīra king (son of

---

[1] *A.I.H.T.*, p. 284.

[2] See Chap. on *Surāṣṭras*, and McCrindle's *Ptolemy*, pp. 136, 139-40.

[3] 188–90 A.D., according to Prof. Bhandarkar; but Rapson assigns Īśvaradatta to the period after 236 A.D.

[4] 'It is also suggested that this dynasty of Īśvarasena is identical with the Traikuṭaka line of Aparānta, and that the establishment of the Traikuṭaka era in A.D. 248 marks the date at which the Ābhīras succeeded the Sātavāhanas in the

Śivadatta), who became Mahākṣatrapa of W. India and wrested from the Sātavāhanas, probably in the third century A.D., portions at least of Mahārāṣṭra, which was ruled over by them up till the reign of Yajñaśrī Sātakarṇī.

The Ābhīras are next mentioned in the celebrated Allahabad Iron Pillar Inscription of Samudragupta (2nd quarter of the fourth century A.D.) as one of the tribal states of W and S.W. India who paid homage to the great Gupta emperor, and who were thus a semi-independent people living outside the borders of his empire.

If the traditional and legendary history of Nepal as contained in the Vaṃśāvalis has any historical value, the Ābhīras or Āhīrs had a settlement in Nepal in very early times. The traditional history of Nepal as recorded in the Vaṃśāvalis begins with a long line of legendary kings, after which the country was taken possession of by a line of Kirāta pretenders, whose passing away probably marks the entry of Nepal into the domain of fairly precise historical tradition. These Kirātas were succeeded by eight princes belonging to the Gopāla dynasty. The Gopālas in their turn were supplanted by the Ābhīras.

The tribe seems to have had another settlement in the South or Dakṣiṇāpatha. According to the *Mārkaṇḍeya Purāṇa*,[1] the Ābhīras are classed with the Puṇḍrakas, Keralas, Kaliṅgas, Pulindas, Andhras, Vidarbhas, Kuntalas and others, all of whom are said to be *Dakṣiṇāpatha-vāsinaḥ*, or dwelling in the southern country. The *Vāyupurāṇa* also records the same tradition (Chap. 45, 126), and describes the Ābhīras, Ātabyas, Śabaras, Pulindas, Vaidarbhas and Daṇḍakas as '*Dakṣiṇāpatha-vāsinaḥ*'.

---

government of northern Mahārāṣṭra and the adjoining region. The last known rulers of the Traikuṭaka line were Indradatta, his son, Dharasena and his son, Vyāghrasena' —Ray Chaudhuri, *P.H.A.I.*, 4th Ed., p 418, f.n. 2.

[1] Chap. 57, vv. 45–8, Chap. 58, v. 22.

# CHAPTER XVI

## THE ŚIBIS

The Śibis (or Śivas) seem to have been a very ancient people. They were a petty tribe occupying some tract in the Western Punjab, whence they seem later to have migrated or sent offshoots south-westwards to Sind and Rajputana and southwards as far as the Chola country.

They are probably alluded to for the first time in the *Ṛgveda* (VII, 18, 7) where the Śivas, doubtless the same people as the Śibis, are grouped together with four other minor tribes, viz. the Aliṇas, Pakhtas, Bhalānasas and Viśāṇins, who were all defeated by the combined army of King Sudās.[1] But whatever the fate of the other four tribes after their defeat, the Śivas seem to have maintained their independent existence for some considerable time, for they are referred to not only by the Greek geographers and historians of Alexander's time, but also by the Scholiast on *Pāṇini* (IV, 2, 109). Their King Śivi, son of Uśīnara, is mentioned in Baudhāyana's *Śrauta Sūtra* (III, 53, 22). There can hardly be any doubt as to the identity of the *Rgvedic* Śivas with the Sibai or Siboi of the Greeks[2] who dwelt between the Indus and the Akesines (= Asiknī of the *R.V.*; mod. Chandrabhāgā or Chenab) in Alexander's time.

'When the army of Alexander', states Arrian, 'came among the Sibai, an Indian tribe, and noticed that they wore skins, they declared that the Sibai were descended from those who belonged to the expedition of Herakles, and had been left behind; for besides being dressed in skins, the Sibai carry a cudgel, and brand on the backs of their oxen the representation of a club, wherein the Macedonians recognised a memorial of Herakles.' (Arrian, *op. cit.*) He continues: 'If any one believes all this, this must be another Herakles, not the Theban, but either the Tyrian or the Egyptian, or even some great King who belonged to the upper country which lies not far from India'. It seems reasonable to suppose, from the above description of their dress and weapons, that the tribe belonged to a racial group not distinctly Aryan. They are said to have had 40,000 foot-soldiers at the time of Alexander.

[1] The 'war of the ten kings' is sometimes interpreted as a struggle between the Aryans (under Sudās) and the pre-Aryans; in which case the Śivas or Śibis were not Aryans, but probably Sumerians.

[2] Arrian, *Indica*, V, 12; Diodorus, XVII, 96.

An earlier reference to this people is found in the *Aitareya Brāhmaṇa* (VIII, 23, 10), where mention is made of Amitratapana, a king of the Śivis. A place called Śivapura or 'town of the Śivas' is mentioned by the Scholiast on *Pāṇini*[1] as situated in the northern country. Śivapura must be identical with Śibipura, mentioned in a Shorkot Inscription (*Ep. Ind.*, 1921, p. 16); and Dr. Vogel takes the mound of Shorkot to be the site of the city of the Śibis. Another scholar points out that local tradition also connects Shorkot with Śiva.[2] Thus we may conclude that the Śivas or Śibis were a people inhabiting the Shorkot region in Jhang in the Punjab, lying between the Irāvatī and the Chandrabhāgā, and therefore included in the northern region or Uttarāpatha.

The Śivas or Śibis seem to have migrated, or rather sent one or more of their offshoots southwards to Rajputana. It is difficult to say exactly when this movement took place, but early references to a geographical location of the tribe other than in the Punjab are found in the Jātakas and in the *Mahābhārata*. The Jātakas[3] mention a Śivi king and his country with two of its cities, Ariṭṭhapura and Jetuttara. Ariṭṭhapura (Skt. Ariṣṭapura) is probably identical with Ptolemy's Aristobothra in the north of the Punjab[4] and may perhaps be the same as Dvārāvatī.[5] Jetuttara or Jettuttara is identified by N. L. Dey with Nāgari, a locality 11 miles north of Chitore.[6] It is evidently the Jattararur of Alberuni,[7] the capital of Mewar. That the Śibis had a habitat near Chitore is attested by other sources as well; a number of coins inscribed with the legend *Majhamikāya Sivijanapadasa*' have been discovered in the territory near Nāgari,—indicating that the janapada or country of the Śibis was located in Madhyamikā, near Chitore in Rajputana. On the testimony of these coins we also learn that the Śibis formed a gaṇa-rāṣṭra or some sort of republican state. This seems to have some support from the *Vessantara Jātaka*, where we read that the king of the Śibis[8] was compelled to banish prince Vessantara in obedience to the demand of his people,—indicating that if not an absolute republic, this community at least had what we may call democratic institutions.

---

1 See *Patañjali*, IV, 2, 2; *Vedic Index*, II, pp. 381-2.

2 Mazumdar, *C.A.G.I.*, p. 669; Sivapura = Siaura = Shor. *C.A.S.R.*, V, pp. 97-103.

3 *Śivi Jātaka*, No. 499; *Ummadantī Jātaka*, No. 527; *Vessantara Jātaka*, No. 547.

4 N. L. Dey, *Geographical Dictionary*, p. 11.

5 *Jātaka* (Fausböll), VI, p. 421; cf. Dey, p. 187.

6 *Geographical Dictionary*, p. 81.

7 Alberuni's *India*, I, p. 202.

8 Cf. also Sivikarāja, which was the Tathāgata's name in a previous birth, referred to in Beal's *Records of the Western World*, I, pp. xvi-cvii, 125.

The Śivas or Śibis were intimately associated with the Uśīnaras, who are assigned by the *Aitareya Brāhmaṇa* to the Madhyadeśa or 'Middle Country', together with the Kurus, the Pañcālas, and the Vasas or Vatsas. The Anukramaṇī of the *Ṛgveda* ascribes one hymn (X, 119) to Śivi Auśīnara, i.e. the Śivi who is descended from Uśīnara; while the *Mahābhārata* refers not only to a king Uśīnara Śibi (*Mbh.*, *Śāntiparvan*, Chap. 29, 39) but also to a Śibi-rāṣṭra or kingdom of the Śibis ruled by King Uśīnara (III, 130-1). It is, therefore, likely that the Uśīnara country was at one time the habitat of the Śibis. According to the tradition as recorded in the Epics and Purāṇas, Śivi was one of the five sons of King Uśīnara, each of whom founded a city. The city of Śivi was known as Śivapura. Śivi had four sons who came to be known as Śivis, giving their name to the tribe to which they belonged. According to Pargiter, Śivi Auśīnara not only originated the Śivis in Śivapura but, extending his conquests westwards, founded through his four sons (Vṛṣadarbha, Suvīra, Kekaya, and Madraka) the kingdoms of the Vṛṣadarbhas, Suvīras (or Sauvīras), Kekayas, and Madras, thus occupying the whole of the Punjab except the north-western corner.[1]

King Śivi Ausīnara bears a legendary name for piety and humanity. The well-known and very popular fable of the hawk and the pigeon immortalises this king's spirit of self-sacrifice.[2]

In the *Mahābhārata* description of the tribes, kings, and princes, who were ranged on Duryodhana's side in the Kuruksetra war, the Śivis are grouped with the foreign tribes, Śakas, Kirātas, Yavanas and Vasātis. As the Yavanas and Śakas did not appear in Indian history before the fifth and second centuries B.C. respectively, the passage in which the mention of these tribes occurs, must be regarded as a later interpolation; but however that may be, the fact that the Śivis are grouped with the 'foreigners' is significant, and it is not unlikely that the tradition has a historical foundation.

Still later, the Śivis seem to have migrated to the extreme south of India. The *Daśakumāracaritam* (*Madhya*, Chap. VI) refers to a settlement of the Śivis on the banks of the Kāverī. The southern

[1] See Chap. on *Uśīnaras*, and Pargiter, *Ancient Indian Historical Tradition*, pp 41 and 264.

[2] *Mbh.*, III, Chap. 196, Chap. 207; XIII, Chap. 67, XIV, Chap. 90. In the *Droṇaparvan* version (Chaps. 130-131) Śivi's father, Uśīnara, is the hero of the fable. Both Fā-Hien and Hsuan Tsang place the scene of the story in Udyāna now called the Swat Valley where a steatite relief (now in the British Museum) representing the fable as given in the *Mbh.* has been discovered. It is, therefore, probable that the present Swat Valley represents the ancient kingdom of Śivi. But according to the *Mahā-Ummaga Jātaka* the Śivi country was situated between the kingdoms of Videha and Pañcāla (Dey, *Geographical Dicty.*, pp. 187-8).

Śivis, according to Dr. H. C. Ray Chaudhuri,[1] are probably to be identified with the Chola ruling family.[2] The Śivi country of the south may be identical with the Śivikā country which is placed among the southern countries by Varāhamihira in his *Bṛhatsaṃhitā* (Chap. XIV, verse 12).

[1] *Political History of Ancient India*, 4th Ed., p. 205, f n 5.

[2] Keilhorn, List of Southern Inscriptions, No. 685.

## CHAPTER XVII

# THE DARADAS

The Daradas were a tribe of N.W. India, well-known both to indigenous and to foreign traditions. They are referred to in the *Mahābhārata* as having joined the Kaurava forces, and as having been defeated by Vāsudeva, along with the Khaśas, Śakas, Yavanas, Trigarttas, Mālavas and others.[1] The *Viṣṇupurāṇa* associates them with the Ābhīras and Kāśmīras[2]; while in the *Matsyapurāṇa*[3] the country of the Daradas is linked with Gandhāra, Śivapura, Urja, Aurasa and other districts forming the basin of the Sindhu (= Indus). The Epic and Puranic traditions seem therefore to locate the Daradas in the north-west along the north-west frontier of Kashmīr, and contiguously with the realm of the Khasas in the upper Punjab. They were probably a mountainous tribe, for 'mountain is the commonest meaning of the word *darad* from which they appear to have derived their name'.

The Greek writers knew this people by various names. Strabo mentions them as Derdai, Pliny as Dardae; while in Dionys. Periêg. (V, 1138) their name is given as Dardanoi. Ptolemy refers to the same people as Daradrai, the additional *r* evidently being inserted by mistake. He locates them east of the Lambatai (= Lampāk or Lamghan) and of Sonestane (= basin of the Swat river), and to the north of the uppermost course of the Indus. The mountains in the country of the Daradas, he says, are of surpassing height.

The Daradas were an important factor in the history of Kashmīr, and are often referred to in the *Rājataraṅgiṇī*.

The country once inhabited by the Daradas still retains clear traces of the ancient name, being known as Dardistan, the district of the Dardo.

[1] *Droṇaparvan*, Chap. 10, 18.
[2] Wilson's Ed., II, p. 184.
[3] CXXI, 45-51.

# CHAPTER XVIII

## THE KĀRŪṢAS OR KARŪṢAS

The Kārūṣas or Karūṣas were a well-known tribe of ancient India, who are often referred to in the Epics, particularly in the *Mahābhārata* and the Purāṇas. Throughout the whole range of early and later Vedic literature they are scarcely mentioned, and their sudden emergence in the period of the Epics and Purāṇas suggests that they had been an insignificant tribe inhabiting a region included in or continuous with the *janapada* of the Cedis, with whom they are constantly associated in the *Mahābhārata*.[1] The *Padmapurāṇa* (IV, Chap. 274, 16-17) moreover, tells us that Dantavakra, King of Karūṣa, was of Caidya lineage. The evidence as recorded in the *Mahābhārata* and the Purāṇas seems to point to the fact that Dantavakra and his father Vṛddhaśarman had been reigning in the time of the Pāṇḍavas.[2] According to the *Viṣṇupurāṇa* (Bk., IV, Chap. XIV) Vṛddhaśarman married Srutadevī, who bore him the fierce Asura Dantavakra. The *Vāyupurāṇa*, however, does not call him an Asura, but King of the Karūṣas. According to the *Padmapurāṇa* (*Pātala*, Chap. 35) Dantavakra was killed by Kṛṣṇa in Mathurā (vide also N. L. Dey, *G.D.A.M.I.*, p. 2). King Dantavakra is said to have had a foster-daughter named Pṛthā, who was married to Pāṇḍu.[3] Their contemporaries in the contiguous territories were Dāmaghoṣa, his son Śiśupāla Sunītha, and grandson Dhṛṣṭaketu, kings of Cedi; and Virāṭa, king of Matsya.[4] The Karūṣa royal family was connected by marriage not only with that of the Cedis but also with those of the Yādavas (i.e. Vāsudeva, Kṛṣṇa and all his relations, and the Pauravas).[5]

We must turn to the Purāṇas for the legendary account of the origin of the Kārūṣas. All the Purāṇas agree in saying that Vaivasvata Manu had nine sons[6]: namely Ikṣvāku, Nābhāga

---

[1] *Bhīṣmaparvan*, Chap. 47, 4, Chap. 54, 8; Chap. 56, 9, *Droṇaparvan*, Chap. 8, 28; Chap. 20, 23; *Karṇaparvan*, Chap. 56, 2, etc.

[2] *Mbh.*, II, Chap. 13, 575, 577; *Vāyu Purāṇa*, Chap. 96, 255; *Viṣṇu P.*, IV, Chap. 14, 11; *Brahmāṇḍa P.*, III, Chap. 71, 156, etc.

[3] *Brahma P.*, Chap. 14, 122.

[4] Pargiter: *A.I.H.T.*, p. 119.

[5] *Ibid.*, 166-7, f.n. 1; *Vāyu Purāṇa*, Chap. 96, 148–159; *Matsya P.*, Chap. 46, 3–9; *Viṣṇu P.*, IV, Chap. 14, 10–13, etc.

[6] According to the *Mahābhārata*, I, Chap. 75, Manu had fifty other sons, all of whom perished through mutual dissensions.

(= Nabhāga or Nṛga), Dhṛṣṭa, Saryāti, Narisyanta, Praṃśu, Nābhānediṣṭha, Karūṣa, and Pṛṣadhra.[1] From Karūṣa were descended the numerous Kṣatriya clans of the Kārūṣas. They were all determined fighters, and are said to have protected N. India,—perhaps from southern inroads as Pargiter suggests (*A.I.H.T.*, p. 255 and f.n. 14).[2]

The Kārūṣas had different settlements at different periods; the location of the principal ones may be described as follows:—

I. (A) In the *Mahābhārata* they are often mentioned along with the Matsyas, Kāśīs, Cedis, and Pañcālas (*Bhīṣmaparvan*, Chap. 47, 4; Chap. 56, 13; Chap. 54, 8; *Droṇaparvan*, Chap. 8, 28; Chap. 20, 23, etc.). The *Viṣṇupurāṇa* mentions them together with the Matsyas, Cedis, and Bhojas (Wilson, II, pp. 156–90). Pargiter therefore suggests that the country of the Kārūṣas lay to the south of Kāśī and Vatsa, between Cedi on the west and Magadha on the east enclosing the Kaimur hills,—i.e. it was equivalent to the country of Rewa, from the Ken river in the west to the confines of Bihar in the east.[3]

(B) The *Bālakāṇḍa* (XXVII, 18–23) of the *Rāmāyaṇa* would seem to indicate a slight difference of locality; it seems to locate the tribe in the district now known as Shahabad (Bihar),—whence they probably migrated south-west to the region indicated by the *Mahābhārata*. According to tradition, the southern district of Shahabad between the river Son and Karmanāśā was called Karukhdeśa or Karushadeśa.[4] This tradition is supported by a modern local inscription found at Masār in the Shahabad district, designating the territory as Karūṣadeśa.[5] Moreover, Vedagarbhapurī or modern Buxar is referred to in the *Brahmāṇḍapurāṇa* (*Purvakhaṇḍa*, Chap. 5) as being situated in Karūṣa.

II. The Kārūṣas probably had another settlement in the territory known in ancient times as Puṇḍra, or Puṇḍravardhana, roughly identical with N. Bengal; for according to the *Bhāgavatapurāṇa* (X, Chap. 66) Karūṣa seems to have been another name for Puṇḍra.

III. In the *Vāyu* (Chap. 45), *Matsya* (Chap. 114, 54), and *Mārkaṇḍeya* (Chap. 57, 53–5) *Purāṇas*, the Kārūṣas are said to have occupied the ridge of the Vindhyas (*Vindhapṛṣṭha-nivāsinaḥ*). In the

---

[1] *Vāyu P.*, Chap. 85, 3-4; *Brahma P.*, Chap. 7, 1-2; *Śiva P.*, VIII, Chap. 60, 1-2; *Kūrma P.*, I, Chap. 20, 4–6, etc.

[2] For references to Karūṣas, see *Vāyu P.*, Chap. 86, 2-3; *Garuḍa P.*, Chap. 142, 4; *Viṣṇu P.*, IV, Chap. I, 14; *Śiva P.*, VII, Chap. 60, 31; *Bhāgavata P.*, XX, 2, 16.

[3] *J.A.S.B.*, 1895, p. 255; *J.R.A.S.*, 1914, p. 271; *Pāṇini*, IV, 1, 178.

[4] Martin's *Eastern India*, Vol. I, p. 405; cf. Dey, *Geographical Dictionary*, p. 95.

[5] Cunningham, *A.S.R.*, III, pp. 67–71.

*Mārkaṇḍeya Purāṇa*, they are mentioned along with the Keralas and Utkalas, and in the *Brahmāṇḍapurāṇa* with the Mālavas, Utkalas, and Daśārṇas (all dwelling in the Vindhya region); while in the *Viṣṇupurāṇa* (Bk. II, Chap. III) they are associated with the Arbudas and Mālavas. Further, the *Viṣṇupurāṇa* definitely refers to them as dwelling along the Pāripātra hills. In the *Bālakāṇḍa* of the *Rāmāyaṇa* (XXIV, 18) the Karūṣas and the Maladas are named together; the Maladas are probably the Molindae of Pliny, whereas the Kārūṣas may be identified with the Chrysei.[1]

The Kārūṣas figure in the Kurukṣetra war along with the Kekayas, Pañcālas, Matsyas, Cedis and Kosalas, who rallied on the side of the Pāṇḍavas.[2] At one time during the war, the Cedi, Kāśī, and Kārūṣa peoples seem to have been led by Dhṛṣṭaketu, King of the Cedis.[3] Another King of the Cedis was Vasu, a descendant of Kuru, who having conquered the Yādava kingdom of Cedi, extended his conquests eastwards as far as Magadha, and apparently north-west also, over Matsya. He divided his territories of Magadha, Cedi, Kauśāmbī, Karūṣa, and Matsya among his five sons (see Chap. on Cedis).

1 M. V. St. Martin's *Etude sur la Geog. Grecque*, p. 199.
2 See *Udyoga*, *Bhīsma* and *Droṇa Parvans*.
3 *Udyogaparvan*, Chap. 198, 2, *Bhīsmaparvan*, Chap. 56, 13

## CHAPTER XIX

# KULAṬAS OR KULŪṬAS

The Kūrmanivesa section of the *Mārkaṇḍeya Purāṇa* (LVII, 49) mentions a tribe called Kulaṭas, and another named Kuruṭas (LVII, 51). Both seem to be results of a confusion with the well-known tribe or people known in history as the Kulūṭas. The *Karṇaparvan* of the *Mahābhārata* refers to the latter which seems to be identical with the Kolūta or Kolūka of the *Kiṣkindhyā Kāṇḍa* of the *Rāmāyaṇa* (XLIII, and annotations). Pargiter (*Mārk.*, p. 382, note) long ago identified the land of the Kulūṭas with the modern Kulu near the source of the Beas which is upheld by a reference to them in later literature of more reliable historical import.

The Kulūṭas seem to have been a tribal republic. Inscriptions and coins testify to the existence of many such republics even in the days of Scythian invasions, among whom the Mālavas, Yaudheyas and Ārjunāyanas were the most important, the Audumbaras Kulūṭas, Kunindas and the Uttamabhadras being only second in rank (*Camb. Hist. of India*, Vol. I, pp. 528-9).

Yuan Chwang, the celebrated Chinese pilgrim, refers to a country named Ku-lu-to (Watters, I, p. 298) which place he reached from Jālandhara after having travelled north-east, across mountains and ravines, by hazardous paths, for above 700 li. The region, says he, was entirely surrounded by mountains. Its capital was 14 or 15 li in circuit. It had a rich soil and yielded regular crops, and it had a rich vegetation. The climate grew gradually cold and there was little snow. There were in the country twenty Buddhist monasteries with above 1,000 brethren of whom the most were Mahāyānists, a few adhering to the Hīnayāna school. Of Deva temples, there were fifteen, and the professed non-Buddhists lived pell-mell. Cunningham long ago identified this Kiu-lu-to country of Yuan Chwang 'with the position of the Kullu district in the Upper valley of Byās river'. The position is roughly identical with the modern Kangra district.

Another important reference to the Kulūṭa people is also found in the introduction of *Bālabhārata* or *Pracaṇḍapāṇḍava* of Rājaśekhara wherein the poet describes the victories of Mahīpāla of the Pratihāra dynasty. Mahīpāla is there credited with having defeated the Kulūṭas along with the Muralas, Mekalas, Kaliṅgas, Keralas, Kuntalas and the Ramaṭhas (Nirṇayasāgar Press Ed. of *Bālabhārata*, I, 7-8).

## CHAPTER XX

# THE KULINDAS

The Kulindas were a small N. Indian tribe, sometimes confounded with the Pulindas. They are mentioned in the *Mahābhārata* [1] along with the Paiśācas, Ambaṣṭhas and Barbaras, who are all described as mountainous people. McCrindle informs us that in another passage of the *Mahābhārata* they are mentioned in a long list of tribes 'dwelling between Meru and Mandāra and upon the Śailodā river, under the shadow of the Bambu forests, whose kings presented lumps of ant-gold at the solemnity of the inauguration of Yudhiṣṭhira as universal emperor'.[2]

The country of the Kulindas is referred to by Ptolemy as Kulindrine. He locates it near the mountainous region where the Vipāśā, Śatadru, Yamunā and Gaṅgā have their sources. Cunningham identifies Kulindrine with the kingdom of Jālandhara (Jullundur),[3] but this is not accepted by Saint-Martin. A territory of the name of Kuluta, which was formed by the upper part of the Vipāśā basin, and which may be included in Ptolemy's Kulindrine, is mentioned in a *Varāha Saṃhitā* list. It was visited by the Chinese pilgrim Hsüan Tsang, who calls it K'in-lu-to. The name still exists under the slightly modified form of Koluta.[4]

The Kulindas were probably identical with the Kunindas, a tribe known from coins,[5] and located in the W. Punjab along with the Mālavas, Yaudheyas, Ārjunāyanas, Udumbaras, Kulūtas and Uttamabhadras.

[1] *Dronaparvan*, Chap. 119, 14.

[2] McCrindle's *Ptolemy*, p. 110.

[3] *C.A.G.I.*, p. 157.

[4] McCrindle, *Ptolemy*, p. 110.

[5] *Cambridge History of Ancient India*, I, pp. 528-9.

# CHAPTER XXI

## THE BARBARAS

The Barbaras, a 'barbarian' tribe, are associated in the *Mahābhārata*[1] with the Ambaṣṭhas, Paiśācas, Kulindas, etc., and also with the Yaunas, Kāmbojas, Gandhāras and Kirātas, in a passage which definitely states that these tribes were located in the Uttarāpatha or northern country.[2] The *Matsyapurāṇa* associates them with the Tuṣāras, Pahlavas, Pāradas, Śakas, Urjas, Aurasas and other tribes whose countries are said to have been watered by the Cakṣu stream of the Ganges before it entered the sea (CXXI, 45–51). The *Mārkaṇḍeya Purāṇa* (LVII, 39) places them in the Sindhu country, and the *Bṛhatsaṃhitā* refers to them as a north or north-west tribe.

The commentary on Kauṭilya's *Arthaśāstra* has some interesting remarks on the Barbara country, and its river Srotasī, which was a source of pearls. Alakanda, a city famous for its pearls, stood on this river. There was also a lake named Śrīghanta in a corner of the sea of Barbara.[3] S. N. Mazumdar sees in Alakanda a remnant of Alexander's name, and he identifies the city with Alexander's Haven.[4] V. A. Smith (*Early History of India*, p. 110, 4th Ed.) points out that the large lake at the mouth of the river where Alexander's Haven stood (near Karachi) still exists. This lake may be identified with the lake Śrīghanta mentioned in the *Arthaśāstra* commentary.

Mazumdar remarks[5] that Barbara is mentioned in an Āyurvedic work called *Rājanighaṇṭu*; and Barbarika, evidently a city of the Barbaras, in another Āyurvedic work, *Dhanvantarīyanighaṇṭu*. This Barbarika (the Barbarei of Ptolemy[6]) is evidently the Barbaricum or Barbaricon emporium mentioned in the *Periplus of the Erythraean Sea* (prob. *circa* 80 A.D.). It was at that time a market town and port, was situated on the middle mouth of the Indus, and included in the Śaka country whose metropolis was Minnagar. Barbarika and Patala (the latter identified by V. A. Smith[7] with Bahmanābād) formed the two towns of the islands of the Indus delta.

---

[1] *Sabhāparvan*, Chap. 31, 199, etc.; *Droṇaparvan*, Chap. 119, 14.

[2] *Mbh.*, XII, 207, 43. '*Uttarāpatha-janmānaḥ kīrtayiṣyāmi tān api Yauna Kāmboja Gāndhārāḥ Kirātā Barbaraiḥ saha.*'

[3] *Arthaśāstra*, Eng. Trsl., p. 86, f.n. 7, 8; p. 90, etc.

[4] *C.A.G.I.*, pp. 692–4.

[5] *Ibid.*, pp. 694-5.

[6] McCrindle's *Ptolemy*, p. 148.

[7] *Early History of India*, 4th Ed., p. 107.

## CHAPTER XXII

# THE MURUṆḌAS

The Muruṇḍas were probably a foreign tribe. They are mentioned for the first time by Ptolemy (second century A.D.), under the name Moroundai. Ptolemy's description would place them on the western border of the 'Gangaridai'. They seem to have occupied an extensive territory, probably the whole of N. Bihar on the east of the Ganges, as far as the head of the delta. They had six important cities, all to the east of the Ganges: Boraita, Koryagaza, Kondota, Kelydna, Aganagora and Talarga. These places are difficult to identify, but to Saint-Martin Kelydna appeared to have some relation with the Kālinadī or Kālindī river, and Aganagora with Aghadīp (Agradvīpa) on the eastern bank of the Ganges, a little below Kātwā (Ptolemy's *Ancient India* by McCrindle, pp. 215-6). According to Cunningham, the name of the Marundai is still preserved in the country of the Muṇḍās, a hill-tribe scattered over Chota-Nagpur and Central India. He says: "The name of Muṇḍa is found in the *Viṣṇupurāṇa* as the appellation of a dynasty of eleven princes who succeeded the Tushāras or Tokhari. In the *Vāyupurāṇa*, however, the name is omitted, and we have only Maruṇḍa'[1] (= Muruṇḍa, the Sanskrit name for Ptolemy's Marundai). Cunningham also suggests that the Moroundai of Ptolemy are identical with the Moredes of Pliny who are mentioned in conjunction with the Surari or Śavaras. It may, however, be mentioned that the Maruṇḍas are referred to in the *Vāyupurāṇa* as one of the Mleccha tribes.

Ptolemy also speaks of a city called Morounda as an inland town of the Aioi. The country of the Aioi was probably some region south of the Kerala country, but the city Morounda has not been identified. It is probable, however, that it was a city of the Maroundai = Muruṇḍas; and in that case the Moroundai had another settlement in the farthest south.

The *Abhidhānacintāmaṇi* of Hemacandra (IV, 26)[2] identifies the Muruṇḍas with the Lampākas, the Lambatai of Ptolemy. The latter were located near the source of the modern Kabul river in the region around Laghmān, and it, therefore, follows that the Muruṇḍas had a settlement in this region as well.

---

[1] Cunningham, *Ancient Geography of India*, Mazumdar's Ed., pp. 581-2.

[2] *Lampākāstu Maruṇḍāḥ syuḥ.*

Among the foreign potentates who came of their own accord to offer allegiance to Samudragupta (fourth century A.D.) were the 'Śaka-Muruṇḍas' [1]; while a 'Muruṇḍa-Svāminī' is mentioned in a Central Indian inscription of the sixth century A.D.

[1] According to Dr. Sten Konow, 'muruṇḍa' is the later form of a Śaka word meaning 'lord' or 'master'. The term '*Śaka-Muruṇḍas*' possibly stands, therefore, for those Śaka lords or chieftains who were ruling in the regions of Surāṣṭra and Ujjain at the time of Samudragupta. (Cf. *Allahabad Pillar Inscription of Samudragupta.*)

## CHAPTER XXIII

# THE ĀRJUNĀYANAS AND THE PRĀRJUNAS

The Allahabad Pillar Inscription of Samudragupta (fourth century A.D.) (i, 22) refers to a host of tribes—Mālavas, Ārjunāyanas, Yaudheyas, Madrakas, Ābhīras, Prārjunas, Sanakānīkas, Kākas, Kharaparikas, and others—that obeyed the imperial commands and paid all kinds of taxes. Research has ascertained that all these tribal states were located along the north-western, western and south-western fringes of the N. Indian kingdom of Samudragupta. The Mālavas, Yaudheyas, Madrakas and Ābhīras are more or less wellknown, but very little is known about the other tribes.

The names of the two tribes, Ārjunāyanas and Prārjunas, apparently have some connection with the name of the Epic hero, Arjuna, though this is not certain. The Allahabad Pillar Inscription, as we have seen, connects the Ārjunāyanas with the Yaudheyas, which is significant, inasmuch as the *Ādiparvan* (95, 76) of the *Mahābhārata* gives the name of one of Yudhiṣṭhira's sons as Yaudheya; so that the connection of the Yaudheyas and Ārjunāyanas appears to be warranted by the Epic.

The author of the *Bṛhatsaṃhitā* also connects these two tribes, and locates them both in the northern division of India. Ray Chaudhuri [1] locates the Yaudheyas in the Bharatpur State of Rajputana; and the Ārjunāyanas may have occupied a contiguous position. The Ārjunāyanas are also known from coins, which do not, however, give any clue to their geographical location.

Vincent Smith [2] places the Prārjunas in the Narasiṃhapur district of the Central Provinces, but a more plausible location is Narasiṃhagarh in Central India,[3] inasmuch as three other tribes which are coupled with the Prārjunas, the Sanakānikas, Kākas and Kharaparikas, seem to have occupied regions more or less within the bounds of Central India.

[1] *Political History of Ancient India*, 4th Ed., p. 458.
[2] *J.R.A.S.*, 1897, p. 892.
[3] *I.H.Q.*, Vol. I, p. 258.

## CHAPTER XXIV

# THE AMBAṢṬHAS

The Ambaṣṭhas [1] as a tribe existed at least as early as the time of the *Aitareya Brāhmaṇa*, when they were probably settled in the Punjab; and they can be traced up to the present day in parts of Bengal and Bihar, whither they migrated in later times. In the *Aitareya Brāhmaṇa* (VIII, 21–3), King Āmbaṣṭhya (= 'of Ambaṣṭha') is mentioned as having been consecrated with the Aindra Mahābhiṣeka along with nine other kings. The *Mahābhārata* [2] mentions the Ambaṣṭhas along with the Śivis, Kṣudrakas, Mālavas and other north-western tribes. In the *Bhīṣma* (Chap. 20, 10) and *Droṇa* (Chap. 119, 14) *Parvans*, the Ambaṣṭhas are referred to as having taken part in the Kurukṣetra war, on the side of the Kurus; while in the *Karṇaparvan*,[3] Śrutāyuḥ, the valiant Kṣatriya, who was killed by Arjuna, is described as a king of the Ambaṣṭhas. The Ambaṣṭhas were also once defeated by Nakula, the fourth Pāṇḍava, along with the Śivis, Trigarttas and Mālavas [4]; and Śrutāyuḥ was among those who did homage to Yudhiṣṭhira after the defeat.[5]

In the Purāṇas, the Ambaṣṭhas are represented as Āṇava Kṣatriyas, and are said to have originated from Suvrata, son of Uśīnara; they were thus intimately related to the Yaudheyas and the Śivis,[6] and were settled on the eastern border of the Punjab.[7] The country is mentioned in the Bārhaspatya *Arthaśāstra*,[8] where it is associated with Sind (*Kāśmīra-Hūna-Ambaṣṭha-Sindhavaḥ*); while the tribe is included in the list derived by Colonel Wilford [9] from the *Varāha Saṃhitā*.

The Purāṇas seem to represent the Ambaṣṭhas as Kṣatriyas, descended as they were from Uśīnara; and, as we have seen, the *Mahābhārata* refers to their King Śrutāyuḥ as 'the best of Kṣatriyas'. But the evidence of Smṛti literature seems to point to their mixed origin. According to the *Gautama-Dharmasūtra* (IV, 16), children born of wives of the next, second or third lower castes become

[1] According to Goldstücker, the older denomination of the tribe was probably Āmbaṣṭha, not Ambaṣṭha.

[2] II, 52, 14-15.

[3] Chap. 5, 18.

[4] *Sabhāparvan*, Chap. 32, 7.

[5] *Ibid.*, Chap. 52, 14-15.

[6] Pargiter, *Ancient Indian Historical Tradition*, p. 109.

[7] *Ibid.*, p. 264.

[8] Ed. F. W. Thomas, p. 21.

[9] *Asiatic Researches*, Vol. VIII, pp. 344, 346.

Sabarṇas, Ambaṣṭhas, Ugras, Niṣādhas, Dauṣyantas or Pārāśaras. The Ambaṣṭhas would thus be descendants of Brāhmaṇas by Kṣatriya, Vaiśya or Śūdra wives. In the *Ambaṭṭha Sutta*,[1] an Ambaṭṭha (= Ambaṣṭha) is called a Brāhmaṇa; but, according to the Jātakas,[2] the Ambaṣṭhas were farmers, while Manu describes them as a people who practised the art of healing.[3] S. N. Mazumdar thinks[4] that 'they were a tribe of Brahma Kṣatriyas' (i.e. Brahmins by descent but warriors by profession); while Ray Chaudhuri[5] is of the opinion that they were a 'tribe who were at first mainly a fighting race, but some of whom took to other occupations, viz. those of priests, farmers, and, according to the Smṛti writers, physicians'.

The Ambaṣṭhas are the same as the Abastanoi (Arrian), Sambastai (Diodoros), Sabarcae (Curtius) or Sabagrae (Orosius) of Alexander's historians.[6] In Alexander's time the tribe was settled on the lower Akesines (Asiknī), and had a democratic government, and an army consisting of 60,000 foot, 60,000 cavalry and 500 chariots.[7] The Ambaṣṭhas are referred to by Ptolemy as Ambastai, a tribe which is described as settled in the east of the country of the Paropanisadai,—Paropanisadai being 'a collective name for the tribes that were located along the southern and eastern sides of the Hindukush'.[8] Lassen[9] thinks that the Ambastai may have been connected in some way with the Ambastai, another tribe mentioned by Ptolemy as dwelling 'along the country of the Bettigoi' and the mountain range of the same name (i.e. southern portion of the Western Ghats).

The Ambaṣṭhas seem to have migrated in later times to some place near the Mekala hill which is the source of the Narmadā (see Mekala chapter). In the Kūrmavibhāga of the *Bṛhatsaṃhitā* (XIV, 7) they are associated with the Mekalas who dwelt on the Mekala hill; and the mention of Mekhalāmuṣṭa (which is in all probability a misreading for Mekalāmbaṣṭha) in the *Mārkaṇḍeya Purāṇa* (LVIII, 14) would seem to prove that the two were neighbouring tribes. The tribe seems to have migrated eastwards as well, however, for even today a class of Kāyasthas known as Ambaṣṭha Kāyasthas can be traced in Bihar; while the Vaidyas of Bengal claim to be designated as Ambaṣṭhas.[10]

---

1 *Dīgha*, I, p. 88; *Dialogues of the Buddha*, I, p. 109. 2 *Jātaka*, IV, No. 363.
3 *Manu*, X, 47: '*Ambaṣṭhānāṃ cikitsitām*'.
4 *C.A.G.I.*, notes, p. 670. 5 *P.H.A.I.*, 4th Ed., p. 207.
6 McCrindle's *Invasion of Alexander*, pp. 292ff. 7 *Ibid.*, p. 252.
8 McCrindle, *Ancient India as described by Ptolemy*, Majumdar's Ed., pp. 311-12.
9 *Indische Alterthumskunde*, pp. 159, 161.
10 They are described as such in Bharata Mallika's commentary on the *Bhaṭṭikāvya*.

CHAPTER XXV

# THE NIṢĀDAS

The Niṣādas are referred to for the first time in the later *Saṃhitās* and the *Brāhmaṇas*.[1] The word Niṣāda 'seems to denote not so much a particular tribe, but to be the general term for the non-Aryan tribes who were not under Aryan control, as the Śūdras were . . .' (*Vedic Index*, Vol. I, p. 453). This is supported by the evidence supplied by Aupamānyava[2] who distinguishes the Niṣādas from the other four varṇas or 'colours' (castes). The word Nisada (Niṣāda) of the *Vājasaneyī Saṃhitā* (XVI, 27) is explained by the commentator Mahīdhara to mean a Bhīl or Bhilla, a tribe that still exists in the hills of Central India and the Vindhyan tracts. Macdonell and Keith point out that 'a village of the Niṣādas is mentioned in the *Lāṭyāyana Śrauta Sūtra* (VIII, 2, 8), and a Niṣāda Sthapati, a leader of some kind of craft, is referred to in the *Kātyāyana Śrauta Sūtra* (1, 1, 12; Weber, *Indische Studien*, 10, 13) and in a *Brāhmaṇa* cited by the scholiast on that passage'.[3] According to Weber,[4] the Niṣādas were settled aborigines. In the opinion of the authors of the *Vedic Index*, this view is supported 'by the fact that the ritual of the Viśvajit Sacrifice (*Kauṣītaki B.*, XXV, 15; *Lāṭ. Ś.S.*, VIII, 2, 8; *Pañ. B.*, XVI, 6, 8, etc.) requires a temporary residence with the Niṣādas; for the Niṣādas who would permit an Aryan to reside temporarily amongst them must have been partially amenable to Aryan influence. But the name might easily be applied to the whole body of aborigines outside the Aryan organisation' (*Vedic Index*, Vol. I, p. 454).[5] The Law-giver, Manu, however, explains the origin of the Niṣādas as 'the offspring of a Brāhmaṇa father and a Śūdra mother'.[6] In his chapter on Mixed Castes, Manu says that the son of a Niṣāda by a Śūdra female becomes a Pulkasa by caste, but the son of a Śūdra by a Niṣāda female is declared to be a Kukkuṭaka.[7] The social duty enjoined on the Niṣādas was to kill

[1] *Taittirīya S.*, IV, 5, 4, 2; *Kāṭhaka S.*, XVII, 13; *Maitrāyaṇī S.*, II, 9, 5; *Vājasaneyī S.*, XVI, 27; *Aitareya B.*, VIII, 11; *Pañcaviṃśa B.*, XVI, 6, 8, etc.

[2] Yāska's *Nirukta*, III, 8.

[3] *Vedic Index*, I, p. 454.

[4] *Indische Studien*, 9, 340. Cf. 10, 13, 16.

[5] Von Schrœder seeks to identify (*Indiens Literatur und Cultur*, p. 366) the Niṣādas with the Nysæana of Greek geographers. This, however, is doubtful. In this connection, see also 'Indo-Aryan Races' by Ramaprasad Chanda who says that the Niṣādas were a non-Aryan race.

[6] *Manu*, X, 8; Muir's *Sanskrit Texts*, I, p. 481.

[7] X, 18.

7B

and provide fish for consumption by the people.[1] According to the Pāli texts as well, they were wild hunters and fishermen.[2] That they were a tribe 'of rude culture or aboriginal stock' (*A.I.H.T.*, p. 290) and outside the Aryan organisation is also attested by the *Rāmāyaṇa* story of Guha, king of the Niṣādas who are described as a wild band.[3]

During the period represented by Epic and Paurāṇic traditions the Niṣādas seem to have had their habitat among the mountains that form the boundary of Jhalwar and Khandesh in the Vindhya and Satpura ranges.[4] This is proved by a reference in the *Mahābhārata*[5] to a Niṣāda *rāṣṭra* in the region of the Sarasvatī and the Western Vindhyas, not very far from Pāriyātra or Pāripātra.[6] The *Mahābhārata* seems to connect the Niṣādas with the Vatsas and Bhargas or Bhaggas:

> '*Vatsabhūmiñca Kaunteyo vijigye balavān balāt*
> *Bhargānāmadhipañcaiva Niṣādādhipatiṃ tathā.*'[7]

The Niṣādas seem also to have had a settlement in the east. The *Bṛhatsaṃhitā* of Varāhamihira (XIV, 10) seems to recognise a kingdom or '*rāṣṭra*' of the Niṣādas in the south-east of the Madhyadeśa. A Niṣāda kingdom whose capital was Śṛṅgaverapura (on the north side of the Ganges opposite Prayāga) is also referred to in the *Rāmāyaṇa* (II Canto, 50, 33 to Canto, 52, 11); and it is not improbable that this Niṣāda kingdom is identical with the one referred to in the *Bṛhatsaṃhitā*.

The first epigraphic mention of the tribe is found in the Junāgaḍh Rock Inscription of the year 72 of Mahākṣatrapa Rudradāman (i.e. 150 A.D.). Rudradāman is there credited with having conquered the Niṣāda country along with E. and W. Malwa, the ancient Māhiṣmatī region, the district round Dwārkā in Gujrat, Surāṣṭra, Aparānta, Sindhu-Sauvīra and others. Thus the Niṣāda country in the middle of the second century A.D. was under the suzerainty of the Western Kṣatrapas.[8]

[1] *Manu*, X, 48.

[2] Fick, *Die Sociale Gliederung*, 12, 160, 206, etc.; cf. Muir's *Sans. Texts*, 301, 303, 366, n. 164, 403, 481.

[3] *Ādikāṇḍa*, Canto I; *Ayodhyā Kāṇḍa*, Canto 51.

[4] Malcolm, *Memoirs of Central India*, Vol. I, p. 452.

[5] III, 130, 4. [6] *Ibid.*, XII, 135, 3-5. [7] II, 30, 10-11.

[8] The Chitorgarh Inscription of Mokala or Mewad of the Vikrama year 1485 (*Ep. Ind.*, Vol. II, pp. 416ff.) states in a general way (verse 46) that Mokala subdued the Aṅgas, Kāmarūpas, Vaṅgas, Niṣādas, Cīnas and Turuṣkas; 'but there can be no doubt that the verse has been put in solely for the sake of poetical ornamentation'.

## CHAPTER XXVI

# THE NIṢADHAS

The Niṣadhas were a different race from the Niṣādas with whom they are often confounded; and we may conclude that they belonged to the Aryan fold. According to the Epic and Paurāṇic tradition, the Niṣadhas are said to have sprung from the primeval King Pṛthu, son of Veṇa.[1] The tribe seems to have derived its name from Niṣadha who is described in the Purāṇas and *Bhagavadgītā* to have been the son of Atithi, grandson of Kuśa, and father of Nala.[2] According to the *Viṣṇupurāṇa* (IV, Chap. 24, 17), the ten kings of the Mekala country and nine of the Sapta Kośala country are said to have been succeeded by the nine kings of the Niṣadhas, while, according to the *Vāyupurāṇa*, the kings of the Niṣadha country held sway till the end of the days of Manu. They were all descendants of King Nala, and lived in the country of Niṣadha (*Vāyu P.*, Chap. 99, 376). This King Nala of the Purāṇas must be identical with the King Nala whose story is referred to in the *Mahābhārata* (III).[3]

But notwithstanding the celebrity of the Niṣadha country as the kingdom of Nala, it is difficult to ascertain exactly where it was situated. It is, perhaps, permissible to conjecture that it was not very far from Vidarbha, the country of Nala's queen, Damayantī. From the directions given by Nala to Damayantī, Wilson thinks[4] that it was near the Vindhyas and Payoṣṇī river, and that it was near the roads leading from it across the Ṛkṣa mountain to Avanti and the south, as well as to Vidarbha and to Kośala. Lassen places Niṣadha, the kingdom of Nala, along the Satpura hills to the north-west of Berar. Burgess also places it to the south of Malwa.[5]

The Purāṇas locate the Niṣadhas in the upper and lower regions of the Vindhya ranges.[6] According to the *Mahābhārata*, the capital of the Niṣadhas was Giriprastha (III, 324, 12).

---

[1] *Vāyu P.*, 62, 137-48; *Brahmāṇḍa P.*, II, 36, 158-73, *Kūrma P.*, I, 1, 6; *Ibid.*, 14, 12, *Śiva P.*, VII, 56, 30-1; *Mbh.*, XII, 59, 2233-4, etc.

[2] *Kūrma P.*, 21, 58, *Bhagavadgītā*, 9, 12, 1; *Saura P.*, 30, 69; *Śiva P.*, *Dharma*, 61-9; *Brahma P.*, 8, 88

[3] The Nala story itself seems to have been much older than the *Mahābhārata*, for it is referred to by Sītā in the *Rāmāyaṇa* (Ray Chaudhuri, *Studies in Indian Antiquities, Chap. on Interrelation of the two Epics*).

[4] *Viṣṇupurāṇa*, Vol. II, pp. 156-90.

[5] *Antiquities of Kathiawar and Kacch*, p. 131.

[6] *Brahmāṇḍa P.*, 49; *Vāyu P.*, 45; *Vāmana P.*, 13, etc.

The Niṣadhas seem to have played a prominent part in the Kurukṣetra war in which they ranged themselves on the side of the Pāṇḍavas, along with the Mekalas, Kośalas, Madras and Daśārṇas.[1] They were at one time defeated by Karṇa.[2]

[1] *Karṇaparvan*, Chap. 22, 3, *Bhīsmaparvan*, Chap. 54. 8.
[2] *Karṇaparvan*, Chap. 8, 19; *Droṇaparvan*, Chap. 4, 8.

CHAPTER XXVII

# THE KĀŚIS

Kāśī was the ancient name of the kingdom of which the chief city was Bārāṇasī, the modern Benares, which is situated 80 miles below Allahabad on the north bank of the Ganges, at the junction between that river and the river Baraṇā.[1] From the joint name of the two streams which bound the city to the north and the south,—the Baraṇā and the Asi,—the Brāhmaṇas derive Varāṇasī or Bārāṇasī.[2] The Barāṇa or Varaṇā is a considerable rivulet which rises to the north of Allahabad and has a course of about 100 miles; while the Asi is a mere brook. The former is probably identical with the river Varaṇāvatī, the water of which is said in the *Atharvaveda* (IV, 7, 1) to have had the property of removing poison. We agree with Macdonell and Keith that, though Kāśī is a late word, it is quite possible that the town is older, as the river Varaṇāvatī may be connected with the later Bārāṇasī.[3]

According to the Jātakas, Bārāṇasī had other names in previous ages, i.e. in previous incarnations of the Buddha: e.g. Surundhana,[4] Sudassana,[5] Brahmavaddhana,[6] Pupphavatī,[7] Rammanagara[8] and Molinī.[9] In the Chinese versions of Buddhist works, the terms Kāśī and Vārāṇasī are generally given in transcription, but the former term is sometimes translated by Ti-miao, meaning 'reed-sprouts'. Ti-miao may have been intended to translate Kāśī, as supposedly connected with Kāśi,[10] a certain kind of grass. Bārāṇasī is also called Kāśīnagara and Kāśīpura (e.g. *Jātaka*, V, 54; VI, 165; *Dhammapada Comm.*, 1, 87).

The city proper, as Rhys Davids says, included the land between the Baraṇā and the Asi. 'Its extent including the suburbs, is often stated to have been, at the time when it was the capital of an independent kingdom (that is some time before the rise of Buddhism) 12 leagues or about 85 miles.'[11] In the Jātakas we find the extent

1 Rhys Davids, *Buddhist India*, p. 34.
2 Cunningham, *Ancient Geography of India* (S. N. Majumdar), p. 500.
3 *Vedic Index*, Vol. I, p. 154.
4 *Jātaka* (Fausböll), IV, p. 104.
5 *Ibid.*, IV, p. 119; V, p. 177.
6 *Ibid.*, IV, p. 119; V, p. 312.
7 *Ibid.*, VI, p. 131.
8 *Ibid.*, IV, pp. 119, 26, etc.
9 *Ibid.*, IV, p. 15.
10 Watters, *On Yuan Chwang*, Vol. II, pp. 58-9.
11 *Buddhist India*, p. 34.

of the city mentioned as 12 yojanas.[1] Nowadays, Benares extends four miles along the bank of the river, which here descends to the water with a steep brink. Down this brink are built flights of steps known as ghats, at the foot of which pilgrims bathe and dead bodies are burnt.[2]

Although the capital of Kāśī (Pāli, Kāsī) is generally given as Bārāṇasī, it is said that when Aśoka was king of Kāśī, his capital was in Potali[3]; and another king, Udaya Bhadda, had his seat of government in Surundha.[4] It is possible that these cities did not form part of the regular kingdom of Kāśī, but became annexed to it during the reigns of some of the more powerful kings.[5]

The little kingdom of Kāśī, whose extent is given in the Jātaka (V, 41; III, 304, 391) as three hundred leagues, was bordered by Kośala on the north, Magadha on the east, and Vatsa on the west.[6] It was a wealthy and prosperous country, having 'an abundance of the seven gems',[7] and the *Bhojājānīya Jātaka* (*J.*, I, 178) tells us that 'all the kings around coveted the kingdom of Benares'. It often served as a bone of contention between its three powerful neighbours, as we shall see.

Kāśī is mentioned several times in Vedic literature and in the Epics. The *Sāṅkhāyana Śrauta Sūtra*[8] mentions Kāśya, the king of Kāśī, and Jala, son of Jātukarṇī, who became the king's chaplain. Kāśya was a warrior, as the *Bṛhadāraṇyaka Upaniṣad* (III, 8, 2) informs us. From the *Śatapatha Brāhmaṇa* (XIII, 5, 4, 19) we learn that Śatānīka, son of Satrājita, took the horse of King Kāśya and performed the Govinata Yajña. Afterwards, the king too performed this sacrifice. The *Bṛhadāraṇyaka* and *Kauśītakī Upaniṣads* speak of Ajātaśatru, another king of Kāśī[9]; while the *Baudhāyana Śrauta Sūtra*[10] tells us that Āyu, son of Purūravas, renounced the world and wandered in the countries of Kāśī, Kuru and Pañcāla.

Purūravas is mentioned in the *Rāmāyaṇa*[11] as king of Kāśī. Mitradeva said to the nymph Urvaśī: 'Go to Purūrava, king of Kāśī. He will be your husband'. In the same *kāṇḍa* (59, 19), Puru, son of Yayāti, is represented as residing in Pratiṣṭhāna and ruling over the kingdom of Kāśī. We are told in the *Ādikāṇḍa* (13th sarga) that

---

[1] *Jātaka*, VI, p. 160; IV, p. 377; *Majjhima Nikāya Comm.*, II, p. 608; B. C. Law, *India as described in early texts of Buddhism and Jainism*, pp. 41 foll.

[2] *Cambridge History of India*, Vol. I, p. 14.

[3] *Jātaka*, II, p. 155.

[4] *Ibid.*, IV, pp. 104ff.

[5] Malalasekera, *Dictionary of Pāli Proper Names*, Vol. I, article on '*Kāsī*'.

[6] *Cambridge History of India*, Vol. I, p. 316.

[7] *Aṅguttara Nikāya*, Vol. I, p. 213; Vol. IV, pp. 252, 256, 260; see also *Dīgha Nikāya*, II, p. 75.

[8] XVI, 29, 5.

[9] *Bṛh. Up.*, II, 1, 1; *Kauś. Up.*, IV, 1.

[10] XVIII, 44.

[11] *Uttarakāṇḍa*, 56th sarga, śl. 25.

Vaśiṣṭha asked Sumantra to invite many pious kings, including the king of Benares, together with one thousand Brahmins, Kṣatriyas, Vaiśyas and Śūdras. In the *Kiṣkindhyākāṇḍa* (40th sarga) we read that Sugrīva sent the monkey king Vinata to Kāśī, among other countries, in quest of Sītā.

Kāśī figures even more prominently in the *Mahābhārata*. Haryaśva, king of Benares, was killed by the relations of king Vītahavya in a battle fought on the land between the Ganges and the Jumna. His son Sudeva was then installed on the throne of Kāśī. Sudeva ruled righteously, but he also was defeated by the Vītahavyas, and his son Divodāsa became king. Divodāsa built the city of Benares which became populated by people of the four castes. The city lay between the north bank of the Ganges and the south bank of the river Gomatī. Big markets were opened, and the city seemed likely to prosper, but the Vītahavyas again attacked, and a great war ensued, lasting for a thousand days. Divodāsa was defeated, and fled to a forest, taking shelter in the hermitage of the sage Bharadvāja, eldest son of Bṛhaspati. This sage assured the king that he would perform a sacrifice so that Divodāsa might be blessed with a son who would kill thousands of the Vītahavyas. This son was duly born, and was named Pratardana. He studied the Vedas and archery, and was sent in due course to conquer the Vītahavyas. A fierce fight ensued, in which the Vītahavyas were defeated.[1] Another passage of the *Mahābhārata* tells us that Divodāsa, the son of Bhīmasena, king of Kāśī, had a son named Pratardana by Mādhavī, daughter of Yayāti.[2] When Pratardana came to the throne of Kāśī, he established his capital in Benares and acquired great fame by offering his own son in charity to a Brahmin.[3]

We have yet another version of Divodāsa's life story in the Purāṇas and the *Harivaṃśa*. Saunihotra, a certain king of Kāśī, had a son named Dhanvantarī who studied the Āyurveda with Bharadvāja,[4] and later became king of Kāśī. He is celebrated as the author of the Āyurveda and killer of all diseases.[5] Divodāsa was the great-grandson of this Dhanvantarī. It is said that in his time, Benares, owing to a curse, was deserted, and infested by a Rākṣasa named Kṣemaka. Divodāsa left Benares and founded his kingdom on the banks of the river Gomatī.[6] Once Bhadraśreṇya,

[1] *Anuśāsanaparvan*, Chap. 30, pp. 1899-1900.
[2] *Udyogaparvan*, Chap. 117, p. 746.
[3] *Anuśāsanaparvan*, Chap. 137, pp. 1995-6.
[4] *Harivaṃśa*, Chap. 31.
[5] *Vāyupurāṇa*, Chap. 92.
[6] *Harivaṃśa*, Chaps. 31-2; cf. *Brahmapurāṇa*, Chap. 13, śl. 75. Genealogical tables of the family of Divodāsa are given in the *Hariv.*, Chaps. 31-2, *Brahmapurāṇa*, Chap. 13, and *Vāyupurāṇa*, Chap. 92.

son of Mahiṣmān [1] and king of the Yadu dynasty, acquired Benares. His sons were defeated by King Divodāsa who recovered the city, sparing the life of Bhadraśreṇya's youngest son, Durdama. Later, however, this Durdama again took Benares which was then recovered by Pratardana, son of Divodāsa. Elsewhere,[2] we read that Ālarka Saunati (grandson of Pratardana) re-established the city of Benares, after killing the Rākṣasa Kṣemaka.

We return to the *Mahābhārata* references to Kāśī. A certain king of Kāśī gave his daughter Sārvasenī in marriage to Bharata, son of Duṣmanta (Duṣyanta), king of the Kuru dynasty, and Śakuntalā, daughter of Viśvāmitra.[3] Kāśya, another king of Kāśī, had three daughters, Ambā, Ambikā and Ambālikā, who were won by Bhīṣma for his brother Vicitravīrya in a Svayaṃvara.[4] Suvāhu, a king of Kāśī, was conquered by Bhīṣma.[5] On the occasion of the marriage ceremony of Abhimanyu, the king of Kāśī and others were invited by Yudhiṣṭhira to a city named Upaplavya near Virāṭa.[6] The king of Kāśī was an ally of Yudhiṣṭhira, and helped the Pāṇḍavas in the Kurukṣetra war.[7] In battle he rode horses decorated with gold and garlands [8]; Śaivya and he guarded the centre of the Pāṇḍava army with 30,000 chariots.[9] The king of Kāśī is mentioned as the best archer.[10] Kāśī, Karūṣa and Cedi armies were under the leadership of Dhṛṣṭaketu.[11]

The Purāṇas contain several stories about kings of Kāśī. We have mentioned the account of Divodāsa. Another king mentioned in the *Vāyupurāṇa*[12] is Kāśa who was the son of Dharmavṛddha of the Nahuṣa family. The sons of Kāśa were Kāśara, Rāṣṭra and Dīrghatapas, and Dīrghatapas' son was the learned Dharma. According to the *Harivaṃśa* (Chap. 29), the sons of Kāśa, a king of the Anenāḥ dynasty, were known as Kāśīs. Dīrghatamas (=Dīrghatapas?) was the eldest son.

Benares, the capital of Kāśī, figures in the story of Kṛṣṇa's quarrel with Puṇḍva. King Puṇḍva, aided by the king of Benares, fought with Kṛṣṇa Vāsudeva who defeated and killed Puṇḍva, and burnt the city of Benares.[13]

According to the Jainas, Pārśvanātha was born in Benares about 817 B.C. His father Aśvasena was the king of Benares, and

[1] *Padmapurāṇa*, Sṛṣṭi, Chap. 12.
[2] *Vāyupurāṇa*, Chap. 92.
[3] *Ādiparvan*, Chap. 95, p. 105.
[4] *Udyogaparvan*, Chaps. 172–94, pp. 791-806.
[5] *Sabhāparvan*, Chap. 30, pp. 241-2.
[6] *Virāṭaparvan*, Chap. 72, śl. 16.
[7] *Udyogaparvan*, Chap. 72, p. 714.
[8] *Droṇaparvan*, Chap. 22, śl. 38.
[9] *Bhīsmaparvan*, Chap. 50, p. 924.
[10] *Ibid.*, Chap. 25, p. 834.
[11] *Udyogaparvan*, Chap. 198, p. 807.
[12] Chap. 92.
[13] *Viṣṇupurāṇa*, 5th Aṃśa, Chap. 34.

he himself attained perfect knowledge (kevala-jñāna) seated under a certain tree near the city.[1]

Kāśī also figures in the stories of Mahāvīra and his disciples.[2] For example, there lived in Benares a householder named Culanipiyā who was prosperous and had no equal. His wife was called Samā. At a certain time Mahāvīra came and a congregation went out from Benares to hear him preach. Culanipiyā lived in conformity with the teaching which he received from Mahāvīra.[3] Among other disciples of Mahāvīra who were connected with Benares were Sūrādeva, a prosperous householder,[4] Āryarakṣita[5] and Jayaghoṣa.[6] We are told also that the king of Kāśī named Nandana, the seventh Baladeva, son of King Agniśikha, abandoned all pleasures and hewed down his karma like a forest, as it were.[7]

On the night in which Mahāvīra died, the king of Kāśī instituted an illumination, it being a day of fasting (Poṣadha); for he said, 'When the light of intelligence is gone, let us make an illumination of material matter'.[8]

There is a reference in Kauṭilya's *Arthaśāstra* to the poisoning of a king of Kāśī by his own queen.

Although, as we have seen, Kāśī and Benares feature fairly prominently in Hindu and Jain sources, it is the Buddhist books, and particularly the Jātakas, which give us fuller information on the subject. In the Purāṇas, Kāśī is mentioned as a janapada or country. In the Pāli canon,[9] however, it is referred to as one of the sixteen 'Mahājanapadas,' and its capital, Bārāṇasī, was one of the four places of pilgrimage for the Buddhists, and was included in the list of great cities suggested by Ānanda as suitable places for the *parinibbāna* of the Buddha.[10]

Although Kāśī was no longer an independent kingdom in the Buddha's day, the memory of its independence seems to have been still fresh, for it is frequently mentioned as such in the Jātakas and elsewhere. To begin with, it is said that Kāśī was once ruled by the Bhāratas one of whom, Dhataraṭṭha, was its king in the time of Reṇu.[11] The traditional name of the king of Kāśī was evidently Brahmadatta, and references to kings of that name abound in the Jātakas.

---

1 S. Stevenson, *Heart of Jainism*, pp. 48-9.

2 B. C. Law, *Mahāvīra: His Life and Teachings*, sec. I.

3 *Uvāsagadasāo*, Vol. II, pp. 90–8. (B.I.S.)

4 *Ibid.*, p. 100.

5 *Heart of Jainism*, p. 78.

6 *Jaina Sūtras*, S.B.E., II, pp. 136-7. See also *ibid.*, p. 50, for the story of the Jaina monk Bala, and Bhadrā, daughter of King Kauśalika.

7 *Sūtrakṛtāṅga*, *Jaina Sūtras*, II, p. 87.

8 *Jaina Sūtras*, I, p. 266.

9 *Aṅguttara Nikāya*, I, pp. 213, etc.

10 *Dīgha Nikāya*, II, 146.

11 *Ibid.*, II, 135f. Here (*Mahāgovinda Sutta*) the foundation of Bārāṇasī is attributed to Mahāgovinda, its first king being Dhataraṭṭha.

Brahmadatta was probably the dynastic name of the kings of Benares; for instance, in the *Gaṅgamāla Jātaka* (*J.*, III, 452) Udaya, king of Benares, is addressed as Brahmadatta. Elsewhere in the *Jātaka* (III, pp. 406ff.), we read that a certain prince Brahmadatta became king of Benares. He married the exquisitely beautiful daughter of the king of Kośala, and made her his chief queen. He held a parasol festival, and the whole city was decorated so splendidly as to seem like a city of the gods. The king went around the city in procession, and then mounted his throne on the dais in the palace. The throne was surmounted by a white parasol. Brahmadatta looked down on all the persons who stood in attendance, 'on one side the ministers, on another the Brahmins and householders resplendent in the beauty of varied apparel, on another the townspeople with various gifts in their hands, on another troupes of dancing girls to the number of sixteen thousand, like a gathering of the nymphs of heaven in full apparel', and reflected that all his splendour was due to 'an alms-gift of four portions of gruel given to four paccekabuddhas '.

One King Brahmadatta told the inhabitants of Kāśī that there would be a famine lasting for twelve years, and that only those inhabitants might remain who had provision for that period. Many people died at Benares on account of this famine. One very wealthy person, however, gave alms to a paccekabuddha who granted three boons in return. The almsgiver himself prayed that his granary should always be filled with paddy; his wife prayed that one pot of rice cooked by her would be sufficient for hundreds of thousands of people; and their son prayed that his treasure-house should always be full of wealth.[1]

There seem to have been frequent wars between the two kingdoms of Kāśī and Kośala, first one side being victorious, and then the other. We are told,[2] for instance, that a certain Brahmadatta was a wealthy king of Benares. He was rich in treasure, revenue, troops and vehicles. The king of Kośala at that time, named Dīghīti, was not so wealthy as he was. Brahmadatta waged war against Dīghīti, defeated him, and took possession of his treasuries and storehouses. The king of Kośala and his consort escaped, went to Benares, and lived there in disguise in a potter's house. The queen bore a son, Dīghāyu (or Dīghāvu), who was sent away for safety. The king of Kāśī some time afterwards learnt that the king and queen of Kośala were dwelling in his kingdom, and they were captured, and were being led to the place of execution when Dīghāyu, who was on a

[1] *Divyāvadāna*, 132ff.
[2] *Vinaya*, I, 343ff.; *Dhammapada Comm.*, I, 56ff.; *Jātaka*, III, 211ff., 487.

visit to the city, saw them. Dīghīti gave out his dying advice to his son: 'Look not too far nor too near.' Understanding this advice, Dīghāyu entered the service of the king of Kāśī. One day the king ascended a chariot driven by Dīghāyu. Travelling at high speed, he left the royal retinue far behind. The king became tired, stopped the chariot, and fell asleep. Dīghāyu thought of killing him, but remembering his father's advice he desisted. When Brahmadatta awoke, however, Dīghāyu revealed his identity, and promised the king his life. His father's kingdom was restored to him, and he married Brahmadatta's daughter.

On another occasion, the king of Benares attacked the kingdom of Kośala and took its king prisoner. He set up royal officials as governors in the conquered country, and himself having collected all their available treasure, returned with his spoils to Benares. The king of Kośala had a son named Chatta who fled when his father was taken prisoner, and went to Taxila to complete his education. On his way back from Taxila, Chatta came to a wood where dwelt five hundred ascetics. Chatta joined them, and eventually became their leader. He came to Benares with the ascetics, and spent a night in the king's garden. The next morning the ascetics, in their quest for alms, came to the door of the palace. The king was charmed with their deportment, and particularly with Chatta, who answered all his questions to his satisfaction; and he asked the ascetics to stay in his garden. Chatta knew a spell whereby he could bring to light buried treasure. He repeated this spell, and discovered that the treasure which had belonged to his father was buried in that very garden. He then told the ascetics that he was the son of the king of Kośala, and they agreed to help him. Chatta removed the treasure which was taken to Śrāvastī by the ascetics. He then had all the king's officers seized, recovered his kingdom, made the city invincible against invasion, and took up his residence there.[1]

In the *Mahāsīlava Jātaka* we read that the kingdom of Benares was once seized by the king of Kośala who buried the king of Kāśī (Mahāsīlava) and his soldiers alive, up to the neck. The king of Kāśī managed to get out of the pit, and to rescue his soldiers; and by the magic power of two yakṣas who happened to be there disputing over a corpse, he secured his sword of state, and went to the usurper's bedside at dead of night and frightened him. On being told the story of the king of Kāśī's escape, the usurper praised him, begged his pardon, and on the morrow gave back his kingdom, and himself with his troops and elephants returned to his own country.[2]

[1] *Jātaka*, III, pp. 115ff.

[2] *Ibid.*, I, pp. 262 *et seq.*; see also I, 409; *Udāna Comm.*, 123.

In the *Asātarūpa Jātaka*, we read that the kingdom of Benares was once seized by the king of Kośala who marched with a great force against Benares, killed the king, and carried off his queen. But the king's son escaped, and later collected a mighty force and came to Benares. He pitched his camp close to the city, and sent a message to the king of Kośala, demanding that he should surrender the kingdom or else give battle. The king informed him that he would give battle. But the young prince's mother sent word to her son advising him not to fight, but to blockade the city on every side, so that the citizens would be worn out for want of food and water. The prince acted on this advice, and the citizens were famished and on the seventh day they beheaded their king and brought his head to the prince. Thus the prince succeeded in regaining his paternal kingdom.[1] On another occasion the kingdom of Benares was seized by a king of Sāvatthī (Śrāvastī) named Vaṅka, but was soon restored.[2]

There seems to have been friendly intercourse between the chieftains of Benares and the kings of Magadha, as instanced by the fact that King Bimbisāra sent his own physician Jīvaka to attend the son of the Treasurer of Benares, when the young man had twisted his internal organs through practising acrobatics.[3]

The *Cambridge History of India* (p. 316) informs us that at different periods Kāśī came under the sway of the three successive suzerain powers of N. India the Purus of Vatsa, the Ikṣvākus of Kośala and the kings of Magadha; but it seems to have enjoyed independent power between the decline of Vatsa and the rise of Kośala, when King Brahmadatta conquered Kośala, possibly about a century and a half before the Buddha's time.

As we have seen, in the early days, Kāśī and Kośala are represented as two independent countries whose kings fought with each other.[4] Kāśī and Kośala are frequently mentioned together in literature (e.g. *Aṅguttara Nikāya*, V, 59). In the Buddha's time, Kośala was already the paramount power in India. We have seen how several successful invasions of Kāśī had been carried out by the kings of Kośala. Kāśī's absorption into Kośala was an accomplished fact before the accession of Pasenadi, for Pasenadi's father Mahākośala gave his daughter a village of Kāśī (Kāsigāma) as 'bath money', on the occasion of her marriage with King Bimbisāra of Magadha.[5]

---

1 *Jātaka*, I, p. 409.
2 *Ibid.*, III, pp. 168-9.
3 *Vinaya Texts*, Pt. II, pp. 184-5 (*Mahāvagga*, VIII, 1).
4 D. R. Bhandarkar, *Car. Lec.*, 1918, p. 55.
5 *Jātaka*, IV, 342; II, 403.

After Bimbisāra's death, Pasenadi withdrew the gift from Ajātaśatru, and this led to a war between Kośala and Magadha. Pasenadi was defeated in three campaigns, but in another battle he avenged his defeat, and took possession of Kāśī. However, Pasenadi treated Ajātaśatru generously, giving him his daughter in marriage, and even bestowing the disputed village on her as a wedding gift.[1] In the *Dīgha Nikāya* we read that Pasenadi, king of Kāśī, used to collect taxes from the inhabitants of these two countries. He used to share the income with his subordinates.[2] The *Mahāvagga*,[3] however, mentions a Kāsika-rājā (king of Kāśī) who sent a robe to Jīvaka. Buddhaghoṣa says[4] that this was a brother of Pasenadi and son of the same father. He was probably a sub-king of Pasenadi.[5] Later, when Ajātaśatru succeeded in establishing his sway over Kośala, Kāśī too was included in his dominions (see Chapter on Kośala).

The *Sumaṅgalavilāsinī*,[6] referring to the more ancient period of Kāśī, mentions a certain Rāma, king of Kāśī, who had an attack of leprosy, in consequence of which he became distasteful to the members of his harem, and the dancing girls. Being much distressed, he left his kingdom in charge of his eldest son, went to a forest, and was soon cured of the disease by living on leaves and fruits. His body now appeared like gold. He dwelt in a tree-hole, and later married the daughter of King Okkāka (Skt. Ikṣvāku). Thirty-two sons were born to him; and these sons afterwards built the city named Kola, and became known as Koliyas. There were intermarriages between the Koliyas and the Śākyas (other descendants of Okkāka) down to the time of the Buddha Gautama.

The names of several other kings of Benares are mentioned in the Jātakas, among them being those of Aṅga, Uggasena, Udaya, Dhanañjaya, Vissasena, Kalābu (*Jātaka*, III, 39), and Saṃyama. The *Suttanipāta Commentary* on the *Khaggavisāṇa Sutta* contains the names of several kings of Benares who renounced the world and became *paccekabuddhas*. The *Ceylon Chronicles*[7] mention the names of others who reigned in Benares, e.g. Duppasaha and sixty of his descendants; Aśoka, son of Samaṅkara, and 84,000 of his descendants; also sixteen kings, ancestors of Okkāka. Sometimes the king is referred to merely as Kāśī-rājā. In the Jātaka (III, p. 28) we are told that a king of Benares used to learn Vedic hymns from his family priest (*purohita*).

---

1 *Saṃyutta Nikāya*, I, pp. 82–5.
2 I, pp. 228-9.
3 *Vin.*, I, 281.
4 *Vinaya Texts*, II, 195, n. 2.
5 Malalasekera, *Dictionary of Pāli Proper Names*, s.v. *Kāśī*.
6 *Sumaṅgalavilāsinī*, Pt. I, pp. 260–2; vide also chapter on *Koliyas*.
7 *Mahāvaṃsa Ṭīkā*, 127, 129, 130.

The king of Benares at the time of the Buddha Kassapa is said to have been Kikī. When Kassapa Buddha arrived in Benares, the king, having listened to his sermons, entertained the Buddha and his monks at the palace.[1] One of Kikī's daughters was Uracchadā, who attained arahatship at the age of sixteen. He had seven other daughters, and a son Pathavindhara, who succeeded him (*Divyāvadāna*; 22, *Sujāta*). During the life of the Buddha Kassapa, Kikī waited on him with many kinds of gifts,[2] and at his death built one of the four gates outside the Buddha's cetiya. This gate was a league in width.[3] In the Sanskrit books he is called Kṛkī,[4] and is mentioned as owning a palace called Kokanada.

From the Jātakas we learn that Benares was ruled with justice and equity. The ministers of the king were just; no false suit was brought to court, and sometimes true cases were so scanty that ministers had to remain idle for lack of litigants. The king of Benares was always on the alert to know his own faults. Once a certain king of Benares went outside the city to find out whether there was anyone who might know anything against him. The king of Kośala was out on a similar mission, and the two kings met at a place where the road was too narrow for two carriages to pass. Each of the drivers spoke of the virtues of his king, and finally the king of Kośala and his driver gave place to the king of Benares.[5]

There was a belief current amongst the people of Benares that when kings rule with justice and equity, when they reign peacefully, all things retain their respective nature and character; but that when kings rule with injustice and inequity, when their reign becomes one of terror and tyranny, all things lose their respective nature. Oil, honey, molasses and the like, and even the wild fruits lose their sweetness and flavour.[6]

In spite of good government, the country was not entirely free from crime. For instance, a physician named Cakkhupāla in anger gave one of his women patients, who had tried to cheat him out of his promised reward for curing her, a drug which made her blind.[7] There were also instances of highway robbery and house-breaking. In the *Satapatta Jātaka* (*Jātaka*, II, pp. 387-8) we read that the Bodhisattva in a former life gathered 500 robbers together and became their chief, living by highway robbery and house-breaking.

1 *Majjhima Nikāya*, II, pp. 49ff.
2 *Suttanipāta Comm.*, I, 281, 283.
3 *Ibid.*, 194.
4 E.g. *Mahāvastu* (ed. Senart), I, 325; *Divyāvadāna*, 22f.; *Avadāna Śataka*, I, 338, etc.
5 *Jātaka*, II, pp. 1–5.
6 *Ibid.*, III, pp. 110-11.
7 *Dhammapada Comm.*, Vol. I, p. 20.

Kāśī was evidently a great centre of trade and industry, and a most populous and prosperous country. Frequent mention is made of caravans leaving Kāśī to travel for trade. One highway went through Kāśī to Rājagṛha,[1] and another to Śrāvastī[2]; and there was also direct trade between Kāśī and Takṣaśilā.[3] We read of a trader of Benares who went with 500 carts to a frontier country and bought sandal wood[4]; and of another trader who was going to Śrāvastī with five hundred carts full of red cloth, but could not cross the river as it was in flood, and had to stay on the near side to sell his goods.[5] The merchants of Benares used to go about hawking goods, which were carried by donkeys.[6] Horse dealers from northern districts used to bring horses to Benares for sale.[7] Sindh horses were available in Benares, and were used as the royal horses of ceremony.[8] In Benares, too, there were skilled elephant trainers,[9] and corn merchants.[10]

In Benares fine cloths widely known as Kāśī cloths were manufactured, and Kāśī robes were most highly esteemed as gifts, each robe being valued at one hundred thousand.[11] Mention is also made of the perfumes of Kāśī [*Kāsi-vilepana—Jātaka*, I, 355; and *Kāsi-candana—Aṅguttara Nikāya*, III, 391; *Udāna Comm.* (P.T.S.), 332].

At Benares there was a rich banker named Mahādhanaseṭṭhi. His parents taught him dancing and music, and he married the daughter of another rich banker, and of similar education. Mahādhana became addicted to drink and gambling, with the result that he lost his own wealth as well as his wife's, being finally reduced to begging for alms.[12] In general, however, the merchants of Benares must have been highly respected, for we read in the *Divyāvadāna* (p. 100) that after the death of Priyasena, the chief merchant, Brahmadatta, king of Kāśī, appointed Supriya chief merchant of the royal court; and after Brahmadatta's death, the ministers anointed Supriya king (p. 121).

There was in Benares a market known as the ivory workers' bazar, where ivory articles were sold.[13] There were also stone cutters or experts in working stone-quarrying and shaping stones.[14]

---

[1] *Vinaya*, I, 212.
[2] *Ibid.*, II.
[3] *Dhammapada Comm.*, III, 445.
[4] *Suttanipāta Comm.*, Vol. II, pp. 523ff.
[5] *Dhammapada Comm.*, Vol. III, p. 429.
[6] *Jātaka*, II, p. 109; *Dhammapada Comm.*, Vol. I, p. 123.
[7] *Jātaka*, II, p. 287.
[8] *Ibid.*, II, 338.
[9] *Ibid.*, II, p. 221.
[10] *Ibid.*, III, p. 198.
[11] *Ibid.*, V, p. 377; *Lalitavistara* (Lefmann), p. 215. *Buddhist Suttas*, S.B.E., XI, p. 92; *Jātaka*, VI, 151, 450.
[12] *Dhammapada Comm.*, Vol. III, p. 429.
[13] *Jātaka*, II, p. 197.
[14] *Ibid.*, I, p. 478.

Five hundred carpenters lived in a village in Kāśī.[1] There was in Benares a great carpenter-quarter containing a thousand families. These carpenters avowed publicly that they could make a bed or a chair or a house; but when they took a large advance from the people, they proved themselves to be liars. They were then so much harassed by their customers that they had to leave the town.[2] A certain carpenter of Benares prepared mechanical wooden birds (airships), by means of which he conquered a tract of land in the Himalayas. His capital was known as Kaṭṭhavāhananagara. He sent valuable presents to the king of Benares who in return sent him the news of the advent of the Buddha Kassapa in Benares.[3]

In Benares, there was a village of hunters on the banks of the river (=Ganges), and another on the farther side. Five hundred families dwelt in each.[4] The Nesāda of the *Māra Jātaka* (II, 36), who was ordered by the king to catch a golden peacock, practised the profession of a hunter in a Nesāda village near Benares.

There were snake-charmers in Benares (*Jātaka*, III, p. 198). An elephant festival was held in the city, in which Brahmins had to chant elephant lore (*Hastisūtram*). In this festival five score elephants with pure white tusks were used.[5] There was also a time-honoured drinking festival, at which people used to drink strong liquor and quarrel with one another. Sometimes their legs and arms were broken, crowns were cracked, and ears were torn off.[6]

From the Jātakas it is evident that the people of Benares were charitable, especially to hermits.[7] Visayha, a great merchant of Benares, had alms-halls built at the four city-gates, besides one in the heart of the city and one at the door of his own house. He distributed alms at these six points, and everyday 600,000 men came there to beg.[8] In the *Lalitavistara* there is a reference to *Ratnacūḍa* (*Ratnaśikhī*), a charitable king of Kāśī.[9]

Enthusiastic young men of Benares used to go to Taxila, for their education.[10] We read in the *Dhammapada Commentary* (I, 251ff.) how a certain king of Benares paid 1,000 *kahāpaṇas* to a young Brahmin for teaching him a mantra (spell) which afterwards proved the means of saving his life, when his barber and senāpati (general) plotted to kill him; and how another king of Benares paid

---

1 *Jātaka*, II, p. 18.

2 *Ibid.*, IV, p. 159.

3 *Suttanipāta Comm.*, II, pp. 575ff.

4 *Jātaka*, VI, p. 71.

5 *Ibid.*, II, p. 48.

6 *Ibid.*, IV, p. 115.

7 *Ibid.*, I, p. 361; p. 239 (Fausböll).

8 *Ibid.*, III, p. 129. Cf. the almost identical stories of Saṅkha, *Jātaka*, IV, p. 15; *Jātaka*, I, p. 262; and of Prince Jarāsandha, *Jātaka*, IV, p. 176.

9 Lefmann, p. 171.

10 *Dhammapada Comm.*, I, pp. 250-51; *Jātaka*, II, 47.

8

1,000 *kahāpaṇas* to a young Brahmin for a spell which enabled him to read people's evil thoughts, so that he could learn whether any of his subjects spoke ill of him. There seem to have been educational institutions at Benares also, some of which were even older than those of Taxila (*Khuddakapāṭha Comm.*, 198). We find for instance that Saṅkha, a Brahmin of Taxila, sent his son Susīma to Benares to study.[1]

A knowledge of spells formed an important part of a young man's education in the days when Kāśī was an independent kingdom; and it is natural that we should read of numerous superstitions which were current in Benares. We read in the Jātakas of the skill of the Brahmins of Benares in '*Lakkhaṇamantam*', or charms for discovering the auspicious signs of various creatures.[2] In Benares there was a Brahmin who professed to be able to tell whether the swords (of warriors) were lucky or not.[3] There was a superstitious belief current in Kāśī, as in other countries, that it was an evil omen if the wind touching the body of a *caṇḍāla* (outcaste) touched that of a person of another caste.[4] Slaughter of deer, swine and other animals for offerings to goblins was in vogue in Benares.[5]

Besides those already referred to, names of places mentioned in literature as belonging to Kāśī are Vāsabhagāma, Macchikāsaṇḍa, Kīṭāgiri and Dhanapālagāma.[6] The place which was most intimately associated with the several visits that the Buddha paid to Benares was Isipatana Migadāva, a famous Deer Park near the city. It was eighteen leagues from Uruvelā, and it was there that the Buddha preached his first sermon after his enlightenment, to his friends the Pañcavaggiya monks.[7] There also the Buddha spent his first rainy season; and he mentioned Isipatana as one of the four places of pilgrimage which his devout followers should visit.[8] 'Isipatana was so called because sages, on their way through the air (from the Himalayas) alight here or start from here on their aerial flight'.[9] Several other incidents connected with the Buddha, besides the preaching of his first sermon, are mentioned in the texts as having taken place in Isipatana.[10]

---

[1] *Dhammapada Comm.*, III, 445. [2] *Jātaka*, IV, p. 335.
[3] *Ibid.*, I, p. 455. [4] *Ibid.*, III, p. 233. [5] *Ibid.*, IV, p. 115.
[6] B. C. Law, *India as described in early texts of Buddhism and Jainism*, p. 42.
[7] *Dīgha Nikāya*, III, p. 141, *Majjhima Nikāya*, I, pp. 170ff.; cf. *Saṃyutta Nikāya*, V, pp. 420ff.; *Kathāvatthu*, pp. 97, 559.
[8] See *Buddhavaṃsa Comm.*, p. 3; *Dīgha Nikāya*, II, p. 141.
[9] Malalasekera, *Dictionary of Pāli Proper Names*, s.v. *Isipatana*.
[10] E.g. *Vinaya Piṭaka* (ed. Oldenberg), I, p. 15f.; *Dīpavaṃsa*, pp. 119-20; *Therīgāthā Comm.*, p. 220; *Aṅguttara Nikāya*, I, pp. 110ff., 279-80; III, pp. 392ff., 399ff.; *Saṃyutta Nikāya*, I, pp. 105-6; V, pp. 406–8.

Some of the most eminent members of the Buddhist community seem to have resided at Isipatana from time to time; among recorded conversations at Isipatana are several between Sāriputta and Mahākoṭṭhita,[1] and one between Mahākoṭṭhita and Citta-Hatthisāriputta.[2]

According to the *Mahāvaṃsa*, there was a large community of monks at Isipatana in the second century B.C. For we are told that at the foundation ceremony of the Mahā Thūpa in Anurādhapura, twelve thousand monks from Isipatana were present.[3] Isipatana was still a monastic centre in Hsüan-Tsang's time, for he found 1,500 monks studying the Hīnayāna there.[4] He quotes the *Nigrodhamiga Jātaka* (*Jāt.*, I, 145ff.) to account for the origin of the Migadāya or Deer Park at Isipatana. According to him, the Deer Park was the forest which was given by the king of Benares for the deer to wander in it unmolested.

Isipatana is identified with the modern Sāranāth, six miles from Benares. Cunningham[5] found the Migadāya represented by a fine wood, covering an area of about half a mile, extending from the great tomb of Dhamek on the north to the Chaukundi mound on the south.

Near Benares, too, was a grove of seven sirīsaka-trees where the Buddha preached to the Nāga-king Erakapatta[6]; and also the Khemiyambavana where Udena met Ghoṭamukha.[7] On the other side of the river was Vāsabhagāma, and beyond that another village called Cundaṭṭhila.[8] The Buddha is several times spoken of as staying in Benares, where he preached several sermons,[9] and converted many people, including Yasa, whose home was in Benares,[10] and his friends Vimala, Subāhu, Puṇṇaji and Gavampati, all members of eminent families.[11]

In the Buddha's time, the *Santhāgārasāla* (Council-Hall) of Benares was no longer being used so much for the transaction of public business as for public discussion on religious and philosophical

1 *Saṃyutta Nikāya*, II, pp. 112–14; III, pp. 167–9, 173–7; IV, pp. 384–6.

2 *Aṅguttara Nikāya*, III, p. 392f.

3 *Mahāvaṃsa*, XXIX, p. 31.

4 Beal, *Records of the Western World*, II, pp. 45ff.

5 *Arch. Reports*, I, p. 107.

6 *Dhammapada Comm.*, III, p. 230.

7 *Majjhima Nikāya*, II, p. 157.

8 *Petavatthu Comm.*, p. 168; B. C. Law, *India as described in early texts of Buddhism and Jainism*, p. 42; see also Barua and Sinha, *Barhut Inscriptions*.

9 E.g. *Aṅguttara Nikāya*, I, pp. 110f., 279f.; III, pp. 392f., 399f.; *Saṃyutta Nikāya*, I, p. 105; V, p. 406; *Vinaya Piṭaka*, I, pp. 189, 216f., 289; *Samantapāsādikā* (P.T.S.), I, p. 201.

10 *Vinaya Piṭaka*, I, p. 15.

11 *Ibid.*, p. 19.

questions.[1] Ascetics who came to the city found lodging for the night in the Potters' Hall.[2]

Many venerable Buddhist monks, e.g. Sāriputta, Mahāmoggallāna, Mahākaccāna, Mahākoṭṭhita, Mahācunda, Anuruddha, Revata, Upāli, Ānanda and Rāhula journeyed through the country of Kāśī.[3] The Buddha's converts in Benares included Aḍḍhakāsī, the daughter of a rich banker of Kāśī, who became a courtesan, whose fee was fixed by the king at half of the daily income of Kāśī (this explains her name, Aḍḍhakāsī). After her conversion by the Buddha, Aḍḍhakāsī is said to have become an arahat.[4] For other references to nuns who were connected with Kāśī, see, e.g. *Therīgāthā Comm.*, p. 106 and pp. 151-2. Elsewhere in the same work (pp. 71-2) it is said that Bhaddā Kapilānī became the chief queen of the king of Benares on account of her approving the offering of cloth to the Buddha in a previous birth.

[1] E.g. *Jātaka*, IV, p. 74. [2] E.g. *Dhammapada Comm.*, I, p. 39.
[3] *Vinaya Texts*, Pt. II, pp. 359-60.
[4] *Therīgāthā Comm.*, pp. 30-1. See also *Vinaya Texts*, III, p. 360, n. 3; II, pp. 195-6, n. 3.

## CHAPTER XXVIII

# THE KOŚALAS

In the earliest Vedic literature, no mention is made of Kośala as the name of a people. It is only in some of the later Vedic works, like the *Śatapatha Brāhmaṇa* and the *Kalpasūtras*, that we find Kośala referred to as a country. Kośala is also mentioned in the Pāli Buddhist literature as one of the sixteen great countries (*Mahājanapadas*) of Jambudīpa or India.[1] Pāṇini, too, mentions Kośala in one of his Sūtras.[2] In the *Atthasālinī*,[3] mention is made of Kośala as one of the great Kṣatriya tribes in Buddha's time.[4]

Kośala lay to the east of the Kurus and Pañcālas, and to the west of the Videhas, from whom it was separated by the river Sadānīrā, probably the great Gaṇḍak.[5] In the *Cambridge History of India*,[6] we read that the northern frontier of Kośala must have been in the hills in what is now Nepal; its southern boundary was the Ganges; and its eastern boundary was the eastern limit of the Śākya territory. According to Macdonell and Keith, Kośala lay to the north-east of the Ganges, and corresponds roughly to the modern Oudh.[7] Rhys Davids states that the Kośalas were the ruling clan in the kingdom whose capital was Sāvatthī (Śrāvastī), in what is now Nepal, seventy miles north-west of the modern Gorakhpur. He thinks that it included Benares and Sāketa, and probably had the Ganges for its southern, the Gaṇḍak for its eastern, and the mountains for its northern boundary.[8]

In the *Cambridge History of India*,[9] we read that the Kośalans were almost certainly of the Aryan race, in the main at least. They belonged to the solar family, and were supposed to have derived directly from Manu through Ikṣvāku. A family of princes bearing this name is known from Vedic literature, and it is quite possible

---

[1] *Aṅguttara Nikāya*, Vol. I, p. 213; IV, pp. 252, 256, 260; cf. *Viṣṇupurāṇa*, Chap. IV, Aṃśa 4.

[2] VI, 1, 17.

[3] *Khuddakapāṭha Comm.*, pp. 110-11; cf. *Papañcasūdanī* (P.T.S.), Vol. I, pp. 59-60. Kośala is mentioned as a beautiful place, attractive, pleasant, full of good things, and prosperous as the home of the gods.

[4] *Atthasālinī* (P.T.S.), p. 305.

[5] *Cambridge History of India*, Vol. I, p. 308; cf. *ibid.*, p. 117, and Rapson, *Ancient India*, p. 164; also *Śatapatha Brāhmaṇa*, 1, 4, 11.

[6] Vol. I, p. 178.

[7] *Vedic Index*, Vol. I, p. 190.

[8] *Buddhist India*, p. 25.

[9] Vol. I, p. 190.

that the solar dynasties of Kośala and other kingdoms to the east of the middle country were descended from this family. If so, Ikṣvāku must be regarded as an eponymous ancestor; and as his superhuman origin had to be explained, a myth founded on a far-fetched etymology of his name was invented, viz. that he was so called because he was born from the sneeze of Manu.[1] Vedic literature points out that the Ikṣvākus were originally a branch of the Purus.[2] Kośala is known to the Buddhists as the land of the Kośala princes,[3] tracing their descent from Ikṣvāku. The descent of those ruling princes of Kośala from Ikṣvāku is borne out by the genealogies in the *Rāmāyaṇa* as well as the Purāṇas.[4] Buddhaghoṣa narrates an anecdote giving a fanciful origin of the name of Kośala, from 'kuśala' (well, healthy, in good condition).[5]

In the *Śatapatha Brāhmaṇa* (I, 4, 11), the Kośala-Videhas appear as coming later than the Kuru-Pañcālas under the influence of Brahmanism. In the same work,[6] the Kauśalya or Kośala king, Para-āṭnāra Hiraṇyanābha, is described as having performed the great Áśvamedha or horse sacrifice. Hiraṇyanābha Kauśalya and Āśvalāyana Kauśalya figure in the *Praśna Upaniṣad* (1, 1) as two contemporary seekers of truth belonging to Kośala. The connection between Hiraṇyanābha of the *Praśna* and Para-āṭnāra Hiraṇyanābha of the *Śatapatha* is uncertain.[7] A passage in the *Sāṅkhyāyana Śrauta Sūtra* (XVI, 9, 13) shows the connection of Kośala with Kāśī and Videha.

It is in the Epic period that Kośala emerges into importance. The scene of action of the *Rāmāyaṇa* is in Kośala, the princes of which country carried Aryan civilisation to the south as far as the island of Ceylon. Pargiter observes that it is remarkable that in the *Rāmāyaṇa* the friendliest relations of Kośala were with the eastern kingdoms of Videha, Aṅga and Magadha, the Punjab kingdoms of Kekaya, Sindhu and Sauvīra, the western kingdom of Surāṣṭra, and the Dākṣiṇātya kings, for these are especially named among the monarchs who were invited to Daśaratha's sacrifice, and no mention is made of any of the kings of the middle region of N. India except Kāśī.[8] Pargiter is of the opinion that it was under

[1] *Cambridge History of India*, Vol. I, p. 305.

[2] *Ibid.*, p. 308.

[3] *Sumaṅgalavilāsinī*, I, p. 239.

[4] Ray Chaudhuri's *Political History*, 4th Ed., p. 86.

[5] *Sumaṅgalavilāsinī*, I, 239.

[6] XIII, 5, 4, 4.

[7] In the dynastic list of kings, occurring in the Purāṇas of doubtful authority, Hiraṇyanābha is mentioned as the immediate predecessor of Prasenajit (Pasenadi) who was a contemporary of Buddha. According to Buddhist tradition, Mahākosala was the father and immediate predecessor of Pasenadi.

[8] *Ancient Indian Historical Tradition*, p. 276.

King Dilīpa II and his immediate descendants that the country acquired the name of Kośala.[1]

We may form some idea of the extent of the Kośala country in the Epic period from the story of the exile of Rāma. Therein we find that, after setting out from Ayodhyā (then the capital of Kośala), the young princes accompanied by Sītā proceeded in a chariot. Evidently, then, there were good roads in the Kośala country, as we may also gather from the Jātaka stories, where we read that merchants loading as many as 500 wagons with their merchandise went from Magadha and the Licchavi countries through Kośala up to the western and north-western frontiers of India. Rāma made his first halt at the river Tamasā (the modern Tons). On the other side of the Tamasā, his chariot reached the Mahāmārga or the 'great road', which was evidently a trade-route. Following this, the party reached the river Śrīmatī Mahānadī. After crossing the river Vedaśruti, Rāma turned his course towards the south. After proceeding a long distance, he crossed the Gomatī and the Syandikā. Having crossed the Syandikā, Rāma pointed out to Sītā the wide plain given by Manu to Ikṣvāku. This region was evidently considered by the people of Kośala as the cradle of their race, the country with which Ikṣvāku began his career of conquest. This country was highly prosperous (*sphītā*) and populous (*rāṣṭravṛtā*). Proceeding through the extensive Kośalan plains, Rāma left behind him the country of the Kośalas, and reached the Ganges, up to which river the Kośala dominion evidently extended. Here he arrived at Śṛṅgaverapura which was the seat of the Niṣāda king Guha. Sir Alexander Cunningham has identified Śṛṅgaverapura with the modern Singror or Singor on the left bank of the Ganges and 22 miles to the north-west of Prayāga or Allahabad.[2]

In the *Ādiparvan* of the *Mahābhārata*[3] we read that Janamejaya, one of the earliest kings of the Paurava family, was the son of Puru and Kauśalyā. Most probably this Kauśalyā was the daughter of a king of Kośala. When Yudhiṣṭhira was about to perform his Rājasūya sacrifice, setting himself up as paramount sovereign over the whole of N. India, and his brothers went out on their expeditions of conquest, it is said that Arjuna, Kṛṣṇa and Bhīma started from the Kuru kingdom and reached Mithilā after crossing pūrva (eastern) Kośala.[4] Afterwards, the second Pāṇḍava brother, Bhīmasena, conquered Bṛhadbala, king of Kośala,[5] and this Bṛhad-

---

[1] *Ancient Indian Historical Tradition*, p. 275.

[2] *Arch. Survey Report*, Vols. XI, 62 and XXI, 11. For further geography of Rāma's exile, see Pargiter, *J.R.A.S.*, 1894, pp. 231 *et seq.*

[3] Chap. 95, p. 105.

[4] *Sabhāparvan*, Chap. 25, p. 240.

[5] *Ibid.*, Chap. 30, pp. 241-2.

bala attended the Rājasūya sacrifice.[1] Karṇa, too, conquered Kośala and proceeded southwards after exacting tribute from the country.[2] Evidently the conquest of Kośala by Karṇa was later than that by Bhīmasena, for we find the Kośala king Bṛhadbala, led by Duryodhana, marching against the Pāṇḍavas.[3] Perhaps it was because the Kośalas were smarting under the defeat inflicted on them by Bhīmasena that they embraced the Kaurava side in the Kurukṣetra war, in the course of which we find ten warriors including King Bṛhadbala of Kośala fighting in the van of the Kuru army.[4] Bṛhadbala fought with Abhimanyu against whom the greatest leaders of the Kuru army led a united attack[5]; and in the *Karṇaparvan*[6] we read that Bṛhadbala was killed by Abhimanyu. Sukṣetra, the son of the king of Kośala, also fought in the great war between the Kurus and the Pāṇḍavas.[7] After the war was ended, Kośala was again attacked and conquered by Arjuna before the performance of the Aśvamedha by Yudhiṣṭhira.[8]

As in the Epics, so also in the Purāṇas, the Kośalas are given great prominence among the Aryan Kṣatriya tribes of N. India. According to Purāṇa and Epic accounts, the Kośala line of kings derived from Ikṣvāku produced a large number of sovereigns who held the glory of the family very high, and some of them, like Māndhātā, Sagara, Bhagīratha and Raghu, occupied the highest position amongst the kings of ancient India.

Most of the Purāṇas[9] state that Ikṣvāku had a large number of sons who divided the whole of India amongst themselves. The *Viṣṇupurāṇa* says that Ikṣvāku had a hundred sons of whom fifty, with Śakuni at their head, became the protectors of N. India, and forty-eight established themselves as rulers over S. India.[10] The *Vāyupurāṇa* says that it was not the sons of Ikṣvāku who divided the country among themselves, but the children of Ikṣvāku's son Vikukṣi. Though the number of Ikṣvāku's immediate descendants as given in the Purāṇas is obviously fanciful, yet it seems worthy of credence that the family sprung from Ikṣvāku spread their rule far and wide over India, as many of the ruling families of India trace their descent to him.

---

1 *Sabhāparvan*, Chap. 34, p. 545.
2 *Vanaparvan*, Chap. 253, p. 513.
3 *Udyogaparvan*, Chap. 97, p. 807.
4 *Bhīṣmaparvan*, Chap. 16, pp. 827-8.
5 *Ibid.*, Chap. 45, p. 916. See also *ibid.*, Chap. 57, pp. 924-5; Chap. 87, p. 957.
6 Chap. 5, pp. 1167-8.
7 *Droṇaparvan*, Chap. 22, pp. 1012-13.
8 *Aśvamedhaparvan*, Chap. 42, p. 2093.
9 E.g., *Viṣṇupurāṇa*, IV, 2, 3; *Vāyupurāṇa*, 88, 8–11.
10 *Viṣṇupurāṇa*, IV, 2, 3.

The Purāṇas state that Vikukṣi incurred the displeasure of his father, Ikṣvāku, by the violation of some ceremonial rule, but later ascended the throne and reigned according to law and custom (*dharmataḥ*). A mythical story is related of the next king, Parañjaya. It is said that his aid was sought after by the Devas who were hard pressed by the Asuras; but the king imposed the condition that he would do so if borne on the shoulders of Indra himself. The king thus obtained the name of Kakutstha.

Sixth in descent from Kakutstha was King Śrāvasta, the founder of the city of Śrāvastī[1] which afterwards became the capital of northern Kośala. Śrāvasta's grandson, Kuvalayāśva, is credited with the overthrowing of an Asura, Dhundhu, which seems to signify the control of a natural phenomenon. According to the account given in the Purāṇas and the *Mahābhārata*,[2] the Ṛṣi Utaṅka complained to king Bṛhadaśva that his hermitage, which was situated on the sea-coast in the west, was disturbed by the Asura Dhundhu, who caused him much trouble, from a subterranean retreat (*antarbhūmigataḥ*). From the description that follows, it is manifest that this subterranean retreat (*asura*) was really a small volcanic pit near the western sea-coast which occasionally caused earthquakes and emitted smoke, ashes and fire. The old king Bṛhadaśva sent his son Kuvalayāśva to destroy the 'asura'. The prince went to the spot with an army of 21,000 men, who are said to be his sons, and whom he set to dig up the earth all around. After the excavation had proceeded for a week, the flaming body of Dhundhu became visible to all, but with disastrous consequences to the soldiers, who perished in the smoke and flames, only three surviving. The excavation, however, appears to have opened a subterranean channel or reservoir of water, which rushed into the volcanic pit and extinguished it for ever; for we read that after Dhundhu had reduced to ashes the 21,000 sons of Kuvalayāśva, streams of water flowed out of his body, and by means of this water the prince put out the fire, and acquired the appellation of Dhundhumāra for this achievement.[3]

A few generations after Kuvalayāśva came the great monarch, Māndhātā, who became a cakravartin or emperor exercising suzerain sway. In Māndhātā's dominions, it was said, the sun never set: 'From where the sun rises to where it sets, all this is the land of Māndhātā, the son of Yuvanāśva.'[4] As in the cases of Ikṣvāku and Kakutstha, fanciful stories based on a literal derivation of the name are narrated in the Purāṇas, which state that the name Māndhātā was

[1] *Viṣṇupurāṇa*, IV, 2, 12.
[2] *Vanaparvan*, Chaps. 201–3.
[3] *Vāyupurāṇa*, Chap. LXXXVIII.
[4] *Viṣṇupurāṇa*, IV, 2, xviii.

due to what Indra said[1] when the prince was born. The *Bhāgavata-purāṇa* adds that Māndhātā acquired the designation of Trasadasyu on account of the fear that he struck into the minds of the Dasyus. Māndhātā's daughters were given in marriage to the Ṛṣi Sauvari, and Purukutsa, one of the king's sons, married a Nāga girl (evidently a girl of a non-Aryan tribe).

Trasadasyu, the son of this Nāga queen, ascended the throne on his father's death. His son Anaraṇya is said to have been killed by Rāvaṇa. Several generations after this, Prince Satyavrata, son of the Kośala king, Trayyāruṇa, was in disfavour with his father as well as with the family priest Vaśiṣṭha, and was given the name of Triśaṅku. Vaśiṣṭha's rival, Viśvāmitra, however, espoused his cause, and placed him on the throne of Kośala. Triśaṅku's son Hariścandra was a very great monarch of the Kośalas; he celebrated a Rājasūya sacrifice and became famous as a *samrāṭ* or emperor.[2] The story of how Hariścandra promised to sacrifice his son to Varuṇa, and how finally Śunaḥśepa, a Brāhmaṇ lad, was sacrificed instead, is told in the *Aitareya Brāhmaṇa* and *Bhāgavatapurāṇa*. The latter also adds that there was a long-standing quarrel between Vaśiṣṭha and Viśvāmitra over this Kośala king Hariścandra. The *Mahābhārata*[3] also speaks of the surpassing glories of King Hariścandra of Kośala.

With Vāhu, who came to the throne of Kośala several generations after Hariścandra, the Kośala power suffered a great reverse. Vāhu was defeated by his enemies, a confederacy of the Haihayas, Tālajaṅghas and other allied Kṣatriya tribes, and was forced to abdicate. He repaired to the forest where after his death his wife gave birth to a son, who was reared with great care by Ṛṣi Aurva, near whose hermitage the king had taken refuge and built his woodland home. This young prince, Sagara, had in him the making of a great king, and when he came of age he sought to revive the glories of Kośala and place it once more in the high position of suzerain power in India. Sagara almost exterminated the Haihayas. A fanciful Purāṇa story says that Sagara had one son Asamañjas by one of his queens, and sixty thousand sons by another. Abandoning Asamañjas on account of his bad conduct, Sagara employed the sixty thousand sons to defend against all aggressors the horse of the Aśvamedha in its unbridled career over the earth. In the course of their journey, they insulted Ṛṣi Kapilā, and, as a result, they were reduced to ashes by him. Sagara then sent Asamañjas' son,

---

1 '*Māṃ dhātā*', 'he will suck me'.

2 *Vāyupurāṇa*, Chap. 88, verse 118.

3 III, Chap. 12. See also *Mbh.*, *Anuśāsanaparvan*, XIII, 65; XII, 20, XIII, 3.

Aṃśumān, in quest of the horse; he appeased the wrath of Kapila, succeeded in bringing back the horse, and obtained a promise from the Ṛṣi that his uncles would be purged of their sins when his grandson would bring down the heavenly Ganges to the pit which the uncles had excavated in their search for the horse. Thus the sacrifice was completed by Sagara who, pleased by the achievements of Aṃśumān, made over the Kośala throne to his son Asamañjas.

The grandson of Aṃśumān was the great Bhagīratha who made his prowess felt far and wide and became a cakravartin, as the *Mahābhārata*[1] tells us. A pretty story is told of him, in connection with the origin of the Ganges. Coming to know of his duty of rescuing his ancestors from their evil fate, Bhagīratha left the government of his vast empire in the hands of his ministers and succeeded by the severest penances in bringing the divine river down from the Himalayas, and thus filled up the pit excavated by his ancestors. The holy stream thereby acquired the designation of 'Bhāgīrathī'.[2]

Further down in the list of Kośala sovereigns, we meet with Ṛtuparṇa who was a contemporary of the celebrated Vidarbha monarch, Nala. Ṛtuparṇa employed Nala as his charioteer when the latter suffered a reverse of fortune, and taught Nala the secret art of dice-playing, acquiring from him in exchange the science of training horses.[3] Ṛtuparṇa's son was Sudāsa who is identified by some with the king of the same name in the *Ṛgveda*. Sudāsa's son was Mitrasaha Saudāsa,[4] who became famous afterwards as Kalmāṣapāda.

It is said in the Purāṇas that when Paraśurāma was carrying out his terrible vow of exterminating the Kṣatriyas, Vālika, grandson of Saudāsa, was saved from his wrath by being surrounded by a number of naked women. He thus became known as Nārīkavaca, i.e. 'protected by women,' and, as he was the source (*mūla*) from which future generations of Kṣatriyas sprang up, he also acquired the designation of Mūlaka (see Mūlaka chapter).

In the fourth generation after Mūlaka, we come to a Kośala sovereign Khaṭvāṅga who is spoken of as a *samrāṭ* whose great prowess led to the gods asking him to help them in their fight with the Asuras.[5] The *Bhāgavatapurāṇa* (IX, 9) adds that Khaṭvāṅga, within the remaining short period of his life, devoted himself to meditation on the supreme spirit with such zeal as to obtain liberation

---

[1] III, 108.

[2] *Rāmāyaṇa* (I, 39–44) and *Mahābhārata* (III, 106–9) give the story at great length.

[3] *Mahābhārata*, III, 71ff.

[4] See Aśmaka chapter.

[5] *Viṣṇupurāṇa*, IV, 4, 39.

(*mokṣa*). Khaṭvāṅga's grandson was the great Raghu, and Raghu's grandson was Daśaratha, the father of Rāma, in whom the glory of the Kośalan royal house reached its culmination.

After Rāma, the extensive Kośalan empire is said to have been divided amongst the sons of himself and his three brothers. The sons of the youngest brother, Śatrughna, ruled at Mathurā; the sons of Lakṣmaṇa established two kingdoms in the far north, in the neighbourhood of the Himālayas, while Bharata's sons founded the cities of Takṣaśilā and Puṣkarāvatī in the Gandhāra country, as the *Vāyupurāṇa*[1] tells us. The Kośala country proper is said to have been divided into two. In southern Kośala, Kuśa, the elder of the two sons of Rāma, became king, and transferred his capital from Ayodhyā to Kuśasthalī which he built on the Vindhya range.[2] Lava, the younger, became the ruler of the northern Kośala country and set up his capital at the city of Śarāvatī or Śrāvastī which was still the seat of the Kośala sovereigns in the Buddha's time.

Among the kings that followed Kuśa in the main line of the Kośala monarchs we do not meet with any great name until we come to Hiraṇyanābha Kauśalya who is said to have been a disciple of Ṛṣi Jaimini, from whom he learnt the science of Yoga, and imparted it in his turn to Yājñavalkya.[3] This distinction of proficiency in the Yogaśāstra is, however, transferred by some of the Purāṇas to Hiraṇyanābha's son, whom the *Vāyupurāṇa*[4] calls Vaśiṣṭha, and the *Viṣṇupurāṇa*,[5] Puṣya. The fifth in descent from Puṣya was Maru or Manu who is said to be living in the village of Kalāpa in a state of *yoga*, waiting to be the progenitor of the Kṣatriyas in the next cycle. Several generations down from this monarch was Bṛhadbala who led the Kośala troops to the Kurukṣetra war.

Many of the Purāṇas end their enumeration of the Kośala kings with Bṛhadbala, while some others, like the *Bhāgavata*,[6] add a few more names of men who are called the future kings of the Ikṣvāku family. The *Vāyupurāṇa* also in a later chapter (Chap. 99) gives a list of the kings in the Ikṣvāku line after Bṛhadbala, whom it calls here Bṛhadratha. Five generations after this Bṛhadratha, the *Vāyupurāṇa* says that Divākara 'is at present ruling the city of Ayodhyā', and after Divākara it speaks of the so-called future kings of the line. This list is substantially the same as the one in the *Bhāgavata*, and one peculiar feature of these lists is that they

1 88, 189-90.
2 *Vāyupurāṇa*, 88, 198: '*Vindhya-parvata-sānuṣu.*'
3 *Bhāgavatapurāṇa*, IX, 12.
4 88, 207-8.
5 IV, 4, 48.
6 IX, 12, 16.

include Śuddhodana and Rāhula, of Buddhist fame. The list in the *Matsyapurāṇa* (Chap. 12) from Kuśa to the Bhārata war is considerably shorter than the others already referred to. It speaks of Śrutaya as the king who fell in the Bhārata war.

The history of Kośala in later times is known chiefly from Jaina and Buddhist literature. In the *Jaina Kalpasūtra* we read that on the death of Mahāvīra, the eighteen confederate kings of Kāśī and Kośala, the nine Mallakis and nine Licchavis, on the day of the new-moon instituted an illumination on the Posada (fasting day)[1]. Jacobi observes[2]: 'According to the Jainas, the Licchavis and the Mallakis were the chiefs of Kāśī and Kośala. They seem to have succeeded the Aikṣvākas who ruled there in the time of the *Rāmāyaṇa*.'

The Pāli Buddhist literature is full of information about Kośala, which occupied a very prominent position at the time of the Buddha, though it was already being eclipsed by the growing power of Magadha.

The Pāli legends preserve the memory of kings of Kośala such as Kālasena, Dīghiti, Dīghāyu, Mallika and Vatika. One of these had his capital at Ayodhyā, some at Sāketa and the rest at Śrāvastī.[3] No connected chronology of Kośalan kings can as yet be made out of these stray names; but the legends are nevertheless important, first, as clearly indicating a succession of three capitals in the kingdom of Kośala, Ayodhyā, Sāketa and Śrāvastī; and, secondly, as broadly outlining the four main stages in the historical process which culminated at about the time of the rise of Buddhism in the unquestioned supremacy of Kośala over Kāśī.

With regard to the first of these questions, we have already seen that Ayodhyā is mentioned in the *Rāmāyana* as the earlier capital of Kośala, and Śrāvastī as its later capital.[4] Ayodhyā was an unimportant town in Buddha's time, while both Sāketa and Śrāvastī stood out prominently among the six great cities of India.[5]

The story of the rivalry between Kāśī and Kośala has already been treated at some length in our chapter on the Kāśīs, so that a summary will suffice here. In the first stage, as brought out in the canonical legend of Dīghīti and his son Dīghāyu Kumāra, King Brahmadatta appears as the powerful king of Kāśī invading the kingdom of Kośala, led by a love of conquest, easily defeating the Kośalan king Dīghīti, and ordering the execution of the Kośalan

---

1 *Kalpasūtra*, §128, S.B.E., Vol. XXII, p. 266.
2 *Jaina Sūtras*, Pt. II, p. 321, n. 3.
3 Ray Chaudhuri's *Political History*, 4th Ed., p. 90.
4 *Ibid.*, p. 90. Cf. *Ghata Jātaka* (No. 454) and *Nandiyamiga Jātaka* (No. 385).
5 *Dīgha Nikāya*, II, p. 146. Ray Chaudhuri, *op. cit.*, p. 90.

king and queen when they were detected in the realm of Kāśī living harmlessly in disguise.[1] We then see how the Kośalan prince Dīghāyu, after having gained the favour of the king of Kāśī and risen to the position of a general, tried to avenge his parents, and was re-established in his father's kingdom.[2]

In the second stage, as portrayed in the *Rājovāda Jātaka* (Fausböll, No. 334), Kāśī and Kośala appear as two equally powerful kingdoms, flourishing side by side, each with its inner circle, outer districts, and border-lands, one ruled over by its king, Brahmadatta, and the other by King Mallika. We see the ruler of Kāśī following the religious principle of 'conquering wrath by wrathlessness' (*akkodhena jine kodhaṃ*), and the ruler of Kośala following the strong administrative principle of 'applying hardness for the hard and softness for the soft' (*daḷhaṃ daḷhassa khipati Malliko mudunā muduṃ*).

In the third stage, as disclosed in the *Mahāsīlava Jātaka* (Fausböll, No. 51), the king of Kośala appears as taking advantage of the goodness of the king of Kāśī and invading the neighbouring kingdom, and the king of Kāśī as remaining passive in the consciousness of his superior dignity and religious security.[3]

Finally, in the fourth stage, Kāśī was absorbed by Kośala, and we find King Mahākośala, father and immediate predecessor of Pasenadi, wielding sovereign power over the extended realm of Kāśī-Kośala. Mahākośala gave his daughter Kosaladevī in marriage to King Bimbisāra of Magadha, and gave her a village in Kāśī yielding a revenue of a hundred thousand for bath and perfume money.[4] When Ajātaśatru put his father Bimbisāra to death, Kosaladevī died of grief. For some time after her death, Ajātaśatru continued to enjoy the revenues of the village, but Pasenadi, king of Kośala, resolved that no parricide should have a village which had been given to his sister and so confiscated it. A war ensued between Ajātaśatru and Pasenadi, in which Ajātaśatru was at first victorious, but was afterwards taken prisoner by the Kośalan king. After he had been subdued, however, he was treated generously by Pasenadi who gave him his daughter in marriage, and even bestowed the disputed village on her as a wedding gift.[5]

---

[1] *Vinaya Piṭaka, Mahāvagga*, pp. 342–9.

[2] See also *Jātaka*, III, 211f., 487; and Kāśī chapter of the present work, where this story and the similar one of Prince Chatta are dealt with.

[3] *Jātaka* (Fausböll), I, 262f.; see also I, 409; *Udāna Comm.*, 123; and see Kāśī chapter.

[4] *Jātaka*, II, p. 237; IV, 342ff.

[5] *Saṃyutta Nikāya*, I, pp. 82–5. See Kāśī and Magadha chapters, and *Jātaka*, Vol. IV, p. 343.

In addition to the stories of the rivalry between Kāśī and Kośala which we have already dealt with in the Kāśī chapter, two more may be mentioned,—the stories of Dabbasena, king of Kośala, who seized a holy king of Benares, and was discomfited by a mystic experience [1]; and of Manoja, king of Benares, and a king of Kośala. The latter story is related in the *Sonananda Jātaka*. Manoja pitched his camp near the city of Kośala (i.e. Śrāvastī?), and sent a message to the king of Kośala asking him either to give battle or to surrender. The king accepted the challenge, and a fierce fight ensued, in which the king of Kośala was defeated, but he was allowed to retain his kingdom.[2]

From the Jātaka stories of the two neighbouring countries of Kāśī and Kośala, it is evident that there was great mutual jealousy between the two kingdoms actuated by a constant spirit of hostility. Each was looking out for an opportunity to inflict a defeat on the other, and annex either the whole or at least a part of the other's dominions. Sometimes they also appear to have been connected by matrimony, and it is probable that the two countries were united sometimes by conquest and sometimes perhaps by a common heir succeeding to the throne of both countries. Even in Vedic times they were closely associated, as is shown by the phrase Kāśī-Kośala, which occurs in Vedic literature.

In the *Dīgha Nikāya* we read that Pasenadi, king of Kāśī-Kośala, used to collect taxes from the inhabitants of these two countries. He used to share his income with his subordinates. The *Mahāvagga*, however, mentions a Kāsika-rājā (king of Kāśī?) who sent a robe to Jīvaka.[3] Buddhaghoṣa says that he was a brother of Pasenadi, and son of the same father.[4] He was probably a sub-king of Pasenadi,[5] who managed to extend his rule so far as to reign as a supreme monarch with four sub-kings under him.[6] Later, before the end of Ajātaśatru's reign, some parts of Kośala were annexed to the kingdom of Magadha,[7] and Kośala finally disappears from history as an independent kingdom, evidently being absorbed by Magadha.[8] There is nothing surprising about this course of events, for, as the *Cambridge History of India* [9] points out, India appeared as a number of kingdoms and republics with a constant tendency towards amalgamation.

---

[1] *Jātaka*, III, p. 13.
[2] *Ibid.*, V, pp. 315-16.
[3] *Vin.*, I, 281.
[4] *Vinaya Texts*, II, 195, n. 2.
[5] Malalasekera, *Dictionary of Pāli Proper Names*, s.v. *Kāśī*.
[6] See article, '*Kośala*', B. C. Law, *Indian Culture*, Vol. I, No. 3.
[7] Bhandarkar, *Carmichael Lectures*, 1918, p. 79.
[8] Smith, *Early History of India*, 4th Ed., p. 45.
[9] I, p. 190.

In the north, the Kośala country bordered on the region occupied by the Śākyas, and there were mutual jealousies between the two peoples, often developing into war. When Pasenadi was at the height of his power, the Śākyas became his vassals, and he received homage from them.[1] The story of how Pasenadi acquired a Śākyan bride (Mallikā, a Vāsabhakhattiyā) has been related in our Śākya chapter. Pasenadi had a great admiration for the Buddha, and many stories are told of his dealings with the Buddha and his disciples. The king became the Buddha's disciple after meeting him at Jetavana.[2]

Pasenadi was famous for his charity. While Buddha was residing at Śrāvastī in the *ārāma* of Anāthapiṇḍika at Jetavana, the king made gifts for a week on an immense scale. These gifts were known as *asadisadāna* (incomparable charity).[3] The king of Kośala provided Kuṇḍa-Dhāna with all necessaries when the latter left the world after hearing the Buddha preach.[4] A great preaching hall (*Saddhamma Mahāsālā*) was built by Pasenadi for the Buddha. On another occasion, Pasenadi performed a great sacrifice in which 500 bulls, 500 calves, 500 goats, and other animals were offered. Buddha, when requested to attend, expressed his disapproval of this sacrifice, as he was against the taking of life by slaughter.[5]

After the death of his wife, Mallikā, Pasenadi went to the Buddha at Jetavana, and He consoled him in his grief.[6] Pasenadi was also consoled by the Buddha when his grandmother died.[7]

The Buddhist texts contain many stories about eminent men and women of Kośala, and many of these are in some way associated with Pasenadi. For instance, Mallikā, queen of Pasenadi, built an *ārāma* at the Kośala capital, Srāvastī, known as Mallikārāma, where the teacher Poṭṭhapāda went to live.[8] The *Dīgha Nikāya* tells us that Pokkharasādi, a famous Brāhmaṇ teacher of Kośala, enjoyed some property given to him by Pasenadi. The king did not allow him to enter his presence, but used to consult him behind a screen.[9] Buddhaghoṣa also furnishes some details about this sage. Pokkharasāti or Pokkharasādi, says he, was a Brāhmaṇa, living at Ukkaṭṭhanagara, which had been given him by the king of Kośala, Pasenadi, as Brahmadeyya (i.e. as a Brahmin's fee). He was well versed in the Vedas and in the arts, and the king bestowed Ukkaṭṭhanagara upon him because he was satisfied by a display

1 *Dīgha Nikāya*, II, p. 83.
2 *Saṃyutta Nikāya*, I, pp. 68–70.
3 *Piṭhavimāna*, *Vimānavatthu Comm.*, pp. 5-6.
4 *Psalms of the Brethren*, pp. 19-20.
5 *Saṃyutta Nikāya*, I, p. 76.
6 *Aṅguttara Nikāya*, III, p. 57.
7 *Saṃyutta Nikāya*, I, p. 97.
8 *Dīgha Nikāya*, I, pp. 178ff.
9 *Ibid.*, I, p. 103.

of his learning.[1] A certain Aggidatta was the purohita or royal chaplain of Mahākosala, father of Pasenadi, and Pasenadi also accepted him as his purohita. Later, Moggallāna converted Aggidatta and his disciples to Buddhism.[2]

Another chaplain of Pasenadi was Bāvarī who was the son of the chaplain of Pasenadi's father. Pasenadi bestowed honour and wealth upon Bāvarī, and learnt the arts (*sippa*) from him in his youth. Bāvarī later took ordination and lived in the royal garden, many Brāhmaṇas becoming his disciples. Pasenadi served him daily with the four requisites. Afterwards Bāvarī and his disciples went to the Deccan.[3] Pasenadi also invited two prominent merchants, Meṇḍakaseṭṭhi and Dhanañjayaseṭṭhi, to settle in Kośala.[4]

The story of the conversion of the Kośala country to the Buddhist faith is told in some detail in the *Majjhima Nikāya*. Here we read that, in the course of his journey over N. India, on one occasion, the Buddha was sojourning in Kośala, and went to Sālā, a Brahmin village of Kośala. The Brahmin householders of Sālā went to see him and asked him various metaphysical questions which he answered to their satisfaction, and they became his life-long disciples.[5] Once the Buddha went to Nagaravinda, a Brahmin village of Kośala. There many Brahmaṇa householders came to see him, attracted by reports of his fame as a great teacher. After listening to his preaching, they became converted to the new faith.[6] Another Brahmin village visited by the Buddha in Kośala was Venāgapura. Here, too, the Brāhmaṇa householders went to pay their respects to him and talk with him.[7] Buddha spent much of his time at Śrāvastī and most of his sermons were delivered there.[8]

As we have seen, the capital cities of Kośala were Śrāvastī (Pāli Sāvatthī) and Sāketa. Many fanciful explanations of the name Sāvatthī have been suggested. For instance, it was said that Sāvatthī was so called because the sage Sāvattha resided there. The author of the *Papañcasūdanī* holds that everything required by human beings is to be found there: hence it is called Sāvatthī (*sabba* and

---

[1] *Sumaṅgalavilāsinī*, I, pp. 244-5.

[2] *Dhammapada Comm.*, Pt. III, pp. 241ff.

[3] *Suttanipāta Comm.*, II, pp. 579ff.

[4] *Dhammapada Comm.*, Pt. 1, pp. 384ff. For further references to Pasenadi, see *Dhammapada Comm.*, II, pp. 1ff.; *Saṃyutta Nikāya*, I, pp. 78–93; *Aṅguttara Nikāya*, V, pp. 65ff.

[5] *Majjhima Nikāya*, I, pp. 400ff. For another story of the Buddha and Kośala, see *Majjhima Nikāya*, II, pp. 45ff., and *Aṅguttara Nikāya*, I, pp. 205ff.

[6] *Majjhima Nikāya*, III, pp. 290ff.

[7] *Aṅguttara Nikāya*, I, pp. 180ff. See also *Saṃyutta Nikāya*, V, pp. 352ff.

[8] *Saṃyutta Nikāya*, V, pp. 349ff.

*atthi*).[1] According to the Purāṇas, Śrāvastī is said to have been built by king Śrāvasta, eighth in descent from Vivakṣu, son of Ikṣvāku.[2]

Sāvatthī was situated in what is now the province of Oudh.[3] It is now known as Maheṭh of the village group Saheṭh-Maheṭh on the borders of the Gonda and Bahraich districts of the United Provinces.[4]

The Pāli Buddhist literature is full of facts regarding the glories of Sāvatthī. Many of the Buddha's most edifying discourses were delivered at the Kośala capital, which was the place of residence of two of the most munificent benefactors of the Buddhist Saṃgha, viz. Anāthapiṇḍika, the great merchant, and Visākhā Migāramātā, the most liberal-hearted of the ladies figuring in the Buddhist literature. Sāvatthī is mentioned in the *Mahāparinibbāna Suttanta* of the *Dīgha Nikāya* as a great city. It was the resort of many wealthy nobles, Brahmins, heads of houses and believers in the Tathāgata. In one of the Jātakas we read that there was at Sāvatthī a rich merchant who was worth eighteen crores[5]; in another we read that at Sāvatthī, in the house of Anāthapiṇḍika, food was always ready for 500 brethren, and the same thing is told about Visākhā and the king of Kośala.[6] In the *Vimānavatthu* we read that the Kosalas and especially the inhabitants of Sāvatthī were remarkable for their charity, which, they believed, was one of the principal ways of obtaining heavenly bliss.

References to the connection of the Buddha and his disciples with Sāvatthī are too numerous to be dealt with in full. Some famous names in the annals of Buddhism which are associated with the Kośalan capital are those of Nandaka,[7] Mahāpajāpatī Gotamī,[8] Sāriputta[9] and Ānanda.[10] Sāvatthī contributed a fair number of bhikkhus and bhikkhuṇīs to the Order. For instance, Mahāsuvaṇṇa, a banker of Sāvatthī, had two sons, the elder of whom became a bhikkhu under the Buddha and was known as Cakkhupāla.[11] Thul-

---

[1] *Papañcasūdanī*, I, pp. 59-60; B. C. Law, *Śrāvastī in Indian Literature*, *M.A.S.I.*, No. 50, p. 19.

[2] *Viṣṇupurāṇa*, Chap. 2, Aṃśa 4; cf. *Bhāgavatapurāṇa*, 9th skandha, Chap. 6, śl. 21; *Matsyapurāṇa*, Chap. 21, śl. 30; *Kūrmapurāṇa*, Chap. 23, śl. 19; *Liṅgapurāṇa*, Chap. 95.

[3] Edkins, *Chinese Buddhism*, p. 290.

[4] *Carmichael Lectures*, 1918, p. 51.

[5] *Jātaka*, VI, p. 68.

[6] *Ibid.*, IV, p. 144; see also pp. 236-7.

[7] *Majjhima Nikāya*, III, pp. 270ff.; *Aṅguttara Nikāya*, I, pp. 193ff.

[8] *Ibid.*

[9] *Aṅguttara Nikāya*, I, pp. 63ff., 118ff.

[10] *Ibid.*, pp. 215ff.; *Dīgha Nikāya*, I, pp. 204ff.

[11] *Dhammapada Comm.*, I, pp. 3ff.

latissa, the Buddha's cousin, lived at Sāvatthī as a bhikkhu.[1] Paṭācārā was the daughter of a rich banker of Sāvatthī. She afterwards became a bhikkhuṇī.[2] Kisāgotamī, also the daughter of a seṭṭhi of Sāvatthī, became a bhikkhuṇī after the death of her only child.[3] Nanda, the son of Mahāpajāpatī Gotamī, was made a bhikkhu by the Buddha at Sāvatthī.[4] Others who became bhikkhus were Anitthigandhakumāra,[5] Vakkali,[6] Kaṅhārevata,[7] Vīra,[8] Kuṇḍadhāna[9] and Ajita.[10] In the *Therīgāthā* we read that Sumanā was born at Sāvatthī as the sister of the king of Kośala. She heard the Master preach the doctrine to King Pasenadi. She put faith in the Buddha, entered the Order, and afterwards became an arahant.[11] In the *Suttanipāta Commentary* we read that there lived at Sāvatthī a *paribbājaka* named Pasura who was a great disputant. He held discussions with Sāriputta, Lāludāyi and the Buddha, and was finally converted to Buddhism.[12]

As we may gather from the various accounts, there were many merchants at Sāvatthī. They used to go to Videha with cartloads of merchandise to sell there, and take Videhan commodities in exchange.[13] Some merchants of Sāvatthī went to Suvarṇabhūmi in a ship,[14] and others went to the northern regions (*Uttarāpatha*), taking with them 500 cartloads of merchandise.[15]

Śrāvastī was visited by the two famous Chinese Pilgrims, Fā-Hien, and Hsüan Tsang, but the glories of the once splendid capital of Kośala had departed at the time of their visit. When Fā-Hien went to Śrāvastī (in the fifth century A.D.), the inhabitants of the city were few, amounting in all to little more than two hundred families. The pilgrim refers to King Prasenajit of Kośala, and he saw the place where the old vihāra of Mahāpajāpatī Gotamī was built, the wells and walls of the house of Anāthapiṇḍika, and the site where Aṅgulimāla attained arahantship. Topes were built at all these places.[16]

Cunningham points out on the authority of Hsüan Tsang that five centuries after Buddha or one century after Kaniṣka, Vikramāditya, king of Śrāvastī, became a persecutor of the Buddhists, and the famous Manorhita, author of the *Vibhāsaśāstra*, committed suicide after being defeated in argument by the Brāhmaṇas. During the reign of Vikramāditya's successor, the Brāhmaṇas were over-

---

1 *Dhammapada Comm.*, I, pp. 37ff. 2 *Ibid.*, II, pp. 260ff. 3 *Ibid.*, pp. 270ff.
4 *Ibid.*, I, pp. 115ff. 5 *Ibid.*, III, pp. 281ff. 6 *Ibid.*, IV, p. 118.
7 *Psalms of the Brethren*, p. 7. 8 *Ibid.*, pp. 13 14.
9 *Ibid.*, pp. 19-20. 10 *Ibid.*, p. 25.
11 *Psalms of the Sisters*, pp. 19-20. 12 *Suttanipāta Comm.*, II, pp. 538ff.
13 *Buddhist Conception of Spirits*, 2nd Ed., p. 63. 14 *Ibid.*, p. 64.
15 *Ibid.*, p. 96. 16 Legge, *Travels of Fā-Hien*, pp 55-6.

come by Vasubandhu, the eminent disciple of Manorhita. In the third century A.D., Śrāvastī seems to have been under the rule of its own kings, for we find Khīradhāra and his nephew mentioned as rājās between A.D. 275 and 319. Still later, Śrāvastī was a dependency of the powerful Gupta dynasty of Magadha, as the neighbouring city of Sāketa is especially said to have belonged to the Guptas. From this time Śrāvastī gradually declined.

A famous Buddhist site at Śrāvastī was the Jetavana, where Anāthapiṇḍika built a vihāra which was originally of seven storeys. This vihāra was dedicated to Buddha and the Buddhist Church by Prince Jeta.[1]

In later times, North Kośala itself came to be known as Śrāvastī in order to distinguish it from South Kośala. Hsüan Tsang, who visited India in the seventh century A.D., says that Śrāvastī, i.e. North Kośala, was about 600 li in circuit. Although it was mostly in ruins, there were some inhabitants. The country had good crops and an equable climate, and the people were honest in their ways, and given to learning, and fond of good works. There were some hundreds of Buddhist monasteries, most of which were in ruins. The brethren, who were very few, were Sammatiyas. There were a hundred deva-temples, and the non-Buddhists were very numerous. The preaching hall built by Pasenadi for the Buddha still survived, and there were several topes,[2] many Buddhist monasteries, and many Mahāyānist brethren.[3]

Another important town of Kośala was Sāketa, which was the capital in the period immediately preaching the Buddha's time.[4] The road from Sāketa to Śrāvastī was haunted by robbers, who were dangerous to passers-by. Even the bhikkhus, who had very little in their possession, were robbed of their belongings and sometimes killed by the robbers. Royal soldiers used to come to the spot where robbery was committed, and used to kill those robbers whom they could arrest.[5]

Besides Sāvatthī and Sāketa, we find mention of other towns in the Kośala country, e.g. Daṇḍakappaka, Nalakapāna, Setavya and Paṅkadhā. Once the Buddha gave a discourse to Ānanda at Daṇḍakappa,[6] and he also visited Nalakapāna, where he dwelt at Palāsavana, and gave religious instruction to the bhikkhus on an uposatha night.[7] On another occasion Kumārakassapa went to Setavya with a large number of bhikkhus. The chief of Setavya,

[1] Legge, *Travels of Fā-Hien*, pp. 56-7; *Khuddakapāṭha Comm.*, pp. 110–2.
[2] Watters, *On Yuan Chwang*, Vol. I, p. 377.
[3] *Ibid.*, Vol. II, p. 200.
[4] *Carmichael Lectures*, 1918, p. 51.
[5] *Vinaya Texts*, Pt. I, pp. 220-1.
[6] *Aṅguttara Nikāya*, III, pp. 402ff.
[7] *Ibid.*, V, pp. 122ff.

Pāyāsi, enjoyed enormous wealth which had been given him by King Pasenadi. He was a false believer, but was converted by Kumāra-kassapa.[1] The Buddha visited Paṅkadhā, and gave instruction to Kassapagotta, a bhikkhu who was dwelling there.[2]

In the *Saṃyutta Nikāya*[3] we find mention of a village named Toraṇavatthu, between Sāvatthī and Sāketa. In this village, the bhikkhuṇī Khemā was observing lent, when Pasenadi spent one night there on his way from Sāketa to Sāvatthī. Hearing of Khemā, he went to her, and she answered to his satisfaction questions regarding life after death.[4]

The Jātakas and Vinaya texts are full of details about Kośala. In one Jātaka there is a vivid description of a drought in Kośala, when the crops were withered, and ponds, tanks and lakes were dried up.[5] Gangs of burglars, highwaymen and murderers were not unknown in Kośala,[6] and the inhabitants were often carried away and killed by them.[7] Their activities could not easily be checked, for the Kośala country included the forest-clad hills and valleys of the outer spurs of the Himālayas.

In the *Pabbajjā Suttanta* of the *Suttanipāta* (p. 73), we read that the inhabitants of Kośala were healthy and powerful. One Jātaka story[8] says that in Kośala there was a Brahmin who by simply smelling a sword could say whether it was lucky or not.

The Kośalan kings and princes received a good education, usually being 'finished' at Taxila. For instance, in the *Brahāchatta Jātaka* we read that Chatta, a son of the king of Kośala, fled to Taxila when his father was taken prisoner, and there he mastered the three Vedas and eighteen *vijjās*. While at Taxila he also learnt the science of discovering hidden treasure, and on his return he acquired his deceased father's buried wealth, engaged troops and reconquered the lost kingdom.[9] King Pasenadi was also educated at Taxila; Mahāli, a Licchavi prince, and a Malla prince of Kusīnārā were his class-mates.[10]

Rhys Davids points out[11] that a conversational dialect, probably based on the local dialect of Śrāvastī, was in general use among Kośala officials, among merchants and among the more cultured classes, not only throughout the Kośala dominions but east and west

[1] *Dīgha Nikāya*, II, pp. 316ff.
[2] *Aṅguttara Nikāya*, I, p. 236.
[3] Vol. IV, pp. 374ff.
[4] *Saṃyutta Nikāya*, IV, pp. 374ff.
[5] *Jātaka*, Vol. I, p. 329.
[6] *Ibid.*, Vol. II, p. 139.
[7] *Vinaya Texts*, Pt. I, p. 312.
[8] *Jātaka*, Vol. I, p. 455.
[9] *Ibid.*, Vol. III, pp. 115-6.
[10] *Dhammapada Comm.*, Pt. I, pp. 337-8.
[11] Rhys Davids, *Buddhist India*, p. 153.

from Delhi to Patna, and north and south from Śrāvastī to Avanti. Jacobi observes that the *Rāmāyaṇa* was composed in Kośala on the basis of ballads popularly recited by rhapsodists throughout the district. Kośala was also the very centre of Buddhist literary activity.[1]

[1] Rhys Davids, *Buddhist India*, p. 183.

## CHAPTER XXIX

# THE VATSAS

The Vaśas or Vatsas were one of the peoples of Vedic Aryandom from the earliest period. A certain Vaśa Aśvya is mentioned in several hymns of the first and eighth maṇḍalas of the *Ṛgveda*, and also once in the tenth, as a protégé of the Aśvins.[1] He is also mentioned in the *Sāṅkhāyana Śrauta Sūtra*.[2] It would seem that this Vaśa Aśvya was a Brahmin Ṛṣi and not a Kṣatriya. He is said to have been the author of the Vaśa hymn in the *Brāhmaṇas* and the *Āraṇyakas*.[3] It is possible to take Vaśa as a personal name, but it is equally likely that Vaśa here is a tribal designation and Aśvya the personal proper name.

Vaśa is mentioned as the name of a people in the *Aitareya Brāhmaṇa*[4] which says, '. . .Therefore, in this firm middle established quarter (Dhruva-madhyamā), whatever kings there are of the Kuru-Pañcālas with the Vaśas and Uśīnaras, they are anointed for kingship. . .' Here we observe that the Vaśas are spoken of as one of the Vedic tribes living in the *Dhruva-madhyamā dik* or the Madhyadeśa of Manu, along with the Kurus, Pañcālas and Uśīnaras. Their connection with this last tribe appears also to be proved by the *Gopatha Brāhmaṇa* (I, 2, 9) where Oldenberg reads *Sa-vaśa-Uśīnareṣu* instead of Śavasa in the printed edition. In the *Kauśītaki Upaniṣad*, too,[5] we have mention of the Vaśas together with the Uśīnaras, Matsyas, Kurus and Pañcālas. The Pāli *Aṅguttara Nikāya* mentions the land of the Vaṃśas (identified by Oldenberg with the Vaśas) as one of the sixteen *Mahājanapadas*, along with the Cedis, Kurus, Pañcālas, Matsyas, Śūrasenas, etc., who appear to have been their close neighbours. The *Janavasabha-Suttanta* associates the Vaṃśas rather with the Cedis than with the Uśīnaras, and mentions the powerful ruling peoples of the time in such groups as Kāśī-Kośala, Vajji-Mallā, Cedi-Vaṃsā, Kuru-Pañcālā and Maccha-Sūrasenā.

In the Pāli Buddhist canon, King Udena of the Vaṃśas is said to have been a contemporary of the Buddha, and to have survived him. Both in Pāli Buddhist and in Brahmanic Sanskrit literature,

[1] *R.V.*, I. 112, 10; 116, 21; VIII, 8, 20; 24, 14; 46, 21, 23; 50, 9; X, 40, 7.

[2] XVI, 11, 13.

[3] *Śatapatha Brāhmaṇa*, VIII, 6, 2, 3; IX, 3, 3, 19; *Aitareya Āraṇyaka*, I, 5, 1, 2; *Sāṅkhāyaṇa A.*, II, 10, 11.

[4] VIII, 14, 3.

[5] IV, 1.

stories are recited about this King Udena of the Vaṃsas (Pāli) or Udayana of the Vatsas (Sanskrit). His capital is mentioned as Kosambī or Kauśāmbī respectively, so evidently the Vaṃśas and Vatsas are identical. In the Jaina books the same people are spoken of as Vacchas.[1]

The country of the Vaṃśas or Vatsas must therefore have been located round about Kauśāmbī, the position of which has been identified by Cunningham with Kosāṃ, not very far from Allahabad. According to the *Bṛhatsaṃhitā*, the land of the Vatsas was in the middle region. It probably lay to the north-east of Avanti along the bank of the Jumna, southwards from Kośala [2] and to the west of Allahabad.[3] The Chinese pilgrim Hsüan Tsang, who speaks of the land of the Vatsas as the Kauśāmbī country, says that it was about 6,000 li in circuit.[4]

The *Mahābhārata* contains certain items of traditional information regarding the Vatsa-bhūmi or land of the Vatsas. In one passage,[5] we are told that, prior to the Rājasūya sacrifice performed by Yudhiṣṭhira, Bhīmasena led an expedition towards the east and conquered the Vatsa-bhūmi; while in the *Vanaparvan*,[6] it is stated that Vatsa was conquered by Karṇa. Elsewhere [7] we read that the Haihayas of the Cedi country seized the capital of the Vatsas after killing Haryaśva who must have been a king of Vatsa. In the *Bhīṣmaparvan*,[8] it is said that in the Kurukṣetra war, the Vatsa army took the side of the Pāṇḍavas. Nakula and Sahadeva along with the Vatsas and others guarded the left side of the Pāṇḍava army.

According to the tradition in the *Harivaṃśa*, the Vatsa-bhūmi was founded by a royal prince of Kāśī, while, according to the *Mahābhārata* proper, its capital Kauśāmbī was founded by the Cedi prince Kusāmba. The Pāli tradition in the *Mahāvaṃsa Commentary* [9] suggests that fourteen pre-Ikṣvāku kings of the Solar dynasty, headed by Baladatta, ruled the Vatsa kingdom with their capital at Kauśāmbī.

The Purāṇas tell us that after Hastināpura was carried away by the Ganges, Nicakṣu who was the fifth in descent from the Puru prince Parikṣit, grandson of Arjuna, transferred his capital to Kauśāmbī where altogether twenty-five Puru kings,[10] from Nicakṣu to

---

1 *Uvāsagadasāo*, Hoernle, Vol. II, Appendix I, p. 7.

2 *Buddhist India*, p. 3.

3 N. L. Dey, *Geographical Dictionary*, p. 100.

4 Watters, *On Yuan Chwang*, Vol. I, p. 365.

5 Chap. 30, pp. 241-2.

6 Chap. 253, pp. 513-14.

7 *Anuśāsanaparvan*, Chap. 30, p. 1899.

8 Chap. 50, p. 924.

9 *Vaṃsatthappakāsinī*, I, pp. 128, 130.

10 Rhys Davids (*Camb. Hist.*, I, p. 308) says: 'The later list contains the names of 29 Puru kings who lived after the war. They reigned first at Hastināpura, the

Kṣemaka, reigned.[1] In this genealogy we are given the succession of the kings of Vatsa from Nicakṣu to Kṣemaka without the length of their reigns. Udayana, who was a contemporary of the Buddha, is represented as the son and successor of Śatānīka; and the four successors of Udayana as Vahīnara, Daṇḍapāṇi, Nirāmitra and Kṣemaka. The evidence of Buddhist literature in general, and of the Pāli canon in particular, clearly proves the contemporaneity of Udayana, the king of Vatsa, with Caṇḍa Pradyota (Pāli Caṇḍa Pajjota) of Avanti, Prasenajit (Pasenadi) of Kośala, and Bimbisāra and Ajātaśatru of Magadha. It is interesting to find that the Purāṇas mention just four kings who succeeded to the throne of Avanti after Caṇḍa Pradyota, and four kings who succeeded to the throne of Kośala after Prasenajit.[2] The total length of the reigns of the five kings of Avanti from Pradyota to Nandivardhana is given as 138 years, Pradyota's four successors having reigned altogether for 115 years.[3] Among the kings of N. India who were contemporaries of the Buddha, Bimbisāra pre-deceased him by about 8 years, and Ajātaśatru survived the Buddha by 16 years; Prasenajit, who was of the same age as the Buddha, died almost in the same year; and though both Pradyota and Udayana survived the Buddha, they could not have lived or reigned for more than 10 or 15 years after the Buddha's demise. Thus, on the whole, it may be surmised that Avanti, Kośala and Vatsa retained their independence for about a century after the Buddha's death, and lost it only during the period of the Nandas. We know that when King Aśoka Maurya ascended the throne of Magadha, the three ancient kingdoms of Kośala, Vatsa and Avanti were already included in the Maurya empire. Ujjenī or Avanti was placed under a Viceroy of Aśoka, while Kauśāmbī or Vatsa was governed by a Mahāmātra.[4]

The *Lalitavistara* contains a tradition according to which King Udayana was born on the same day as the Buddha.[5] He appears to have strengthened his political position by matrimonial alliances

---

ancient capital of the Kuru princes, which is usually identified with a ruined site in the Meerut district on the old bed of the Ganges, lat. 29° 9′ N., long 78° 3′ E. (Pargiter, *Mārk. Pur.*, p. 355); but when this city was destroyed by an inundation of the Ganges in the reign of Nichakshu, they removed the seat of their rule to Kauśāmbī.... Another of their capitals was Indraprastha in the Kuru plain, the ancient city of the Pāṇḍu princes ...'

[1] For the genealogy in full, see Pargiter, *Dynasties of the Kali Age*, pp. 65-6.

[2] *Ibid.*, pp. 67-8.

[3] *Ibid.*, p. 68.

[4] Aśoka's *Kauśāmbī Schism Pillar Edict.*

[5] *Vide* Foucaux, Tr. of the Tibetan version of the *Lalitavistara*; cf. Rockhill, *The Life of the Buddha*, pp. 16-17.

with the neighbouring kings, particularly with King Caṇḍa Pradyota of Avanti. Stories of Udayana and his queens abound in Sanskrit and Pāli literature, and provide the themes for no less than four dramas.[1] The Pāli legends tell us that Udayana ascended the throne of Vatsa by the assertion and establishment of his rightful claim as the son and successor of his father Parantapa.[2] In the *Udenavatthu*, Vatsa is described as a *paveṇirajja*, i.e. a kingdom in which succession to the throne was determined by the law of primogeniture.[3] In most of the other references, whether Brahmanical, Jaina, or Buddhist, Śatānīka (better, Śatānīka II) is represented as Udayana's father.[4] In the *Skandapurāṇa* alone, Sahasrānīka is represented as the father and Śatānīka as the grandfather of Udayana.[5] The *Skandapurāṇa* speaks of Śatānīka as a king of Kauśāmbī who belonged to the family of Arjuna, was powerful and intelligent, beloved by his subjects, and who was killed in a war between the Devas and the Asuras.[6] According to the Jaina tradition, Udayana's father Śatānīka II invaded Campā, the capital of Aṅga, during the reign of King Dadhivāhana.[7] According to the *Skandapurāṇa* and *Vividhatīrthakalpa*, Udayana's mother was Queen Mṛgāvatī, granddaughter of Kṛtavarmā, king of Ayodhyā.[8] In the plays of Bhāsa, Udayana is described as Vaidehīputra, which indicates that his mother was princess of Videha.[9]

Udayana was a warlike king who kept a strong army noted for its elephants. Envious of his fellow-monarch's wealth and prosperity, Caṇḍa Pradyota of Avanti laid a trap for Udayana when he was visiting the frontier of his kingdom, and succeeded in taking him captive. He made his escape from captivity with the help of Vāsuladattā or Vāsavadattā, daughter of Caṇḍa Pradyota, who eloped with Udayana and became his chief queen.[10]

[1] Bhāsa's *Svapnavāsavadattā* and *Pratijñāyaugandharāyaṇa*; Harṣa's *Ratnāvalī* and *Priyadarśikā*. The legends of Udayana are also to be found in the *Brahmakhaṇḍa* of the *Skandapurāṇa*, the Jaina *Vividhatīrthakalpa*, the *Lalitavistara*, Tibetan Buddhist literature, Pāli *Udenavatthu*, Sanskrit *Mākandika Avadāna*, and the *Si-yu-ki* of Hsüan Tsang.

[2] *Dhammapada Comm.*, I, pp. 165 foll.

[3] *Ibid.*, I, p. 169.

[4] *Vividhatīrthakalpa*, ed. Jina Vijaya Sūri, p. 23.

[5] Cf. *The Romantic Legend of Śākya Buddha*, p. 28, in which King Pih-Shing or 'Hundred Excellences', i.e. *Śatānīka*, is represented as the son of Tsien-Shing ('Thousand Excellences' or *Sahasrānīka*). It should be noted that 'anīka' can also mean 'army, host', it would appear that Parantapa, Śatānīka and Sahasrānīka may all be taken to refer to the valour and martial strength of the king of Vatsa.

[6] Chap. 5, *Brahmakhaṇḍa*.

[7] *J.A.S.B.*, 1914, p. 321.

[8] *Skandapurāṇa*, Chap. V, *Brahmakhaṇḍa*.

[9] *Vividhatīrthakalpa*, p. 23; Bhandarkar, *Carmichael Lectures*, 1918, p. 59.

[10] *Dhammapada Comm.*, I, pp. 191–9, and *Svapnavāsavadattā*.

According to the Pāli legend, Udayana was born and brought up in the Himalayan region, in the hermitage of a sage who was previously a native of Allakappa. He was named Udena or Udayana because of his birth, just at sunrise, on the top of a hill, and under a clear sky.[1] According to another Buddhist legend in the Tibetan *Dulva*, 'as the world was illuminated at his birth, as with the sun, he was called Udayana'.[2]

Udayana is said to have married Sāmāvatī (Śyāmāvatī), daughter of a banker of Bhaddavatī, who was brought up in the family of the banker Ghosita of Kauśāmbī. Another of his wives was Māgandiyā or Mākandikā, an exquisitely beautiful Brahmin girl from the Kuru country,[3] and yet another was Padmāvatī, daughter of King Ajātaśatru of Magadha.[4] The *Ratnāvalī* represents Udayana as having also married Sāgarikā, a princess from Ceylon. In the *Udenavatthu*, each of his three queens Vāsuladattā, Sāmāvatī and Māgandiyā, is said to have been attended by 500 dancing girls. The *Priyadarśikā* also speaks of a matrimonial alliance made by Udayana with Dṛḍhavarman, king of Aṅga. We are told that Udayana once helped Dṛḍhavarman to regain his throne.

In the Jaina *Vividhatīrthakalpa* (p. 23), Udayana is praised as an expert in the science of music (*gandhabbaveya-niuṇo*). He ruled despotically and sometimes recklessly. When his queen Māgandiyā was found guilty of putting her co-wife Sāmāvatī to death, Udayana ordered her to be buried alive. According to one Buddhist tradition, a hermit fled to Śrāvastī when his life was threatened by Udayana.[5] On one occasion, in a fit of drunken jealousy, Udayana tortured the Buddhist Thera Piṇḍola Bhāradvāja by causing a nest of brown ants to be tied to his body. Later, however, he consulted this same Piṇḍola about various spiritual matters,[6] and ended by professing himself his disciple. We have no evidence that he proceeded very far along the path, but his fame has lasted in a curious way in Buddhist legends. Udayana is said to have made a golden image of the Buddha,[7] and Hsüan Tsang brought back from India many things including a statue of the Buddha carved out of sandal-wood on a transparent pedestal. This figure is described as a copy of the statue which Udayana, king of Kauśāmbī,

1 *Dhammapada Comm.*, I, p. 165.
2 Rockhill, *Life of the Buddha*, p. 17. Cf. Watters, *On Yuan Chwang*, I, p. 368.
3 *Udenavatthu*, pp. 161 foll.
4 *Svapnavāsavadattā*, *Pratijñāyaugandharāyaṇa*.
5 Watters, *On Yuan Chwang*, I, p. 368.
6 *Saṃyutta Nikāya*, IV, pp. 110–2.
7 Edkins, *Chinese Buddhism*, p. 49, 2nd Ed.

had made.[1] It is said in the *Si-yu-ki* that in the city of Kauśāmbī, within an old palace, there was a large vihāra about 60 feet high, containing a figure of the Buddha carved out of sandal wood above which was a stone canopy. It was the work of the King U-to-yen-na (Udayana). By its spiritual qualities it produced a divine light, which from time to time shone forth. The princes of various countries had used their power to try to carry off this statue, but although many men tried, none could move it. They therefore worshipped copies of it, and pretended that their likeness was a true one, the original of all such figures.[2] The *Petavatthu* records the erection of a vihāra by one Uttara, a wood-carver, in the service of King Udayana.[3] The figure was known to have been made for King Udayana by a distinguished artist of the time.[4] But nowhere in the earlier tradition is Udayana mentioned as the builder of any such temple or statue.

Immediately prior to the rise of Buddhism, there were four powerful monarchies in N. India, each of which was enlarged by the annexation of a neighbouring territory. Thus Aṅga was annexed to Magadha, Kāśī to Kośala, Bharga to Vatsa, and Śūrasena to Avanti. The kingdom of Vatsa must have served as a buffer State between Magadha and Avanti on the one hand, and Kośala and Avanti on the other. Bhāsa in his *Svapnavāsavadattā* tells us that an upstart named Aruṇi ousted Udayana and seized the throne of Vatsa.[5]

As in earlier days, so during the reign of Aśoka in the third century B.C., Kauśāmbī stood on the high road connecting Vidisā and Ujjayinī with Benares and Pāṭaliputra. Aśoka appears to have been an overlord of Vatsa, and to have placed its administration in charge of Mahāmātras with their headquarters at Kauśāmbī. Kauśāmbī was probably the place of residence of Aśoka's second queen Kāluvākī, and her son Prince Tīvala; the edict on her donations was promulgated only at Kauśāmbī.

However that may be, Vatsa was finally absorbed into the Magadhan empire,[6] probably during the reign of Śiśunāga. We may infer from the inscriptions at Pabhosā that in the second century

[1] Beal, *Records of the Western World*, Vol. I, Intro., p. xx.
[2] *Ibid.*, Vol. I, p. 235.
[3] This Uttara had friendly relations with Mahākaccāyana and various Buddhist Theras, but his mother was a believer in false doctrines, see *Paramatthadīpanī on the Petavatthu*, pp. 140–4; cf. also B. C. Law, *The Buddhist Conception of Spirits*, 2nd Ed., pp. 89-90.
[4] Watters, *On Yuan Chwang*, I, p. 368.
[5] *Svapnavāsavadattā*, Sukthankar's trsl., p. 64.
[6] Bhandarkar, *Carmichael Lectures*, 1918, pp. 81 and 84.

B.C., Vatsa (Kauśāmbī) and Pañcāla (Ahicchatra) were governed by branches of the same royal family, and that both kingdoms acknowledged the suzerainty of the Śuṅgas.[1] Dhanabhūti, a Śuṅga feudatory, is called Vacchiputa, son of a princess of Vatsa.[2] It may be that King Dhanabhūti, the donor of Bharhut gateways, his father Āgaraju and grandfather Viśvadeva were all local chiefs of Vatsa under the Śuṅgas.[3] However that may be, the stūpa of Bharhut was erected in the Vatsa country not earlier than the second century B.C., the first pillar of its main railing being donated by Chāpādevī, wife of Revatīmitra, of Vidiśā.[4] Revatīmitra was in all probability a member of the Śuṅga-Mitra family, stationed at Vidiśā. If this is so, we can say that when the Bharhut railing was erected, the Śuṅga dominions extended as far west as Vatsa and Avanti. As clearly proved by the inscriptions, when the Bharhut gateways were erected by King Dhanabhūti not earlier than the first century B.C., the Vatsa country was included in the Śuṅga empire (*Suganaṃ raje*).[5]

An inscription on the gateway on the fort of Kara, dated Saṃvat 1093 (1036 A.D.), records the grant of the village of Payalāsa (modern Prās) 'in the Kauśāmbī-maṇḍala to one Māthura-vikaṭa of Pabhosā together with its customary duties, royalties, taxes, gold and tithes in perpetuity to his descendants by Mahārājādhirāja Yaśaḥpāla',[6] who was the last Pratihāra king of Kanauj. The history of Vatsa or the country of Kauśāmbī as a political unit ended with the rule of Yaśaḥpāla of Kanauj.

As we have seen, the Bhagga or Bharga State was a dependency of the Vatsa kingdom. We learn from the preface to the *Dhonasākha Jātaka*, No. 353, that Prince Bodhi, the son of Udayana, king of the Vatsas (by his queen Vāsuladattā or Vāsavadattā), dwelt on the Suṃsumāragiri and built a palace called Kokanada. Suṃsumāragiri, according to Buddhist tradition, was the capital of the Bharga kingdom; so evidently in the sixth century B.C. the territory of the Bhargas was a dependency of the Vatsa kingdom, governed by a Viceroy of the royal family of Kauśāmbī. Bhikṣu Rāhula Sam-

1 *Cambridge History of India*, Vol. I, pp. 525-6.

2 *Ibid.*, Vol. I, p. 523.

3 Barua, *Barhut*, Bk. I, pp. 41-2, inclines tentatively to connect King Dhanabhūti and his predecessors with Mathurā or a nearby locality. Rapson, in *Camb. Hist.*, *loc. cit.*, observes: 'We may conclude that this family ruled at Bharhut, and that it was connected in some way with the royal family at Mathurā, more than 250 miles to the north-west.'

4 Barua and Sinha, *Barhut Inscriptions*, p. 3.

5 *Ibid.*, No. I, p. 1. See B. C. Law, *Kauśāmbī in Ancient Literature*, *M.A.S.I.*, No. 60, pp. 12-13, for a further discussion on the subject.

6 *J.R.A.S.*, 1927, p. 694.

krityāyana proposes to identify the Bharga country with the present Mirzapur district, and its capital Suṃsumāragiri with the present Chunar hill.[1] Buddhaghoṣa suggests, however, that Suṃsumāragira (not Suṃsumāragiri) was the name of the principal town in the Bhagga country. Originally the Vatsas and Bhārgavas (or Bhaggas) were two ruling clans that settled down and founded kingdoms side by side. Vatsa and Bhṛgu, from whom the Vatsas and Bhārgavas respectively claimed their descent, are said to have been sons of King Pratardana of Kāśī.[2]

The country of Kauśāmbī (i.e. Vatsa) is described as follows by the Chinese pilgrim Hsüan Tsang: ''This country is about 6,000 li in circuit, and the capital about 30 li. The land is famous for its productiveness; the increase is very wonderful. Rice and sugar-cane are plentiful. The climate is very hot, the manners of the people hard and rough. They cultivate learning and are very earnest in their religious life and in virtue'.[3]

The *Aṅguttara Nikāya*[4] speaks of the land of the Vaṃsas as a country which abounded in seven kinds of gems and was consequently regarded as very rich and prosperous. Kauṭilya's *Artha-śāstra* mentions Vatsa as one of the countries of which the cotton fabrics were of the very best quality.[5]

From the earliest times, the Vatsas, as the *Aitareya Brāhmaṇa* clearly attests, established a monarchical form of government in their land. They formally anointed their kings in accordance with the prescribed Vedic rites, and they are not known to have deviated from this practice at any period of their history. Ordeal by walking through fire was applied as a test of purity of descent of the kings.[6] Capital punishment by impaling on a stake was inflicted on a culprit even for a light offence, as illustrated by the Jātaka story of 'Maṇḍavya with the Peg'. When King Kosambika ruled over Kosambī in the kingdom of Vatsa, a robber committed a theft and, being chased, left the stolen goods near the door of an ascetic named Maṇḍavya, and himself escaped. When the owner of the property came there, he took the ascetic to be the robber, and brought him before the king. The king without enquiry said, 'Off with him,

---

[1] *Buddhacaryā*, pp. 75, 175; Ghosh, *Early History of Kauśāmbī*, p. 32.

[2] Ray Chaudhuri, *Political History of Ancient India*, 4th Ed., pp. 112-13 and 159. The *Mahābhārata* and the *Harivaṃśa* testify to the close connection between the Vatsas and the Bhargas.

[3] Beal, *Records of the Western World*, I, p. 235. See also Watters, *On Yuan Chwang*, I, p. 366.

[4] IV, pp. 252, 256, 260.

[5] *Arthaśāstra*, Shāma Śāstrī's trsl., p. 94.

[6] *Cambridge History of India*, I, p. 134.

impale him upon a stake'. Stakes of acacia and nimb wood did not pierce him, so concluding that the ascetic was innocent, the king ordered the stake to be drawn out. This was found to be impossible, however, so at Maṇḍavya's suggestion the stake was cut off with the skin. Thenceforward he was called Maṇḍavya with the Peg. The king asked his pardon and settled him in the royal park.[1]

According to the Buddhist legendary tradition, the Vatsa country was among those considered by the Devaputras in the Tuṣita heaven when a suitable birthplace for the Buddha was under discussion. The defects of the Vatsas and their royal family were then pointed out. For instance, it was said that the Vaṃsas were rude and rough, and their king an 'Ucchedavādin'; and, finally, it was decided that the royal family of Vatsa was unsuited for the honour of the Buddha's birth.[2] However, when the Buddha was about to pass away, Ānanda mentioned Kauśāmbī of the Vatsas as one of six great cities suitable for the Buddha's *parinibbāna*.[3]

Kauśāmbī, the capital of the Vatsas, is identified by Cunningham with Kosāṃ on the Jumna, about 30 miles south-west of Allahabad.[4] The *Cambridge History*, following Cunningham, says that Kauśāmbī seems to have been on the south bank of the Jumna, at a point about 400 miles by road from Ujjain, and about 230 miles upstream from Benares.[5] The Chinese pilgrims, Fā-Hien and Hsüan Tsang, give discrepant accounts of the situation of Kauśāmbī. Fā-Hien arrived there from the Deer Park to the north of Benares, after walking north-west for 13 yojanas (about 91 miles), as he says. This would make Kauśāmbī lie to the north or north-west of Prayāga, as St. Martin thinks[6]; but Hsüan Tsang, who visited Kauśāmbī twice, arrived there by going from Prayāga 'south-west through a forest infested by wild elephants and other fierce animals, and after a journey of above 500 li (about 100 miles).'[7]

The question of the site of Kauśāmbī has been much debated, chiefly because of the impossibility of reconciling Cunningham's identification with the descriptions of the Chinese pilgrims. But such descriptions may either have been incorrect originally or may have been subsequently misinterpreted. For instance, there is nothing in the actual records of Hsüan Tsang to suggest that the

[1] *Jātaka* (Fausböll), Vol. IV, pp. 28 foll.

[2] See the *Romantic Legend of Śākya Buddha*, p. 28; and *Lalitavistara*, ed. Lefmann, p. 21.

[3] *Dīgha Nikāya*, pp. 146, 169.

[4] *Ancient Geography of India*, p. 454. See also Rapson, *Ancient India*, p. 170.

[5] *Cambridge History*, Vol. I, pp. 187-8.

[6] Watters, *On Yuan Chwang*, Vol. I, pp. 366-7.

[7] *Ibid.*, p. 365.

distance given was the actual distance between Prayāga and the city of Kauśāmbī. It is likely that the pilgrim went to Kauśāmbī by a roundabout route from Prayāga. The distance and direction of Kauśāmbī from Sārnāth as given by Fā-Hien may be taken as fairly correct. The distance of 13 yojanas (about 90 or 104 miles) is almost the present distance by road from Benares to Kosam. The fact that Fā-Hien placed Kauśāmbī to the north-west of Benares may perhaps be due to his having walked along a road following a north-west direction for some distance.

Vincent Smith considers that the site of Kauśāmbī is to be looked for near the Sutnā railway station in the valley of the Tons river.[1] As for earlier evidence, the *Brāhmaṇas* generally assert that Kauśāmbī stood either on the Ganges or close to it, and the discovery of the name 'Kosāmbimaṇḍala' in an inscription over the gateway of the fort of Khara seems to confirm this, although the south-west bearing from Prayāga or Allahabad as recorded by Hsüan Tsang points unmistakably to the line of the Jumna.[2]

The *Śatapatha Brāhmaṇa* (XII, 2, 2, 13) mentions Proti Kausurubindi as a pupil undergoing *brahmacarya* under Uddālaka Āruṇi (of Upaniṣadic fame) and bearing the local epithet of Kauśāmbeya which the commentator Harisvāmin explains as meaning 'a native of Kauśāmbī.'[3] The *Gopatha Brahmana* (I, 4, 24) contains the same reference, but the name of Uddālaka's pupil is here given as Predi Kausurubindu. Kosaṃbeyaka, a Prākrit form of Kauśāmbeya, occurs in one of the Bārhut Inscriptions, being employed to mean 'a person from Kauśāmbī.'[4]

Thus, from the employment of Kauśāmbeya as a local epithet of a person in the *Brāhmaṇas*, it may be safely inferred that the name Kauśāmbī was current as early as the *Brāhmaṇa* age. The Pāli canon abounds in references to Kauśāmbī as a well-known city in N. India, the capital of the Vatsa country of King Udayana. The high antiquity of Kauśāmbī as a royal city is equally proved by traditions not only in the two great Sanskrit Epics and the Purāṇas, but also in the *Vamsatthappakāsinī* (commentary on the *Mahāvaṃsa*). The *Mahābhārata*[5] attributes the foundation of the city of Kauśāmbī to Prince Kuśāmba, third son of the Cedi king Uparicara Vasu. In the *Rāmāyaṇa* story, however, Prince Kuśāmba is described as the eldest son of an ancient king named Kuśa, who

---

1 *J.R.A.S.*, 1898, p. 503.

2 For a fuller discussion of the problem, see B. C. Law, *Kauśāmbī in Ancient Literature* (*Memoirs of the Archaeological Survey of India*, No. 60).

3 Ray Chaudhuri, *Political History of Ancient India* (4th Ed.), p. 58.

4 Barua and Sinha, *Barhut Inscriptions*, p. 12.

5 *Ādiparvan* (Vaṅgavāsī Ed.), Chap. 63, pp. 69–71.

had four sons by his queen Vaidarbhī, the youngest of them being Vasu.[1] According to the *Matsyapurāṇa*, when Hastināpura was swept away by a Ganges flood, the Kuru or Bhārata king Nicakṣu, who was fifth in descent from Parikṣit, the grandson of Arjuna, abandoned Hastināpura and dwelt in Kauśāmbī.[2] There is, however, no suggestion made in the Purāṇa that Nicakṣu was himself the founder of the city. We are told in McCrindle's *Ptolemy*[3] that Kauśāmbī was a famous city on the river Jumna, which became the Pāṇḍu capital after Hastināpura had been swept away by the Ganges, and which was noted as the shrine of the most sacred of all the statues of the Buddha. Its fame began only with the reign of Cakra, the eighth in descent from Arjuna the Pāṇḍava.[4] It is stated in the Purāṇas that the three sons of Adhisāmakṛṣṇa, named Nirvakta, Nemicakra and Vivakṣu, lived in Kauśāmbī after the destruction of Hastināpura by the inundation of the Ganges.[5]

Several explanations have been suggested to account for the name Kauśāmbī or Kosambī. Different traditions suggest (1) that the city was named after Prince Kuśāmba[6]; (2) that it was originally the dwelling place of the sage Kosamba[7]; (3) that the city came to be called Kosambī because when it was founded, numerous Kosamba trees were uprooted on the site,[8] or because the town abounded in shady Kosamba trees.[9]

Indian literature consistently refers to Kauśāmbī as a royal city, i.e. the capital of a kingdom; but in the *Si-yu-ki* of Hsüan Tsang, Kauśāmbī (Kiao-shang-mi) is represented rather as a country with its capital, which was 'evidently named Kauśāmbī.'[10] The Chinese pilgrim must have followed the later usage which represented Kauśāmbī as a political unit instead of as a mere city.[11]

Kauśāmbī is described in the *Trikāṇḍaśesa* (2, 1, 14) as Vatsa-paṭṭana, 'the capital of Vatsa'.[12] In the Buddhist literature, too,

---

1 *Rāmāyaṇa* (Bombay Ed.), I, 32, 1–6.

2 Ray Chaudhuri, *Political History of Ancient India* (4th Ed.), p. 58.

3 McCrindle, *Ancient India as described by Ptolemy*, p. 72.

4 Cunningham, *Ancient Geography*, p. 391.

5 *Matsyapurāṇa*, Chap. 50; cf. *Vāyu* and *Bhāgavata Purāṇas*.

6 See B. C. Law, *Kauśāmbī in Ancient Literature*, p. 2.

7 *Paramatthajotikā*, Vol. II, p. 300. Aśvaghoṣa in his *Saundarananda Kāvya* (B. C. Law's trsl., p. 9) refers to the hermitage (*āśrama*) of Kuśāmba, where the city of Kauśāmbī was built.

8 *Papañcasūdanī*, Pt. II, pp. 389-90.

9 *Vividhatīrthakalpa*, p. 23.

10 Watters, *On Yuan Chwang*, I, pp. 365-6.

11 E.g., Inscription of Yaśapāla, dated Saṃvat 1093 (A.D. 1037)—Kauśāmbī is mentioned as *Kosambamaṇḍala*.

12 Ghosh, *Early History of Kauśāmbī*, Introd., p. xvii.

Kauśāmbī is described as the capital of the Vatsa country, as also in the *Kathāsaritsāgara*.[1] The *Vividhatīrthakalpa* (p. 23) definitely states that the forests of Kauśāmbī were reached along the course of the Kālimdī (i.e. Yamunā or Jumna).[2]

According to the description in the *Suttanipāta* of a journey of Bāvarī's disciples from Patiṭṭhāna to Rājagaha, Kauśāmbī was one of the halting places on the same high road which led to Sāketa and Śrāvastī. The *Vinaya Mahāvagga*[3] gives a description of a somewhat different route that lay between Kauśāmbī and Śrāvastī. Kauśāmbī was the most important entrepôt for both goods and passengers coming to Kośala and Magadha from the south and west. The route from Kauśāmbī to Rājagṛha was down the river,[4] and Kauśāmbī was also one of the chief stopping places on the way from Śrāvastī to Patiṭṭhāna.[5]

Kauśāmbī had great military strength. The remains at Kosaṃ include those of a vast fortress with eastern ramparts and bastions, four miles in circuit, with an average height of 30 to 35 feet above the general level of the country. The fact that the city was an important commercial centre, is indicated by the extraordinary variety of the coins found there.[6] Cast coins were issued at the close of the third century by the kingdoms of Kauśāmbī, Ayodhyā and Mathurā, some of which bear the names of local kings in the Brāhmī script.[7] There is little foreign influence traceable in the die-struck coins, all closely connected in point of style, which were issued during the first and second centuries B.C. from Pañcāla, Ayodhyā, Kauśāmbī and Mathurā. A number of these bear Brāhmī Inscriptions. The coins of Kauśāmbī have a tree within a railing on the obverse.[8] The coinage of the kings of Kauśāmbī seems to begin in the third century B.C., and to extend over a period of about 300 years.[9]

In the Buddha's time, there were four establishments or settlements of the Order in or near Kauśāmbī, each of them having a group of huts under trees. Buddhaghoṣa informs us that the three banker friends, Ghosita, Kukkuṭa and Pāvārika, were the great business magnates of Kauśāmbī in the Buddha's time. All of them went on

[1] II, 1.
[2] Spence Hardy, *Manual of Buddhism*, p. 501. Cf. *Manorathapūraṇī*, I, pp. 306-7.
[3] Vol. I, p. 352 foll.
[4] Rhys Davids, *Buddhist India*, p. 36.
[5] *Ibid.*, p. 103.
[6] *Cambridge History of India*, Vol. I, p. 524.
[7] Brown, *Coins of India*, p. 19.
[8] *Ibid.*, p. 20. See also *Prācīna Mudrā*, p. 105.
[9] *Cambridge History of India*, Vol. I, p. 525.

elephant-back from Kauśāmbī to Śrāvastī to wait upon the Buddha at Jetavana, and it was at their invitation that the Buddha agreed to visit Kauśāmbī. Each of the bankers built a suitable retreat for the Buddha in the neighbourhood of the city. Regarding Ghositārāma, Hsüan Tsang tells us that it was situated 'outside the city on the south-east side with an Aśoka tope over 200 feet high'.[1] Within the city, at the south-east angle of it, there were the ruins of an old habitation, the house of Ghosita (Ghosira) the nobleman. In the middle there was a vihāra of the Buddha and a stūpa containing hair and nail relics. There were also ruins of the Tathāgata's bathing-house.[2] The pilgrim has also left hints as to the location of the remaining two *ārāmas*. Kukkuṭārāma was situated to the south-east of Ghositārāma. At the time of his visit, it was 'a two-storeyed building with an old brick upper chamber'.[3] Pāvārika's mango-grove was situated to the east of Ghositārāma, where the old foundations of a building were visible.[4]

Besides the three retreats built by the three bankers, we read of another Buddhist retreat in or near Kauśāmbī, which was known as Badarikārāma.[5] The Deer Park in Bhesakaḷāvana or Kesakaḷāvana[6] in the neighbourhood of Suṃsumāragira, the principal town in the Bhagga province, then ruled by Prince Bodhi as Viceroy, was the other important Buddhist retreat and early centre of Buddhist activity in the Vatsa dominion. The Park evidently belonged to Prince Bodhi, who became an ardent lay supporter of Buddhism. The story of a cordial entertainment of the Buddha and his disciples in the famous 'Lotus Palace' then built by Prince Bodhi is narrated in the *Majjhima Nikāya*.[7]

In the time of Hsüan Tsang, there were more than ten Buddhist monasteries (in or near Kauśāmbī), but all in utter ruins. The brethren, who were above 300 in number, were adherents of the Hīnayāna system. There were more than fifty deva-temples, and the non-Buddhists were very numerous.[8]

[1] Watters, *On Yuan Chwang*, I, p. 369. The Aśoka pillar on which Samudragupta recorded the history of his reign is supposed to have been erected originally at Kauśāmbī, which was no doubt honoured at times by the residence of the monarch (see Smith, *Early History of India*, p. 310, 4th Ed.).

[2] Beal, *Buddhist Records of the Western World*, Vol. I, p. 236.

[3] Watters, *On Yuan Chwang*, I, p. 370.

[4] *Ibid.*, p. 371.

[5] *Tipallatthamiga Jātaka* (Fausböll, No. 16).

[6] *Bodhirājakumāra Sutta, Majjhima Nikāya*, II, 91; *Jātaka* (Fausböll), III, 157.

[7] Vol. II, pp. 91 foll.

[8] Watters, *On Yuan Chwang*, Vol. I, p. 366. See also Legge, *Fā-Hien*, p. 96.

The Buddha's favourite retreat at Kauśāmbī was undoubtedly the Ghositārāma where he stayed on several occasions.[1] For instance, we read in the *Majjhima Nikāya*[2] that once while the Buddha was staying at the Ghositārāma, he tried to prevent the Kauśāmbīan monks, who were divided into two parties, from quarrelling. From the *Surāpāna Jātaka* we learn that the Buddha, after staying for a long time at Bhaddavatika, went to Kauśāmbī where he was cordially received by the townsfolk, some of whom invited him to a meal. On this occasion the Buddha condemned the drinking of intoxicants.[3] While dwelling at the Badarika monastery in Kauśāmbī, the Buddha related the *Tipallatthamiga Jātaka* about the elder Rahula.[4]

In the *Dhammapadaṭṭhakathā*,[5] we read that there lived at Kauśāmbī a householder's son, Kosambivāsī Tissathera, who took ordination from the Buddha. One of the Buddha's chief disciples, Ānanda, also delivered several sermons at Kauśāmbī.[6] Among famous followers of the Buddha who stayed at Ghositārāma were Sāriputta and Upavāṇa.[7] After the passing away of the Master, and when the First Great Council was over, Mahākaccāyana lived near Kauśāmbī in a forest hermitage with twelve bhikkhus.[8]

Some of the Kosambians entertained a great respect for the Buddha and the Buddhist faith, and were converted; while we are told that others went so far as to enter the Order and attain arahatship,—e.g. Gavaccha the Less.[9] At the time of the Buddha, Sāmāvatī Therī was born in a rich householder's family at Kauśāmbī. She was the favourite friend of Queen Sāmāvatī, wife of King Udayana. After the death of the queen, she was very much grieved, and became a bhikkhuṇī. Her grief was so bitter that she was unable to attain the *ariyamagga*. Afterwards listening to the instruction of Ānanda, she became free from sorrow by developing insight, and became an arahat.[10]

When the Vajjian monks carried out the act of excommunication against Yasa, he is said to have risen up into the sky and descended

[1] See, e.g. *Vinaya Texts*, Pt. II, p. 285; *Ibid.*, Pt. III, p. 233; *Majjhima Nikāya*, I, pp. 513ff.; *Saṃyutta Nikāya*, III, pp. 94-5; V, pp. 224, 229-30; *Sumaṅgalavilāsinī*, Pt. I, pp. 317-19; *Cullavagga* (*Vinaya Texts*, Pt. II, pp. 370ff).

[2] *Majjhima Nikāya*, I, pp. 320 foll; Vol. III, p. 153.

[3] *Jātaka* (Fausböll), Vol. I, pp. 360 foll.

[4] *Ibid.*, Vol. I, pp. 160 foll.; Vol. III, pp. 64 foll.

[5] Vol. II, pp. 182-5.

[6] *Saṃyutta Nikāya*, III, pp. 133 foll.; II, pp. 115 foll.; IV, pp. 113-14.

[7] *Ibid.*, V, pp. 76-7.

[8] See *Paramatthadīpanī on the Petavatthu*, pp. 140–144.

[9] *Psalms of the Brethren*, p. 16.

[10] *Therīgāthā Comm.*, P.T.S., pp. 44-5.

at Kauśāmbī.[1] The *Mahāvaṃsa* tells us, however, that the venerable Yasa is said to have fled from Vaiśālī to Kauśāmbī just before the assembly of the second Buddhist Council.[2]

The Pārileyyaka forest, where the Buddha is said to have spent one rainy season, and the location of which is unknown, was probably not very far from Kauśāmbī.[3] The town of Bhaddavatika which lay on the way from the Pārileyyaka forest to Śrāvastī was another place in the Vatsa kingdom which became associated with the life of the Buddha.[4] Somewhere in the neighbourhood of Kauśāmbī and Ghositārāma was a cave called Pilakkhaguhā, where a Parivrājaka or wandering ascetic named Sandaka used to live with his 500 followers during the summer season. The venerable Ānanda is said to have converted Sandaka to the Buddhist faith, with all his following.[5] In the *Dīgha Nikāya*[6] we read that the city of Kauśāmbī was visited by two wanderers named Maṇḍissa and Jāliya, who interviewed the Buddha at Ghositārāma.

The *Mahāvaṃsa* attests that some 30,000 bhikkhus of the Ghositārāma, headed by Thera Urudhammarakkhita, visited Ceylon in about the first century B.C., during the reign of King Duṭṭhagāmaṇi.[7]

In the second year of the reign of King Kaniṣka, the Buddhist nun Buddhimitrā or Buddhamitrā installed a Bodhisattva image in Kauśāmbī, which was then known to have been 'sanctified by the Buddha's several visits'.

The records of the influence of religion over Vatsa and Kauśāmbī prior to the introduction of Buddhism and Jainism are few and far between. The people were supposed to have been preoccupied with worldly thoughts, but we read even in the *Brāhmaṇas* of hermits such as Proti Kausurubindi who had considerable influence. The main supporters of such hermits were the bankers of Kauśāmbī, all of whom were members of the Vaiśya caste.[8] The introduction of Buddhism, too, was due to the religious tendencies of persons belonging to this caste, as we have seen from the story of the bankers Ghosita, Kukkuṭa, and Pāvārika. According to the Buddhist tradition in the Tibetan *Dulva*, the Buddha visited Kauśāmbī when King Udayana was busy planning a military expedition to the city of Kanakavatī. The appearance of the messenger of peace was naturally

1 Kern, *Indian Buddhism*, p. 104.
2 Geiger, *Mahāvaṃsa*, p. 22. See also *Vinaya Texts*, Pt. III, p. 394.
3 *Saṃyutta Nikāya*, III, pp. 94-5.
4 *Jātaka* (Fausböll), I, p. 360.
5 *Majjhima Nikāya*, I, pp. 513 foll.
6 *Dīgha Nikāya*, I, pp. 157, 159-60.
7 P.T.S., p. 228.
8 *Dhammapada Comm.*, I, p. 203.

looked upon and dreaded as the appearance of a bad omen.[1] It was evidently not easy to convert Udayana and members of the royal family to the new faith. There seems to be some truth in the Buddhist legends that the devotion of Queen Sāmāvatī and her attendants, and the martyrdom suffered by them, were greatly instrumental in bringing about a change of heart in Udayana and making him a supporter of Buddhism.[2] Here again the banker Ghosita is indirectly concerned, for Sāmāvatī was brought up with his family.

The influence of Jainism over Kauśāmbī does not appear to have been extensive. However, Kauśāmbī is known to the Jainas as the sacred place where Vardhamāna Mahāvīra was worshipped even by the Sun and Moon; and where Chandanā attained to Kaivalya. Kauśāmbī is also known to the Jainas as the place hallowed by the birth, career and death of Jina Prabha Sūri. The Pabhosā rock cave was excavated in about the first century B.C. for the residence of the Kāśyapīya arahats.

In the inscription of the goldsmiths of Kauśāmbī, dated Saṃvat 1621 (1565 A.D.) we find that six of them call themselves Vaiṣṇavas, although the record itself contains only the prayers of five leading goldsmiths and of thirteen of their employees to Ganeśa and the god Bhairava 'for favour'.

[1] Rockhill, *Life of the Buddha*, p. 74.
[2] *Dhammapada Comm.*, I, pp. 208ff.

# CHAPTER XXX

## THE VĀṬADHĀNAS—THE ĀTREYAS—THE BHARADVĀJAS—THE LAMPĀKAS

### THE VĀṬADHĀNAS

The Vāṭadhānas are mentioned in the *Mārkaṇḍeya Purāṇa*, once along with the Vāhlīkas, the Ābhiras, the Aparāntakas and the Śūdras, all grouped in the north-west (LVII, 36), and at another place, along with the Śiviḍas, Dāserakas, Śavadhānas, Puṣkalas, Kairātas, etc., all grouped as peoples of the north (LVII, 44). The *Vāyupurāṇa*, erroneously no doubt, reads Vāḍhadhānas (XLV, 115).

That they were a Punjab tribe is also borne out by the evidence of the *Mahābhārata*. There the Vāṭadhānas are said to be derived from an eponymous king Vāṭadhāna who belonged to the same *Krodhavaśa* group as the eponymous kings of the Vāhlīkas, Madras and Sauvīras (*Ādiparvan*, LXVII, 2695–9). The *Sabhāparvan* locates their country in the western region (XXXI, 1190-1), and the *Udyogaparvan* seems to suggest that they joined the side of the Kurus in the great Bhārata War (XVIII, 569–601). The people are mentioned elsewhere in the Epics as well, e.g. *Sabhāparvan*, I, 1826; *Udyogaparvan*, III, 86; *Bhīṣmaparvan*, IX, 354 and *Droṇaparvan*, XI, 398. Vāṭadhāna-dvijas were amongst those who were conquered by Nakula (*Sabhāparvan*, XXXI, 1190-1).

According to Manu, Vāṭadhāna was the offspring of an outcaste Brāhmaṇa woman (X, 21), but Pargiter points out that this 'is no doubt an expression of the same arrogance which in later times stigmatised all the Punjab races as outcastes' (*Mārkaṇḍeya Purāṇa*, p. 312, notes).

### THE ĀTREYAS

The *Mārkaṇḍeya Purāṇa* list mentions the Ātreyas along with the Bharadvājas, Puṣkalas, Kuśerukas, Lampākas, etc., as peoples of the north (LVII, 39-40). The *Matsyapurāṇa* reads Atris who are undoubtedly the same as the Ātreyas (CXIII, 43).

The Ātreyas are also mentioned in several places in the *Mahābhārata*. They are represented as a family of Brāhmaṇas dwelling in the Dvaitavana (*Vanaparvan*, XXVI, 971) not far from the Sarasvatī (*Vanaparvan*, CLXXVII, 12354–62). They are also mentioned in the *Bhīṣmaparvan* list (IX, 376), and the *Harivaṃśa* seems to suggest that the people originated from the Ṛṣi Prabhākara of Atri's race (XXXI, 1660–8) whence came the name of the tribe Ātreya.

### The Bharadvājas

What is true of the Ātreyas seems to be equally true of the Bharadvājas or Bhāradvājas. The *Mārkaṇḍeya* list (LVII, 39-40) mentions the tribe along with the Ātreyas, Puṣkalas, Lampākas, etc., and locates them in the north. They are also mentioned in the *Bhīṣmaparvan* list (IX, 376) in the same context as that of the Ātreyas; the Great Epic tradition connects Bhāradvāja with the upper Gangetic region near the hills (*Ādiparvan*, CXXX, 5102–6; CLXVI, 6328–32; *Vanaparvan*, CXXXV, 10700–28; *Śalyaparvan*, XLIX, 2762–2824), and Bhāradvāja, the Ṛṣi, was evidently the originator of the race or tribe. Like the Ātreyas, it is tempting to connect the people of various caste divisions of present-day India claiming to belong to the Bhāradvāja gotra with the Bhāradvāja tribe.

### The Lampākas

The Lampākas are mentioned in the *Mārkaṇḍeya* list (LVII, 40) along with the Kuśerukas, Śūlakāras, Culikas, Jāguḍas, etc. as a people of the north. The *Matsyapurāṇa* reads (CXIII, 43) Lampākas instead, which is no doubt wrong. The *Mahābhārata* (*Droṇaparvan*, CXXI, 4846-7) also mentions the tribe and seems to suggest that they were a rude mountain tribe like the Daradas and Pulindas. Long ago Cunningham identified the region of the Lampākas with modern Lamghan, hundred miles to the east of Kapisene, north-east of Kabul, which practically upholds Lassen's identification of the place with Lambagae, south of the Hindu Kush in modern Kafiristan.

If the tradition contained in Hemacandra's *Abhidhāna-cintāmaṇi* is to be believed, then Lampāka seems to have once been the centre of the Sai-wang or the Śaka-Muraṇḍa people (*Lampākāstu Muraṇḍāh syuḥ*).

## CHAPTER XXXI

# THE YONAS

The Yonas or Yavanas, literally 'Ionians', a people or peoples of Greek descent, may be traced in Indian literature and inscriptions[1] from the third century B.C. to the second century A.D. They were 'manifestly a factor of no small importance in the political history of Northern and Western India'.[2]

In the *Mahābhārata* we find them taking part in the Bhārata War at Kurukṣetra as allies of the Kurus along with other peoples of North-Western India like the Kāmbojas, Śakas, Madras, Kaikeyas, Sindhus and Sauvīras.[3] Indian tradition, however, regards them as aliens or outcastes. Thus the *Sūtras* mention the Yavanas (Greeks) as the most esteemed of foreigners, but all Yavanas are regarded as sprung from Śūdra females and Kṣatriya males. Gautama says that this view is held by some.[4] The *Rāmāyaṇa*[5] refers to the struggles of the Hindus with mixed hordes of Śakas and Yavanas (cf. *Śakān Yavanamiśritān*). In the *Kiṣkindhyā Kāṇḍa* (IV, 43, 11-12), Sugrīva places the country of the Yavanas and the cities of the Śakas between the country of the Kurus and the Madras and the Himālayas.[6] In the *Mahābhārata*, the Yonas or Yaunas are classed with other peoples of Uttarāpatha or Northern India like the Kāmbojas, Gandhāras, Kirātas and Barbaras.[7] In the *Mārkaṇḍeya Purāṇa*, we also find a list of peoples where the Gabalas or Yavanas are classed with some other people of Northern or North-Western India like the Gandhāras, Sindhu-Sauvīras and Madrakas. Instead of Gabalas, the *Vāyu* and the *Matsya Purāṇas* read Yavanas which seems to be the correct reading.[8] The Yonas or Yavanas thus seem to be one of the ancient tribes settled in some part of India. A Yona or Greek State is, therefore, mentioned along with Kamboja

[1] *Indian Culture*, Vol. I, pp. 343 foll.

[2] *Cambridge History of India*, Vol. I, p. 225.

[3] *Ibid.*, p. 274.

[4] *Gautama Dharmaśāstra*, IV, 21; *Cambridge History of India*, Vol. I, 240 f.n.

[5] I, 54, 21.

[6] *Political History of Ancient India* (4th Ed.), p. 3.

[7] Cf. *Uttarāpathajanmānaḥ Kīrtayīshyāmi tān api Yauna Kāmboja Gāndhārāḥ Kirātā Barbaraiḥ saha. Mbh.*, XII, 207, 43.

[8] Cf. *Gāndhārā Yavanaścaiva Sindhu-Sauvīra-Madrakāḥ* (*Mārkaṇḍeya Purāṇa*, Chap. 57, 36).

in the *Majjhima Nikāya* (II, 149) as flourishing in the time of Gautama Buddha and Assalāyana.[1]

The *Milinda-Pañho* refers to the land of the Yonas as the place fit for the attainment of *Nibbāna* (Trenckner ed., p. 327). The *Mahāvastu* speaks of the assembly of the Yonas where anything which was decided was binding on them (Vol. I, p. 171). Hence D. R. Bhandarkar in his *Carmichael Lectures* [2] observes that there is nothing strange in Pāṇini flourishing in the sixth century B.C. and in his referring also to *Yavanānī*, the writing of the Greeks. When Alexander invaded India he found a large number of autonomous tribes and principalities in the North-Western Frontier Province and the Punjab. Among these we find mention of the Nysaeans forming a small hill-state with a republican constitution. They had Adouphis then as their President and they had a Governing Body of three hundred members. Holdich in discussing the site of Nysa [3] shows that the lower spurs and valleys of Koh-i-Mor are where the ancient city of Nysa once stood. According to Bhandarkar,[4] Nysa was situated between the Kophen and the Indus. In the Fifth Book of Arrian's work,[5] we find two relevant passages in this connection. Arrian says, 'The Nysaeans are not an Indian race, but descended from the men who came into India with Dionysus.'[6] The deputies of Nysa, who waited upon Alexander, themselves told the Macedonian monarch that their city was founded by Dionysus; for Dionysus, the Greeks believed, had gone conquering across Asia, at the head of his revellers, in the old heroic days. 'The Greeks', Bevan says,[7] 'always experienced a keen joy of recognition, when they could connect foreign things with the figures of their own legends, and they were delighted with the suggestion.' In the legend the name Nysa was specially connected with Dionysus—it was the name of his nurse, or of the place where he was born or of his holy hill—and the name of this little town in the Hindu Kush, as it was pronounced to Alexander, had a similar sound. Again the legend said that Dionysus had been born from the thigh (*mēros*) of Zeus, and a neighbouring summit, the Greeks discovered, was called *Meru*. When, moreover, the Greeks saw the sacred plants of the same god, viz. vine and ivy (which grew nowhere else in the land of the Indians), running wild over the mountain, as they knew them at home, no doubt could be left. So hostilities with these interesting kinsmen

[1] Cf. *Yona Kambojesu . . . dveva vaṇṇā, ayyo c'eva dāsoca.*

[2] 1921, p. 29.

[3] *Gates of India*, p. 122.

[4] *Carmichael Lectures*, 1921, p. 32.

[5] Cf. McCrindle's *Ancient India : its invasion by Alexander the Great*, pp. 79-80.

[6] Chinnock's edition, p. 399.

[7] *Cambridge History of India*, Vol. I, p. 354.

could not be thought of, and the Nysaeans themselves joined with Alexander. Three hundred of them on their mountain horses joined the army of the Yavana king and followed him to battle in the plains of the Punjab.[1] The evidence furnished by Arrian's account of Nysa shows that Nysa was a Greek colony before the advent of Alexander to India.[2] In the inscription of Aśoka,[3] we find mention of the Yonas along with Kāmbojas.[4] The question here arises—Who were these Yonas? Bhandarkar in his *Carmichael Lectures*, 1921 (pp. 28ff.), points out that it is impossible to identify the Yonas of Rock Edict XIII with the Greeks of Bactria because the same edict was promulgated when Antiochus Theos, King of Syria, was living, his name being actually specified therein. In Aśoka's time Bactria was included in the Syrian empire of Antiochus Theos. We learn from Greek historians, Trogus, Justin and Strabo, that it was Diodotus who first made Bactria independent. He was a Satrap of this province under Antiochus Theos. The death of Antiochus probably caused disturbance when Diodotus made himself independent in Bactria. So the Yonas of the Aśokan inscription are to be located elsewhere. Bhandarkar therefore concludes: 'I suspect that it has to be identified with Aria or Arachosia which were the two provinces ceded by Seleucuos to Chandragupta and which must have been inherited intact by Aśoka. I admit it is not possible to locate these Yonas exactly, but this much is certain that they were outside the kingdom of Antiochus Theos, and lived in Aśoka's empire in a territory adjoining Gandhāra but outside India.'[5] Bhandarkar[6] therefore holds the view that in all likelihood, the Yavanas of Rock Edict XIII must have come and settled in large numbers in some outlying province of India long before Alexander. Numismatic evidence also lends support to such a view. Coins similar to those of the earliest type of Athens are known to have been collected from the north-west frontiers of India. They bear head of Athena on the obverse and owls on the reverse.[7] These owls of Athens have been picked up in Southern Arabia Felix. But none of the owls found in the east are of the types known from Athens. The coins found in Arabia might have travelled there as a result of commercial intercourse, for they are generally counter-marked on the obverse with Sabaean letters or are scratched on the reverse with a

[1] *Cambridge History of India*, Vol. I, p. 354.

[2] *Carmichael Lectures*, 1921, p. 32.

[3] Rock Edict XIII.

[4] Cf. '*Yona-Kamboyeshu Nabhake Na(bhi)tina Bhoja-Pitinikeshu Aṃdhra-Puli(de) shu savatra devanam priyasa dhramanuśasti anuvataṃti.*' (Shabhazgarhi text—*Inscriptions of Aśoka*, edited by Bhandarkar and Majumdar, pp. 53-4.)

[5] *Carmichael Lectures*, 1921, p. 26.

[6] *Ibid.*, p. 27.

[7] *Numismatic Chronicle*, XX, 191.

Sabaean monogram. Bhandarkar argues when a foreign money for the first time comes into circulation along with the native coinage of a country, all the new specimens are tested, and those, which are found not deficient in weight or quality of metal, are sanctioned by marking them with an official stamp which may consist of a single letter or symbol. These official stamps which are found on the owls of Athens, discovered in South Arabia, are conspicuous by their absence on those found on the frontiers of India. The practice of putting such counter-marks on coins was not unknown in or near India also, for the silver Persian sigloi which were current in the Punjab bear Indian counter-marks.[1] When there is no counter-mark, it is not reasonable to say that they were brought there in course of trade. Bhandarkar[2] therefore concludes: 'The natural inference must be that they were native to some outlying district of India which was peopled by the Yavanas or Greeks. And as the original owls of Athens have been assigned to *circa* 594–560 B.C., a Greek colony, it is possible to infer, may have been established near India about 550 B.C.' Ray Chaudhuri[3] also notes that the exact situation of the Yona territory has not yet been determined. In the *Mahāvaṃsa* (XII) we find that the Thera Mahārakkhita was sent to the country of the Yonas. This work also refers to its chief city, Alasanda, which Geiger identifies with the town of Alexandria founded by the Macedonian conqueror near Kabul.[4] Not only the Yonas are mentioned in the inscriptions of Aśoka, we also find a Yavana official or a vassal Yavanarāja called Tushāspha ruling as governor of Surāṣṭra with his capital at Girinagara (Girnar) during the days of Aśoka, as we learn from the Junāgadh Rock Inscription of Mahākshatrapa Rudradāman. Vincent Smith argues that the form of the name shows that the Yavanarāja must have been a Persian. But Ray Chaudhuri contends that if Greeks and other foreigners adopted Hindu names there is no wonder that some of them assumed Iranic appellations. There is, then, no good ground for assuming that Tushāspha was not a Greek, but a Persian. After the death of Aśoka, a Yavana army crossed the Hindu Kush, which was the northern frontier of Aśokan empire on the ruins of which an Indo-Greek kingdom arose. The *Yuga Purāṇa* section of the *Gārgī Saṃhitā* points to the decline of Maurya power in the Madhyadeśa when it says: 'Tataḥ Sāketam ākramya Pañcālaṃ Mathurāṃstathā । Yavanaḥ duṣṭavikrāntaḥ prāpsyati Kusuma-

[1] *J.R.A.S.*, 1895, 874 and ff.
[2] *Carmichael Lectures*, 1921, p. 29.
[3] *Political History of Ancient India*, 4th Ed., p. 253.
[4] *Mahāvaṃsa*, Geiger's translation, p. 194.

dhvajam ‖ Tataḥ Puṣpapure prāpte Karddame prathite hite । Ākulā viṣayā sarve bhaviṣyanti na saṃśayaḥ ‖ '[1] In Patañjali's *Mahābhāṣya* there is a similar line: 'Arunad Yavanaḥ Sāketaṃ: Arunad Yavano Madhyamikām.' According to Sir R. G. Bhandarkar this shows that a certain Yavana or Greek prince had besieged Sāketa or Ayodhyā and another place called Madhyamikā (near Chitor) when Patañjali wrote this. Kālidāsa in his *Mālavikāgnimitram* refers to a conflict between the Śuṅga prince Vasumitra and a Yavana on the southern bank of the Sindhu. The name of this invader, however, is not given in the *Mahābhāṣya* or the *Mālavikāgnimitram*.[2] It is clear at any rate that the extension of Yavana power to the interior of India was thwarted in the first instance by the Śuṅgas. In Western India the rising power of the Andhras, Andhrabhṛtyas or Sātavāhanas caused the last vestige of Yavana power to disappear. Thus from the Nāsik Cave Inscription of Gautamīputra Śātakarṇi we learn that he destroyed the Śakas, Yavanas and Pahlavas. While in the north-west of India the Yavanas were swept away by the onrush of the Parthians or Pahlavas, as we learn from Chinese sources.

---

1 Kern, *Bṛhatsaṃhitā*, p. 37.

2 *Political History of Ancient India*, 4th Ed., p. 316.

## CHAPTER XXXII

# THE KALIṄGAS

The Kaliṅgas as a tribe are almost always associated with the Aṅgas and Vaṅgas in ancient Indian literature. These three tribes along with the Puṇḍras and Suhmas are said to have been named after the five sons of Bali, Aṅga, Vaṅga, Kaliṅga, Puṇḍra and Suhma who were called Bāleya Kṣatra and also Bāleya Brāhmaṇas.[1] These five tribes evidently then lived conterminously and had their distinct entities within respective geographical boundaries to which they gave the names of their respective tribes. The tradition referred to above is contained in the Purāṇas and the Great Epic, according to which, the sage Dīrghatamas had married King Bali's Śūdra nurse and had Kakṣivant and other sons; and at Bali's desire begot on the queen Sudeṣṇā the aforesaid five sons. According to the Great Epic again,[2] King Jarāsandha is said to have extended his supremacy over the Aṅgas, Vaṅgas, Kaliṅgas and the Puṇḍras. In the *Droṇaparvan*,[3] Vāsudeva is said to have once routed in battle the Aṅgas, Vaṅgas, Kaliṅgas and the Pauṇḍras along with other peoples. A town named Kaliṅganagara, evidently one of the cities of the Kaliṅga people, is mentioned in the *Rāmāyaṇa*, on the west of the Gomatī and not far from it.[4] A Kaliṅga tribe is also referred to in the *Mārkaṇḍeya Purāṇa*[5] as having their settlement on the Śatadru. Pargiter suggests that the reading is erroneous, for there seems to be no ground for thinking that the Kaliṅgas lived in N. India.[6] Moreover, the *Vāyupurāṇa*[7] in the same context reads Kulindas instead, which seems to be the correct reading. The *Mārkaṇḍeya Purāṇa*[8] mentions another people named the Ārkaliṅgas along with the Kuntalas, Kāśīs, Kośalas, Ātharvas and the Malakas. Pargiter doubts this reading as well, because of the *Vāyupurāṇa* reading which is different in the same context.[9] The *Matsyapurāṇa* reads Avantas and Kaliṅgas instead,[10] but this is also hardly satisfactory in view of the fact that the Kaliṅgas are hardly known to have been associated with the Avantas and moreover that the Kaliṅgas are elsewhere

---

[1] Puranic tradition as contained in a number of Purāṇas, the *Mahābhārata* and the *Harivaṃśa*. See the Dīrghatamasa story and its sequel. Compare Pargiter, *A.I.H.T.*, p. 158.

[2] *Mahābhārata*, XII, Chap. 5, 6607.

[3] *Ibid.*, Chap. 10, 15.

[4] *Ayodhyā K.*, LXXIII, 14, 15.

[5] LVII, 37.

[6] *Mārkaṇḍeya Purāṇa*, p. 316 n.

[7] XLV, 116.

[8] LVII, 33.

[9] *Mārkaṇḍeya Purāṇa*, p. 308 n.

[10] CXIII, 36.

described not only in the same Purāṇa but also in other Purāṇas as a people of the southern region. The *Mārkaṇḍeya*, for example, says that they dwelt in the southern region along with the Mahārāṣṭras, Mahiṣakas, Ābhīras, Vaiśikyas, Savaras, Pulindas and others.[1] A number of famous Kaliṅga or Kāliṅga kings are mentioned in the Ādiparva of the *Mahābhārata*[2] and they are credited with having contracted matrimonial relations with princesses of the Aryan royal families of the north (e.g. *Ādiparvan*, XCV, 3774-5, 3780; *Droṇaparvan*, LXX, 2436). According to epic evidence as contained in the *Mahābhārata*,[3] the Kaliṅga country comprised the entire tract of country lying along the coast of Vaitaraṇī in Orissa to the borders of the Āndhra country.[4]

The country of the Kaliṅgas is mentioned by Pāṇini.[5] According to Baudhāyana, the country was branded as an impure one and was included in his list of *Saṃkīrṇa yonayaḥ*.[6] According to Kauṭilya's *Arthaśāstra*,[7] elephants of Aṅga and Kaliṅga belonged to the best of their types, while those of Karūṣa, Daśārṇa and Aparānta were only second in order of classification, those of the Saurāṣṭras and allied tribes (Saurāṣṭrikāḥ pañcajanāḥ) having been the worst.

The Jātakas contain a number of references to the Kaliṅga country and its kings. Thus, for example, according to the *Kumbhakāra Jātaka*, Karaṇḍu was a Kaliṅga and he was a contemporary of Nimi, king of Videha. The *Mahāgovinda Suttanta* makes Sattabhū, king of Kaliṅga, a contemporary of Reṇu, king of Mithilā and of Dhataraṭṭha or Dhṛtarāṣṭra, king of Kāśī and Aṅga. The Jātakas also refer to the capital city of Kaliṅga which was Dantapuranagara which is probably identical with Dantakura mentioned in the *Mahābhārata*,[8] Dantapura of inscriptions.[9] Other cities of the Kaliṅga country are also known, e.g. Rājapura,[10] Siṃhapura,[11] which is probably identical with Singupuram near Chicacole,[12] Kāñcanapura of the Jainas,[13] and Kaliṅganagara which has been identified with Mukhaliṅgaṃ on the river Vaṃśadharā.[14] Kaliṅga (Kāliṅga) is mentioned in the *Niddesa*.[15] From Kaliṅga the Buddha's tooth was brought to Ceylon at the time of King Sirimeghavaṇṇa. A Kaliṅga king picked up a quarrel with Aruṇa, the Assaka king of Potali, but was defeated and had to surrender.[16]

---

1 LVII, 46-7.
2 LXVII, 2701.
3 III, 114, 4.
4 Ray Chaudhuri, *P.H.A.I.*, 4th Ed., p. 75.
5 IV, 1, 170.
6 I, i, 30-1.
7 II, 2.
8 V, 48–76.
9 *Epigraphia Indica*, XIV, p. 361.
10 *Mahābhārata*, XIII, 4, 3.
11 *Mahāvastu*, Senart's Ed., p. 432.
12 Dubreuil, *A.H.D.*, p. 94.
13 *Indian Antiquary*, 1891, p. 375.
14 *Epigraphia Indica*, IV, 187.
15 *Cullaniddesa*, ii, 37.
16 *Jātaka* (Fausböll), III, 3f.

Susīmā, a Kaliṅga princess, was married to a king of Vaṅga.[1] Vijayabāhu I married a Kaliṅga princess named Tilokasundarī.[2] Māgha, a prince of Kaliṅga, did a great mischief to Ceylon.[3] Asoka's brother Tissa spent his retirement in the Kaliṅga country with his teacher Dhammarakkhita.[4]

Important light on the history of the Kaliṅga people is thrown by Pliny, the classical historian. From the accounts of Diodoros Curtius and Plutarch, we know that at the time of Alexander's invasion, there were two very powerful peoples in the lower Gangetic valley, the Parasii (Braisioi) and the Gangaridai whose king was Xandrammes or Agrammes. The capital city of the Prasii was Palibothra or Pāṭaliputra, while that of the Gangridai was Gange at the mouth of the Ganges, according to the author of the *Periplus of the Erythraean Sea*, or at the junction of the Ganges leading to the Maga and Kamberikhon mouths respectively. Pliny adds a third important people of E. India at that time, namely the Kaliṅgas. He says: 'The tribes called Kaliṅgas are nearest the sea, and higher up are the Mandaei and the Malli, in whose country is mount Mallus, the boundary of all that district being the Ganges . . . the final part of its course is through the country of the Gangaridaes. The royal city of Kaliṅga is called Parthalis. Over their king 60,000 foot-soldiers, 1,000 horsemen and 7,000 elephants keep watch and ward.' An alternative reading of Pliny's text makes Gangaridae-Kaliṅga one people, having a king, a capital city, and an army of their own. Pliny further mentions two more tribes which must have been allied with the Kaliṅga people proper, e.g. the Maccokaliṅgae (cf. modern Mukhaliṅgam referred to above, or is it Mukhya Kaliṅgāḥ, the main Kaliṅgas?) and the Modokaliṅga, both inhabiting an island in the Ganges. The capital city Parthalis of the Kalingae has been identified with Pūrvasthali, a large village about 20 miles from the present Burdwan town,[5] which, however, is not above criticism. In any case, from the description of Pliny, it is certain that the countries of the Gangaridae and the Kalingae were adjacent territories.

Agrammes or Xandrammes has been usually identified with Mahāpadma Nanda who was king of both Prasii and Gangaridae. Mahāpadma was supplanted by Candragupta Maurya who is referred to by Greek writers as having been king of Prasii but nowhere is he mentioned as king of Gangaridae as well. The well-known Kaliṅga expedition of Aśoka was, perhaps, directed against a probable

---

[1] *Mahāvaṃsa*, VI, 1; *Dīpavaṃsa*, IX, 2ff.
[2] *Cūḷavaṃsa*, LIX, 30.
[3] *Ibid.*, LXXX, 58f.
[4] *Theragāthā Commentary*, I, 506.
[5] *I.H.Q.*, IV, p. 55.

Kalingae-Gangaridae combination of forces, suggested by an alternative reading of Pliny referred to above. In any case, the Kaliṅga resistance must have been a very stiff one, as is evident from the description in the thirteenth Rock Edict.

Kaliṅga is again lifted to historical prominence when Khāravela of the Ceta dynasty became anointed, when he had completed his twenty-fourth year, as Mahārāja of Kaliṅga. In his Hathigumpha Cave Inscription Kaliṅga finds mention for more than once and it is said in that very inscription that in the first year of his reign he repaired the gates and ramparts of his capital Kaliṅganagara identified with Mukhaliṅgam.

We do not hear of the Kaliṅgas or their country, so far at least as N. India history is concerned, for a long time, in fact not until we reach the time when Yuan Chwang visited the country in about the second quarter of the seventh century A.D. Kālidāsa, however, in his *Raghuvaṃśam* mentions both Utkala and Kaliṅga, from which it is evident that they were two distinct countries. Yuan Chwang travelled from Oḍra to Kangoda whence he travelled through jungle and forest, dense with huge trees, south-west for 1,400 or 1,500 li, to Kaliṅga (Ka-long-ka). According to him, 'the country was above 5,000 li in circuit, its capital being above 20 li. There were regular seed-time and harvest, fruits and flowers grew profusely, and there were continuous woods for some hundreds of li. The country produced dark wild elephants prized by neighbouring countries. The climate was hot . . . The people were . . . fast and clear in speech; in their talk and manners they differed somewhat from "Mid-India". There were few Buddhists, the majority of the people being of other religions. There were above ten Buddhist monasteries, and 500 brethren students of the Mahāyānist Sthavira School System. There were more than 100 Deva temples, and the professed adherents of the various sects were very numerous, the majority being nirgranthas.'[1]

Earlier, however, by about two centuries (i.e. fifth century A.D.) there is the well-known Komarti grant[2] which introduces us to a Śrī Mahārāja named Candravarman who is described as Kaliṅgādhipati (lord of Kaliṅga). To his dynasty, probably, also belonged Umavarman and Viśākhavarman who were both evidently lords of Kaliṅga. To about the same date as that of the Komarti grant, may be ascribed the inscription of a certain Kaliṅgādhipati Vāsiṣṭhīputra Śaktivarman of the Māṭhara family who granted from Piṣṭapura (= Pithāpuram) the village of Rākaluva in the Kaliṅga-

1 Watters, *On Yuan Chwang*, Vol. II, p. 198.
2 Sewell, *Historical Inscriptions of Southern India*, p. 18.

viṣaya.[1] In the Aihole Inscriptions (634-35 A.D.) Pulakesin II claims to have subdued the Kaliṅgas along with the Kośalas and took the fortress of Piṣṭapura.[2] One at least of the Vākāṭaka kings is credited with having conquered the Andhra and Kaliṅga countries; he was Hariṣena, the father-in-law of Mādhavavarman the Viṣṇukundin.[3] Towards the middle of the seventh century Kaliṅga seems to have come, for a time at least, under the sway of Kāmarūpa. One of her kings, Harṣadeva or Śrī Harṣa, is described in a contemporary Nepalese inscription to have been the king of Gauḍa, Oḍra, Kaliṅga, Kośala and other countries.[4]

Another reference to Kaliṅga we find in the Bheraghat Inscription of Alhaṇadevī, the queen of Gayā-Karṇa of the Kalacuri dynasty, the grandson of the famous Lakṣmīkarṇa. It informs us that when Lakṣmīkarṇa gave full play to his heroism, Vaṅga trembled with Kaliṅga.[5] King Rāmapāla of the Pāla dynasty also seems to have inflicted a defeat on Kaliṅga as well as on Utkala and Kāmarūpa.[6] King Vijayasena of the Sena dynasty is credited with having inflicted a defeat on the Kaliṅgas whose king at that time was evidently Rāghava.[7] The Madhainagar grant of Lakṣmaṇasena informs us that the Gauḍeśvara (i.e. Lakṣmaṇa) in his youth took his pleasures with the females of Kaliṅga.

The reference to Trikaliṅga in some of the old records is very interesting. The S. Indian dynasties that ruled in the northern districts of Madras, C.P., and Orissa assumed the title 'Lord of Trikaliṅga' or 'Trikaliṅgādhipati'.[8] Kaliṅga, evidently in a narrow sense, has always been distinguished in literature and sometimes also in epigraphs from Oḍra and Utkala and Kośala; but we must also take the Puranic statement into consideration that the Amarakaṇṭaka hill was situated in the western half of Kaliṅga (*Kaliṅgadeśe paścārdhe parvate Amarakaṇṭake*). Mention may also be made in this connection to Pliny's reference to three Kaliṅgas in his time, already mentioned: (i) the Gangaridae-Calingae, the Kaliṅgas who lived conterminously with the Gangaridae, (2) the Macco-Calingae, either the Mekala-Kaliṅgas or (Macco = Muka =

---

1 *Ep. Ind.*, XII, pp. 1ff.

2 *Ibid.*, VI, pp. 4ff.

3 *J.R.A.S.*, 1914, p. 137.

4 *Ind. Ant.*, 1880, Vol. IX, p. 179; *J.R.A.S.*, 1898, pp. 384–5; *I.H.Q.*, 1927, p. 841.

5 *Ep. Ind.*, Vol. II, p. 11.

6 *Rāmacarita*, II, 45 and 47.

7 *Deopara Inscription.*

8 E.g., the Sonpur grant of Mahāśivagupta Yayāti where the king is described as such. The same king is described in one of his grants as having been elected king of Kaliṅga, Kaṅgoda, Utkala and Kośala. Kaṅgoda is certainly the Kung-Yū-t'u of Yuan Chwang, when the pilgrim went to Ḳaleng-ka, cf. the Narasapatam grant of Trikaliṅgādhipati Vajrahastadeva.

three) the Muka-Kaliṅgas (perhaps identical with Mukhaliṅgam) and (3) the Calingae proper. The word Tilang which we meet with in some Arabic records[1] evidently is a corruption of this Trikaliṅga which is also responsible for the term Talaing used to designate the ancient people of Lower Burma or Ramaññadeśa who must have originally migrated from the Trikaliṅga countries. The term Kliṅg applied to the people of Malay Peninsula must have originally been derived from Kaliṅga which seems to have been the original home of the Kliṅg people.

---

[1] E.g., see Elliot, *History of India as told by her own Historians*, Vol. III, p. 234.

# CHAPTER XXXIII

## THE ANDHRAS

The earliest mention of the Andhras as a tribe is to be found along with the Śavaras, Pulindas and probably also the Mūtibas, in the *Aitareya Brāhmaṇa* where all these tribes are referred to as *dasyus* or non-Aryans.[1] In the *Śatapatha Brāhmaṇa* also, the Andhras are mentioned along with the Puṇḍras, Śavaras, Pulindas and the Mūtibas.[2] Vincent Smith is of opinion that the Andhras were a Dravidian-speaking people and were evidently the progenitors of the modern Telegu-speaking people occupying the deltas of the Godāvarī and the Kṛṣṇā,[3] while P.T.S. Iyangar also holds that the Andhras were originally a Vindhyan tribe that extended its political power from the west gradually to the east down the Godāvarī and the Kṛṣṇā valleys.[4] That the Andhras were indigenous to the Deccan is attested to by both the epics; the *Mahābhārata* says that they were Dakṣiṇā-patha-janmānaḥ, while the *Rāmāyaṇa* connects them with the Godāvarī:

*Dakṣiṇā-patha-janmānaḥ sarve naravarāndhrakāḥ,*
*Guhāḥ Pulindāḥ Śavarāś Cukukā Madrakaiḥ* (?) *saha.*
(*Mbh.*, XII, 207, 42.)

*Nadīṃ Godāvarīṃ caiva sarvamevānupaśyataḥ,*
*Tathaivāndhrāṃśca Puṇḍrāṃśca colān Pāṇḍrāṃścakebalān.*
(*Rām.*, Kish. Kāṇ., 41, Chap. 11.)

That the Andhras occupied the Godāvarī-Kṛṣṇā valley is further upheld by one of the earliest records of the Pallava dynasty that flourished in the Andhra region. The Mayidavolu plates of the early Pallava ruler Śivaskandavarman prove that the Andhrāpatha or the region of the Andhras embraced the Kṛṣṇā district with Dhaññakada or Bezwada as its capital.[5]

The *Mārkaṇḍeya Purāṇa*[6] mentions in the list of peoples inhabiting the eastern countries a tribe called the Andhrarakas which is substituted by the Andhravākas.[7] But both seem to be misreadings for the Andhras who were always a people of the southern regions, as also in view of the fact that the same *Mārkaṇḍeya Purāṇa*

---

[1] *Aitareya Br.*, VII, 18.

[2] '*Antān vaḥ prajāḥ takṣiṣṭa iti*, etc. *Andhrāḥ Puṇḍrāḥ Śavarāḥ Pulindāḥ Mūtibāḥ iti uddyantāḥ vahaboḥ bhavanti.*'

[3] *Ind. Ant.*, 1913, pp. 276–8.

[4] *Ibid.*, 1918, p. 71.

[5] *Ep. Ind.*, VI, p. 88.

[6] Canto LVII, 42.

[7] XLV, 122.

places a people called the Andhas along with the Maulikas, Aśmakas, Bhogavardhanas, Naiṣikas, Kuntalas, etc., in the southern region.[1] The reading Andhas is also corrected in the *Vāyupurāṇa* as Andhras.[2] These peoples are mentioned in the *Mahābhārata* in the *Udyogaparvan* and *Bhīṣmaparvan* as Andhakas and Andhras respectively.[3] According to the *Sabhāparvan* and *Vanaparvan*,[4] the Andhas or Āndhras were a rude uncivilised people.

The earliest epigraphic mention of the Andhra people is made in some of the edicts (XIII, R.E.) of Aśoka where the Andhras, Palidas (Pāladas, Parimdas = the Pulindas, or the Pāradas), Bhojas and Rāṭhikas (Rāṣṭrikas) are said to have been vassal tribes of the great Maurya. The Andhra people are also referred to by Pliny who says that the Andarae or Andhras possessed a very large number of villages, thirty towns defended by walls and towers, and supplied their king with an army of 100,000 infantry, 2,000 cavalry and 1,000 elephants.[5]

The founder of the great Sātavāhanas, Simuka, who is credited by the Purāṇas to have assailed the Kāṇvāyanas and destroyed the remains of the Śuṅga power in about the first century B.C. is said to have started a dynasty that ruled over the Dakṣiṇāpatha, for about 250 years. The Sātavāhanas are claimed by the Purāṇas to have been Andhras or Andhrabhṛtyas. The exact significance of this appellation cannot, however, be determined but doubtless they ruled over the whole of Andhradeśa and the adjoining regions.

In the Harāhā Inscription of the Maukhari king Kumāragupta III (554 A.D.) a certain 'lord of the Andhras' (Andhrādhipati) is said to have given the Maukhari king a great trouble by his 'thousands of three-fold rutting elephants'.[6] Dr. H. C. Ray Chaudhuri suggests that the Andhra king referred to was probably Mādhavavarman (I, Javāśraya) of the Polamuru plates belonging to the Viṣṇukuṇḍin family.[7] This suggestion seems to be in agreement with the fact that the Jaunpur Inscription of Īśvaravarman, father of Īśānavarman Maukhari, refers to victory over the Andhras on behalf of Īśvaravarman.[8] The Vākāṭaka king Harisena, father-in-law of Mādhavavarman of the Viṣṇukuṇḍin family referred to above, also claims to have conquered the Andhra and Kaliṅga regions.[9]

The Ikṣvākus succeeded the Sātavāhanas in the rule of the Andhra region where almost all the records of the dynasty have

---

1 LVII, 48-9.
2 XLV, 127.
3 XVIII, 586 and X, 357 respectively.
4 IV, 119; XXX, 1175; XXXIII, 1270 and *Vanaparvan*, LI, 1988.
5 *Ind. Ant.*, 1877, p. 339.
6 *Ep. Ind.*, XIV, pp. 110ff.
7 *P.H.A.I.*, 4th Ed., p. 509.
8 *C.I.I.*, III, p. 230.
9 *J.R.A.S.*, 1914, p. 137.

been found. At the time of Pallava Śivaskandavarman, the Andhrāpatha or the Andhra country seems to have come under the sway of the Pallava dynasty whose headquarters at this time were at Dhaṃnakada (Dhānya-kaṭaka). According to the Purāṇas, the Andhra (i.e. the Sātavāhana) dynasty had five different branches.[1] In fact, one of these five branches, namely, the Cutusātakarṇi branch, is known from inscriptions, coins and literary references to have ruled in the Kuntala country before the Kadambas.[2] The *Vāyu-purāṇa* in the same context referred to above mentions the Ābhiras who ruled after the Andhras (i.e. the Sātavāhanas).

In about the second quarter of the seventh century A.D., the celebrated Chinese pilgrim Hsüan Tsang visited the An-to-lo or the Andhra country. The nearest transcription of An-to-lo is Andara which is comparable to Pliny's Andarae referred to above, though doubtless it means the Andhra country. From Kosala (evidently South Kośala), the pilgrim travelled south, through a forest, for above 900 li to the An-to-lo country which 'had a rich fertile soil with a moist hot climate; the people were of violent character; their mode of speech differed from that of "Mid-India", but they followed the same system of writing. There were twenty odd Buddhist monasteries with more than 3,000 brethren. Near the capital was a large monastery with a succession of high walls and storeyed terraces . . .'.[3]

The name of the capital of the country as given by the pilgrim was Ping-ki-lo which does not seem to have as yet been correctly identified, though Cunningham sought to equate it with Warangal.

We have seen above that in the time of Pallava Śivaskandavarman, Dhāryakaṭaka was the capital of the Andhrāpatha, but Hsüan Tsang seems to refer to Dhānyakaṭaka as a region separate from Andhra. The pilgrim proceeds to relate that from Andhra he continued his journey south, through wood and jungle, for over 1,000 li, and reached the Te-na-ka-che-ka country which was above 6,000 li in circuit, and its capital was above 40 li in circuit. Te-na-ka-che-ka has been equated with Dhānyāyakaṭaka or Dhanakaṭaka.[4]

---

[1] E.g. *Vāyu P.*, 99, 358. '*Andhrānāṃ saṃsthitāḥ pañca teshāṃ vaṃśāḥ samāḥ punaḥ.*'

[2] Sircar, *Successors of the Sātavāhanas*, pp. 218ff. For a summary of the historical vicissitudes of Andhradeśa after the Sātavāhanas, see *ibid.*, pp. 3–5 of the introduction.

[3] Watters, *On Yuan Chwang*, Vol. II, p. 209.

[4] Watters, *ibid.*, Vol. II, pp. 214ff. But there are scholars who hold that Yuan Chwang's description of the city and its surroundings does not suit the identification. Fergusson, Burgess and Sewell therefore locate the city at Bezwada. Cunningham, *A.G.I.*, Majumdar's Ed., notes, p. 737.

'The country had a rich soil and yielded abundant crops; there was much waste land and the inhabited towns were few; the climate was warm, and the people were of black complexion, violent disposition, and fond of the arts. There was a crowd of Buddhist monasteries but most of them were deserted, about 20 being in use, with 1,000 brethren mostly adherents of the Mahāsaṅghika system. There were about 100 Deva temples and the followers of the various sects were numerous . . .'

Stray references to the Andhra country and people are made in later epigraphic records as well. Thus the Indian Museum inscription of the ninth year of Nārāyaṇapāladeva of the Pāla dynasty refers to the Andhra-vaiṣayika Sākyabhikṣu Sthavīra Dharmamitra who erected an image, evidently of the Buddha.

The Pāli Buddhist literature is not wanting in references to the Andhras. The *Apadāna*,[1] a book of the Pāli Canon, mentions Andhakas along with the Muṇḍakas, Kolakas and Cīnas who came to show respect to a banker's son named Jatukannika in the town of Haṃsavatī.

A young brahmin after completing his education at Takkasīlā (Taxila), then a great seat of learning, came to the Andhra country to profit by practical experience.[2] Assaka and Aḷaka or Muḷaka were the two Andhaka kings.[3] A brahmin well versed in mantras belonging to the kingdom of Kośala came to live in the kingdom of Assaka on the banks of the Godāvarī.[4]

[1] Pt. II, p. 359.

[2] *Jāt.* [I, pp. 356ff (Fausböll)]. Cowell means *Mahiṁsakaraṭṭha* by Andhradeśa (Cowell, *Jāt.*, I, p. 203).

[3] *Suttanipāta Commentary*, II, p. 581.

[4] *Suttanipāta*, p. 190.

## CHAPTER XXXIV

# THE DAMIḶAS

The Damiḷas,[1] commonly known as the Tamils, were a powerful S. Indian tribe, frequently mentioned in Buddhist texts, particularly the Ceylon Chronicles (*Dīpavaṃsa, Mahāvaṃsa, Cūḷavaṃsa*). It is interesting to note that a Vinaya Commentary called *Vimalivinodanī* was written by Kassapa Thera, an inhabitant of the kingdom of Damiḷa.[2] In the *Mahāvaṃsa Ṭīkā*, however, we are told that the Damiḷas were disrespectful to the Buddhist stūpas.[3]

From the Pāli Chronicles we find that the Damiḷas were a warlike people. From early times they made incursions into Ceylon, and we frequently find Damiḷa rulers on the throne at Anurādhapura. For instance, in 177 B.C., two Damiḷas, Sena and Gutta, are said to have conquered King Suratissa (187–177 B.C.) and ruled the island of Laṅkā (= Ceylon) for twenty-two years.[4] In the second and first centuries B.C. the island of Laṅkā was very much troubled by the Damiḷas who became very turbulent. A Damiḷa king named Eḷāra reigned in Laṅkā from 145 B.C. till 101 B.C., and was then defeated and dethroned by the famous Duṭṭhagāmaṇī, 'himself a great warrior, accompanied by ten great heroes'.[5] In the *Mahāvaṃsa Ṭīkā* we read that Duṭṭhagāmaṇī fought with the Damiḷas,[6] killing large numbers of them,[7] and made a single realm of Ceylon.[8] This story is elaborated in the *Sumaṅgalavilāsinī* (p. 640).[9] Here we read that 'Duṭṭhagāmaṇī Abhaya', after defeating 32 Damiḷa kings and being crowned at Anurādhapura as undisputed ruler of Ceylon, was so highly delighted that he did not sleep for a month. The *Thūpavaṃsa* (p. 59) further says that Duṭṭhagāmaṇī defeated the Damiḷas at Mahiyaṅgana, where he built a golden cetiya

---

1 We may note that the word 'Dravidian' comes from the ethnic name '*Draviḍa*', or '*Dramiḍa*', or '*Damiḷa*'.

2 *Sāsanavaṃsa*, 33.

3 *Mahāvaṃsa Ṭīkā*, p. 447 (P.T.S. Ed.).

4 *Dīpavaṃsa*, 18, 47.

5 *Mahābodhivaṃsa*, p. 133.

6 *Mahāvaṃsa Ṭīkā*, p. 24.

7 *Ibid.*, p. 489—the phrase is '*ghātetvā Damiḷe sabbe*', 'killing all the Damiḷas', but this is probably poetic licence.

8 '*Ekarajjaṃ katvā*'—*ibid.*, p. 437; and see p. 100.

9 Cf. *Thūpavaṃsa* (P.T.S. Ed. by B. C. Law), p. 63, and B. C. Law, *History of Pāli Literature*, Vol. II, p. 577.

and worshipped it. On another occasion, he conquered the Damiḷas 'on the other side of the Ganges' (Gaṅgāya paratīre).[1]

Many Damiḷas were also killed by Veḷusumano, a general of Duṭṭhagāmaṇī, after they had taken refuge in the city called Vijitanagara (or Vijitapura). Thereupon Duṭṭhagāmaṇī's troops went to Giriloka, where a Damiḷa general named Giriya was slain.[2] King Kākavaṇṇa Tissa, Duṭṭhagāmaṇī's father, had also fought with the Damiḷas at Mahiyaṅgana, where he built a golden stūpa.[3] In order to put a check on the Damiḷas he kept guards at the fords of the Mahāgaṅgā.[4]

In 43 B.C., in the fifth month of Vaṭṭagāmaṇī's reign, a Brahmin named Tissa rose against him, but was defeated by seven Damiḷas who landed at Mahātittha. Then these Damiḷas waged war against Vaṭṭagāmaṇī and defeated him at Kolambālaka. For fourteen years, Vaṭṭagāmaṇī and his queen Anulā were exiled, and during this period five Damiḷas ruled in succession at Anurādhapura. First came Pulahattha who ruled this city for three years, and appointed a Damiḷa named Bāhiya as his commander (senāpati).[5] Bāhiya succeeded Pulahattha, and was followed in his turn by Panayamāra, Piḷayamāra, and Dāṭhika.[6] Meanwhile, Vaṭṭagāmaṇī was staging a comeback, and in 29 B.C. he attacked and slew Dāṭhika, regained his throne, and reigned until 17 B.C.

Some years later (between 12 and 16 A.D.), the wicked queen Anulā poisoned all her husbands in succession; among them were two Damiḷas, namely Vaṭuka and Niliya.[7] Though there must have been Damiḷa incursions during the succeeding four centuries, we have no definite dates until 433 A.D. when a Damiḷa usurper named Paṇḍuka reigned in Ceylon for five years, after killing King Mittasena.[8] A little later, another Damiḷa usurper named Pīṭhiya ruled at Anurādhapura for seven months, and was then killed in battle.[9]

More Damiḷas were killed by Māna,[10] eldest son of Kassapa II (641–650 A.D.). We then have another gap in the chronology, until

---

[1] *Mahāvaṃsa Ṭīkā*, p. 476. The Ganges in this case is the 'Great River' of Ceylon (= Mahāvālukagaṅgā).

[2] *Thūpavaṃsa* (P.T.S. Ed. by B. C. Law), p. 62; *Mahāvaṃsa Ṭīkā*, pp. 475, 479; and see Malalasekera, *Dictionary of Pāli Proper Names*, s.v. *Veḷusumano*, *Duṭṭhagāmaṇī*, and *Giriya*.

[3] *Thūpavaṃsa*, p. 58.

[4] *Mahāvaṃsa Ṭīkā*, p. 448.

[5] *Ibid.*, p. 617.

[6] This Dāṭhika must be identical with the Sāṭhika or Dāṭhika who is mentioned in the *Dīpavaṃsa* (19, 16) as having been killed by 'Abhaya, son of Saddhātissa', i.e. by *Vaṭṭagāmaṇī*.

[7] *Mahāvaṃsa Ṭīkā*, p. 626.

[8] *Cūḷavaṃsa* (P.T.S.), p. 22.

[9] *Ibid.*, p. 24.

[10] *Ibid.*, p. 71.

the time of Parakkamabāhu I of Ceylon (1153–1186 A.D.). During this period, Kulasekhara, a Cholian king of S. India, besieged the Pāṇḍyan king, Parakkama of Madhurā, and the latter appealed for help to Parakkamabāhu who sent an expeditionary force to S. India where they carried on a prolonged campaign against Kulasekhara and his allies, in the course of which the fortress of Semponmāri was conquered by the Sinhalese.[1] Meanwhile, the Pāṇḍyan king had been killed, but the Sinhalese defeated Kulasekhara and installed Parakkama's son on the throne of Madhurā.[2] About a century later, a powerful Damiḷa general named Āriyacakkavattī laid waste the kingdom of Ceylon, entered the town of Subhagiri, seized all its sacred treasures, including the Buddha's tooth relic, and returned with them to the Paṇḍu kingdom, then ruled over by another Kulasekhara (1268–1308 A.D.).[3]

A study of the Buddhist texts clearly shows that the Damiḷas were a fighting people, engaged in constant strife with the Sinhalese. They are described as 'anāriyā' or uncultured. They were defeated and mercilessly massacred in almost all their battles with the Sinhalese; on one occasion, as we read in the *Mahāvaṃsa Commentary*,[4] the Damiḷas were killed in such large numbers that the water of a pond became red on account of the profuse flow of Damiḷa blood. They are said to have used red-hot iron balls and molten pitch against their enemies.[5]

The literary tradition of Ceylon does not clearly indicate who these Damiḷa invaders were. But, as we have seen above, the general Āriyacakkavattī, for example, came from the Paṇḍu kingdom, i.e. the land of the Pāṇḍyas in the southernmost part of India; and we may perhaps conclude from this that the Damiḷas who made predatory excursions into the island of Ceylon from time to time were natives of Pāṇḍya. We cannot tell, however, whether those Damiḷas who invaded Ceylon in early times were sent on their expeditions by the king of Pāṇḍu, or whether they were a race of marauders who undertook those expeditions on their own initiative. The Commentaries of Buddhaghosa distinguish the Damiḷas from the Yavanas and Kirātas on the one hand, and from the Andhras on the other.

The relations between the Damiḷa country and Ceylon were not always inimical. For instance, the account of Vijaya in the *Mahāvaṃsa*[6] distinctly brings out that a matrimonial alliance

---

[1] *Cūḷavaṃsa* (P.T.S.), p. 402.

[2] See Malalasekera, *op. cit.*, s.v. *Kulasekhara*.

[3] *Cūḷavaṃsa*, p. 512.

[4] p. 482.

[5] *Ibid.*, p. 477.

[6] VII, 72.

existed between the rulers of Laṅkā and Pāṇḍya. It is also mentioned that there was a very early settlement in Ceylon of skilled craftsmen and families of the eighteen guilds, all from Pāṇḍya. There existed a close cultural relationship and constant intercourse between S. India and Ceylon; notable centres of Buddhist learning mentioned in Pāli works being Kāverīpaṭṭaṇa, Madhurā and Kāñcipura (modern Conjeeveram).

CHAPTER XXXV

# THE ŚAVARAS

The Śavaras or Śabaras referred to in both the Great Epics were a non-Aryan tribe. The earliest mention of them is to be found in the *Aitareya Brāhmaṇa* (VII, 18), where it is stated that the elder sons of Viśvāmitra were cursed to become progenitors of such servile races as Andhras, Puṇḍras, Śavaras, Pulindas and Mūtibas.[1] The implication of this passage seems to be that the Śavaras were a non-Aryan people dwelling somewhere in the Dakṣiṇāpatha. The *Matsya* and *Vāyu Purāṇas* definitely locate them in the south, describing them as Dakṣiṇāpathavāsinaḥ.[2] The *Mahābhārata* (XII, 207, 42) also places them in the Deccan along with the Andhras and Pulindas:—

*Dakṣiṇāpathajanmānaḥ sarve naravarāndhrakāḥ*
*Guhāḥ Pulindāḥ Śavarāś Cucukā Madrakaiḥ* (?) *saha.*

Ptolemy [3] mentions a country called Sabarai which is generally held to be identical with the region inhabited by the Śavaras. Cunningham identifies the Sabarai of Ptolemy with Pliny's Suari, and further identifies both with the aboriginal Śavaras or Suars, a wild race who lived in the woods and jungles without any fixed habitations, and whose country extended as far southward as the Pennār river. These Śavaras or Suars are only a single branch of a widely spread race found in large numbers to the south-west of Gwalior and Marwar and S. Rajputana where they are known as Surrius.[4]

The *Rāmāyaṇa* story of the Śavara women who were deeply attached to Rāmacandra also seems to indicate that the Śavaras were a wild tribe inhabiting the forest regions of the south.[5]

---

1 Roth, *Zur Litteratur und Geschichte des Weda*, p. 133.
2 *Matsya P.*, 144, 46–8; *Vāyu P.*, 45, 126.
3 McCrindle: *Ptolemy's Ancient India*, Ed. S. N. Majumdar, p. 173.
4 *Ibid.*, p. 173.
5 See *Rāmāyaṇa*, I, 1, 55 sq. (Cf. *Rām.*, III, 77, 6 sq.)

## CHAPTER XXXVI

# THE MŪTIBAS

The Mūtibas were a non-Aryan barbarian (Dasyu) tribe, mentioned in the *Aitareya Brāhmaṇa* (VII, 18) along with the Andhras, Pulindas and Śavaras. They are also probably referred to in the *Sāṅkhāyana Śrauta Sūtra* (XV, 26, 6) under the name Mūcīpas or Mūvīpas.[1]

The location of the Mūtibas is not definitely known, but as they are mentioned along with the Śavaras and Pulindas who, according to the Purāṇas[2] and the *Mahābhārata*,[3] were 'dakṣiṇāpathavāsinaḥ' or located in the south, it may be surmised that the Mūtibas also were a southern tribe. This is also indicated by the fact that the Andhras with whom they are associated were also a southern people.

The Mūtibas were probably the same as the Modubae of Pliny, who are said to have dwelt beyond the Modo-Galingae, a tribe occupying a large island in the Ganges; though it is difficult to account for the Mūtibas evidently a southern tribe, coming to occupy a region not very far from the Ganges.

The Mūtibas do not seem to have been an important tribe; they are scarcely mentioned in the historical period.

---

[1] 'It is not altogether improbable that the Mūcīpas are the people who appear in the *Mārkaṇḍeya Purāṇa* (57, 46) under the designation of Mūshika. A comparison of the *Aitareya Brāhmaṇa* with the *Sāṅkhāyana Śrauta Sūtra* betrays a good deal of confusion with regard to the second and third consonants of the name. It was, therefore, perfectly natural for later generations to introduce further variations. The Mūshikas were probably settled on the banks of the river Musi on which Hyderabad now stands' (*P.H.A.I.*, 4th Ed., p. 80).

[2] *Vāyu P.*, 45, 126; *Matsya P.*, 114, 46–8.

[3] XII, 207, 42.

## CHAPTER XXXVII

# THE PULINDAS

The Pulindas were a people belonging to the aboriginal stock, and have often been classed with such non-Aryan tribes as the Śabaras, Ābhīras, Pulkusas, etc. They are usually definitely stated to be a southern tribe, but there seems to have been a northern branch of the Pulindas as well.

The association of the Pulindas with the Andhras and Śavaras, as also with the Puṇḍras and Mūtibas, is as old as the *Aitareya Brāhmaṇa* (VII, 18), where it is stated that the elder sons of Viśvāmitra were cursed to become progenitors of such races as the Andhras, Puṇḍras, Śavaras, Pulindas and Mūtibas.[1]

The *Mahābhārata*[2] places the Pulindas in the Dakṣiṇāpatha (Deccan), along with the Andhras, Guhas, Śavaras, Cucukas and Madrakas. The *Matsya* and *Vāyu Purāṇas*[3] also describe them as *Dakṣiṇāpatha-vāsinaḥ* (dwelling in the Deccan), along with the Vaidarbhas, Daṇḍakas, Vindhyas and others. The *Mārkaṇḍeya* Purāṇa[4] too places the Pulindas in the Deccan, and classes them with the Puṇḍrakas, Keralas, Kaliṅgas, Ābhīras, Andhras, Vidarbhas and Kuntalas. The *Śrīmad-Bhāgavatam* (2, 4, 18) associates them with the Kirātas, Hūṇas, Andhras, Pukkusas, Ābhīras, Suhmas, Yavanas and Khaśas, all of whom sought the protection of Śrī Kṛṣṇa.

In the Bengali recension of the *Rāmāyaṇa* (*Kiṣkindhyā K.*, XLI, 17; XLIV, 12), the Pulindas appear both in the south and in the north. The northern recension knows only of the northern Pulindas (*Kiṣkindhyā K.*, XLIII). The *Viṣṇupurāṇa*[5] associates the Pulindakas (probably identical with the Pulindas) with the Sindhus: the two peoples are coupled in a compound—Sindhu-

---

[1] Roth, *Zur Litteratur und Geschichte des Weda*, p. 133.

[2] XII, 207, 42.

[3] *Teṣām pare janapadā Dakṣiṇāpatha-vāsinaḥ*
*Kārūṣāśca sahaiṣīkā Āṭavyāḥ Śavarāstathā*
*Pulindā Vindhyapuṣikā Vaidarbhā Daṇḍakaiḥ saha* (*Matsya*, 114, 46–8).
*Ābhīrāḥ saha caiṣīkāḥ Āṭavyāḥ Śavarāśca ye*
*Pulindā Vindhyamulīkā Vaidarbhā Daṇḍakaiḥ saha* (*Vāyu*, 45, 126).

[4] 57, 45–8. The Pulindas are also mentioned in the *Brahmāṇḍa Purāna* (see *Pūrva Bhāga*, 16, 40ff.), *Brahma P.* (27, 41ff.), *Vāmana P.* (13, 35ff.), *Garuḍa P.* (55, 10ff.).

[5] See Wilson, *Viṣṇu P.* tr., Vol. 2 (1865), pp. 156ff.

Pulindakas--and are mentioned together with the Kārūṣas, Bhojas, Daśārṇas, Mekalas, Utkalas and other tribes. The compound Sindhu-Pulindaka also occurs in the *Mahābhārata* (6, 346ff.) and *Padmapurāṇa* (III, 6, 4ff.). The Pulindas are alluded to in the *Raghuvaṃśa* as well (XVI, 32), but there is hardly any clue to their geographical location.

The capital of the (southern) Pulindas was Pulindanagara which lay to the south-east of Daśārṇa, i.e. in the Vidiśā or Bhilsa region, and may have been identical with Rupnāth, the find-spot of one recension of Minor Rock Edict I of Aśoka.[1]

At the time of Aśoka, the Pulindas, together with the Andhras, Bhojas and Rāṣṭrikas, formed a group of vassal tribes within the Emperor's dominions,[2] which extended as far south as the Pennar river in the Nellore district, just stopping short of the Tamil kingdoms, which are referred to as Pracaṃta or frontier states.

Some interesting information about the Pulindas is supplied by Ptolemy. According to him, the Pulindas seem to have been located along the banks of the Narmadā, to the frontiers of Lārike or Lāṭa = Gujarat; for he describes them as occupying a region northward of Nasik, Ozene (= Ujjain), Minnagara, Lārika or Lāṭadeśa (= Gujarat), Barygaza (= Bharukaccha = Broach), etc. His epithet for the tribe is 'Agriophagoi', - a Greek word indicating that they were a tribe that subsisted on raw flesh and wild roots and fruits.

Yule in his map locates the Pulindas to the north-east of the Gulf of Cutch.

---

[1] *P.H.A.I.*, 4th Ed., pp. 79, 258.

[2] Rock Edict, V and XIII.

## CHAPTER XXXVIII

# THE KUNTALAS

The Kuntalas are twice mentioned in the *Mārkaṇḍeya Purāṇa* list of tribes, once in connection with the peoples of Kāśī and Kośala (LVII, 33), which means that they were a Madhyadeśa tribe, and elsewhere (LVII, 48) along with the Aśmakas, Bhogavardhanas, Naiṣikas, Andhras, etc., which suggests that they were a people of the Deccan. The *Bhīṣmaparvan* of the *Mahābhārata*, however, seems to locate the people in three different regions. One verse (IX, 347) seems to locate them in the Madhyadeśa, while another (IX, 367) in the Deccan which is also upheld by a reference apparently to the same people in the *Karṇaparvan* (XX, 779). A third reference in the *Bhīṣmaparvan* (IX, 359) suggests location of the tribe somewhere in the western region. Cunningham points out (*A.S.R.*, XI, 123) that the country of the Kuntalas of the Madhyadeśa should be identified with the region near Chunar which he calls Kuntila. Whatever be the merit of the identification, the Kuntalas of the Madhyadeśa do not seem to have attained to any historical eminence. The Kuntalas of the west also have hardly any place in history. But the Kuntalas of the Deccan appear to have risen to considerable importance in historical times as will be evident from subsequent details.

Literary and epigraphic references have now proved beyond doubt that there were several families of the Śātakarṇis of the Deccan, and one or more of these families ruled over Kuntala of the Kanarese districts before the Kadambas (Ray Chaudhuri, *P.H.A.I.*, 4th Ed., 339-40). One member mentioned in the *Matsyapurāṇa* list is actually called Kuntala Śātakarṇi, a name that is commented upon by the commentator of Vātsyāyana's *Kāmasūtra*. He takes the word 'Kuntala' in the name Kuntala Śātakarṇi to mean 'Kuntalaviṣaye jātatvāt tatsamākhyaḥ'. A Śātavahana of Kuntala is also referred to in the *Kāvyamīmāṃsā* of Rājaśekhara. This king ordered the use of Prākrit to the exclusion of every other language by the ladies of his inner apartments. He has often been identified with king Hāla who hailed from Kuntala (*Kāvyamīmāṃsā* notes, p. 9).

According to certain Mysore Inscriptions,[1] the Kuntala region included the southern part of the Bombay Presidency and the

[1] Rice, *Mysore and Coorg from Inscriptions*, p. 3; Fleet, *Dynasties of the Kanarese Districts*, p. 284, f.n. 2.

northern portion of Mysore, and it was ruled at one time by the kings of the Nanda dynasty.

Kuntala figured in history also in later times. An Ajantā Inscription credits the Vākāṭaka king Pṛthivīsena I with having conquered the lord of Kuntala. Another Vākāṭaka king Hariṣeṇa claimed victories over Kuntala along with Lāṭa, Avanti, Andhra, Kaliṅga, etc.

## CHAPTER XXXIX

# THE RĀṢṬRIKAS

The Rāṣṭrikas are mentioned for the first time in the Rock Edicts of Aśoka (V and XIII), along with the Andhras, Pulindas and Bhojas who were included as vassal tribes within Aśoka's dominions. The Andhras, Pulindas and Bhojas were known as early as the time of the *Aitareya Brāhmaṇa*, but the Rāṣṭrikas find no mention there. The tribe had evidently not come into importance at that time.

Even after Aśoka's time the Rāṣṭrikas continued to be associated with the Bhojas. In the Hāthigumphā Inscriptions of King Khāravela of Kaliṅga (*c.* 150 B.C.), that monarch is said to have defeated the Bhojakas and Rāṭhikas (i.e. the Bhojas and Rāṣṭrikas of Aśokan inscriptions) in the fourth year of his reign, and to have compelled them to do him homage.

The Sātavāhana records refer to two tribes, Mahābhojas and Mahāraṭhis (Smith, *Aśoka*, 4th Ed., p. 225), who were evidently identical with the earlier Bhojas and Rāṣṭrikas, and it is clear that the Rāṣṭrikas or Mahāraṭhis were the ancestors of the present Mahārāṣṭra people or Mārāṭhas (cf. R. G. Bhandarkar, *Anc. History of the Deccan*).

The Bhojas were located in the Vidarbha or modern Berar region, which is included within modern Mārāṭhi-speaking districts. The Rāṣṭrikas who were so frequently associated with them must have occupied the adjoining tracts, and it may be assumed that they were located in the very region where the present Mārāṭhas dwell.

# CHAPTER XL

## THE NĀSIKYAS

The Purāṇas make a mess in the mention of this people. The *Mārkaṇḍeya Purāṇa* in one context reads it as Naiṣikas (LVII, 48), but in the same canto in another context reads it as Nāsikyāvas (LVII, 51), and still in another place correctly as Nāsikyas (LVIII, 24). There is no doubt that at all these places one and the same people of ancient Nasik is meant. The *Vāyupurāṇa* reads Nairṇikas (XLV, 127) which the *Mārkaṇḍeya Purāṇa* reads Naiṣikas, and instead of Nāsikyāvas of the same source, it reads Nāsikyas. The *Matsyapurāṇa* reads Vāsikas (CXIII, 50). This confusion makes it evident that the people and the region were not so widely celebrated. This people moreover does not seem to have been known to the authors of the Epics.

## CHAPTER XLI

# THE AŚMAKAS

The Aśmakas or Assakas formed one of the Kṣatriya tribes of ancient India. They are not mentioned in the Vedic literature, but we find them referred to in the Epics and Purāṇas. In an enumeration of the countries in 'Bhāratavarṣa', the land of the Aśmakas is mentioned along with those of the most prominent Kṣatriya peoples of ancient India, such as the Kurus and Śūrasenas.[1] In the different recensions of the *Mahābhārata*, the name of the tribe varies, being spelt either Aśmaka or Aśvaka. In Pāli Buddhist literature, the name is Assaka which, as Rhys Davids points out, may be the vernacular equivalent of either Aśmaka or Aśvaka. He continues: 'Either there were two distinct tribes so called, or the Sanskrit form Aśvaka is a wrong reading or a blunder in the Sanskritization of Assaka'.[2] The Greek writers mention a people called the Assakenoi in eastern Afghanistan and the Kunar valley, with their chief town at Massaga or Maśakāvatī.

In the *Mahābhārata*, there is some confusion between the Aśmakas and the Aśvakas, and some of the passages appear to contradict one another. In the *Jayadrathavadhaparvādhyāya*,[3] the Aśmakas are found ranged on the Pāṇḍava side in the Kurukṣetra war; on the other hand, an 'Aśmaka-dāyàda', or a relative of the Aśmaka monarch, is said to have been killed in battle by Abhimanyu (VII, 37, 1605); and the same person is also referred to as 'Aśmakasya suta' (son of Aśmaka) in the verse immediately following (VII, 37, 1606). An Aśmakeśvara (king of Aśmaka) is also spoken of here (VII, 37, 1608). In a list of the tribes conquered by Karṇa, the Aśmakas are mentioned along with the Vatsas, Kaliṅgas, Ṛsikas, etc. (VIII, 8, 237). In the *Ādiparvan*, a Rājarṣi Aśmaka, son of Vaśiṣṭha and Madayantī, wife of Kalmāṣapāda, is mentioned, and the story of his birth is referred to.[4] The same king, who is called a Vāśiṣṭha, is said to have founded Paudanya (I, 177, 6791).

Pāṇini mentions Aśmaka in one of his Sūtras (IV, I, 173).

The *Aṅguttara Nikāya*,[5] like the Purāṇas,[6] tells us that Assaka was one of the sixteen *Mahājanapadas* of Jambudīpa (India). It

---

[1] *Bhīṣmaparvan*, Chap. 9, p. 822.
[2] *Buddhist India*, p. 28.
[3] VII, 85, 3049.
[4] I, 122, 4737.
[5] I, p. 213; IV, pp. 252, 256, 260.
[6] *Padmapurāṇa*, *Svargakhaṇḍa*, Chap. III; *Viṣṇudharmottaramahāpurāṇa*, Chap. IX.

had an abundance of food and gems, and was wealthy and prosperous. From the *Mahāgovinda Suttanta*, we learn that Potana was the (capital) city of the Assakas.[1]

In the *Suttanipāta*,[2] one of the oldest works of the Pāli Buddhist literature, the Assaka or Aśmaka country is associated with Mūlaka with its capital Patiṭṭhāna (Paithan), and mentioned as situated on the bank of the river Godāvarī, immediately to the south of Patiṭṭhāna. The same passage speaks of a Brāhman guru called Bāvarī who, having left the Kośala country, settled near a village on the Godāvarī in the Assaka territory in the Dakṣiṇāpatha.[3]

Rhys Davids points out that the country is mentioned together with Avanti, in the same way as Aṅga is with Magadha, and its position in the list of *Mahājanapadas*, between Śūrasena and Avanti, makes it appear probable that when the list was drawn up, Aśmaka was situated immediately north-west of Avanti. In that case, the settlement on the Godāvarī was a later colony, and this is confirmed by the fact that there is no mention of Potana (or Potali) in the list.[4] Further, Asaṅga in his *Sūtrālaṅkāra* mentions an Aśmaka country in the basin of the Indus; and we have already noted that the Greek writers knew of a people called the 'Assakenoi' in eastern Afghanistan.

The legendary story of the origin of Aśmaka, founder of the tribe, barely mentioned in the *Mahābhārata*, is narrated in full in the *Bṛhannāradīya Purāṇa*. Once Sudāsa, who is often identified with the Ṛgvedic hero who won the battle of the ten kings, went to the forest to hunt. He killed a tiger, and the dying animal took the shape of a terrible monster bent on wreaking vengeance on the king. An occasion soon presented itself. When Vaśiṣṭha, the king's priest, had departed after performing a sacrifice for Sudāsa, the monster assumed the form of the priest, appeared before the king, and asked him to prepare meat for him to eat. The monster once more changed his appearance, and appeared before King Sudāsa in the guise of a cook. When ordered by the king to prepare a dish of meat for Vaśiṣṭha, he cooked human flesh; and the king offered the dish to the genuine Vaśiṣṭha when he arrived. Vaśiṣṭha thought the king to be wicked in offering him meat; and when, after meditation, he discovered that it was actually human flesh, he cursed the king, saying that he would become a monster, greedy for human flesh. When the king told him that it was (supposedly) by Vaśiṣṭha's own order that the dish had been prepared, the Ṛṣi meditated once more, learnt the

---

1 *Dīgha*, II, p. 235.
2 Verses 976-7.
3 D. R. Bhandarkar, *Carmichael Lectures*, 1918, p. 4; and p. 53, n. 5.
4 *Buddhist India*, pp. 27-8.

whole truth, and modified his curse to have effect for twelve years only. The king, in his turn, was about to curse Vaśiṣṭha, but his queen Madayantī entreated him to forbear, and appeased his wrath. The king washed his feet with the curse-water; his legs turned black, and thenceforward he was famous as Kalmāṣapāda ('having speckled feet').

Every third night thenceforth the king took the shape of a rākṣasa, and strolling about the forest, used to kill human beings. One night he ate a Brāhmaṇī's husband, and the Brāhmaṇī cursed him, saying, 'You will die at the time of union with your wife'. After twelve years, the king was duly freed from the curse of Vaśiṣṭha. He desired an heir, but recollecting the Brāhmaṇī's curse, requested Vaśiṣṭha to act as his proxy. Queen Madayantī conceived, and a son was born to her after the lapse of seven years. According to the legend, the boy was named Aśmaka because his mother smote her womb with a stone (*aśman*) before he was born, in order to hasten delivery. Aśmaka's son was Mūlaka,[1] and his great-grandson is said to have been Dilīpa, the forefather of Rāma. Thus a connection is established between the Ikṣvākus and the Aśmakas.[2]

The *Matsyapurāṇa* (Chap. 272) gives us a list of twenty-five Aśmaka kings, contemporaries of the Śiśunāgas who reigned in Magadha before the Nandas.

One of the Jātakas relates the following story. In Potali, the capital of Assaka, there reigned a king Assaka who had a queen of unique beauty. When she died, the king was overwhelmed with grief. The Bodhisattva, then dwelling at the foot of the Himālayas, got to know of the king's sorrow, and appeared before him. He showed the king his queen, reincarnated as a tiny dungworm. The king made himself known to his queen who told him in human voice that she no longer loved him,—the worm was now dearer to her. Thus the king was consoled.[3]

In another Jātaka,[4] we read that Assaka was the king of Potali in the Assaka country. At this time Kaliṅga was reigning in the city of Dantapura in the Kaliṅga kingdom. Kaliṅga had four daughters of surpassing beauty, whom he ordered to sit in a covered carriage to be driven to every village, town and city with an armed escort. Kaliṅga declared that if any king were desirous of taking them into his harem, he would join battle with him. Passing through various countries, the princesses reached Potali in the Assaka country. The gates were opened by order of Nandisena,

---

[1] For the connection between the Aśmakas and Mūlakas, see *Mūlaka chapter*.

[2] *Bṛhannāradīya Purāṇa*, Chap. 9.

[3] *Jātaka* (Fausböll), Vol. II, pp. 155 foll.

[4] *Ibid.*, III, pp. 3 foll.

the minister of the king of Assaka; and the four princesses were brought before the king who, acting on Nandisena's advice, made them his queen-consorts and sent a message to King Kaliṅga informing him of this. Keeping his threat, Kaliṅga set out for Assaka with a large army, and a great battle was fought. Through Nandisena's diplomacy, Assaka defeated Kaliṅga who fled to his own city. Assaka demanded from Kaliṅga a portion of the dowry of his daughters. King Kaliṅga sent a befitting dowry to Assaka, and thenceforth the two kings lived amicably. According to this story, the countries of the Assakas and the Kaliṅgas bordered on each other. Evidently it is the southern Aśmaka country, on the Godāvarī, that is here referred to.

The *Vimānavatthu Commentary* tells us that a king named Assaka, whose capital was Potananagara, reigned in the country of Assaka. In fulfilment of a promise to grant a boon to his younger wife, he reluctantly sent Sujāta, his son by his first wife, to the forest, so that his younger wife's son should succeed him on the throne. Whilst in the forest, Sujāta met the Elder Mahākaccāyana, was instructed in the Dhamma by him, and afterwards became a bhikkhu.[1]

[1] *Vimānavatthu Commentary*, pp. 259ff.

## CHAPTER XLII

# THE MŪLAKAS

The Mūlakas were a small tribe, very closely related with the Aśmakas of the South [1] (= Aśvakas of the *Mahābhārata*, Assakas of Pāli literature). They were perhaps situated to the south of Avanti, and according to Bhaṭṭasvāmī, the commentator of Kauṭilya's *Arthaśāstra*, their country was identical with Mahārāṣṭra. The position of the Aśmakas and Mūlakas may be determined by two references in the *Suttanipāta*. From verse 977 we gather that the Assakas and Mūlakas [2] occupied the region on the banks of the Godāvarī; while in verse 1011 the capital of the Mūlakas is described as being located at Patiṭṭhāna (Sans. Pratiṣṭhāna), i.e. Paithan (= Baithan of Ptolemy) on the north bank of the Godāvarī in the Aurungabad district of the Nizam's dominions.

Some scholars are of opinion that the Mūlakas occupied the same tract of country as that of the Aśmakas, and that the two tribes were identical.[3] This is, however, doubtful. In the *Vāyupurāṇa*, both Aśmakas and Mūlakas are no doubt stated to be scions of the Ikṣvāku family (Chap. 88, 177-8); and if we are to believe the Pauranic tradition as contained in the *Garuḍapurāṇa* (Chap. 142, 34), Mūlaka, the originator of the Mūlaka tribe, was the son of King Aśmaka, a descendant of Bhagīratha. The Aśmakas and the Mūlakas were thus intimately related, but that the two tribes were different and lived in separate regions is revealed not only by the Brahmanical sources of the Epics and Purāṇas, but by Buddhist sources as well.

In early Pāli literature, Assaka is distinguished on the one hand from Mūlaka in the north and on the other from Kaliṅga in the east.[4] According to the *Paramatthajotikā* (II, Pt. II, p. 581), the Godāvarī formed the border line between the territories of two Andhra kings (that is to say, between Assaka and Aḷaka). That the two countries were distinguished from each other is also upheld by the Pauranic tradition as contained in the *Viṣṇudharmottara*

---

[1] As distinguished from the Aśmakas of N.W. India, identical with the Assakenoi of the Greeks.

[2] It should be noted, however, that Mūlaka occurs only in the Burmese reading of the S.N. The Singhalese has 'Aḷaka', which seems to be identical with Mūlaka (Law, *Geography of Early Buddhism*, p. 21).

[3] Dey, *Geographical Dictionary*, pp. 13 and 133.

[4] Bhandarkar, *Carmichael Lectures*, 1918, pp. 53-4.

(Pt. I, Chap. 9). D. R. Bhandarkar, however, suggests that in later times Mūlaka came to be included in Assaka. In the *Sonadaṇḍa Jātaka*,[1] the Assaka country is associated with Avanti; this contiguity, according to Bhandarkar, can only be explained if it is assumed that Mūlaka was included in Assaka, and that the latter country was thus contiguous with Avanti.[2]

In giving the genealogy of the kings of Ayodhyā who belonged to the Ikṣvāku or 'solar' race, some of the Purāṇas[3] mention the names of six kings, namely, Aśmaka, Mūlaka, Śataratha, Iḍaviḍa (with variations), Vṛddhaśarman and Viśvasaha, who came after King Saudāsa Kalmāṣapāda. The list differs from that given in the other Purāṇas, but Pargiter considers it more authentic (*Anc. Ind. Hist. Tradition*, pp. 94 and 147). King Mūlaka is referred to in the Purāṇas enumerated above as reigning contemporaneously with one King Rāma. Mūlaka was afraid of Rāma and lived protected by a guard of women (nārī-kavaca). A similar statement occurs in the *Mahābhārata*.[4] In the historical period, Aśmaka and Mūlaka were no longer connected with Ayodhyā.[5]

As late as the second quarter of the second century A.D., the Mūlakas are distinguished from the Aśmakas. The Nāsik Inscription of Gautamī, the Sātavāhana Queen, states that her son conquered the Śakas, Yavanas and Pahlavas, and that her dominions extended not only over Asika, Asaka (= Aśmaka) and Mūlaka, but also over Surattha, Kukkura, Aparānta, Anupa, Vidarbha and Ākara-Avanti.

[1] *Jātaka* (Fausböll), V, p. 317.

[2] *Carmichael Lectures*, 1918, pp. 53-4.

[3] *Vāyu P.*, Chap. 88, 178-9; *Brahmāṇḍa P.*, Pt. III, Chap. 63, 178-9; *Liṅga P.*, Pt. I, Chap. 66, 29; *Kūrma P.*, Pt. I, Chap. 21, 14; *Bhāgavata P.*, Pt. IX, Chap. 9, 40.

[4] XII, Chap. 49, 1770–8 and 1792-3; for the historicity of these tales, see Pargiter, *op. cit.*, p. 152, f.n. 2.

[5] The country of the Mūlakas seems to have been mentioned as Maulika in Varāhamihira's *Bṛhatsaṃhitā*, XIV, 4.

## CHAPTER XLIII

# CŌḶAS

In the earliest time of which we have any record, the Tamiḻagam or Tamil realm, as Dr. Barnett thinks, extended over the greater part of the modern Madras Presidency, its boundaries being on the north a line running approximately from Pulicat on the coast to Venkatagiri (Tirupati), on the east the Bay of Bengal, on the south Cape Comorin, and on the west the Arabian Sea as far north as the 'White Rock' near Badagara, to the south of Mahi. Malabar was included in it.[1] It consisted of three kingdoms, those of the Pāṇḍyas, Cōḷas and Chêras or Keralas. The Cōḷa kingdom stretched along the eastern coast, from the river Penner to the Vellār, and on the west reaching to about the borders of Coorg. According to tradition, the Cōḷa country comprised the land between two streams having the same name, Veḷḷāṟu, in the north and the south, the sea on the east and Kōṭṭaikkarai in the west. The area included the modern districts of Trichinopoly and Tanjore and part of the Pudukkottah State.[2] Its capital was Uraiyūr (old Trichinopoly). Kāvirī-paṭṭinam or Pugar on the northern bank of the river Kāverī was its great port while Kāñchī (modern Conjeeveram) was one of its chief towns. Uraiyūr corresponds to Sanskrit Uragapūra.

Negapatam, about 10 miles south of Kāraikkāl, also on the seaboard, was perhaps known to Ptolemy as an important town; at any rate it became a centre of trade and of many religions including Buddhism long before it attracted the attention of European merchants and missionaries. Tanjore, Trichinopoly and Kumbakonam are the present notable cities of the former Cōḷa country. Gangaikoṇḍa-Cōḷapuram, at the meeting point of the modern districts of Trichinopoly, S. Arcot and Tanjore, rose to prominence as the Cōḷa capital in the eleventh and twelfth centuries.

The Cōḷa country was thus drained by the river Kāverī and comprised the districts of Trichinopoly and Tanjore.[3] The river Kāverī is often alluded to and associated with the name of the Cōḷas in South Indian inscriptions. Thus we learn from a South Indian inscription[4] that Hara asked Gunabhara: 'How could I, standing in

---

[1] *Cambridge History of India*, Vol. I, p. 595.
[2] K. A. Nilakanta Sastri, *The Cōḷas*, Chap. 11, p. 22.
[3] Ray Chaudhuri, *Political History of Ancient India*, 4th Ed., p. 271.
[4] Hultzsch, *South Indian Inscriptions*, Vol. I, p. 34.

a temple on earth, view the great power of the Cōḷas or the river Kāverī?' From another inscription we learn that the Cālukya king Pulakesin II crossed the river Kāverī with his victorious army to enter the Cōḷa country when 'the Kāverī had her current obstructed by the causeway formed by his elephants'. The glory of the Kāverī forms an inexhaustible theme of early Tamil poetry. According to the *Maṇimēkhalai*,[1] this noble stream was released from his water-pot by the sage Agastya in response to the prayer of the king Kānta and for the exaltation of the 'children of the sun'. She was the special banner of the just race of the Cōḷas, and she never failed them in the most protracted drought. The yearly freshes in the Kāverī formed the occasion of a carnival in which the whole nation from the king down to the meanest peasant took part.[2] The origin of the name Cōḷa is uncertain. The *Parimēlaḷagar* is inclined to make it the name, like Pāṇḍya and Cēra, of a ruling family or clan of antiquity. The story of the eponymous brothers Cēran, Śōḷan and Pāṇḍiyan is indeed suggestive. The name Cōḷa, however, indicated from the earliest times the people as well as the country subject to the Cōḷa dynasty of rulers. Col. Gerini wrongly connects the word Cōḷa with the Sanskrit Kāla (black) and with Kōla which denoted in the early days the black or dark coloured pre-Aryan population of Southern India in general. The effort to derive it similarly from Tamil 'Cōḷam' (millet) or Sanskrit 'Cōra' (thief) seems unsound. Other names generally used for the Cōḷas are Kiḷḷi, Vaḷavan and Śembiyan. Kiḷḷi probably comes from 'Kil' (dig) meaning a 'digger'; this word forms an integral part of early Cōḷa names like Neḍungilli and so on which is not found in later Cōḷa names. Vaḷavan probably comes from 'Vaḷam' (fertility) and means owner of a fertile country, like the land of the Kāverī. Śembiyan is generally taken to mean a descendant of Śibi, a legendary hero whose self-sacrifice in saving a dove from the pursuit of a falcon figures among the early Cōḷa legends and forms the theme of the *Sibi Jātaka* among the Jātaka stories of Buddhism.[3]

The Cōḷa kings were alleged to belong to the tribe of Tiraiyar or 'Men of the Sea'. Their connection with the sea is probably indicated by the following reference of Aelian to the realm of Soras (Chola?) and its chief city: 'There is a city which a man of royal extraction called Soras governed at the time when Eukratides governed the Bactrians, and the name of that city is Perimuda. It is inhabited by a race of fish-eaters who go off with nets and catch oysters.'[4] During the age of the *Periplus of the Erythraean Sea*,

---

[1] I, 9–12; 23-4. [2] *Maṇimēkhalai*, p. 23. [3] *Ibid*., p. 25.
[4] Ray Chaudhuri, *Political History of Ancient India*, 4th Ed., 271, f.n. 2.

as Dr. Ray Chaudhuri shows in Appendix B (p. 387) of his work, the kingdom of Argaru (= Uragapura) was included in Damirica. The geographer Ptolemy refers to the kingdom of Sora (Chola) ruled by Arkatos and the kingdom of Malanga (probably Kāñchī, according to Dr. Ray Chaudhuri), ruled by Basaronagas. In the *Mārkaṇḍeya,*[1] *Vāyu*[2] and *Matsya*[3] *Purāṇas*, the Cōḷas are mentioned along with the Pāṇḍyas and Keralas. In the *Rāmāyaṇa,*[4] Sugrīva is described as sending his monkey followers to the countries of the Cōḷas, Pāṇḍyas and Keralas in quest of Sītā. Kātyāyana in his *Vārttikas* or aphorisms to Pāṇini's Sūtras or grammatical rules mentions the Cōḷas and the Pāṇḍyas.[5] Patañjali in his *Mahābhāṣya*[6] mentions Kāñchīpura. Aśoka in his Rock Edicts II and XIII mentions the Cōḷas, Pāṇḍyas, Ketalaputras and Satiyaputras as forming 'prachaṃta' or outlying provinces outside his empire. They were on friendly terms with him. The Cōḷas, like the Pāṇḍyas, are spoken of in the plural in all the versions of the Asokan edicts, and this has been held to imply that 'in Aśoka's time there were more than one Cōḍa and one Pāṇḍya King'.[7] Two or three poets of the Śaṅgam make references to an invasion of the south by the Mōriyar (Mauryas). Māmūlanār also speaks of the wealth of the Nandas hidden under the Ganges at Pāṭaliputra. He says that the Vaḍugar formed the vanguard of the invading Mauryas (*Aham* 281). He further says that the Kōśar undertook the subjugation of the south and as the Mōhūr chieftain continued defiant, the Mauryas came down with their great forces on a warlike expedition to the south (*Aham* 251). The above account thus confirms the story of Bindusāra's conquest of Southern India as recorded by the Tibetan historian Tārānāth. It is evident thus that Maurya empire in Southern India probably received some setback before the date when Rock Edicts II and XIII were promulgated.[8] Allusions to the land of the Cōḷas and Kāveripaṭṭinam are found in the *Mahāvaṃsa*. The *Milinda-Pañho*[9] mentions Kola-Paṭṭana, which according to Rhys Davids, must be some place on the Coromandel Coast. Here is a reference probably to Kāveripaṭṭinam. In the Jātaka story[10] Akitti to escape from his admirers is said to have left the neighbourhood of Benares for the Tamil country where he spent some time in a garden near Kāveripaṭṭana. The *Mahāvaṃsa* shows that towards the middle of the second century B.C., a Damiḷa of noble descent, Eḷāra

---

1 Chap. 57, V. 45.
2 Chap. 45, V, 124.
3 Chap. 112, V. 46.
4 IV. Chap. 41, Bombay Ed.
5 R. G. Bhandarkar, *Early History of the Dekkan*, p. 6.
6 IV, 2, Second Āhnika.
7 Cf. Bhandarkar, *Aśoka*, p. 41.
8 *Ibid.*, p. 28.
9 Trenckner Ed., p. 359.
10 *Jātaka* (Fausböll), IV, 237 foll.

by name, came to Ceylon from the Cōḷa country (Coḷaraṭṭha) overpowered Asela,[1] the then king of the island, and himself reigned as king for forty-four years with even justice towards friends and foes on occasions of disputes at law. He sentenced his only son to death for unwittingly causing the death of a young calf. In Tamil literature also we find the story of the prince and the calf which is placed in the reign of Manu.

The early history of the Cōḷa country is obscure. About the beginning of the Christian era the Cōḷa king was Peru-nar-Killi. His son was Iḷanjet-Senni whose son was Karikāl, a vigorous ruler, under whom the Cōḷas became the leading power of the south. He defeated an allied army of the Cheras and Pāṇḍyas and made an expedition to the north. At home he suppressed the turbulent Āyar, Aravāḷar, Kurumbar and Oḷiyar. He made his capital at Kāveri-paṭṭinam on the Kāverī and he secured it from flood by raising the banks of the river as well as by making canals. From the Cōḷas the hegemony of the south passed to the Cheras and later still to the Pāṇḍyas who were ousted by the Pallavas who later on became the suzerain power of Southern India.

[1] *Mahāvaṃsa* (Geiger), p. 166.

# CHAPTER XLIV

## PĀṆḌYAS

The Pāṇḍya kingdom comprised the greater part of the modern Madura and Tinnevelly Districts and in the first century of the Christian era Southern Travancore also. It had its capital originally at Kolkai on the Tāmraparṇi river in Tinnevelly and later at Madura (Dakṣiṇa Mathurā).[1] According to Dr. H. C. Ray Chaudhuri the Pāṇḍya country corresponded to the Madura, Ramnad and Tinnevelly districts and perhaps the southern portion of the Travancore State. It was watered by the rivers Tāmraparṇi and Kṛtamālā or Vaigai. Kātyāyana in his *Vārttika* derives Pāṇḍya from Pāṇḍu. In the *Mahābhārata* and in several Jātakas the Pāṇḍus are spoken of as the ruling race of Indraprastha. In the statement of Kātyāyana regarding the connection of the Pāṇḍyas with the Pāṇḍus who are mentioned in the Epic tale, we find an interesting clue for the name of Madura, the Pāṇḍya capital. Madura or Dakṣiṇa Mathurā is in a sense the same as Mathurā or Muttra, the capital of the Śūrasena kingdom. Now, according to Epic tradition, the Pāṇḍus of Indraprastha were closely connected with the ruling family of the Śūrasena country by ties of friendship and marriage. The geographer Ptolemy (*circa* 150 A.D.) speaks of the country of the Pandoouoi in the Punjab. The association of the Pāṇḍyas of the south with the Śūrasenas of Mathurā and the Pāṇḍus of Northern India is probably alluded to in the confused statement of Megasthenes regarding Heraklcs and Pandaia. Megasthenes, who visited the court of Candragupta Maurya towards the end of the fourth century B.C., has left on record some rumours concerning these southern States. He thus notes a legend that Heracles placed the south under the rule of his daughter 'Pandaia'. The Sanskrit Epics mention them vaguely as foreign lands outside their purview. Thus in the *Mahābhārata* [2] Sahadeva, the youngest of the Pāṇḍu princes, is represented in his career of conquest to have gone to Dakṣiṇāpatha after having conquered the king of the Pāṇḍyas. In the same way the country of the Pāṇḍyas is mentioned in the *Rāmāyaṇa* where Sugrīva is said to have sent his monkey-soldiers in quest of Sītā, Rāma's consort.[3] In the Purāṇas also as in the case of the

---

[1] *Cambridge History of India*, Vol. I, p. 595.
[2] *Sabhāparvan*, Chap. 31, V. 17.
[3] *Rāmāyaṇa*, IV, Chap. 41.

*Mārkaṇḍeya,*[1] *Vāyu*[2] and *Matsya,*[3] we find mention of the Pāṇḍyas. In Rock Edicts II and XIII, Aśoka mentions the Pāṇḍyas whose territory lay outside his empire. The relations between the Damiḷas and the natives of Ceylon form one of the main strands in the narrative of the *Mahāvaṃsa*. Though on several occasions the Chronicle speaks only of Damiḷas in general, still the distinction between the Pāṇḍya and Cōḷa divisions of the Tamil country is well known and clearly observed in it. A careful study of the Buddhist texts shows that the Damiḷas were a fighting people always engaged in constant strifes with the Ceylonese. They are described as *anāriyā* or uncultured. 'Might is right' was their policy with the result that they were defeated and mercilessly massacred in almost all their battles with the Sinhalese as we find in the *Mahāvaṃsa Commentary* (p. 482). It is only in connection with a particular Damiḷa general named Āriyacakkavattī that we are told that he returned with all booties to the Pāṇḍu country, the land of the Pāṇḍyas in the south. The literary tradition of Ceylon keeps us entirely in the dark as to whether those Damiḷas were sent with expeditions by the king of Pāṇḍu or they were a race of marauders who undertook those expeditions on their own initiative. The account of Vijaya distinctly brings out that there existed a matrimonial alliance between the ruler of Laṅkā and that of Pāṇḍya. It is also mentioned that there was a very early settlement in Ceylon of skilled craftsmen and families of the eighteen guilds, all from Pāṇḍya.[4] There existed similarly a close cultural relationship and constant intercourse between South India and Ceylon; the notable centres of Buddhist learning mentioned in Pāli works being Kāveripaṭṭana, Madhurā, and Kāñcipura.[5]

Strabo (XV, 4, 73) makes mention of an embassy sent to Augustus Caesar about the year 22 B.C. by a king 'Pandion', possibly a Pāṇḍya of the Tamil country.[6] In the *Periplus of the Erythraean Sea*, the Pandian kingdom is mentioned which was included in Damirica.[7] From the Hāthigumphā Inscription of the Cheta king Khāravela of Kaliṅga, it appears that in his eleventh year 'he had had Pithuḍa ploughed with a plough drawn by an ass', and seems to have pushed his conquest further south and made his power felt even by the king of the Pāṇḍya country.[8]

We have very little information regarding the early history of the Pāṇḍya country. Meagre references in the pages of classical

---

1 Chap. 57, V. 45.
2 Chap. 45, V. 124.
3 Chap. 112, V. 46.
4 *Mahāvaṃsa*, Chap. 7.
5 B. C. Law, *Geographical Essays*, Vol. 1, pp. 79-80.
6 *Cambridge History of India*, Vol. I, p. 597.
7 Ray Chaudhuri, *Political History of Ancient India*, 4th Ed., App. E, p. 541.
8 *Ibid.*, 4th Ed., p. 349.

writers like Pliny supplemented by the data collected from ancient Tamil literature are the only materials for a study of their history. From these we can gather that Neḍun-jeliyan II was the first conspicuous Pāṇḍya ruler who made the Pāṇḍyas the leading power of the south. But the supremacy of the south ultimately passed to the Pallavas.

## CHAPTER XLV

# KERALAS OR CHERAS

The Keralaputra (Ketalaputra or Chera) is 'the country south of Kūpaka (or Satya), extending down to Kanneti in Central Travancore (Karunagapalli Taluk). South of it lay the political division of Mūshika'. It was watered by the river Periyār on the banks of which stood its capital Vañji (near Cochin) and at its mouth the seaport of Muziris (Kranganur).[1] According to L. D. Barnett[2] the Chera or Kerala territory comprised Travancore, Cochin and the Malabar District; the Koṅgu-deśa (corresponding to the Coimbatore District and the southern part of Salem District), which at one time was separate from it and later annexed to it. Its capital was originally Vañji (now Tiru-Karūr, on the Periyār river, near Cochin), but later Tiru-Vañjikkalam (near the mouth of the Periyār). It had important trading centres on the western coast at Tondi on the Agalappulai, about five miles north of Quilāndi, Muchiri (near the mouth of the Periyār), Paḷaiyūr (near Chowghāṭ), and Vaikkarai (close to Kottayam).

The three Tamil kingdoms, viz. Cōḷa, Chera and Pāṇḍya, are vaguely mentioned in the Sanskrit Epics and Purāṇas. Thus in the Purāṇas, as Sir R. G. Bhandarkar points out,[3] the term Dakṣiṇāpatha or Dakṣiṇa is used to denote the whole peninsula to the south of the Narmadā. The *Mārkaṇḍeya Purāṇa* (Chap. 57, 45) reads Kevalas. The *Vāyupurāṇa* (XLV, 124) and the *Matsyapurāṇa* (CXIII, 46) as well as the *Bhīṣmaparvan* of the *Mahābhārata* (IX, 352 and 365) give the correct reading Kerala. According to the *Mahābhārata*,[4] the Keralas seem to have been a forest tribe. In historical times they are associated with the Cōḷas and Pāṇḍyas. This is upheld by *Harivaṃśa* as well (XXXII, 1836). The *Mārkaṇḍeya*, *Vāyu* and *Matsya Purāṇas* mention the Cōḷas, Pāṇḍyas and Keralas among the peoples of the Dakṣiṇāpatha. In the *Mārkaṇḍeya Purāṇa*,[5] the reading of the second line, as R. G. Bhandarkar says, is wrong. He gives his reading as follows: 'Pāṇḍyāś ca Keralāścaiva Coḷāḥ Kulyās tathaiva ca'. In the *Rāmāyaṇa*,[6] we read that Sugrīva, the

---

1 *Political History of Ancient India*, 4th Ed., p. 273.
2 *Cambridge History of India*, Vol. I, p. 595.
3 *Early History of the Dekkan*, p. 1.
4 *Sabhāparvan*, XXX, pp. 1174-5.
5 Chap. 57, 45 (ed. *Bibliotheca Indica*).
6 IV, Chap. 41, Bom. Ed.

monkey-king, is described as sending his followers to the different quarters in search of Rāma's wife, Sītā, and Rāvaṇa, her ravisher. The monkey-soldiers are directed to go to the countries of the Andhras (Telugu people), the Pāṇḍyas, the Cōḷas and the Keralas, in the south, and are told that they will there see the gate of the city of the Pāṇḍyas adorned with gold and jewels. In the *Mahābhārata*[1] Sahadeva in his career of conquest is represented to have subdued the Pāṇḍyas, Drāviḍas, Udras, Keralas and Andhras. Patañjali in his *Mahābhāṣya* shows an intimate acquaintance with the south. In *Mahābhāṣya*[2] Kerala (or Malabar) is mentioned. The same work mentions Māhiṣmatī, Vaidarbha and Kāñcīpura (Conjeeveram).[3] In the second and thirteenth rock edicts of Aśoka, the outlying provinces of the Cōḷas, Pāṇḍyas, Satiyaputras, Ketalaputras (Chera or Kerala), and the Andhras and Pulindas are mentioned.

Damirica is shown in the age of the *Periplus* as including Cerobothra (i.e. Keralaputra). During the age of Ptolemy the kingdom of Karoura was ruled by Kerobothros (Keralaputra).

After the Cōḷas, the Cheras for a time became the leading power of the south. After them the Pāṇḍyas became the supreme power for some time in Southern India and then the Pallavas.

1 *Sabhāparvan*, Chap. 31.
2 IV, I, 4th Āhnika.
*Early History of the Dekkan*, p. 7.

## CHAPTER XLVI

# THE MAGADHAS

The Magadhas occupied a prominent position in very ancient times. Though the *Ṛgveda* does not mention them as such, yet Vedic literature generally contains innumerable references to them as a people. In the *Atharvaveda Saṃhitā*,[1] the Māgadha is said to be connected with the Vrātya as his Mitra, his Mantra, his laughter and his thunder in the four quarters. In the *Lāṭyāyana Śrauta Sūtra* [2] (which belongs to a school of the *Sāmaveda*), Vrātya-dhana or the property of the Vrātya is directed to be given either to a bad Brahmin or to a Brahmin of Magadha; but the *Pañcaviṃśa Brāhmaṇa* (XVII, 1, 16), which also belongs to the *Sāmaveda*, does not say anything on the point.

In the *Taittirīya Brāhmaṇa* (III, 4, 1, 1) we read that the people of Magadha were famous for their loud voice. The fact that Māgadha in later times often stands for 'minstrel' is easily accounted for by the assumption that the country was the home of minstrelsy and that wandering bards from Magadha were apt to visit the more western provinces of ancient India. The minstrel character of the Magadhas also appears from the *Mānava Dharmaśāstra* which mentions them as bards and traders.[3] The *Brahmapurāṇa* tells us that the first great Samrāṭ or Emperor Pṛthu gave Magadha to Māgadha, being highly pleased with his song in praise of himself.[4]

The later texts recognise the Māgadhas as a special caste, inventing their origin from intermarriage among the old established castes. In the *Gautama Dharmaśāstra* (IV, 17) and *Manusaṃhitā*,[5] the Māgadha is not a man of Magadha, but a member of a mixed caste produced by the union of a Vaiśya man and a Kṣatriya woman.

In the *Sāṅkhyāyaṇa Āraṇyaka* it is said that Madhyama, son of Prātibodhi, was a resident of Magadha (Magadhavāsin).[6] In the *Āpastamba Śrauta Sūtra* (XXII, 6, 18), the Magadhas are mentioned along with other peoples both of E. and of W. India, viz. the Kāliṅgas, the Gandhāras, the Pāraskaras and the Sauvīras.

---

1 *Harvard Oriental Series*, p. 774.

2 VIII, 6, 28. Cf. *Kātyāyana Śrauta Sūtra*, XXII, 4, 22.

3 *Manusaṃhitā*, X, 47.

4 Chap. IV, śl. 67; *Vāyupurāṇa*, Chap. 62, śl. 147.

5 X, 47.

6 Keith, *Sāṅkhyāyaṇa Āraṇyaka*, p. 46.

They are also mentioned in the *Śatapatha Brāhmaṇa*,[1] where it is said that neither Kośala nor Videha was fully brahmanised at an early date,—much less Magadha.

Coming down to the Epic age, we find the Magadhas frequently mentioned, and much information about the country and the people may be culled from the Great Epics. For instance, the *Rāmāyaṇa* [2] tells us that Vaśiṣṭha asked Sumantra to invite many pious kings, including the Magadhan king, who was well versed in all the śāstras. King Daśaratha tried to appease his irate queen Kaikeyī by offering to present her with 'articles manufactured in Magadha'.[3] The *Kiṣkindhyā Kāṇḍa* [4] informs us that Sugrīva sent monkeys in quest of Sītā to all parts of India, and even beyond its boundaries. Here Magadha is mentioned as one of the countries in the east.

Pargiter has sought to show on the evidence of the Purāṇas that the dynasties of Magadha and the adjoining countries were descended from Kuru's son Sudhanvan. Vasu, the fourth in succession from Sudhanvan, conquered Cedi from the Yādavas, thereby obtaining the title Caidyoparicara, and also annexed the adjoining countries as far as Magadha. When he offered to divide his five territories among his five sons, the eldest son Bṛhadratha took Magadha with Girivraja as its capital and founded the famous Bārhadratha dynasty there.[5] We read in the *Rāmāyaṇa* that 'Vasu, the fourth son of Brahmā, built Girivraja, the ancient capital of Magadha'.[6]

The Purāṇas assert that the successors of Jarāsandha ruled over Magadha for a thousand years. Two of these kings, Kuśāgra and Vṛṣabha, are commemorated in early names of Rājagṛha (Girivraja, Kuśāgra-pura, Vṛṣabha-pura). Ripuñjaya was the last king of this dynasty. He was killed by his minister Sunīka (? Pulika, Muṇika, Suṇaka), who installed his son Pradyota on the throne of Magadha. Five kings of the Pradyota dynasty ruled over Magadha for 138 years, after which the Śiśunāgas came into power.[7] Twelve kings of this dynasty reigned in Magadha for 162 years, Mahānandin being the last king. Mahāpadma Nanda, son of Mahānandin by his Śūdra wife, destroyed the Kṣatriya race and established Śūdra rule in Magadha. Thereafter eight sons of Nanda ruled over Magadha for

[1] I, 4, I, 10.
[2] *Ādi Kāṇḍa*, 13th Sarga.
[3] *Ayodhyā Kāṇḍa*, śl. 37, 10th Sarga.
[4] 48th Sarga, śl. 23.
[5] Pargiter, *Ancient Indian Historical Tradition*, pp. 118, 282.
[6] *Ādi Kāṇḍa*, canto 32, verse 7.
[7] The famous King Bimbisāra is said to have been the fifth of the Śiśunāga line, which was established before 600 B.C.; but the *Mahāvaṃsa* makes Śiśunāga the founder of a dynasty which succeeded that of Bimbisāra.

a hundred years,[1] and then the Nandas were destroyed in their turn by Kauṭilya who installed Candragupta Maurya on the throne. Ten kings of the Maurya dynasty are said to have ruled over Magadha for 137 years. Bṛhadratha was the last king of this dynasty, which was followed by the Śuṅgas, founded by Puṣyamitra. Ten kings of this dynasty ruled for 112 years, Devabhūti being the last monarch of the Śuṅga family; he was killed by Vāsudeva Kāṇva, who founded the Kāṇva dynasty, and four kings of this family ruled in Magadha for 45 years. Then Sipraka, a royal servant, murdered King Suśarman, usurped the throne and founded the Andhra dynasty, thirty kings of which reigned in Magadha for 456 years.[2] The *Viṣṇupurāṇa* gives us a long list of the ancestors of Jarāsandha as well as of the monarchs who succeeded him.[3]

Kālidāsa, who seems to have derived his materials from the Purāṇas and Epics, speaks of the intermarriage of the early kings of Kośala with the ruling family of Magadha. He says that Dilīpa, the father of Raghu, married Sudakṣiṇā, daughter of the king of Magadha.[4] In his beautiful account of the Svayaṃvara of Indumatī, Kālidāsa also refers to the prominent position occupied by the Magadhan king.[5] We have a description of Magadha in the *Daśa-kumāracaritam* of Daṇḍin who belongs to about the same period as Kālidāsa. Daṇḍin there speaks of a monarch, Rājahaṃsa, who was a powerful king of Magadha, and who defeated Mānusāra, king of Mālava.[6] Bhāsa's *Svapnavāsavadattā* also speaks of Magadha and its king, whose daughter Padmāvatī married the king of Vatsa, Udayana.[7]

The *Samantapāsādikā* mentions two other kings of Magadha, viz. Anuruddha, and his son Muṇḍa. The latter is also referred to in the *Aṅguttara Nikāya*. Here we read that King Muṇḍa was overwhelmed with grief at the death of his queen, Bhaddā, and asked his treasurer to embalm her body in an oil pot, so that he might continue to look at her. The treasurer besought Muṇḍa to go to the sage Nārada who was dwelling at the Kukkuṭārāma near Pāṭaligāma

---

[1] Twenty-two years according to the more reliable account of the *Samanta-pāsādikā* (72); cf. *Mahāvaṃsa*, Chap. IV.

[2] *Viṣṇupurāṇa*, IV, 24. The Buddhist *Samantapāsādikā* (Vol. I, pp. 72-3) gives the following summary of Magadhan dynasties. Udaya Bhadda reigned for sixteen years. He was succeeded by Susunāga (i.e. Śiśunāga) who ruled for eighteen years. Then came the Nandas who reigned in Magadha for the same period. The Nanda dynasty was overthrown by Candagutta who ruled the kingdom for twenty-four years, and he was succeeded by Bindusāra who reigned for twenty-eight years, and was succeeded by Aśoka.

[3] *Viṣṇupurāṇa*, IV, Chap. 19, Chap. 23; *Matsyapurāṇa*, Chap. 50, Chap. 271.

[4] *Raghuvaṃśa*, I, 31.

[5] *Ibid.*, VI.

[6] *Saṅkhiptakathā*, Pūrvapīṭhikā, pp. 4-5.

[7] See *Vatsa chapter*.

(later Pāṭaliputra), and listen to his doctrine. Muṇḍa went to Nārada who instructed him and brought him solace. The king then asked his treasurer to burn the dead body of his queen, and thereafter attended to his duties as usual.[1]

Before passing on to a more detailed account of the Magadhan dynasties, it may be as well to summarise what is known of the location of Magadha. According to Parāśara and Varāhamihira, Magadha was situated in the eastern division of the nine portions into which the sub-continent of India was divided.[2] Magadha was bounded by the Ganges on the north, by the district of Benares on the west, by Hiraṇyaparvata or Monghyr on the east, and by Kiraṇa Supavana or Singhbhum on the south. Cunningham infers that in ancient times Magadha must have extended to the Karmanāsā river on the west and to the sources of the Dāmoodar river on the south.[3] Rhys Davids gives as probable boundaries: the Ganges to the north, the Son to the west, the country of Aṅga to the east, and a dense forest reaching the plateau of Chota Nagpur to the south.[4]

Magadha was a narrow strip of country of some considerable length from north to south, and of an area greater than that of Kośala. Just as Kośala corresponded very nearly to the present province of Oudh, but was somewhat larger, so Magadha corresponded at the time of the Buddha to the modern district of Patna, but with the addition of the northern half of the modern district of Gayā. The inhabitants of this region used to call it Magā, a name doubtless derived from Magadha.[5] According to the Siamese and other Buddhist books, as Spence Hardy shows, Magadha or Madhyamaṇḍala was supposed to be situated in the centre of Jambudvīpa. It is generally regarded as answering to Central Bihar. It is called Makata by the Burmese and Siamese, Mo-ki-to by the Chinese and Makala Kokf by the Japanese.[6] All these are no doubt phonetic variations of the name Magadha. Rapson says[7] that Magadha or Southern Bihar comprises the districts of Gayā and Patna; while Dr. H. C. Ray Chaudhuri places Magadha to the west of Aṅga, being separated from the latter kingdom by the river Campā.[8]

One of the earliest and most famous kings of Magadha was Jarāsandha of Epic fame. The *Mahābhārata* speaks of Jarāsandha, son of King Bṛhadratha, as a very great and powerful king of Magadha who reigned in the city of Girivraja or Rājagṛha, 'well guarded by

---

1 *Aṅguttara Nikāya*, III, pp. 57ff.
2 Cunningham, *Ancient Geography*, p. 6.
3 *Ibid.*, pp. 518ff.
4 *Cambridge History of India, Ancient India*, p. 182.
5 *Ibid.*, pp. 182-3.
6 Spence Hardy, *Manual of Buddhism*, p. 140.
7 *Ancient India*, p. 166.
8 *Political History*, p. 53.

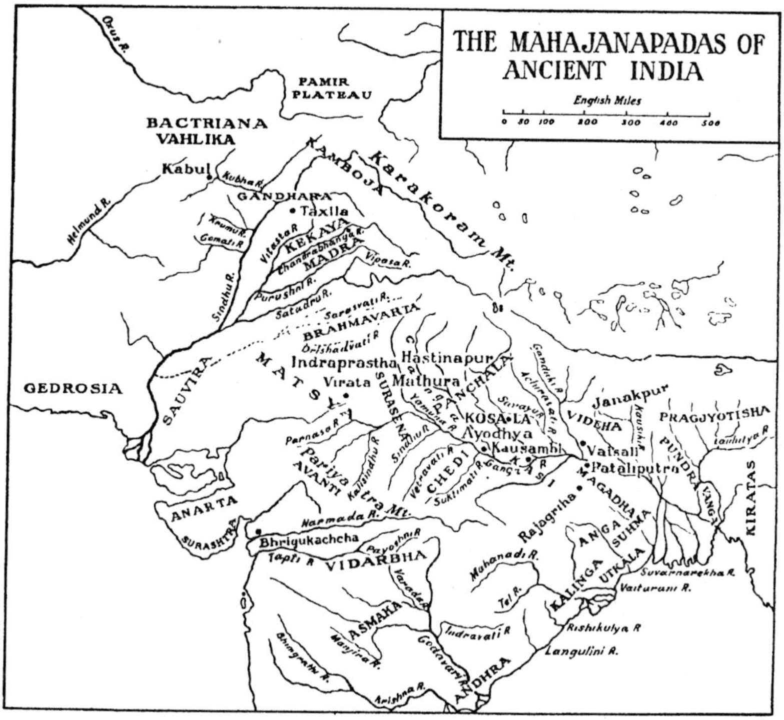


THE MAHAJANAPADAS OF ANCIENT INDIA

mountains on all sides'.[1] One of the ancient names of Rājagṛha was Bārhadrathapura, after Jarāsandha. According to the *Viṣṇu-purāṇa*, Jarāsandha gave his two daughters in marriage to Kaṃsa, king of Mathurā, and when Kaṃsa was killed by Kṛṣṇa, Jarāsandha marched with his army to Mathurā to destroy Kṛṣṇa with all the Yādavas, only to be repulsed with heavy loss.[2] From other sources, however, we learn that Jarāsandha besieged Mathurā with his large army of 23 akṣauhiṇīs, defeated many of the kings of N. India, and kept them imprisoned in Girivraja, it is said in a temple of Śiva, in order to sacrifice them to the god.[3] According to the *Śāntiparvan* of the *Mahābhārata*, Jarāsandha, hearing of the valour of Karṇa, fought with him, but was defeated, and being pleased with his great skill in arms, made him king of the city of Mālinī.[4] In the *Ādiparvan*, Jarāsandha is represented as a reincarnation of Vipracitti, a chief of the demons.[5] Jarāsandha exercised such great power that without defeating him it was not possible for Yudhiṣṭhira to assume the status of a paramount sovereign and perform the Rājasūya sacrifice. The *Bhāgavatapurāṇa* narrates that Bhīma, Arjuna, and Kṛṣṇa went to Girivraja where Bhīma killed Jarāsandha, and Kṛṣṇa made Sahadeva (Jarāsandha's son) king of Magadha, and released all the kings imprisoned by Jarāsandha.[6] The *Sabhāparvan* relates that Bhīma proceeded again to Girivraja where he forced Sahadeva to pay taxes to him; and at the Rājasūya sacrifice, Sahadeva was present as one of the vassals of the Pāṇḍavas.[7] In the Kurukṣetra battle, Dhṛṣṭaketu, son of Jarāsandha, helped the Pāṇḍavas with a fourfold army.[8] After the battle of Kurukṣetra, when the horse let loose at the Aśvamedha sacrifice of Yudhiṣṭhira was proceeding towards Hastināpura, Meghasandhi, son of Sahadeva of Magadha, offered battle to Arjuna, but was defeated by him.[9]

After Ripuñjaya, the last king of Jarāsandha's line, came the Pradyotas, of whom there is not much to relate; and then followed the Śiśunāgas. The Śiśunāga dynasty was established before 600 B.C. (perhaps in 642 B.C.) by a chieftain of Benares named Śiśunāga who fixed his capital at Girivraja or Rājagṛha. Bimbisāra, said to

---

[1] *Sabhāparvan*, Chap. 21.

[2] *Viṣṇupurāṇa*, Aṃśa 5, Chap. 22. The Khila-Harivaṃśa (*Viṣṇuparvan*, Chap. 35, śls. 92ff. and Chap. 36, śl. 40) informs us that Jarāsandha, king of Magadha, killed the horses yoked to the chariot of Balarāma, but was ultimately defeated by the Vṛṣṇis.

[3] *Mahābhārata*, II, 14-5; *Brahmapurāṇa*, Chap. 195, śl. 3.

[4] *Śāntiparvan*, Chap. 5.

[5] *Ādiparvan*, Chap. 67, v. 4.

[6] *Bhāgavatapurāṇa*, Skandha 10, Chap. 72, śls. 16, 46.

[7] *Sabhāparvan*, Chap. 30, v. 18.

[8] *Udyogaparvan*, Chap. 57, v. 8.

[9] *Aśvamedhaparvan*, Chap. 82.

have been the fifth of his line, came to the throne about 528 B.C. The *Mahāvaṃsa*, however, makes Śiśunāga the founder of a dynasty which succeeded that of Bimbisāra; and the Purāṇas are self-contradictory. The first Pradyota, namely, Caṇḍa Pradyota Mahāsena, was a contemporary of Bimbisāra according to the early Pāli texts; but the Purāṇas, as we have seen, make Śiśunāga an ancestor of Bimbisāra.[1] The fact that Vārāṇasī was included within Śiśunāga's dominions[2] supports the view that Śiśunāga came after Bimbisāra and Ajātaśatru, who were the first to establish Magadhan authority in Kāśī. The *Mālālaṃkāravatthu*[3] tells us that Rājagṛha lost its rank as a royal city from the time of Śiśunāga. This also goes to show that Śiśunāga came after the flourishing days of Rājagṛha, i.e. the period of Bimbisāra and Ajātaśatru.

The *Mahāvaṃsa* (Geiger Ed., p. 15) records some facts regarding King Bimbisāra of Magadha, telling us that he was 15 years old when he was anointed king by his father, and that he reigned for 52 years. The father of Bimbisāra was probably Bhaṭṭiya[4] who was defeated by Brahmadatta, king of Aṅga. As we shall see, this defeat was later avenged by Bimbisāra.[5] Dr. Bhandarkar, however, makes Bimbisāra the founder of a dynasty, and says that he was a general who carved out a kingdom for himself at the expense of the Vajjis.[6]

There are several more or less fanciful explanations of Bimbisāra's name. The *Suttanipāta Commentary* relates that he was called Māgadha because he was the lord of the Magadhas. He was the possessor of a large army, hence he was called Seṇiya; and he was called Bimbisāra because his colour was like that of excellent gold.[7] In Rockhill's *Life of the Buddha* (p. 16), it is said that Bimbisāra was so called because he was the son of Bimbi, queen of King Mahāpadma of Rājagṛha. Jaina works represent Bimbisāra as a Jain by religion, and sometimes in Jaina tradition his name is coupled with that of Aśoka's grandson Samprati, as a notable patron of the creed of Mahāvīra.[8] All the Buddhist books, however, represent him as a devoted patron of the Buddha, and a great benefactor of the Buddhist Order.

[1] *Vāyupurāṇa*, 99, 314; Ray Chaudhuri, *Political History of Ancient India*, 4th Ed., p. 98, and his article on *Seṇiya Bimbisāra*, *Ind. Hist. Quar.*, Vol. I, No. 1, March, 1925, p. 87.

[2] *Dynasties of the Kali Age*, p. 21.

[3] S.B.E., XI, p. 16.

[4] *J.A.S.B.*, 1914, 321.

[5] Ray Chaudhuri, *Political History of Ancient India*, 4th Ed., pp. 98-9.

[6] *Carmichael Lectures*, 1918, p. 72.

[7] *Ibid.*, p. 448.

[8] Smith, *Ancient and Hindu India*, p. 45.

Bimbisāra is said to have built the new Rājagṛha, the outer town to the north of the ring of hills encircling the ancient fort. We shall return later to the history of Rājagṛha.

King Bimbisāra annexed Aṅga to his kingdom. Aṅga was a small kingdom to the east, corresponding to the modern district of Bhagalpur and probably including Monghyr.[1] The Jātaka stories contain several references to Aṅga, both as an independent kingdom and as a vassal of Magadha. It is stated in one Jātaka story that at one time the king of Benares conquered Aṅga and Magadha,[2] and in another that the Magadhan kingdom once came under the suzerainty of Aṅga.[3] The *Campeyya Jātaka* records a fight between the two neighbouring countries of Aṅga and Magadha. The river Campā flowed between Aṅga and Magadha, and a Nāga king named Campeyya used to live in that river. From time to time Aṅga and Magadha were engaged in battle. Once the Magadhan king was defeated and pursued by the army of Aṅga, but he escaped by jumping into the river Campā. Again, with the help of the Nāga king, he defeated the king of Aṅga, recovered his lost kingdom, and conquered Aṅga as well. He became intimately associated with the Aṅga king and used to make offerings to him on the bank of the river Campā every year with great pomp.[4]

While this story is evidently fanciful, the *Mahāvagga*[5] offers reasonable evidence to prove that Aṅga came under Bimbisāra's sway, while the *Sonadaṇḍa Suttanta* of the *Dīgha Nikāya*, by mentioning the bestowal of Campā, the capital of Aṅga, as a royal fief on the Brahman Sonadaṇḍa, indirectly proves the same.[6] The Jaina works[7] tell us that a Magadhan prince governed Aṅga as a separate province with Campā as its capital. During Bimbisāra's lifetime, his son Ajātaśatru acted as Viceroy at Campā.

The annexation of Aṅga was the turning point in the history of Magadha. As V. A. Smith says, it marked 'the first step taken by the kingdom of Magadha in its advance to greatness and the position

---

1 Smith, *Early History of India*, 4th Ed., p. 32.

2 *Jātaka* (Fausböll), V, 316.

3 *Ibid.*, VI, 272. See also Ray Chaudhuri, *Political History of Ancient India*, 4th Ed., p. 91.

4 *Jātaka* (Fausböll), IV, pp. 454-5. In the *Mahāvastu* (I, pp. 288ff.) a story is narrated of how once Rājagṛha was suffering from a very severe pestilence. The king sent to the king of Aṅga for a bull with supernatural powers, owing to which the Aṅga kingdom was prosperous and healthy. This bull was lent by the king of Aṅga, and when it was brought within the boundary limits of the Magadhan capital, all pestilences due to attack by superhuman beings vanished.

5 S.B.E., XVII, p. 1.

6 *Dīgha Nikāya*, I, pp. 111ff.

7 Hemchandra, *Sthavīrāvalī-charita*; cf. the *Bhagavatī Sūtra* and the *Nirayāvalī Sūtra*.

of supremacy which it attained in the following century, so that Bimbisāra may be regarded as the real founder of the Magadhan imperial power. He strengthened his position by matrimonial alliances with the two neighbouring states, viz. Kośala and Vaiśālī. He took one consort from the royal family of Kośala and another from the influential Licchavi clan at Vaiśālī'.[1] A third queen of Bimbisāra, as mentioned in the *Therīgāthā Commentary* (p. 131) was Khemā, daughter of the king of Madda (Madra) in the Punjab. According to the Jaina *Nirayāvalīya Sutta*, the mother of Vehalla or Vihalla, one of the sons of Bimbisāra, was a daughter of Ceṭaka, the then king of Videha.[2] There is also mention of Udumbarikā-devī, a royal lady, whose relation with Bimbisāra is not precisely known. The Jātakas tell us that Bimbisāra married Mahākośala's daughter, Kosaladevī, to whom her father gave as a wedding gift a village of Kāśī yielding a revenue of a hundred thousand, for bath and perfume money.[3] The *Mahāvagga* says that Bimbisāra had 500 wives.[4]

Thus the marriages of Bimbisāra paved the way for the expansion of Magadha both westward and northward, and enabled Bimbisāra to add a part of Kāśī to his dominions and to launch Magadha on that career of conquest and aggrandisement which only ended when Aśoka sheathed his sword after the conquest of Kaliṅga.[5]

The *Vinaya Piṭaka* (I, p. 179) tells us that Bimbisāra was the lord of 80,000 villages, and the *Mahāvagga* also states that Bimbisāra's dominions embraced 80,000 townships, the overseers (*Gāmikas*) of which used to meet in a grand assembly.[6]

Bimbisāra had many sons, of whom we know the names of several, viz. Kūṇika Ajātaśatru, Abhaya,[7] Vimala-Koṇḍañña,[8] Vehalla (or Vihalla), Sīlavat, Megha, Halla, and Nandisena.[9] King Bimbisāra's eldest son, Ajātaśatru, murdered his father. Many are the myths surrounding this dreadful deed.[10] Devadatta, the recalcitrant cousin of the Buddha, is said to have performed a miracle and thereby succeeded in persuading Ajātaśatru to become his follower. It was he, it is said, who induced the prince to torture his father to death. During the lifetime of Bimbisāra, Ajātaśatru was made king, but at the instigation of Devadatta, he killed his

---

1 Smith, *Early History of India*, pp. 31-2. See *Licchavi chapter*.
2 *Jaina Sūtras*, I, S.B.E., p. xiii.
3 Nos. 239, 283, 492. See *Kośala and Kāśī chapters*. 4 VIII, 1, 15.
5 Ray Chaudhuri, *Political History of Ancient India*, 4th Ed., pp. 166-7.
6 Cf. *Vinaya Piṭaka*, Pt. II, p. 1. 7 See *Licchavi chapter*.
8 *Psalms of the Sisters*, p. 120; *Psalms of the Brethren*, p. 65.
9 *Jaina Vividha-tīrtha-kalpa*, p. 22.
10 See e.g., *Sumaṅgalavilāsinī*, Pt. I, p. 134.

father by starving him, in spite of the efforts of Queen Kośaladevī to provide her husband with sustenance.

On the day that Bimbisāra died, a son was born to Ajātaśatru. The reports conveying the news of the death of his father and the birth of his child were received by his ministers simultaneously. They first handed to Ajātaśatru the letter conveying the news of the birth of his son. Forthwith the king's mind was filled with filial affection, and all the virtues of his father rose up before his mind's eye, and he at once ordered Bimbisāra's release. But it was too late. The ministers handed him the other letter, and on learning of his father's death, he wept, went to his mother, and asked her whether his father had any affection for him. Kośaladevī told him a story illustrating his father's love for him. Hearing this, Ajātaśatru wept hot tears.[1]

The *Vinaya* (II, 490) gives a short account of an attempt made by Ajātaśatru to kill his father with a sword, and in the concluding portion of the *Sāmaññaphala Sutta*, there is an allusion to the actual murder which he afterwards committed.[2] The details may or may not be true, but the fact that Bimbisāra was put to death by Ajātaśatru appears to have been a historical truth, the tradition is so strong and persistent with regard to this matter. According to the Ceylonese Chroniclers, this event took place 8 years before the death of Buddha, when Bimbisāra had been on the throne for 52 years.[3] According to other accounts, Bimbisāra reigned for 28 or 38 years, and Ajātaśatru for 25 years.[4]

After Bimbisāra's death, Queen Kośaladevī died of grief. Ajātaśatru then began to enjoy the revenues of the Kāśī village, the dowry of his mother. But Pasenadi of Kośala determined that no parricide should possess a village which had been presented to his sister, and he accordingly waged war upon his nephew. Pasenadi was defeated in three campaigns, but in another battle he avenged his defeat, and took possession of Kāśī. However, he treated Ajātaśatru generously, giving him his daughter Vajirā in marriage, and even bestowing the disputed village on her as a wedding gift. Thus Kāśī once again came under the sway of Ajātaśatru, and the two kingdoms of Magadha and Kośala were once more closely united by matrimonial alliance.[5]

Ajātaśatru afterwards succeeded not only in permanently annexing Kāśī, but also in absorbing the land of the Licchavis. At

---

1 *Sumaṅgalavilāsinī*, Pt. I, pp. 138-9.

2 *Dīgha Nikāya*, I, p. 86.

3 *Dīpavaṃsa*, III, 50–60; *Mahāvaṃsa*, II, 28–31.

4 Pargiter, *Purāṇa Text of the Dynasties of the Kali Age*, pp. 67–9.

5 *Saṃyutta Nikāya*, I, 82–5. See *Kāśī and Kośala chapters*, and cf. *Vaḍḍhaki-sūkara*, *Kummāsapiṇḍa*, *Taccha-sūkara* and *Bhaddasāla Jātakas*.

any rate, the Licchavis were obliged to accept Ajātaśatru's suzerainty and to pay him revenue, but they were in all probability independent in their internal politics. Ajātaśatru is said to have made use of two deadly weapons, the Mahāsilākaṇṭaga and the Ra(t)hamusala, in his war with the Licchavis. The first seems to have been some engine of war of the nature of a catapult which hurled big stones. The second was a chariot to which a mace was attached and which, when in motion, effected a great slaughter of men. It may be compared to the modern tank.[1]

Kūṇika Ajātaśatru is represented throughout Jaina literature as a king of Aṅga who reigned in Campā. But the fact is that he was only the *Uparāja* or Viceroy of Aṅga which formed part of the kingdom of Magadha. While Viceroy of Aṅga, Kūṇika-Ajātaśatru picked a quarrel with the Vṛji-Licchavis of Vaiśālī over the possession of a mineral mine on the boundary of the two territories. The Pāli commentatorial tradition indicates that Ajātaśatru was jealous of the Vṛji-Licchavis on account of their national solidarity and numerical strength. Accordingly, after he had ascended the throne of Magadha, he became bent upon destroying them and uprooting their power. He deputed his minister Varṣakāra to wait upon the Buddha and learn his opinion regarding the future of the Vṛjis. On coming to know that the Buddha laid much stress on unity as the source of their national strength, Ajātaśatru employed two of his ministers, Sunīdha and Vassakāra, to build a fort at Pāṭaligāma with a view to repelling the Vṛjis.[2] He also proceeded to weaken them by treacherous means, and eventually succeeded in conquering them.[3]

The *Mahāvaṃsa*[4] assigns a reign of 32 years to Ajātaśatru, while the Vinaya Commentary, *Samantapāsādikā*, puts his reign at 24 years, and the Puranic tradition indicates that he reigned for 25 years.[5] Ajātaśatru suffered the same miserable fate as his father, being put to death by his son Udāyi Bhadda.[6] According to the genealogical lists given in the Purāṇas, Ajātaśatru was succeeded by Darśaka.[7] Bhāsa's *Svapnavāsavadattā* mentions a Magadhan king named Darśaka, but makes no mention of any fact that might lead us to believe that Darśaka was the successor of Ajātaśatru.

---

[1] Ray Chaudhuri, *Political History of Ancient India*, 4th Ed., pp. 172-3.

[2] *Sumaṅgalavilāsinī*, II, pp. 516-7; *Dīgha Nikāya*, II, 87.

[3] For a fuller account, see *Licchavi chapter*.

[4] II, vv. 29, 31, 32.

[5] Pargiter, *Purāṇa Text of the Dynasties of the Kāli Age*, pp. 67–9.

[6] *Mahāvaṃsa*, Chap. IV, v. 1.

[7] Pargiter, *Purāṇa Text of the Dynasties of the Kāli Age*, pp. 67–9. 'Ajātaśatru was followed by Darśaka who reigned for 25 or 27 years. After Darśaka, Udāyin became king and made Kusumapura (Pāṭaliputra) his capital, situated on the south bank of the Ganges.'

Dr. Bhandarkar identifies him with Nāga Dāsaka who is represented by the Ceylonese Chronicles as the last king of Bimbisāra's line. The Pāli Canon and Jaina tradition do not warrant us in holding that Darśaka was the immediate successor of Ajātaśatru. The former asserts that Udāyi Bhadda was the son of Ajātaśatru and probably also his successor, and the latter[1] represents Udāyi as the immediate successor of Kūṇika Ajātaśatru. The Ceylonese Chronicles[2] also inform us that Udāyi Bhadda succeeded his father Ajātaśatru on the throne, and reigned for 16 years. That Udayabhadda or Udāyibhadda was the son and successor of Ajātaśatru is borne out by the *Sāmaññaphala Sutta* of the *Dīgha Nikāya* (I, p. 50), by the *Samantapāsādikā* (p. 72) and the *Sumaṅgalavilāsinī* (Vol. I, pp. 153-4).

Before his accession to the throne, Udāyi Bhadda seems to have acted as his father's Viceroy at Campā.[3] The Jaina work *Pariśiṣṭaparvan* tells us that it was Udāyin who founded on the bank of the Ganges a new capital which came to be known as Pāṭaliputra, though the first beginning of a garrison town appears to have been made during the Buddha's lifetime. The *Vāyupurāṇa* bears testimony to this fact and says that Udaya built the city of Kusumapura in the fourth year of his reign.[4]

The successors of Udāyi Bhadda, according to the Purāṇas, were Nandivardhana and Mahānandin. The Purāṇa account does not tally with the *Samantapāsādikā*[5] which tells us that Udāyi Bhadda was succeeded by his son Anuruddha who reigned for 18 years, and was succeeded by his son Muṇḍa who reigned for the same period. Then came Nāga Dāsaka who reigned for 24 years. Nāga Dāsaka was banished by the citizens who anointed the minister, Śiśunāga, as king. This was probably because the people had become disgusted with the succession of parricides from Ajātaśatru to Nāga Dāsaka. Śiśunāga reigned for 18 years, and was followed by his son Kālāśoka, who reigned for 28 years. Kālāśoka had ten sons who ruled for 22 years.[6]

Then came in succession the nine Nandas who took possession of the throne of Magadha and are said to have reigned for 22 years. According to the Purāṇas, the founder and first king of the Nanda dynasty was Mahāpadma Nanda, son of Mahānandin by a Śūdra woman. He usurped the throne of Magadha in or about 413 B.C.[7]

---

1 Jacobi, *Pariśiṣṭaparvan*, p. 42.

2 *Dīpavaṃsa*, V, 97; *Mahāvaṃsa*, IV, 1.

3 Jacobi, *Pariśiṣṭaparvan*, p. 42.

4 Ray Chaudhuri, *Political History of Ancient India*, 4th Ed., p. 176. Cf. Vincent Smith, *Early History of India*, 4th Ed., pp. 38-9, and *Samantapāsādikā*, pp. 72-3.

5 *Ibid.*, pp. 72-3.

6 Cf. *Dīpavaṃsa*, V.

7 Smith, *Early History of India*, 4th Ed., p. 41.

We learn from Kauṭilya's *Arthaśāstra*, Kāmaṇḍaka's *Nītisāra*, the Purāṇas and the *Mudrārākṣasa* that the Nanda dynasty was overthrown by Candragupta Maurya with the help of his wily and astute minister, Kauṭilya.

Candragupta was the son of the chief queen of the Moriya king of Pipphalivana,[1] and founder of the Imperial Maurya dynasty of Magadha. He was advised by his minister Kauṭilya to seek the help of the Licchavis who were then living under a saṅgha form of government. The Licchavis enjoyed a great deal of independence under Candragupta. It will be remembered that they had been forced by Ajātaśatru to acknowledge the suzerainty of Magadha. Candragupta appears to have liberated the Punjab from foreign rule. He inherited from his Nanda predecessor a huge army which he increased until it numbered 30,000 cavalry, 9,000 elephants, 600,000 infantry, and a multitude of chariots. With this irresistible force, he overran and subdued all the northern States, probably as far south as the Narmadā or even farther.[2] Plutarch [3] tells us that he brought under his sway the whole of India. Justin also says that Candragupta was in possession of India. Vincent Smith states that 'the dominions of Candragupta, the first historical paramount sovereign or emperor in India, extended from the Bay of Bengal to the Arabian Sea'.[4] Justin [5] informs us that while India was under Candragupta, Seleukos (Seleucus), a general of Alexander the Great, made an expedition into India (about 305 B.C.). Appianus says that he crossed the Indus and waged war on Candragupta, king of the Indians, until he made friends and entered into relations of marriage with him.[6] The hosts of Candragupta, however, proved too strong for the invader to overcome, and Seleukos was perforce obliged to retire and to conclude a humiliating peace. This treaty may be dated in or about 303 B.C. It was ratified by a 'matrimonial alliance', which is taken to mean that Seleukos gave a daughter to Candragupta. Seleukos was not only compelled to abandon all thought of conquest in India, but also to surrender a large part of Ariana to the west of the Indus. In exchange for the comparatively trifling equivalent of 500 elephants, Candragupta received the Satrapies of the Paropanisadai, Aria and Arachosia, the capitals of which were known as Kabul, Herat and Kandahar respectively. The Satrapy of Gedrosia with its capital Makran seems also to have been ceded. The inscriptions of Aśoka prove the inclusion of the

---

[1] See *chapter on Bulis, Moriyas, etc.*
[2] Smith, *Early History of India*, 4th Ed., p. 124.
[3] *Alex.*, LXII.
[4] Smith, *op. cit.*, p. 124.
[5] Watson's Ed., p. 143.
[6] *Indian Antiquary*, Vol. VI, p. 114.

Kabul Valley within the Maurya empire. After the war, the Syrian and Indian emperors lived on friendly terms. Seleukos sent an envoy, Megasthenes, to Candragupta's court. Megasthenes stayed at Pāṭaliputra for a considerable time, and wrote a history of India. Unfortunately this work, which would have been invaluable for the ancient history of India, has been lost. The fragments which survive in quotations by later authors such as Strabo and Arrian have been collected by Schwanbeck, and translated by McCrindle.

Great soldier and conqueror as Candragupta admittedly was, he was no less great as an administrator. We have a beautifully complete and detailed account of the system of administration in vogue in his time from the *Arthaśāstra* of Kauṭilya who is generally supposed to have been his chief minister, and the few fragments of Megasthenes which have survived amply corroborate this picture. The edicts of Aśoka again confirm in many respects the particulars of the organisation of the empire given by Kauṭilya and Megasthenes. The supreme government, it appears from Kauṭilya's work, consisted of two main parts: (1) The *rājā*, on the one hand, and (2) the *Mahāmātras*, *Amātyas* or *Sacīvas* (ministers) on the other. At the head of the State was the sovereign (*rājā*) who had military, judicial, and legislative as well as executive functions, but was never the spiritual head. In addition to the *Mantrins*, there was the *Mantripariṣad* or Assembly of Imperial Councillors. In several passages of the *Arthaśāstra*, the *Mantrins* are sharply distinguished from the *Mantripariṣad*. The members making up the latter body evidently occupied an inferior position, their salary being 12,000 *paṇas*, while that of a *Mantrin* was 48,000 *paṇas*.[1]

Kauṭilya's *Arthaśāstra* has been so largely utilised by scholars that any attempt to present anew an account of Candragupta's government would be futile and a mere repetition of what has already been said on the subject. The *Early History of India*[2] and the *Political History of Ancient India*[3] give us a systematic and critical account of the government of the great Maurya Emperor, while Jayaswal's work on Hindu Polity illuminates many obscure points of ancient Indian statecraft and administration.

Historians differ in presenting an account of the last days of Candragupta. According to Jain tradition, Candragupta abdicated the throne and became a Jain ascetic. He is said to have repaired to Mysore, where he died.[4] According to Vincent Smith, 'Chandragupta either abdicated or died in the year 298 B.C.'.[5]

---

[1] Ray Chaudhuri, *Political History of Ancient India*, 4th Ed., p. 230.
[2] By Vincent Smith. [3] By Hemchandra Ray Chaudhuri.
[4] Rice, *Mysore and Coorg from Inscriptions*, pp. 3-4.
[5] V. Smith, *Early History of India*, 4th Ed., p. 126.

Candragupta was succeeded by his son Bindusāra, surnamed Amitraghāta (slayer of foes),—an epithet which is quoted, perhaps with reference to this king, in the grammatical work of Patañjali.[1] It is uncertain whether Bindusāra earned, or merely assumed, his sobriquet. The Purāṇas attribute to Bindusāra a reign of 25 years, and the Ceylonese Chroniclers a reign of 28 years. The *Samantapāsādikā*,[2] on the other hand, says that he ruled for 18 years only. According to Smith's chronology, Bindusāra's reign terminated about 273 B.C.[3] The *Divyāvadāna*[4] tells us that Taxila revolted during his reign, and that he sent his son Aśoka to quell the rebellion. When the prince approached Taxila with his troops, all disturbance was allayed. The people came out to meet him and said: 'We are not opposed to the prince, nor even to King Bindusāra, but the wicked ministers insult us.' Aśoka alludes to the high-handedness of the Maurya officials in his Kaliṅga Edict.[5] Nothing of political importance is known to have happened during Bindusāra's reign, but it is clear that he maintained intact the dominions inherited from Candragupta. The friendly relations between India and the Hellenistic powers, which had been initiated by his father Candragupta and the Greek empire-builder Seleukos, continued unbroken throughout his reign.[6]

Bindusāra was succeeded by his son Aśoka, who is said to have won undivided sovereignty over all Jambudvīpa after slaying all his brothers except the youngest, Tissa. Aśoka reigned without coronation for four years,[7] and then consecrated himself as king in the city of Pāṭaliputra.[8] He assumed the title of *Devānampiya*[9] ('dear to the gods'), and loved to speak of himself as *Devānampiyadasi*. The name Aśoka is found only in literature, and in two inscriptions, viz. the Maski Edict of Aśoka himself, and the Junāgaḍh Inscription of the Mahākṣatrapa Rudradāman. Aśoka was at first called Caṇḍāsoka on account of his evil deeds, but he later became known as Dhammāsoka on account of his meritorious deeds.[10] The Sarnath Inscription of Kumāradevī mentions the name Dharmāśoka.

During the first thirteen years of his reign, Aśoka appears to have followed the traditional Maurya policy of expansion within India and of friendly co-operation with foreign powers. In the thirteenth year of his reign, he conquered the kingdom of the Three Kaliṅgas or Kaliṅga, and annexed it to his empire. The annexation of Kaliṅga, like that of Aṅga by Bimbisāra, was a great landmark

[1] *Mahābhāṣya*, III, 2, 88. [2] Vol. I, p. 73. [3] *Aśoka*, p. 73.
[4] *Ibid.*, pp. 371-2. [5] *Ibid.*, 3rd Ed., pp. 194-5.
[6] Smith, *Early History of India*, 4th Ed., pp. 156 foll.
[7] *Samantapāsādikā*, I, p. 41. *Cattāri vassāni anabhisitto'va rajjaṃ kāretvā.*
[8] Smith, Aśoka, p. 232. [9] Cf. Rock Edicts. [10] *Mahāvaṃsa*, Chap. V.

in the history of Magadha and of India. But the unavoidably heavy loss of life and property involved in the conquest of Kaliṅga made a deep impression on Aśoka and awakened in him feelings of profound compunction and sorrow. About this time he appears to have come under the influence of Buddhist teachers. This opened a new era—an era of peace and kindness to all animate beings, of social progress, of religious propaganda, and it marked the close of a career of conquest and aggression. 'The martial spirit of Magadha began to die out for want of exercise.' Thus came to an end the era of political '*digvijaya*' begun by his mighty grandfather, giving place to the sacred 'era of *Dhammavijaya*' or conquest by the spiritual force of non-violence. Aśoka's change of religion after the Kaliṅga war resulted in a change of the monarch's internal as well as foreign policy. He maintained friendly relations with the S. Indian and Hellenistic powers. He renounced once for all the old policy of violence, of conquering peoples, suppressing revolt by force and annexing territory. In Edict IV he says with a spirit of exultation: 'the reverberation of the war drums (*Bherīghoṣo*) has become the reverberation of the Law (*Dhammaghoṣo*)'. He called upon his future successors—sons and grandsons—to shun new conquests. This change of policy darkened the political horizon of the Magadhan empire in its heyday. Magadha which, before Bimbisāra was merely a tiny State in South Bihar, had, during the interval from the time of Bimbisāra to the Kaliṅga war of Aśoka, expanded to a gigantic empire from the foot of the Hindu Kush to the borders of the Tamil country. After the Kaliṅga war, the political destiny of Magadha was reversed. The empire gradually became smaller and smaller till it sank to its pre-Bimbisarian area and position.

At one time King Bindusāra used to give alms to 60,000 Brahmins and heretics. Aśoka also followed his father for some time in making donations to non-Buddhist ascetics and institutions. But becoming displeased with them he stopped further charities to them and gave charities to the Buddhist bhikkhus.[1] Aśoka sent missionaries all over India and also to Ceylon to preach the Buddhist *dhamma*. Almost all of these missionaries were natives of Magadha.[2]

Aśoka continued the Council Government of his predecessors. The inscriptions bear ample testimony to the fact that he also retained the system of provincial administration in vogue under his forefathers. The emperor, and the princes who often acted as Viceroys in charge of the provinces, were helped by a number of officials who, according to the Edicts, may be classed as (1) The *Mahāmātras*,

---

[1] *Samantapāsādikā*, I, p. 44.

[2] *Ibid.*, I, p. 63.

(2) The *Rājūkas*, (3) The *Prādeśikas*, (4) The *Yutas* (the *Yuktas* of the *Arthaśāstra*, p. 59), (5) *Pulisā* (*Purushas*), (6) *Paṭivedakā* (*Prativedakas*), and (7) *Vachabhumikā* (*Vrajabhūmikas*).[1]

Aśoka was succeeded by Daśaratha who was followed by a succession of weak Maurya kings who had only a vestige of the great power that Aśoka wielded. Bṛhadratha, the last of the Maurya dynasty, was treacherously murdered by his commander-in-chief, Puṣyamitra Śuṅga, who established himself upon the throne of his master and set up the Śuṅga dynasty. The *Divyāvadāna* (p. 434) tells us that the emperor continued to reside in Pāṭaliputra. Puṣyamitra ruled over Magadha for thirty-six years from about 185 to 149 B.C. During his reign the *Mantripariṣad* (Assembly of Councillors) continued to be an important element of the governmental machinery. The viceregal princes were assisted by *pariṣads*.[2] The historical events worth mentioning during Puṣyamitra's reign were the Vidarbha war and the Greek invasion. The former resulted in the splitting up of the kingdom of Vidarbha into two States, between which the river Varadā formed the boundary. The latter is referred to in Patañjali's *Mahābhāṣya* and Kālidāsa's *Mālavikāgnimitra*. Unfortunately, the name of the Greek invader is not given in either of these works. Historians differ as to the identity of the invader, but they agree that he was a Bactrian Greek. Dr. Ray Chaudhuri[3] adduces strong evidence to identify Demetrius with the Yavana invader referred to by Patañjali and Kālidāsa. Puṣyamitra died in or about 149 B.C., as the Purāṇas affirm. He was followed by nine kings who ruled for 76 years. The Śuṅga dynasty probably lasted for 112 years. The last of the Śuṅga monarchs was Devabhūti who was a young and dissolute prince. The Purāṇas state that he was overthrown by his Minister, Vāsudeva Kāṇva. Rapson[4] says that the Śuṅgas were a military power, but in later times they became puppets in the hands of their Brahmin councillors. They probably ruled originally as feudatories of the Mauryas at Vidiśā, the modern Besnagar, on the Vetravatī (Betwa) near Bhīlsā, and about 120 miles east of Ujjain. The Śuṅga dynasty probably came to an end about 73 B.C., and was succeeded by the Kāṇva dynasty which lasted till 27 B.C., when the Andhras came into power. For some time, Pāṭaliputra may have acknowledged their supremacy, but later on, it must have re-asserted its independence. After the period of the Andhras, the history of Pāṭaliputra passes into oblivion.

[1] For a full account of this reign, see Vincent Smith's *Aśoka*.
[2] Ray Chaudhuri, *Political History of Ancient India*, 4th Ed., pp. 324-5.
[3] *Ibid.*, pp. 308ff.
[4] *Cambridge History of India*, Chap. XXI, pp. 522-3.

At the beginning of the fourth century A.D. the Magadhan monarchy again rose into prominence under the Guptas. I-tsing mentions a king Mahārājā Śrīgupta of Magadha who may be placed in about the second century A.D. (175 A.D.). But the first independent sovereign (Mahārājādhirāja) was Candragupta, son of Mahārāja Ghaṭotkacha Gupta, and grandson of Mahārāja Gupta. Candragupta ascended the throne in 320 A.D., the initial date of the Gupta era. Like Bimbisāra he strengthened his position by a matrimonial alliance with the Licchavis of Vaiśālī, who appear to have continued to occupy an influential position in N. India, though for a time their glory was eclipsed by the rising State of Magadha. The union of Candragupta I with the Licchavis is commemorated by a series of coins, and by the Allahabad inscription. Through his Licchavi connection, Candragupta was elevated from the rank of a local chief, and he proceeded to lay the foundations of the second Magadhan empire.

His son and successor Samudragupta often felt pride in describing himself as the son of the daughter of the Licchavis. Before his death, Candragupta selected Samudragupta, his son by the Licchavi princess, as his successor. It is clear from the Allahabad *praśasti* and from the epithet '*tatpādaparigṛhīta*' applied to Samudragupta in other inscriptions that the prince was selected by Candragupta I from among his sons, as the best fitted to succeed him. It was the aim of Samudragupta to bring about the political unification of India and to make himself an *Ekarāṭ* (sole sovereign) over this united empire; but his only permanent annexation was that of portions of Āryāvarta, the Gangetic plain.[1] Samudragupta made the rulers of the Āṭavika *rājyas* ('forest kingdoms') his servants, led an expedition to the south, and made his power felt by the powerful rulers of the Eastern Deccan. Here he defeated the kings, but following the pre-Mauryan Hindu policy he did not annex their territory. According to Dr. Fleet,[2] the Āṭavika *rājyas* were closely connected with Dabhāla, i.e. the Jabbalpur region.[3] The Eran inscription of Samudragupta bears testimony to the conquest of this region and to the fact that the Vākāṭakas of the Western Deccan were deprived of their possessions in Central India by the Emperor.[4] The kings (mostly of Dakṣiṇāpatha) who came into conflict with the great Gupta conqueror were Mahendra of Kośala, Vyāghrarāja of Mahākāntāra, Maṇṭarāja of Kaurāla, Svāmidatta of

[1] Ray Chaudhuri, *Political History of Ancient India*, 4th Ed., p. 447.
[2] *Corpus Inscriptionum Indicarum*, Vol. III, p. 114.
[3] *Epigraphia Indica*, VIII, pp. 284–7.
[4] Ray Chaudhuri, *Political History of Ancient India*, 4th Ed., pp. 455-6.

Piṣṭapura and of Koṭṭūra of Mahendragiri, Damana of Eraṇḍapalla, Viṣṇugopa of Kāñcī, Nīlarāja of Avamukta, Hastivarman of Veṅgī, Ugrasena of Palakka, Kuvera of Devarāṣṭra, and Dhanañjaya of Kusthalapura.[1] The tribal States of the Punjab, W. India and Malwa are also said to have obeyed his compelling mandate or decree (pracaṇḍa-śāsana) 'by giving all kinds of taxes, obeying his orders and coming to perform obeisance'. The most important among the eastern kingdoms which submitted to the mighty Gupta emperor were Samataṭa (part of E. Bengal bordering on the sea), Davāka (not yet satisfactorily identified) and Kāmarūpa (in Assam).[2] The Dāmodarpur plates inform us that Puṇḍravardhana or N. Bengal formed an integral part of the Gupta empire and was governed by a line of Uparika Mahārājas as vassals of the Gupta emperor. The dominion under the direct government of Samudragupta in the middle of the fourth century comprised all the most populous and fertile provinces of N. India. It extended from the Brahmaputra on the east to the Jumna and Chambal on the west, and from the foot of the Himalayas on the north to the Narmadā on the south. Beyond these wide limits, the frontier kingdoms of Assam and the Gangetic delta, as well as those on the southern slopes of the Himalayas, and the free tribes of Rājputāna and Mālwā, were attached to the empire by bonds of subordinate alliance; while almost all the kingdoms of the south had been overrun by the emperor's armies and compelled to acknowledge his irresistible might.[3]

The exact year of Samudragupta's death is not yet ascertainable. Dr. Ray Chaudhuri states[4] that he died some time after 375 A.D. He was succeeded by his son Candragupta II (born of Queen Dattadevī), who assumed the title of Vikramāditya ('Sun of Power'). He was also called Siṃhacandra and Siṃha Vikrama. Certain Vākāṭaka inscriptions and the Sāñchi inscription of 412 A.D. call him Devagupta or Devarāja.[5]

The greatest military achievement of Candragupta Vikramāditya was his advance to the Arabian Sea through Malwa and Gujarat, and his subjugation of the peninsula of Surāṣṭra or Kathiawaḍ, governed for centuries by rulers known as Śaka Satraps.[6] As a result of the western expedition, Malwa and Surāṣṭra were added to the Gupta dominions. Another event of political importance was the Emperor's matrimonial alliance with

---

[1] Ray Chaudhuri, *Political History of Ancient India*, 4th Ed., p. 452.
[2] Ibid., p. 456. [3] Smith, *Early History of India*, 4th Ed., p. 303.
[4] *Political History of Ancient India*, 4th Ed., p. 464.
[5] *Indian Antiquary*, 1913, p. 160.
[6] Smith, *Early History of India*, 4th Ed., p. 307.

the Vākāṭaka king of the Deccan, by the marriage of the Emperor's daughter Prabhāvatī with King Rudrasena II, son of Pṛthivīsena I. The original capital of Magadha under Candragupta II was Pāṭaliputra, but after his western conquests, Ujjain was made a second capital. Smith says: 'Ajodhyā enjoyed a more favourable situation and appears to have been at times the headquarters of the government of both Samudragupta and his son. the latter of whom probably had a mint for copper coins there. There is reason to believe that during the fifth century Ajodhyā rather than Pāṭaliputra, was the premier city of the Gupta empire.' [1]

Detailed information regarding the administrative history of the Magadhan empire under Candragupta II is not available, but the narrative of Fā-Hien and the inscriptions that have hitherto been discovered throw much light on the character of his administration, and on the social and religious condition of India at the time.

The Rājā was the head of the State. He was apparently nominated by his predecessor, both primogeniture and capacity being taken into consideration. A body of high ministers whose office was very often hereditary used to assist him. There was no distinction between civil and military officials.

After Candragupta II, the Gupta power in Magadha was temporarily eclipsed by the Puṣyamitras.[2] Then followed the Hūna invasion, in which the Emperor Skandagupta, according to Dr. Ray Chaudhuri,[3] was presumably victorious, and, according to Smith,[4] was unable to continue the successful resistance which he had offered in the earlier days of his rule, and was forced at last to succumb to the repeated attacks of the foreigners.

But the Magadhan empire did not wholly perish on the death of Skandagupta. It was ruled by Puragupta, Narasiṃhagupta, Kumāragupta II, and Buddhagupta.

Then the imperial line passed on to a dynasty of eleven Gupta princes known as the 'later Gupta monarchs of Magadha'. The Damodarpur plates, Sarnath inscriptions, the Erāṇ epigraph of Buddhagupta, and the Betul plates of the Parivrājaka Mahārāja Saṃkṣobha, dated in the year 518 A.D., testify to the fact that the Gupta empire continued to exert sovereign rights in the latter half of the fifth as well as the sixth and seventh centuries A.D.

In the first half of the seventh century, Harṣa, the great Kanouj monarch, overshadowed the Gupta power, which was revived by Ādityasena, who assumed the titles of Paramabhaṭṭakāra

---

[1] Smith, *Early History of India*, 4th Ed., p. 310.

[2] Ray Chaudhuri, *Political History of Ancient India*, 4th Ed., p. 478.

[3] *Ibid.*, p. 488.

[4] *Early History of India*, 4th Ed., p. 328.

and Mahārājādhirāja. Ādityasena and his successors, as proved by Aphsaḍ and Deo-Baraṇark inscriptions, were the only N. Indian sovereigns who laid claim to the imperial dignity during the last quarter of the seventh century A.D., and appear actually to have dominated Magadha and Madhyadeśa. The last king of the line of Ādityasena was Jīvitagupta II, who reigned early in the eighth century A.D.

About this time, the throne of Magadha was occupied by a Gauḍa king named Gopāla, as the Pāla inscriptions seem to indicate.[1] Then the great Magadhan empire decayed politically, being included in the Gauḍa empire of the Pālas and Senas, but it continued to remain the centre and headquarters of Buddhist learning up to the time of the Muhammadan conquests at the close of the twelfth century, when the monasteries with their well-stocked libraries were reduced to ashes.[2]

Magadha and its ancient capital Rājagṛha were intimately associated with the Buddha. Magadha was the scene of the real birth of Buddhism.[3] The Buddha's chief disciples, Sāriputta and Moggallāna, were natives of Magadha, and it was at Rājagṛha that they were converted by the Buddha.[4] Their conversion, and the consequent desertion of the school of Sañjaya the Wanderer, must have created a sensation among the citizens of Rājagṛha.[5] Another notable conversion was that of Mahākāśyapa, who formerly belonged to another religious sect. Persons of many well-known families either became monks or lay supporters of the new doctrine. For want of accommodation in Veṇuvana, the bhikkhus passed the night in grottoes and caverns of the hills surrounding the city. This induced Anāthapiṇḍika, the great banker of Rājagṛha, to undertake, with the permission of the Buddha, to build some 60 vihāras for them.

Rājagṛha was the first place visited by the Bodhisattva after his adoption of ascetic life at Anupiyā in the Malla territory. It was here that he begged his food from door to door for the first time.[6] It was somewhere in Magadha, between Rājagṛha and Uruvelā, that he met and placed himself under the training of Ārāḍa Kālāma and Udra Rāmaputra in the method of Yoga.[7] He

[1] *Early History of India*, 4th Ed., p. 413.
[2] Smith, *Early History of India*, 4th Ed., p. 420.
[3] Malalasekera, *Pāli Proper Names Dicty.*, II, s.v. *Magadha.*
[4] *Kathāvatthu*, I, 97; *Vinaya Piṭaka*, I, 37ff.
[5] *Vinaya*, *Cullavagga*, p. 14.
[6] *Suttanipāta*, pp. 72ff.; Fausböll, *Jātaka*, I, pp. 65ff.
[7] *Majjhima Nikāya*, I, pp. 163ff.; *Mahāvastu*, II, 118; III, 322; *Lalitavistara*, VII, v. 54; Fausböll, *Jātaka*, I, pp. 66ff.

eventually selected Uruvelā in Magadha as the most fitting place for meditation and the attainment of enlightenment. Shortly after his attainment of Buddhahood, it was suggested to him that his primary task was the reformation of the religions of Magadha, which had all become corrupt.[1]

A notable triumph of the Buddha in Magadha was the conversion of the three great leaders of the Jaṭilas with their thousand followers. With all these new converts, he proceeded towards Rājagṛha and halted on the way at Laṭṭhi or Yaṣṭi-vana, a beautiful palm-grove belonging to King Bimbisāra. He was received with ovations by all the citizens of Rājagṛha and the inhabitants of Aṅga-Magadha, headed by King Bimbisāra.[2]

The conversion of the king (who was the Buddha's junior in age by five years) to the new faith proved a great incentive to the people at large to welcome it. King Bimbisāra made a gift of his bamboo grove, Veluvana-Kalandaka-Nivāpa to the Buddha and his disciples.[3] With the formation of the order of Bhikkhuṇīs at Vaiśālī, many women of Rājagṛha, headed by Kṣemā, the gifted queen of Bimbisāra, joined the Order.[4] Bhaddā Kuṇḍalakesī, who was converted by the Buddha, went to Magadha after she became a therī, and lived in Gijjhakūṭa for some time.[5] Therī Cālā was born in Magadha at Nālakagāma, in an influential Brahmin family. She, Upacālā, and Sisupacālā were the sisters of Sāriputta. They obtained ordination from the Buddha when they learnt that Sāriputta had been ordained.[6] Other Magadhan ladies who entered the order were Mettikā and Subhā, the daughters of an eminent Brahmin of Rājagṛha,[7] Dhammadinnā,[8] Cittā,[9] and Subhā, a goldsmith's daughter.[10]

The *Theragāthā* records the influence of the Buddha's teachings. For instance, once the Buddha gave instruction to Visākha, the son of a rājā in Magadha, and as a result Visākha renounced the world.[11] The *Divyāvadāna*[12] gives an account of a journey from Śrāvastī to Rājagṛha, which was undertaken by the Buddha and his monks. In the course of this journey, the Buddha six times saved some merchants of Śrāvastī from being robbed. Velaṭṭha Kaccāna was another trader who, on his way to Rājagṛha from Andhakavindha,

1 *Majjhima Nikāya*, I, p. 168; *Vinaya, Mahāvagga*, p. 5.
2 Watters, *On Yuan Chwang*, II, p. 146; *Mahāvastu*, III, 441ff.
3 *Vinaya, Mahāvagga*, p. 39; Fausböll, *Jātaka*, I, p. 85.
4 *Therīgāthā Comm.*, pp. 127-8.
5 *Ibid.*, pp. 106-7.
6 *Ibid.*, pp. 162-3.
7 *Therīgāthā*, pp. 28 and 148.
8 *Ibid.*, p. 16.
9 *Ibid.*, p. 27.
10 *Ibid.*, p. 142.
11 *Psalms of the Brethren*, p. 152.
12 pp. 55, 94-5.

met the Buddha and his pupils, and offered each bhikkhu a pot of molasses.[1]

The *Dīgha Nikāya*[2] narrates that at Rājagṛha the Buddha summoned all the bhikkhus and prescribed several sets of seven conditions of welfare for the Saṅgha. Once the Buddha, while sojourning amongst the Magadhas, went to a Brahmin village named Khānumata, and took up his abode in the Ambalaṭṭhikā grove (mango-grove). An influential Brahmin named Kūṭadanta, the owner of the village, together with many Brahmin householders, was converted to the Buddhist faith after conversing with the Buddha.[3]

The Pāli Texts abound with references to the Buddha's experience and converts in Magadha, and especially at Rājagṛha.[4] One of the best-known stories is that of the Buddha and Bharadvāja, the Brahmin ploughman of Ekanālā, a Magadhan village.[5] The *Dīgha Nikāya* and *Sumaṅgalavilāsinī* give a beautiful account of the visit paid to the Buddha by the parricide monarch of Magadha, Ajātaśatru. Territorial expansion could not satisfy Ajātaśatru or bring peace to his perturbed mind. After murdering his father he could not sleep soundly, but dreamed dreadful dreams; and he devised various means of spending the night without sleep. On one occasion, the whole of Rājagṛha was illumined and decorated and was full of festivities and enjoyments. Ajātaśatru with his ministers went on the terrace and saw the festivities going on in the city, so that he might not fall asleep. The moon-lit night by its soft beauty elevated his soul, and the thought arose within him of approaching a 'Samaṇa or Brāhmaṇa' who could bring solace to his tortured mind.[6] Hearing of the great virtues of the Buddha from Jīvaka, the greatest physician of the day, Ajātaśatru came to the mango-grove where the Buddha was staying,[7] and asked whether he could show him the effect of leading the life of a Samaṇa. The Buddha did so by delivering to the repentant king a discourse on various virtues of the ascetic life as narrated in the *Sāmaññaphala Suttanta* of the *Dīgha Nikāya*.[8]

---

1 *Vinaya Piṭaka*, I, pp. 224-5.

2 II, pp. 76–81.

3 *Dīgha Nikāya*, I, pp. 127ff.

4 See, e.g. *Dīgha Nikāya*, I, pp. 150ff.; II, pp. 202-3, 218; III, pp. 36ff., 58, 99, 194ff.; *Saṃyutta Nikāya*, I, pp. 8ff., 27-8, 52, 55, 65–7, 106-7, 160–4, 166-7, 185ff.; *Aṅguttara Nikāya*, II, pp. 29-30, 181-2; II, pp. 366ff., 374ff., 383ff.; *Majjhima Nikāya*, III, 237ff.; *Jātaka*, I, 65-6, 86, 156.

5 *Saṃyutta Nikāya*, I, pp. 172-3; *Suttanipāta*, I, 3.

6 *Sumaṅgalavilāsinī*, I, 141-2.

7 *Ibid.*, I, 151-2.

8 *Ibid.*, I, pp. 158ff. See also *Dīgha Nikāya*, I, 47ff.

Once Vassakāra (later the chief minister of Ajātaśatru) began the work of repairing the fort at Rājagṛha. He needed timber for the purpose, and went to the reserved forest, but was informed that the wood was taken by a bhikkhu named Dhaniya. Vassakāra complained to King Bimbisāra, and the incident was brought to the notice of the Buddha who ordered the bhikkhus not to take anything which was not offered or presented to them.[1]

The Buddha passed away in the eighth year of Ajātaśatru's reign.[2] It was from Rājagṛha that he started on his last journey to Kuśīnārā, stopping on the way at Ambalaṭṭhikā, Nālandā and Pāṭaligāma, and delivering fruitful discourses to all who came in contact with him.[3] After the Buddha's *parinirvāṇa*, his relics were distributed among various clans. Ajātaśatru obtained a share and enshrined it with great respect and honour, instituting a worship of the relics on a grand scale.[4] He built Dhātu Caityas all round Rājagṛha, his capital,[5] and at his own cost repaired 18 *mahāvihāras* at Rājagṛha which had been deserted by the bhikkhus after the Buddha's death.[6] The bhikkhus headed by Mahākassapa performed the funeral ceremony of the Buddha, and resolved to hold a council at Rājagṛha.[7] Accordingly, Rājagṛha is famous in the history of Buddhism as the place where 500 distinguished theras met under the leadership of the Venerable Mahākassapa to recite the doctrine and discipline of the Buddha, and fix the Buddhist canon.[8] All later traditions, whether in Pāli or Sanskrit, tell us that the First Council was convoked in front of the Saptaparṇī or Saptaparṇa cave on a slope of the Vaibhāra or Vaihāra hill, and under the auspices of king Ajātaśatru, who constructed a suitable *maṇḍapa* (tent) for the purpose; but the Vinaya account distinctly says that the main reason for selecting Rājagṛha for the purpose was that it could afford spacious accommodation for the 500 theras.

The shady slopes and caverns of the hills around Rājagṛha were fitting places for the lonely meditation of bhikkhus and bhikkhuṇīs, theras and therīs. The sombre beauty of the hills and the retreats was much praised by the Buddha.[9]

The *Vimānavatthu Commentary* points out that Rājagṛha was much frequented by Gautama Buddha and his disciples. The people of Rājagṛha were always ready to satisfy the needs of the

[1] *Vinaya Piṭaka*, III, pp. 41–5.
[2] *Samantapāsādikā*, I, p. 72.
[3] *Dīgha Nikāya*, II, pp. 72–89.
[4] *Paramatthadīpanī on the Petavatthu*, p. 212.
[5] *Mahāvaṃsa*, p. 247. *Ekatiṃsatimoparicchedo*, v. 21.
[6] *Samantapāsādikā*, I, pp. 9-10.
[7] *Mahāvaṃsa*, Chap. 3, pp. 16 foll.
[8] *Vinaya Cullavagga*, XI.
[9] *Dīgha Nikāya*, II, p. 116.

bhikkhus.[1] Buddhaghosa records various facts about Rājagṛha. For instance, two chief disciples of the Buddha went to the city, and the inhabitants showered charities upon them. A silk robe was also given in charity to Devadatta (the Buddha's wicked cousin).[2] The *Samantapāsādikā* records that Rājagṛha was a good place, having accommodation for a large number of bhikkhus.[3] We may also mention two Jātaka references to legends regarding Rājagṛha.[4]

It is not possible to refer to all of the stories told of the Buddha's disciples and their connection with Magadha, and particularly Rājagṛha. We have already mentioned the fact that Sāriputta was a native of Magadha; he is often referred to in the Pāli literature.[5] It was at Rājagṛha that Anāthapiṇḍika, the great banker of Śrāvastī, was converted by the Buddha.[6] The *Manorathapūraṇī* relates that Piṇḍola Bharadvāja, one of the Buddha's foremost disciples, was born at Rājagṛha in a rich Brahmin family.[7] It further narrates that Cullapanthaka and Mahāpanthaka, grandsons of Dhanaseṭṭhi, a banker of Rājagṛha, could by their supernatural power create as many bodies as they liked.[8] Kumārakassapa, foremost of the orators amongst the Buddha's pupils, was born at Rājagṛha.[9] While the Buddha was at Rājagṛha at Kalandakanivāpa, a party of six bhikkhuṇīs went to attend the Giraggasamajja, a kind of festival.[10] Apparently such festivals were common in the Magadhan capital, for we read in the *Jātaka* (I, 489) that there was a festival at Rājagṛha where people drank wine, ate flesh, danced and sang; and in the *Visuddhimagga*[11] we read of a festival at Rājagṛha in which five hundred virgins offered Mahākassapa-thera a kind of cake which he accepted. Another celebration known as Nakkhattakīḷam, 'sport of the stars', in which the rich took part, used to be held at Rājagṛha, and lasted a week.[12]

The *Divyāvadāna* contains several stories about Rājagṛha. For instance, a householder went to sea with merchandise[13]; on another occasion 500 merchants came to Rājagṛha, but could not buy merchandise as there was a festival going on at the time.[14] Once a childless merchant of Rājagṛha died. The inhabitants of the town put seeds of various colours into a pot and declared that the

[1] *Vimānavatthu Comm.*, pp. 250-1; and see *ibid.*, pp. 246-7, 27-8.
[2] *Dhammapada Comm.*, I, pp. 77ff.
[3] Vol. I, P.T.S., pp. 8-9.
[4] *Jātaka* (Fausböll), No. 445, IV, pp. 37 foll., No. 311, IV, pp. 33 foll.
[5] See, e.g. *Aṅguttara Nikāya*, V, pp. 120-1; *Saṃyutta Nikāya*, IV, pp. 251-60.
[6] *Saṃyutta Nikāya*, I, pp. 55-6.
[7] Sinhalese Ed., p. 122.
[8] *Manorathapūraṇī*, Sinhalese Ed., pp. 130ff.
[9] *Ibid.*, pp. 173ff.; and see *Dhammapada Comm.*, III, pp. 144 foll.
[10] *Vinaya Piṭaka*, IV, 267.
[11] Vol. II, p. 403.
[12] *Vimānavatthu Comm.*, pp. 62-74.
[13] p. 301.
[14] p. 307.

person who was able to pick out seeds of one colour only would become the merchant (i.e. his heir).[1]

A certain merchant of Rājagṛha built a vihāra for the bhikkhus.[2] The *Vinaya Piṭaka*[3] tells us a story of a trader who had made preparations to go on a journey from Rājagṛha to Patiyāloka, when a bhikkhu on his begging tour came to the trader's house for alms. The trader exhausted the food which he had collected for the journey, by giving it to several bhikkhus. Not being able to start his journey when he had intended, he set out late and was killed by robbers on the way.

It is apparent from the foregoing references that many people of Magadha, and more especially of Rājagṛha, were engaged in trade and commerce. There are numerous references in the Jātakas to big bankers of Magadha in the Buddha's time. In the *Asampadāna Jātaka*, for instance, we find that a Magadhan seṭṭhi or banker named Saṅkha was the master of eighty crores of wealth. He had a friend in Benares who was also a banker, having the same amount of riches. Saṅkha helped his friend greatly, but was repaid by base ingratitude. Hearing of this ingratitude, the king caused the seṭṭhi of Benares to give all his wealth to his benefactor; but the Magadhan banker was so honest that he refused to take back more than his own money.[4] The *Petavatthu Commentary* tells us that there was a merchant at Rājagṛha who was so very wealthy that his immense riches could not be exhausted even if 1,000 coins were spent every day.[5]

Rājagṛha, the ancient capital of Magadha, had many names in the course of its long history; and many explanations of these names have been put forward by various authorities, indigenous and foreign. By some it was said that Rājagṛha (Pāli Rājagaha) was so called because it was founded by a king, and every house in it resembled a palace.[6] Buddhaghosa says, however, that the town was called Rājagaha because it was used as a residence (lit. seized) by Mandhātā, Mahāgovinda, and the rest.[7] Dhammapāla refers to another opinion accounting for the name Rājagaha as a prison for inimical kings (paṭirājūnaṃ gahabhūtattā).[8] The town was also called Kuśāgrapura, 'the city of the superior reed-grass' which abounded there,[9] or 'city of (King) Kuśāgra' and Girivraja,

[1] p. 309. [2] *Vinaya Piṭaka*, II, p. 146. [3] IV, pp. 79-80.
[4] *Jātaka* (Fausböll), I, pp. 466-7. [5] pp. 2-9.
[6] Spence Hardy, *Manual of Buddhism*, p. 162, note.
[7] *Sumaṅgalavilāsinī*, I, p. 132.
[8] *Udāna-vaṇṇanā*, Siamese Ed., p. 32. Cf. *Bhāgavatapurāṇa*, X, Chap. 7, according to which Jarāsandha imprisoned several kings in Rājagṛha.
[9] Watters, *On Yuan Chwang*, II, 148.

because it was surrounded by mountains.[1] Girivraja is the name which was given in the *Rāmāyaṇa* and the *Mahābhārata* to the old capital of Jarāsandha, king of Magadha. Dhammapāla says that the place was originally built or planned by Mahāgovinda, the famous architect,[2] while in the *Sāsanavaṃsa* we read that King Mandhātā was the founder of Rājagaha,[3] and in the *Suttanipāta Commentary* it is stated that Rājagaha was ruled by famous kings like Mandhātā and Mahāgovinda.[4] In the Jātakas it is mentioned as a great city.[5]

The *Mahābhārata* describes Girivraja or Rājagṛha, the capital of Jarāsandha, as a city which had a teeming population and was noted for hot springs (*tapodas*). Jinaprabha-sūri tells us that it contained 36,000 houses of merchants, half of which belonged to the Buddhists, while the other half belonged to the Jainas, shown forth in the middle as a row of magnificent buildings.[6] Buddhaghosa too mentions Rājagaha as a city, the inner and outer areas of which contained each nine crores of people. The city had 32 gates and 64 posterns.[7] According to the Chinese pilgrims' accounts, high mountains surrounded it on every side and formed its external ramparts, as it were. On the west it could be approached through a narrow pass, while on the north there was a passage through the mountains. The town was extended (i.e. broad) from east to west, and narrow from north to south. It was about 150 li in circuit. The remaining foundations of the wall of the inner city were about 30 li in circuit. Kaṇika trees with fragrant bright golden blossoms were on all the paths, and these made the woods in late spring all golden-coloured.[8]

Hsüan Tsang would have us believe that the name Rājagṛha was strictly applicable only to the new city built either by Bimbisāra or by Ajātaśatru, not far to the north-east from Veṇuvana[9] (the old city being known as Girivraja). Fā-Hien too speaks of the 'old city' and the 'new city'. By the old city Hsüan Tsang distinctly means Kuśāgrapura, and by the new city he means the city which King Ajātaśatru made his capital.

---

[1] *Mbh.*, *Sabhāparvan*, Chap. XXI, v. 3. For a detailed description of the mountains surrounding Rājagṛha, see B. C. Law, *Rājagṛha in Ancient Literature*, *M.A.S.I.*, No. 58.

[2] *Vimānavatthu Comm.*, p. 82. *Mahāgovindapaṇḍitena Vatthuvijjāvidhinā sammadeva nivesite, sumāpite.*

[3] p. 152. [4] p. 413. [5] I, 391.

[6] *Vividha-tīrtha-kalpa*, p. 22.

[7] Spence Hardy, *Manual of Buddhism*, p. 323.

[8] Beal, *Buddhist Records of the Western World*, II, 150; Watters, *On Yuan Chwang*, II, 148.

[9] Watters, *On Yuan Chwang*, II, 162.

The Jaina *Vividha-tīrtha-kalpa* speaks of Rājagṛha as the residence of such kings and princes as Jarāsandha, Śreṇika, Kuṇika, Abhaya, Megha, Halla, Vihalla and Nandisena.[1] Śreṇika was no other than King Seṇiya Bimbisāra of Pāli literature, and Kuṇika was King Ajātaśatru. Abhaya, Megha, Halla, Vihalla and Nandisena we have already referred to as sons of Bimbisāra.

During the reigns of Bimbisāra and Ajātaśatru, the city of Rājagṛha was at the height of its prosperity. Aṅga formed an integral part of the kingdom of Magadha, which comprised an area covered by the districts of Gayā and Bhāgalpur. The Jaina texts describe Rājagṛha as a city which was rich, happy and thriving[2]; but some two centuries after the death of Mahāvīra a terrible famine visited Magadha.[3] Rājagṛha must have lost its glory with the removal of the capital to Pāṭaliputra or Kusumapura by Udāyibhadda, some 28 years after the Buddha's demise. But the Hathigumpha Inscription lifts the veil for a moment, and shows that when Bṛhaspatimitra was king of Magadha (second century B.C.), King Khāravela of Kaliṅga marched towards Magadha after having stormed Gorathagiri, and brought pressure to bear upon Rājagṛha (Rājagahaṃ upapīḍāpayati).[4] Rājagṛha must have been used by the then king of Magadha, if not as a capital, at least as a strong fortress against foreign inroads. As was the case with most if not all ancient cities, Rājagṛha was walled; we read in the *Vinaya Piṭaka* (IV, pp. 116-7) that the city-gate of Rājagṛha was closed in the evening, and then nobody, not even the king, was allowed to enter the city. The same inscription refers to Aṅga and Magadha as united into one kingdom.

When Fā-Hien visited the place in the fifth century A.D., he found the sites still there as of old, 'but inside the city all was emptiness and desolation, no man dwelt in it'.[5] The Karanda Veṇuvana monastery was still in existence, tenanted by a 'company of monks'.[6] At the time of Hsüan Tsang's visit in the seventh century A.D., 'the old inhabitants of the city were 1,000 Brahmin families', and many Digāmbaras lodged on the Pi-pu-lo (Vaibhāra) mountain and practised austerities.[7]

Rājagṛha was intimately associated not only with the development of Buddhism, but also with its rival religion, Jainism, and with earlier popular creeds such as Nāga- and Yakkha- worship. Nāgas and Yakkhas were popular objects of veneration in Rājagṛha

---

[1] p. 22. [2] *Jaina Sūtras*, Pt. II, p. 419.
[3] Mrs. Sinclair Stevenson, *Heart of Jainism*, p. 10.
[4] Barua, *Old Brāhmī Inscriptions in the Udayagiri and Khandagiri Caves*, p. 17.
[5] Legge's *Fā-Hien*, p. 82. [6] *Ibid.*, p. 84.
[7] Watters, *On Yuan Chwang*, II, pp. 154, 162.

in early times; while old ruined temples of Gaṇeśa and Śiva still remain on Vaibhāra-giri. Rājagṛha was popularly known to have been so much under the influence of such malevolent spirits as Nāgas and Yakṣas that even the Buddhist bhikkhus had to be furnished with a Paritta or 'saving chant' in the shape of the *Mahā-āṭānāṭiya Suttanta* for their protection against them.[1] The *tapodas* or hot springs and the Tapodā or Sarasvatī carrying water from those hot springs were popularly regarded as puṇyatīrthas or places for holy ablutions.[2] The hot springs of Rājagṛha survive today.

Rājagṛha was the earliest known stronghold of heresy and heterodoxy of the age.[3] The early records of Buddhism bring before us six powerful teachers, Purāṇa Kassapa, Makkhali Gosāla, Pakudha Kaccāyana, Ajita Kesakambalī, Sañjaya Belaṭṭhiputta and Nigaṇṭha Nātaputta (i.e. Mahāvīra), who proved founders of schools (titthakaras) and leaders of thought. Makkhali Gosāla was the leader of the Ājivikas, and Nigaṇṭha Nātaputta the leader of the Nirgranthas or Jainas. The beginnings of their career are bound up with the history of Rājagṛha.

Vardhamāna Mahāvīra was born in Magadha,[4] and he once preached at the court of Bimbisāra with so much force and good logic that the heir, prince Nandisena, was converted.[5] Mahāvīra spent fourteen rainy seasons in Rājagṛha.[6] The eleven Gandharvas of Mahāvīra died in Rājagṛha after fasting for a month.[7] Jaya, son of King Samudravijaya of Rājagṛha, renounced the world and practised self-restraint.[8]

Rājagṛha was one of the three places selected by the Chabbaggiyas (Ṣaḍvargikas) of Vinaya notoriety, for planting centres of their mischievous activities. Rājagṛha, too, was the place where Devadatta fell out with the Buddha, tried to do personal harm to him, fomented schism in the Saṅgha, and eventually created a division in it.[9] The *Dhammapada Commentary* records the jealousy of other sects towards Buddhism. Moggallāna, for example, was struck by certain fanatics with the help of some hired men.[10] In the *Petavatthu Commentary*, we read that many heretics of the

[1] *Dīgha Nikāya*, III, pp. 194ff.; *Saṃyutta Nikāya*, II, pp. 259–62.
[2] Watters, *On Yuan Chwang*, II, pp. 154, 162.
[3] The Wanderer Mahāsakuladāyi informed the Buddha that Aṅga and Magadha were full of sophistic activities (*Majjhima Nikāya*, II, pp. 1–22).
[4] Mrs. Sinclair Stevenson, *Heart of Jainism*, p. 8.
[5] *Ibid.*, p. 126.
[6] *Jaina Sūtras*, S.B.E., Vol. I, p. 264.
[7] *Ibid.*, p. 287.
[8] *Ibid.*, II, pp. 86-7. For other mentions of Rājagṛha and Jainism, see *ibid.*, II, pp. 31ff., 383 f.n.
[9] *Vinaya Cullavagga*, VII.
[10] III, pp. 65ff.

Saṃsāramocaka caste lived in some villages of Magadha.[1] Somewhere in Magadha, between Rājagṛha and Uruvela, not far from the Mahānadī (Mohānā) lived two teachers, Ārāḍa Kālāma and Udra Rāmaputra, who founded schools for the training of pupils in yoga.[2]

The Brahmins who lived in Rājagṛha and around it were mostly of the Bhāradvāja-gotra. Some of them were agnihotris, some upholders of the cult of purity by birth, morals and penance. They were generally opposed to the conversion of any of their number to the Buddhist and other such non-Brahmanical faiths.[3] In the Buddha's time, Rājagṛha was surrounded by many Brahmin villages or settlements.[4]

What actually happened to the Buddhist Saṅgha at Rājagṛha as a consequence of the transfer of the capital to Pāṭaliputra, we cannot precisely say. But we can tell from glimpses of fact here and there that the process of history was one of decay. Hsüan Tsang tells us that 'two or three li to the north-west of this (the Kalanda Tank to the north of the Veṇuvana monastery) was an Aśoka tope beside which was a stone pillar, above 50 feet high, surmounted by an elephant, and having an inscription recording the circumstances leading to the erection of the tope.[5] The circumstances that led to the erection of the tope at Rājagṛha by Aśoka are also narrated by the Pāli scholiasts and chroniclers. The *Mahāvaṃsa* says that the Venerable Indagutta (Indragupta) went from all places around Rājagṛha as a representative to take part in the grand celebration of a Mahāthūpa in Ceylon during the reign of King Duṭṭhagāmaṇi (second century B.C.).[6] As some of the images recently discovered at Rājagṛha indicate, there was some amount of new vigour in Buddhist activities at the place under the patronage of the Pāla kings, after which the history of Buddhism at Rājagṛha became practically closed for ever.

We have already indicated that Rājagṛha was surrounded by mountains. The Ṛṣigiri or Isigili, as its name shows, was a favourite hermits' retreat,[7] as indeed were the other mountains which encircled

[1] pp. 67–72.

[2] *Majjhima Nikāya*, I, pp. 163ff.; Fausböll, *Jātaka*, I, pp. 66ff.; *Lalitavistara*, pp. 243ff.; *Mahāvastu*, Vol. II, p. 118; Vol. III, p. 322; *Buddhacarita*, VI, v. 54; Watters, *On Yuan Chwang*, II, p. 141.

[3] *Saṃyutta Nikāya*, I, pp. 160–7. See also Watters, *On Yuan Chwang*, II, p. 162; *Saṃyutta Nikāya*, II, pp. 238-9; *ibid.*, IV, p. 230.

[4] E.g., *Ekanālā Ambasaṇḍa, Khānumata.*

[5] Watters, *On Yuan Chwang*, II, p. 162.

[6] Ed. Geiger, pp. 227-8.

[7] *Majjhima Nikāya*, III, pp. 68–71; and see B. M. Barua's *Historical Background of 'Jinalogy and Buddhalogy'*, in the *Calcutta Review*, 1924, p. 61.

the city.[1] The most famous of these mountains was the Gṛdhrakūṭa or Gijjhakūṭa peak, so called either because it was shaped like vulture's beak, or because it was frequented by vultures.[2] Dhaniya, a potter's son, made a beautiful hothouse at the foot of the Gijjhakūṭa hill, and many people came to see it.[3]

The Vepullapabbata, which was once known as the Vaṅkakapabbata, was another of the hills surrounding Rājagṛha. King Vessantara was banished to this mountain, which was also called Supassa. It took three days to reach its summit.[4]

Among the villages which lay near Rājagṛha was Ekanālā, a Brahmin village in Dakkhiṇagiri, an important locality which lay to the south of the hills of Rājagṛha. A Buddhist establishment was founded there.[5] The *Saṃyutta Nikāya* distinctly places it in the kingdom of Magadha, outside the area of Rājagṛha.[6]

Nāla, Nālaka, Nālagāma or Nālakagāma was a village in Magadha, where Sāriputta died.[7] The *Vimānavatthu Commentary* [8] locates Nālakagāma in the eastern part of Magadha. The village of Kolika is also associated with Sāriputta.[9]

Khānumata was a prosperous Brahmin village somewhere in Magadha, where a Vedic institution was maintained on a land granted by King Bimbisāra.[10] The garden Ambalaṭṭhikā in the vicinity of Khānumata became the site of a Buddhist establishment. The Rājagāraka at Ambalaṭṭhikā was a garden house of King Bimbisāra.[11] Ambalaṭṭhikā stood midway between Rājagṛha and Nālandā,[12] and was the first halting place on the high road which extended in the Buddha's time from Rājagṛha to Nālandā and further east and north-east.[13]

The place where King Ajātaśatru is said to have built a stūpa for the enshrinement of his share of the Buddha's relics [14] is an important site from the Buddhist point of view. Hsüan Tsang definitely tells us that this stūpa stood to the east of Veṇuvana.[15]

[1] For a full account of these mountains, and indeed for everything regarding Rājagṛha, see B. C. Law, *Rājagṛha in Ancient Literature*, No. 58 of *Memoirs of the Archaeological Survey of India.*

[2] *Suttanipāta Comm.*, p. 413.

[3] *Vinaya Piṭaka*, III, 41-2.

[4] *Ibid.*, II, 191-2.

[5] *Sāratthappakāsinī*, I, p. 242.

[6] *Saṃyutta Nikāya*, I, p. 172.

[7] *Ibid.*, V, p. 161.

[8] p. 163.

[9] Watters, *On Yuan Chwang*, II, p. 171. Kolika was located eight or nine li (1½ miles) south-west of the Nālandā monastery.

[10 & 11] *Sumaṅgalavilāsinī*, I, p. 41.

[12] *Dīgha Nikāya*, I, p. 1; *Sumaṅgalavilāsinī*, I, p. 35.

[13] *Dīgha Nikāya*, II, pp. 72ff.

[14] *Ibid.*, II, p. 166. See also *Sumaṅgalavilāsinī*, II, pp. 611 and 613. *Mañjuśrīmūlakalpa*, p. 600.

[15] Watters, *On Yuan Chwang*, II, p. 158.

The Veluvana or Veṇuvana was a charming garden, park or grove at Rājagṛha, surrounded by bamboos.[1] The name may be translated 'Bamboo Grove' or 'Bamboo Park'. The land was received as a gift by the Buddha. The fuller name of the site was Veluvana Kalandakanivāpa, the second part of the name indicating that here the Kalandakas or Kalakas (squirrels or jays) roamed about freely and found a nice feeding ground. In the Pāli accounts King Bimbisāra figures as the donor of the garden. It is certain that the site was outside the 'inner city'. Fā-Hien definitely informs us that the Karanda Bamboo Garden stood to the north of the old city, over 300 paces from the gate, on the west side of the road.[2] Hsüan Tsang adds further details regarding its site.[3]

Another grove which was presented to the Buddha and his Order was the Jīvaka-Ambavana, a mango-grove which Jīvaka converted into a vihāra, and gave to the Buddha and his Order. King Ajātaśatru had to go out of the city of Rājagṛha to reach this orchard.[4] In the commentary on the *Sāmaññaphala Sutta*, Buddhaghosa says that the king proceeded by the eastern gate of the city, the 'inner city of Rājagaha', under the cover of the Gijjhakūṭa mountain, because the mango-grove stood somewhere between the mountain and the city wall.[5] Fa-Hien places it at the 'north-east corner of the city in a (large) curving (space)'.[6] Hsüan Tsang, too, locates the site 'in a bend of the mountain wall', north-east from the (old) city.[7] According to Watters' suggestion, based upon a Chinese account in the *Fo-shuo-sheng-ching*, Chap. II, the orchard 'was apparently in the inclosure between the city proper and the hills which formed its outer defences on the east side'.[8]

Other sites in or near Rājagṛha, which find mention in Pāli literature, were the deer-park at Maddakucchī,[9] Pippali- or Pipphali-guhā a cave which became a favourite resort of Mahākassapa,[10] and which was visited by the Buddha,[11] Ambasaṇḍa (Skt. Āmrakhaṇḍa), a Brahmin village,[12] and the Laṭṭhivana (Skt. Yaṣṭivana), the royal park of Bimbisāra where the Buddha arrived from Gayāsīsa (the

[1] Cf. *Suttanipāta Comm.*, p. 419.
[2] Legge's *Fā-Hien*, pp. 84-5.
[3] Watters, *On Yuan Chwang*, II, pp. 162-3.
[4] *Dīgha Nikāya*, I, pp. 47, 49.
[5] *Sumaṅgalavilāsinī*, I, p. 150; cf. *ibid.*, p. 133.
[6] Legge's *Fā-Hien*, p. 82.
[7] Watters, *On Yuan Chwang*, II, p. 150.
[8] *Ibid.*, II, p. 151.
[9] *Sāratthappakāsinī*, I, pp. 77-8; *Saṃyutta Nikāya*, I, p. 110.
[10] *Udāna*, I, p. 4; *Dhammapada Comm.*, II, pp. 19–21; D. N. Sen, *Rājgīr and its neighbourhood*, p. 5; *Udāna-vaṇṇanā*, Siamese Ed., p. 77; *Mañjuśrī-Mūlakalpa*, Paṭala LIII, p. 588.
[11] Legge, *Fā-Hien*, p. 85; Watters, *On Yuan Chwang*, II, p. 154; *Saṃyutta Nikāya*, V, p. 79.
[12] *Dīgha Nikāya*, II, p. 263; *Sumaṅgalavilāsinī*, III, p. 697.

main hills of Gayā) and halted with the Jaṭila converts on his way to the city of Rājagṛha.[1] The Pāsānaka-cetiya (Pāsāna-caitya) is famous in Buddhist tradition as the place where the Buddha had delivered the Pārāyaṇa Discourses,[2] now embodied in the concluding book of the *Suttanipāta*.[3] Other places which find mention in Pāli literature are Macalagāma,[4] Maṇimālaka-cetiya[5] and Andhaka-vindha.[6]

The *Majjhima Nikāya* describes Senānigāma, one of the villages of Magadha, as a very nice place having a beautiful forest and a river with transparent water. It was a prosperous village, alms being easily obtainable there.[7]

As already indicated, the later capital of Magadha was Pāṭaliputra, near Patna of the present day, the seat of the Government of Bihar. Its ancient Sanskrit names were Kusumapura and Puṣpapura, from the numerous flowers which grew in the royal enclosure. The Greek historians call it Palibothra, and the Chinese pilgrims Pa-lin-tou.

Hsüan Tsang, the great Chinese traveller, gives the following account of the legendary origin of the name of the city. Once upon a time, a very learned Brahmin had a large number of disciples. On one occasion a party of these disciples were wandering in a wood, and one youth among them appeared unhappy and disconsolate. To amuse the gloomy youth, his companions arranged a mock marriage for him. A man and a woman were chosen to represent the bridegroom's parents, and another couple, the parents of the imaginary bride. They were all near a Pāṭali tree, which was chosen to symbolise the bride. All the ceremonies of marriage were gone through, and the man acting as father of the bride broke off a branch of the Pāṭali tree and gave it to the bridegroom. When all was over, his companions wanted the pseudo-bridegroom to go with them, but he insisted on remaining near the tree. Here at dusk an old man appeared with his wife and a young maiden, whom he gave

[1] *Vinaya, Mahāvagga*, I, p. 35; Fausböll, *Jātaka*, I, pp. 83–5; *Samantapāsādikā*, Ceylonese Ed., p. 158; D. N. Sen, *Rājgīr and its neighbourhood*, p. 13; *Mahāvastu*, III, p. 441; Watters, *On Yuan Chwang*, II, pp. 146–8; see also *Ancient Geography of India*, p. 529.

[2] *Commentary on the Cullaniddesa*, Siamese Ed., p. 270.

[3] *Suttanipāta*, pp. 218ff.

[4] Fausböll, *Jātaka*, I, pp. 199–206; *Dhammapada Comm.*, I, pp. 265–80; *Sumaṅgalavilāsinī*, III, pp. 710ff.

[5] *Saṃyutta Nikāya*, I, p. 208.

[6] *Vinaya, Mahāvagga*, I, p. 109. Andhakavinda was connected with Rājagaha by a cart-road.

[7] I, pp. 166-7.

to the young student to be his wife. The couple lived together in the forest for a year, when a son was born to them. The student, now tired of the lonely life of the woods, wanted to go back to his home, but the old man, his father-in-law, induced him to remain by promising him a properly built establishment. Afterwards, when the seat of government was removed to this place, it received the name Pāṭaliputra, because it had been built by gods for the son of the Pāṭali tree.[1]

According to Jaina tradition, Pāṭaliputra was built by Udaya, son of Darśaka, but the first beginnings were made by Ajātaśatru, for the Buddha, when on his way to Vaiśālī from Magadha, saw Ajātaśatru's ministers measuring out a town.[2]

Pāṭaliputra was originally a village of Magadha, known as Pāṭaligāma, which lay opposite to Koṭigāma on the other side of the Ganges, which formed a natural boundary between Magadha and the territory of the Vṛji-Licchavis of Vaiśālī. The Magadhan village was one of the halting stations on the high road which extended from Rājagṛha to Vaiśālī and other places. The fortification of Pāṭaligāma which was undertaken in the Buddha's lifetime by the two Brahmin ministers of Magadha, Sunīdha and Vassakāra, led to the foundation of the city of Pāṭaliputra,[3] to which the capital of Magadha was removed by Udāyi or Udāyibhadda, the son and successor of Ajātaśatru. Thus it may be established that Ajātaśatru was the real builder of Pāṭaliputra, which was in fact the new Rājagṛha or new capital of Magadha, as distinguished from the old Rājagṛha or Girivraja with its outer area.

This tradition somehow became twisted and led the Chinese pilgrims Fā-Hien and Hsüan Tsang to speak of the 'old city' and the 'new city' of Rājagṛha, both with reference to Girivraja, crediting Ajātaśatru with the building of the 'new city'. Fā-Hien says that a yojana to the west from Nāla, the place of birth and death of Sāriputra, brought him to 'New Rājagṛha, the new city which was built by King Ajātaśatru'. There were then (fifth century A.D.) two monasteries in it. It was enclosed by a wall with four gates. Three hundred paces outside the west gate was the stūpa erected by Ajātaśatru over a portion of the relics of Buddha. Some four li (less than a mile) south from the south gate was the old city of King Bimbisāra, 'a circular space formed by five hills'.[4]

---

1 Watters, *On Yuan Chwang*, Vol. II, p. 87.

2 See a paper on *Pāṭaliputra* by H. C. Chakladar in the *Modern Review*, March, 1918, where the traditions about the foundation of Pāṭaliputra are discussed at some length.

3 *Dīgha Nikāya*, II, pp. 86ff.; *Sumaṅgalavilāsinī*, II, p. 540.

4 Legge, *Fā-Hien*, pp. 81-2.

There may be some truth in the suggestion made by Hsüan Tsang that the cause of removal of the capital was a fire which broke out in the old capital.[1]

Pāṭaliputra was built near the confluence of the great rivers of Mid-India, the Ganges, Son and Gaṇḍak, but now the Son has receded some distance away from it. The city was protected by a moat 600 ft. broad and 30 cubits in depth. At a distance of 24 ft. from the inner ditch there stood a rampart with 570 towers and 64 gates. The *Samantapāsādikā* informs us that Pāṭaliputra had four gates, Aśoka's income from them being 400,000 kahāpaṇas daily. In the *Sabhā* (council), he used to get 100,000 kahāpaṇas daily.[2]

Pāṭaliputra was the capital of the later Śiśunāgas, the Nandas, and also of the great Mauryan emperors, Candragupta, and Aśoka, but it ceased to be the ordinary residence of the Gupta sovereigns after the completion of the conquests made by Samudragupta.[3]

Fā-Hien came to Pāṭaliputra in the fifth century A.D. The Chinese pilgrim was so much impressed by the glory and splendour of the city that he says that 'the royal palace and halls in the midst of the city were all made by spirits which Aśoka employed, and which piled up the stones, reared the walls and gates, and executed the elegant carving and inlaid sculpture-work in a way which no human hands of this world could accomplish'. There was in the city a Brahmin named Rādhasāmi, a professor of the Mahāyāna system of Buddhism. By the side of the tope of Aśoka there was also a Hīnayāna monastery. The inhabitants of the city were rich, prosperous and righteous.[4] Fā-Hien further gives an interesting description of a grand Buddhist procession at Pāṭaliputra.[5]

Hsüan Tsang says that south of the Ganges lay an old city above 70 li (about 14 miles) in circuit, the foundations of which were still visible, although the city had long been a wilderness. He notes that it was first called Kusumapura, and then Pāṭaliputra.[6] The poet Daṇḍin speaks of Pāṭaliputra as the foremost of all the cities, and full of gems.[7]

During the reign of Candragupta Vikramāditya, Pāṭaliputra was still a magnificent and populous city, and was apparently not ruined until the time of the Hun invasion in the sixth century. Harṣavardhana, when he ruled N. India as a paramount sovereign (612–47

---

[1] Watters, *On Yuan Chwang*, II, pp. 161-2.
[2] *Samantapāsādikā*, I, p. 52.
[3] V. A. Smith, *Early History of India*, 4th Ed., p. 309.
[4] Legge, *Fā-Hien*, pp. 77-8.
[5] *Ibid.*, Chaps. X–XVII.
[6] Watters, *On Yuan Chwang*, Vol. II, p. 87.
[7] *Daśakumāracaritam*, 1st Ucchvāsa, śl. 2, Pūrvapīṭhikā.

A.D.), made no attempt to restore the old Magadhan Imperial capital, Pāṭaliputra.[1] About 600 A.D. Śaśāṅka Narendragupta, king of Gauḍa and Karṇasuvarṇa, destroyed the 'Buddha's footprints' at Pāṭaliputra, and smashed many Buddhist temples and monasteries.[2] Dharmapāla, the most powerful of the Pāla kings of Bengal and Bihar, took some steps to renew the glory of Pāṭaliputra, but the interests of the Pāla monarchs seem to have been centred in Bengal rather than in Magadha.[3]

As might be expected, the Pāli Buddhist literature has references to Pāṭaliputra, but as it had not grown up into a city in the Buddha's lifetime, it does not find such frequent mention as Rājagṛha, the ancient capital. However, on one occasion, the upāsakas of Pāṭaligāma, as it then was, built an Āvasathāgāra (living-house), and they invited the Buddha on the occasion of its opening ceremony.[4] An influential Brahmin householder of Benares named Ghoṭamukha built a vihāra at Pāṭaliputra for Udena, a bhikkhu, and the vihāra was called Ghoṭamukhī.[5] Another bhikkhu, Bhadda, dwelt at Kukkuṭārāma near Pāṭaligāma, and had conversations with Ānanda, the Buddha's famous disciple.[6]

The *Dāṭhāvaṃsa* contains a long story concerning King Pāṇḍu of Pāṭaliputra, the heretical Nigaṇṭhas, and King Guhasīva, a vassal of Pāṇḍu. In brief, the Nigaṇṭhas went to Pāṇḍu to complain that Guhasīva worshipped the tooth-relic of the Buddha, instead of Pāṇḍu's gods Brahmā, Śiva and the rest. Pāṇḍu, angered, sent a subordinate king called Cittayāna to arrest and bring Guhasīva to him with the tooth-relic. However, Cittayāna was converted by Guhasīva to be a follower of the Buddha, and together they went to Pāṭaliputra, where a series of miracles ensued, as every effort made by Pāṇḍu to destroy the relic failed. Finally, King Pāṇḍu was convinced of the relic's miraculous properties, and gave up his false belief.[7]

Sthūlabhadra, leader of some of the Jaina bhikkhus, summoned a council at Pāṭaliputra (about 200 years after Mahāvīra's death), in the absence of Bhadrabāhu and his party, to collect the Jaina sacred literature. Bhadrabāhu on his return refused to accept the work of the Council of Pāṭaliputra.[8]

---

[1] Smith, *Early History of India*, 4th Ed., p. 310.
[2] S. C. Vidyābhūṣaṇa, *History of Indian Logic*, p. 349.
[3] Smith, *Early History of India*, 4th Ed., pp. 310-11.
[4] *Vinayapiṭaka*, I, pp. 226–8.
[5] *Majjhima Nikāya*, II, pp. 157 foll.
[6] *Saṃyutta Nikāya*, V, pp. 15-16, 171-2.
[7] See B. C. Law, *Dāṭhāvaṃsa*, Intro., pp. xii–xiv.
[8] Mrs. Sinclair Stevenson, *Heart of Jainism*, p. 72.

Pāṭaliputra coins had their own individual marks.[1] The discoveries of punch-marked coins give the death-blow to the theory that all symbols on them 'were affixed haphazard by shroffs and moneyers through whose hands the coins passed', and give rise to the incontestable conclusion that they constitute 'coinages' peculiar to three different provincial towns, one belonging to Taxila, the second to Pāṭaliputra, and the third to Vidiśā (Bhilsā) of Central India.[2]

The following are the interesting discoveries made by the Archaeological Department of the Government of India at the site of Pāṭaliputra:—

1. Remains of wooden palisades at Lohanipur, Bulandibagh, Mahārājganj and Mangle's tank.
2. Punch-marked coins found at Golakpur.
3. Didarganj statue.
4. Durukhia Devī and Perso-Ionic capital.
5. The railing pillar probably belonging to the time of the Śuṅgas.
6. Coins of Kushan and Gupta kings.
7. Votive clay tablet found near Purabdarwaza.
8. Remains of Hīnayāna and Mahāyāna monasteries at the time of Fā-Hien, the temples of Sthūlabhadra and other Jaina temples and the temples of Choti and Bari Patan Devīs.[3]

Nālandā[4] was a famous seat of learning in ancient India. It was a village which Cunningham identifies with modern Baragaon, seven miles north of Rājgir in Bihar.[5] Nālandā is mentioned in the *Mahāvastu Avadāna*[6] as a very prosperous place at no great distance from Rājagṛha.

After the *nirvāṇa* of the Buddha, five kings, named Śakrāditya, Buddhagupta, Tathāgatagupta, Bālāditya and Vajra, built five *saṅghārāmas* or monasteries at Nālandā.[7] In the Buddha's time, Nālandā was one of the halting stations on the high road connecting Rājagṛha with Pāṭaligāma, Koṭigāma, Vaiśālī, etc. Buddhaghosa knew it as a town at a distance of one yojana (about 7 miles) from

---

[1] *Carmichael Lectures*, 1921, p. 100.

[2] *Ibid.*, p. 99.

[3] *Pāṭaliputra* by Manoranjan Ghosh, pp. 14-15.

[4] For an interesting account of Nālandā vide *Nālandā* (*J.M.U.*, Vol. XIII, No. 2) by K. A. Nilakanta Śāstrī, A. Ghosh, *A Guide to Nālandā* (Delhi, 1939), *Nālandā in Ancient Literature* (5th Indian Oriental Conference, 1930) and *Harsha* (Oxford) by Dr. R. K. Mookerji.

[5] Cunningham, *Ancient Geography*, p. 537.

[6] Vol. III, p. 56.

[7] Watters, *On Yuan Chwang*, II, pp. 164-5.

Rājagṛha.[1] Cunningham identifies the ancient site with the modern village of Baragaon which lies at the northern end of the precincts of the Nālandā Mahāvihāra. The Pāli texts, however, refer not so much to Nālandā itself as to Pāvārika's mango-grove in its vicinity, as the real place of importance both to the Buddhists and the Jainas.[2] According to the tradition recorded by Hsüan Tsang, 'in a Mango Wood to the south of this monastery was a tank the dragon of which was called Nālandā, and the name was given to the monastery. But the facts of the case were that Ju-lai (Buddha) as a P'usa (Bodhisattva) had once been a king with his capital here, that as king he had been honoured by the epithet Nālandā or 'Insatiable in giving' on account of his kindness and liberality, and that this epithet was given as its name to this monastery'. The grounds of the establishment were originally a mango park bought by 500 merchants for ten koṭis of gold coins and presented by them to the Buddha.[3]

Nālandā was often visited by the Buddha.[4] Mahākassapa, who was at first a follower of a heretical teacher, met the Buddha for the first time while he was seated on the road between Rājagṛha and Nālandā. He declared himself a follower of the Buddha.[5] The *Majjhima Nikāya* tells us that once Nigaṇṭha Nātaputta was at Nālandā with a large retinue of his followers. A Jaina named Dīghatapassī went to the Buddha, who was in the Pāvārika *ambavana* at Nālandā, and the Buddha converted many of Mahāvīra's followers.[6] In the *Jaina Sūtras* we read that there was at Nālandā a householder named Lepa who was rich and prosperous. Lepa had a beautiful bathing hall containing many hundreds of pillars. There was a park called Hastiyāma. Once Gautama Buddha lived at Nālandā. He had a discussion with Udaka, a nigaṇṭha and follower of Pārśva, who failed to accept Gautama's views as to the effect of *karma*.[7] It was at Nālandā that Mahāvīra spent the second year of his asceticism, and here, too, that he found many rich supporters. The *Kalpa-sūtra* (p. 122) informs us that Mahāvīra spent as many as fourteen rainy seasons at Rājagṛha and Nālandā.

According to Tibetan accounts, the quarter in which the Nālandā University, with its grand library, was located, was called Dharmagañja (Piety Mart). It consisted of three grand buildings called

---

[1] *Sumaṅgalavilāsinī*, III, p. 873; I, p. 35: *Rājagahato pana Nālandā yojanaṃ eva*.

[2] *Majjhima Nikāya*, I, p. 371.

[3] Watters, *On Yuan Chwang*, II, p. 164.

[4] See, e.g. *Dīgha Nikāya*, I, pp. 1ff., 211; *ibid.*, II, pp. 81–4; *Saṃyutta Nikāya*, IV, p. 110, 311ff., 314–7.

[5] *Saṃyutta Nikāya*, II, pp. 219ff.

[6] *Majjhima Nikāya*, I, pp. 371ff.

[7] S.B.E., II, pp. 419-20.

Ratnasāgara, Ratnodadhi and Ratnarañjaka respectively.[1] Dharmapāla, a native of Kañcipura in Drāviḍa (modern Conjeeveram in Madras) studied at the University of Nālandā and acquired great distinction. In course of time he became the head of the University.[2] Śīlabhadra, a Brahmin, came of the family of the king of Samataṭa (Bengal). He was a pupil of Dharmapāla, and in course of time he too became the head of the University.[3] The Chinese pilgrim, I-tsing, who started for India in 671 A.D., arrived at Tāmralipti at the mouth of the Hooghly in 673 A.D. He studied Buddhist literature at Nālandā.[4] He relates that venerable and learned priests of the Nālandā monastery used to ride in sedan chairs, never on horseback.[5]

According to Dr. S. C. Vidyābhūṣana, the year 450 A.D. is the earliest limit which we can roughly assign to the royal recognition of Nālandā.[6]

Besides Nālandā, Magadha had other great seats of Buddhist learning which attracted students from all parts of India and beyond, such as the Universities of Odantapuri and Vikramaśilā. In the eighth century A.D., Gopāla, the founder of the Pāla dynasty of Bengal, founded a great monastery at Uddandapura or Otantapuri in Bihar.[7] As a University, the glories of Vikramaśilā were hardly inferior to those of Nālandā. Hither too came students from Tibet, and Tibetan works tell us how Dīpaṅkara or Śrījñāna Atīsa, a native of Bengal, who was at the head of the University from 1034–8 A.D., was induced to go to Tibet and establish the Buddhist religion there.[8]

The Vikramaśilā Vihāra was a Buddhist monastery situated on a bluff hill on the right bank of the Ganges, and had sufficient space within it for a congregation of 8,000 men with many temples and buildings. On the top of the projecting steep hill of Pātharghāṭā, there are the remains of a Buddhist monastery, and the space covered by the ruins is large enough to hold an assembly of many thousands of people. This Pātharghāṭā was the ancient Vikramaśilā.[9] It is said to have included 107 temples and 6 colleges.[10] This University was known for its output of numerous commentaries. It was a centre

---

1 *History of Indian Logic*, p. 516; see also H. D. Sankalia, *The University of Nālandā* (Madras, 1934).

2 *Ibid.*, p. 302; Beal, *Buddhist Records of the Western World*, II, p. 110.

3 Beal, *Buddhist Records of the Western World*, II, p. 110.

4 I-tsing, *Records of the Buddhist Religion*, Intro., p. xvii.

5 *Ibid.*, p. 30.

6 *History of Indian Logic*, pp. 514-5.

7 Smith, *Early History of India*, 4th Ed., p. 413; cf. Eliot, *Hinduism and Buddhism*, Vol. II, p. 111.

8 *Journal of the Buddhist Text Society*, Vol. I.

9 *J.A.S.B.*, New Series, Vol. V, No. I, pp. 1–13.

10 Smith, *Early History of India*, 4th Ed., p. 414.

not only of tāntric learning but of logic and grammar, and is interesting as showing the connection between Bengal and Tibet.[1] King Dharmapāla endowed the University with rich grants sufficing for the maintenance of 108 resident monks, besides numerous non-resident monks and pilgrims. At the head of the University, there was always a most learned and pious sage. Thus, at the time of Dharmapāla, Ācārya Buddhajñānapāda directed the affairs of the University. Grammar, metaphysics (including logic) and ritualistic books were especially studied at Vikramaśilā. On the walls of the University were painted images of *paṇḍitas* (learned men) eminent for their learning and character. The distinguished scholars of the University received diplomas of *paṇḍita* from the king himself. The most erudite sages were appointed to guard the gates of the University, which were six in number.

The University of Vikramaśilā is said to have been destroyed by the Mohammedan invader, Bakhtiar Khalji, about 1203 A.D., when Śākya Śrī Paṇḍita of Kashmir was at its head.[2]

Like princes of most other Indian States, Magadhan princes were frequently educated at Taxila. One Magadhan prince, Duyyodhana, as we learn from the *Jātaka*, went to Taxila to learn the arts. He later became king, and used to give alms to Śramaṇas, Brāhmaṇas and others, observe the precepts and perform many meritorious deeds.[3] The *Dārimukha* and *Saṅkhapāla Jātakas* have references to the education of Magadhan princes at Taxila.[4]

Magadha was the birthplace of Jīvaka, the famous physician, who educated himself at Taxila and on his return to his native city was appointed physician to the royal family.[5] His success in operating on King Bimbisāra won for him the post of royal physician, and the king later appointed him physician to the Buddha and the congregation of bhikkhus. Once, we are told, Magadha was badly attacked by five kinds of diseases, and Jīvaka had to treat the suffering bhikkhus.[6]

The Jātakas are full of interesting information about Magadha. From them we learn that Magadha was famous for conch shells[7]; that white elephants were used there by the royal family[8]; that agriculture was prosperous, and that some Brahmins used to cultivate

---

[1] Eliot, *Hinduism and Buddhism*, Vol. II, p. 111.

[2] S. C. Vidyābhūṣaṇa, *History of Indian Logic*, pp. 519-20.

[3] *Jātaka* (Fausböll), V, pp. 161-2.

[4] III (Fausböll), pp. 238–40. Needless to say, the *Jātaka* contains many stories of supposed previous incarnations of the Buddha, in the course of which he was born in Magadha, e.g. III, pp. 238–40; I, pp. 199, 213, 373.

[5] *Vinaya Piṭaka*, I, pp. 71 foll.

[6] *Ibid.*, I, p. 71.

[7] *Jātaka* (Fausböll), VI, p. 465.

[8] *Ibid.*, I, p. 444.

land themselves in Magadha.[1] The *Vinaya Piṭaka* states that the fields of Magadha were well divided for the purpose of cultivation.[2] We have already noted that there were stated to be 80,000 villages in Magadha in King Bimbisāra's time. A story reminiscent of the Fools of Gotham is that of a particular village inhabited by fools who once went to the forest where they used to work for their livelihood. They had to pay the penalty for their foolishness by losing their lives while trying to destroy mosquitoes with bows and arrows.[3]

The *Lakkhaṇa Jātaka* refers to the destruction of paddy by deer which used to come to the field during the harvest. The Magadhans laid traps and devised various other means to capture and kill them.[4]

The *Aṅguttara Nikāya* mentions Magadha as one of the sixteen great *janapadas* or provinces of ancient India, stating that it was full of seven kinds of gems, and had immense wealth and power.[5] Hsüan Tsang gives a fair account of Magadha in the seventh century A.D. According to him, the country was 5,000 li in circuit. There were few inhabitants in the walled cities but the other towns were fully populated. The soil was rich and yielded luxurious crops. It produced a kind of rice with large grain of extraordinary fragrance. The land was low and moist, and the towns were on plateaux. From the beginning of summer to the middle of autumn, the plains were flooded, and boats could be used. The climate was hot, and the inhabitants were honest, esteemed learning, and revered Buddhism. There were above 50 Buddhist monasteries and more than 10,000 ecclesiastics, for the most part adherents of the Mahāyāna system. There were some deva temples, and the adherents of the various sects were numerous.[6]

On account of Magadha's predominant political position, the language spoken there obtained recognition all over India in very early times. The *Mahāvaṃsa* goes so far as to tell us that the Māgadhī language is the root of all Indian languages.[7] It was in this Māgadhī language that Buddhaghosa translated the Sinhalese commentary on the *Tripiṭaka*.[8] At the time of Aśoka, as the numerous inscriptions scattered all over India show, the dialect of Magadha must have been understood over the greater part of India.

---

[1] *Jātaka* (Fausböll), IV, pp. 276-7. Cf. the Story of Bharadvāja.
[2] *Vinaya Piṭaka*, I, p. 287. [3] *Makasa Jātaka*; *Jātaka*, I, p. 246.
[4] *Jātaka* (Fausböll), I, p. 143; cf. *ibid.*, p. 154.
[5] I, 213; IV, 252, 256, 260. Cf. *Mahāvastu*, ed. Senart, II, p. 419.
[6] Watters, *On Yuan Chwang*, II, pp. 86-7; Beal, *Buddhist Records of the Western World*, II, pp. 82-3.
[7] *Cūlavaṃsa*, 37, vs. 230, 242–4: *Sabbesaṃ mūlabhāsāya Māgadhāya niruttiyā.*
[8] B. C. Law, *The Life and Work of Buddhaghosa*, p. 37.

## CHAPTER XLVII

# THE VIDEHAS

The Videhas are mentioned in the Brāhmaṇa portion of the Vedas as a people in a very advanced stage of civilisation. The part of the country where they lived appears to have been known by the name of Videha even in the still more ancient times of the Saṃhitās, for the *Yajurveda Saṃhitās* mention the cows of Videha, which appear to have been particularly famous in ancient India.[1]

According to Julius Eggeling, a confederacy of kindred peoples known as the Kośala-Videhas, occupying a position of no less importance than that of the Kuru-Pañcālas, lived to the east of the Madhyadeśa at the time of the redaction of the *Brāhmaṇas*. The legendary account is that these people claimed Videgha Māthava as their common ancestor, and the two branches are said to have been separated from each other by the river Sadānīrā (corresponding either to the Rāpti or to the Gandak). In Eggeling's opinion, the Videha country in those days constituted the extreme east of the land of the Aryans.[2] Dr. Weber notes that the Aryans, led by Videgha Māthava and his priest, apparently pushed up the river Sarasvatī as far east as the river Sadānīrā which formed the western boundary of the Videhas, or more probably the Gandak (?=Sadānīrā) which was the boundary between the Kośalas and the Videhas.[3]

The Videha country, as we have seen, is said to have derived its name from this King Videgha Mathāva or Videha Mādhava, who introduced the sacrificial fire; and according to some, this introduction of the sacrificial fire is symbolical of the inauguration of the Brahmanical faith in the region. This legend, which is of importance in connection with the question of Aryan settlement in the Videha country, may be read in full in the *Śatapatha Brāhmaṇa*. According to this account, King Māthava Videgha carried Agni Vaiśvānara (=fire) in his mouth. When invited to do so, Agni sprang forth, and started to flash over the ground, burning it up. Starting from the river Sarasvatī, he went burning along towards the east, drying up all the rivers. Only he did not burn over the river Sadānīrā,

---

[1] The commentator of the *Taittirīya Saṃhitā* explains the adjective *Vaidehī* by *Viśiṣṭa-deha-sambandhinī*, 'having a splendid body' (see *Vedic Index*, Vol. II, p. 298 and Keith's *Veda of the Black Yajus' School*, Vol. I, p. 138).

[2] *Śatapatha Brāhmaṇa*, S.B.E., Vol. XII, Intro. XLII-XLIII.

[3] S.B.E., Vol. XII, p. 104 f.

flowing from the Northern (Himalaya) mountain. 'That one of the Brāhmaṇas did not cross in former times, thinking, "It has not been burnt over by Agni Vaiśvānara". Nowadays, however (i.e. in the time of the *Śatapatha Brāhmaṇa*), there are many Brāhmaṇas to the east of it....Māthava, the Videgha, then said (to Agni), "Where am I to abide?" "To the east of this (river) be thy abode", said he. Even now this (river) forms the boundary of the Kośalas and the Videhas; for these are the Māthavas (or descendants of Māthava).'[1]

Great importance has rightly been attached to this passage which, since the days of Professor Weber, has been taken by scholars to indicate the progress of Vedic Aryan civilisation from N.W. India towards the east. Though we cannot be sure about this point, yet it shows at least that in which times the *Śatapatha Brāhmaṇa* considers ancient, the Videha country had received Vedic civilisation, and the cult of offering sacrifices in fire had developed there. According to tradition, the *Śatapatha Brāhmaṇa* was compiled in the Videha country by Yājñavalkya who flourished at the court of the Emperor (Samrāṭ) Janaka, though parts of it bear testimony to its having originated like the other great *Brāhmaṇa* in the country lying farther to the west.

In the later Mantra period, Videha must have been organised so far as to take a leading part in Vedic culture, and the *Śatapatha Brāhmaṇa* clearly indicates that the great spiritual and intellectual lead offered by Samrāṭ Janaka and Ṛṣi Yājñavalkya was accepted by the whole of N. India. Ṛṣis from the Kuru-Pañcāla regions flocked to the court of Janaka and took part in the discussions held about the supreme Brahman; and they had to admit the superior knowledge of Yājñavalkya. In our opinion, the Videha country must have received Vedic culture long before the time of the compilation of this *Brāhmaṇa*, for we find in the *Bṛhadāraṇyaka Upaniṣad* which forms a part of it, that Samrāṭ Janaka of Videha was a great patron of Vedic culture, and that Ṛṣis from the whole of N. India repaired to his court.[2]

From the *Bṛhadāraṇyaka* account, it would seem that at the time of the *Śatapatha Brāhmaṇa* the Videha Brāhmaṇas were superior to the Kuru-Pañcālas as regards the Upaniṣadic phase of the development of Vedic culture.

In other works of the *Brāhmaṇa* period as well as of the *Sūtra* period that followed, other celebrated kings of Videha are mentioned (vide *Vedic Index*, II, 298), so that there can be no question but that

[1] *Śatapatha Brāhmaṇa*, transl. Eggeling, S.B.E., XII, pp. 104–6.
[2] Cf., for example, the story of Yājñavalkya and the cows, *Bṛh. Up.*, III, 1–9.

the Videhas maintained a high position in Vedic society at least in the *Brāhmaṇa* period, and from the superior intellectual position that they had attained in this period it is legitimate to assume that Vedic Aryan culture had taken its root in Videha long before the *Brāhmaṇa* age, and most probably in the early *Saṃhitā* age of the *Ṛgveda*.

The Jātaka stories, too, refer to sacrifices performed by the Videhan kings, saying that goats were sacrificed in the name of religion.[1] We are told in the Purāṇas that Nimi, Ikṣvāku's son, performed a sacrifice for a thousand years, with the help of Vaśiṣtha who had previously officiated as high-priest at a certain Yajña performed by Indra.[2]

The evidence of the *Adhyātma Rāmāyaṇa* also testifies to the sacrificial activities of the Videhan royal family. Viśvāmitra is represented as saying to Rāma: 'We are going to Mithilā, of which Janaka is the ruler. After attending the great Yajña of Janaka we shall make for Ayodhyā'.[3]

Coming to the Epic age, we find Rāmacandra, the hero of the *Rāmāyaṇa*, marrying Vaidehī (= Sītā), the adopted daughter of Janaka, king of Mithilā.[4] This Janaka is probably not the same person as the patron of Yājñavalkya; it appears that several sovereigns of the dynasty bore that name which had been rendered glorious by the intellectual and political powers of the Vedic king. The *Rāmāyaṇa* gives a splendid picture of the Videhan capital and the wide and richly equipped sacrificial ground of King Janaka.

The distance between Mithilā and Ayodhyā may be gauged from the fact that during the reign of Janaka, king of Videha, it took Viśvāmitra, together with Rāma and Lakṣmaṇa, four days to reach Mithilā from Ayodhyā. On the way they rested for one night only, at Viśālā.[5] The messengers sent by Janaka reached Daśaratha's capital in three days of very fast travelling; while Daśaratha on his journey to the Videhan capital in his chariot took four days. Mithilā is identified by tradition with the modern Janakapura in the hills in the present Nepalese territories; a large number of pilgrims visit it every year.

Videha, its capital, Mithilā, and its King Janaka are mentioned many times in the *Mahābhārata*.. After Yudhiṣṭhira's accession to the throne of Indraprastha, before the Rājasūya sacrifice, Bhīma

---

1 *Jātaka* (Fausböll), Vol. I, pp. 166ff.

2 *Viṣṇupurāṇa*, p. 246 (Vaṅgavāsī edition).

3 *Adhyātma Rāmāyaṇa*, *Bālakāṇḍa*, Chap. VII, p. 68, Kāli Śaṅkara Vidyāratna's edition.

4 *Rāmāyaṇa*, *Bālakāṇḍa* (Bombay edition), Chap. 73.

5 *Rāmāyaṇa* (Vaṅgavāsī edition), 1–3.

defeated the king of the Videha people in the course of his *digvijaya.*[1] Karṇa also conquered Mithilā, the Videha capital, during his *digvijaya.*[2] The celebrated sacrifice of Janaka is referred to in several places,[3] while a conversation between Janaka and Yājñavalkya is related in the *Śāntiparvan* (Chap. 311). There are many references to Janaka's spiritual enlightenment, his talks with Pañca-śikha, with Sulabhā and others, and the teaching imparted by him to the young Śuka.[4] Kṛṣṇa, together with Bhīmasena and Arjuna, visited Mithilā on his way from Indraprastha to Rājagṛha.[5] The Videhas are mentioned twice in the list of peoples in the *Bhīṣmaparvan*: once as Videhas along with the Magadhas, and once as Vaidehas along with the Tāmraliptakas.

The *Viṣṇupurāṇa* also mentions the Videha country, furnishes a list of its rulers from ancient times, and gives a fanciful account of the origin of the name of Videha and also that of Mithilā, the capital. The story goes that Vaśiṣṭha, having performed the sacrifice of Indra, proceeded to Mithilā to commence the sacrifice of King Nimi. On reaching there he found that the king had engaged Gautama to perform the sacrificial rites. Seeing the king asleep he cursed him thus: 'King Nimi will be bodiless (*videha, vi-vigata-deha*), inasmuch as he having rejected me has engaged Gautama'. The king on awakening cursed Vaśiṣṭha, saying that he too would perish, as he had cursed a sleeping king. Ṛṣis churned the dead body of Nimi, and as a result of the churning a child was born, afterwards known as Mithi[6] (supposedly from manth, to churn). According to the *Bhaviṣyapurāṇa*, Nimi's son Mithi founded a beautiful city which was named Mithilā after him. From the fact of his having founded the city, he came to be known as Janaka ('begetter, creator').[7] The *Mahāgovinda Suttanta* of the *Dīgha Nikāya* gives another account of the origin of Mithilā, stating that it was built by Govinda.[8]

Undoubtedly the most important Videhan king was Janaka, but we find references to other kings in ancient literature, namely Sāgaradeva, Bharata, Aṅgīrasa, Ruci, Suruci,[9] Patāpa, Mahāpatāpa,

---

[1] *Sabhāparvan*, Chap. 30.
[2] *Vanaparvan*, 254.
[3] *Ibid.*, Chaps. 132, 134, etc.
[4] *Śāntiparvan*, Chap. 327, etc.
[5] *Sabhāparvan*, 20.
[6] *Viṣṇupurāṇa*, pp. 388ff. See also *Bhāgavatapurāṇa*, IX, 24, 64.
[7] *Bhaviṣyapurāṇa*: '*Nimeḥ Putrastu tatraiva . . purijanana sāmarthāt Janakaḥ sa ca kīrtitaḥ*'. See also *Bhāgavatapurāṇa*, IX, 13, 13, where the story of the founding of Mithilā is also related.
[8] P.T.S., Vol. II, p. 235.
[9] For the story of Suruci's childless queen, see *Jātaka* (Fausböll), IV, pp. 314 foll.

Sudassana, Neru, Mahāsammata, Mucala, Mahāmucala, two Kalyāṇas,[1] Śatadhanu of ill-fame,[2] Makhādeva, Sādhina and others.

Kings of Videha usually maintained friendly relations with neighbouring powers. We have already referred to the marriage of Sītā and Rāmacandra, son of Daśaratha, king of Kośala. Instances of matrimonial alliances concluded by the kings of Videha with the neighbouring royal families occur also in later literature. Dr. D. R. Bhandarkar points out that in the plays of Bhāsa, Udayana is called Vaidehīputra, indicating that his mother was a princess of Videha.[3] In the Buddhist literature we have a reference to a Videhan princess (no doubt a queen of Bimbisāra), who was the mother of Ajātaśatru. Her name was Vāsavī.[4]

Vardhamāna Mahāvīra, the great founder of Jainism, 'a Videha, son of Videhadattā, a native of Videha, a prince of Videha, had lived thirty years in Videha when his parents died'.[5] Mithilā was his favourite resort, and he spent six monsoons there.[6]

At the time when the Buddha preached his gospel, we find the ancient Videha country cut up into parts, the Licchavis occupying the foremost position. Eight peoples are named as making up the Vajjian confederacy, the Licchavis and the Videhas occupying a prominent position. The confederacy, according to Kauṭilya, was a '*rājaśabdopajīvī*' Saṅgha.[7] Videha was twenty-four yojanas in length from the river Kauśikī to the river Gaṇḍak, and sixteen yojanas in breadth from the Ganges to the Himalayas.[8] The capital of Videha, Mithilā, was situated about thirty-five miles north-west from Vesālī.[9]

It is stated in the Jātakas that the city of Mithilā was seven leagues, and the kingdom of Videha 300 leagues in extent.[10] It was the capital of the kings Janaka and Makhādeva, in the district now called Tirhut.[11] The city of Mithilā in Jambudvīpa had plenty of elephants, horses, chariots, oxen, sheep and all kinds of wealth of this nature, together with gold, silver, gems, pearls and other precious things.[12] From a Jātaka description, we learn that the

---

1 *Mahāvaṃsa*, P.T.S., Chap. II, p. 12. *Kalyāṇakāduve.*

2 *Viṣṇu Purāṇa*, Pt. III, Chap. XVIII, p. 217. (Vaṅgavāsī Ed.)

3 *Carmichael Lectures*, 1918, pp. 58, 59. Udayana is addressed as Vaidehīputra (*S.V.*, Act 6, p. 68, Gaṇapati Śāstrī's Ed.).

4 Rockhill, *Life of the Buddha*, pp. 63-4.

5 *Jaina Sūtras*, S.B.E., Vol. XXII, Pt. 1, p. 256.

6 *Ibid.*, p. 264.

7 *Arthaśāstra*, trsl. Shāma Śāstri, p. 455. See also *Licchavi chapter.*

8 *Bṛhat Viṣṇupurāṇa.*

9 Rhys Davids, *Buddhist India*, p. 26.

10 *Jātaka* (Fausböll), Vol. III, p. 365: *Tiyojanasatike.*

11 Rhys Davids, *Buddhist India*, p. 37.

12 Beal, *Romantic Legend of Śākya Buddha*, p. 30.

kingdom of Videha had 16,000 villages, storehouses filled, and 16,000 dancing girls.[1] Magnificent royal carriages could be seen, drawn by four horses; and the Videhan king was driven in state around his capital.[2]

In the *Si-Yu-Ki* (Buddhist Records of the Western World) we find that the Chinese traveller Hsüan Tsang, describing the kingdom of Fo-li-shi (Vṛji), says that the capital of the country was Chen-shu-na. Beal quotes V. de St. Martin who connects the name Chen-shu-na with Janaka and Janakapura (= Mithilā).[3]

From very early times, Videha was frequented by merchants. At the time of Buddha Gautama we find people coming from Śrāvastī to Videha to sell their wares.[4]

The Videhas were a charitable people. Many institutions of charity were in existence in their country, and we are told that six hundred thousand pieces were spent daily in alms-giving.[5]

The Jātaka stories often make extravagant demands upon popular credence, as when they relate how the average length of human life at the time of the Buddha Gautama was thirty thousand years. More fortunate than the average mortal, King Makhādeva of Mithilā had a lease of life of eighty-four thousand years,[6] in the earlier portion of which he amused himself as a royal prince. Later on, he was appointed a Viceroy, and last of all became king. We come to a more sober estimate when we find it related that there lived in Mithilā a Brāhmaṇ named Brahmāyu, aged one hundred and twenty years, who was well versed in the Vedas, Itihāsas, Vyākaraṇa, Lokāyata, and was endowed with all the marks of a great man.[7]

Polygamy appears to have been in vogue among the kings of Videha. Brahmadatta, king of Benares, had a daughter named Sumedhā whom he declined to give in marriage to a Videhan prince who had a large number of wives, fearing that her co-wives would make her life miserable.[8]

Many writers bear testimony to the devotion and faithfulness of Videhan princesses. The story of Sītā is too well-known to be repeated. Again, it is stated in the *Amitāyurdhyāna Sūtra* that when Ajātaśatru arrested his father Bimbisāra at the instigation of

---

[1] *Jātaka* (Fausböll), Vol. III, p. 365. [2] *Ibid.*, Vol. II, p. 39.

[3] Beal, *Records of the Western World*, Vol. II, p. 78, n. The actual words are: '. . . *Janaka and Janakapura*, capital of Mithilā'; but, as we have seen, Mithilā is identified with Janakapura.

[4] See, e.g. Dhammapāla's *Paramatthadīpanī on the Theragāthā*, Pt. III, pp. 277-8.

[5] *Jātaka* (Fausböll), Vol. IV, p. 355. See also *Makhādeva Jātaka.*

[6] *Ibid.*, Vol. I, p. 139.

[7] *Majjhima Nikāya*, Vol. II, pp. 133-4.

[8] *Jātaka* (Fausböll), Vol. IV, pp. 314 foll.

Devadatta, and confined him in a room with seven walls, declaring that none must approach him, Vaidehī (i.e. Videhan princess), the queen-mother, kept him alive (until she was discovered), by concealing food and drink for him.[1]

We read in one of the Jātakas that the people of Videha once reproached their king for his childlessness.[2]

The kings of Mithilā were men of high culture. We have already referred to Janaka, the great Rājarṣi of the Brahmanic period. In the Buddhist age, we find Sumitra, king of Mithilā, devoted to the practice and study of the 'true law'.[3] King Videha of Mithilā had four sages to instruct him in law[4]; and we read[5] that the son of this King Videha was educated at Taxila, the usual seat of learning for young men of noble birth.[6]

Stories regarding the religious tendencies of the royal family of Videha are frequently found in ancient literature,—see, e.g. the story of King Nimi and the hawk, *Jātaka*, III, p. 230. Another Jātaka story relates that Videha, king of Videha, and the Bodhisattva, then king of Gandhāra, were on friendly terms, although they had never met. Once, on the fast day of the full-moon, the king of Gandhāra took a vow to keep the five moral precepts, and delivered before his ministers a discourse on the substance of the law. At that moment the demon Rāhu was overshadowing the full-moon's orb so that the moon's light was dimmed by an eclipse. The king observing the phenomenon thought that all trouble came from outside; he considered his royal retinue was nothing but a trouble, and that it was not proper that he should lose his light like the moon seized by Rāhu. He thereupon made over his kingdom to his ministers, took to a religious life, and having attained transcendental powers, spent the rainy season in the Himalayan regions, devoting himself to the delights of meditation.

When the king of Videha heard of the religious life of the king of Gandhāra, he abdicated his throne, went to the Himalayan region and became a hermit. The two ex-kings lived together in peace and friendliness without knowing each other's antecedents. The ascetic of Videha waited upon the ascetic of Gandhāra. One day, they witnessed an eclipse of the moon, and this was the indirect cause of their recognising each other as former fellow kings.[7]

---

[1] S.B.E., Vol. XLIX, pp. 161–201.

[2] *Jātaka* (Fausböll), V, pp. 279-80.

[3] Beal, *Romantic Legend of Sākya Buddha*, p. 30.

[4] *Jātaka* (Fausböll), VI, p. 333.

[5] *Ibid.*, Vol. II, p. 39.

[6] See my paper: '*Taxila as a seat of learning in the Pāli Literature*', *J.A.S.B.*, Vol. XII, 1916.

[7] *Jātaka* (Fausböll), Vol. III, pp. 365-6.

We have already referred to the long life of King Makhādeva of Mithilā. One day this king, on his barber showing him a grey hair from his head, thought that his days were numbered. Handing over his kingdom to his son, the old king became a recluse, and developed very high spiritual powers.[1]

Sādhina, a righteous king in Mithilā, kept the five *sīlas* and observed the fast-day vows. His virtue was praised by the princes of heaven who sat in the 'Justice Hall' of Śakra, and all the gods desired to see him. Accordingly, Śakra ordered Mātali to bring Sādhina to heaven in his own chariot. Mātali went to the kingdom of Videha on the day of the full-moon, driving his celestial chariot side by side with the moon's disc. All the people shouted, 'See, two moons are in the sky'. Then, when the chariot came nearer, they saw what it was, and concluded that it had come for their virtuous king. Mātali went to the king's door and made a sign that he should ascend the chariot. After arranging for the distribution of alms, the king went with Mātali. One-half of the city of gods and twenty-five millions of nymphs, and a half of the palace of Vaijayanta were given to Sādhina by Śakra; and the king lived there in happiness for seven hundred years. But when his merits were exhausted, dissatisfaction arose in him, and he did not wish to remain in heaven any longer. The king was carried back to Mithilā, where he distributed alms for seven days. On the seventh day he died, and was reborn in the heaven of the thirty-three (gods).[2]

Śakra is concerned in another legendary story about the Videhan royal family. Suruci, king of Mithilā, had a wife named Sumedhā who was childless. Sumedhā prayed for a son. She took the eightfold sabbath vows (*aṭṭhasīlanī*), and sat meditating upon the virtues; and Śakra appeared to her and granted her boon.[3]

[1] *Jātaka* (Fausboll), I, pp. 137-8. In the *Makhādeva Sutta* (*Majjhima Nikāya*, Vol. II, pp. 74–83) we find the same story with slight variations. Nimi, a later king, was like Makhādeva. Indra with other gods came to him and praised him. When Nimi reached the Assembly Hall of the gods, he was received cordially by Indra, and sent back to his kingdom in a celestial chariot.

[2] *Jātaka* (Fausböll), Vol. IV, pp. 355-6.

[3] *Ibid.*, Vol. IV, pp. 315 foll.

## CHAPTER XLVIII

# THE JÑĀTṚKAS

The Jñātṛkas (also known as the Nātha or Nāya clan) gave India one of its greatest religious reformers, Mahāvīra, the last Tīrthaṅkara of the Jains, and this is their sole claim to fame among ancient Indian tribes.

The Jñātṛkas, or Kṣatriyas of the Jñātri (or Nāya) clan, used to dwell in Vaiśālī (Basārh), Kuṇḍagrāma and its suburb Kollāga, and Vāṇijyagrāma.[1] The *Cambridge History of India*[2] states that Kuṇḍagrāma was a suburb just outside Vaiśālī, probably surviving in the modern village of Basukuṇḍ. Mrs. Sinclair Stevenson (*Heart of Jainism*, pp. 21-2) says that some 2,000 years ago, in Basārh, the same divisions existed as would be found today, and there, in fact, the priestly (Brāhmaṇa), warrior (Kṣatriya) and commercial (Vāṇiyā or Vāṇijyā) communities lived so separately that their quarters were sometimes spoken of as though they had been distinct villages, as Vaiśālī, Kuṇḍagrāma and Vāṇijyagrāma. Strangely enough, she adds, it was not in their own but in the Kṣatriya ward that Mahāvīra was to be the great hero of the commercial class. We are not prepared to accept Mrs. Stevenson's statement that Vaiśālī was exclusively a Brahmin settlement, in the absence of positive evidence.

The Jain writers give an idealised picture of the Jñātṛkas, telling us that they were afraid of sin, abstained from wicked deeds, did no mischief to any being, and therefore did not partake of meat.[3] Dr. Hoernle says[4]: 'Outside their settlement at Kollāga, the Jñātṛkas possessed a religious establishment (or Cheïya) which bore the name Duïpalāsa. Like most Cheïyas,[5] it consisted of a park enclosing a shrine, hence in the *Vipāka Sūtra* it is called the Duïpalāsa Park (Ujjāna)'. The Nāya clan seems to have supported a body of monks who followed Pārśvanātha, an ascetic, who lived some 250 years before Mahāvīra.[6] It is stated in the *Uvāsagadasāo* that Mahāvīra's parents (and with them probably the whole clan of Nāya Kṣatriyas) are said to have been followers of the tenets of Pārśvanātha. When Mahāvīra, who was taken to be the successor of Pārśvanātha, appeared, the members of his clan became his devoted followers.

---

1 *Uvāsagadasāo* (Hoernle), Vol. II, p. 4, f.n.

2 Vol. I, p. 157.

3 *Jaina Sūtras*, Pt. II, S.B.E., Vol. XLV, p. 416.

4 *Uvāsagadasāo*, Vol. II, pp. 4 and 5, f.n.

5 = Skt. *Chaitya*, shrine.

6 Mrs. Stevenson, *Heart of Jainism*, p. 31.

Dr. Hoernle says that Vaiśālī, one of the settlements of the Jñātṛkas, was an oligarchic republic, the government of which was 'vested in a senate composed of the heads of the resident Kṣatriya clans and presided over by an officer who had the title of king and was assisted by a Viceroy and a Commander-in-chief'.[1] Mrs. S. Stevenson says that the government of Vaiśālī seems to have resembled that of a Greek State.[2]

In the early sixth century B.C., the chief of the Kṣatriya Ñātha clan was Siddhārtha who married Triśalā, sister of Ceṭaka, the most eminent among the Licchavi princes. Siddhārtha and Triśalā were the parents of Mahāvīra, who lived from approximately 570-500 B.C. (See B. C. Law, *Mahāvīra: His Life and Teachings*, p. 53). Of Siddhārtha Dr. Hoernle says: 'Though, as may be expected, the Sacred Books of the Jains speak of him in exaggerated terms, they do not, I believe, ever designate him as "the king of Kuṇḍapura or Kuṇḍagāma"; on the contrary, he is, as a rule, only called the Khattiya Siddhattha (Siddhatthe Khattiye) and only exceptionally he is referred to simply as King Siddhattha. This is perfectly consistent with his position as the chief of the Kshatriyas of Kollāga. Accordingly, Mahāvīra himself was born in Kollāga and naturally when he assumed the monk's vocation, he retired to the Cheïya of his own clan, called Duïpalāsa and situated in the neighbourhood of his native place, Kollāga.'[3] Mahāvīra, on renouncing the world, probably first joined Pārśva's sect of which, however, he soon became a reformer and chief himself.[4]

A detailed sketch of the life and work of Mahāvīra would fill a volume and is beyond the scope of the present treatise.[5] We may, however, mention the fact that it was Mahāvīra who brought the Jñātṛkas into intimate touch with the neighbouring communities of eastern India and developed a religion which is still professed by millions of Indians. Another celebrity of the Jñātṛka clan was Ānanda, a staunch follower of Mahāvīra. The story of Ānanda and his wife Śivanandā is related in the *Uvāsagadasāo*.[6]

[1] *Uvāsagadasāo*, Ed. Hoernle, Vol. II, p. 6.
[2] *Heart of Jainism*, p. 22.
[3] *Uvāsagadasāo*, Vol. II, pp. 5-6.
[4] *Ibid.*, p. 6.
[5] For an account of Mahāvīra, see B. C. Law: *Mahāvīra: His Life and Teachings*.
[6] Vol. II, tr. pp. 7–9.

## CHAPTER XLIX

# THE ŚĀKYAS

The Śākyas have acquired great importance in Indian history owing to the Buddha having been born among them. Before the birth of the founder of Buddhism, the Śākyas were comparatively little known; yet in the rugged fastnesses of the lower Himalayas, they had already built up a remarkable though not a very powerful principality.

The traditional story of the Buddha's birth starts with a discussion among the Devaputras in the Tuṣita heaven, as to which of the great royal families of India the Bodhisattva should honour with his birth. In this discussion, the Śākyas were not mentioned. The Devaputras pondered over the merits of the sixteen *Mahājanapadas* of Jambudvīpa (India), and analysed the claims of all the important royal families of the day, but found them all stained with one black spot or another. Being at a loss to find a people worthy of claiming him as their congener, the Devaputras at length had recourse to the Bodhisattva himself, and when finally the Śākyas were chosen as the recipient of that great honour, it was rather on account of their moral qualities.[1]

The Śākyas of Kapilavastu claimed to be Kṣatriyas. As soon as they heard the news of the Buddha's passing away, they demanded a portion of his relics, saying, '*Bhagavā amhākaṃ ñāti-seṭṭho*'[2] ('the Blessed One was the chief (or best) of our kinsmen'). While all the other Kṣatriya clans that claimed a portion of the Buddha's ashes did so on the grounds of their belonging to the same caste (*Bhagavā pi Khattiyo, mayampi Khattiyā*), in the case of the Śākyas the claim was founded upon a closer relationship, that of consanguinity.

The origin of the Śākyas is traced back to King Okkāka, i.e. Ikṣvāku. It is stated in the *Sumaṅgalavilāsinī*[3] that King Okkāka had five queens. By the chief queen, he had four sons and five daughters. After the death of the chief queen, he married another lady who extorted from him the promise to place her son upon the throne. The king thereupon requested his other sons to leave the kingdom. The princes, accompanied by their sisters, accordingly

---

[1] *Lalitavistara*, Ed. Lefmann, pp. 26-7.
[2] *Dīgha Nikāya* (P.T.S.), Vol. II, p. 165.
[3] *Sumaṅgalavilāsinī*, Pt. I, pp. 258–60.

left the kingdom, and going to a forest near the Himalayas, they began to search for a site to build a city. In the course of their search, they met the sage Kapila who said that they should build a town in the place where he lived. The princes duly built the town, and named it Kapilavatthu (Kapilavastu). In course of time, the four brothers married four of the sisters (excepting the eldest one), and the family came to be known as the Śākyas.

This story is evidently fanciful. Sister-marriage was not in vogue in ancient India even in the earliest times of which we have any record, as the story of Yama and Yamī in the *Ṛgveda* amply demonstrates. The descent from King Okkāka, however, may be based on fact. The *Mahāvaṃsa* too traces the origin of the Śākyas to Okkāka, and gives their genealogy in great detail, going back to Mahāsammata of the same dynasty.[1]

There can be no doubt that King Okkāka in this genealogy is no other than Ikṣvāku of the so-called solar dynasty of the Purāṇas. Comparing the names with those in the Paurānic list, we find that the lists do not agree in every detail, but there is agreement with regard to some of the more prominent names. Thus, for example, in the long history of the solar dynasty given in the *Viṣṇupurāṇa*, Pt. IV, we find many of the names in the *Mahāvaṃsa* list, like Māndhāta (Mandhātā), Sagara (Sāgara), etc. The *Viṣṇupurāṇa* states that King Bṛhadvala (Bṛhadbala) of this dynasty was killed in the Kurukṣetra war,[2] and next proceeds to trace the descent of King Śākya from the Bṛhadvala.[3]

The source of the accounts given in the *Mahāvaṃsa* and the *Sumaṅgalavilāsinī* is not, however, the Purāṇas, but such ancient Buddhistical works as the *Mahāvastu*. This latter work gives a detailed account of the foundation of Kapilavastu and the settlement of the Śākyas there. The story of the sister-marriage is given there, and, as in the *Mahāvaṃsa*, the Śākya family is traced back to Mahāsammata. The names of the kings that succeeded him agree in the two accounts, for the most part. The following story[4] is told of Sujāta, king of the Śākyas, who reigned in the city of Sāketa. The king had five sons and five daughters, and also another son by a concubine, Jentī. Being pleased with Jentī, he promised her a boon. She demanded that her son, Jenta, should be recognised as heir-apparent; and the king, thought loath to consent, could not break his word. The five princes, his legitimate sons, went into

[1] For the complete genealogy of the Śākyas, according to Sinhalese tradition, see *Mahāvaṃsa*, Chap. II, verses 1–24.

[2] *Visnupurāṇa*, Pt. IV, Chap. IV, verse 48.

[3] Wilson, *Viṣṇupurāṇa*, Vol. IV, Chap. XXII, pp. 167–72.

[4] Obviously corresponding to the story of King Okkāka.

exile, followed by many thousands of citizens. They were received by the king of Kāśī-Kośala, and the people of Kāśī-Kośala were delighted with the bearing of the princes. The king, however, became envious and drove the princes out of his kingdom. At the foot of the Himalayas there lived a wise sage called Kapila. His hermitage was vast and charming, with fruits and flowers, adorned with a good many plants and with a dense forest. The princes went to the dense forest and lived there. Traders used to pass through there on their way to Kāśī and Kośala. When asked whence they came, these traders replied that they had come from a certain part of the forest called Sākoṭavana.

The people of Sāketa as well as the traders of Kośala visited the Sākoṭavana. The princes took their brides from among their sisters by the same mother, because they did not wish their race to be contaminated by a mixture of blood. Hearing of this, King Sujāta asked his purohitas and learned Brahmins whether such a custom was permissible, and they replied in the affirmative.

Meanwhile the princes decided to build a town. They went to the sage Kapila and said that they desired to build a city and name it after him. The princes built a city, making the sage's hermitage a royal residence. As the hermitage was given by Kapila the sage, the city became known by the name of Kapilavastu. Kapilavastu was prosperous, wealthy and peaceful; there alms were easily obtainable, and the people were fond of trade and commerce, sociable, and fond of taking part in festivities.

The names of the five princes were Opura, Nipura, Karaṇḍaka, Ulkāmukha and Hastikaśīrṣa. Opura was the eldest, and he was elected king of Kapilavastu.[1]

The story given in the *Mahāvastu* and the *Sumaṅgalavilāsinī* about the origin of the Śākyas by sister-marriage is referred to in the introduction to the *Kunāla Jātaka*. Here the story of the origin of the Śākyas exactly tallies with that in the *Mahāvastu*, but there is some difference in the story of the Koliyas. While the *Mahāvastu* says that they resided in a cave of a hill, the Jātaka story relates that they received the name Koliya because of having resided in the hollow of a Koli or jujube tree.

In the *Mahāvastu* the Śākyas are called *ādityabandhus* or 'kinsmen of the sun'. This refers to their descent from the Solar

[1] *Mahāvastu*, Ed. Senart, Vol. I, pp. 348–52. It will be observed that Opura, Nipura, Karaṇḍaka, Ulkāmukha and Hastikaśīrṣa are represented in a former passage of the *Mahāvastu* as sons of King Sujāta. Here, however, the relationship between each prince and the one next mentioned is represented as that of father and son.

dynasty to which the Ikṣvākus belonged.[1] The *Mahāvastu* also speaks of King Śuddhodana, father of the Buddha, as born in the Ikṣvāku family.[2] Another passage in the same work speaks of the Buddha as a Kṣatriya of the Ādityagotra and of the Ikṣvākukula, i.e. born in the family of the Ikṣvākus who derived their descent from the sun.[3] The *Lalitavistara* (p. 112) also speaks of the Buddha as born in the royal family of Ikṣvāku.

The Śākyas were Kṣatriyas of the Gotama gotra, as is seen from the fact that the Buddha had the surname Gotama, while the Licchavis and Mallas who also belonged to the same race, bore the gotra name of Vaśiṣṭha. The gotra of a Kṣatriya family was derived from the gotra name of the purohita or family priest; so evidently the Śākyas had adopted the Gotamas as their priests at an early date. The Gotama gotra is described in the Pāli books[4] as occupying a very high position among the gotras, no doubt from its association with the founder of Buddhism.

Kapilavastu, the Śākya capital, is sometimes called Kapilavāstu. The *Lalitavistara* calls it Kapilavastu, and sometimes Kapilapura (p. 243) or Kapilāhvayapura (p. 28, etc.); and these names are also found in the *Mahāvastu*.[5] The *Divyāvadāna* also connects Kapilavastu with the sage Kapila.[6] In the *Buddhacarita*, the city is described as Kapilasya-vastu.[7]

Kapilavastu is said to have been surrounded by seven walls.[8] A clue to the identification of the city is furnished by the discovery of the famous Rummindei Pillar which marks the site of the ancient Lumbini garden, the traditional scene of Śākyamuni's birth. Smith is inclined to identify the Śākya capital, which lay not far from the Lumbinigrāma, with Piprawa in the north of the Basti district on the Nepalese frontier.

The Chinese pilgrim, Fā-Hien, who visited India early in the fifth century A.D., says that the neighbourhood of Kapilavastu was infested by white elephants and lions, against which the people had to be on their guard.[9] The country was thinly populated. He noticed towers at Kapilavastu, set up at various places, viz. where prince Siddhārtha left the city by the eastern gate, where his chariot was made to turn back to the palace, where his horoscope was cast

1 *Mahāvastu*, II, p. 303.
2 *Ibid.*, III, p. 247.
3 *Ibid.*, III, p. 246.
4 E.g. *Suttavibhaṅga*, *Pācittiya*, II, 2; *Vinaya Piṭaka*, Oldenberg, Vol. IV, p. 6.
5 Vol. II, p. 11, line 3.
6 *Divyāvadāna*, p. 548, lines 20–2. Kapilavastu, *ibid.*, pp. 90, 390; Kapilavāstu, *ibid.*, p. 67.
7 *Buddhacarita*, Book I, verse 2.
8 *Mahāvastu*, Vol. II, p. 75.
9 *Travels of Fā-Hien and Sung-Yun*, by S. Beal, pp. 88–98.

by the sage Asita, where the elephant was struck by Nanda and others, where the arrow going thirty li in a south-easterly direction penetrated into the earth and produced a fountain of water which quenched the thirst of travellers in later generations, where Śuddhodana was met by his son when the latter had acquired supreme wisdom, where five hundred Śākya converts honoured Upāli, and where the children of the Śākyas were massacred by King Viḍūḍabha.[1]

Hsüan Tsang, who visited India in the seventh century A.D., narrates that Kapilavastu, the country of the Śākyas, was about four thousand li in circuit. The royal precincts built of brick were within the city, measuring fourteen or fifteen li round.[2] He says that, long after the passing away of the Buddha, topes and shrines were built in or near Kapilavastu.[3] The villages were few and desolate. The monasteries (*saṅghārāmas*) which were then in ruins, were more than one thousand in number. There still existed a *saṅghārāma* near the royal precincts which contained thirty (3,000 according to one text) followers who read 'the little vehicle of the Sammatiya school'. There were two deva-temples where different sectarians worshipped. There were some dilapidated foundation walls, the remains of the principal palace of King Śuddhodana, above which a vihāra (monastery) was built containing a stūpa of the king. Near it was a foundation in ruins, representing the sleeping palace of Queen Mahāmāyā. Above it a vihāra was built containing a figure of the queen. Close by stood a vihāra, on the spot where the Bodhisattva was supposed to have entered the womb of his mother. A stūpa was built to the north-east of 'the palace of spiritual conception' of the Bodhisattva.[4] To the north-west of the capital, a stūpa was built where King Viḍūḍabha massacred the Śākyas.[5] The cultured land was rich and fertile and the climate of the country was bracing.

According to Rhys Davids, there were villages around the rice-fields, and the cattle roamed about in the outlying forest. The jungles, which were occasionally resorted to by robbers, divided one village from another.[6]

Mention is made of several other Śākya towns besides Kapilavastu, viz. Chātumā, Sāmagāma, Ulumpā, Devadaha, Sakkara,

[1] *Travels of Fā-Hien*, by Beal, pp. 85–7.
[2] Beal, *Records of the Western World*, Vol. II, pp. 13-14.
[3] Watters, *On Yuan Chwang*, Vol. II, p. 4.
[4] Beal, *Records of the Western World*, Vol. II, pp. 14-15.
[5] *Ibid.*, Vol. II, p. 12.
[6] *Buddhist India*, pp. 20-21.

Sīlāvatī, and Khomadussa.[1] The latter was so called on account of its abundant produce of linen cloth.[2]

It is stated in the *Jātaka* that the Śākyas were a haughty people, and did not do obeisance to Siddhārtha on the ground that he was younger in age, but were afterwards made to do so on seeing a miracle performed by him.[3] Hsüan Tsang, however, says that the manners of the people were 'soft and obliging',[4] while in Rockhill's *Life of the Buddha* it is said that they did not kill any living thing, 'not even a black beetle'.[5] The produce of their cattle and rice-fields supplied their only means of livelihood. The villages were grouped around the rice-fields, and the cattle wandered through the outlying forest over which the peasantry had rights of common.[6]

The Tibetan Buddhist Books as translated by Rockhill[7] relate that the Śākya law allowed a man one wife only. This law is rather remarkable inasmuch as polygamy was in vogue in India from the Vedic age downwards,—especially among the Kṣatriyas who were rich and powerful. We may, however, account for the existence of this law among the Śākyas on the ground of their special constitution and position. They were a small tribe, and very proud of their birth. They would not give one of their girls in marriage even to such a powerful prince as Pasenadi of Kośala. Among such a people, marriage was generally confined within the tribe itself, and the number of marriageable girls being limited, many adult males would have to go without a wife if polygamy prevailed. Hence the law had grown up among them limiting the number of wives to one. But that the Śākyas had no objection to polygamy as such on religious or other grounds, is clear from the fact narrated by the same Tibetan works that the rigorous provision of the law was relaxed in the case of Śuddhodana, the father of the Buddha; in consideration of a great public service rendered by him when, as a young prince, in subduing the hillmen of the Pāṇḍava tribe, he was allowed by the Śākyas to have two wives.

The *Lalitavistara* seems to suggest that Śuddhodana had a crowded harem, when it says that Māyādevī was his chief queen, being at the head of a thousand ladies.[8] But this appears to be a mere poetic exaggeration, for the Pāli books speak of only two

[1] *Cambridge History of India*, Vol. I, p. 175.
[2] *The Book of the Kindred Sayings*, Pt. I, p. 233.
[3] *Jātaka* (Fausböll), Vol. VI, pp. 479 foll.
[4] Beal, *op. cit.*, Vol. II, p. 14.
[5] Rockhill, *Life of the Buddha*, p. 117.
[6] Rhys Davids, *Buddhist India*, p. 20.
[7] *Life of the Buddha*, p. 15.
[8] '*Suddhodanassa pramadā pradhānā nārīsahasreṣu hi sāgraprāptā*'. *Lalitavistara*, p. 28.

wives of the king. Prince Siddhārtha had only one wife according to all accounts, and, according to the *Lalitavistara*, even the hand of this girl was not granted to him, although he was a prince, until he could satisfy the proud Śākya father of his knowledge of the *śilpas* or arts, by an open exhibition of skill in warfare as well as the finer arts.[1] Siddhārtha's wife is named Yaśodharā in the *Mahāvastu*, and her father is called Mahānāma.[2]

How proud and aristocratic the Śākyas were when asked to give away their daughters in marriage to any one outside their clan will appear from the following story of King Pasenadi of Kośala, who desired to have a Śākya girl as his consort. The king considered that if he married a Śākya girl, the Brethren (i.e. Bhikkhus) would be his friends, as he would then be related to them by marriage. So, rising from his seat, he returned to the palace, and sent a message to Kapilavatthu to this effect: 'Please give me one of your daughters in marriage, for I wish to become connected with your family'. On receipt of this message the Śākyas gathered together and deliberated: 'We live in a place subject to the authority of the king of Kośala; if we refuse to give him one of our daughters, he will be very angry; and if we give her, the custom of our clan will be broken. What are we to do?' Then Mahānāma said to them, 'I have a daughter named Vāsabhakhattiyā. Her mother is a slave woman named Nāgamuṇḍā; the girl is sixteen years old, of great beauty and auspicious prospects, and noble on her father's side. Let us send her, as a girl nobly born.' The Śākyas agreed, and, sending for the king's messengers, said that they were willing to give a daughter of the clan, and that they might take her with them at once. But the messengers reflected: 'These Śākyas are desperately proud in matters of birth. Suppose they should send a girl who is not one of them, and say that she is so. We will take none but one who eats along with them.' However, by a ruse, Mahānāma avoided eating more than one mouthful with his daughter, and Pasenadi's messengers did not discover the secret.

'So Mahānāma sent away his daughter in great pomp. The messengers brought her to Śrāvastī, and said that this maiden was the true-born daughter of Mahānāma. The king was pleased, and caused the whole city to be decorated, and placed her upon a pile of treasure, and by a ceremonial sprinkling made her his chief queen. She was dear to the king, and beloved.'[3]

The Tibetan books have preserved a story of Pasenadi. Once Pasenadi, king of Kośala, carried away by his horse, reached Kapila-

[1] *Lalitavistara*, pp. 243ff.; and see *Mahāvastu*, II, 73. [2] *Mahāvastu*, II, 48.
[3] *Jātaka* (Fausböll), Vol. IV, pp. 146 foll.

vastu alone, and roaming about hither and thither, came to the garden of Mahānāman. Here he saw the beautiful Mallikā, who was well versed in the Śāstras, and asked her whose garden it was, and was told that it belonged to the Śākya Mahānāman. The king dismounted, and asked for water for washing and drinking. Mallikā brought water for him, and then she was desired by the king to rub his feet, which she willingly did. Hardly had she touched his feet than he fell asleep. Mallikā thought that the king might have enemies, and did not open the gate when instructed to do so by a multitude of people. The king awoke and asked her what the matter was, and she told him what she had done. Her shrewdness and wisdom were admired by the king. Coming to know that she was a slave girl of Mahānāman, he went to her master and expressed his desire to marry her. The master agreed, and the king took her with him in great pomp to Śrāvastī. The king's mother was highly displeased that her son had married a slave girl, but when Mallikā went to pay respects to her and touched her feet, she immediately fell asleep. When she awoke, she thought that such a touch could not but be that of a maiden of noble birth, worthy of the family of Kośala. Shortly afterwards a son was born to Mallikā, and was called Virudhaka or the high-born.[1] It is evident that this story is a Tibetan version of the story of Pasenadi and Vāsabhakhattiyā.

We learn, then, that the Śākyas contracted marriages within their own tribe, and even their ruling house did not enter into matrimonial relations with any of the numerous princely houses in N. India,—unlike the royal houses of Kośala, Magadha and Videha, for example. When the marriage of Prince Siddhārtha was decided upon at the council of five hundred Śākya elders, these proceeded to select a bride for him from among themselves. This clannish custom among the Śākyas perhaps gave rise to the idea that they married their sisters.[2]

In Hsüan Tsang's times, when a Śākya child was born, it was carried to the temple of Īśvaradeva to be presented to the god. The temple contained a stone image of the god in the posture of rising and bowing.[3]

The women appear to have enjoyed a greater amount of independence and freedom of thought among the Śākyas than among the people of the plains, perhaps owing to the scarcity of women. Thus, according to all Buddhist accounts, the Śākya ladies were the

---

[1] Rockhill, *Life of the Buddha*, pp. 75–7. According to Pāli canonical literature, Virudhaka was the son of Pasenadi by another wife named Vāsabhakhattiyā, who was given in marriage to Pasenadi by the Śākyas.

[2] *Vide ante.*

[3] Watters, *On Yuan Chwang*, Vol. II, p. 13.

first to cut themselves off from the world, and to institute the order of nuns, the foster-mother of the Buddha, Mahāpajāpatī Gotamī, taking the lead.[1] Some of the Śākya ladies who left the world and adopted the life of the female ascetic have left behind them poems and songs that are preserved in the Psalms of the Sisters (*Therīgāthā*). Among these ladies were Tissā, Abhirūpanandā and Mittā. Tissā was born at Kapilavastu among the Śākyas. She renounced the world with Mahāpajāpatī Gotamī, and attained Arahatship.[2] Abhirūpanandā was the daughter of Khemaka the Śākya. She was called Nandā the Fair for her great beauty and amiability. Her beloved kinsman, Carabhūta, died on the day on which she was to choose him from amongst her suitors. She had to leave the world against her will, and though she entered the Order, she could not forget that she was beautiful. Fearing that the Buddha would rebuke her, she used to avoid his presence. At last, however, she was compelled to come to him for instruction, and by his supernatural power the Buddha conjured up a beautiful woman who became transformed into an old and fading figure. This had the desired effect, and Nandā became an Arahat.[3] Mittā, born in the royal family of the Śākyas at Kapilavastu, left the world with Mahāpajāpatī Gotamī, and like the other two, soon attained Arahantship.[4]

There was a technical college of the Śākyas in the mango-grove. 'It was a long terraced mansion made for the learning of crafts.'[5] The learning of one or other of the arts was incumbent upon every Śākya youth, for, as we have seen, no father would give his daughter in marriage to an idler or ignoramus. There was also a school for archery at Kapilavastu, where the Śākyas were trained.[6] The Śākyas being a Kṣatriya tribe devoted to warlike pursuits, and surrounded on all sides by warlike tribes, the school of archery was necessarily a flourishing institution. The *Lalitavistara* describes in details the various sciences and arts, beginning with the arts of writing, that the young Siddhārtha had to learn. But the whole description is that of an ideal school which the poet imagined, no doubt basing the account on the condition of education in India at the time in which he wrote. There is nothing in the description that might be called particularly Śākya.

The minds of the Śākya royal princes and nobles were so enlightened by the Buddha that they were able to realise 'the perfect

---

[1] *Vinaya Texts*, S.B.E., Vol. XX, Pt. III, pp. 320–6, 1, 2, 3, 4, 1st paragraph, and paragraphs 5 and 6.

[2] *Psalms of the Sisters*, pp. 12-13.

[3] *Ibid.*, pp. 22-3, and see also *ibid.*, pp. 55–7 (Sundarī Nandā).

[4] *Ibid.*, p. 29.

[5] *Sumaṅgalavilāsinī*, Vol. III, p. 905.

[6] Watters, *On Yuan Chwang*, Vol. II, p. 13.

fruit of righteousness'.[1] Nandupananda and Kuṇḍadana, two principal nobles, and other persons of the Śākya clan became recluses.[2] Upāli, son of Atalī, followed their example. Then the other princes and the sons of the chief minister renounced the world.[3] At the request of the Buddha, many Śākyas became recluses, and were well provided for.[4] The life of the Śākya recluse was so attractive that Sumaṅgala (reborn in a poor family) became a recluse. The recluses were respected for their simplicity of life.[5] There was a residence at Kapilavastu provided by the community for recluses of all schools.[6]

The administrative and judicial business of the Śākya clan was carried out in their *santhāgāra* or Council-Hall at Kapilavastu.[7] A young Brahmin named Ambaṭṭha who went to Kapilavastu on business had the opportunity of visiting the *santhāgāra* of the Śākyas, where he saw the young and the old seated on grand seats.[8] The '*saṃsthāgāra*' is spoken of in the *Mahāvastu* and the *Lalitavistara*, and we are told there that 500 Śākyas usually took their seats in the Hall. The *Mahāvastu* describes how thirty-two princes, the sons of a Śākya girl and Rājā Kola of Benares, came to settle in Kapilavastu, and presented themselves before the Śākya council (*Śākya-pariṣad*), where 500 Śākya leaders sat together to transact some important business. A new Council-Hall of the Śākyas was raised at Kapilavastu when the Buddha was dwelling at the Nigrodhārāma in the Mahāvana which was close to it. At their request, the Buddha inaugurated the hall, and a series of ethical discourses lasting the whole of the night were delivered by him, Ānanda and Moggallāna.[9]

The *Lalitavistara* also gives 500 as the number of the members of the Śākya Council.[10] The *Pariṣad* of the Licchavis appears to have been larger, but the system of administration seems to have been very much the same, though there was this difference, that while at Vaiśālī everyone called himself a *rājā*, at Kapilavastu there was one distinct headman called the *rājā* who was elected by the people. According to Rhys Davids, he had to preside over the sessions and when no sessions were held, he had to conduct the business of the State. But we hear that once Bhaddiya, a young cousin of the Buddha, took the title of *rājā*; and in one passage, Śuddhodana is styled a *rājā*, although he is elsewhere spoken of as a simple citizen.[11]

[1] *S.B.E.*, Vol. XIX, p. 226.
[2] *Ibid.*, pp. 226-7.
[3] *Ibid.*, p. 227.
[4] *Ibid.*, pp. 226-7; *Psalms of the Brethren*, p. 81.
[5] *Psalms of the Brethren*, p. 47.
[6] *Buddhist India*, p. 20.
[7] *Ibid.*, p. 19.
[8] *Dīgha*, I, p. 91. '*Uccesu āsanesu nisinnā*'.
[9] *Buddhist India*, p. 20.
[10] *Lalitavistara*, Ed. Lefmann, pp. 136-7.
[11] *Buddhist India*, p. 19.

In Prof. Rhys Davids' opinion, no doubt all the more important places had a 'Mote-Hall' or 'pavilion covered with a roof but with no walls in which to conduct their business'. The local affairs of the villages were conducted in open assembly consisting of the householders, 'held in the groves which, then as now, formed so distinctive a feature of each village in the long and level alluvial plain'.[1] In the time of the Chinese travellers, Fā-Hien, Sung-Yun and Hsüan Tsang, there was no central government at Kapilavastu. There existed a congregation of priests and about ten families of laymen.[2] Each town appointed its own ruler and there was no supreme ruler.[3]

D. R. Bhandarkar says that *kula* or clan sovereignty was prominent among the Śākyas. *Kula*, which was more extensive than the family, was the lowest political unit amongst the political *saṅghas*. To quote his words, *kula* 'denotes not simply the domination of a chief over his clan, but also and principally his supremacy over the territory occupied by that clan'.[4]

It appears from the *Mahāvastu*[5] that Koliya and Licchavi young men also showed their prowess at the tournament held to test the knowledge of Prince Siddhārtha before his marriage. It seems that the Koliyas and Licchavis were on terms of close relationship with the Śākyas. The Koliyas were of kindred origin, and the Licchavis, from their living in the country to the south-east of the Śākya territory, most probably often became intimate with the Śākyas.

The Kośala country bordered on the region occupied by the Śākyas, and there were mutual jealousies between the two peoples that often developed into war. Thus we are told that the Śākyas became the vassals of King Pasenadi of Kośala who received homage from them. At first Pasenadi was scornful of and disrespectful towards the Buddha, but he later repented of his attitude, developed a great admiration for the Buddha, and paid his respects to him.[6] We have already seen how he desired to establish a connection with the Buddha's family by marriage.

When Viḍūḍabha, the son of Pasenadi and Vāsabhakhattiyā, came of age, he found out that the Śākyas had deceived his father, and he resolved to take revenge upon them. In order to do this, he decided to get possession of the throne for himself, and with the aid of his commander-in-chief, Dīrgha Cārāyana or Dīgha Kārāyana,

[1] *Buddhist India*, p. 20.
[2] Beal, *Travels of Fā-Hien and Sung-Yun*, pp. 85–7.
[3] Beal, *Records of the Western World*, Vol. II, p. 14.
[4] *Carmichael Lectures*, 1918, pp. 162–4.
[5] Vol. II, p. 76.
[6] *Majjhima Nikāya* (P.T.S.), Vol. II, Pt. I, pp. 118–24.

he deposed his father who fled from Śrāvastī, the Kośala capital, and set out for Rājagṛha, the capital of Magadha. But 'it was late when he came to the city, and the gates were shut and lying down in a shed, exhausted by exposure to wind and sun, he died there'.[1] After ascending the throne, Viḍūḍabha invaded the Śākya country, took their (capital) city and slew many of them without any distinction of age or sex. He then took 500 Śākya girls for his harem, to celebrate his victory. Full of rage and hatred, the girls declared that they would never submit to the king. On hearing this, the king was enraged, and gave orders that they should be killed. According to the king's orders, the officers cut off their hands and feet and threw them into a ditch. The girls invoked the Buddha who saw their plight through his divine insight, and ordered a bhikkhu to go to them and preach his doctrine. Having heard the instruction, they attained 'purity of the eyes of law', died, and were all reborn in heaven.[2] Viḍūḍabha himself is said to have perished by a sudden flood, along with numerous Kośalan followers.

There is a different version of this account in the *Viḍūḍakāvadānaṃ* of the *Avadānakalpalatā*.[3] According to this, Viḍūḍaka ( = Viḍūḍabha) slaughtered seventy-seven thousand Śākyas and stole one thousand boys and girls. One day when he was eulogising his own prowess in his court, the stolen Śākya girls said, 'Wherefore this pride when death is inevitable to a man bound by action?' The king heard this, became angry, and ordered his men to cut off the hands of the girls.

Rhys Davids says that the real motives which led Viḍūḍaka to attack and conquer the Śākyas were most probably similar to the political motives which led Ajātaśatru to attack and conquer the Licchavis of Vaiśālī. Viḍūḍaka perhaps used the arrogance of the Śākyas as a pretext.[4]

It is stated in the *Mahāvaṃsa Ṭīkā* that during the lifetime of the Buddha some Śākyas, being oppressed by Viḍūḍabha, fled to the Himalayas, where they built a beautiful city, which was known as Moriyanagara (Mauryanagara), because the spot always resounded with the cries of peacocks.[5] The Buddhists hold that Aśoka and the Buddha were of the same family, as the former was descended from Candragupta, who was a son of the queen of one of the kings of Moriyanagara.[6]

---

1 *Jātaka* (Fausböll), Vol. IV, p. 152.
2 Beal, *Buddhist Records of the Western World*, Vol. II, pp. 11-12.
3 11th Pallava (*Bibl. Indica series*).
4 Rhys Davids, *Buddhist India*, pp. 11-12; and see also *Licchavi chapter*.
5 *Mahāvaṃsa Ṭīkā* (Ceylonese edition), pp. 119–21.
6 Beal, *Records of the Western World*, Vol. I, Intro., p. xvii.

CHAPTER L

# THE MALLAS

The Mallas were a powerful people of E. India at the time of Gautama Buddha, and are often mentioned in Buddhist and Jaina works.

The country of the Mallas is spoken of in many passages of a Buddhist work as one of the sixteen 'great countries' (*Mahājanapadas*).[1] It is also mentioned in the *Sabhāparvan* of the *Mahābhārata*, where we are told that the second Pāṇḍava, Bhīmasena, during his expedition to E. India, conquered the chief of the Mallas, besides the country of Gopālakakṣa and the northern Kośala territories.[2] The *Bhīṣmaparvan* mentions the Mallas along with such E. Indian peoples as the Aṅgas, the Vaṅgas and the Kaliṅgas.[3]

At the time of which we are speaking, the Mallas appear to have been divided into two confederacies, 'one with headquarters at Pāvā, and the other with headquarters at Kuśīnārā', as we see from the *Mahāparinibbāna Suttanta*.[4] There is reason to believe that in the Buddha's time Kuśīnārā was not a city of the first rank, like Rājagṛha, Vaiśālī, or Śrāvastī. When the Lord expressed to Ānanda his desire to die at Kuśīnārā, Ānanda said to him, 'Let not the Exalted One die in this little wattle-and-daub town, in this town in the midst of the jungle, in this branch township....' The fact that the Buddha hastened to Kuśīnārā from Pāvā during his last illness indicates that the distance between the two towns was not great; but the description in the *Mahāparinibbāna Suttanta* does not enable us to make any accurate estimate. Kuśīnārā has been identified by Cunningham with the village of Kāsiā in the east of the Gorakhpur district,[5] and this view has recently been strengthened by the fact that in the stūpa behind the Nirvāṇa temple, near this village, a copperplate has been discovered, bearing the inscription '(parini)rvāṇa-caitya-tāmra-patta', or 'the copperplate of the parinirvāṇa-caitya'. This identification appears to be correct, although V. A. Smith would prefer to place Kuśīnārā in Nepal, beyond the first range of hills.[6] Rhys Davids expresses the opinion

---

1 *Aṅguttara Nikāya*, Vol. IV, p. 252.
2 Vaṅgavāsī Ed., Vol. I, p. 241; *Sabhāparvan*, Chap. XXX, śl. 3.
3 *Ibid.*, *Bhīṣmaparvan*, Chap. IX, śl. 46.
4 *Dīgha Nikāya*, Vol. II, p. 165.
5 *Ancient Geography of India*, pp. 430–3.
6 *Early History of India*, 4th Ed., p. 167, f.n. 5; *J.R.A.S.*, 1913, p. 152.

that, if we may trust the Chinese pilgrims, the territory of the Mallas of Kuśīnārā and Pāvā was on the mountain slopes to the east of the Śākya land and to the north of the Vajjian confederation. But some would place their territory south of the Śākyas and east of the Vajjians.[1] It is a considerable distance from Kāsiā in the Gorakhpur district to Pāwāpuri of the Jainas in the Patna district, and one so ill as the Buddha was not likely to go such a distance on foot. Therefore Pāvā of the Buddhist books appears to have been distinct from Pāwāpuri, and situated not very far from Kāsiā.

The Cullavagga of the *Vinaya Piṭaka* mentions another town of the Mallas named Anupiyā,[2] where the Buddha resided for some time. This Anupiyā may be the same as the mango-grove called Anupiya, where Gautama spent the first seven days after his renunciation, on his way to Rājagṛha.[3]

A fourth town of the Mallas, called Uruvelakappa, where the Buddha stayed for some time, is mentioned in the *Aṅguttara Nikāya*.[4] In its neighbourhood a wide forest called Mahāvana appears to have existed, where the Buddha went alone for midday rest after his meal, and met the *gahapati* Tapusa.

From the *Mahāparinibbāna Suttanta* account of the Buddha's death and cremation,[5] it is evident that the Mallas belonged to the Kṣatriya caste; and they are repeatedly addressed by the Buddha as well as by Ānanda and others as Vāseṭṭhas or Vāśiṣṭhas,[6]—showing that, like the Licchavis, they belonged to the Vaśiṣṭha gotra. Like the Licchavis again, the Mallas are described by Manu (X, 22) as 'born of a Kṣatriya mother and of a Kṣatriya father who was a *vrātya*,' i.e. who had not gone through the ceremony of Vedic initiation at the proper age.

According to Kauṭilya, the Mallas were a *saṅgha* or corporation of which the members called themselves *rājās*, just as the Licchavis did. Buddhaghosa also calls them *rājās*.[7] A passage in the *Majjhima Nikāya* mentions the Licchavis and Mallas as examples of *saṅghas* and *gaṇas*. The Mallas of Pāvā and Kuśīnārā, then, had their respective *Santhāgāras* or Council-Halls, where all matters, both political and religious, were discussed. The *Saṅgīti Suttanta* of the *Dīgha Nikāya*[8] tells us that when the Buddha came to the Mallas, a new Council-Hall named Ubbhaṭaka had just been built at Pāvā.

---

[1] *Buddhist India*, p. 26.
[2] *Cullavagga*, VII, 1, 1; *Vinaya Texts*, S.B.E., Pt. III, p. 224.
[3] *Jātaka* (Fausböll), Vol. I, pp. 65-6.
[4] *Saṃyutta Nikāya*, Pt. V, p. 228; *Aṅguttara Nikāya*, Vol. IV, p. 438.
[5] *Dīgha Nikāya*, II, p. 165.
[6] *Ibid.*, III, p. 209.
[7] *Sumaṅgalavilāsinī*, III, p. 971; and see *Licchavi chapter*.
[8] *Dīgha*, Pt. III, p. 207.

The Mallas invited the Buddha to this hall, saying, 'Let the Lord, the Exalted One, be the first to make use of it. That it has first been used by the Exalted One will be for the lasting good and happiness of the Pāvā Mallas'. At their request, the Buddha gave a discourse on his doctrine to the Mallas of Pāvā, until the late hours of the night. The Mallas were in assembly and had been doing business in their Council-Hall when Ānanda went to them with the message of the impending death of the Master; and again they gathered in assembly, evidently in the same *Santhāgāra*, to discuss the procedure to be followed in the disposal of the body, and afterwards to discuss the claims put forward by the various Kṣatriya kings and peoples.

In the *Mahāparinibbāna Suttanta*, there is mention of a set of officers called *Purisas* among the Mallas of Kuśīnārā, about whose functions we are quite in the dark. Rhys Davids [1] takes them to be a class of subordinate servants. It is not unlikely that they are the same as the *Pulisas* mentioned in the edicts of Aśoka.

It seems that the Mallas were a martial race and were devoted to such manly sports as wrestling.[2] It is probable that the word 'Malla' denoting a professional wrestler was derived from the tribal name of this people. But the Mallas cultivated learning as well as physical culture. We read in one of the Buddhist texts, for example, that Bandhula, a son of a king of Kuśīnārā, went to Taxila for his education. There he studied with a great teacher, along with Pasenadi of Kośala, and Mahāli, a Licchavi prince of Vaiśālī. After completing his education he came back to this realm.[3] We often find the Mallas discussing philosophical problems, as may be seen, e.g. from *Saṃyutta Nikāya*, IV, pp. 327ff.; V, pp. 228-9, 349ff.

Before the advent of Jainism and Buddhism, the Mallas seem to have been *caitya*-worshippers like their neighbours, the Licchavis. One of their shrines called Makuṭa Bandhana, to the east of Kuśīnārā, is mentioned in connection with the death of the Buddha: his dead body was carried thither for cremation. There is no indication of the kind of worship that was performed at this place.

Jainism found many followers among the Mallas. The accounts in Buddhist Literature of the schism that appeared in the Jaina Church after the death of Mahāvīra amply prove this. At Pāvā, the followers of Nigaṇṭha Nātaputta were divided after the death of their great Tīrthaṅkara. There were both ascetics and lay devotees among these Jainas, for we read that on account of the disputations among the ascetics, 'even the lay disciples of the white robe, who

---

1 *Buddhist India*, p. 21. 2 *Jātaka* (Fausböll), Vol. II, p. 96.
3 Fausböll, *Dhammapadaṃ* (old edition), p. 211.

followed Nātaputta, showed themselves shocked, repelled and indignant at the Nigaṇṭhas.'[1] These lay Jainas appear from this passage to have been draped in white robes, just as the *Śvetāmbaras* are at the present day. The Buddha seems to have taken advantage of the schism that overtook the Jaina church on the death of its founder, for the propagation of the rival faith. In the *Pāsādika Suttanta*, we find that Cunda, the novice of Pāvā, brought the news of the death of Mahāvīra to Ānanda at Sāmagāma in the Malla country. Ānanda forthwith reported it to the Buddha who delivered a long discourse.[2]

The Mallas were much attached to the founder of Jainism. We are informed by the *Kalpa Sūtra* that to mark the passing away of the great Jina, nine Mallakis or Malla chiefs were among those that instituted an illumination on the day of the New-moon, saying, 'Since the light of intelligence is gone, let us make an illumination of material matter.'[3]

Buddhism also attracted many devotees among the Mallas some of whom, like the venerable Dabba, attained a high and respected position among the brethren.[4] On account of his virtues, he was appointed, after due election by the Buddhist *Saṅgha*, a regulator of lodging places and apportioner of rations. He was so successful in the discharge of these duties, which required a great deal of patience and tact, that he was considered by the *Saṅgha* to be possessed of miraculous powers. But there were some who were envious of him, and preferred charges against him to bring about his expulsion from the *Saṅgha*. The venerable Dabba, however, was exculpated from these charges.

Another Malla, Khaṇḍasumana, born in the family of a Malla rājā of Pāvā, entered the Buddhist Order and acquired six-fold Abhiññā.[5]

Once, Buddha was in the country of the Mallas at Uruvelakappa. One day he asked Ānanda to remain there, while he left for Mahāvana to spend the day. While Ānanda was at Uruvelakappa, a householder named Tapussa, probably a Malla, came to him, and Ānanda took him to the Buddha whose teachings cured Tapussa of his desire for sensual pleasures.[6] Another Malla, Roja, asked Ānanda whether the Buddha would accept potherbs and meal from him, and the Buddha asked him to hand them over to the bhikkhus.[7] A certain Sīha was born in the country of the Mallas, in the family of a rājā.

---

[1] *Dīgha*, III, p. 210.

[2] *Ibid.*, III, p. 118.

[3] *Jaina Sūtras*, Pt. I, S.B.E., XXII, p. 266.

[4] *Vinaya Texts*, Pt. III, pp. 4ff.

[5] *Psalms of the Brethren*, p. 90.

[6] *Aṅguttara Nikāya*, Vol. IV, pp. 438–48.

[7] *Vinaya Texts*, Pt. II, S.B.E., Vol. XVII, p. 139.

As soon as he saw the Buddha, he was attracted to him. The Buddha taught him the Dhamma, and he entered the Buddhist order and eventually developed insight and acquired Arhatship.[1]

It was at the Mallian city of Pāvā that the Buddha ate his last meal at the house of Cunda, the smith, and fell ill. Though in pain, the Buddha went to the rival Mallian city of Kuśīnārā. When he felt that his last moment was fast approaching, he sent Ānanda with a message to the Mallas of Kuśīnārā who had then assembled in their *Santhāgāra* (Council-Hall) for some public affair. On receipt of the news, they flocked to the Sāla grove where the Buddha was, with their young men, girls and wives, 'being grieved and sad and afflicted at heart'. The venerable Ānanda caused them 'to stand in groups, each family in a group,' and presented them to the Buddha.[2] After his last exhortations to the assembled brethren to work out their salvation with diligence, the Buddha entered into *parinirvāṇa*.

The Mallas then met together in their Council-Hall to devise some means of honouring the earthly remains of the Lord in a suitable manner, and carried them with music to the shrine of the Mallas, called the Makūṭa-bandhana, to the east of their city. They treated the remains of the Tathāgata as they would treat the remains of a king of kings (Cakravarttirājā).[3] When the cremation was over, they extinguished the funeral pyre with water scented with all sorts of perfumes, and collected the bones, which they placed in their Council-Hall, surrounding them 'with a lattice work of spears and with a rampart of bows.'[4]

As they had a separate principality, the Mallas of Pāvā were among the various clans that pressed their claims for a share of the remains. They sent a messenger to the Mallas of Kuśīnārā, saying: 'The Exalted One was a Kṣatriya and so are we. We are worthy to receive a portion of the relics of the Exalted One. Over the remains of the Exalted One will we put up a sacred cairn, and in his honour will we celebrate a feast.' Both the Mallas of Pāvā and of Kuśīnārā erected stūpas over their respective shares, and celebrated feasts.

The Mallas appear to have usually been on friendly terms with their neighbours, the Licchavis, with whom they had many ties of kinship, though, as was inevitable, there were occasional rivalries between the two States, as, for instance, the story of Bandhula, a Mallian general, shows.[5] Bandhula drove to Vaiśālī, the Licchavi capital, where he arrogantly misused the water of a tank where the members of the king's families were in the habit of obtaining water

---

1 *Psalms of the Brethren*, p. 80.
2 *Dīgha*, II, pp. 148 foll.
3 *Ibid.*, p. 161.
4 *Ibid.*, p. 164.
5 Fausböll, *Dhammapadaṃ* (old ed.), pp. 218–20.

for ceremonial purposes. Five hundred Licchavi Rājās set forth to capture Bandhula, but the latter 'sped a shaft and it cleft the heads of all the chariots and passed right through the five hundred kings,'—who forthwith died in gruesome circumstances.

The Mallas appear to have lost their independence to that ambitious monarch of Magadha, Ajātaśatru, and their dominions were annexed to the Magadhan empire.[1]

---

[1] D. R. Bhandarkar, *Carmichael Lectures*, 1918, p. 79.

## CHAPTER LI

# THE VAṄGAS

It is not difficult for the philologist to recognise the present Bengal in the tribal name 'Vaṅga'. But Vaṅga in ancient days denoted only a portion of present-day Bengal; it is distinguished in ancient literature and epigraphic records not only from Rāḍha which included Suhma[1] or was conterminous with it[2] and Gauḍa which at one time included Karṇasuvarṇa[3] and a portion of Rāḍha,[4]—all making up what is now roughly known as Western Bengal,—but also from Puṇḍra or Puṇḍravardhana which included Varendra or Varendri,[5] making up what is roughly identical with present Northern Bengal. Vaṅga thus stood for what is now known as Eastern Bengal comprising the modern Dacca and Chittagong divisions. Among the important divisions of Vaṅga in ancient days were included Samataṭa (mod. Faridpur), according to Watters, and for some time even Tāmralipta or Tāmalitti (mod. Tamluk).[6] Hemacandra in his *Abhidhānacintāmaṇi* (IV, 23), however, identifies the country of the Vaṅga with that of a tribe called the Harikelas.[7] In the eleventh century Cola Inscription (Tirumalai Rock Ins. of Rājendra Cola) as well as in the Goharwa Plate of Karṇadeva, king of Cedi (*c.* 1040–1070 A.D.), the Vaṅga country is referred to as Baṅgāla-deśam, which, in the thirteenth century, came to be called Baṅgāla (Wright's Marco Polo) and in Mohamedan times Bāṅglā. The Tirumalai Inscription distinguishes Vaṅga from South Rāḍha (Takkana Lāḍham) and North Rāḍha (Uttila Lāḍham). Thus Vaṅga which at one time denoted Eastern Bengal has now given its name to the entire province of modern Bengal, the English rendering of the name being derived from Baṅgāla or Bāṅglā.[8]

---

[1] *I.H.Q.*, Vol. VIII, No. 3, pp. 525–9.

[2] S.B.E., Vol. XXII, pp. 84-5, Nilakaṇṭha's commentary on the *Sabhāparvan* of the *Mahābhārata*. 'Suhmāḥ Rāḍhāḥ' = The Suhmas are the Rāḍhas.

[3] M. Chakravarti, *J.A.S.B.*, 1908, p. 274. [4] *Prabodhacandrodaya*, Canto II.

[5] Tarpaṇdighi Grant of Lakṣmaṇasena, *Inscriptions of Bengal*, III, pp. 99ff. But in some of the Sena records Vaṅga is included in Puṇḍravardhanabhukti.

[6] *I.H.Q.*, Vol. VIII, No. 3, p. 533.

[7] According to I-tsing (I-tsing, Takakusu, p. xlvi), Wuhing, another Chinese pilgrim, visited Harikela, which was the eastern limit of E. India. Harikela is also mentioned in an illustrated manuscript of *Aṣṭasahasraprajñāpāramitā* in the Camb. Univ. Library (MSS. Add. 1643).

[8] In a Nālandā Inscription recently edited by N. G. Majumdar (*Ep. Ind.*, Vol. XXI, Pt. III, pp. 97ff.) the name *Vaṅgāla deśa* appears.

In the time of Baudhāyana[1] (fourth century B.C. ?), the Vaṅgas were distinguished from the Puṇḍras, while in the Epics and Purāṇas, Vaṅga is distinguished from Puṇḍra and Suhma, as well as from Aṅga and Kaliṅga. According to the Purāṇas and the *Mahābhārata*,[2] King Bali's queen, Sudeṣṇā, and the sage Dīrghatamas had five sons (with Bali's consent): Aṅga, Vaṅga, Kaliṅga, Puṇḍra, and Suhma. These five were called the Bāleya Kṣatras or Bāleya Brāhmaṇas, and are said to have been the founders of the five countries bearing their respective names. In the *Matsyapurāṇa*, Vaṅga and Suhma are included in a list of the eastern countries (Chap. 114, 43–45).[3] According to the *Mahābhārata* (XII, Chap. 5, 6607), King Jarāsandha is said to have extended his supremacy over the Aṅgas, Vaṅgas, Kaliṅgas, and Puṇḍras. Karṇa is also once said to have conquered the Suhmas, Aṅgas and Vaṅgas (*Karṇaparvan*, Chap. 8, 19), while Vāsudeva is said to have once routed in battle the Aṅgas, Vaṅgas, Kaliṅgas and Pauṇḍras along with other peoples. In the *Sabhāparvan*, the Pāṇḍavas are described as having subjugated the Puṇḍras and the Vaṅgas, and led their victorious army to Suhma (*Sabhāparvan*, Chap. XXX, 23–5).

It, therefore, seems that in the period represented by the Epics and the Purāṇas, Vaṅga, Puṇḍra (or Pauṇḍra) and Suhma were the three important divisions of Bengal, but it is difficult to define with any degree of exactitude the geographical positions of these divisions. We may, however, assume that Puṇḍra and Suhma were two adjacent tracts, identical roughly with the modern Rajshahi and Burdwan divisions respectively. In the *Sabhāparvan* of the *Mahābhārata* Aṅga and Vaṅga are mentioned as forming one *Viṣaya* or kingdom. This is supported by a reference in the *Rāmāyaṇa* (Bk. II, Chap. X) where the Vaṅgas are mentioned along with the Aṅgas; they are, moreover, nearly always associated in ancient literature with the Aṅgas and Kaliṅgas.

The Vaṅgas as a tribe are not mentioned in earlier Vedic literature, unless we recognise them in the curious word 'Vaṅga-Vāgadhāḥ' which occurs in the *Aitareya Āraṇyaka* (II, I, I). 'Vaṅga-Vāgadhaḥ' has often been amended into 'Vaṅga-Māgadhāḥ',

[1] *Dharmasūtra*, I, I, 14; cf. Oldenberg, *Buddha*, 394, n.

[2] *Vāyu P.*, Chap. 99, 26–34, 47–97; *Brahmāṇḍa P.*, III, Chap. 74, 25–34, 47–100; *Matsya P.*, Chap. 48, 23–9, 43–89; *Brahma P.*, IV, Chap. 18, 1; *Bhāg. P.*, IX, Chap. 23, 5; *Mbh.* I, Chap. 104, 4193–221, with variations; XII, Chap. 343, 13177–84, cf. Pargiter, *Anc. Ind. Hist. Tradition*, pp. 109 and 158.

[3] Cf. also *Mbh.* (*Bhīṣmaparvan*, Chap. 9, 46) where the Aṅgas, Vaṅgas and Kaliṅgas are mentioned as East Indian peoples (Law, '*Some Kṣatriya Tribes of Ancient India*', p. 147). Cf. also *Rāmāyaṇa* (*Kiṣkindhyā Kāṇḍa*, Canto xlii) where the Puṇḍras are mentioned as an Eastern people.

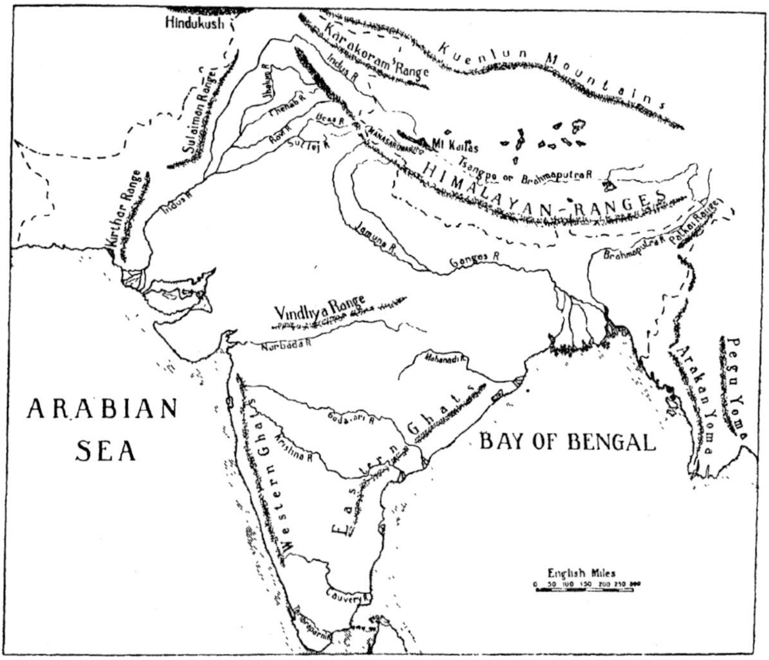


The physical map of India

i.e. the Vaṅgas and the Magadhas, who were neighbouring peoples. The amendment is doubtful; but if it be correct, the Vaṅgas along with the Magadhas must have been branded by the Aryans as an impure people, probably a pre-Aryan tribe; for the two tribes are described as 'pakṣī-viśeṣāḥ', or like certain species of birds. Baudhāyana too brands Vaṅga as an impure country, along with Puṇḍra, Kaliṅga and Sauvīra. An Aryan who had been to any of these countries was required to perform a certain sacrificial rite to become free from the impurities attaching to residence there. Even in the time of Patañjali (second century B.C.) the Vaṅgas and their country were excluded from Āryāvarta. The country was, however, Aryanised before Manu wrote his Dharmaśāstra (between 200 B.C. and 200 A.D., acc. to Bühler), for the *Manusaṃhitā* extends the eastern boundary of Āryāvarta to the sea.[1] In the early Buddhist literature where detailed lists appear of many countries and peoples, the Vaṅgas and their country are conspicuous by their absence. They are, however, mentioned in the *Jain Prajñāpāṇā*,[2] which ranks Aṅga and Vaṅga in the first group of Aryan peoples, and in the *Milinda-Pañho*,[3] where Vaṅga is described as a trading-place to be reached by sea. The mother of Sīhabāhu and Sīhasīvalī, of *Mahāvaṃsa* and *Dīpavaṃsa* fame, was a Vaṅga princess, the daughter of a king of Vaṅga who had married the daughter of the king of Kaliṅga.[4]

The first epigraphic mention of the Vaṅgas is probably made in the Maharauli Iron Pillar Inscription (*C.I.I.*, Vol. III, pp. 141ff.), where the mighty King Candra is said to have 'in battle in the Vaṅga countries turned back with his breast the enemies who uniting together came against him.' H. P. Śāstrī identified this King Candra with King Candravarman of the Allahabad Pillar Inscription, and with the king of the same name of Pokhrana, which he located in Marwar

[1] For early references to Vaṅga see Lévi, *Pre-Aryan et Pre-Dravidian dans l'Inde*.

[2] It is interesting to see what accounts we may get of the ancient Vaṅga people out of some records of non-Aryan activities of a time when the Aryans disdained to notice the tribes outside the pale of Āryāvarta. For a detailed study vide B. C. Majumdar, *History of the Bengali Language*, pp. 38–41. Glimpses of the ancient relation of Bengal with the Tamils are reflected in at least one place-name of ancient Bengal Tāmralipti, which was once called Dāmalipti or Dāmilitti, i.e. the city of the Dāmala people. The Dāmalas are the same as the Tāmala people or the Tāmila; and Bengal must once have been a home of these people.

H. P. Śāstrī, *Mānasī*, Vaiśākh, 1321 B.S., pp. 356-8.

[3] P. 359 (Trenckner).

[4] *Mahāvaṃsa*, VI, 1ff.; *Dīpavaṃsa*, IX, 2. We may note here that *Lāḷa*, which is mentioned in this story has been proved by H. C. Ray, in an interesting note, to be identical with Rāḍha (H. C. Ray, '*Lāḷa*—A Note', *J.A.S.B.* (new series), Vol. XVIII, 1922, No. 7).

in Rajputana. H. C. Ray Chaudhuri and S. K. Chatterjee, however, identify Pokhrana or Puṣkaraṇa with a village of the same name on the Dāmodara river in the Bankura district of Bengal, some 25 miles east of the Susunia Hill on which the record of Candravarman is inscribed.[1] The Vaṅgas are mentioned in Kālidāsa's *Raghuvaṃśa,* where Raghu is said to have conquered the Vaṅgas after he had finished his task with the Suhmas, and then to have planted his victorious banner in the midstream of the Ganges (Canto IV, 35-6). This passage shows that in the age of Kālidāsa (*c.* 400 A.D.) the Vaṅgas were distinguished, as in earlier days, from the Suhmas. It is likely that the realm of the Vaṅgas abutted on the Ganges, which probably formed the dividing line between the two countries.

The Vaṅga country is also referred to in the Mahākuṭa Pillar Inscription (*Ep. Ind.*, Vol. V), which tells us that in the sixth century A.D., Kīrtivarman of the Cālukya dynasty gained victories over the kings of Vaṅga, Aṅga and Magadha, which were three neighbouring countries. Another reference to the realm of the Vaṅga people is made in the '*Gauḍavaho*', a Marathi Prakrit poem that records the exploits of King Yaśovarman of Kanauj (first half of the eighth century A.D). The identity of Yaśovarman has been sufficiently established by his mention in Chinese records (as I-chafon-mo), and also in the *Rājataraṅgiṇī* of Kalhaṇa; but the exploits recorded in the '*Gauḍavaho*', with the exception of the main topics, i.e. the defeat and death of the Gauḍa king, are of doubtful historical value. We are told that Yaśovarman, bent on conquest, first came to the river Son, whence he proceeded to the Vindhyas with his army. Fearing his approach, the Gauḍa king, who was also the king of Magadha, fled, and Yaśovarman entered his territory and fixed his camp there. The Gauḍa king returned, and a battle was fought in which he was killed. Yaśovarman next proceeded to the Vaṅga kingdom, whose king also submitted to him.[2] Not long after Yaśovarman's victories, Odivisa, Vaṅga and five other countries of the east (which seem to have included Gauḍa, Suhma, Puṇḍra, etc.) seem, according to the celebrated Tibetan historian Tārānāth (*Ind. Ant.*, Vol. IV, pp. 365-6), to have been plunged into a chaos which has been described as '*Mātsya-nyāya*',—i.e. the system where the strong destroy the weak, like the big fish eating up the small frog. This was ended when Gopāla, the first of the Pāla dynasty, was elected king from amongst the people sometime in the middle of the eighth century A.D.

---

[1] Ray Chaudhuri, *P.H.A.I.*, p. 448 (4th Ed.); S. K. Chatterjee, *The Origin and Development of the Bengali Language*, II, p. 1061. See also *I.H.Q.*, I, Pt. II, p. 255.

[2] N. Ray, *The Maukharis of Kanoj*, *Cal. Rev.*, 1928, Feb., pp. 216-7.

From the above account we see that the Vaṅga country seems to have been distinguished from that of the Gauḍas in the eighth century A.D.; and this distinction seems to have been maintained as late as the twelfth century A.D. In the Pithāpuram plates of Prithvīsena (A.D. 1186) King Malla is said to have subdued among others the kings of the Vaṅgas, Magadhas and Gauḍas. In the Tirumalai Rock Inscription[1] of King Rājendra Cola (1025 A.D.) *Vaṅgāladeśam*, i.e. the realm of the Vaṅgālas or Vaṅgas (at that time ruled over by Govinda Candra) is distinguished from Uttira-Lāḍam or Uttara-Rāḍha (= the Brahma country of the *Kāvya-mīmāṃsā*),[2] ruled over by Mahipāla, and from Takkana-Lāḍam or Dakṣiṇa Rāḍha (= Suhma of the Epics, the Purāṇas and the *Kāvya-mīmāṃsā*), ruled over by Raṇaśūra. The *Kāvyamīmāṃsā*,[2] a work of the tenth century A.D., mentions Aṅga, Vaṅga, Suhma, Brahma, Puṇḍra, etc., as janapadas of the east. The Vaṅga country is also referred to not only in the copperplate grant of Vaidyadeva of Kāmarūpa (twelfth century), who is said to have been victorious in southern Vaṅga (*Ep. Ind.*, Vol. II, p. 355), but also in the Edilpur plate of Keśavasena, the Madanpāḍa plate of Viśvarūpasena, and the Sāhitya Parishad plate of the same king (*Inscriptions of Bengal*, Vol. III, pp. 119, 133 and 141).

It thus appears that from the fall of the later Guptas (eighth century) to the break-up of the Sena dynasty (twelfth century), the more important divisions of Bengal were Vaṅga, Puṇḍra, Gauḍa and Suhma (which latter, according to one authority, was identical with Rāḍhā-Nīlakaṇṭha's commentary on the *Mahābhārata*, and, according to another, stood for a portion, i.e. the southern portion of Rāḍhā, the northern portion being called Brahma).[3] Other important divisions were Karṇasuvarṇa and Varendra, Tāmralipti, Bāgḍī, Samataṭa and Harikela (of which the last two were included in or identical with Vaṅga). Tāmralipti was included in Suhma and Varendra in Puṇḍra or Puṇḍravardhana, while Karṇasuvarṇa seems to have stood for some region perhaps identical with some portion of the northern Rāḍha country. Some scholars have identified it with Rāṅgāmāṭi in the Murshidabad district.[4] Others think that Karṇasuvarṇa was situated to the west of the Bhāgīrathi and included Murshidabad, Bankura, Burdwan and Hughli.[5] Bāgḍi, one of the four divisions of the ancient Bengal, according to Vallālasena (Gopāla Bhaṭṭa's *Vallāla-Charitaṃ*,—a book of doubtful

---

1 *Ep. Ind.*, Vol. IX, p. 231.

2 Chaps. 3 and 17.

3 See P. Sen, *Some Janapadas of Ancient Rāḍha*, *I.H.Q.*, Vol. VIII, No. 3, pp. 521–9.

4 *J.A.S.B.*, XXII, p. 281; *Kubjika Tantra*, Chap. 7.

5 Dey's *Geographical Dicty.*, p. 94.

value—Pūrva-khaṇḍa, verses 6 and 7) comprised the delta of the Ganges and the Brahmaputra, and may be identified with what is now known as the 24-parganas and the Sunderbans (*C.A.G.I.*, Ed. Majumdar, pp. 730-1).

Samataṭa, as we have already said, was included in the larger divisions of Vaṅga. Some scholars are of opinion that it was distinct from Vaṅga, which lay between the Meghna on the east, the sea on the south, and the old Buḍigaṅgā course of the Ganges on the north. The western boundary of Vaṅga appears always to have been indefinite (vide Bhaṭṭasāli, *Sculptures in the Dacca Museum*, pp. 4–6).[1] Samataṭa is mentioned for the first time in the Allahabad Pillar Inscription[2] of Samudragupta as one of the most important among the north-east Indian frontier kingdoms which submitted to the mighty Gupta emperor. It is also mentioned in the *Karmavibhāga* of the *Bṛhatsaṃhitā* (Chap. XIV) as an eastern country, and was visited by the Chinese travellers, Hsüan Tsang, I-tsing and Seng-chi. Hsüan Tsang describes it as 'the country of which the rivers have flat and level banks of equal height on both sides'. According to him, it was much to the south of Kāmrūpa and east of Tāmralipta; it was low, moist and on the sea side. Samataṭa thus seems to have been identical with the delta of the Ganges and Brahmaputra and must have comprised, according to epigraphic evidence, the modern districts of Tipperah, Noakhali, Sylhet (*J.A.S.B.*, 1915, pp. 17, 18), and probably portions of Barisal. That it included Tipperah is proved also by Nos. 19 and 59 of the *Cambridge MSS.*, Add., 1643, and Foucher, *Iconographie Bouddhique*, Vol. I; also Bhaṭṭasāli, *op. cit.*, pp. 12-13.

When Hsüan Tsang visited the country (*c.* 640 A.D.), Samataṭa was an important kingdom. There were about 30 Buddhist Saṁghārāmas with about 2,000 priests in the country, while the temples of Brahmanical gods were also numerous, and there were also many Jain (Nigaṇṭha) ascetics. During the visits of Hsüan Tsang and Seng-chi, Samataṭa seems to have been under the rule of the Khaḍga dynasty.[3] The Asrafpur copperplates of the Khaḍgas (*Mem., A.S.B.*, Vol. I, No. 6) were issued from a place called Karmānta, which has been identified with Baḍ-Māmtā, 12 miles west of Comilla. Karmānta has often been identified as the capital of Samataṭa (Dey, *Geog. Dicty.*, p. 175; Bhaṭṭasāli, *op. cit.*, p. 6). Later on,

[1] Regarding Vaṅga, Vaṅgāla and Samataṭa, mention may be made here of H. C. Ray Chaudhuri's Bengali article, '*Vaṅga kon deśa*' in his *Studies in Indian Antiquities*, Cal. Univ., pp. 184-192.

[2] *C.I.I.*, Vol. III, No. 1.

[3] *Memoirs of A.S.B.*, Vol. I, No. 6; also Beal, *Life of Hiuen Tsang*, Introduction, p. xi, No. 40.

Samataṭa came to be ruled over by the Candra dynasty of Vaṅga (cf. Govindacandra of Vaṅgāla deśam of the Tirumalai Inscription). The Rampal plate of Śrīcandradevaṃ (*Ep. Ind.*, Vol. XII, p. 136) informs us that a Candra dynasty held sway over the Rohita hill (identified by Bhaṭṭasāli with a range of hillocks in the Tipperah district, see *Sculptures in the Dacca Museum*, pp. 9-10), and appears to have mastered the whole of Vaṅga including Samataṭa. Śrīcandradeva's father Trailokyacandra is described as having been the mainstay of the king of Harikela. The Candras were ousted from their possession of Samataṭa in the beginning of the eleventh century by the Varmans, who in their turn gave place to the Senas towards the end of the same century. During their rule Vaṅga was included in the Puṇḍravardhanabhukti.

## CHAPTER LII

# THE GAUḌAS

The earliest literary reference to the country of the Gauḍas is made by the celebrated grammarian Pāṇini who seems to locate the country in the east (*Pāṇini*, VI, ii, 99-100). The country is also referred to in the *Arthaśāstra* of Kauṭilya as well as in the *Kāmasūtra* of Vātsyāyana (*nakhacchedya prakaraṇam*, ii, 13). Varāhamihira (sixth century A.D.) probably refers to the Gauḍa country when he places 'Gauḍaka' in the eastern division of India. But the first epigraphic mention of the tribe is made in the Harāhā inscription of A.D. 554 (*Ep. Ind*, XIV, pp. 110ff.), where King Īśānavarman of the Maukhari dynasty claims victories over the Andhras, the Śūlikas (prob. = the Cālukyas) and the Gauḍas, who are described as living on the seashore (*Gauḍān samudrāśrayān*). It is difficult to define with any amount of certainty the exact region which the Gauḍas occupied at that time. H. C. Ray Chaudhuri, however, suggests that their 'proper realm' was Western Bengal as it bordered on the sea, and included Karṇasuvarṇa and Rāḍhāpurī (*P.H.A.I.*, 4th Ed., p. 509). This may find confirmation in the combined testimony of Bāṇa and Hsüan Tsang who state that Śaśāṅka or Karṇasuvarṇa (identified with Rāṅgāmāṭi in Murshidabad, W. Bengal) was the Gauḍa king, the great rival of Rājyavardhana and Harṣavardhana, the kings of Thāneśvar (seventh century).

The fight with the Maukharis seems to have brought the Gauḍas into the forefront of Eastern Indian politics. At first the Gupta-Maukhari struggle effected the serious discomfiture of the Guptas; in fact they were obliged to give up Magadha to their enemies and retire to Mālava.[1] During the reign of Rājyavardhana of Kanauj, the king of Mālava was Devagupta,[2] and the king of the Gauḍas was Śaśāṅka who was also the king of Karṇasuvarṇa, according to Hsüan Tsang. Devagupta allied himself with Śaśāṅka, and defeated and killed Grahavarman, the Maukhari king, who had married Rājyaśrī, sister of Rājyavardhana and Harṣavardhana. Rājyavardhana, who came to the rescue of his widowed sister, and succeeded in defeating Devagupta, was treacherously slain

---

[1] N. Ray, *The Maukharis of Kanoj*, *Cal. Rev.*, 1928, Feb.

[2] Bāṇa's *Harṣacarita*; cf. also *the Madhuvan and Banskhera Inscriptions of Harṣavardhana*.

by the latter's ally, Śaśāṅka, king of Gauḍa[1] (606 A.D.). Though the murdered king's brother Harṣavardhana sought to avenge his death, Śaśāṅka is known to have been still in power as late as the year 619; but his kingdom probably became subject to Harṣa at a later date.[2]

After the death of Śaśāṅka, the Gauḍas seem to have faded out of history for a time; but in the first half of the eighth century they again appear on the stage, and a Gauḍa king is seen to occupy the throne of Magadha. This appears from the *Gauḍavaho*, a Prākrit poem by Vākpatirāja, which records the slaying of the Gauḍa king, who was also the king of Magadha, by Yaśovarman, king of Kanauj. The Gauḍa country in Vākpatirāja's account is distinguished from the Vaṅga country. As its king was also the king of Magadha, it may be assumed that it was contiguous with Magadha.

The sequel to the story of Yaśovarman is given in the *Rājataraṅgiṇī* of Kalhaṇa. Yaśovarman was defeated in his turn by Lalitāditya, king of Kāśmīr, who had launched out on a career of conquest. Lalitāditya is also credited by Kalhaṇa with having defeated another Gauḍa king and compelled the latter to give him his whole elephant force. We are not told who this Gauḍa king was or which region he ruled over. According to Kalhaṇa, Lalitāditya had the Gauḍa king killed in spite of a promise given not to harm him and sworn by his favourite god Parihāsa Keśava. When the Gauḍas heard of this treachery, they at once started for Kāśmīr, and entering the capital, they threw down the idol of the Rāmasvāmī temple, broke it into pieces and strewed them on the road. While they were thus engaged, the royal army from Śrīnagar arrived and attacked them. Undaunted, the Gauḍas continued in their work of destruction until they were annihilated by the army. Even in the time of Kalhaṇa (twelfth century A.D.) the Rāmasvāmī temple was empty, and the heroism of the Gauḍas was sung all over the valley. But it is difficult in the absence of other records to ascertain the elements of historic truth underlying this romantic story, and sober history would hardly agree to recognise it.[3]

Lalitāditya's grandson Jayāpīḍa (close of the eighth century) is also described by Kalhaṇa as having had some relations with the Gauḍas. He is said to have once gone to Bengal *incognito*.

---

[1] V. A. Smith, *Early History of India* (4th Ed.), p. 350.

[2] The Gauḍa country is referred to in the Apshad Inscription of Ādityasena (*c.* 655 A.D.), where Sūkṣmaśiva, the engraver of the inscription, is mentioned as being a native of the Gauḍa country.

[3] After Yaśovarman's defeat Kalhaṇa makes Lalitāditya start on a march of triumphal conquest round the whole of India, which is manifestly legendary (Stein, *Chronicles of the Kings of Kāsmīr*, Vol. I, p. 90).

Having killed a tiger which had become a terror to the city of Pauṇḍravardhana, he came to the notice of the king who ruled there, one Jayanta. Jayanta gave him his daughter in marriage, and Jayāpīḍa is then said to have subdued five kings of the Gauḍa country (which probably meant the major portion of the province of Bengal with Monghyr and Bhagalpur of the province of Bihar) on behalf of his father-in-law, and then returned to Kāśmīr in triumph with his bride. The whole story reads more as fiction than history, and serious criticism has doubted its authenticity.[1]

The Gauḍas are twice mentioned in Rājaśekhara's *Kāvyamīmāṃsā*, where it is said that they spoke Sanskrit, but could not speak Prākrit well (Chap. X, p. 57; Chap. 7, p. 33).

The Pāla kings of Bengal are often described as 'Lords of Gauḍa' (*Gauḍendra* or *Gauḍeśvara*) as well as '*Vaṅgapati*', in the contemporary epigraphic records of the ninth century A.D. Dharmapāla and Devapāla had often to measure swords with the Gurjara Pratihāras on the one hand and the Rāṣṭrakūṭas on the other. Thus the Rādhanpur plates of Rāṣṭrakūṭa Govinda III (*Ep. Ind.*, VI, p. 248) as well as the Wani grant of the same monarch refer to a defeat inflicted by the Rāṣṭrakūta king Dhruva upon Vatsarāja, the Gurjara king, who had already defeated the king of Gauḍa. The Sanjan Copperplate of Amoghavarṣa I tells us that Dhruva took away the white umbrellas of the king of Gauḍa, which were destroyed between the Ganges and the Jumna (*Ind. Ant.*, Vol. XII, p. 159). That Dhruva actually advanced so far is also proved by a verse in the Baroda plates of Kakkarāja. This proves almost conclusively that the kingdom of Gauḍa in the ninth century stretched at least as far as Allahabad at the confluence of the Ganges; and Vatsarāja's son Nāgabhaṭa is stated in the Gwalior Inscription of Bhoja to have defeated the king of Bengal (*c.* 810 A.D.). The Jodhpur Inscription of Bauka informs us that his father Kakka 'gained renown by fighting with the Gauḍas at Madgagiri (or Monghyr)' (Majumdar, *Gurjara Pratihāras*, p. 60). The Sirur and Nilgund Inscriptions (*Ep. Ind.*, Vol. VI) of Amoghavarṣa I (866 A.D.) refer to the Rāṣṭrakūṭa Govinda III, who imprisoned not only the Keralas and Mālavas, but also the Gauḍas, whose king at that time was Devapāla who is described in the Garuḍa Pillar Inscription of Bādal (*Ep. Ind.*, Vol. II, pp. 160ff.) as the Lord of Gauḍa. It was probably during the reign of Devapāla's grandson

[1] Stein, *Chronicles of the Kings of Kāsmīr*, Vol. I, p. 94. 'But the romantic tale of his visit *incognito* to the capital of Pauṇḍravardhana, then the seat of government of a king named Jayanta, unknown to sober history, seems to be purely imaginary' (Smith, *Early History of India*, 4th Ed., p. 387).

Nārāyaṇapāla that the Rāṣṭrakūṭa king Krishna II inflicted a defeat on the Gauḍas. In the Deoli Plates he is said to have 'taught humility to the Gauḍas'. The Gauḍas are represented as having been humiliated by Krishna III as well (Karhad Plates of Krishna III, *Ep. Ind.*, IV, p. 287). The Kāmarūpa copperplate of Vaidyadeva also refers to the Lord of Gauḍa, evidently meaning the Pāla king[1] who appointed Vaidyadeva as ruler (*Ep. Ind.*, Vol. II, p. 348).

After the fall of the Pālas, the Gauḍa country seems to have passed into the hands of the Senas. Vijayasena (c. 1060 A.D.), one of the early kings of the Sena dynasty, is described in the Deopara Inscription (*Ep. Ind.*, Vol. I, pp. 305–15) as having defeated Nānya, Vīra, and the kings of Gauḍa, Kāmarūpa, and Kaliṅga. The Madhainagar copperplate of Lakṣmaṇasena (*J.A.S.B.*, N.S., Vol. V, pp. 467ff.) describes Lakṣmaṇasena (early twelfth century) as having suddenly seized the kingdom of Gauḍa, and raided Kaliṅga. He is referred to as *Gauḍeśvara*, i.e. Lord of Gauḍa, and his sons Keśavasena and Viśvarūpasena are also referred to as Lords of Gauḍa (*J.A.S.B.*, N.S., Vol. X, pp. 99–104). During the rule of the Senas the Gauḍa country seems to have more than once been attacked. In the Nagpur Stone Inscription of the rulers of Mālava (1104-5 A.D.), Lakṣmadeva, the Paramāra king, is said to have defeated the Lord of Gauḍa—an unhistorical claim, says Kielhorn (*Ep. Ind.*, Vol. II, p. 193). The Piṭhapuram Inscription of Prithivīśvara (Prithivīsena) points out that King Malla is credited with having subdued among others the Lord of the Gauḍas.[2]

The Gauḍas at one time or another must have inhabited other countries and localities than the region with which they were primarily associated. The late A. M. T. Jackson pointed out that Thāneśwar was called Guḍa (a corruption of Gauḍa) in Alberuni's day (*J.R.A.S.*, 1905, pp. 163-4). He was supported by B. C. Majumdar (*J.R.A.S.*, 1906, p. 442), who cites a verse from the *Matsyapurāṇa* to the effect that Rājā Śrāvasta founded Śrāvastī in Gauḍadeśa—the evident conclusion being that 'Gauḍa must have been lying to the north of Kośala and to the north-west of Mithilā'. The reference is supported by similar references in the *Kūrma* and *Liṅga Purāṇas*[3]; and R. C. Majumdar[4] was led to conclude that there was more than one Gauḍa. It is more

---

[1] Kumārapāla, acc. to Smith, *Early History of India*, p. 416 (4th Ed.).
[2] See *chap. on the Vaṅgas*.
[3] *Matsya P.*, XII, p. 30; *Liṅga P.*, I, p. 65; *Kūrma P.*, I, 20, 19.
[4] *Gurjara Pratihāras*, p. 34, f.n. 2.

likely, however, that Śrāvastī which is referred to in the Purāṇas is the same Śrāvastī which is mentioned in the Silimpur Inscription of Prahās (*Ep. Ind.*, Vol. XII, pp. 283–95), and which is to be located somewhere in North Bengal, i.e. in the Varendra country of Gauḍa.

Gonda, a subdivision of Uttara Kośala, 42 miles south of the Kośala Śrāvastī, is, according to Cunningham, a corruption of Gauḍa.[1] The term *Pañca Gauḍa*, often used to designate the entire territory of Northern India as far as Kanauj and the river Sarasvatī, is however late, and is probably 'reminiscent of the Gauḍa empire of Dharmapāla and Devapāla, and cannot be equated with the ancient realm of the Gauḍas in the early centuries of the Christian era' (*P.H.A.I.*, 4th Ed., p. 537). The ruins of the ancient city of the Gauḍas, which was situated at the junction of the Ganges and the Mahānandā, can still be seen near Maldah in North Bengal, at a distance of 10 miles from the town.

---

[1] Cunningham, *Anc. Geography*, p. 408; Dey's *Geographical Dictionary*, p 63.

CHAPTER LIII

# THE SUHMAS

The land of the Suhmas is mentioned for the first time probably in the *Āyāraṅga-sutta*, one of the oldest sacred books of the Jainas. It is stated therein that Mahāvīra 'travelled in the pathless countries of the Lāḍhas, in Vajjabhūmi and Subbhabhūmi', where he was very rudely treated by the people. This Lāḍha [1] is doubtless identical with what later came to be known as Rāḍha, and Subbhabhūmi with the country of the Suhma people. The Suhma country was thus a portion of the more comprehensive region which was later known as Rāḍha. According to the Epics and the Purāṇas, the Suhma country is distinguished from Vaṅga and Puṇḍra, the two other important divisions of Bengal. The Epic account of Bhīma's eastern conquests makes the country of the Suhmas distinct from Vaṅga and Tāmralipta. In the *Daśakumāracaritam* (Chap. VI), Damalipti or Tāmralipti (mod. Tamluk in Midnapur) is described as having been a city of the Suhmas, while according to the *Matsyapurāṇa* (Chap. 114) Suhma and Tāmralipti were different countries. The Jain *Prājñāpāṇā* includes Tāmalitti in Vaṅga (see chapter on the Vaṅgas).

The distinction between Suhma and Vaṅga (and Puṇḍra) is supported by the Epic and Pauranic tradition, which distinguishes Suhma, one of the eponymous 'Bāleya Kṣatras', from his brothers Aṅga, Vaṅga, Kaliṅga and Puṇḍra.[2] In the *Sabhāparvan* (Chap. 30, 16) of the *Mahābhārata*, the Pāṇḍavas are described as having subdued the Puṇḍras and Vaṅgas, and led their victorious army to Suhma. In Kālidāsa's *Raghuvaṃśa* also, Suhma is distinguished from the sea coast and the country of the Vaṅgas (Canto IV, 35-6). According to the *Pavanadūta* of Dhoyīka, the Suhma country seems to have been situated on the Ganges (verse 27). In Rājaśekhara's *Kāvyamīmāṃsā*, the Suhma country along with Brahma to the north, Vaṅga and Puṇḍra, was included in a list of the *Janapadas* of the east. In the *Bṛhatsaṃhitā* it is located between Vaṅga and Kaliṅga.

According to Epic tradition, Suhma was once conquered by Pāṇḍu (*Mbh.*, *Ādiparvan*, Chap. 113), and at another time by Karṇa (*Mbh.*, *Karṇaparvan*, Chap. 8, 19). It was in Sumbha

---

[1] *J.A.S.B.* (New Series), Vol. XVIII, 1922, No. 7.

[2] See *chapter on the Vaṅgas*.

or Suhma that the Buddha delivered the *Janapada-kalyānī Sutta*, while dwelling in a forest near the town of Desaka[1] (*Telapatta Jātaka*, Jātaka No. 96, Vol. I, p. 393).

According to Nīlakaṇṭha's commentary on the *Mahābhārata*, the Suhmas and the Rāḍhas were one and the same people (see Vaṅga Chap.); but from the *Āyāraṅga-sutta*, one may gather that the Suhma country formed a part of the Rāḍha (Lāḍha) country, the other important part having been called Brahma (cf. Brahmottara of the Purāṇas and Brahma of the *Kāvyamīmāṃsā*).

In the fourth Jain Upāṅga, called the *Prājñāpāṇā* (or *Paṇṇavanā*), as well as in the fifth Jain Aṅga, called the *Bhagavatī*, Lāḍha is described as having been one of the 16 great *Janapadas*, and one of the Ariya *Janapadas* of India. But the name Rāḍha is not traceable in the Epics or any other Sanskrit record before the tenth century A.D. 'The reason for this fact seems to be that in all Sanskrit records of the period including the Great Epic, the names Suhma and Brahma have always been used to denote the Rāḍha country which was almost fully covered by these two *Janapadas*.'[2] By the end of the tenth century A.D. Rāḍha which seems to have comprised the whole of Western Bengal, bounded on the north and east by the Ganges and the Bhāgīrathī, had come to be divided into two parts: Uttara Rāḍha and Dakṣiṇa Rāḍha: for Śrīdhara Bhaṭṭa, the author of the philosophical work, *Nyāyakaṇḍali*, composed in 991 A.D., is said to have been born in a village called Bhūrisṛṣṭi in Dakṣiṇa Rāḍha. Moreover, the Tirumalai Rock Inscription of Rājendra Cola (1025 A.D.) mentions Uttara Rāḍha and Dakṣiṇa Rāḍha as two distinct *Janapadas* (see Vaṅga Chap.); and Uttara Rāḍha is also mentioned in the Belava copperplate of Bhojavarman as well as in the Naihati copperplate of Vallālasena, as a *maṇḍala* (district) included in the *bhukti* (limit) of Vardhamāna. It is highly probable that the two *Janapadas*, Brahma and Suhma, of the Epics, the Purāṇas, the *Kāvyamīmāṃsā*, and other Sanskrit sources are identical with the two divisions of Rāḍha (Uttara and Dakṣiṇa) alluded to in the *Nyāyakaṇḍali*, the Tirumalai Inscription, the *Prabodhacandrodaya* (Canto II), and finally in the Sena records. The Rāḍha country seems to have comprised the modern districts of Hooghly, Howrah, Burdwan, Bankura, and the major portions of Midnapur; Uttara and Dakṣiṇa Rāḍha being separated by the river Ajaya.

---

[1] Sedaka, acc. to *Saṃyutta Nikāya*, V, 89.

[2] For a most interesting and original discussion of this subject, see Sen, *Some Janapadas of Ancient Rāḍha* (*I.H.Q.*, Vol. VIII, No. 3, pp. 521ff.).

## CHAPTER LIV

# THE PUṆḌRAS

The Puṇḍras seem to have been a very ancient people. They are mentioned in the *Aitareya Brāhmaṇa* (VII, 18), where they are described as outcaste descendants of Viśvāmitra. Viśvāmitra, so the story goes, had many sons; but he adopted the Bhārgava Sunaḥśepa, calling him Devarāta, and made him the chief of all his sons. But the other sons did not all accept Devarāta's headship; and it is said that Viśvāmitra cursed those who repudiated it to become *mlecchas* or dog-eaters[1] such as Āndhras, Puṇḍras and Śabaras.[2]

The Puṇḍras are mentioned in the *Sūtras* as well (cf. *Baudhāyana*, 1, 2, 14), and in Manu's *Dharmaśāstra* (10, 43-4)—here in the form Pauṇḍraka. But they are most frequently mentioned in the Purāṇas and Epics by the name of their originator, Puṇḍra, one of the eponymous 'Bāleya Kṣatras'[3] (see Vaṅga Chap.). It is said that Vāsudeva defeated the Puṇḍras along with the Aṅgas, Vaṅgas, Kaliṅgas, Kāśīs, Kośalas, Karūṣas and others (*Mbh.*, *Droṇaparvan*, XI). Jarāsandha, king of Magadha, is referred to in the *Harivaṃśa* (Chap. 116) as having once held sway over the Puṇḍras as well as over the Aṅgas, Vaṅgas and Kaliṅgas. In the *Rāmāyaṇa* (*Kiṣkindhyā Kāṇḍa*, XLI, 12), Puṇḍra is referred to as a southern country, but, according to the Purāṇas and the *Mahābhārata*, the realm of the Puṇḍras seems to have been situated in the eastern division, as they are always associated with the Vaṅgas, Aṅgas and Kaliṅgas, as also with the Suhmas. This is also supported by Rājaśekhara's *Kāvyamīmāṃsā*, which places the Puṇḍra country in the east along with Prāgjyotiṣa and Tāmralipta.[4] This determines the correctness of the usually accepted identification of the ancient Puṇḍra country with what later came to be known as Puṇḍravardhana.

The Puṇḍras are sometimes referred to as Pauṇḍras, Pauṇḍrakas (cf. *Manusaṃhitā*), or even Pauṇḍrikas. In the *Mahābhārata*,

---

1 *Mahābhārata*, XIII, Chap. 3.

2 Cf. also *Sāṅkhyāyana Śr. Sūtra*, XV, 26; vide Pargiter, *Ancient Indian Historical Tradition*, p. 235.

3 *Brahma P.*, Chap. 13, 30-1; *Agni P.*, Chap. 278; *Matsya P.*, Chap. 48, 19; *Viṣṇu P.*, IV, Chap. 18, 1-2; *Mbh.*, *Ādiparvan*, Chap. 104; *Garuḍa P.*, Chap. 143, v. 71.

4 Chap. 17.

these names are sometimes used as equivalents, but sometimes a distinction is made between the Pauṇḍras and Puṇḍras.[1] Pargiter[2] holds that they were two different tribes occupying two different countries. According to this theory, the Puṇḍras, linked as they were with the Vaṅgas and Kirātas (*Sabhāparvan*, XIV) and with the Aṅgas and Vaṅgas (*Sabhāparvan*, IV), occupied some intermediate position between the Aṅgas, the Vaṅgas, and the hilly countries of the Himalayas. Accordingly, the Puṇḍra country should be identified with Maldah, portions of Purnea, east of the Kosi, and parts of Dinajpur and Rajshahi. The Pauṇḍras, however, linked as they were with the Udras, Utkalas, Mekalas, Kaliṅgas and Āndhras (*Bhīṣmaparvan*, IX; *Droṇaparvan*, IV), occupied the modern district of Santal Parganas and Birbhum and northern portion of Hazaribagh.[3] But as the enumeration of the countries and peoples in the Epics and Purāṇas is often loose, the distinction cannot be pushed very far, and in fact it is hardly ever accepted. In later literary and epigraphic records the distinction between Puṇḍra and Pauṇḍra is never maintained.

According to the *Divyāvadāna* (pp. 21-2), Puṇḍravardhana was the eastern boundary (of the Middle Country). In the Sumāghadhāvadāna of the *Avadāna Kalpalatā* (Chap. 93, v. 10), Puṇḍravardhana is described as being situated 160 yojanas (or 640 miles) to the east of Śrāvastī.

It is not improbable that Puṇḍravardhana formed a part of the Magadhan empire during the time of the Mauryas. This is suggested by the testimony of Hsüan Tsang, who saw stūpas of Aśoka near Tāmralipta and Karṇasuvarṇa in Samataṭa, as well as in Pun-na-fa-tan-na (Puṇḍravardhana). Travelling east, Hsüan Tsang 'crossed the Ganges, and after a journey of above 600 li reached the Pun-na-fa-tan-na country. This country was above 4,000 li in circuit and its capital was more than 30 li in circuit. Twenty li to the west of the capital was a magnificent Buddhist establishment, the name of which is given in some texts as Po-shih-po. Near it was an Aśoka tope at the place where the Buddha had preached for three months'. (Watters, *On Yuan Chwang*, II, 184-5.)

On the authority of Hsüan Tsang's description of the Po-shih-po monastery in Puṇḍravardhana, Cunningham identified the capital of Puṇḍravardhana with Mahāsthān, saying that the Buddhist remains of Bhāsu Vihāra, 4 miles to the west of Mahāsthān, corresponded with those noted by Hsüan Tsang at

---

[1] *Bhīṣmaparvan*, IX; *Sabhāparvan*, LII. [2] *J.A.S.B.*, 1897, p. 85.

[3] Cunningham, *Ancient Geography of India*, Majumdar, Notes, pp. 723-4.

the Po-shih-po monastery, situated just 4 miles to the west of the capital city of Puṇḍravardhana.[1] This conclusion is confirmed by the mention of 'Puṇḍanagala' (= Puṇḍranagara, the city of the Puṇḍras) in a fragmentary Maurya Brāhmī Inscription paleographically dated in the second century B.C., which has been discovered at Mahāsthān, 7 miles north of the modern town of Bogra.[2]

About the second century B.C., then, the Puṇḍras had their chief city at Puṇḍranagara. Not long after, they had spread over a wider area, which came to be known as Punavaḍhana (= Puṇḍravardhana), for the name Punavaḍhana occurs in at least two inscriptions (Nos. 102 and 217, *Ep. Ind.*, Vol. II, pp. 108 and 380) of the Sānchi stūpa. Its inhabitants, Dhamatā (Dharmadattā) and Isinadana (Ṛṣinandana), made gifts of architectural pieces that went to the building up of the Sānchi stūpa and its walls and *toraṇas*. The Mahāsthān fragmentary inscription proves that the district of Bogra was certainly included in what later came to be known as Puṇḍravardhana. That it also included the district of Rajshahi, or at least portions of it, is proved by the recently discovered Pāhārpur copperplate (478-9 A.D.) which purports to have been issued from Puṇḍravardhana city itself.[3] But contemporaneously the term appears as the name of a *bhukti* or provincial division. Thus, in the Damodarpur (a village in the Dinajpur district) Copperplate Inscriptions (*Ep. Ind.*, XV, pp. 113ff.) of Kumāragupta I (443 and 448 A.D.) and of Budhagupta, the Puṇḍravardhanabhukti is referred to as being governed successively by Cirātadatta, Brahmadatta and Yayadatta, all provincial governors. In all these records, Koṭivarṣaviṣaya is recorded as a subdivision of the Puṇḍravardhanabhukti. But naturally enough it is in the epigraphic records of the Pālas and Senas of Bengal that the name most frequently occurs. Puṇḍravardhana continued as in the days of the Guptas to be a provincial division of Bengal. Among the Pāla records, it is referred to in the Khalimpur grant of Dharmapāla, the Nālandā grant of Devapāla, the Bāngarh grant of Mahīpāla I, the Amgachi grant of Vigrahapāla III and

[1] *A.S.R.*, XV, p. 110.

[2] This inscription has been edited by D. R. Bhandarkar for the *Ep. Ind.* Cf. also 'Mahāsthān and its environs' (monograph No. 2); and also D. R. Bhandarkar's 'Important Fragmentary Inscription found at Mahāsthān (Bogra district) belonging to the Varendra Research Society', published in the *Indian Antiquary*, September, 1933.

[3] In the Sangli copperplates (Śaka year 855) of the Rāṣṭrakūṭa king Govinda Suvarṇa-varṣa, Pauṇḍravardhananagara is mentioned as the place from which the donee, Keśava Dīkṣita, is said to have come (*Ind. Ant.*, XII, pp. 251ff.).

the Manhali grant of Madanapāla.[1] Among the Sena grants it is referred to in the Barrackpur grant of Vijayasena, the Anulia, the Tarpanadighi, the Madhainagar and the Sunderban copperplates, all of Lakṣmaṇasena, the Edilpur copperplate of Keśavasena, the Madanapāḍā and the Sāhitya Parishad copperplates of Viśvarūpasena (for Sena records, see *Inscriptions of Bengal*, Vol. III, Varendra Research Society).

During the rule of the Guptas, the Puṇḍravardhanabhukti included as we have seen Koṭivarṣaviṣaya, which must have included the whole or a part of Dinajpur. It is certain that by that time (*c.* 535–720 A.D.) Puṇḍravardhana stood for the greater part of North Bengal, including at least the modern districts of Rajshahi, Bogra, Dinajpur, and portions probably of Maldah and Rungpur. But in the time of the Pālas (*c.* 730–1060 A.D.), the Puṇḍravardhanabhukti must have comprised a larger area, while the Senas must have ruled over a still larger division. We are led to this conclusion by the fact that the records of these two dynasties refer to the following subdivisions as included in the larger division of Puṇḍravardhanabhukti: The Koṭivarṣaviṣaya (Dinajpur), the Vyāghrataṭi maṇḍala (Maldah), the Khāḍiviṣaya (identical with the Sunderbans and the 24-Parganas), Varendri (roughly identical with Rajshahi, Bogra, Rungpur and Dinajpur), and Vaṅga (Eastern Bengal, more particularly the Dacca division). That Puṇḍravardhana included Varendri as well as Gauḍa (Maldah and Dinajpur) is also proved by a reference in Puruṣottama's lexicon (eleventh century A.D.), where we have 'Puṇḍrāh syur Varendri-Gauḍa-nivṛti', i.e. 'the Puṇḍras include the Varendri and Gauḍa (countries)'.

The capital city of the Puṇḍravardhanabhukti is referred to in the *Rāmacaritam* of Sandhyākara Nandi (eleventh century A.D.), as well as in the *Karatoyā Māhātmyam* (sixteenth century A.D.) as Śrī Puṇḍravardhanapura, and also as Puṇḍranagara. According to the *Rāmacaritam* (Kavipraśasti, v. 1), Śrī Puṇḍravardhanapura seems to have been situated in Varendri, for it is there stated that Varendri was the foremost place of the east, and Puṇḍravardhanapura was its 'crest jewel', or the most beautiful ornament.

Puṇḍravardhana is also referred to in a picture label of a manuscript of the Pāla period now in the Cambridge University Library[2]; and the name occurs in the *Devī-bhāgavata*, *Padma*, *Matsya*, *Brahmāṇḍa* and *Mārkaṇḍeya Purāṇas*, as well as in the *Jñānārṇava Tantra*. According to the *Rājataraṅgiṇī*, Pauṇḍra-

---

[1] For Pāla Inscriptions see *Gauḍalekhamālā* (in Bengali), Varendra Research Society.

[2] Foucher, *Iconographie Bouddhique de l'Inde*, p. 190.

vardhana was the seat of government of Jayanta, a vassal chief of the kingdom of Gauḍa, when Jayāpīḍa, king of Kāśmīr, is said to have visited it in the eighth century A.D.; but Jayanta is not recognised as historical by present-day scholars.[1] Pauṇḍrabhukti, a shortened form of Puṇḍra-vardhana-bhukti, is referred to in the Rāmpāl copperplate of Śrīcandradeva, Belava copperplate of Bhojavarman, and Dhulla plate of Śrīcandra (for these records see *Inscriptions of Bengal*, Vol. III).

[1] See *Gauḍa chapter; Chronicles of the Kings of Kāsmīr*, pp. 93-4.

## CHAPTER LV

# THE KIRĀTAS

The Kirātas were a non-Aryan mountain tribe, possessing a rude culture. They are referred to in the *Mahābhārata* (XII, 207, 43) together with the Yaunas or Yavanas, Kāmbojas, Gāndhāras, and Barbaras, who all dwelt in the northern region or Uttarāpatha; while the *Rāmāyaṇa* mentions them along with the Mlecchas, or 'barbarians', another non-Aryan tribe. That the Kirātas were outside the Aryan fold is evident from a passage in the *Śrīmad-bhāgavatam* (II, 4, 18) which states that the Kirātas along with the Hūṇas, Andhras, Pulindas, Pulkasas, Ābhīras, Suhmas, Yavanas, Khasas, and other impure tribes purified themselves by offering their allegiance to Śrī-Kṛṣṇa. The Kirātas are mentioned in the *Viṣṇupurāṇa* (Wilson's Ed., II, pp. 156–90), in a long list of Indian peoples and countries, where they also seem to have been located in the northern region.

That the Kirātas were located in the Uttarāpatha seems also to have been attested to by Ptolemy who includes the Kirrhadai (or Kirrhodoeis) among the tribes of Sogdiana (present-day Soghd), which was divided from Baktriana by the river Oxus (see McCrindle, *Ancient India*, p. 277). Kirrhadia, the country of the Kirrhadai, is mentioned in the *Periplus of the Erythraean Sea* as lying west from the mouth of the Ganges. This reference seems to suggest that the Kirātas had settlements in the eastern region as well. Ptolemy's Kirrhadoi or Airrhadoi spread widely not only over Gangetic India, but also over countries farther east. The *Mahābhārata*, too, seems to point to a settlement of the Kirātas in Kāmarūpa; we are told that Bhagadatta, the powerful ruler of Prāgjyotiṣa (= Kāmarūpa), led a mighty *Mleccha* army of Kirātas and Cīnas in the battle of Kurukṣetra. For further remarks on the location of the Kirātas or Kirrhadoi, see Lassen's *Indisches Alterthum*, Vol. III, pp. 235–7. L. Pliny and Megasthenes also mention the tribe under the name Skyrites. According to Megasthenes, they were a nomadic people 'who instead of nostrils have merely orifices'. They were probaly a flat-nosed people of primitive origin dwelling in forests and mountains and *living by hunting*.

Long assures us[1] that there is still a tradition in Tripurā, precisely where Ptolemy places his Kirrhadia, that the first name

[1] *J.A.S.B.*, XIX, 'Chronicles of Tripurā', p. 536.

of the country was Kirāt. The Kirātas had an influential settlement in Nepal, and a Kirāta dynasty of kings held the valley in sway in succession to the Ābhīras. Sylvain Levi has pointed out that the Nepalese usage still gives the name Kirāta to the country between the Dudh-kosi and the Arun, and that there is evidence that the Kirātas once occupied a much more extensive area in Nepal.[1]

[1] *Lé Nepal*, II, pp. 72–8.

CHAPTER LVI

# THE PRĀGJYOTIṢAS

If the story of Kṛṣṇa's fight with the demons Muru and Naraka, as told in the *Viṣṇupurāṇa*,[1] the *Mahābhārata*,[2] and the *Harivaṃśa*,[3] can be interpreted as having an ethnological significance, then undoubtedly the Prāgjyotiṣas were a people of non-Aryan extraction. The Epics definitely describe the country of Prāgjyotiṣas as an *Asura* or *Dānava* kingdom ruled over by the demons, Naraka and Muru, with whom the leaders of Aryanism were in frequent conflict. The Pauranic description of Naraka, the *Asura* leader, attributes to him immense power and a strength that baffled and perplexed even Indra. The environs of his capital city called Prāgjyotiṣapura were defended by nooses constructed by the demon Muru. Of course, the Aryan leader, Kṛṣṇa, is described as having got the better ot the fight with the demons, which may be interpreted as one of the exploits in the history of the spread of Aryan influence in the east.

The *Mahābhārata* in other places[4] refers to Prāgjyotiṣa as a Mleccha kingdom ruled over by a king named Bhagadatta who is always spoken of in respectful and even eulogistic terms. Bhagadatta is styled a Yavana,[5] probably denoting that he did not belong to the Aryan fold. The *Udyogaparvan* describes him as the son of Naraka, the Prāgjyotiṣa king, and as an ally of Duryodhana.[6] Among his retinues Bhagadatta counted the Cīnas (the people of China),[7] and if the Kālayavana of the *Viṣṇupurāṇa* refers to the same king, as Wilson seems to think,[8] he also 'assembled many myriads of Mlecchas and barbarians' among his followers. The *Mahābhārata* mentions him as a king of boundless might (*aparyanta-bala*) ruling over (the country of) Muru and Naraka.[9]

---

[1] Wilson's Ed., 5, XXIX, 88ff.

[2] *Vanaparvan*, XII, 488; *Udyogaparvan*, XLVII, 1887–92.

[3] CXXI, 6791–9; CXXII, 6873, etc.

[4] *Sabhāparvan*, XXV, 1000-1; *ibid.*, L, 1834; *Udyogaparvan*, CLXVI, 5804; *Karṇaparvan*, V, 104-5.

[5] *Sabhāparvan*, XII, 578–80; *ibid.*, L, 1834–6.

[6] Chap. IV.

[7] *Udyogaparvan*, XVIII, 584-5.

[8] Wilson's *Viṣṇupurāṇa*, Bk. V, pp. 54-5.

[9] *Sabhāparvan*, I, 578-9:

> '*Muruṃ ca Narakaṃ caiva śāsti yo Yavanādhipaḥ*
> *aparyantabala-rājā pratīcyāṃ Varuṇo yathā.*
> *Bhagadatto mahārājo Vṛddhastavapituḥ sakhā*
> *sa vacā praṇatastasya karmaṇā ca viśeṣataḥ.*'

According to the *Mahābhārata*, Prāgjyotiṣa was situated in the northern region of India[1]; but the *Mārkaṇḍeya Purāṇa* places it in the eastern region, together with the Brahmottaras (or Suhmottaras), Pravijayas (perhaps Prāvṛṣeyas), Bhārgavas, Jñeyamallakas, Madras, Videhas, Tāmraliptakas, Mallas and Magadhas; or together with the Candreśvaras, Khaśas, Magadhas, and Lauhityas.[2] The mountainous regions called Antar-giri, Vahir-giri, and Upa-giri in the *Mahābhārata*[3] appear to comprise the lower slopes of the Himalayas and the Nepalese Terai; and it is not unlikely that the Prāgjyotiṣas lived contiguously, as Bhagadatta is called Śailālaya ('one whose abode is in the mountains').[4] According to the *Abhidhānacintāmaṇi*, Prāgjyotiṣa was the same as Kāmarūpa,[5] though in the *Raghuvaṃśa* the Prāgjyotiṣas and Kāmarūpas are described as two different peoples. Generally speaking, the two countries came in later times to be regarded as one and the same. In the *Kālikāpurāṇa*,[6] for example, the capital of Kāmarūpa is called Prāgjyotiṣapura, which has been identified with Kāmākhyā or Gauhātī. The *Raghuvaṃśa* seems to locate Prāgjyotiṣa beyond the Brahmaputra,[7] but Kālidāsa's knowledge of distant geographical locations is not always satisfactory. For all practical purposes, Prāgjyotiṣa may, therefore, be identified with the whole of Assam proper, along with Northern Bengal as far as Rungpur and Cooch Behar, which is the territory comprised by Kāmarūpa, according to the *Yoginītantra*.[8]

King Bhagadatta, as we have seen, was a Mleccha, and his people also Mlecchas or Yavanas, i.e. non-Aryans, but the *Rāmāyaṇa* ascribes the foundation of the kingdom to Amūrtarājas, one of the four great sons of King Kuśa—a significant Aryan name.

According to the *Brahmāṇḍapurāṇa* and the *Rāmāyaṇa*, there seems to have been another Prāgjyotiṣapura on the river Vetravatī or Betwa.[9]

The later kings of Kāmarūpa, who claimed to have been descended from the line of Narakāsura and Bhagadatta, figured prominently in Indian history. Most important of them was Kumāra Bhāṣkaravarman, an ally of Harṣavardhana Śilāditya, and referred to both by Bāṇa (in his *Harṣacarita*) and by Hsüan Tsang, the celebrated Chinese pilgrim.

---

1 *Sabhāparvan*, XXV, 1000; *Vanaparvan*, CCLII, 15240–2.

2 Pargiter's Ed., pp. 327–30, 357.

3 *Sabhāparvan*, XXV, 1000—XXVI, 1012.

4 *Strīparvan*, XXIII, 644.

5 *Prāgjyotiṣaḥ Kāmarūpaḥ*, IV, 22. The name Kāmarūpa seems to have come into use later.

6 Chap. 38.

7 IV, 81.

8 *Imp. Gaz. India*, XIV, p. 331.

9 *Brahmāṇḍapurāṇa*, Chap. 27; *Rāmāyaṇa*, *Kiṣkindhyā Kāṇḍa*, Chap. 42.

King Prālamba of Kāmarūpa (*c.* 800–825 A.D.)[1] is described in the Tezpur plates of his grandson as 'Prāgjyotiṣeśa', i.e. 'ruler of Prāgjyotiṣa'. His grandson Vanamāla claims to belong to the line (*anvaya*) of the lords of Prāgjyotiṣa, and so also does Balavarman, another king of the same dynasty (*c.* 975 A.D.). During the earlier half of the eleventh century A.D., the capital city of Prāgjyotiṣa seems to have attained great eminence under the kingship of Ratnapāla. In the Bargaon grant of this king, the city is referred to as impregnable, and rendered beautiful by the Lauhitya (= Brahmaputra river?).[2]

The Kamauli grant of Vaidyadeva[3] (*c.* 1100) refers to the Maṇḍala of Kāmarūpa and the Viṣaya of Prāgjyotiṣa, which implies that the latter was the larger administrative division, including Kāmarūpa.

Rājyamatī, a daughter of King Harṣavarman Prāgjyotiṣa (according to the stray plate of King Harjara),[4] is described as Bhagadattarājakulajā,[5] i.e. born of the family of King Bhagadatta.

[1] *J.A.S.B.*, 1840, IX, 2, pp. 766ff.
[2] *Ibid.*, 1898, LXVII, pp. 115-8.
[3] *Ep. Ind.*, XII, pp. 37ff.
[4] *I.H.Q.*, Dec. 1927, p. 841, f.n. 1.
[5] *Ind. Ant.*, 1880, IX, p. 179; *J.R.A.S.*, 1898, pp. 384-5.

## CHAPTER LVII

# THE BULIS—THE KOLIYAS—THE MORIYAS—THE BHAGGAS—THE KĀLĀMAS

We may group together a number of lesser tribes which are occasionally referred to in the Buddhist texts, particularly in the *Mahāparinibbāna Suttanta*. They may be enumerated as follows:-

(1) The Bulis of Allakappa.
(2) The Koliyas of Devadaha and Rāmagāma.
(3) The Moriyas of Pipphalivana.
(4) The Bhaggas of Suṃsumāra Hill.
(5) The Kālāmas of Kesaputta.[1]

These five clans or tribes are mere passing shadows in the early Buddhist records, there being scarcely any data for an historical account of them. The *Mahāparinibbāna Suttanta* mentions the Bulis of Allakappa, the Koliyas of Rāmagāma and the Moriyas of Pipphalivana, along with the Licchavis of Vesāli, the Śākyas of Kapilavatthu and others, as so many distinct clans or corporations, all of whom claimed shares of the bodily remains of the Buddha Gautama on the ground that, like the deceased master, they were of the Kṣatriya caste.[2] The claimants are said to have obtained their respective shares of relics, which they enshrined with customary ceremonies. The Bulis of Allakappa and the Koliyas of Rāmagāma had the good fortune to obtain one share each of the bodily remains, while the Moriyas of Pipphalivana had to be satisfied with a share of the ashes, as they were rather late in sending their messenger to Kuśīnārā. One of their descendants (or at least a namesake of theirs)—a Moriya of Pāṭaliputra—was more fortunate. The existing Buddhist traditions all agree on the fact of the redistribution of the relics of the Buddha (with the exception of those enshrined at Rāmagāma by the Koliyas) in the time of King Aśoka Moriya (Maurya).

The legend from the *Aśokāvadāna*, as summarised by the late Dr. Vincent Smith, is as follows: 'When King Aśoka desired to distribute the sacred relics of the body of Buddha among the eighty-four thousand stūpas erected by himself, he opened the stūpa of the Urn, wherein King Ajātaśatru had enshrined the

---

1 Rhys Davids, *Buddhist India*, p. 22.
2 *Dīgha Nikāya*, II, pp. 164ff., *Buddhist Suttas*, S.B.E., Vol. XI, p. 132.

cremation relics collected from seven of the eight original stūpas. The eighth, that at Rāmagāma, was defended by the guardian Nāgas, who would not allow it to be opened. The relics thus withdrawn from the stūpa of the Urn were distributed among eighty-four thousand stūpas, "resplendent as the autumn clouds" which were erected in a single day by the descendant of the Mauryas.'[1] A similar legend can be gathered from the Sinhalese chronicles and other late Pāli works, particularly Buddhaghosa's commentary[2] on the *Mahāparinibbāna Suttanta*; while the epilogues attached to the *Mahāparinibbāna Suttanta* and the *Buddhavaṃsa* indicate that the sacred relics of the Buddha's body were, after their re-distribution, enshrined all over Northern India from Gandhāra to Kaliṅga.[3]

The *Mahāvaṃsa Commentary*[4] furnishes us with some interesting information about the origin of the Moriyas of Pipphalivana and their connection with the Maurya rulers of Magadha. We are told that there are two theories about the derivation of the name Moriya. According to one theory, the name is derived from 'modiya', meaning pleasing or delightful; the Moriyas were a people who lived in a delightful land. According to the other, the name is connected with 'mora', peacock, and the people came to be known as Moriyas from the fact that the place where they founded their city always resounded with the cries of peacocks. Further, the city which they founded had buildings of blue stone, like the neck of the peacock. It is said that the Moriyas were originally Śākyan princes of Kapilavatthu, who escaped to the Himālaya regions to save themselves from the attacks of Viḍūḍabha, the ambitious and cruel usurper of the throne of Kośala, and established a city there, building it around a lake in a forest tract abounding in peepul trees.

When the Moriyas are introduced to us in the *Mahāparinibbāna Suttanta*, they are contemporaries and powerful rivals of the Śākyas of Kapilavastu. Viḍūḍabha's invasion of Kapilavastu and the carnage committed upon its citizens took place, if the tradition is to be believed, shortly before the demise of the Buddha. There may be some truth in the suggestion that the Moriyas were in some way connected with the Śākyas of Kapilavastu, and with the advance of ethnological researches it may be found that the matri-

---

[1] Vincent Smith, *Aśoka*, 2nd Ed., pp. 251-2.

[2] *Sumaṅgalavilāsinī*, Burmese edition, Pt. II, pp. 183ff.; P.T.S. Ed., II, 609ff.

[3] *Dīgha Nikāya*, II, p. 167; *The Buddhavaṃsa and the Cariyāpiṭaka*, J.P.T.S., 1882, p. 68; *The Minor Anthologies of the Pali Canon*, Pt. III, translated by B. C. Law, p. 87.

[4] *Mahāvaṃsa Ṭīkā* (Sinhalese edition), pp. 119ff.

monial alliance of the Śākyas with the neighbouring hill peoples brought some new tribes into existence.

Moreover, the *Mahāvaṃsa Commentary* traces the origin of the Maurya rulers of Magadha to the Moriyas of Pipphalivana. According to this account, Candragupta, the founder of the Maurya dynasty, was born of the chief queen of the Moriyan king of Pipphalivana. This conflicts with the evidence of Viśākhadatta's *Mudrārākṣasa*, where Candragupta is represented as a Vṛṣala,[1] a person of low birth, an illegitimate son of the last Nanda king by a Śūdra woman named Murā. How far Viśākhadatta's account represents the true state of things is a controversial point. But there are many instances of a misconception of history resulting from a conjectural etymology of personal and dynastic names. It appears, however, that the royal family of the Nandas was connected by matrimonial alliance with the Moriyas of Pipphalivana; and Aśoka's mother, Dhammā, was also a Moriyan princess.[2]

As regards the Kālāmas of Kesaputta, our information is very meagre. There is a bare mention of them in the Nikāyas, but no doubt they existed at the time of the Buddha as a distinct tribe or clan. Their home was probably in a mountain fastness, not far from the upper Gangetic valley. The etymology of the name 'Kesaputta' indicates that the tribe traced its descent from the Keśins, a tribe connected with the Pañcālas.[3]

Among members of the Kālāma clan specially mentioned by name are Bharaṇḍu-Kālāma,[4] who was once a co-disciple of the Buddha (as Bodhisattva), and Āḷāra-Kālāma, a renowned religious teacher, who is mentioned frequently in the *Mahāparinibbāna Suttanta* [5] and in other Buddhist texts, ancient and modern. One caravan merchant named Pukkusa, a young Mallian, was a disciple of Āḷāra-Kālāma. Pukkusa laid much emphasis on the spiritual attainments of Kālāma. He said that his preceptor's ecstatic trance was so very deep and profound that a long train of heavily laden carts passed by him without his perceiving them.[6] The Buddhist texts represent the Kālāmas as worshippers of the Buddha Gautama, who was a disciple of Āḷāra-Kālāma, before his enlightenment.[7] The Buddha preached a famous sermon when on a visit to Kesaputta.[8]

Little is known of the Bulis, apart from the fact that they claimed and obtained one-eighth share of the Buddha's relics and

---

1 Act III, pp. 134–6, 141–3, etc.

2 *Vaṃsatthappakāsinī* (*Mahāvaṃsa Ṭīkā*), P.T.S., 189.

3 *Vedic Index*, Vol. I, p. 468.

4 *Aṅguttara Nikāya*, I, 277 f.

5 *Dīgha Nikāya*, II, pp. 130–1.

6 *Buddhist Suttas*, S.B.E., Vol. XI, p. 76.

7 Kern, *Manual of Indian Buddhism*, p. 18.

8 *Aṅguttara Nikāya*, I, 188 f.

raised a stūpa over them in their city of Allakappa.[1] Their territory was probably near Veṭhadīpa, for the king of Allakappa is mentioned[2] as being in intimate relationship with the king of Veṭhadīpa.

The Koliyas were one of the republican clans in the time of the Buddha, and owned two chief settlements—one at Rāmagāma and the other at Devadaha. The commentaries contain accounts of the origin of the Koliyas. For instance, the *Sumaṅgalavilāsinī*[3] states that the eldest of the five daughters of Okkāka contracted leprosy (*kuṭṭharoga*). Her four brothers, being afraid of infection, took her to a forest and there confined her in an underground chamber. Rāma, king of Benares, contracted the same complaint at this time, entered the forest, and cured himself by eating wild fruits and leaves. Hearing the voice of a woman one night, he discovered the princess in her underground chamber. He cured her by means of the fruits and leaves which had cured him, and then married her. He built a town in the forest, removing a big Kola tree in order to do so. Inasmuch as the town was built on the site of the Kola tree, it came to be called Kolanagara, and the king's descendants were known as Koliyas.

We find a variant of the story in the *Mahāvastu*,[4] which tells us that the daughter of a certain Śākya noble was attacked with leprosy. The physicians failed to cure her; sores appeared all over her body, and the people began to hate her. She was taken by her brothers in a palanquin to a spot close to the Himālayas. They dug out a subterranean room, and she was left there with plenty of food and water. They blocked up the entrance to the cave with planks, and put a large heap of dust in front of it, and then returned to Kapilavastu. After living in the stuffy room for some time, she resumed her former beauty, for the heat had cured her of leprosy. Now, not far from the cave lived a royal sage named Kola.[5] While wandering about in the vicinity of his hermitage, Kola came to the cave where the Śākya girl lived, and saw a tiger scratching up the heap of dust with its feet. His curiosity was aroused; the sage drove away the tiger, removed the planks, and opened the door of the cave, revealing the Śākya girl. Seeing her exquisite beauty, the sage became very much attached to her, and took her along to his hermitage. Sixteen pairs of twin sons were born to the couple. When these sons were grown up, they were sent to Kapilavastu by their mother, who told them

---

1 *Dīgha Nikāya*, II, p. 167.
2 *Dhammapada Comm.*, I, 161.
3 Pt. I, pp. 260–2.
4 Vol. I, pp. 352–5.
5 A variant of Rāma; Kola also is stated to have been a king of Benares.

that they would there be provided for by their uncles, who were Śākya nobles. She trained them in the manners of the Śākyas, and they were then allowed to set out. They saluted their parents and went to Kapilavastu. On arriving, the sons of the sage, surrounded by a vast crowd, went to the assembly hall of the Śākyas, where five hundred Śākyas were assembled and transacting business. They approached the assembly in the way their mother had taught them. The Śākya assembly was astounded to see the Śākya manners in them, and asked them whence they came. They answered as they had been instructed, 'We are sons of Kola, the royal sage, who has his hermitage somewhere at the foot of the Himālayas. Our mother is the daughter of a certain Śākya.' Hearing this, the Śākyas were pleased to learn that the youths were born of the royal sage, and not of some one of inferior rank. Recognising them as Śākyas, they said, 'Let them be given Śākya girls and appointments.' They were given Śākya brides, cultivable lands, and villages. As the princes were sons of the sage Kola, they were known as Koliyas.

It is stated in the Introduction to the *Kunāla Jātaka* [1] that the Koliyas used to dwell in the Kola tree. Hence they came to be called 'Koliyas' or dwellers in Kola (jujube) trees. When the Śākyas wished to abuse the Koliyas, they said that the latter had once 'lived like brute beasts in a hollow Kola tree'. The territories of the Śākyas and Koliyas were adjacent, being separated by the river Rohiṇī. A bitter quarrel once arose between the two tribes regarding the right to the waters of the river which irrigated the land on both sides. Incensed by insulting remarks as to their respective origins, the two tribes got themselves ready for battle, and sallied forth at eventide. Now at this time, so the story goes, the Buddha came to the spot from Sāvatthī, and sat cross-legged in the air between the two hosts. The Śākyas recognised him and at once threw down their arms with the words, 'Let the Koliyas slay us or roast us alive.' The Koliyas, on seeing the Buddha, acted in the same way. The Lord instructed them, quelled the feud and brought about a reunion. In gratitude, each tribe dedicated some of its young men to the membership of the Order, and during the Buddha's stay in the neighbourhood, he lived alternately in Kapilavastu and in Koliyanagara.[2]

---

[1] *Jātaka*, Fausböll, V, p. 413.

[2] For details of the quarrel and its results, see *Jātaka*, V, 412ff.; *Dhammapada Comm.*, III, 254ff.; *Sumaṅgalavilāsinī*, II, 672ff. A variant of the river-motif runs as follows: 'When the female slaves of the Śākyas and Koliyas came to the river to fetch water, and throwing the coils of cloth that they carried on their heads upon the ground, were seated and pleasantly conversing, a certain woman

The *Mahāvastu* tells us that there was a Koliya prince who aspired to rival the Buddha in the art of arrow-shooting, but he, together with others, was defeated.[1]

In the *Udāna* we read of Suppavāsā, daughter of the king of the Koliyas ('*Koliyadhitā*'), who was helped by the Buddha when she was suffering, and who, after a healthy son had been born to her, entertained the Buddha and Sāriputta at her house.[2]

It is stated in the *Mahāparinibbāna Suttanta* that the inhabitants of Rāmagāma belonged to the serpent race.[3] According to Cunningham,[4] Rāmagāma (Rāmagrāma) is identical with Deokāli; some scholars hold that the Koliyas of Rāmagāma originally came from the same ethnic group as the Koliyas of Devadaha. There are no historical data for ascertaining the political relations of the Koliyas of Rāmagāma and the Śākyas.

Several other townships of the Koliyas, visited by the Buddha or by his disciples, are mentioned in literature; e.g. Uttara, the residence of the headman Pāṭaliya[5]; Sajjanela, residence of Suppavāsā[6]; Sāpūga, where Ānanda once stayed[7]; Kakkarapatta, where Dīghajānu lived[8]; and Haliddavasana, residence of the ascetics Puṇṇa Koliyaputta and Seṇiya.[9]

The Bhaggas (or Skt. Bhargas) were a republican tribe of Northern India in the Buddha's time (sixth century B.C.). They are mentioned not only in Buddhist works, but also in Sanskrit works of the *Brāhmaṇa* and Epic periods. The earliest mention of the Bhargas is made in the *Aitareya Brāhmaṇa* (VIII, 28) where reference is made to a Bhargāyana prince named Kairiśi Sutvan. They are also referred to by Pāṇini in his *Aṣṭādhyāyī* (IV, i, 178), where they are associated with the Yaudheyas ('*na prācya Bhargādi Yaudheyādibhyaḥ*'). In the *Bhīṣmaparvan*[10] of the *Mahābhārata*, mention is made of the Bhargas along with other tribes, e.g. the Andhras, Kirātas, Kośalas, Gandhāras, Sauvīras, Sindhus, etc. In both the *Mahābhārata* proper[11] and the *Harivaṃśa*,[12] the

took another's cloth, thinking that it was her own; and when owing to this a quarrel arose, each claiming the coil of cloth as hers, gradually the people of the two cities, the serfs and the labourers, the attendants, herdsmen, councillors and viceroys, all of them sallied forth ready for battle.'

1 *Mahāvastu*, ed. Senart, II, pp. 76-7.
2 *Udāna*, P.T.S., pp. 15-18.
3 *Dīgha Nikāya* (P.T.S.), Vol. II, p. 167.
4 *Anc. Geography of India*, p. 423.
5 *Saṃyutta Nikāya*, IV, 340.
6 *Aṅguttara Nikāya*, II, 62.
7 *Ibid.*, 194.
8 *Ibid.*, IV, 281.
9 *Majjhima Nikāya*, I, 387; see also *Saṃyutta Nikāya*, V, 115.
10 Chap. 9, p. 822.
11 *Vatsabhūmiñca Kaunteyo vijigye balavān balāt*
*Bhargāṇāmadhipañcaiva Niṣadādhipatiṃ tathā.*—*Mbh.*, II, 30, 10, 11.
12 29, 73.

Bhargas are associated with the Vatsas, as well as with the Niṣādas (II, 30, 10-11). The *Harivaṃśa* tradition describes the Bharga and the Vatsa as the two sons of Pratardana. Attention may also be drawn here to the mention of a people called 'Bhārgavas' in the Purāṇas, e.g. in the *Mārkaṇḍeya Purāṇa* (LVII, 43). The Bhārgavas are also mentioned in the *Bhīṣmaparvan* (IX, 358) where the Bhargas also find mention (cf. Pargiter, *Mārk. P.*, pp. 310 note and 327-8, note). It is likely that the Bhaggas, Bhargas and Bhārgavas are one and the same people.

The epic tradition of the close association of the Bhargas with the Vatsas is corroborated by the Buddhist tradition as recorded in the *Jātakas*. The *Dhonasākha Jātaka* (No. 353) states that Prince Bodhi, son of Udayana, king of the Vatsas, had his dwelling-place on the Suṃsumāra Hill, where he built a palace called Kokanada. It seems that in Udayana's time (i.e. the sixth century B.C.), the Bhagga State was under the suzerainty of the Vatsa king.

The Bhaggas of the Suṃsumāra Hill are casually referred to in some suttas of the *Majjhima* and *Saṃyutta Nikāyas*.[1] There is no doubt that the Suṃsumāra Hill, their capital, was used as a fort. It was situated in a deer park at Bhesakaḷāvana. In the lifetime of the Buddha, Prince Bodhi, son of Udena (Udayana), ruled over the Bhaggas, apparently as his father's Viceroy. He became a follower of the Buddha.[2] When the Buddha was amongst the Bhaggas, the householder Nakulapitā came to him and asked for instruction, afterwards becoming one of the devotees of the Master at Bhesakaḷāvana.[3] The Bhagga country lay between Vesālī and Sāvatthī.[4] In the *Apadāna*,[5] the Bhaggas are mentioned with the Kārūsas.

The social customs, religious beliefs, laws and administrative systems of these minor clans were in all likelihood the same as, or similar to, those of the more important tribes dealt with in other chapters.

---

[1] *Majjhima Nikāya*, Vol. I, pp. 332–8; Vol. II, Pt. I, pp. 91–7; *Saṃyutta Nikāya*, Pt. III, pp. 1–5; Pt. IV, p. 116.

[2] *Bodhirājakumāra Sutta, Majjhima Nikāya*, Vol. II, p. 91; Fausböll, *Jātaka*, Vol. III, p. 157.

[3] *Saṃyutta Nikāya*, Pt. III, pp. 1–5.

[4] Malalasekera, *Dictionary of Pali Proper Names*, s.v. Bhaggā. *The Cambridge History of India* (I, 175) says that the Bhaggas were members of the Vajjian confederacy.

[5] II, 359. Other references to the clan are: *Aṅguttara Nikāya*, II, 61; IV, 85, etc.; *Vinaya Piṭaka*, II, 127; IV, 115, 198; V, 145; *Theragathā Comm.*, I, 70. See also B. C. Law, *Countries and Peoples of India* (Epic and Pauranic sources), *A.B.O.R.I.*, Vol. XVII, Pt. III, April, 1936.

## CHAPTER LVIII

# THE LICCHAVIS

### Name and Origin

The Licchavis were a great and powerful people of Eastern India in the sixth century B.C. Their peculiar form of government, their free institutions, their manners and customs, their religious views and practices afford us glimpses of India of the transition period, when the ancient Vedic culture was developing in new directions, and undergoing a transformation under the influence of the speculative activity out of which emerged the two great religions of Jainism and Buddhism. Fortunately for us, Buddhist literature, and to a lesser extent the Jaina sacred books, have preserved for us facts and comments, which, though fragmentary, are yet sufficient to give us a living picture of this interesting people. From the account of their political institutions that can be gleaned from the Pāli Buddhist Canon, we obtain an insight into the democratic ideas of statecraft and government that prevailed among the majority of the Aryan clans that peopled Northern India before the imperialistic policy grew and developed.

In Indian literature we find the name of this people in slightly varying forms—Licchavi, Licchivi, Lecchavi, Lecchaī and so on. Throughout the Pāli Canon, the name occurs in the form 'Licchavi'. In some of the Buddhist Sanskrit texts, e.g. the *Divyāvadāna*,[1] the name is found in this form, but in others, e.g. the *Mahāvastu*, the usual form is Lecchavi.[2] In the Chinese translations of the Buddhist sacred books, the name occurs in both forms, Licchavi and Lecchavi,[3] as is to be expected, since these translations are based on the Buddhist Sanskrit texts. The *Mahāvastu* form Lecchavi answers very well to the Prākrit form Lecchaī, which we find in another set of works claiming to be contemporaneous in origin with the Buddhist Canon, namely, the Jaina sacred literature which, according to some scholars, began to be composed perhaps by the direct disciples of Mahāvīra in the first century after his death, or at the latest in the next century, by the time

[1] *Divyāvadāna*, ed. E. B. Cowell and R. A. Neil, pp. 55-6, 136.
[2] *Mahāvastu*, ed. E. Senart, Vol. I, p. 254, etc.
[3] T. Watters, *On Yuan Chwang*, Vol. II, p. 77.

of Candragupta Maurya, when the first Council of the Jains was held at Pāṭaliputra.[1]

In the *Sūtrakṛtāṅga*, one of the earliest works of the Jaina sacred literature, we meet with the name Lecchaī,[2] and the same form occurs in the *Kalpasūtra* attributed to Bhadrabāhu, who is considered to have been a contemporary of Candragupta (*c.* 321–297 B.C., according to Rapson, *Ancient India*, p. 182). The Jain commentators equate the Prākrit Lecchaī with Sanskrit Lecchakī.[3] In the form Lecchakī, however, the name never occurs in Sanskrit literature, in which the earliest mention of the tribe, so far as we have been able to ascertain, is in Kauṭilya's *Arthaśāstra*, where they are called Licchivis. Here we read that the corporations of Licchivi, Vṛji, Malla, Madra, Kukura, Kuru, Pañcāla and others were 'rājaśabdopajīvinaḥ', i.e. enjoyed the status of rājās or kings.[4] We next find the Licchavis mentioned in the *Mānava Dharmaśāstra* (X, 22). Here there are some *variæ lectiones*; the anonymous Kashmirian comment on the text reads Lichavi which approximates very closely to the Buddhistic form. Medhātithi and Govindarāja, the two earliest commentators, read Licchivi, and this reading tallies exactly with the name as given by Kauṭilya; this form, therefore, represents the earliest spelling of the word in the Brahmanic Sanskrit literature. Kullūka Bhaṭṭa, the Bengali commentator, however, reads Nicchivi, and Rāghavānanda, another

[1] M. Winternitz, *Geschichte der Indischen Litteratur*, II, p. 295.

[2] *Kalpasūtra*, paragraph 128. *Śrīkalpasūtram*, Bhavnagar edition, p. 192; see also *Jaina Sūtras* by H. Jacobi, S.B.E., Vol. XXII, p. 266, f.n. 1; Vol. XIV, part II, p. 321, f.n. 3.

[3] *Jaina Sūtras*, Jacobi, S.B.E., Vol. XXII, part I, p. 266, f.n. 1.

[4] See Kauṭilya's *Arthaśāstra*, translated by R. Shāma Shāstrī, p. 455. The Sanskrit text has: '*Licchivika-Vṛjika-Mallaka-Madraka-Kukura-Kuru-Pañcālādayo rājaśabdopajīvinaḥ.*' The '*ka*' at the end of Licchivi, etc., is adjectival. It will be noted that Kauṭilya distinguishes the Licchivis from the Vṛjis. Regarding this H. Panday ('Notes on the Vajji country and the Mallas of Pāvā', *J.B.O.R.S.*, Vol. VI, pt. II, June 1920, pp. 259 *et seq.*) says that it appears from the Pāli Suttas that the names Vajji and Licchavi are interchangeable to some extent. The accounts of Chinese pilgrims, however, point to a different conclusion. Fā-Hien calls the country of which Vaiśālī was the capital, 'the kingdom of Vaiśālī', and the people of the country, 'Licchavis'. He does not mention Vṛji or Vajji. Hsüan Tsang describes Vaiśālī and Vṛji as two distinct countries, and Watters is inclined to doubt the accuracy of his description of the Vṛji country. Ray Chaudhuri reconciles the evidence of the Pāli literature with that of Kauṭilya and Hsüan Tsang, saying: 'Vajji was not only the name of the confederacy but also of one of the constituent clans. But the Vajjis like the Licchavis are sometimes associated with the city of Vesālī which was not only the capital of the Licchavi clan, but also the metropolis of the entire confederacy.'—(*Political History of Ancient India*, 4th Ed., p. 101.)

commentator, follows him in this as in other matters; and the ordinary printed editions of the *Manusaṃhitā* have generally adopted this reading.[1] Both Jolly and Bühler have accepted the form Licchivi, but Jolly cites two MSS. and five printed editions with the form 'Nicchivi'. Kullūka, who probably wrote in the fifteenth century, i.e. about 600 years later than Medhātithi, and about 300 years later than Govindarāja, was probably misled by the similarity of the letters 'N' and 'L' as they were written in Bengali in the fifteenth century, and as they are still written even in modern Bengali manuscripts.[2]

The Sanskrit inscriptions of the early Gupta emperors favour the form 'Licchavi'. In the Allahabad Stone Pillar Inscription of Samudragupta, that monarch is described as '*Licchavidauhitra*', 'the son of the daughter of the Licchavis',[3] so we have here the same form as in the Pāli Buddhist works. The same form occurs in many other inscriptions of the Guptas, for example, in the Mathurā Stone Inscription of Candragupta II,[4] the Bilsād Stone Pillar Inscription of Kumāra Gupta of the year 96[5] and the Bihar Stone Pillar Inscription of Skandagupta.[6] On the other hand, the variant Licchivi occurs in the Bhitarī Stone Pillar Inscription of Skandagupta[7] and the Gayā Copperplate Inscription of Samudragupta[8] (which is considered to be spurious). Some coins of Candragupta I bear the name Licchavi. Moreover, in the inscriptions of the Nepal kings, who claim to be descended from the family of the Licchavis, the expression used is always *Licchavikula-ketu*, 'the banner (or glory) of the Licchavi family'.[9] We have seen that in the Chinese translations which are based on Sanskrit Buddhist texts, the form is Licchavi or Lecchavi; Fā-Hien speaks of them as Licchavis,[10] while in Hsüan Tsang (Beal's *Records of the Western World*) the form is Li-ch'e p'o, which would correspond to the form Licchavi.[11] The Tibetans, who began to have

[1] For the various readings see *Mānava Dharmaśāstra*, ed. J. Jolly, p. 325. See also *Laws of Manu*, Bühler, S.B.E., Vol. XXV, p. 406, n.

[2] R. D. Banerjee, *The Origin of the Bengali Script*, Cal. Univ., 1919, p. 82, pp. 108-9. It is clear, however, that the form Nicchivi is a very old reading, as it occurs in the Sinhalese *Aṭṭhakathā*, which forms the basis of Buddhaghosa's story.

[3] *Inscriptions of the Early Gupta Kings*, ed. J. F. Fleet—*Corpus Inscriptionum Indicarum*, Vol. III, p. 8.

[4] *Ibid.*, p. 27.

[5] *Ibid.*, p. 43.

[6] *Ibid.*, p. 50.

[7] *Ibid.*, p. 53.

[8] *Ibid.*, p. 256.

[9] *Ibid.*, p. 177 f.n.; *Indian Antiquary*, Vol. IX, pp. 168ff.

[10] Legge, *Fā-Hien*, pp. 71, 76.

[11] *Buddhist Records of the Western World*, by S. Beal, Vol. II, p. 73.

the Buddhist books translated into their own language from the eighth century A.D., also have the form Licchavi.[1]

There is clear evidence in the Buddhist literature to show that the Licchavis belonged to the Aryan ruling caste—the Ksatriya. In the *Mahāparinibbāna Suttanta* we read that after the decease of the Buddha, the Licchavis claimed a share of the remnants of his body. They sent a messenger to the Mallas of Kuśīnara, where he had died, saying: 'The Exalted One was a Kṣatriya and so are we. We are worthy to receive a portion of the relics of the Exalted One.'[2] Here we see that the claim of the Licchavis was based on the fact that they were Kṣatriyas or people of the same caste as the Buddha.

Moreover, we are told that a Licchavi named Mahāli says, 'I am a Khattiya (Kṣatriya), so is the Buddha'[3]; while in the introduction to the *Sigāla Jātaka* we read of a Licchavi girl, 'the daughter of a Kṣatriya and high-born'.[4] Dr. Richard Fick in his work, *The Social Organisation in North-East India in Buddha's Time,* is rather sceptical as to whether the word Kṣatriya as used in the Pāli texts has exactly the same connotation as in the ancient Brahmanical literature; but Professor Oldenberg observes[5] that there is no ground for this scepticism.

That the Licchavis were Kṣatriyas appears also from the Jaina sacred literature. Just as the Licchavis of Vaiśālī honoured the Buddha at his death by erecting a noble monument (*stūpa*) over their share of the remnants of his body, so they had, before this, done honour to the memory of Mahāvīra, the founder of Jainism. The *Kalpasūtra* narrates: 'In that night in which the venerable ascetic Mahāvīra died. . . . , the eighteen confederate kings of Kāśī and Kośala, the nine Mallakis and nine Licchavis, on the day of new moon, instituted an illumination on the Poshadha, which was a fasting day. . . .'[6] The Jaina works further tell us, as Professor Jacobi points out, that these nine Licchavis were tributary to Ceṭaka, king of Vaiśālī and maternal uncle of Mahāvīra,[7] who was

1 Tibetan *Dulva*, quoted by Rockhill in his *Life of the Buddha* (pp. 97 *et seq.*); Tārānātha's *Geschichte des Buddhismus in Indien*, translated into German by Anton Schiefner, pp. 9, 41, 146.

2 *Dīgha Nikāya*, P.T.S., Vol. II, pp. 164 *et seq.* Trsl. Prof. and Mrs. Rhys Davids, in *Dialogues of the Buddha*, Vol. III, p. 187.

3 *Sumangalavilāsinī*, Pt. I, P.T.S., p. 312.

4 *Jātaka*, ed. V. Fausböll, Vol. II, p. 5.

5 Prof. H. Oldenberg, *On the History of the Indian Caste System*, *Z.D.M.G.*, Vol. LI; translated into English by Prof. H. C. Chakladar, *Ind. Ant.*, Vol. XLIX, December, 1920, p. 227.

6 *Kalpasūtra*, paragraph 128, trsl. Prof. H. Jacobi, S.B.E., Vol. XXII, p. 266.

7 Jacobi, *op. cit.*, note 1, p. 266.

a Jñātri Kṣatriya of the Kāśyapa *gotra*, as we read in the *Kalpasūtra*. There are reasons to believe that Mahāvīra was a native of a suburb of Vaiśālī.[1] That the Licchavis were looked upon as persons of high pedigree appears from a passage in another Jaina work, the *Sūtrakṛtāṅga*, where we read of the 'renowned *gotra*' (family) of the Licchavis.[2]

The Licchavis were Kṣatriyas of the Vāśiṣṭha *gotra*, and were addressed as 'Vāśiṣṭhas' by the Buddha (*Mahāvastu-Avadāna*, ed. Senart, Vol. I, p. 283, and elsewhere) and by Maudgalāyana, one of the pillars of the Buddhist Church (Rockhill, *Life of the Buddha*, pp. 97ff.). Further, the Jaina sacred works state that the Kṣatriyāṇī Triśalā, mother of Mahāvīra, and sister of Ceṭaka, one of the kings of Vaiśālī, belonged to the Vāśiṣṭha *gotra*.[3]

In the *Nepal Vaṃśāvalī*, the Licchavis are allotted to the Sūryavaṃśa or solar race of the Kṣatriyas.[4] This is quite in agreement with the fact elicited from the Buddhist records that they were Vāśiṣṭhas by *gotra*, for we know from the *Aitareya Brāhmaṇa* that the *gotra* or *pravara* (family) of a Kṣatriya is the same as that of his purohita or family priest.[5] Sir R. G. Bhandarkar also points out that the *gotra* of a Brāhmaṇa 'could be assumed for sacrificial purposes by a Kṣatriya, for, according to *Āśvalāyana* (*Śr. S.*, XII, 15), the *gotra* and the ancestors of the Kṣatriyas invoked are those of their priests or chaplains, and the only Ṛṣi ancestors that all the Kṣatriyas have, are Mānava, Aila and Paurūravasa. The names of these do not distinguish one Kṣatriya family from another, and to answer the purposes of such a distinction, the *gotra* and ancestors of the priest are assumed'.[6] The Vāśiṣṭha *gotra* was, therefore, the *gotra* of their family priest, and we know that the Vāśiṣṭhas were the family priests of the kings of the solar race, especially of the Ikṣvākus. In this connection it is interesting to note Prof. Jacobi's observation: 'According to the Jainas, the Licchavis and Mallakis[7] were the chiefs of Kāśī and Kośala. They seem to have succeeded the Aikṣvākas who ruled there in the times

[1] *Kalpasūtra*, pp. x–xii.

[2] Jacobi, *Jaina Sūtras*, Part II, S.B.E., Vol. XLV, p. 321.

[3] S.B.E., Vol. XXII, p. xii. See Jacobi, *Jaina Sūtras*, S.B.E., Vol. XXII, p. 193 (*Āyārāṅga-sūtra*, 11.15.15).

[4] *Indian Antiquary*, Vol. XXXVII, p. 79.

[5] *Aitareya Brāhmaṇa*, Ch. 34, *Kāṇḍa* 7, verse 25.

[6] Sir R. G. Bhandarkar, *Vaiṣṇavism, Śaivism, and minor Religious Systems*, p. 12.

[7] The kinship of Licchavis and Mallas is confirmed by the *Mahāparinibbāna Suttanta* (*Buddhist Suttas*, S.B.E., Vol. XI, pp. 121-2), and the *Saṅgīti Sutta* of the *Dīgha Nikāya* (*Dialogues of the Buddha*, Pt. III, p. 202), where the Mallas are likewise addressed as 'Vāseṭṭhas' (=Vāśiṣṭhas).

of the *Rāmāyaṇa*.'[1] The *Rāmāyaṇa* tells us that the city of Vaiśālī was founded by Viśāla, a son of Ikṣvāku and the heavenly nymph Alamvuṣā,[2] while the *Viṣṇupurāṇa* substitutes Tṛṇabindu, a later member of the Ikṣvāku family, as the father of the eponymous hero who founded the city. This shows that the ruling family of Vaiśālī was traditionally believed to have been descended from the Ikṣvākus.

The Licchavis were also associated with the Śākyas. We read in the *Karma-Śataka*[3] that Prabodha, king of the Vṛjis, gave away his two daughters, Māyā and Mahāmāyā, as brides to Śuddhodana, son of Siṃhahanu, and father of the Buddha. Rockhill in his *Life of the Buddha* (derived from Tibetan works) speaks of a tradition, according to which the Śākyas and the Licchavis were branches of the same people.[4]

We now come to the mythical account of the origin of the Licchavis, which can be gathered from Buddhaghosa's *Paramatthajotikā* on the *Khuddakapātha*. It came to pass that the chief queen of the king of Benares was with child. When her time came, she was delivered, not of a child, but of a lump of flesh, 'of the colour of lac and of bandhu and jīvaka flowers'. Fearing the displeasure of the king if he should hear of this, the other queens put the lump of flesh into a casket marked with the royal seal and placed it on the flowing waters of the Ganges. However, a certain god, wishing to provide for its safety, wrote with a piece of cinnabar on a slip of gold the words 'The child of the chief queen of the King of Benares', tied it to the casket, and replaced it in the river. The casket was discovered by an ascetic, and taken by him to his hermitage, where he cared for the lump of flesh. After the lapse of some time, the lump broke up into two pieces of flesh, which gradually assumed shape, till finally one of them became a boy resplendent like gold, and the other a girl. Whatever entered the stomach of these two infants looked as if put into a vessel of precious transparent stone (maṇi), so that they seemed to have no skin (nicchavi). Others said: 'The two were attached to each other by their skin (līnā-chavi) as if they had been sewn together'; so that these infants came to be designated 'Licchavis'. The ascetic, having to nurse these two children, had to enter the village in the early morning for alms and to return when the day was far advanced. Accordingly the neighbouring cowherds, seeing

[1] Jacobi, *Jaina Sūtras*, Pt. II, p. 321, note 3.
[2] *Rāmāyaṇa*, Bombay edition, *Bāla Kāṇḍa*, Chap. 47, verses 11-12.
[3] *Karma-Śataka*, 20, ii, 7, trsl. from Tibetan by M. L. Feer. Reprint, p. 40.
[4] Rockhill, *Life of the Buddha* (popular edition), p. 203, note.

his difficulty, offered to look after the children for him. The ascetic gladly agreed, and handed over the two children with these words: 'The children are possessed of great virtue and goodness, bring them up with great care and when they are grown up, marry them to each other; please the king and getting a piece of land, measure out a city, and instal the prince there.' But the children, when grown big, used to beat and kick the children of the cowherds. Then the parents of these other children would say, 'These children harass the others and trouble them, they are not to be kept, they must be abandoned (*Vajjitabbā*).' Thenceforward that country measuring 300 yojanas is called Vajji. Then the cowherds securing the king's permission, obtained that country, and measuring out a town there, they anointed the boy king. After giving the girl in marriage to the boy, who was then sixteen years of age, the old king made it a rule that no bride was to be brought in from outside, nor any girl from within the settlement to be given away outside. Sixteen pairs of twins were born to the couple (a boy and a girl each time), and as these children were growing up, and there was no room in the city for their gardens, pleasure groves, residential houses and attendants, three walls were thrown up round the city at a distance of a quarter of a yojana from each other; as the city was thus again and again made larger (Visālikatā), it came to be called Vesālī. This is the history of Vesālī.[1]

The *Pūjāvaliya*,[2] a Ceylonese Buddhist work, gives the same account with slight variations. These stories are, of course, entirely mythical and must have grown up in recent times, there being no evidence in the sacred canon itself to corroborate any part of them.

The two derivations of the name Licchavi which are suggested by Buddhaghosa are entirely fanciful. Licchavi is the name of a race or tribe. The people must have acquired that name long before they come to our notice in the pages of the Buddhist or Jaina literature, or in the *Arthaśāstra*. Buddhaghosa's derivations must have been invented much later, when the Licchavis had acquired renown and power, and it was thought necessary to find some meaning for the word, which defies easy analysis. It should be observed that the two derivations suggested by Buddhaghosa are almost identical with those given in Chinese Buddhist works,[3] indicating a common source.

It is clear that at the time the Buddha and Mahāvīra lived and preached, the Licchavis were recognised as Kṣatriyas with

---

[1] *Paramatthajotikā* on the *Khuddakapāṭha*, ed. H. Smith, P.T.S., pp. 158–60.
[2] Spence Hardy, *Manual of Buddhism*, 2nd Ed., 1880, pp. 242-3.
[3] *Shan-hsien-lü* (Chap. 8), T. Watters, *On Yuan Chwang*, Vol. II, p. 77.

whom the highest-born princes of eastern India considered it an honour to enter into matrimonial alliance. The powerful king Ajātaśatru was always designated 'Vedehiputto', the family name of his mother in the Pāli Buddhist Tripiṭaka. Even two centuries later, in the time of Candragupta Maurya, the Licchavis were of equal rank and position with the great Kṣatriya peoples of Northern India, viz. the Madras in the north-west, the Kuru-Pañcālas in the central region, and the Mallas and others in the east--the tribes who were organised as corporations of warriors and lived upon their position as *rājās*, that is as owners of land deriving an income from their tenants.

At the time when the present code of Manu was composed, we find that the Licchavis were still looked upon as Kṣatriyas, though of the Vrātya variety.[1] Regarding the Vrātyas, Manu says: 'Those (sons) whom the twice-born have by wives of equal caste, but who, not fulfilling their sacred duties, are excluded from the Sāvitrī, one must designate by the appellation Vrātyas.'[2] Here 'not fulfilling their sacred duties' stands for '*avratāḥ*', which means 'not being initiated at the proper time', on the authority of what Manu himself states in an earlier chapter, where he fixes the upper limits of the age before which the initiation of the twice-born castes must take place. After those periods, men of the three upper castes who had not received the sacrament become *Vrātyas* (outcastes) excluded from the Sāvitrī (initiation) and despised by the Aryans. Here Manu is in agreement with the earlier lawgivers, Gautama, Āpastamba, Vaśiṣtha and Baudhāyana.[3] There is no question, then, that the Licchavis were pure Kṣatriyas by origin but were not very careful in obeying the regulations about initiation and perhaps similar other matters.[4]

From what we know of the religious history of the Licchavis as a people, it is natural to expect that they would depart from the strict observance of the Brahmanic regulations. We have seen that Mahāvīra, the founder of Jainism, was of their very kin, and we also know that he had many followers among the residents of Vaiśālī, even among the highest officers. Then again, between the sixth century B.C. and 200 B.C., the earliest estimated date

1 *Manu*, X, 22; Bühler, *Laws of Manu*, p. 406.

2 *Manu*, X, 20; Bühler, *Laws of Manu*, pp. 405-6.

3 See Bühler, *Laws of Manu*, pp. 405-6, note 20; Gautama, XXI, 11; Āpa., I, 1, etc.; Vaś., XI, 74-9; Baudh., I, 16, 16.

4 For further information regarding the Vrātyas, see J. W. Hauer, *Der Vrātya: Untersuchungen Über die nichtbrahmanische Religion Altindiens*; and Haraprasad Sastri's *Annual Address*, *J.A.S.B.*, 1921, No. 2 (Vol. XVII, New Series).

of the *Manusaṃhitā*,[1] the Licchavis had won the good graces of the Buddha as well as of the followers of the religion he preached, as we shall see later. During this long interval, when the two great 'heretic' faiths flourished in their country, it is but natural to expect that the Licchavis were not over-particular about initiation and similar other ceremonies and practices that the regulations of the orthodox Brahmins required. Hence we can understand how Manu, the great Brahmin law-giver, came to refer to the Licchavis as Vrātyas. To claim the authority of this passage of Manu in support of a theory of non-Aryan origin of the Licchavis is quite unwarranted.

The above discussion, we hope, will also explain what the lexicographers and the author of the *Vaijayantī*, following Manu, declare regarding the origin of the Licchavis, viz. that they were sons of a Kṣatriya Vrātya and a Kṣatriyā.[2]

Before leaving the question of origin, we must refer to the two theories about the Tibetan and Persian affinities of the Licchavis, originated by the late Drs. V. A. Smith and Satis Ch. Vidyābhūṣaṇa respectively. Dr. Smith's conclusion about the Tibetan affinity rests on the agreement that is observed between the Tibetans and the Licchavis in the custom of exposure of the dead and in judicial procedure. We shall discuss these two points separately.

The prevalence among the Licchavis of the practice of exposing the dead to be devoured by wild animals is vouched for by a passage in Beal's *Romantic Legend of Śākya Buddha*,[3] derived from Chinese sources. There we have a description of a visit paid by the Bodhisattva (future Buddha) to a cemetery at Vaiśālī, where the Ṛṣis are stated to have told him: 'In that place the corpses of men are exposed to be devoured by the birds; and there also they collect and pile up the white bones of dead persons....; they burn corpses there also, and preserve the bones in heaps. They hang dead bodies also from the trees; there are others buried there, such as have been slain or put to death by their relatives, dreading that they should come to life again; whilst others are left there upon the ground that they may return, if possible, to their former bodies.' Dr. Smith argues that this passage 'proves a belief that the ancient inhabitants of Vaiśālī disposed of their dead sometimes by exposure, sometimes by cremation, and sometimes by burial. The tradition is supported by the discoveries made at prehistoric cemeteries in

---

[1] According to Bühler, the *Manusmṛti* was compiled at some time between 200 B.C. and 200 A.D. (Bühler, *Manu*, Introduction, p. cxvii).

[2] Monier Williams, *Sanskrit-English Dictionary*, 1899, p. 902; *Vaijayantī*, ed. Gustav Oppert, p. 76.

[3] pp. 159-60.

other parts of India, which disclose very various methods of disposing of the dead.'[1] He then concludes from the similarity between these customs of the disposal of the dead, and those of Tibet, that the Licchavis had Tibetan affinities. But we need not go to Tibet for these customs, inasmuch as they were prevalent among the Vedic Aryans from whom the Licchavis were descended. We read in the well-known funeral hymn of the *Atharvaveda*[2]: 'They that are buried, and they that are scattered (*vāp*) away, they that are burned and they that are set up (*uddhita*)—all those Fathers, O Agni, bring thou to eat the oblation'.[3] Whitney, whose translation of the verse we have quoted here, observes on the expression *Uddhitāh*, 'it evidently refers to exposure on something elevated, such as is practised by many people'.[4] Whitney also refers to an analogous passage in *Āpastamba* (I, 87) which contains a further reference to the customs of burial and exposure on a raised platform.[5] The Vedic literature shows that cremation was one of the methods of the disposal of the dead. Methods other than cremation were in vogue, it seems, in particular localities and among particular classes or peoples; and the custom of exposure of the dead was most probably brought into India by the Vedic Aryans, as we find the same custom among the closely allied Iranians. To seek for the origin of this ancient Aryan custom in Tibet is absolutely unwarranted. The other argument of Dr. Smith, that the ancient judicial procedure at Vaiśālī as given in the *Aṭṭhakathā* is substantially identical with the modern procedure at Lhāsā as observed by the Bengali traveller in Tibet, the late Rai Bahadur Sarat Chunder Das, C.I.E., need not detain us very long. This procedure the Tibetans may well have imbibed along with Buddhism from the province of Tirhut, which was nearest to their frontiers, and which was inhabited by the descendants of the Licchavis of old.

Satis Chandra Vidyābhūṣaṇa held that the Licchavis were of Persian origin. His strongest argument is the verbal coincidence between Nisibis in the Persian Empire, and the word Nicchivi which occurs in *Manu*. He continues: 'It appears to me very probable that while about 515 B.C., Darius, king of Persia, sent an expedition to India, or rather caused the Indus to be explored

[1] *Indian Antiquary*, Vol. XXXII, 1903, p. 234.

[2] XVIII, 2, 34. '*Ye nikhātā ye paroptā ye dagdhā ye coddhitāḥ sarvāṃstānagna āvaha pitrīn haviṣe attave.*'—*Atharvaveda Saṃhitā*, ed. Roth and Whitney, p. 339.

[3] *Atharva Saṃhitā*, trsl. W. D. Whitney, revised and ed. C. R. Lanman, Harvard Or. Series, Vol. VIII, p. 840.

[4] *Ibid.*, p. 841.

[5] With regard to this passage see also Zimmer, *Altindisches Leben*, p. 402; and Macdonell and Keith, *Vedic Index*, Vol. I, p. 8.

from the land of the Pakhtu (Afghans) to its mouth, some of his Persian subjects in Nisibis (off Herat) immigrated to India, and having found the Punjab over-populated by the orthodox Brāhmaṇas, came down as far as Magadha (Bihar) which was at that time largely inhabited by Vrātyas or outcaste people.'[1] This is absurd on the face of it. The Licchavis were already a flourishing people, long established in the Videha country, and had built up a splendid capital at Vaiśālī at the time of the Buddha's death; and whether we take the date of this event to be 487 B.C., as the late V. A. Smith thought, or 544 B.C., the traditional date maintained by the Ceylonese Buddhist monks, it is absurd to identify the Licchavis with the followers or subjects of Darius who were exploring the Indus about 515 B.C.

It remains for us to refer to another theory about the foreign origin of the Licchavis, started by Beal, viz. that they were 'Yue-chi'.[2] It hardly requires to be refuted, as the Yue-chi came to India about the beginning of the Christian era, and the Licchavis were a highly civilised and prosperous people in the fifth and sixth centuries B.C. when the Ephathalites or White Huns had not started from their original home in the east.

### Vaiśālī, the Capital of the Licchavis

Vaiśālī, 'the large city' *par excellence*, is renowned in Indian history as the capital of the Licchavi rājās and the headquarters of the powerful Vajjian confederacy.[3] This great city is intimately associated with the early history of both Jainism and Buddhism.

Vaiśālī claims the founder of Jainism as its citizen. The *Sūtrakṛtāṅga*,[4] a Jaina canonical work, says of Mahāvīra, the last Tīrthaṅkara of the Jains: 'Thus spoke the Arahat Jñātṛputra, the reverend, famous native of Vaiśālī, who possessed the highest knowledge and the highest faith.'[5] Mahāvīra is spoken of as Vesālie or Vaiśālika, i.e. a native of Vaiśālī.[6] Moreover, Abhayadeva in his commentary on the *Bhagavatī* (2, 1, 12, 2) explains Vaiśālika by Mahāvīra and speaks of Viśālā as Mahāvīrajananī or 'the mother of Mahāvīra'.[7] Besides, from a comparison of the

[1] *Indian Antiquary*, Vol. XXXVII, 1908, p. 79.
[2] *The Life of Hiuen-Tsiang* by Beal, Intro. p. xxii.
[3] Rhys Davids, *Buddhist India*, p. 40.
[4] Jacobi, *Jaina Sūtras*, S.B.E., Pt. II, p. 261 (*Sūtrakṛtāṅga*, 1, 2, 3, 22).
[5] *Ibid.*, Pt. II, Lecture VI, 17, p. 27 (*Uttarādhyayanasūtra*).
[6] Jacobi, *Jaina Sūtras*, Pt. I, Introduction, xi.
[7] Weber, *Indische Studien*, Band XVI, p. 263: 'Auch Abhayadeva zu Bhag. 2, 1, 12, 2 erklärt Vaiçālika durch Mahāvīra, und zwar als Metronymicum (!); Viçālā Mahāvīrajananī.'

Buddhist and Jaina scriptures, it appears that Kuṇḍagrāma, the birthplace of Mahāvīra, was a suburb of Vaiśālī.[1] As we have already seen, Mahāvīra's mother Triśalā was a sister of Ceṭaka, one of the rājās of Vaiśālī. The Jaina *Kalpasūtra* speaks of the connection of Mahāvīra with the Videha country and its capital Vaiśālī.[2] During his later ascetic life Mahāvīra did not neglect the city of his birth, and we are told that out of the 42 rainy seasons of this period of his life, he passed no less than 12 at Vaiśālī.[3]

The connection of the Buddha with Vaiśālī is no less close. Many of his immortal discourses were delivered here either at the mango-grove of Ambapālī, on the outskirts of the city, or at Kūṭāgāraśālā in the Mahāvana, the great forest stretching out up to the Himalayas. The Buddha was charmed with the conduct of the Vajjis or Licchavis residing within the town, and looked upon them with kindness and approbation. The seven points of excellence,[4] with which he characterised the Licchavis in answer to the queries put to him by the ministers sent by King Ajātaśatru of Magadha, are very well known.

One hundred years after the Buddha's Nirvāṇa, Vaiśālī again drew to itself the care and attention of the Buddhist Church,—but this time not on account of the many good qualities of character and powers of organisation of its citizens, but because of the secular tenets held by the Vaiśālī monks (*Vajjiputtaka bhikkhus*), who were not carrying out the Master's precepts conscientiously. The second general council of the Buddhist Church, known as the Sattasatika or the Convention of the 700, took place at Vaiśālī in order to suppress the heresies of these pleasure-seeking monks.[5]

We have already referred to the fanciful accounts of Buddhaghosa, the *Rāmāyaṇa* and the *Viṣṇupurāṇa* regarding the origin of Vaiśālī. The *Rāmāyaṇa* further tells us that when Rāma and his brother Lakṣmaṇa, guided by the sage Viśvāmitra, crossed the river Ganges on their way to Mithilā, they had a view of the city of Vaiśālī. It does not tell us that it was exactly on the bank of the river, but says that 'while seated on the northern shore they saw the town'.[6] Then, the story goes on, the travellers went to the city of Viśālā which was an excellent town, 'charming and

---

[1] Jacobi, *Jaina Sūtras*, S.B.E., Vol. XXII, pp. x-xi.

[2] *Ibid.*, Vol. I, p. 256, *Kalpa Sūtra*, paragraphs 110, 111.

[3] Jacobi, *Kalpasūtra*, paragraph 122.

[4] *Dīgha Nikāya*, II, 73f.; *Aṅguttara Nikāya*, IV, 15f.

[5] *Dialogues of the Buddha*, Pt. II, pp. 131ff.; Kern, *Manual of Indian Buddhism*, pp. 103-9. *Examination of the Pāli Buddhistical Annals*, Vol. VI, Pt. II, p. 729, *J.A.S.B.*, 1837 (Sept.).

[6] *Rāmāyaṇa* (Bombay edition), Chap. 45, verse 9.

heavenly, in fact a veritable svarga'.[1] Viśvāmitra here narrates a long mythological story to show the importance of the locality. He goes on to say that the Ikṣvāku prince then ruling over the country was named Sumati, and adds that, by favour of Ikṣvāku, the father of the eponymous founder of the city and ancestor of the ruling dynasty, all the kings of Vaiśālī (*sarve Vaiśālikā nṛpāḥ*) were long lived, high souled, possessed of strength and power and highly virtuous.[2]

From all these mythical stories, it is apparent that the name of the city had something to do with the word *viśāla* or 'extensive', and from what we read of the description of the ruins that Hsüan Tsang saw in the seventh century A.D., there can be no doubt of its wide extent. The Chinese traveller relates, 'The foundations of the old city Vaiśālī were sixty or seventy li in circuit, and the "palace city" (i.e. the walled part of the city) was four and five li in circuit.'[3] This would mean an area of about twenty miles in circumference for the outer town; and the 'palace city' perhaps represents the earliest of the three cities which, according to Buddhaghosa, were built to accommodate the Licchavis as they rapidly increased in numbers; but its area would not in that case agree with the statement that each of the three walls was at a distance of a *gāvuta* (*gavyuti*) or a quarter yojana, that is roughly a league from the other.

Buddhaghosa's description is also supported by the *Aṭṭhakathā* to the *Ekapaṇṇa Jātaka*, where we are told, 'At the time of the Buddha, the city of Vesāli was encompassed by three walls at a distance of a *gāvuta* from one another, and at three places there were gates with watch-towers and buildings.'[4] The three walls are also referred to in the *Aṭṭhakathā* to the *Lomahaṃsa Jātaka*.[5]

The Tibetan *Dulva* (iii, f. 80) gives the following description: 'There were three districts in Vaiśālī. In the first district were seven thousand houses with golden towers, in the middle district were fourteen thousand houses with silver towers, and in the last district were twenty-one thousand houses with copper towers; in these lived the upper, the middle and the lower classes according to their positions.'[6]

---

[1] *Rāmāyaṇa* (Bombay edition), Chap. 45, verses 10 and 11.

[2] *Ibid.*, Chap. 47, verse 18. Whether *nṛpāḥ* can here be taken to mean the oligarchy of rājās referred to elsewhere is uncertain.

[3] Watters, *On Yuan Chwang*, Vol. II, p. 63.

[4] *Jātaka* (Fausböll), Vol. I, p. 504. '*Vesālinagaraṃ gāvutagāvutantare tīhi pākārehi parikkhittaṃ tīsu ṭhānesu gopuraṭṭālokayuttaṃ.*'

[5] *Ibid.*, Vol. I, p. 389.

[6] Rockhill, *Life of the Buddha*, p. 62.

Hoernle in his English translation of the Jaina work, *Uvāsagadasāo*, advances the suggestion that the three districts referred to in the *Dulva* and in the *Aṭṭhakathā*, 'may very well have been Vesāli proper, Kuṇḍapura and Vāṇiyagāma occupying respectively the south-eastern, north-eastern and western portions of the area of the total city. Beyond Kuṇḍapura, in a further north-easterly direction lay the suburb (or 'station', *sannivesa*) of Kollāga which appears to have been principally inhabited by the Kṣatriyas of the Nāya (or Jñātṛ) clan, to which Mahāvīra himself belonged; for it is described as the Nāya-kula'.[1] He further observes that the phrases used in the *Āyārāṅga-sūtra* like '*Uttara-Khattiya-Kuṇḍapura-sannivesa* or *dahiṇa-māhaṇa-Kuṇḍapura-sannivesa*', 'do not mean the northern Kṣatriya (resp. Southern Brahmanical) part of the place Kuṇḍapura, but the Northern Kṣatriya, etc., suburb of Kuṇḍapura, i.e. that suburb (*sannivesa*) of the city of Kuṇḍapura, which lay towards the north and was inhabited by the (Nāya clan of) Kṣatriyas; it was distinguished from the southern suburb of the same city (Kuṇḍapura or Vesālī) which was inhabited by the Brahmins. This interpretation is confirmed by the parallel phrases in Kap. §22 (*et passim*), Khattiya-Kuṇḍagāme Nayare and Māhaṇa-Kuṇḍagāme Nayare, which are rightly translated as the Kṣatriya (resp. the Brahmanical) part of the town Kuṇḍagāma'.[2] He also points out that 'the phrase *ucca-nīya majjhimāiṃ kulāiṃ*, "upper, lower and middle classes", applied to the town of Vāṇiyagāma in sections 77, 78 (of the *Uvāsagadasāo*) curiously agrees with the description of Vesālī given in the *Dulva*'.[3]

The Buddha must have paid many visits to the Licchavi capital, and reports of at least two besides that already referred to are preserved in Buddhist books. The earliest of his visits is described at length in the *Mahāvastu*.[4] We are told there, how the people of Vaiśālī were troubled by a frightful pestilence which was laying their country waste, and how all their efforts to stay the plague proved fruitless. In their distress they sent for various well-known holy men, but these failed to afford them any relief. As a last resort the people of Vaiśālī sent a deputation headed by Tomara, a Licchavi chief, to Rājagṛha to bring the Buddha to their city. King Bimbisāra himself secured the Buddha's consent to help the Licchavis, and insisted on accompanying him to the boundaries of his territory.

---

[1] Hoernle, *Uvāsagadasāo*, Vol. II, translation, p. 4, note 8.

[2] *Ibid.*, Vol. II, p. 5.

[3] *Ibid.*, Vol. II, translation, p. 6.

[4] *Le Mahāvastu*, ed. E. Senart, Vol. I, pp. 253ff. See also Buddhaghosa's introduction to commentary on *Ratana-sutta*.

To impress the Licchavis with an idea of his power and wealth, the king of Magadha had the road from Rājagṛha to the Ganges, which formed the boundary between the two dominions, levelled, cleaned, decorated, and sprinkled with flowers; while the smoke of rich incense perfumed its whole length. He himself followed the Buddha, with his whole court and numerous retinue. The Licchavis, both the Abhyantara-Vaiśālakas, those living within the walls of the city, and the Bāhira-Vaiśālakas, the people living in the suburbs and surroundings, came in all their splendour and magnificence, in dazzling garments of all colours. Even the Buddha was impressed by their appearance, and compared them to the Tāvatiṃsa gods. The Licchavis decorated the road from the Ganges to Vaiśālī with a magnificence that far outdid the preparations made by the Magadhan king, and they provided for the comfort of the Buddha and the congregation of monks on a still more lavish scale. As soon as the Buddha crossed over to the northern side of the river and stepped on Licchavi soil, all malign influences that had hung over the country vanished, and the sick and the suffering were restored to health. The Buddha did not wish to live in the city or its suburbs, but he accepted the invitation[1] of Bhagavatī Gośṛṅgī to live in the Mahāvana, the great forest extending from the city far away to the north.

The Licchavis built the Kūṭāgārasālā monastery for the Buddha in the forest, and offered it to him and to the Buddhist congregation; and the Buddha permitted the bhikkhus to reside there. One day the Licchavis on coming to the Mahāvana learnt that the Buddha had repaired to the Cāpāla-Caitya to spend the day; thereupon they presented it to him and to the congregation of monks. Similarly, finding the Buddha spending the day at the Saptāmra-Caitya, Bahuputra-Caitya, Gautama-Caitya, Kapinahya-Caitya and Markaṭahrada-tīra-Caitya respectively, the Licchavis made a gift of all these places of worship to him and to the Buddhist Church. Even the courtesan Āmrapālī made a gift of her extensive mango-grove to the congregation; and similarly Bālikā made over Bālikāchavi,[2] which is evidently the same as the Bālikārāma of the Pāli Buddhist books.[3] On this visit to their city, the Buddha delivered many discourses to the people of Vaiśālī, and established the Buddhist faith on a strong foundation at the capital of the Licchavis.

We read in the *Vinaya* (*Mahāvagga* and *Cullavagga*) and other Pāli texts of the Buddha's visits to the Kuṭāgārasālā and other

[1] *Le Mahāvastu*, ed. Senart, Vol. I, pp. 295-9. [2] *Ibid.*, Vol. I, p. 300.
[3] *Vinaya Texts*, S.B.E., Pt. III, p. 408.

retreats. On one such occasion the Buddha taught his monks many matters connected with the sort of houses they were to build and dwell in; and he also ordered the Saṃgha to excommunicate Vaddha, a Licchavi, who had brought a false charge against one of the brotherhood; but afterwards relented on Vaddha's making due reparations.[1]

In accounts in the Buddhist books, whether Pāli or Sanskrit, Vaiśālī is represented as a rich and prosperous town.[2] For example, in the *Lalitavistara* we are told that some of the gods of the Tuṣita heaven, in advancing the claims of Vaiśālī for the honour of being the Buddha's birthplace, said, 'This great city of Vaiśālī is prosperous and proud, happy and rich with abundant food, charming and delightful, crowded with many and various peoples, adorned with buildings of every description, with storeyed mansions, buildings with towers, and palaces, with noble gateways and charming with beds of flowers in her numerous gardens and groves. This city, resembling the city of the gods, is indeed fit for the birth of the Bodhisattva.'[3]

We next come to the accounts of the city left by the Chinese travellers. Fā Hien, who visited Vaiśālī at the beginning of the fifth century A.D., i.e. about a thousand years after the Buddha's time, says,[4] 'North of the city is a large forest, having in it the double-galleried vihāra where Buddha dwelt, and the tope over half the body of Ānanda.' The double-galleried vihāra is evidently the Kūṭāgārasālā in the Mahāvana or 'great forest', which stretched right up to the Himalayas as Buddhaghosa explains in his *Sumaṅgalavilāsinī* to the *Mahāli Sutta* in the *Dīgha Nikāya*.[5] With regard to the Kūṭāgārasālā Buddhaghosa says: 'In that forest (i.e. Mahāvana) was established a *saṃghārāma* (monastery). A *pāsāda* (storeyed building) was built on pillars and putting a pinnacle above, it was made into a *kūṭāgārasālā* resembling a chariot of the gods (*devavimāna*). From it, the whole *saṃghārāma* is known as Kuṭāgārasālā.'[6] This agrees with Fā-Hien's description of the double-galleried vihāra. The upper storey was evidently built

[1] *Cullavagga, Vinaya Texts*, Pt. II, S.B.E., pp. 101 *et seq.* See also *Vinaya Texts*, S.B.E., Pt. III, pp. 322 and 408; Pt. II, pp. 210-11.

[2] See, e.g., *Mahāvagga, Vinaya Texts*, Pt. II, S.B.E., p. 171.

[3] *Lalitavistara*, ed. Lefman, Chap. III, p. 21.

[4] Legge, *Fā-Hien*, p. 72.

[5] *Sumaṅgalavilāsinī*, Pt. I (P.T.S.), p. 309.

[6] *Ibid.*, Pt. I, P.T.S., p. 309. '*Tasmin vanasaṇḍe saṅghārāmaṃ patiṭṭhāpesuṃ. Tattha kaṇṇikaṃ yojetvā thambhānaṃ upari Kūṭāgārasālā-saṃkhepena devavimāna-sadisaṃ pāsādaṃ akaṃsu. Taṃ upādāya sakalo pi saṃghārāmo Kūṭāgārasālā ti paññāyittha.*'

upon a large number of pillars instead of walls, and on the top there was a *kūṭa* or peak, so that there were two galleries, one below and the other above, and from the upper storey rose a pinnacle, as we see in the *vimānas* or *rathas* referred to by Buddhaghosa. Hsüan Tsang, who visited the city more than 200 years after Fā-Hien, found this great vihāra in ruins. He adds, 'To the east of the tope of the Jātaka narrative was a wonder-working tope on the old foundations of the "two-storey Preaching Hall",[1] in which Ju-lai delivered the P'u-men-t'o-lo-ni and other sūtras. Close to the remains of the Preaching Hall was the tope which contained the half-body relics of Ānanda.'[2] The story of the *parinirvāṇa* of Ānanda and the division of the remnants of the body has been told by Fā-Hien, and the same account is also given in the Tibetan works.[3]

Hsüan Tsang's account of the country of which Vaiśālī was the capital agrees pretty well with the tradition of its prosperity preserved in the Buddhist books. The Vaiśālī country is described by the pilgrim as being above five thousand li in circuit, a very fertile region abounding in mangoes, plantains and other fruits. The people were honest, fond of good works, lovers of learning, and both orthodox and heterodox in faith.[4]

In the Tibetan works, a similar account is given of the prosperity and opulence of Vaiśālī, which is invariably described in the *Dulva* as a kind of earthly paradise, with its handsome buildings, its parks and gardens, singing birds and continual festivities.[5] The *Romantic Legend of Śākya Buddha*,[6] translated by Beal from Chinese sources, gives an account similar to that in the *Lalitavistara.*

The identification of Vaiśālī, the capital of the Licchavis, has been much discussed by scholars. General Cunningham identified the present village of Basārh in the Muzafferpur district in Tirhut as marking the spot where Vaiśālī stood in ancient days,[7] and M. Vivien de Saint Martin agreed with him. Dr. W. Hoey sought, though on very insufficient evidence, to establish the identity of Vaiśālī with a place called Cherānd, situated on the northern bank of the Ganges about 7 miles south-east from Chāprā.[8] This identification was proved to be untenable by V. A. Smith,[9] who succeeded

[1] Evidently the Kūṭāgāra Hall.
[2] Watters, *On Yuan Chwang*, Vol. II, p. 71.
[3] Legge, *Fā-Hien*, pp. 75–7.
[4] Beal, *Buddhist Records of the Western World*, II, 66.
[5] Rockhill, *Life of the Buddha*, p. 63.
[6] P. 28.
[7] *Arch. S. Report*, Vol. I, pp. 55, 56 and Vol. XVI, p. 6.
[8] *J.A.S.B.*, 1900, Vol. LXIX, Pt. I, pp. 78–80, 83.
[9] V. A. Smith, *J.R.A.S.*, 1902, p. 267, n. 3.

in confirming Cunningham's identification. The identity of Vaiśālī and Basārh was proved still more decisively by the archæological explorations carried out on the site in 1903-4 by T. Bloch. Bloch excavated a mound called Rājā Viśāl kā gaṛh. Three distinct strata were found, the uppermost belonging to the period of Mahomedan occupation of the place, the second, at a depth of about five feet from the surface, related to the epoch of the Imperial Guptas, and the third, at a still greater depth, belonging to an ancient period of which no definite date could be obtained.[1] The finds in the second stratum, however, were of great value, especially a hoard of 700 clay seals evidently used as attachment to letters or other literary documents.[2]

The names of certain Gupta kings, queens and princes on some of these seals, coupled with palæographic evidence, clearly demonstrate that they belonged to the fourth and fifth centuries A.D.[3] Some of the impressions show that the name Tīrabhukti (the original form of Tirhut) was applied to the province even in these early times, and some show the name of the town itself, Vaiśālī.[4] These things go to prove the identity of the site with Vaiśālī, and there seems to be no ground to question this conclusion any longer. But it must be noted that the results so far obtained by excavation are very meagre.

### Manners and Customs

We have already seen that the Licchavis were included in the great Vajjian confederacy. But sometimes Vajji (Skt. Vṛji) and Licchavi were used indiscriminately as synonyms. At the time the Buddha lived, 'the Vajjis were divided into several clans such as the Licchavis, the Vaidehis, the Tīrabhuktis and so on, and the exact number of those clans would appear to have been eight, as criminals were arraigned before the Aṭṭhakūlakā or eight clans, which would appear to have been a jury composed of one member from each of the separate divisions of the tribe'.[5]

All these Vajjis lived in great amity and concord, and this unity coupled with their martial instincts and the efficiency of their martial institutions made them great and powerful amongst the nations of North-Eastern India.[6] Their sympathy for one another was exemplary. If one Licchavi fell ill, the other Licchavis came to see him. The whole clan would join in any auspicious

[1] Sir John H. Marshall, *Arch. Surv. of India, Annual Report*, 1903-4, p. 74.

[2] *Ibid.*, p. 74. [3] *Ibid.*, p. 110. [4] *Ibid.*, p. 110.

[5] Cunningham, *Ancient Geography of India*, p. 447.

[6] *Buddhist Suttas*, S.B.E., Vol. XI, p. 3; see also Turnour, *Pāli Buddhistical Annals*, No. 5, *J.A.S.B.*, Dec. 1838, p. 992.

ceremony performed in the house of one of their number; if any foreigner of rank and power paid a visit to the Licchavi capital, they would all go out in a body to receive him and do him honour.[1]

The young Licchavis were handsome in appearance and fond of brilliant colours in their dress and equipages.[2] We have already seen how their splendour impressed the Buddha when he first met them. We have a detailed account of the attire of the Licchavi nobles in the *Mahāparinibbāna Suttanta*, which describes how the Licchavi nobles went out for the last time to meet the Buddha. Apparently the Licchavis suited the colour of their clothes and ornaments to the tint of their complexions, and dressed themselves in dark blue (*nīla*), yellow (*pīta*), red (*lohita*), or white (*odāta*) accordingly.[3] Exactly the same description of the colours favoured by the Licchavis is given in the *Aṅguttara Nikāya*,[4] which shows that they wore these colours not only on festive occasions but in their ordinary daily life also. Once while the Buddha was staying at the Kūṭāgāraśālā in the Mahāvana, five hundred of the Licchavis were seated around him. Some of them were *nīla* or blue all over in clothes and ornaments, and similarly others were yellow, red or white. We may compare these descriptions with the more detailed account in the *Mahāvastu* of the colours favoured by the Licchavis: 'There are Licchavis with blue horses, blue chariots, blue reins and whips, blue sticks, blue clothes, blue ornaments, blue turbans, blue umbrellas and with blue swords, blue jewels, blue footwears and blue everything befitting their youth.'[5] In the same terms the *Mahāvastu* speaks of the Licchavis decked all in yellow (*pīta*) and in light red, the colour of the Bengal *mādār* (*mañjiṣṭha*), in red (*lohita*), in white (*śveta*), in green (*harita*), and some in variegated colours (*vyāyukta*).[6]

Perhaps the Licchavis were divided into separate septs as Senart suggested, distinguished by the colour worn by each; otherwise it is difficult to explain why the same colours should be preferred for the trappings of the horses and decorations of their carriages, as well as the articles of dress adorning their own persons. There was moreover a profusion of gold and jewels in everything in their equipage—carriages drawn by horses, gold-bedecked elephants, palanquins of gold set with all kinds of precious stones.

[1] *Sumaṅgalavilāsinī* (P.T.S.), II, pp. 517-8.
[2] Watters, *On Yuan Chwang*, Vol. II, p. 79.
[3] *Dīgha Nikāya*, Vol. II, p. 96; *Buddhist Suttas*, S.B.E., Vol. XI, p. 31.
[4] *Aṅguttara Nikāya*, P.T.S., Pt. III, p. 239.
[5] *Mahāvastu*, Vol. I, p. 259.
[6] We have here followed the interpretation, suggested by Senart, of *Vyāyukta* (*Le Mahāvāstu*, note, p. 574); this meaning, however, is very doubtful.

All this bespeaks a prosperous people, and it might be expected that they would be given to luxury and indolence. But this was not their character at the time when the Buddha lived and preached among them. The *Saṃyutta Nikāya* preserves this saying, which is attributed to the Buddha: 'Look ye Bhikkhus here, how these Licchavis live sleeping with logs of wood as pillows, strenuous and diligent (*appamattā*), zealous and active (*ātāpino*) in archery. Ajātasattu Vedehiputto, the Magadhan king, can find no defect in them, nor can he discover any cause of action (against them). Should the Licchavis, O Bhikkhus, in the time to come, be very delicate, tender and soft in their arms and legs, should they sleep in ease and comfort on cushions of the finest cotton until the sun is up in the heavens, then the Magadhan king, Ajātasattu Vedehiputto, will find defects and will discover cause of action.'[1] This testimony of the Buddha goes to show that the Licchavis were hardy and active, ardent and strenuous in their military training.

The Licchavis used to kill animals on the 8th, 14th and 15th day of the lunar months and eat their flesh.[2]

They were fond of manly pastimes such as elephant training and hunting. Among the *Psalms of the Brethren* (*Theragāthā*), we find one composed by Vajjiputtaka, the son of a Licchavirājā at Vaiśālī, who, in his early life, was engaged in training elephants.[3] The *Aṅguttara Nikāya* narrates how a large number of Licchavi youths, armed with bows, ready with strings, set and surrounded by a pack of hounds, were roving about in the Mahāvana, but finding the Buddha seated at the foot of a tree in the forest, threw away their bows and arrows and sending away the pack of hounds sat by the Great Teacher, subdued by his presence. A Licchavi of advanced years, named Mahānāma, who came to pay his respects to the Buddha, expressed his great wonder at the sight of the Licchavi youths, full of life and vivacity, notorious for their insolent and wanton conduct in the city, thus sitting silent and demure, in an attitude of reverence before the Great Teacher. 'The Licchavi youths, O Lord!' he goes on, 'are rude and rough and whatever presents are sent to the families, sugarcane or plums, cakes, sweetmeats or preparations of sugar, these they plunder and eat up, throw dust at the ladies of respectable families and girls of good families; such young men are now all silent and demure, are doing obeisance with joined palms to yourself, O Lord.'[4]

1 *Saṃyutta Nikāya* (P.T.S.), Pt. II, pp. 267-8.
2 *Divyāvadāna* (Cowell and Neil), p. 136.
3 *Psalms of the Brethren*, Mrs. Rhys Davids, p. 106; *Theragāthā*, V, 119.
4 *Aṅguttara Nikāya* (P.T.S.), Pt. III, p. 76.

'In the Buddha's time, the young Licchavis of the City', says Watters, 'were a free, wild, set, very handsome and full of life, and Buddha compared them to the gods in Indra's heaven. They dressed well, were good archers, and drove fast carriages, but they were wanton, insolent and utterly irreligious.'[1] This is an exaggeration and is probably based on the Chinese translations of such passages as the one in the *Lalitavistara*, where some of the Tuṣita gods point out the defects in the character of the Vaiśālians when their city was recommended by others among them as a suitable place of birth for the Bodhisattva.[2] Whatever might have been the opinions of these 'sons of heaven' before the birth of the Buddha, they must later have changed their opinions about the people of Vaiśālī, who showed such remarkable veneration towards the Buddha and received such marked favour from him. We may, however, assume that the Licchavis were rather independent in character and would not easily accept a subordinate position to any one, whether in politics, religion, or ordinary daily life.

Then again the statement that the Licchavis did not respect their elders or were irreligious, is in direct contradiction to what the Buddha said about their regard for elders to Vassakāra, the Magadhan minister.[3]

The Licchavi youths went to distant countries for their education. We read of a Licchavi named Mahāli who went to Taxila to learn *śilpa* or arts. It is said that he in his turn trained as many as 500 Licchavis who also, when educated, took up the same task and in this way education spread far and wide among the Licchavis.[4]

Nor were the fine arts neglected. Artisans such as tailors, goldsmiths and jewellers must have been much in demand in the city of Vaiśālī to furnish the gay robes of the 'seven thousand seven hundred and seven' rājās or nobles. The art of architecture also was much developed in Vaiśālī; the magnificent palaces of the Licchavis are spoken of in the *Lalitavistara*.[5] They were equally enthusiastic in the building of temples, shrines, and monasteries for the Bhikkhus; and we are told that the Bhikkhus themselves superintended the construction of these buildings for the Order. The Licchavis of Vaiśālī built many *caityas* or shrines inside and outside their great city, and we have already seen with what great

[1] Watters, *On Yuan Chwang*, Vol. II, p. 79.
[2] *Lalitavistara*, ed. S. Lefmann, Vol. I, p. 21.
[3] *Dialogues of the Buddha*, Pt. II, p. 80.
[4] Fausböll, *Dhammapada* (old ed.), p. 211.
[5] Chap. 3, p. 23 (*Bibl. Indica Series*).

liberality they gave the best among them to the Buddha and the Buddhist Church. That these *caityas* were beautiful and fine buildings, where people might wish to dwell indefinitely, was the expressed opinion of the Buddha, as we see from a passage in the *Dīgha Nikāya*.[1]

About the marriage rites of the Licchavis, it is said in the Tibetan books that there were rules restricting the marriage of all girls born in Vaiśālī to that city alone. They state, 'The people of Vaiśālī had made a law that a daughter born in the first district could marry only in the first district, not in the second or third; that one born in the middle district could marry only in the first and second; but that one born in the last district could marry in any of the three; moreover, that no marriage was to be contracted outside Vaiśālī.'[2] Certain passages in the *Bhikkhunī Vibhaṅga Saṅghādidesa*[3] indicate that a Licchavi could ask the Licchavi-*gaṇa* or corporation of Licchavis to select a suitable bride for him, or to try a case of adultery. The punishment for a woman who broke her marriage vow was very severe; the husband could even kill her with impunity. But an adulterous woman could save herself from punishment by entering the congregation of nuns.[4] The Licchavis appear to have had a high idea of female chastity; violation of chastity was a serious offence amongst them. The Buddha says that 'no women or girls belonging to their clans are detained among them by force or abduction'.[5] The *Petavatthu Aṭṭhakathā* gives the story of a Licchavi rājā named Ambasakkhara who was enamoured of a married woman, whose husband he engaged as an officer under him; but he was foiled in his attempts to gain her love.[6]

The Licchavis observed various festivals, of which the *Sabbarattivāro* or *Sabbaratticāro* was the most important. At this festival, songs were sung, and drums and other musical instruments were used.[7] When a festival took place at Vaiśālī, all the people used to enjoy it, and there were dancing, singing and recitations.[8]

1 *Buddhist Suttas*, S.B.E., Vol. XI, p. 58.

2 Rockhill, *Life of the Buddha*, p. 62.

3 *Bhikkhunī Vibhaṅga Saṅghādidesa*, II, *Vinaya Piṭaka*, ed. H. Oldenberg, Vol. IV, pp. 225-6.

4 *Ibid.*, p. 225.

5 *Buddhist Suttas*, S.B.E., Vol. XI, pp. 3-4.

6 *Petavatthu Aṭṭhakathā*, Sinhalese edition, Simon Hewavitarana's Bequest Series, No. 1, pp. 154–6; and see B. C. Law, *The Buddhist Conception of Spirits*, 2nd Ed., pp. 73-5.

7 *Saṃyutta Nikāya*, Vol. I, pp. 201-2.

8 *Theragāthā Commentary*, v. 62; *Psalms of the Brethren*, p. 63.

### Views and Practices

All our information about the views and practices of the Licchavis is derived from Buddhist books, and to a smaller extent from Jaina works. From these we learn that the Licchavis, though vigorous, martial, and highly prosperous, were at the same time of a strongly religious bent of mind. Both Jainism and Buddhism found many followers among them. Even before the advent of the two new forms of religion, the Licchavis, or to call them by their wider designation, the Vajjis, appear to have been imbued with a strong religious spirit. The Vajjis appear to have had numerous shrines in their town as well as in the country. Even after Jainism and Buddhism had obtained a strong hold on the Licchavis of Vaiśālī, the great body of the people of the Vajji country as well as of the capital remained staunch followers of their ancient faith, the principal feature of which was *Caitya* worship, although they had due respect for the Jaina or Buddhist sages who wandered over their country preaching the message delivered by their respective teachers. The *Mahāparinibbāna Suttanta* tells us what the Buddha told Vassakāra, the prime minister (*mahāmātra*) of Magadha, when the latter was sent by Ajātaśatru to learn from the Buddha what he would predict with regard to the king's daring plan of exterminating the Vajjis. The Buddha said: 'So long as the Vajjians honour and esteem and revere and respect and support the Vajjian shrines [1] in town or country, and allow not the proper offerings and rites, as formerly given and performed, to fall into desuetude, so long as the rightful protection, defence and support shall be fully provided for the Arahants among them . . . . so long may the Vajjians be expected not to decline but to prosper.' [2] This was said by the Buddha on the eve of his last departure for Vaiśālī. Buddhaghosa in his commentary, the *Sumaṅgalavilāsinī*, also informs us that the Licchavis observed their old religious rites.[3] We must here bear in mind the fact that Buddhism at the early stage of which we are speaking was a form of faith for ascetics only, not a religious creed for all people. The Buddhists at this period formed only one of the numerous ascetic sects of Northern India; thus there was nothing unusual in the fact that many of the

[1] The word in the text is '*Cetiyāni*'. T. W. Rhys Davids' translation seems to be too exclusive for, as Kern points out, the name *Cetiya* was applied not only to shrines, but also to sacred trees, memorial stones, holy spots, images, religious inscriptions (*Manual of Indian Buddhism*, p. 91. See also B. C. Law, *Geography of Early Buddhism*, pp. 79-80).

[2] T. W. and C. A. F. Rhys Davids, *Dialogues of the Buddha*, Pt. II, p. 80.

[3] *Sumaṅgalavilāsinī* (P.T.S.), II, pp. 517-8.

Licchavis who were householders and had not accepted the life of Bhikkhus should remain firm followers of their former faith.

From the meagre mention of the *Caityas* of the Licchavis in the Buddhist books, it is not easy to determine what the principal objects of their worship were; but there is nothing to show that the religious beliefs of the Licchavis were in any way different from the form of faith which obtained in other parts of Northern India. The Vedic religion was still in full vigour in N.E. India, as the references to Vedic sacrifices in the Buddhist books show. We should bear in mind that the country of the Vajjis was the sacred land of Videha, where the great Samrāt Janaka had exercised his sway, and where Yājñavalkya preached the *White Yajurveda*.

The *Caityas* mentioned in the *Mahāvastu* are the Cāpāla, Saptāmraka, Bahuputra, Gautama, Kapinahya, and Markaṭa-hradatīra. In the *Mahāparinibbāna Suttanta*, we find the following names of *Caityas* as mentioned by the Buddha: Gotamaka (= Gautama), Sattambaka (= Saptāmraka), Bahuputtaka (= Bahuputra or Bahuputraka), Sārandada, and Cāpāla. The *Pāṭika Suttanta* seems to indicate that Vaiśālī was bounded by four shrines: Udena (Udayana) on the east, Gotamaka on the south, Sattamba on the west, and Bahuputta on the north.[1] A passage in the *Divyāvadāna* also gives a list of the *Caityas* in almost the same words as the *Mahāparinibbāna Suttanta*; there also the Buddha is represented as speaking of the beauties of the *Caityas* called Cāpāla, Saptāmraka, Bahupatraka and Gautama-nyagrodha.[2] Bahupatraka is evidently the same as the Bahuputraka of the other texts. Buddhaghosa in his commentary on the *Mahāparinibbāna Suttanta* explains *cetiyāni* in the text as Yakkha-*cetiyāni*, and regarding the Sārandada-caitya where the Buddha preached, he says: 'This was a Vihāra erected on the site of a former shrine of the Yakkha (tree deity) Sārandada.'[3] Hence it is reasonable to assume that the Yakkhas were worshipped in some of the *Caityas*. The Buddhist books show further that the Vedic gods, Indra and Prajāpati or Brahmā,[4] were popular deities in the regions where the Buddha preached; while Kauṭilya's *Arthaśāstra*[5] speaks of many gods popularly worshipped, besides the Vedic divinities. Some scholars are of opinion that the *Caityas* were 'shrines of pre-Buddhistic

1 *Dialogues of the Buddha*, Pt. III, p. 14.
2 *Divyāvadāna*, p. 201.
3 *Dialogues of the Buddha*, Pt. II, p. 80, notes 2 and 3.
4 For Brahmā, see *S.N.*, 122 seq.; *Saṃy.*, VI, 1, 1–3, 10, etc.; *M.P.S.*, VI, 15, etc.
5 Ed. R. Shāma Shāstri, 2nd Ed., p. 244.

worship' and that 'they were probably trees and barrows.'[1] Some of the *Caityas*, as their names suggest, might have been named after the trees which marked the spots, but it would be going too far to imagine merely from the name that these shrines consisted of trees and nothing else.

As we have seen, Mahāvīra, the 24th Tīrthaṅkara of the Jains, was a citizen of Vaiśālī. Even before his advent, the faith of which he was the last exponent seems to have been prevalent in Vaiśālī and the surrounding country, in some earlier form. It appears from the Jaina accounts that the religion as fixed and established by Pārśvanātha, the 23rd Tīrthaṅkara, was followed by some at least of the Kṣatriya peoples of N.E. India, especially amongst the residents of Vaiśālī. We read in the *Āyārāṅga-sūtra* that Mahāvīra's parents were 'worshippers of Pārśva and followers of the Śramaṇas'.[2] Similar accounts are given in other Jaina works of the prevalence in the country of a faith which was afterwards developed by Mahāvīra. Śramaṇas or wandering ascetics had been in existence ever since the time of the earlier Upaniṣads, and evidently the Śramaṇas that were followed by the parents of Mahāvīra belonged to one of the numerous sects or classes of Indian ascetics. After Mahāvīra's time, the number of his followers among the Licchavis appears to have been large, even including some men of the highest position in Vaiśālī, as is seen from the Buddhist books. In the *Mahāvagga*[3] we read that Sīha, a general-in-chief of the Licchavis, was a disciple of Nigaṇṭha Nātaputta (= Mahāvīra). When the Buddha visited Vaiśālī, Sīha wished to see him, having heard reports of his greatness; but Mahāvīra dissuaded him, pointing out the defects in the doctrines preached by the Buddha. Sīha's enthusiasm for the Buddha abated for the time, but was again roused by the discussions of the other Licchavis, so that he finally did pay a visit to the Buddha, who gave him a long discourse on the Buddhist doctrine. Sīha was converted to the Buddhist faith. One day he invited the Buddha and the Bhikkhus to take their meal at his house, and procured meat at the market to feed them. But the Jains spread a false report that Sīha had killed an ox and made a meal for the 'Samaṇa Gotama', and that the Samaṇa Gotama was knowingly eating the meat of an animal killed for this very

[1] Prof. and Mrs. Rhys Davids, *Dialogues of the Buddha*, Pt. II, p. 110, f.n. 2. See also R. P. Chanda's *Mediaeval Sculpture in Eastern India*, *Cal. Univ. Journal* (*Arts*), Vol. III.

[2] *Jaina Sūtras*, Pt. I, *Āyārāṅga-sūtra*, trsl. H. Jacobi, S.B.E., Vol. XXII, p. 194.

[3] See *Vinaya Texts*, trsl. Rhys Davids and Oldenberg, S.B.E., Vol. XVII, pp. 108ff.

purpose, and was therefore responsible for the killing of the animal.[1] This false report circulated by them only made Sīha firmer in his zeal for his new faith, but the story shows that the number of the Nigaṇṭhas at Vaiśālī was sufficiently large to defy the influence of such an important man as Sīha, and this is also confirmed by the story of Saccaka, a Nigaṇṭha, who had the hardihood to challenge the Buddha himself to a discussion on philosophical tenets before an assemblage of five hundred Licchavis.

We read in the *Majjhima Nikāya*[2] that the Nigaṇṭhaputta Saccaka told the Licchavis of his intention to defeat the 'Samaṇa Gotama' in argument, and induced 500 of them to go with him to the Mahāvana to listen to the discussion. He approached the place where the Bhikkhus were walking up and down and told them, 'We are anxious to see Gotama, the Blessed One'. The Buddha was seated to spend the day in meditation at the foot of a tree in the Mahāvana. Saccaka with a large number of Licchavis went up to him; then arguments relating to the saṃghas and *gaṇas*, and some knotty points of Buddhist psychology and metaphysics were started between Saccaka and the Buddha. Saccaka, being defeated, invited the Buddha to dinner. The Licchavis were informed of this, and asked to bring whatever they liked to the dinner, which would be held on the following day. At the break of day, the Licchavis brought five hundred dishes for the Buddha. The Nigaṇṭhaputta and the Licchavis became greatly devoted to the Buddha.

The Buddha paid at least three visits, but probably many more, to Vaiśālī; and the Pāli works have recorded many occasions similar to those mentioned above, on which the Licchavis sought his aid for the solution of numerous problems of religion and dogma.

Once when the Buddha was staying in the Kūṭāgārasālā in the Mahāvana, a Licchavi named Bhaddiya paid a visit to him and asked him whether it was true that he employed magic spells to attract converts. Thereupon the Buddha explained his doctrine of '*kusala* and *akusala-dhamma*' saying that his teaching did indeed rest on fact. Bhaddiya, delighted with the exposition, forthwith declared himself a follower of the Buddha.[3]

On another occasion we find that when the Buddha was at Vaiśālī, two Licchavis, named Sāḷho and Abhaya, approached him, and asked his opinion as to the relative merits of 'purity of conduct' (*sīla*) and 'the practice of self-mortification' (*tapa*).[4]

---

1 *Vinaya Texts*, S.B.E., Vol. XVII, p. 116.
2 *Majjhima Nikāya*, Vol. I, pp. 227–37 (*Cūḷasaccaka Sutta*).
3 *Aṅguttara Nikāya* (P.T.S.), Vol. II, pp. 190–94.
4 *Ibid.*, Vol. II, pp. 200–2.

Another time a Licchavi minister (*mahāmātra*) named Nandaka approached the place where the Buddha was, and the Buddha explained to him the four Dhammas.[1] On another occasion when the Buddha was at Vaiśālī, there were 500 Licchavis assembled at the *Sārandada-cetiya*. They had a discussion about the five kinds of 'rare gems' (elephant, horse, jewel, woman, and householder), and asked the Buddha's opinion, whereupon he solved the problem in an unexpected way.[2]

The *Aṅguttara Nikāya* tells of a large number of distinguished Licchavis who went to see the Buddha when he was at Vaiśālī; and also narrates how on another occasion, when the Buddha was at Vaiśālī, he was worshipped by 500 Licchavis arrayed in various coloured garments, ornaments and trappings.[3]

A certain Añjana-Vaniya was born at Vaiśālī in the family of a rājā. During his adolescence, the three-fold panic of drought, sickness and non-human foes afflicted the Vajjian territory. Afterwards, the Buddha put a stop to the panic and addressed a great gathering. Hearing his discourse, the prince attained faith, left the world, and eventually became an Arahat.[4] Another son of a rājā who was converted by the Buddha was Vajjiputta, 'the son of the Vajjis'.[5]

In the *Saṃyutta Nikāya*[6] we read of Mahāli, a Licchavi, who went to the Buddha and told him that Purāṇa Kassapa was of opinion that beings suffered or were purified without cause. The Buddha refuted this theory. The *Aṅguttara Nikāya*[7] also speaks of a Licchavi named Mahāli, at whose request the Buddha expounded the causes of merit and demerit.[8]

The Buddha exercised a remarkable influence even over the fiercest of the Licchavis. For instance, it was said of a certain Licchavi prince that he was so very fierce, cruel, passionate and vindictive that none dared to utter more than two or three words in his presence. At last his parents resolved to bring him to the Buddha for correction. Accordingly he was brought before the Buddha, who painted a convincing picture of the results of cruelty

[1] *Saṃyutta Nikāya* (P.T.S.), Vol. V, pp. 389-90.
[2] *Aṅguttara Nikāya*, Vol. III, pp. 167-8.
[3] *Ibid.*, Vol. V, p. 133.
[4] *Theragāthā*, V, 55 and comm.; *Psalms of the Brethren* (P.T.S.), p. 56.
[5] *Ibid.*, V, 119 and comm.; *ibid.*, p. 106.
[6] Pt. III, pp. 68–70.
[7] Vol. V, pp. 86-7.
[8] For other discussions between the Licchavis and the Buddha or his chief disciples, see *Aṅguttara Nikāya* (P.T.S.), I, pp. 220–22; II, pp. 190–94, 200–02; *Saṃyutta Nikāya* (P.T.S.), Vol. IV, pp. 261-2; Vol. V, pp. 163–5.

and wickedness. After this exhortation, the prince's heart miraculously became filled with love and kindness.[1]

Among the Licchavi women who were converted by the Buddha, we read of Sīhā, Jentī, Vāseṭṭhī, and Ambapālī.

Sīhā, a niece of the Licchavi general Sīha, was born at Vaiśālī at the time of Gotama Buddha. When she attained years of discretion, one day she heard the Master preaching. She became a believer, obtained the consent of her parents to enter the Order, and eventually became an Arahat.[2]

The case of Jentī or Jentā was similar. She was born in a princely family of the Licchavis at Vaiśālī, and won Arahatship after hearing the Dhamma preached by the Buddha.[3] Another Licchavi woman, Vāsiṭṭhī, was born in a clansman's family at Vaiśālī. Her parents gave her in marriage to a clansman's son of equal position. She had a son. When the child was able to run about, he died. Overwhelmed with grief, Vāsiṭṭhī came to Mithilā, and there she saw the Buddha. At the sight of the Buddha she regained her normal mind; and he taught her the outlines of the Dhamma, whereupon she soon attained Arahatship.[4]

We have read of the courtesan Āmrapālī, who gave a vihāra to the Buddha. For further details of her life, see *Therīgāthā*, V, 252ff. (*Psalms of the Sisters*, pp. 120-1, 125).

### Government and Administration of Justice

The Licchavis formed a republic in the sense that there was no hereditary monarch, the power of the State being vested in the assembly of citizens. It does not appear to have been a completely democratic republic, but an oligarchy, citizenship being confined to members of the confederate clans. There is ample evidence to show that in ancient times this form of government, as described in the Buddhist books, was much more in vogue than we are led to imagine from later literature.

The Licchavis formed what was called a *saṃgha* or *gaṇa*, that is, an organised corporation. One of the Buddhist canonical books, the *Majjhima Nikāya*,[5] speaks of the Vajjis and the Mallas as forming *saṃghas* and *gaṇas*, i.e. clans governed by an organised corporation and not by an individual sovereign. The *Mahāvastu* says that when plague raged in Vaiśālī, a Licchavi named Tomara

---

1 *Ekapaṇṇa Jātaka*, Fausböll, *Jātaka*, Vol. I, pp. 504ff.

2 *Therīgāthā*, V, 77ff.; *Psalms of the Sisters*, pp. 53-4.

3 *Ibid.*, V, 21 and 22; *Psalms of the Sisters*, pp. 23-4.

4 *Ibid.*, V, 133ff.; *ibid.*, pp. 79-80.

5 P.T.S., Vol. I, p. 231.

was elected by the *gaṇa* to appeal to the Buddha and bring him to the city.

Kauṭilya says[1] that the Licchavis and various other tribes were '*rāja-śabda-upajīvinaḥ*'. This apparently means that among these peoples each citizen had the right to call himself a rājā, 'king', i.e. a dignitary who did not owe allegiance or pay revenue to any one else. Each citizen not merely looked upon himself as a rājā, but considered that his title should be recognised not only by his fellow clansmen but also by the other people of India. This is corroborated by the description of the Licchavis given in the *Lalitavistara*, which says that at Vaiśālī there was no respect for age, nor for position, whether high or middle or low, each one thinking that he was a rājā.[2] Kauṭilya's account shows that this designation of each individual clansman was not confined to the Licchavis, but was shared by them with many other warrior peoples of Northern India. Śavaraswāmī in his commentary on the *Pūrvamīmāṃsā Sūtra*, Book II, says that the word '*rājā*' is a synonym for Kṣatriya, and states that even in his time the word was used by the Andhras to designate a Kṣatriya. On his authority, it can be said that the word '*rājā*' in early times designated a member of the Kṣatriya caste, and subsequently acquired the specialised meaning of 'king'.

In practice the rank of *rājā* must have been restricted to a comparatively small section of the community, because we learn from the *Ekapaṇṇa Jātaka* that besides the *rājās*, there were the *uparājās*, *senāpatis*, etc. What the real number of *de facto* rājās was, we do not know. The *Mahāvastu*[3] speaks of the twice 84,000 Licchavi rājās residing within the city of Vaiśālī. The Pāli commentaries, e.g. the preambles to the *Cullakāliṅga Jātaka*[4] and the *Ekapaṇṇa Jātaka*[5] speak of seven thousand seven hundred and seven rājās of Vaiśālī. The *Kalpasūtra* speaks of only nine (*Jaina Sūtras*, Pt. I, S.B.E., Vol. XXII, p. 266).

Kauṭilya[6] observes that all these *saṃghas* by virtue of their being united in such corporations, were unconquerable by others. He further observes that for a king, a corporation was the best and most helpful of all allies, because of the power derived from their union which made them invincible. When Ajātaśatru sent his prime minister (*mahāmātra*) to ascertain the views of the Buddha

[1] See *Arthaśāstra*, trsl. R. Shāma Shāstrī, p. 455.

[2] '*Ekaika eva manyate ahaṃ rājā, ahaṃ rājeti.*' *Lalitavistara*, ed. Lefmann, Vol. I, p. 21; *Bibl. Indica Series*, Chap. III, 23.

[3] Vol. I, p. 271.

[4] Fausböll, *Jātaka*, Vol. III, p. 1.

[5] *Ibid.*, Vol. I, p. 504.

[6] *Arthaśāstra* (2nd Ed.), p. 378.

with regard to his proposed extermination of the Vṛjis, the Buddha said to Ānanda, 'So long, Ānanda, as the Vajjians hold these full and frequent public assemblies; so long may they be expected not to decline but to prosper'.[1]

The public hall where the Licchavis used to hold their meetings was called the *Santhāgāra*, and there they discussed both religion and politics. We have seen in the story of the conversion of Sīha that the Licchavis met at the *Santhāgāra* to discuss the teaching of the Buddha. The procedure that was followed in these assemblies may be gathered, as D. R. Bhandarkar[2] has pointed out, from an account of the procedure followed at a ceremony of ordination in the *saṃgha* of the Buddhist Bhikkhus. There can be no doubt that in organising the Buddhist *saṃgha*, the Buddha took as his model the political *saṃghas* of N.E. India, especially that of the Licchavis whose corporation, as we have seen, he esteemed very highly. Fortunately for us, the rules of procedure followed in the Buddhist community or *saṃgha* have been preserved in the description of the *upasampadā* or ordination ceremony in the Pātimokkha section of the *Vinaya Piṭaka*, and from this description we can form an idea of the procedure followed in the political *saṃgha* of the Licchavis. First of all, an officer called the *Āsanapaññāpaka* (regulator of seats) was elected, whose function seems to have been to seat the members of the congregation in order of seniority.[3] As in the Buddhist congregation, so among the Licchavis, the elders of the clans were highly respected, as we see from the *Mahāparinibbāna Suttanta*.[4]

The form of moving a Resolution in the council thus assembled and seated may be gathered from the full description of procedure in the Buddhist *saṃgha*, for which see Rhys Davids and Oldenberg, *Vinaya Texts*, Pt. I, pp. 169-70.

As might be expected in such an assembly, there were often violent disputes and quarrels with regard to controversial topics. In such cases, the disputes were settled by the votes of the majority and this voting was by ballot; voting tickets or *salākās* were served out to the voters, and an officer of approved honesty and impartiality was elected to collect these tickets or voting papers.[5] The appointment of this officer, who was called the *Salākā-gāhāpaka*, was also made by the whole assembly.

1 *Buddhist Suttas*, S.B.E., Vol. XI, p. 3.
2 *Carmichael Lectures*, 1918, p. 181.
3 *Vinaya Texts*, S.B.E., Vol. XX, p. 408, f.n.
4 *Buddhist Suttas*, S.B.E., Vol. XI, p. 3.
5 *Cullavagga*, S.B.E., Vol. XX ; *Vinaya Texts*, Pt. III, p. 25.

There was also a provision for taking the votes of absent members. The *Mahāvagga*[1] mentions an example of a declaration of the consent of an absent member (of the congregation of monks) to an official Act. Such a declaration was called *Chanda.*

A quorum was required, and difficulty was often experienced in securing the right number, so that the Buddha exhorted the Bhikkhus to help to complete the quorum.[2] There are other detailed rules in the *Vinaya Piṭaka* for the regulation of the assembly. This elaboration of the procedure, as well as the use of technical terms for each detail, shows that the organisation of these popular assemblies had already been highly developed among the political *saṃghas* like that of the Licchavis before the Buddha adopted them for the regulation of his religious *saṃgha* or congregation.[3]

The Tibetan works mention a Nāyaka who was the chief magistrate of the Licchavis and 'was elected by the people or rather by the ruling clans of Licchavis'.[4] We do not know exactly what his functions were; perhaps he was an executive officer for carrying out the decisions of the assembly.

There does not appear to have been any outstanding figure among the Licchavis, comparable to Śuddhodana among the Śākyas. The preamble to the *Ekapaṇṇa Jātaka*[5] relates that of the *Rājās* who lived in Vaiśālī permanently exercising the rights of sovereignty, there were seven thousand, seven hundred and seven, and there were quite as many *Uparājās* (subordinate officials), *Senāpatis* (generals), and *Bhāṇḍāgārikas* (treasurers). A passage in the preamble to the *Cullakāliṅga Jātaka*[6] also mentions seven thousand, seven hundred and seven Licchavi rājās, who lived at Vaiśālī. The number seven thousand, seven hundred and seven cannot be the number of all the Licchavis living in the town of Vaiśālī; in fact we are told in the *Mahāvastu* that the Licchavis, who went out of Vaiśālī to meet the Buddha on his first visit to that city, numbered as many as twice eighty-four thousand, which was not an incredible number for such an extensive city as Vaiśālī. But 7,707 is evidently an artificially concocted number, seven being used from the idea that it had some magic potency. It is significant

---

[1] *Mahāvagga*, S.B.E., Vol. XIII, p. 277. [2] *Ibid.*, pp. 307–9.

[3] For the democratic organisation of the Licchavis, see D. R. Bhandarkar, *Carmichael Lectures*, 1918, pp. 179–84.

[4] Rockhill, *Life of the Buddha*, p. 62.

[5] Fausböll, *Jātaka*, Vol. I, p. 504: '*Niccakālam rajjaṃ kāretvā vasantānaṃ yeva rājūnaṃ sattasahassāni satta ca rājāno honti, tattakā yeva uparājāno, tattakā senāpatino, tattakā bhaṇḍāgārikā.*'

[6] *Ibid.*, Vol. III, p. 1.

that none of the canonical texts themselves gives this number, which occurs only in a later commentary, the *Nidānakathā* of the Jātakas.

Bhandarkar says that an *Uparājā* or Viceroy, a *Senāpati* or general, and a *Bhāṇḍāgārika* or treasurer formed the private staff of every Licchavi *Rājā*. He adds that each *Rājā* had personal property of his own which was managed by himself with the help of these three officers. This seems to be likely, because the existence of a *Bhāṇḍāgārika* attached to each *Rājā* necessarily implies that each *Rājā* had his own separate *Bhāṇḍāgāra* or treasury.

There must have been officers who recorded the decisions of the Council. A passage in the *Mahāgovinda Suttanta* of the *Dīgha Nikāya* seems to justify this conclusion. In describing a meeting of the thirty-three gods in the Tāvatiṃsa heaven, it is said that after the deliberations were over, four great kings recorded the conclusions arrived at, and on this passage the translators observe, 'This sounds very much as if the Four Great Kings were looked upon as Recorders of what had been said. They kept the minutes of the meeting. If so (the gods being made in the image of men), there must have been such Recorders at the meetings in the Mote-Halls of the clans.' [1]

A passage in the preamble to the *Bhaddasāla Jātaka* mentions a tank, the water of which was used at the ceremony of *abhiṣeka* or coronation of the *kulas* or families of the *gaṇa rājās* of Vaiśālī.[2] This may refer to the ceremony performed when a Licchavi rājā was elected to a seat in the assembly of the State, or it may denote that the ceremony of coronation was performed when a young Licchavi *kumāra* (prince) succeeded to the title and position of his father.

The *Aṭṭhakathā* on the *Mahāparinibbāna Suttanta* [3] gives an account of the judicial procedure among the Licchavis. When a person who had committed an offence appeared before the Vajjian *rājās*, they surrendered him to the *Viniccaya-Mahāmāttas*, i.e. officers whose business it was to make enquiries and examine the accused with a view to ascertaining whether he was innocent or guilty. If they found the man innocent, they released him; but if they considered him guilty, they made him over to the *Vohārikas*, i.e. persons learned in law and custom. These could discharge

1 *Dialogues of the Buddha*, Pt. II, p. 263.

2 Fausböll, *Jātaka*, Vol. IV, p. 148: '*Vesālīnagare gaṇarājakulānaṃ abhisekamaṅgalapokkharaṇīṃ, ...*' See also D. R. Bhandarkar, *Carmichael Lectures*, 1918, pp. 150-1.

3 *Sumaṅgalavilāsinī*, II, 519 (P.T.S.).

him if they found him innocent; if they held him guilty, they transferred him to certain officers called *Suttadhāras*, that is, officials who kept up the *sūtra* (*sutta*) or thread of (ancient) law and custom. They in their turn made further investigation, and if satisfied that the accused was innocent, they discharged him. If, however, they considered him guilty, he was made over to the *Aṭṭhakūlakā*[1] (lit. 'the eight castes or tribes') which was evidently a judicial institution composed of judges representing the eight *kūlas* or tribes of the confederacy.

The *Aṭṭhakūlakā*, if satisfied of the guilt of the accused, made him over to the *Senāpati* or commander of the army, who delivered him over to the *Uparājā* or sub-king, and the latter in his turn handed him over to the *Rājā*. The *Rājā* released the accused if he was innocent; if he was found guilty, the *Rājā* referred to the *Paveṇipotthaka*, that is, the *pustaka* or book recording the law and precedents, and prescribing the punishment for each particular offence. The *Rājā*,[2] having measured the culprit's offence by means of that standard, used to inflict a proper sentence.[3]

### Political History

It is from the Buddhist literature that we first realise the importance of the Licchavis. In the *Brāhmaṇa* literature, though there is repeated mention of Videha, which in the Buddha's time joined with the Licchavis and formed a confederation, there is no mention of the Licchavis. It is remarkable that while the Mallas, their immediate neighbours, are mentioned in the *Mahābhārata*, the Licchavis are not found among the peoples that were encountered by the Pāṇḍava brothers in their peregrinations, or on their mission of conquest. In the sixth century B.C., however, we find them in the Jaina and Buddhist books as a powerful people in the enjoyment of great prosperity and of a high social status among the ruling races of Eastern India, and, as we have seen, they had already evolved a system of government and polity bearing no small

[1] The Hon. G. Turnour says that no satisfactory explanation can be obtained as to the nature of the office held by these functionaries. It is inferred to be a judicial institution composed of judges from all the eight castes.

[2] It seems that the '*Rājā*' who was the highest authority in the administration of criminal justice was different from the ordinary *rājās* who constituted the popular assembly. He was perhaps the senior amongst the *rājās*, or was one elected from time to time to administer criminal justice.

[3] G. Turnour, *An Examination of the Pāli Buddhistical Annals*, *J.A.S.B.*, December, 1838, pp. 993-4, f.n.

resemblance to some of the democracies[1] of the western world. It must have taken a long time to develop such institutions. But we must not imagine that the system was a creation of the Licchavis; for it seems that the *saṃgha* form of government was the normal form in ancient India even among the peoples that had a king at their head. The earliest Indian tradition of a king is that of a person elected by the people and ruling for the good of the people.[2] The procedure of conducting the deliberations of an assembly must have been developing from the earliest Vedic times, as the *samiti* and the *pariṣad* were well-known institutions in the *Ṛgveda.* The Licchavis must have modelled their procedure on that which was already in vogue among the Indian Aryans, allowing a century for the evolution of the particular form of government of the Licchavis from the already existing system. Their emergence from obscurity may fairly be placed at the beginning of the seventh century B.C. It is true that we do not find the Licchavis among the Vedic peoples, but in the fourth century B.C. (the time of the *Arthaśāstra*) they are mentioned along with the Kuru-Pañcālas and the Madras, i.e. with some of the powerful races of the Brāhmaṇic period.

We know nothing of the history of the Licchavis during the period of their early growth and development. The earliest political fact of any importance that we know of is that a Licchavi girl was given in marriage to Seṇiya or Śreṇika Bimbisāra, king of Magadha. This Licchavi lady, according to the *Nirayāvalī Sūtra,* one of the early Jaina works, was Cellanā, the daughter of Ceṭaka,[3] one of the *Rājās* of Vaiśālī, whose sister Kṣatriyānī Triśalā was the mother of Mahāvīra. In a Tibetan Life of the Buddha, her name is given as Śrībhadrā,[4] and in some places she is named Maddā.[5] She is, however, usually called Vaidehī in the Buddhist books, and her son Ajātaśatru is frequently designated 'Vedehiputto',[6] or the son of the Videhan princess.

[1] It may be argued that the Licchavi constitution was not a democracy, since citizenship was confined to the Licchavi clan, but in reply it may be pointed out that even in the great democracy of Athens, every resident was not a citizen. The Metics and the Slaves, for instance, were excluded from citizenship.

[2] See, e.g., the story of Beṇa and Pṛthu, *Mahābhārata, Śāntiparvan,* Vaṅgavāsī Ed., Chap. 60, verse 94.

[3] Jacobi, *Jaina Sūtras,* S.B.E., Vol. XXII, Introduction, p. xiii.

[4] *Ibid.*, p. xiii, note 3.

[5] Mrs. Rhys Davids and S. Sumaṅgala Thera, *The Book of the Kindred Sayings,* Pt. I, p. 38, n. 1.

[6] *Saṃyutta Nikāya,* Pt. II, p. 268.

The *Divyāvadāna* in one passage[1] speaks of Ajātaśatru as Vaidehīputra, and elsewhere[2] it states that King Bimbisāra reigned at Rājagṛha with his chief queen Vaidehī, and Ajātaśatru, his son. The Tibetan *Dulva* gives the name of Vāsavī to Ajātaśatru's mother, and narrates a story regarding Ajātaśatru's origin which cannot be traced in the Pāli Canon.[3]

D. R. Bhandarkar holds that 'this matrimonial alliance was a result of the peace concluded after the war between Bimbisāra and the Licchavis',[4] and that 'Bimbisāra thus appears to have seized Magadha after expelling the Vajjis beyond the Ganges'.[5] Bhandarkar's theory is based on Rhys Davids' supposition that the expression *Vesālim Māgadhaṃ puraṃ* in verse 1013 of the *Suttanipāta*[6] (P.T.S.) refers to one and the same city, taking *Māgadhaṃ puraṃ* in apposition to Vesālī. But the commentator has taken Māgadhaṃ to be a synonym of Rājagaha (= Rājagṛha).[7] Mention of the Pāsāṇa-cetiya in the same verse also goes to show that *Māgadhaṃ puraṃ* was not Vaiśālī. In several places we find mention of the *caityas* or *cetiyas* round about Vaiśālī, but nowhere do we come across a Pāsāṇa-cetiya. From verse 1014 of the *Suttanipāta* it appears that this *cetiya* was situated on a mountain peak. It is quite possible, therefore, that it was one of the *cetiyas* round about Rājagṛha, and most probably it was the Gṛdhrakūṭa (Pāli Gijjhakūṭa) monastery. There seems to have been some basis, however, for concluding that there was a war between Bimbisāra and the Licchavis, as such a war is referred to incidentally in the Tibetan *Dulva*, in a passage which traces the birth of Abhaya ('fearless'), another son of Bimbisāra, also by the Licchavi woman.[8] This story, which makes Abhaya or Abhayakumāra, as the Jaina books have it, a son of Ambapālī (Āmrapālī), the courtesan of Vaiśālī, is not confirmed by the Pāli books, where her son by Bimbisāra is called Vimala-Koṇḍañña, who became a Bhikkhu.[9]

The Licchavis appear to have been on friendly terms with King Pasenadi (Prasenajit) of Kośala, who speaks of them as his

[1] *Divyāvadāna* (Cowell and Neil), p. 55. [2] *Ibid.*, p. 545.
[3] Rockhill, *Life of the Buddha*, pp. 63-4.
[4] *Carmichael Lectures*, 1918, p. 74. [5] *Ibid.*, p. 73.
[6] P.T.S. (new edition), p. 194.
[7] *Suttanipāta Commentary*, p. 584: '*Māgadhaṃ puranti Magadhapuraṃ Rājagahan-ti adhippāyo*'.
[8] Rockhill, *Life of the Buddha*, p. 64.
[9] *Psalms of the Sisters*, pp. 120-1; *Psalms of the Brethren*, p. 65.

friends.[1] The relation of the Licchavis with their neighbours, the Mallas, also seems to have been friendly in general, as is evidenced by the Mallas standing by the Licchavis against their common foe, Ajātaśatru. The Jaina books also speak of nine Malla chiefs and nine Licchavi chiefs showing reverence to Mahāvīra at the time of his passing. There were, however, occasional hostilities between the two tribes, as is shown by the story of Bandhula, a Mallian prince, who was victorious over the Licchavi chiefs.[2]

We must now speak of the relations of the Licchavis with Ajātaśatru, the son and successor of Bimbisāra. The Magadhan king must have felt that the confederacy formed the greatest bar to the realisation of his idea of Magadhan expansion; and we find him taking the dreadful resolve to root out and destroy the Vajjians.[3]

According to one account,[4] the Vajjians attacked Ajātaśatru many times. This enraged him, and in order to baffle their attempts he had a fort constructed at Pātaligāma, and finally annihilated them. It is probable that Ajātaśatru was partly influenced by his fear of his foster-brother Abhaya, who had Licchavi blood in him. At this time, too, the Licchavis were gaining strength day by day, and no doubt becoming increasingly arrogant. In the *Sumaṅgalavilāsinī* account[5] we read that there was a port near the Ganges extending over a yojana, half of which belonged to Ajātaśatru and half to the Licchavis. There was a mountain not far from it, and at the foot of this mountain was a mine of precious substance (*Mahogghabhaṇḍa*). Once Ajātaśatru was late in arriving there, and the Licchavis took away all the treasure; and this happened again the following year. Having sustained a heavy loss, Ajātaśatru decided on vengeance. He realised, however, that the Licchavis were numerically stronger; so he conceived the idea of destroying their unity by sowing seeds of dissension among them. He sent his prime minister Vassakāra to the Buddha, who predicted that in future the Licchavis would be delicate and pleasure-loving, but that at present they could not be overcome save by propitiating them with tributes, or dissolving their internal unity. When Vassakāra reported this to Ajātaśatru, the king did not agree to propitiate the Vajjians with tributes, so he decided to break up their union, and arranged to bring a trumped-up charge against Vassakāra, whereupon the latter, feigning anger at his disgrace, would go to the Vajjis and offer to betray Ajātaśatru

---

1 *Majjhima Nikāya*, P.T.S., Vol. II, pp. 100-1 (*Aṅgulimāla Sutta*).
2 *Jātaka*, Vol. IV, p. 149 (*Bhaddasāla Jātaka*).
3 *Buddhist Suttas*, S.B.E., Vol. XI, pp. 1 and 2 (*Mahāparinibbāna Suttanta*).
4 *Ibid.*, p. 18.
5 (P.T.S.) II, p. 516.

to them. This plan was duly carried out, and the Vajjis offered Vassakāra the same post as he had held in Magadha, of 'Judicial Prime Minister'. Vassakāra accepted this post, and very soon acquired a reputation for his able administration of justice. After some time he started sowing dissension among the Licchavis, making them suspicious of each other and of their chiefs. In this way he succeeded in the course of three years in bringing about such disunion among the rulers that none of them would tread the same road together. He then sent a mission to Ajātaśatru, telling him that the time to strike had arrived. The king forthwith assembled his forces and set out. The Vajjians, on receiving intimation thereof, sounded the tocsin calling the citizens to action; but no one responded to the call, and Ajātaśatru entered the city and routed the inhabitants.[1] Thus the Magadhan kingdom was very much extended during his reign.

Of the subsequent history of the Licchavis we know very little. But it is certain that they were not completely exterminated by Ajātaśatru. He seems to have succeeded in making the Licchavis acknowledge his suzerainty and pay him revenue, but they must have been independent in the matter of internal management, and maintained their democratic institutions, for Kauṭilya speaks of them two centuries later as living under a *saṃgha* form of government, and advises King Candragupta Maurya to seek the help of these *saṃghas* which, on account of their unity and concord, were almost unconquerable.

It may safely be presumed that the Licchavis acknowledged the suzerainty of Candragupta's grandson Aśoka. After this we next meet them (as Licchivis) in Manu's Code, some time between 200 B.C. and 200 A.D., and then we do not hear of them again until the fourth century A.D., when their name appears in the records of the Imperial Guptas.

At the beginning of the fourth century A.D., Candragupta I, a son-in-law of the Licchavi family and son of Ghaṭotkaca Gupta, established a new kingdom.[2] A gold coin was introduced under the name of Candragupta I by his son, the emperor Samudragupta, who succeeded in establishing his suzerainty over a great part of India. On the obverse of the coin were incised the figures of Candragupta and his queen Kumāradevī. The former is offering an object (which on some coins appears clearly as a ring) to his queen. The words 'Candragupta' and 'Kumāradevī', or 'Śrī Kumāradevī', or 'Kumāradevī Śriḥ' are inscribed in the Brāhmī

[1] *Dīgha Nikāya Comm.* (*Sumaṅgalavilāsinī*), II, 524 (P.T.S.).

[2] R. D. Banerjea, *Prācīna Mudrā*, p. 121.

character of the fourth century A.D., and on the reverse was engraved the figure of Lakṣmī, the goddess of Fortune, seated on a lion couchant, with the legend 'Licchavayaḥ', 'the Licchavis'. With this is to be combined the significant fact that Samudragupta in his Allahabad Inscription takes pride in describing himself as 'Licchavidauhitra', 'the son of a daughter of the Licchavis'. This combined evidence justifies the conclusion that in the fourth century A.D., when the Guptas rose to power, the Licchavis must have possessed considerable political power in N.E. India. It is quite probable that Candragupta's dominions received considerable expansion by the addition of the country which he obtained through his Licchavi wife Kumāradevī, perhaps by succession.

Fleet, in editing the inscriptions in which the Gupta-Licchavi connection is mentioned, observes: 'Proof of friendly relations between the early Guptas and the Licchavis, at an early time, is given by the marriage of Candra Gupta I with Kumāra Devī, the daughter of Licchavi or of a Licchavi king. And that the Licchavis were then at least of equal rank and power with the early Guptas, is shewn by the pride in this alliance manifested by the latter.' [1] Fleet even goes so far as to declare: 'In all probability the so-called Gupta era is a Licchavi era, dating either from a time when the republican or tribal constitution of the Licchavis was abolished in favour of a monarchy; or from the commencement of the reign of Jayadeva I, as the founder of a royal house in a branch of the tribe that had settled in Nepal.[2] The fact that this royal house that was planted by the Licchavis in Nepal about the period 330 to 355 A.D. by Jayadeva I [3] was all along Brahmanical, proves that the Licchavis had not entirely dissociated themselves from the Brahmanic faith.'

Allan [4] presumes that it was to keep up the memory of his father, Candragupta, and his mother, Kumāradevī, that the coin bearing their names and that of the Licchavis was issued by Samudragupta. It is not improbable that the inscription 'Licchavayaḥ' which occurs on Candragupta's gold coins together with the name of his queen Kumāradevī may signify that she belonged to a royal family of the Licchavis previously reigning at Pāṭaliputra [5] (modern Patna), which seems to have been the original capital of the Gupta empire. A similar opinion is held by V. A. Smith, who says that Candragupta, a local rājā at or near Pāṭaliputra, married Kumāradevī, a princess

[1] Fleet, *Gupta Inscriptions—Corpus Ins. Ind.*, Vol. III, Introduction, p. 135.
[2] *Ibid.*, p. 136.
[3] *Ibid.*, p. 135.
[4] Allan, *Gupta Coins*, pp. 8–11.
[5] Rapson, *Indian Coins*, pp. 24, 25.

belonging to the Licchavi clan, in or about the year 308.[1] In ancient times, the Licchavis of Vaiśālī had been the rivals of the kings of Pāṭaliputra, but Candragupta was now elevated through his Licchavi connection from the rank of a local chief.

The Nepal inscriptions point out that there were two distinct houses, one of which, known as the Thākuri family, is mentioned in the *Vaṃśāvalī*, but is not recorded in the inscriptions; and the other was the Licchavi or the Sūryavaṃśī family which issued its charters from the house or palace called Mānagṛha and uniformly used an era with the Gupta epoch.[2]

[1] V. A. Smith, *Early History of India* (4th Ed.), p. 295.
[2] Fleet, *Corpus Inscriptionum Indicarum*, Vol III, p. 135.

## CHAPTER LIX

# THE UTKALAS AND UḌRAS

### THE UTKALAS

Some Purāṇas seem to imply that one of the ten sons of Manu was Ila-Sudyumna, a Kimpurusha [1] who in his turn had three sons, Utkala, Vinatāśva [2] and Gaya who enjoyed respectively the territories of Utkala, an undefined western country and Gayā.[3] These three territories have sometimes been collectively designated in the Purāṇas as *Saudyumnas*.[4] The Saudyumnas thus seem to have occupied the hilly tracts from Gayā to Orissa.

Epic tradition [5] connects the Utkalas with the Uḍras, Mekalas, Kaliṅgas and Āndhras. The *Droṇaparvan* of the *Mahābhārata* would have us believe that Karṇa conquered the Utkalas along with the Mekalas, Pauṇḍras, Kaliṅgas, Āndhras, Niṣadas, Trigarttas and Vāhlikas. In the *Rāmāyaṇa* the Utkala country is associated with the Mekala and Daśārṇa countries. In sending his army of monkeys to the different countries in quest of Sītā, Sugrīva asked Suṣeṇa to send his retinue among other countries of the south to Mekala, Utkala and Daśārṇa (Canto XLII).

From the Epic tradition as contained in the *Mahābhārata* cited above, it is evident that even as early as the period when the tradition was recorded, Utkala was distinguished from Oḍra or Uḍra and the distinction seems to have been maintained throughout in ancient Indian literature and inscriptions. It is equally evident that it was distinguished from Kaliṅga as well, though a verse in the *Vanaparvan* of the *Mahābhārata* [6] seems to suggest that Utkala at one time formed a part of Kaliṅga. The *Raghuvaṃśa* of Kālidāsa,[7] however, represents Utkala as an independent kingdom. The *Brahmapurāṇa* [8] also suggests that Utkala and Kaliṅga were separate kingdoms. According to the *Raghuvaṃśa*, the eastern boundary of

1 For a critical and synthetic study of Paurāṇic legends in this connection, see Pargiter, *A.I.H.T.*, pp. 253-4.

2 Or simply Vinata in most Purāṇas, or Haritāśva according to *Matsyapurāṇa* and *Padmapurāṇa*.

3 *Utkalasya Otkalam rāṣṭram Vinatāśvasya paścimaṃ dik pūrvā tasya rājarṣer Gayasya tu Gayāpurī.*

4 E.g., *Vāyupurāṇa*, pp. 99, 266.

5 *Mbh.*, *Bhīṣmaparvan*, Chap. IX, 348; *Droṇaparvan*, Chap. IV, 122.

6 *Vanaparvan*, Chap. 114.

7 IV, v. 38.

8 47, 7.

Utkala seems to have extended to the river Kapiśā (probably identical with either the modern Suvarṇarekhā, according to Lassen, or with the Kāśāi in Midnapur, according to Pargiter) and to the realm of the Mekalas on the west, with whom they are constantly associated, and who were inhabitants presumably of the Mekala hills. In the *Apadāna* of the *Khuddaka Nikāya* of the *Sutta-piṭaka*, a book of the Pāli Canon, Okkalā or Ukkalā or Utkalas were a tribe mentioned along with the Mekalas.[1] Southward must have extended the realm of the Kaliṅgas. From this, Pargiter deduced that Utkala must have comprised the southern portion of modern Chotanagpur.[2] He further suggests that the reading *Suhmottarāḥ*, a people of the eastern countries, of the *Matsyapurāṇa*,[3] should be amended to Suhmotkalāḥ to mean the 'Suhmas and the Utkalas', in which case the Utkalas become the immediately contiguous southern neighbours of the Suhmas who occupied roughly the modern districts of Bankura, Midnapore, Purulia and Manbhum. The *Mārkaṇḍeya Purāṇa*, however, locates the Utkalas as inhabiting the Vindhya mountains, along with the Karūshas, Keralas (according to *Vāyu* and *Matsya Purāṇas*, the reading here should be Mekalas and not Keralas which is evidently incorrect), the Uttamaraṇas and the Daśārṇas. Roughly speaking, the Utkalas were indeed a Vindhyan people inasmuch as the Chotanagpur hills are just an extension of the Vindhya ranges.

Coming to more definite historical times, we hardly find mention of the Utkalas as a people, though in later inscriptions and literature there are numerous references to Utkaladeśa or Utkalaviṣaya, the country presumably of the Utkala people. Thus a twelfth century epigraph of Gāhaḍavāla Govindachandra refers to a Buddhist scholar Śākyarakṣita, who was a resident of the Utkaladeśa. Another inscription, also of the twelfth century (Bhuvaneswar Stone Inscription of Narasiṃha I) refers to the building of a Viṣṇu temple by Candrikā, sister of Narasiṃha, at Ekāmra or modern Bhuvaneswar, in the Utkalaviṣaya. It is obvious from this inscription that Utkalaviṣaya at this period at least comprised the Puri and Bhuvaneswar regions as well. Earlier, in the Bhagalpur grant of Nārāyaṇapāla, a certain king of the Utkalas (*Utkalānāmādhīśa*) took fright and fled from his capital at the approach of Prince Jayapāla of the Pāla dynasty. The Bāḍal Pillar Inscription of the time of Guḍavamiśra credits King Devapāla with having eradicated the race of the Utkalas along with the pride of the Huṇas and the conceit of the rulers of Drāviḍa and Gurjara. The *Rāmacaritam* of Sandhyākara Nandī in giving a list of foreign countries invaded by

---

[1] Pt. II, p. 359. [2] *Mārkaṇḍeya P.*, p. 327 f.n. [3] Chap. CXIII, 44.

his hero Rāmapāla distinguishes Utkala from Kaliṅga in the eleventh century. A Sonpur grant of Mahāśivagupta Yayāti, of about the same date, also distinguishes Utkaladeśa from Kaliṅga and Kongoda.

The Buddhist literature contains some interesting information about Utkalas or Okkalas. Two merchants, named Tapussa and Bhallika,[1] were on their way from Ukkala to see the Buddha who was at the foot of the Rājāyatana tree near Uruvelā. They were asked by their relative to offer food to the Blessed One who at first refused to accept it, but he afterwards accepted it and ate it up. The two merchants became his disciples.[2] They were wealthy merchants who also visited Majjhimadeśa from Ukkala with five hundred carts.[3] Two inhabitants of Ukkala, named Vassa and Bhañña, did not believe in causation action on reality (*ahetuvādā*, *akiriyāvādā*, and *natthikavādā*).[4]

## The Uḍras

The earliest mention of the Uḍras or Oḍras or Auḍras as a people is, perhaps, found in the following śloka of the *Mānavadharmaśāstra* where the Oḍras are classed as outside the Brahmanical pale (i.e. Mlecchas) along with the Pauṇḍrakas, Drāviḍas, Kambojas, Yavanas, Śakas, Pāradas, Pahlavas, Cīnas, Kirātas, Daradas and Khaśas.

*Sanakaistu kriyālopādimāḥ kshatriyajātayaḥ*
*Vṛṣalatvam gatā loke brāhmaṇādarśanena cha*
*Pauṇḍrakāśchauḍra Drāviḍa Kamboja Yavanāḥ Śakāḥ*
*Pāradaḥ Pahlavaśchaināḥ Kirātā Daradāḥ Khaśāḥ.*

The *Apadāna*, a work of the Pāli Canon, mentions Oḍḍakā who were the same as Oḍrā or Uḍrā.[5]

Pliny in his *Natural History* mentions the Oretes as a people of India in whose country stood Mount Maleus which in another passage he locates amongst the Monedes and Suari. Cunningham identifies the last two peoples as the Mundas and Suars, from which he is led to conclude that the Oretes must be the people of Orissa. But it must be remembered that even then we cannot definitely equate the Greek Oretes with the Sanskrit Oḍra or Uḍra or Auḍradeśa.

Epic tradition connects the Uḍras along with the Poṇḍras, Utkalas, Mekalas, Kaliṅgas and Andhras.[6] According to the

[1] Cf. *Mahāvastu*, III, p. 303, where Ukkalā is mentioned as situated in Uttarāpatha.

[2] *Vinaya Piṭaka*, P.T.S., Vol. I, pp. 3-4.

[3] *Jātaka*, Fausböll, I, p. 80.

[4] *Aṅguttara Nikāya*, II, p. 3; Cf. *Saṃyutta Nikāya*, III, p. 73; *Majjhima Nikāya*, III, 78, and *Kathāvatthu*, I, p. 141.

[5] Pt. II, p. 358.

[6] *Vanaparvan*, LI, 1988; *Bhīṣmaparvan*, IX, 365; *Droṇaparvan*, IV, 122.

*Brahmapurāṇa* (28, 29, 42) which is admittedly very late, the country of the Oḍras extended northwards to Vrajamaṇḍala (Jājpur), and consisted of three *kshetras* called Purushottama or Śrīkshetra, Savitu or Arkakshetra, and Birajākshetra through which flew the river Vaitaraṇī. But it is somewhat strange that nowhere in early inscriptions do we find any mention of the people and their country. The first elaborate account of the people and their country is found in the itinerary of Hsüan Tsang. From Karṇasuvarṇa the pilgrim travelled south-west for about 722 li and came to the Wu-t'u or U-cha country.

'The country was above 7,000 li in circuit, and its capital above 20 li. The people were of violent ways, tall and of dark complexion, in speech and manners different from the people of "Mid-India". They were indefatigable students and many of them were Buddhists. There were above 100 Buddhist monasteries, and a myriad brethren, all Mahāyānists. Of deva temples there were fifty, and the various sects lived pell-mell. Near the shore of the ocean in the south-east of this country was the city Che-li-ta-lo (= Charitrapura = Puri?), above 20 li in circuit which was a thoroughfare and resting-place for sea-going traders and strangers from distant lands.'[1]

About a century later the country of the Oḍras became involved in chaos which has been described as *mātsyanyāya* in contemporary records. The celebrated Tibetan historian Tārānāth in his History of Buddhism records that Oḍiviśa, Vaṅga and five other countries of the east plunged themselves in a chaotic political condition[2] from which they were rescued by the election of King Gopāla on the throne. Oḍiviśa of Tārānāth is certainly a corruption or adaptation of Oḍra-viṣaya. Oḍiviśa is further mentioned by Tārānāth in connection with the reign of Devapāla who is credited by him as having 'brought into submission the kingdom of Varendra in the east and afterwards the province of Oḍiviśa'.

The Tirumalai Rock Inscription of the thirteenth year of King Rājendra Coḷa credits the king as having seized by his great warlike army the Oḍḍa-viṣaya in the course of his northern expedition. This Oḍḍa-viṣaya is certainly identical with Oḍra-viṣaya. The Coḷa king, Rāja-rāja, is also said to have conquered the Oḍḍa country. Doubtless, during this period, Oḍḍa-viṣaya came to mean the whole of the present Orissa country.

[1] Watters, *On Yuan Chwang*, II, pp. 193-4.

[2] 'There was no longer any member of it (the royal family of the Candras) a king; in Odiviśa, in Vaṅga, and the other five provinces to the east, each Kṣatriya, Brāhmaṇa, and merchant, constituted himself king of his surroundings, but there was no king ruling the country.'—Tārānāth, *Ind. Ant.*, IV, 1875, pp. 365-6.

## CHAPTER LX

# THE AVANTIS

In Vedic times, the Avantis do not emerge into importance as a ruling Kṣatriya tribe of ancient India. Their name is not found in the Vedic literature; but in the *Mahābhārata* they are found to be one of the most powerful of the Kṣatriya clans. Their dual monarchs, Vinda and Anuvinda, each led an akṣauhinī of troops to Duryodhana's army, and thus the Avantis made up one-fifth of the entire Kuru host (V, 19, 24).[1] The two monarchs are designated 'mahāratha' ('great warrior'), the highest title given to an epic warrior (VII, 5, 99),[2] and are spoken of as wielding powerful bows.[3] The two Avanti princes figure very prominently in the battle, and many are the glorious and heroic deeds with which they are credited. They rendered useful service to the Kaurava cause by their individual prowess and generalship as well as by the large army consisting of forces of every description which they led to battle.[4] They fought bravely in the field until they were slain,—by Arjuna, according to one account (VII, 99, 3691), and by Bhīma, according to another (XI, 22, 617). We read of the mighty hosts of the Avantis—Sainyaṃ Āvantyānāṃ—in the *Karṇaparvan* and elsewhere (VII, 113, 4408; VIII, 8, 235).

The *Matsyapurāṇa* (Chap. 43) traces the origin of the Avantis to the Haihaya dynasty of which Kārttavīryārjuna was the most glorious ruler, and adds that Avanti was the name borne by one of the sons of this monarch. The *Liṅgapurāṇa* states that out of the hundred sons of Kārttavīryārjuna, five, namely Śūra, Śūrasena, Dṛṣṭa, Kṛṣṇa and Yayudhvaja, ruled Avanti and acquired great renown. The *Viṣṇu-Dharmottara Mahāpurāṇa* (Chap. IX) and the *Padmapurāṇa* (*Svarga Khaṇḍa*, Chap. III) speak of Avanti as one of the *mahājanapadas* or chief provinces of ancient India. The *Skandapurāṇa* has a whole section, the Āvantyakhaṇḍa, dealing with the sacred sites and places of pilgrimage in the country of the Avantis. It is stated (Chap. 43) that the god Mahādeva, after he

---

[1] '*Āvantyau ca mahīpālau mahāvalasaṃvṛtau pṛthagakṣuhiṇībhyāṃ tāvabhiyātau suyodhanaṃ.*'

[2] '*Vindānuvindāvāvantyau rājaputrau mahārathau.*' See also *Mbh.*, V, 166, 5753, Cal. Ed.; *Bhīṣmaparvan*, VI, 99, 4504; VI, 114, 5293, 5309.

[3] VI, 83, 3650; VI, 94, 4195.

[4] *Mbh.*, VI, 16, 622; II, 17, 673, etc.; VI, 59, 2584; VI, 81, 3557; VI, 83, 3650–60; VI, 86, 3823; VI, 102, 4666; VI, 113, 5240; VII, 14, 542; 25, 1083; 32, 1410.

had destroyed the demon Tripura, visited Avantipura, which came to be known as Ujjayinī in honour of his victory. This Purāṇa in the section of Ayodhyā-māhātmya (Chap. I) relates that saints of Ujjayinī, the Avanti capital, came to Kurukṣetra with their disciples to attend the sacrifice of Rāma.

The Purāṇas also speak of intermarriages between the royal family of the Avantis and the ruling dynasty of the Yadus. Thus the *Viṣṇupurāṇa* (IV, 12) and *Agnipurāṇa* (Chap. 275) state that a Yadu princess called Rājyādhidevī was married to the king of Avanti. She was one of the five sisters of the Yadu monarch, Vasudeva, son of Śūra. The *Viṣṇupurāṇa* adds (IV, 14) that Rājyādhidevī bore two sons, Vinda and Upavinda, who are most probably to be identified with the Avanti princes, Vinda and Anuvinda of Epic fame.

The grammarian Pāṇini refers to Avanti in one of his sūtras (IV, 1, 176).

With regard to the location of Avanti, the sage Dhaumya (*Vanaparvan, Mbh.*), in enumerating the places of pilgrimage in W. India, refers to the country of the Avantis,[1] and speaks of the sacred river Narmadā as being situated therein. At the beginning of the *Virāṭaparvan*, Arjuna mentions Avanti along with other kingdoms in W. India, namely, Surāṣṭra and Kunti (IV, 1, 12). The geographical connection between the Avantis and the Kuntis is also shown in the description of 'Bhāratavarṣa' in the *Bhīṣmaparvan* (VI, 9, 350). A path leading to the city of Avanti is referred to in the Nalopākhyāna of the *Vanaparvan* (III, 61, 2317). Mrs. Rhys Davids notes[2] that Avanti lay north of the Vindhya mountains north-west of Bombay. It was one of the four chief monarchies in India when Buddhism arose, and was later absorbed into the Mauryan empire.

Rhys Davids observes: 'The country (Avanti), much of which is rich land, had been colonized or conquered by Aryan tribes who came down the Indus valley and turned west from the Gulf of Kutch. It was called Avanti at least as late as the second century A.D. (see Rudradāman's Inscription at Junāgaḍh) but from the seventh or eighth century onwards, it was called Mālava' (*Buddhist India*, p. 28).

Ujjayinī, which was situated on the Siprā, a tributary of the Carmanvatī (Chambal), is the modern Ujjain in Gwalior, Central India. It was the capital of Avanti or Western Mālava, and the residence of the Viceroy of the western provinces both under the Maurya and the Gupta empires.[3]

---

[1] *Mbh., Vanaparvan*, III, 89, 8354; *Avantiṣu Pratīcyām vai.*

[2] *Psalms of the Brethren*, p. 107, note i.

[3] Rapson, *Ancient India*, p. 175, s.v. *Ujjayinī.*

In the *Dīpavaṃsa*,[1] we read that Ujjenī (Ujjayinī) was built by Accutagāmī. Watters[2] points out that the Avanti capital Ujayana mentioned by Hsüan Tsang is generally supposed to be the well-known Ujain or Ujjen (Ujjain). In some of the canonical scriptures, Ujain is located to the west of Kanoj, which lies between Ujain and Benares.

The Chinese pilgrim Hsüan Tsang thus describes Ujjayinī, which name he gives to the whole country surrounding the capital—'Ujjainī is about 6,000 li in circuit; the capital is some 30 li round. The produce and manners of the people are like those of the country of Surāṣṭra. The population is dense and the establishments wealthy. There are several tens of convents, but they are mostly in ruins; some three or five are preserved. There are some 300 priests; they study the doctrines both of the Great and the Little Vehicle. There are several tens of Deva temples, occupied by sectaries of various kinds. The king belongs to the Brahman caste. He is well-versed in heretical books, and believes not in the true law. Not far from the city is a stūpa; this is the place where Aśoka-rājā made the hell (of punishment).'[3]

Owing to its position, Avanti became a great commercial centre. Three trade-routes met here; from the western coast with its sea-ports, Śūrpāraka (Sopāra) and Bhṛgukaccha (Broach); from the Deccan; and from Śrāvastī in Kośala (Oudh). It was also a great centre of science and literature. Ujjayinī was one of the seven sacred cities of the Hindus, and astronomers reckoned their first meridian of longitude from there. The dramas of Kālidāsa were performed on the occasion of the Spring Festival before the viceregal court of Ujjayinī, *c.* 400 A.D.[4]

An interesting notice of Ujjain is to be found in the *Periplus of the Erythraean Sea* (sec. 48) where we read: 'Eastward from Barygaza (=Bhṛgukaccha) is a city called Ozene, formerly the capital where the king resided. From this place is brought down to Barygaza every commodity for local consumption or export to other parts of India, onyx-stones, porcelain, fine muslins, mallow-tinted cottons and the ordinary kinds in great quantities. It imports from the upper country through Proklais for transport to the coast, spikenard, kostos and bdellium.' The ancient city no longer exists, but its ruins can be traced at a distance of a mile from its modern successor.[5]

---

[1] Oldenberg, p. 57, Text.

[2] *On Yuan Chwang*, Vol. II, pp. 250-1.

[3] *Buddhist Records of the Western World*, Vol. II, p. 270.

[4] Rapson, *Ancient India*, p. 175; and see McCrindle, *Ancient India as described by Ptolemy*, p. 154.

[5] McCrindle, *Ancient India as described by Ptolemy*, p. 155.

Avanti was one of the most flourishing kingdoms of ancient India, mentioned in the *Aṅguttara Nikāya* as one of the sixteen 'mahājanapadas' of Jambudvīpa.[1] From the first, Avanti became an important centre of the new doctrine which we now call Buddhism, and may have been the scene of elaboration of Pāli, the sacred language of the Buddhists.[2] Several of the most earnest adherents of the Dhamma were either born or resided there: Abhaya Kumāra,[3] Isidāsī,[4] Isidatta,[5] Dhammapāla,[6] Sona Kuṭikaṇṇa,[7] and especially Mahākaccāyana.[8]

Many are the stories that are told of Mahākaccāyana. He was born at Ujjayinī in the family of the chaplain of King Caṇḍapajjota. He learnt the three Vedas, and, on his father's death, succeeded him in the chaplainship. Subsequently, both Mahākaccāyana and the king his master were converted by the Buddha, and Mahākaccāyana devoted himself to furthering the Dhamma in his native province.[9] One of his most celebrated converts was Sono Kuṭikaṇṇo (so called because he used to wear ear-jewellery worth a crore). Kuṭikanno, the son of a wealthy councillor of Avanti, became a land-owner, but asked Mahākaccāyana to ordain him, after hearing him preach.[10] Isidatta was another of Mahākaccāyana's converts. He was born at Veḷugāma as the son of a guide to caravans.[11]

Dhammapāla, a Brahman's son of the country of Avanti, was also one of the early converts to the new faith. When he was returning from the university of Takṣaśīlā after completing his education, he met a thera, heard the Dhamma from him, left the world and acquired six-fold abhiññā.[12]

When the first Great Council of the disciples of the Buddha was held after his *parinibbāna*, to compile his teachings, Yasa sent messengers to the bhikkhus of Avanti inviting them to attend and help to perform the task.[13] This shows that at that time

---

[1] *Aṅguttara Nikāya*, Vol. IV, pp. 252, 256, 261.

[2] Eliot, *Hinduism and Buddhism*, Vol. I, p. 282.

[3] *Theragāthā Commentary*, 39.

[4] *Therīgāthā Commentary*, 261–4.

[5] *Theragāthā*, 120.

[6] *Ibid.*, 204.

[7] *Vinaya Texts*, II, 32; *Theragāthā*, 369; *Udāna*, V, 6.

[8] *Saṃyutta Nikāya*, III, p. 9; IV, 117; *Aṅguttara Nikāya*, I, p. 23; V, 46; *Majjhima Nikāya*, III, 194, 223.

[9] *Psalms of the Brethren*, pp. 238-9; also (for further stories of Mahākaccāyana) *Aṅguttara Nikāya*, V, pp. 46-7; *Saṃyutta Nikāya*, III, pp. 9ff.; *ibid.*, Vol. IV, pp. 115-16; *Dhammapada Commentary*, Vol. II, pp. 176-7.

[10] *Dhammapada Commentary*, Vol. IV, p. 101; cf. also *Vinaya Texts*, S.B.E., Pt. II, pp. 32ff.; *Psalms of the Brethren*, pp. 202-3.

[11] *Psalms of the Brethren*, p. 107; *Saṃyutta Nikāya*, IV, pp. 285–8.

[12] *Psalms of the Brethren*, p. 149.

[13] *Vinaya Texts*, Pt. III, p. 394; cf. Geiger, *Mahāvaṃsa*, Tr., p. 21.

(*c.* 480 B.C.) followers of the new faith in the western province of Avanti must have been numerous and influential.

King Bimbisāra of Magadha had a son, Abhaya, by a courtesan of Ujjayinī named Padumavatī.[1]

The great propounder of the Jaina faith, Mahāvīra, is said to have performed some of his penances in the country of Avanti, especially in Ujjayinī.[2] Here, too, the temple of Mahākāla—one of the twelve most famous Śaiva temples in India—was built.[3] One of the sacred places of the Liṅgāyat sect is situated at Ujjain. The Liṅgāyat itinerant ascetics wander over India, frequenting especially the five siṃhāsanas or Liṅgāyat sees.[4]

With regard to the political history of Avanti, we have already referred to King Caṇḍa Pajjota or Pradyota, who was a contemporary of the Buddha, and under whom the new faith became the state religion of Avanti. The Pradyotas were kings of Avanti (Western Malwa), and their capital was Ujjayinī.[5] There is a reference to King Caṇḍa Pajjota in the Chinese Buddhist legends collected by Beal.[6] In Buddha's time, the king of Madhurā (Mathurā) was styled Avantiputta, showing that on his mother's side he was connected with the royal family of Ujjain.[7]

The commentary on verses 21–3 of the *Dhammapada* gives a romantic story of the manner in which a matrimonial alliance was established between the royal families of Kauśāmbī and Avanti. One day, King Pajjota asked his courtiers whether there was any king more glorious than himself, and they told him that King Udena of Kosambī surpassed him. Angered, King Pajjota determined to attack Udena. He caused a wooden elephant to be made, and concealed sixty warriors in it. Knowing that Udena had a great liking for fine elephants, he had him informed by spies that a magnificent elephant was to be found in the frontier forest. King Udena came to the forest, and, in pursuit of the prize, became separated from his retinue and was taken prisoner. While a captive, he fell in love with Vāsuladattā, daughter of King Pajjota. One day, when Pajjota was away on a pleasure jaunt, Udena put Vāsuladattā on an elephant and eloped with her. On his return, King Pajjota sent a force in pursuit, but the wily Udena delayed

1 *Therīgāthā Commentary*, p. 39. For further references in Buddhist texts to Ujjain and Avanti, see, e.g. *Therīgāthā Commentary*, pp. 260-1, *Vimānavatthu Commentary*, pp. 137ff.

2 Mrs. S. Stevenson, *The Heart of Jainism*, p. 33.

3 *Ibid.*, p. 75.

4 Eliot, *Hinduism and Buddhism*, Vol. II, p. 227.

5 *Cambridge History of India*, Vol. I, pp. 310-11.

6 *The Romantic Legend of Śākya Buddha*, S. Beal, p. 29.

7 *Carmichael Lectures*, 1918, p. 53.

his pursuers by scattering coins and gold-dust on the route, and reached his own territory in safety. Udena and Vāsuladattā entered the city in triumph, and with due pomp and ceremony the princess was anointed queen.[1]

In the fourth century B.C., Ujjayinī became subject to Magadha. Later (early third century B.C.), Aśoka was stationed at Ujjayinī as Viceroy of the Avanti country, prior to his accession.[2] We read[3] that Aśoka's son, Mahinda, was born while Aśoka was Viceroy in Ujjayinī, under his father Bindusāra. Aśoka's grandson, Samprati, ruled in Ujjain and figured in Jaina legends.[4] Vikramāditya, the celebrated king of Ujjain, who is usually identified with Candragupta II (*c.* 375 A.D.) is said to have expelled the Scythians and thereafter established his power over the greater part of India.

In later times some of the ruling families of Avanti made their mark on Indian history. The Paramāra dynasty of Malwa, anciently known as Avanti, is especially memorable by reason of its association with many eminent names in the history of later Sanskrit literature. The dynasty was founded early in the ninth century by a chief named Upendra or Kṛṣṇarāja. Upendra appears to have come from Candrāvatī and Achalgarh near Mount Abu, where his clan had been settled for a long time. The seventh rājā, named Muñja, was famous for his learning and eloquence, and was not only a patron of poets but himself a poet of no small reputation. About 1018 A.D., Muñja's nephew, the famous Bhoja, ascended the throne of Dhārā, which was the capital of Malwa in those days, and reigned gloriously for more than forty years.[5] About 1060 A.D., this prince succumbed to an attack by the confederate kings of Gujarat and Cedi; but his dynasty lasted as a purely local power until the beginning of the thirteenth century, when it was superseded by chiefs of the Tomara clan, who were followed in their turn by Chauhan rājās, from whom the crown passed to Muhammadan kings in 1401. The Emperor Akbar suppressed the local dynasty in 1569, and incorporated Malwa in the Mughal empire.[6]

There is generally one distinguishing mark of the coins current in Ujjain; but on some of the rare coins the word 'Ujeniya' is incised in Brāhmī characters of the second century B.C. Generally on one side is a man with a symbol of the Sun and on the other is seen the sign of Ujjain. On some coins, a bull within a fence, or the Bodhi-tree, or Sumeru hill, or the figure of the Goddess of Fortune,

---

[1] Rhys Davids, *Buddhist India*, pp. 4-7. The same story is related in another form by Bhāsa in his drama, *Svapnavāsavadattā*; Dham. Com., Vol. I, pp. 191-2.

[2] V. A. Smith, *Aśoka*, p. 235.

[3] Copleston, *Buddhism*, p. 181.

[4] Mrs. Stevenson, *Heart of Jainism*, p. 74.

[5] Smith, *Early History of India*, 4th Ed., p. 410.

[6] *Ibid.*, p. 411.

is seen on one side. Some coins of Ujjain are quadrangular while others are round.[1] The class of round coins found at Ujjain display a special symbol, the 'cross and balls', known from its almost universal occurrence on the coins of ancient Malwa as the Ujjain symbol.[2] Square copper Mughal coins were struck at Ujjain up to the time of Shah Jahan I.[3]

---

1 R. D. Banerjee, *Prācīna Mudrā*, p. 108.
2 Brown, *Coins of India*, p. 20.
3 *Ibid.*, p. 87.

## CHAPTER LXI

# THE SINDHU-SAUVĪRAS

The Sauvīras seem to have been an ancient people. Their country is mentioned as early as Baudhāyana's *Dharmasūtra*. It was at that time considered an impure country, situated outside the limits of Aryandom proper; and Āryans who happened to go there were required to perform a sacrifice of purification on their return.[1] In later literature, the Sauvīras are often connected with their neighbouring tribe, the Sindhus, and the inclusive name 'Sindhu-Sauvīra', at once determines that the two tribes which were later regarded as one and the same were settled on the Sindhu or Indus.

The Sauvīras and Sindhus seem to have played an important part in the Kurukṣetra war; they are described in the *Bhīṣmaparvan* as having joined the Kauravas, along with the Bhargas, Andhras, Kirātas, Kośalas and Gāndhāras.[2] Elsewhere,[3] the Sauvīras are said to have supported Bhīṣma in the war, together with the Śālvas, Matsyas, Ambaṣṭhas, Traigarttas, Kekayas and Kaitavas. In *Bhīṣmaparvan* (51, 14), the Sindhus and Sauvīras are mentioned together, and are associated with the Śivas, Vaśātis and Gāndhāras. In a late passage of the Epic,[4] mention is made of a Greek overlord (Yavanādhipa) of Sauvīra; he must have been one of those Indo-Bactrian princes who established themselves in the north and western portions of India between about 200 B.C. and 200 A.D. According to the *Rāmāyaṇa* (Bengal recension, *Kiṣ. K.*, 41, 8–10) the Sindhu-Sauvīras were settled in the western division of India.

The Sindhus (or Saindhavas) and Sauvīras are usually conjoined in the Purāṇas, though they are mentioned separately in the *Viṣṇupurāṇa*.[5] According to the *Mārkaṇḍeya Purāṇa*, they were located in the north (LVII, 36; LVIII, 30); but the *Viṣṇupurāṇa* places them in the extreme west along with the Hūṇas, Śālvas, Sākalas, Madras (see Madra Chapter for their location, etc.; Wilson's *Viṣṇu P.*, Hall's Ed. II, III, 133). Puranic tradition seems to point to the intimate relation of the Sauvīras with the Śivis, and therefore with their neighbouring Uśīnaras as well. The Sauvīras were traditionally descended from Suvīra, one of the four sons of Śivi Auśīnara. Śivi and his sons are said to have founded the

[1] *Baud.*, I, 1, 2.

[2] Chap. 9, p. 822.

[3] *Bhīṣmaparvan*, Chap. 18, 13-14.

[4] *Ādiparvan*, Chap. 139, 21–3.

[5] Book II, Chap. III.

kingdoms of the Śibis, Vṛṣadarbhas, Madras, Kekayas and Sauvīras, thus occupying the whole of the Punjab except the north-western corner.[1] According to the *Agnipurāṇa* (Chap. 200), the river Devikā, but, according to the *Bhāgavatapurāṇa* (verse 10), the river Ikṣumatī flowed through Sauvīra.

Other Epic references to the Sauvīras include the mention of a Sauvīra king Śatruñjaya, who received instruction from a priest named Bharadvāja (*Mbh.*, XII, Chap. 140, 5249-50), and of a Sauvīra princess who married Manasyu, the son of Pravīra by a Śaurasena princess, and grandson of Puru (*Mbh.*, *Ādiparvan*, Chap. 49, 3696-7). Sovīra or Sauvīra is also mentioned in early Buddhist literature. The *Mahāgovinda Suttanta*[2] refers to Sovīra whose king was Bharata; while the *Divyāvadāna* in relating a story (pp. 544–86) accounting for the name of Bharukaccha (Broach), refers to Rudrāyaṇa, king of Roruka in Sauvīra. The *Mahābhāṣya* of Patañjali and the *Vyākaraṇa* of Kramadeśvara mention a city named Dattāmitri in Sauvīra.[3] In the *Milinda-Pañho*, Sovīra is described as a great sea-port (Trenckner Ed., p. 359); and it is not unlikely that the country is identical with the famous Sophir or Ophir of the Bible.[4] Alberuni appears to identify Sauvīra with Multan and Jahrawar (*India*, Vol. I, pp. 300, 302); while, according to the *Haimakoṣa* (IV, 26), the Sauvīra country is identical with Kunālaka.

Towards the middle of the second century A.D., the land of the Sindhus and the Sauvīras seems to have been administered by the Kṣatrapa rulers of W. India. The Junāgaḍh Rock Inscription of Rudradāman (*c.* 150 A.D.) refers to the Mahākṣatrapa's conquest of Sindhu-Sauvīra,[5] along with E. and W. Ākara (= mod. Khandesh) and Avanti (Pūrvaparākarāvanti), Anupanivṛt (probably the Māndhātā region), Ānartta, Surāṣṭra, Śvabhra, Maru, Kaccha, Kukura, Aparānta and other countries. The Kṣatrapas seem, however, to have wrested the country from the Kuṣāṇas, probably from one of the successors of Kaniṣka. After the era of the Kṣatrapas, the region probably passed over to the Guptas, and later to the Maitrakas of

[1] Pargiter, *A.I.H.T.*, pp. 109, 264; and Chap. on *Yaudheyas*.

[2] *Dīgha*, II, pp. 235-6.

[3] *Ind. Ant.*, 1911, *Foreign Elements in Hindu Population* (Bhandarkar); *Bomb. Gaz.*, I, ii, 11; *Kramadiśvara*, p. 96.

[4] Cunningham, *A.G.I.*, pp. 569–71.

[5] *P.H.A.I.*, 4th Ed., p. 390. Sindhu is the inland portion lying to the west of the Indus (Watters, *On Yuan Chwang*, II, 252-3 read with 256). Sauvīra includes the inland portion lying to the east of the Indus as far as Multan (*Alberuni*, I, 302; *Ind. Ant.*, 7, 259). See also in this connection Appendix B of *P.H.A.I.*, 4th Ed., dealing with the Chronological relation of Kaniṣka and Rudradāman I (pp. 522–7).

Valabhi. The country of the Sindhus, i.e. Sind, was the first kingdom to feel the impact of the conquering raids of the Arabs. An eighth century copperplate grant of the Gujarat Cālukya Pulakeśirāja [1] refers to the Tājikas (i.e. Arabs), who are described as having defeated the Saindhavas and other tribes of W. India.

---

[1] *Bom. Gaz.*, Vol. I, Pt. I, p. 109.

## CHAPTER LXII

# THE SURĀṢṬRAS

The Surāṣṭras as a tribe must have existed at least as early as the period represented by the Epics. The tribe, together with its country, is mentioned in more than one connection in Vālmīki's *Rāmāyaṇa*.[1] The *Kiṣkindhyā Kāṇḍa* locates the tribe in the west; for, in sending the retinue of monkeys in the western direction in quest of Sītā, Sugrīva asked Suṣena to send his unit to Surāṣṭra (among other countries). There are a number of countries and peoples in this list, e.g. the Kaliṅgas, Andhras, Cholas, Vidarbhas, etc. that cannot be located in the west; but the fact that the Surāṣṭras were included in the west division of India is upheld not only by a reference in the *Mahābhārata*,[2] where they are associated with the countries of the Kuntis and Avantis, but also by the evidence of the Purāṇas. According to the *Viṣṇupurāṇa*,[3] they are definitely located in the extreme west, and associated with the Sūras, Ābhīras, Arbudas and Mālavas, all of whom dwelt along the Pāripātra mountains. The *Mārkaṇḍeya Purāṇa*[4] includes them in W. India (Aparānta), while the *Brahmapurāṇa* associates them with the Aparāntas, Śūdras, Ābhīras and Mālavas, and describes them as dwelling along the Pariyātra (= Paripātra) hills. This geographical location of the tribe is also supported by the evidence of the *Kāvyamīmāṃsā*[5] of Rājaśekhara who includes the Surāṣṭra country in the Paścāddeśa or west division along with Dasoraka, Travana, Bhṛgukaccha, Kacchīya, Ānartta, Arbuda and other countries. At the time of the *Mahābhārata*, the Surāṣṭra country was ruled by the Yādavas.

The Surāṣṭra country is referred to in Baudhāyana's *Dharmasūtra*, where it is coupled with Dakṣiṇāpatha (Deccan). The country came to be included in the Maurya empire as early as the reign of Candragupta; for the Junāgaḍh Rock Inscription of Rudradāman refers to Candragupta's Rāṣṭrīya (= Viceroy) Puṣyagupta the Vaiśya, who constructed the Sudarśana lake. It was included in Aśoka's dominions, for the same inscription refers to Tushāspha, a Persian contemporary and vassal of Aśoka, who carried out supplementary operations on the lake. This Tushāspha

---

1 *Ādi Kāṇḍa*, Canto XII; *Ayodhyā Kāṇḍa*, Canto X; *Kiskindhyā Kāṇḍa*, Canto XLI.

2 *Virāṭaparvan*, Chap. I, 12.

3 Book II, Chap. III, 132–5.

4 Chap. 57, 52.

5 *Gaekwad's Oriental Series*, pp. 93-4.

was Rājā of the Surāṣṭra Saṃgha (community). That Surāṣṭra enjoyed the democratic form of government implied by the use of the word 'Saṃgha' is also testified to by Kauṭilya[1] (*Arthaśāstra*, p. 378), who refers to a number of Saṃghas, among which were included Kamboja and Surāṣṭra.

The records of Greek historians establish that after Aśoka and his successors, Surāṣṭra passed into the hands of the Bactrian Greeks. According to Strabo,[2] the Bactrian conquests were achieved partly by Menander (middle of second century B.C.) and partly by Demetrios, son of Euthydemos (*c.* 190 B.C.). They gained possession not only of Patalene, but of the kingdom of Saraostos and Sigerdis[3] which constitutes the remainder of the coast. Patalene is to be identified with the Indus delta, while Saraostos must certainly be identical with Surāṣṭra (Syrastrēnē of Ptolemy).

Ptolemy[4] refers to a country called Syrastrēnē, which must be identical with Surāṣṭra (= mod. Sorath in Kathiawar) on the Gulf of Kanthi (= Gulf of Kaccha or Cutch). Syrastrēnē, which extended from the mouth of the Indus to the Gulf of Cutch, was one of the three divisions of Indo-Scythia in Ptolemy's time,– the other two being Patalene and Abiria. Syrastrēnē is also mentioned in the *Periplus of the Erythraean Sea* as the sea-board of Aberia (= Abiria = Ābhīra), which is to be identified with the region to the east of the Indus, above the insular portion formed by its bifurcation (McCrindle, p. 140). Pliny, in his enumeration of the tribes of this part of India, mentions the Horatae, –evidently a corruption of Surāṣṭra or Sorath (Lib., VI, c. XX).

The Indo-Scythian or Śaka rule was interrupted by a member of the Āndhra dynasty, Viliyavākura II (Gautamīputra Sātakarṇī, 113–138 A.D.). In the Junāgaḍh Rock Inscription, Rudradāman is stated to have extended his rule over East and West Avanti, Ānartta, Surāṣṭra, Anupa, Sindhu-Sauvīra, Maru, Kaccha, Kukura, Aparānta, etc. Of these, Surāṣṭra, Kukura, Anupa and Aparānta, which formed parts of Gautamīputra Sātakarṇī's dominions, must have been conquered either from him or from one of his sons.

After the Scythian occupation, Surāṣṭra seems to have passed into the hands of the Guptas. It is not improbable that Surāṣṭra was one of the countries whose rulers hastened to buy peace by establishing diplomatic relations with Samudragupta (*c.* 326–375

---

1 *Arthaśāstra*, p. 378.

2 Strabo, Bk. XI, sec. XI, 1, in Falconer's version. (Strabo, Hamilton and Falconer, Vol. II, pp. 252-3, vide also Ray Chaudhuri, *Political History of Ancient India*, 4th Ed., p. 317.)

3 Prob. = Sāgaradvīpa of *Mahābhārata*, II, 31, 66.

4 See McCrindle's *Ptolemy*, pp. 35-6, 136, 140.

A.D.). The Saka-Murundas alluded to in the Allahabad Pillar Inscription (*C.I.I.*, Vol. III) were probably the Kṣatrapas of Indo-Scythia who came to do homage to the great conqueror. His successor Candragupta II (375–413 A.D.) also seems to have led a successful campaign against the Western Kṣatrapas of Surāṣṭra.[1] The fall of the Saka Satrapa is alluded to by Bāṇa, and also proved by coins; while we find decisive evidence of the Gupta occupation of Surāṣṭra in the Junāgaḍh Inscription of Skandagupta (*c.* 455–480 A.D.) which tells us that he (Skanda) 'deliberated for days and nights before making up his mind who could be trusted with the important task of guarding the lands of the Surāṣṭras'.[2] He finally appointed Parṇadatta as governor.

The rule of the Guptas in this territory does not seem to have long survived Skandagupta. Soon the Maitrakas of Valabhi asserted their independence, and established their supremacy over West Malwa, Baroda, Gujrat, Kathiawar and the adjoining region.[3] Accordingly, when Hsüan Tsang visited Su-la-ch'a or Suratha in the seventh century A.D., it was included in the kingdom of Valabhi. According to the pilgrim, Su-la-ch'a touched the river Mo-hi (= Mahi) on the west, and its capital lay at the foot of Mt. Yuh-shan-ta (= Prakrit Ujjanta, Skr. Urjayat of the Junāgaḍh Inscriptions of Rudradāman and Skandagupta), which is to be identified with the Girnar hill near Junāgaḍh.[4]

When the Maitrakas of Valabhi became extinct about the middle of the eighth century A.D., the Surāṣṭras seem to have suffered a reverse at the hands of the Tājikas who are generally identified with the Arabs. Already, during the early years of the eighth century, the Arabs had taken possession of Sind, and it is certainly not unlikely that they attempted a conquest of the neighbouring Surāṣṭra country. In a Nausari Copperplate grant of the Gujarat Cālukyas, Pulakesirāja (eighth century A.D.) is credited with having defeated the Tājikas who are therein reported to have destroyed the Saindhavas, Kacchelas, Surāṣṭras, Cāvotakas, Gurjaras and Mauryas, before they were themselves defeated by the Cālukya king.[5]

---

1 *C.I.I.*, Vol. III—Udaygiri Cave Inscription.

2 *Ibid.*

3 Ray, *Maitrakas of Valabhi*, *I.H.Q.*, Sept., 1928.

4 *C.A.G.I.*, Mazumdar's Ed., pp. 372–4, 697-8.

5 *Bomb. Gazetteer*, Vol. I, Pt. I, p. 109.

## CHAPTER LXIII

# THE ŚŪDRAS

The Śūdras as a tribe (as distinct from the fourth caste) seem to have played some part in Ancient Indian History, and are several times mentioned in the *Mahābhārata* and Purāṇas, as also in the accounts of Greek geographers and historians.

The Śūdras were a fairly important tribe of the north-west at the time when Alexander the Great invaded India (326 B.C.). They were among those who were vanquished by the Macedonian conqueror. Greek writers refer to them as Sodrai, in association with the Massanoi and Mousikaroi, all of whom occupied portions of modern Sind. The next datable reference to the tribe is contained in Patañjali's *Mahābhāṣya* (1, 2, 3), where they are associated with the Ābhīras. In the *Mahābhārata* also they are associated with the Ābhīras,[1] and are said to have occupied the region where the river Sarasvatī vanishes into the desert, i.e. near Vinaśana in Western Rajputana.[2]

In the *Harivaṃśa*,[3] we have 'Madrābhīrāḥ' (Madras and Ābhīras) where we would expect to find 'Śūdrābhīrāḥ'; here Madra may be a misreading for Śūdra, for the Madras are hardly anywhere connected with the Ābhīras.[4]

According to the *Mārkaṇḍeya Purāṇa* (57, 35), the Śūdras were located in the Aparānta region or western country, and were associated with the Vāhlīkas, Vātadhānas, Ābhīras, Pallavas, etc. The *Brahmapurāṇa*[5] also places them in the west, and associates them with the Saurāṣṭras, Ābhīras, Arbudas, Mālavas, etc. The *Viṣṇupurāṇa* (II, 3) has Śūrābhīrāḥ for what obviously should be Śūdrābhīrāḥ. In the *Bhāgavatapurāṇa* (XII, 1, 36) also we have:

'*Saurāṣṭrāvaityabhīrāśca Śūdrā Arbuda-mālavāḥ.*'

---

[1] *Śalyaparvan*, 2119.

[2] *Mbh.*, IX, 37, 1: '*Śūdrābhīrān prati dveṣād yatra naṣṭā Sarasvatī*'.

[3] Cal. Ed., 12, 837.

[4] M. Langolis reads '*Śūrābhīrāḥ*', evidently following the *Viṣṇu*, *Bhāgavata*, and some other Purāṇas. See his translation of the *Harivaṃśa*, Vol. II, p. 401; also Goldstücker's *Dictionary*, p. 299.

[5] 19, 17: '*Tathāparāntyāḥ Saurāṣṭrāḥ Śūdrābhīrāstathārbudāḥ*
*Mārukā Mālavāścaiva Pāriyātranivāsinaḥ.*'

## CHAPTER LXIV

# THE LĀṬAS

The name of the Lāṭas as a people must have been known as early as the beginning of the Christian era, if not earlier, and their country Lāṭa or Lāṭa-viṣaya was well known in Indian history till as late as the seventh and eighth centuries. It is curious, however, that neither the country nor its people is ever mentioned in any of the earlier Purāṇas, or even in the Epics.

The earliest definite mention of the country seems to have been made by Ptolemy. According to his description of India within the Ganges, Lārike lay to the east of Indo-Skythia along the sea-coast.[1] Lāṭadeśa in its Prākrit form Lārdeśa (the country of Lār) seems to have been a very early name for the territory of Gujrat and Northern Konkon,[2] and McCrindle conjectured that Lārike 'may therefore be a formation from Lār with the Greek termination *ike* appended'.[3] The name Lārdeśa probably survived the Hindu period, 'for the sea to the west of that coast was in the early Muhammadan time called the sea of Lār, and the language spoken on its shores was called by Mas'ūdi, Lāri'.[4]

In Ptolemy's Lārike lay the mouth of the river Mōphis, which is identical with the Mahī, a village named Pakidare which is difficult to identify, and the cape Maleo which 'must have been a projection of the land somewhere between the mouth of the Mahī and that of the Narmadā, but nearer to the former if Ptolemy's indication be correct'.[5]

The two great cities of Barygaza and Ozene were also within the political division of Lārike. In Ptolemy's Gulf of Barygaza lay Kamane, doubtless identical with Kamonone of the *Periplus* which places it to the south of the Narmadā estuary, while Ptolemy locates it to the north; Nausaripa, which is the same as modern Nausārī on the coast and Sanskrit Navasārikā, and finally Poulipoula, which in Yule's map is located at modern Sanjam on the coast south from Nausārī. Barygaza itself is the same as Sanskrit Bhṛgukṣetra or Bhṛgukaccha, Pāli Bharukaccha, modern Broach; while Ozene, of course, is Ujjayinī or Ujjain.

---

1 McCrindle, *Ptolemy's Ancient India*, pp. 38, 152-3.

2 Marco Polo, Vol. II, p. 302 n. (Yule).

3 McCrindle, p. 38.

4 *Ibid.*, p. 153; Marco Polo, II, p. 353 n.

5 McCrindle's *Ptolemy*, p. 38.

The Ceylonese chronicles (*Dīpavaṃsa* and *Mahāvaṃsa*) refer to the country of Lāḷa in connection with the first Aryan migration to Ceylon, led by Prince Vijaya. Attempts have been made to identify Lāḷa both with Lāṭa or Lāḍa in Gujrat, and Rāḍha in Bengal, and both countries claim the honour of the first Aryanization of Ceylon. Prince Vijaya is described in the chronicles as having been the great-grandson of a princess of Vaṅga; hence one school of scholars mainly depending on historical evidence proposes to equate Lāḷa with Rāḍha, while the other school finds Lāḷa to be philologically more closely akin to Lāṭa or Lāḍa. It is not impossible that the tradition of two different streams of immigration came to be knit together in the story of Vijaya, as Dr. Barnett thinks.[1]

In the days of the early Imperial Guptas, the Lāṭa country came to be formed into an administrative province as Lāṭa-viṣaya, along with Tripuri-viṣaya, Arikiṇa-viṣaya, Antarvedi-viṣaya, Vālavī-viṣaya, Gayā-viṣaya, etc. These *viṣayas* or *pradeśas* seem to have been subordinate to the larger administrative division, called *bhukti*.

It is likely that the Lāṭa country was the same as the Lāṭeśvara country mentioned in one or two early Gurjara and Rāṣṭrakūṭa records. In the Baroda Copperplate Inscription (verse 11) the capital of the kingdom of Lāṭeśvara is said to have been at Elapur. The inscription also gives the genealogy of the kings of Lāṭeśvara. K. M. Munshi, in his work 'Gujarāta and its literature', gives us some information about Lāṭa. He says: 'From about *c.* A.C. 150, the tract between Khambhāta (Cambay) and Narmadā acquired the name of Lāṭa which, thereafter, came to include the country south of the Narmadā up to the Damaṇagaṅgā. Under the Chalukyas of Aṇahilavāḍa Pātaṇa (A.C. 961), the name Lāṭa was gradually displaced by the name Gurjara Bhūmi . . . . The whole of Lāṭa up to Damaṇagaṅgā became part of Gujarāta in *c.* A.C. 1400.'[2] Lāṭa, then, was evidently the equivalent of South Gujarāta. Lassen, however, identifies Lārike with Sanskrit Rāṣṭrika,[3] in its Prakrit form Lātika, which is easily equated with Lāṭa, though the equation of Rāṣṭrika and Lātika is not convincing enough.

Lāṭa is mentioned twice in Vātsyāyana's *Kāmasūtra*.[4] Vātsyāyana does not give any clue as to location of the country, but contents himself with describing the characteristics of the men and women respectively. Lāṭa is also referred to by the author of

[1] *J.A.S.B.*, Vol. XVIII, 1922, No. 7.
[2] *Ibid.*, pp. 2-3. See also *ibid.*, p. 20 n., p. 36.
[3] See chapter on *Rāṣṭrikas*. It may be that Rāṣṭrika formed the northern part of Gujarat, and Lāṭa, the southern.
[4] *Ibid.*, pp. 103 and 126.

Kuvalayamālā (*c.* 779 A.D.). The inhabitants of Lāṭa are distinguished from those of Gurjara, the Lāṭa people appearing as pleasure-loving and humorous, and those of the north as sterner and of stronger build. Lāṭa appears to have possessed distinctive literary traits. A kind of style, favoured by the authors of Lāṭa, acquired the name of Lāṭī. Rājaśekhara represents the people of Lāṭa as preferring Prākrit to Sanskrit.

## CHAPTER LXV

# THE ŚŪRPĀRAKAS

The Śūrpārakas were evidently the people of Śūrpāraka. The *Mārkaṇḍeya* list (LVII, 49) reads Sūryārakas which is evidently a mistake, but all the Purāṇas agree in placing them in the west where lived the celebrated sage Rāma Jāmadagnya (*Mbh.*, *Vana P.*, LXXXV, 8185). But the *Mahābhārata* also locates them in the south (*Sabhā P.*, XXX, 1169; *Vana P.*, LXXXVIII, 8337) because it bordered on the southern sea in the western region (*Śānti P.*, XLIX, 1778–82). The region situated near Prabhāsa (*Vana P.*, CXVIII, 10221–7) included the country around the mouth of the Narmadā (*Anuśāsana P.*, XXV, 1736). It was the sage Rāma Jāmadagnya who is credited with having built the city of Śūrpāraka (*Harivaṃśa*, XCVI, 50).

Śūrpāraka is mentioned in one of the inscriptions of Śaka Uṣavadāta and is undoubtedly the same as Suppāraka of Pāli literature where it is described as a great sea-coast emporium identified with Sopārā of early Greek geographers.

## CHAPTER LXVI

# THE AUDUMBARAS

The Audumbaras seem to have been a minor oligarchical or republican tribe. They are mentioned in the *Sabhāparvan* of the *Mahābhārata* (II, 1869), where they are located in the Madhyadeśa (midland district). The *Harivaṃśa* refers to certain ascetics, descendants of Viśvāmitra, as Audumbaras, but it is difficult to determine their exact relation with the tribe of the *Sabhāparvan*.

The Purāṇas [1] mention a people called the Udumbaras, along with the Kāpiṅgalas, Kuruvāhyas and Gajāhvayas. The last-named people were connected with Hastināpura, the Kuru capital, and the Kuruvāhyas must also have had some connection with the famous Kuru people. It is, therefore, reasonable to assume that the Udumbaras (presumably identical with the Audumbaras) occupied a district contiguous with, or not far from, the Kuru country. Both Lassen (Ind. Art. map) and Cunningham (*Arch. Surv. Rep.*, XIV, 115 and 135) seem to locate the Udumbaras somewhere in Cutch.

The *Harivaṃśa* [2] mentions a river Udumbaravatī in the south, while the *Mañjuśrīmūlakalpa* [3] refers to a city named Udumbarapura in the Magadhajanapada.

The Audumbaras are also known from coins which come chiefly from the Kangra District of the Punjab, and which belong to about the eighteenth century A.D.[4]

1 See, e.g. *Mārkaṇḍeya Purāṇa*, LVIII, 9.

2 CLXVIII, 9511.

3 Gaṇapati Śāstrī's Ed., p. 633. '*Māgadhaṃ janapadaṃ prāpya pure Udumbarāhvaye*'.

4 Smith, *Cat. of Coins*, pp. 160-1.

## CHAPTER LXVII

# THE KĀKAS, KHARAPARIKAS AND SANAKĀNIKAS

These three tribal peoples are referred to in the Allahabad Pillar Inscription of Samudragupta, along with the Mālavas, Ārjunāyanas, Yaudheyas, Madrakas, Ābhīras and Prārjunas. Recent researches have ascertained that the better-known among these tribes- -i.e. the Mālavas, Yaudheyas, Madras and Ābhīras—inhabited the regions on the western, north-western and south-western fringe of Āryāvarta proper; and it is likely that the Kākas, Kharaparikas and Sanakānikas also occupied this region.

So far as is known, there is no other mention of the Sanakānikas, either in literature or in any other epigraphic record except the Udayagiri Cave Inscription of G.E. 82 which mentions a Mahārāja of the Sanakānika tribe. Udayagiri is just two miles to the north-west of Bhilsa, ancient Vidiśā.

The name Kharaparika does not occur elsewhere in inscriptions or literature; but Dr. D. R. Bhandarkar [1] finds a probable identification of the tribe with Kharpara mentioned in the Bāṭihāgarh Inscription of the Damoh District of the Central Provinces. The *Mārkaṇḍeya Purāṇa* (LVIII, 47) mentions a tribe called Khara-sāgara-rāśis,[2] along with the Gandhāras and the Yaudheyas; and the *Matsyapurāṇa* (CXXI, 56) refers to a country named Kharapatha, watered by the river Nalinī. It is difficult to say whether this people Khara-sāgara-rāśī, and country Kharapatha, had anything to do with the Kharaparikas.

The Kākas [3] are mentioned in the *Mahābhārata* (VI, 9, 64) where they are associated with the Vidarbhas who were a well-known people occupying tracts of territory in what is now known as the Central Provinces. The territory of the Kākas is sometimes identified with Kākūpur near Bithur,[4] while Smith suggests an identification with Kākanāda near Sāñcī.[5]

[1] *I.H.Q.*, I, p. 258; *E.P.*, XII, p. 46, v. 5.

[2] A variant reading is '*Svarasāgararāśī*'.

[3] Var. reading *Kāñcika*.

[4] *Bombay Gazetteer*.

[5] *J.R.A.S.*, 1897, pp. 892–9.

## CHAPTER LXVIII

# THE MATSYAS

The Matsyas appear to have been one of the prominent Kṣatriya tribes that made up the Vedic Aryan people in the earliest period of their residence in India. We read in a hymn of the *Ṛgveda* (VII, 18, 6) that the Matsyas were attacked by Turvaśa, a famous king, in order to extract from them the wealth which he required for the performance of a sacrifice. We observe that the Matsyas were regarded as a wealthy people, their riches most probably consisting of cows which were much in demand for the performance of lengthy and elaborate sacrifices. It is well known that in Epic times the Matsyas were very rich in this wealth of cows, for which the Trigarttas and the Kurus led predatory expeditions against them. In the Rigvedic passage referred to above, the word 'Matsya' in the text has been taken by some scholars to mean 'fish' (its original meaning). Sāyaṇa gives both meanings, and the authors of the *Vedic Index* (Vol. II, p. 121) also think both possible. From the context, however, Matsya clearly refers to the people. There is, moreover, no doubt that cattle made up the wealth here intended, for the verse following the one in question states clearly that Indra recovered the cows (*gavyā*) from the Tritsu plunderers (just as Indra's son, Arjuna, recovered the cattle plundered by the Kurus as described in the *Mahābhārata*). Further, other tribes of Western India, e.g. the Druhyus and the Bhṛgus, are mentioned in the verse (VII, 18, 7) side by side with the Matsyas. So it is evident that the latter is here also a tribal name.

The question arises whether the name Matsya has anything to do with totemism, as suggested by Prof. Macdonell in his *Vedic Mythology*. He says: 'There are possibly in the *Ṛgveda* some survivals of totemism, or the belief in the descent of the human race or of individual tribes or families from animals or plants', and he refers to the Matsyas as an illustration of his statement (*Vedic Mythology*, p. 153). But, as Prof. A. Berriedale Keith points out, 'mere animal names prove little as to totemism, which is not demonstrated for any Aryan stock'.[1] The myth about the birth of a king called Matsya from the womb of a fish along with Matsyagandhā Satyavatī, as related in the *Mahābhārata* (*Ādiparvan*,

[1] *Aitareya Āraṇyaka* (Anecdota Oxoniensia), p. 200, f.n., a.

Chap. 63)[1] cannot be proved to have any connection with the Matsya people. Nor is there anything in the account of the Matsyas to show that the fish was an object of worship among them, or was ever regarded with any special veneration. The fish incarnation of Viṣṇu has nothing specifically to do with the Matsya people. There is, in fact, no valid reason for thinking that such Indo-Aryan tribal names as *Matsya* (fish), *Aja* (goat), and *Vatsa* (calf) have anything to do with totemism.

Coming down to the *Śatapatha Brāhmaṇa*,[2] we find that a Matsya king, Dhvasan Dvaitavana, is mentioned among the great monarchs of ancient times who acquired renown among the Vedic Aryan people owing to their performance of the horse sacrifice. We shall have occasion to mention this king again in connection with the lake to which he gave his name.

In the *Kauṣītaki Upaniṣad*,[3] the Matsyas are mentioned along with other tribes, viz. the Uśīnaras, Kuru-Pañcālas, and Kāśī-Videhas. In the *Gopatha Brāhmaṇa*, they are connected with the Śālvas, a Kṣatriya tribe in their neighbourhood, and mentioned along with other well-known Kṣatriya tribes of the Vedic period, such as the Kuru-Pañcālas, Aṅga-Magadhas, Kāśī-Kośalas and Vaśa-Uśīnaras.[4] The relation of the Matsyas with the Śālvas is also attested by the *Mahābhārata*. King Suśarmā of the Trigarttas, addressing Duryodhana, says: 'We have been defeated more than once by the Matsyas and Śālvas (*Matsya-Śālveyakaiḥ*).'[5] Evidently the Śālvas were neighbours of the Matsyas and their allies in Vedic and Epic times. In the *Padmapurāṇa* (Chap. 3) and the *Viṣṇu-dharmottara Mahāpurāṇa* (Chap. 9), Matsya is mentioned as one of the *Janapadas* of Bhāratavarṣa.

In later times, we find the Matsyas associated with the Cedis and the Śūrasenas. Among the kings who brought about the ruin of their own tribes and families, the *Mahābhārata* (Vol. 74, 16) mentions a King Sahaja who was instrumental in causing the destruction of the Cedi-Matsyas. In the Paurāṇic age the Matsyas are spoken of along with the Śūrasenas and the *Cambridge History of India*[6] observes that the two peoples are constantly associated, and may possibly have been united under one king. In the *Bhīṣma-parvan* of the *Mahābhārata*, the Cedi-Matsya-Karūṣas are grouped together in one passage, the Cedi-Matsyas in another, and the Cedi-

---

[1] The *Vāyupurāṇa* (Chap. 99) also refers to this King Matsya born of Uparicara Vasu and a fish.

[2] *Śatapatha Brāhmaṇa*, XIII, 5, 4, 9; S.B.E., Vol. XLIV, p. 398.

[3] *Kauṣitaki Up.*, IV, I. Trsl. by Max Müller, S.B.E., Vol. I, p. 300.

[4] *Gopatha Brāhmaṇa*, I, 2, 9; *Bibliotheca Indica Series*, ed. Dr. R. L. Mitra, p. 30.

[5] *Mbh.*, *Virāṭaparvan*, Chap. 30, pp. 1-2.

[6] Vol. I, p. 316.

Matsya-Karūṣas in another.[1] Elsewhere in the *Mahābhārata*, in the description of the Kurukṣetra battle, the Cedi-Pañcāla-Karūṣa-Matsyas,[2] Matsya-Pañcāla-Cedis,[3] Cedi-Karūṣa-Matsyas,[4] and Cedi-Matsyas [5] respectively are grouped together.

In the *Manusaṃhitā* we read: "The plains of the Kurus, the (country of the) Matsyas, Pañcālas and Śūrasenakas, these (form) indeed, the country of the Brahmarshis (Brahman sages) which ranks immediately after Brahmāvarta. From a Brāhman born in that country let all men on earth learn their several usages.' [6] From this passage it appears that the Matsyas were regarded by the Indians as belonging to the most orthodox followers of Brahmanism in ancient times. Manu also prescribes, when laying down rules for the marshalling of troops on the battle-field, that '(Men born in) Kurukṣetra, Matsyas, Pañcālas, and those born in Śūrasena, let him (i.e. the king or leader) cause to fight in the van of the battle, as well as (others who are) tall and light'.[7] Apparently the Matsyas occupied a pre-eminent position both because of the purity of their conduct and customs, and through their bravery and prowess on the field of battle.

In the *Kiṣkindhyā Kāṇḍa* of the *Rāmāyaṇa*, we read that when Sugrīva sent his monkey host to search for Sītā, those under Aṅgada made their enquiries throughout the countries of the Matsyas and the Kaliṅgas, two peoples situated 'at the two extremities of India'. When speaking [8] about the country of the Śūrasenas and the Kurus and Bharatas who were the immediate neighbours of the Matsyas, Sugrīva does not refer to the Matsyas at all, although as we have seen, the Śūrasenas and Matsyas were constantly associated in the Paurāṇic age. This omission suggests that at the time of the *Rāmāyaṇa* the Matsyas were not regarded as an important people: perhaps they had lost the importance which they had acquired in the Vedic age.

Among references to Matsya in the Buddhist literature, we may mention *Aṅguttara Nikāya* (I, p. 213; IV, pp. 252, 256, 260), where Matsya is named as one of the *Mahājanapadas* of India. There is a reference to the Matsyas or Macchas (together with the Kāśīs and Śūrasenas) in the *Janavasabha Suttanta* of the *Dīgha Nikāya* in connection with the account of the Buddha's stay in Nādika.[9] In the *Vidhurapaṇḍita Jātaka* we read that the Macchas witnessed the dice-play of the king of the Kurus with the Yakkha Puṇṇaka.[10]

---

1 See *Bhīṣmaparvan*, Chap. 9; Chap. 52, 9; Chap. 54, 8.
2 *Mbh.*, Vaṅgavāsī Edn., 59, 129.
3 *Ibid.*, 118, 52-3.
4 *Ibid.*, VIII, 30, 27, 29.
5 *Ibid.*, VIII, 78, 25.
6 *Manusaṃhitā*, II, 19-20; S.B.E., Vol. XXV, pp. 32-3.
7 *Ibid.*, VII, 193; S.B.E., Vol. XXV, p. 247.
8 *Kiṣkindhyā Kāṇḍa*, 43, 11.
9 *Dīgha Nikāya*, Vol. II, p. 200.
10 *Jātaka* (Fausböll), Vol. VI, pp. 280 foll.

The *Śatapatha Brāhmaṇa* contains a reference to a Matsya king; Dhvasan Dvaitavana, who appears to have given his name to a lake, Dvaitavana. In the *Mahābhārata*, we find mention of an extensive forest named Dvaitavana where the Pāṇḍavas passed a large portion of their exile. In the *Virāṭaparvan* (IV, 5, 4-5), we are told that the Pāṇḍavas went to the Matsya capital (Virāṭa) from lake Dvaitavana, leaving the Daśārṇas to the South and the Pañcālas to the North, passing through the country of the Yakṛllomas and Śūrasenas, and entering the Matsya dominion from the forest. Elsewhere in the same *Parvan* (III, 24), a lake Dvaitavana is mentioned as existing in the Dvaitavana forest (which was supposed to be situated around the Sarasvatī), and this lake appears to have been close to the Sarasvatī (III, 177). Evidently both the lake and the forest were named after Dhvasan Dvaitavana, and were included in the Matsya dominions in early times. From the *Mahābhārata* account, it appears that the forest was outside the Matsya country, though not very far from it.

We have seen that according to Manu the Matsya country formed a part of the Brahmarṣi-deśa, the country of the holy sages which, as Rapson [1] points out, included the eastern half of the State of Patiala and of the Delhi division of the Punjab, the Alwar State and adjacent territory in Rajputana, the region which lies between the Ganges and the Jumna, and the Muttra District in the United Provinces. In this land of the Brahmarṣis, as Cunningham shows, 'In ancient times the whole of the country lying between the Arabali hills of Alwar and the river Jumna was divided between Matsya on the W. and Śūrasena on the E., with Daśārṇa on the S. and S.E. border. Matsya then included the whole of the present Alwar territory, with portions of Jaypur and Bharatpur. Vairāṭ and Māchāri were both in Matsya-deśa . . . To the E. were the Pañcālas . . .' [2]

In later times the Matsya country appears to have been known also as Virāṭa or Vairāṭa. Hsüan Tsang speaks of it as Vairāṭa, and Cunningham points out on his authority that in the seventh century A.D. the kingdom of Vairāṭa was 3,000 li or 500 miles in circuit. It was famous for its sheep and oxen, but produced few fruits or flowers. This is still the case with Jaypur to the S. of Vairāṭa, which furnishes most of the sheep required for the cities of Delhi and Agra, and their English garrisons. Vairāṭa, therefore, may have included the greater part of the present State of Jaypur. Its precise boundaries cannot be determined; but they may be fixed approximately as extending on the north from Jhunjun to Kot Kāsim, 70 miles; on the west from Jhunjun to Ajmer, 120 miles;

[1] *Ancient India*, pp. 50-1.
[2] Cunningham's Report, *Archaeological Survey of India*, Vol. 20, p. 2.

on the south from Ajmer to the junction of the Banās and Chambal, 150 miles; and on the east from the junction to Kot Kāsim, 150 miles; or altogether 490 miles.[1]

The capital of the country is generally called Virāṭanagara in the *Virāṭaparvan* and elsewhere in the *Mahābhārata*[2]; but occasionally it is called Matsyanagara,[3] and also sometimes Matsyasyanagara.[4] Evidently it was this Virāṭanagara which afterwards became known as Vairāṭ. This city was the royal seat of the Epic king Virāṭa, the friend of the Pāṇḍavas. The fourth book of the *Mahābhārata* refers to an attempt made by the Trigarttas to plunder the cows of Virāṭa. Virāṭa heard that the Trigarttas were taking away thousands of his kine. He thereupon collected his army; kings and princes put on their armour. Dreadful, infuriated elephants appeared like rain-bearing clouds, and were driven to battle by trained and skilled heroes. The leading heroes of Matsya, who followed their king, had 8,000 chariots, 1,000 elephants, and 60,000 horses Nevertheless King Virāṭa was taken captive by the Trigarttas, but was rescued by Bhīma, the second Pāṇḍava.[5] The period of exile of the Pāṇḍava brothers concluded with a year's living incognito in the kingdom of Matsya. They then disclosed their identity, and a marriage between Abhimanyu, son of Arjuna, and Uttarā, daughter of King Virāṭa, was arranged and celebrated with great pomp.[6]

So much for the traditional history of Virāṭa and his capital. The earliest historical mention of Vairāṭ is that of the Chinese pilgrim Hsüan Tsang, in 634 A.D. According to him, the capital was 14 or 15 li, or 2½ miles, in circuit, corresponding almost exactly with the size of the ancient mound on which the present town is built. The people were brave and bold and their king, who was of the race of *Fei-she* (either a Vaiśya or a Bais Rajput), was famous for his courage and skill in war.[7]

We next hear of Vairāṭ during the reign of Mahmud of Ghazni, who invaded the country in A.D. 1009. The Matsya king submitted to Mahmud, but his country was again invaded in A.D. 1014, and Vairāṭ taken and plundered by Amir Ali who found an ancient stone inscription at Nārāyaṇ, which was said to record that the temple of Nārāyaṇ had been built 40,000 years previously. As this inscription is also mentioned by the contemporary historian Otbi, we may accept the fact of the discovery of a stone record in characters so ancient that the Brahmins of that day were unable to read them.

1 Cunningham, *Ancient Geography*, pp. 344-5.
2 *Mbh.*, IV, 6, 35; IV, 13, 3. 3 *Ibid.*, IV, 13, 1. 4 *Ibid.*, IV, 14, 1.
5 M. N. Dutt, *Mahābhārata*, *Virāṭaparvan*, Chap. XXXI; also Chap. X, and Chap. XXII.
6 *Ibid.*, Chap. LXXII. 7 Cunningham, *Ancient Geography*, p. 343.

Cunningham thought it highly probable that this was the famous inscription of Aśoka that was afterwards discovered by Major Burt on the top of a hill at Vairāṭ.[1]

The present town of Vairāṭ is situated in the midst of a circular valley surrounded by low bare bed hills, which have all along been famous for their copper mines. It is 105 miles to the south-west of Delhi, and 41 miles to the north of Jaypur. The soil is generally good, and the trees, especially the tamarinds, are very fine and abundant. Vairāṭ is situated on a mound of ruins, about one mile in length by half a mile in breadth, or upwards of 2½ miles in circuit, of which the present town does not occupy more than one-fourth. The old city Vairāṭnagara is said to have been quite deserted for several centuries until it was repeopled about 350 years ago, most probably during the reign of Akbar. The town was certainly in existence in Akbar's time, as it is mentioned by Abul Fazl in the *Ayin-i-Akbari* as possessing very profitable copper mines.[2]

Another city of King Virāṭa's kingdom was Upaplavya, whither, according to the *Mahābhārata* account, the Pāṇḍavas transferred themselves (from Virāṭa) on completion of their exile.[3] This city of Upaplavya is also mentioned in other places. It was hither that Sañjaya, the messenger of the Kurus, was sent by Dhṛtarāṣṭra (*Mbh.*, V, 22, 1). Upaplavya does not appear to have been a capital of the Matsyas as asserted in the *Cambridge History of India* (p. 316), but only one of the towns in the Matsya country. The commentator on the *Mahābhārata*, Nīlakaṇṭha, explains that Upaplavya was the name of 'another (or some) city near Virāṭanagara'[4]; but its exact site is uncertain.

Dr. Ray Chaudhuri points out that Matsya is not mentioned by Kauṭilya as a state having the *saṃgha* form of government. Therefore the probability is that the monarchical constitution lasted throughout the period of Matsya's independence. The kingdom was probably annexed at one time by the neighbouring kingdom of Cedi, and finally absorbed into the Magadhan empire.[5]

---

[1] Cunningham, *Ancient Geography*, pp. 343-4.

[2] *Ibid.*, p. 342.

[3] "*Tatastrayodaśe varṣe nivṛtte pañcapāṇḍavāḥ Upaplavyaṃ Virāṭasya samapadyanta sarvaśaḥ*" (*Mbh.*, IV, 72, 14).

[4] Nīlakaṇṭha on the *Mbh.*, IV, 72, 14: '*Upalavyaṃ Virāṭanagarasamīpasthanagarāntaram*'.

[5] H. C. Ray Chaudhuri, *Political History of Ancient India*, 4th Ed., p. 116. For further references to Matsya, see, e.g. Smith's *Early History of India*, 4th Ed., p. 413 and R. D. Banerjee, *Vāṅgālār Itihāsa*, p. 158.

CHAPTER LXIX

# THE RAMAṬHAS

The Ramaṭhas seem also to have been a northern people living not far from the Kulūṭas. The *Vāyupurāṇa* mentions a people named Ramaṭas (XLV, 117), while the *Matsyapurāṇa* refers to a people named Rāmaṭhas (CXIII, 42), both no doubt meaning the one and the same people, the Ramaṭhas. The *Kūrmapurāṇa* (XLVII, 41) reads Rāmas instead and the *Mārkaṇḍeya* Māṭharas (LVII, 37). The *Bṛhatsaṃhitā* places them in the western division of India along with the Pañcanadas, while the *Vāyupurāṇa* in the reference cited above locates them in northern division along with the Kulindas.

The *Bṛhatsaṃhitā* contention that the Ramaṭhas were a western people is upheld by the *Mahābhārata* (*Sabhāparvan*, XXXI, 1195; *Vanaparvan*, LI, 1991; *Śāntiparvan*, LXV, 2430). The *Bhīṣmaparvan* mentions a people called Ramaṇas who also may be the same people as the Ramaṭhas (IX, 374).

In the same context of the introduction of the *Bālabhārata* or *Pracaṇḍapāṇḍava* of Rājaśekhara where we find Mahipāla of the Pratihāra dynasty is credited with having inflicted a defeat on the Kulūṭas, we find also the Ramaṭhas having shared the same fate at the hands of the Pratihāra king. This will be evident from the following passage:—

> '*Namita-Murala-mauliḥ pākalo Mēkalānāṃ raṇa-Kalita-Kaliṅgāḥ keli-taṭ Kēral-ēndoḥ. Ajani-jita-Kulūtaḥ Kuntalānām, kuṭhāraḥ, haṭha-hṛta-Ramaṭha Śrīḥ Śrī Mahīpāladevaḥ Tena ca Raghuvaṃśa-muktāmaṇinā-Āryāvartamahārājādhirājena. Śrī-Nirbhayanarendra-nandanenādhikṛtāḥ Sabhāsadaḥ sarvān . . . etc.*'

(Nirṇayasāgar Press Ed., I, 7-8.)

CHAPTER LXX

# THE PĀRADAS

The Pāradas, like the Barbaras and Daradas, seem to have been a barbarous hill tribe and are associated in the Puranic and Epic tradition with similar rude tribes of the North (e.g. *Mbh.*, *Sabhāparvan*, L, 1832; LI, 1869; *Droṇaparvan*, CXXI, 4819). In the *Sabhāparvan* of the *Mahābhārata*, they are associated with the Kulindas and Taṅganas (LI, 1858-9). They are mentioned in the *Vāyupurāṇa* (Chap. 88) as well as in the *Harivaṃśa* (I, 14). The *Mārkaṇḍeya Purāṇa* at one place (LVII, 37) locates them along with the Kaliṅgas, the Hārabhūṣikas, Māṭharas (Ramaṭhas), etc., while at another place (LVIII, 31), with the Śūdras, the Barbaras, the Kirātas the Pāṇḍyas, the Pāraśavas, etc. In the *Sabhāparvan* of the *Mahābhārata* (LI, 1858-9), the Pāradas are said to have dwelt on the river Śaliodā along with the Khasas and the Taṅganas. A collation of Epic and Puranic tradition referred to above shows that the tribe is found mentioned in a list of barbarous and rude tribes with the Śakas, Yavanas, Kambojas, Pahlavas, Khasas, Māhiṣikas, Coḷas, Keralas, etc. The *Harivaṃśa* states (XIII, 763-4; XIV, 775-83) that King Sagara degraded them and ordered them to have their hair-locks long and dishevelled; according to the same authority they were *mlecchas* and *dasyus*. They also find mention in *Manusmṛti* where it is said that they were originally Kṣatriyas, but were degraded owing to extinction of sacred rites, etc. (X, 43-4). At least one reference in the Great Epic connects the people with the Ābhiras (*Sabhāparvan*, L, 1832).

The Rock Edicts of Aśoka give a list of territories that were occupied by vassal tribes; among them figures a tribe named Palidas along with the Andhras, Bhojas and Raṭhikas. The Palidas have often been identified with the Pulindas, but Hultzsch does not accept this identification in view of the fact that the Kālsi and Girnar versions of the relevant portion of the Edicts have the variants Pālada and Pāriṃda. H. C. Ray Chaudhuri thinks that these variants 'remind us of the Pāradas'. If that be so, then the association of the Pāradas with the Andhras in Asokan inscriptions would suggest 'that in the Maurya period they may have been in the Deccan. But the matter must be regarded as not definitely settled'.[1]

---

[1] *P.H.A.I.*, 4th Ed., p. 259.

According to ancient Indian historical tradition as contained in the Epics and the Purāṇas, the Pāradas were one of the allies along with others, namely, the Śakas, the Kambojas, the Yavanas and the Pahlavas, of the Haihaya-Tālajaṅghas that drove Bāhu, the eighth king in descent from Hariścandra, from his throne (Pargiter, *A.I.H.T.*, pp. 206, 268 and f.n.). Pargiter places all these tribes in the north-west.

## CHAPTER LXXI

# THE BHOJAS

The Bhojas were a very ancient tribe, who attained to considerable eminence as early as the period represented by the *Aitareya Brāhmaṇa*. The term Bhoja is mentioned even in the *Ṛgveda* (III, 53, 7) though many scholars do not consider it to be a tribal name there, and Sāyaṇa also explains it otherwise. According to the *Aitareya Brāhmaṇa*,[1] the Bhojas were a southern people, a ruling tribe whose princes held the Satvats in subjection. The *Śatapatha Brāhmaṇa* (XIII, 5, 4, 21) seems to imply that the Satvats were located near the Gaṅgā and Yamunā, which was the realm of the Bharatas,[2] for the defeat by Bharata of the Satvats, and his taking away of the horse which they had prepared for an *Aśvamedha* sacrifice are here referred to. It is likely, therefore, that the Bhojas had spread over Central and Southern India in very early times.

According to the Purāṇas,[3] the Bhojas and the Satvats were allied tribes, both belonging to the Yadu-vaṃśa which dwelt at Mathurā (the capital of the Śūrasenas, q.v.) on the banks of the Yamunā. The *Viṣṇupurāṇa*[4] alludes to a branch of the Satvats as Bhojas, and by the Epic period at least the Bhojas and Satvats were indistinguishable.

In the *Mahābhārata*, the Bhojas are declared to have been descended from Druhyu, the third son of Yayāti, the great ancestor of the Kuru-Pāṇḍavas. When King Yayāti proposed to have Druhyu's youth transferred to himself, and was unceremoniously refused, he cursed his son, saying that he would be a king only in name. 'You shall rule over a region where there will be no roads, no passages for either horses or horse-drawn excellent chariots, nor for elephants, asses, goats, bullocks, palanquins and other good vehicles, where the only means of locomotion will be rafts and floats. In such a place will you have to live, and with all your family you will get the designation of Bhoja,—and there will not be a Rājā amongst you.[5] Druhyu's children were the Bhojas.[6]

---

1 VIII, 14: '*Dakṣiṇasyāṃ diśi ye ke ca Satvatāṃ rājāno*
*Bhaujyāyaiva te' bhiṣiñcyante Bhojetyenānabhiṣiktān-ācakṣata.*'

2 *Śatapatha Brāhmaṇa*, XIII, 5, 4, 11.

3 *Matsyapurāṇa*, Chap. 43, p. 48; Chap. 44, pp. 46–8; *Vāyupurāṇa*, Chap. 94, p. 52; Chap. 95, p. 18; Chap. 96, pp. 1-2; *Viṣṇupurāṇa*, IV, 13, 1–6.

4 IV, 13, 1–61.

5 *Mahābhārata*, *Ādiparvan*, Chap. 84, pp. 20–2; Vaṅgavāsī Ed.

6 *Ibid.*, Chap. 85, verse 34.

Though the Bhojas are condemned in the above passage, yet there appear to have been very cordial relations between them and the Pauravas, the children of Puru, Yayāti's favourite son, from whom the Kurus and Pāṇḍavas traced their descent. Thus we find that when Arjuna in the course of his expedition of pilgrimage went to Dvārakā, the Bhojas and their allied tribes, the Vṛṣṇis and Andhakas, hurried to have a look at the great Pāṇḍava hero as he marched along the road. Arjuna was welcomed and honoured by the young men of his own age among the Bhojas, Vṛṣṇis and Andhakas, and went to take up his residence in the house of Kṛṣṇa, who evidently belonged to these people.[1] We then meet with an account of festivities celebrated by the Bhoja-Vṛṣṇi-Andhakas on the hill of Mahendra.[2] When the report of the abduction of Subhadrā, Kṛṣṇa's sister, was proclaimed at the assembly of the allied tribes, then the Bhojas along with the Vṛṣṇis and Andhakas took up arms to recover the princess from the clutches of her abductor.[3] Again we read that Kṛṣṇa, accompanied by a host of Bhoja-Vṛṣṇi-Andhakas, paid a visit to Indraprastha when Arjuna returned there after his exile: and we are further told that Kṛṣṇa paid a formal visit to the Pāṇḍava king, attended by Vṛṣṇis, Andhakas and Bhojas.[4]

It appears from many passages in the *Mahābhārata* that the Bhojas formed a confederacy for offensive and defensive purposes with the Vṛṣṇis, Andhakas, and also the Yādavas. They were evidently descended from the same main stock, and were therefore bound together by consanguinity as well as by mutual interest. Besides the references given above, we may mention *Vanaparvan*, Chap. 120, where the prominent warriors of the Vṛṣṇis, Bhojas and Andhakas are mentioned together; and *Virāṭaparvan*, Chap. 72 and *Udyogaparvan*, Chap. 7, where we are told that a large crowd of Vṛṣṇis, Andhakas and Bhojas followed Kṛṣṇa to Dvārakā.[5] When Kṛṣṇa returned to Dvārakā after the Kurukṣetra war was over, the Bhojas, Vṛṣṇis and Andhakas received him with honour.[6] In the *Mauṣalaparvan*, where the extermination of the relatives and followers of Kṛṣṇa by internecine quarrel is described, we have a mention of the Bhojas who along with the Vṛṣṇis and Andhakas took part in that mutually destructive combat.

In the *Sabhāparvan*, we find Kṛṣṇa telling Yudhisṭhira of the oppressive domination of Jarāsandha, king of Magadha. In this

---

1 *Ādiparvan*, Chap. 218, verses 18–21.
2 *Ibid.*, Chap. 219, verses 2ff.
3 *Ibid.*, Chap. 220, verses 12 and 32.
4 *Ibid.*, Chap. 221, verses 33 and 38.
5 See also *Udyogaparvan*, Chap. 28.
6 *Mahābhārata*, *Aśvamedhaparvan*, Chap. 59.

connection he says that the Bhojas descended from Yayāti had propagated and acquired a high position for themselves, but had been robbed of it by the confederacy under the suzerainty of Jarāsandha.[1] In a later verse (v. 25) of the same chapter, we are told that the eighteen families of the Bhojas that lived in the Udīcya or northern country had, from fear of Jarāsandha, been forced to take refuge far in the west. Kṛṣṇa is also represented as saying that the aged Bhoja kings, being oppressed by Kaṃsa who was in alliance with Jarāsandha, had sought refuge with him (Kṛṣṇa), in order to rescue their relatives; and it appears that the connection between the Vṛṣṇis and the Bhojas was cemented by the marriage of Āhuka's daughter with Akrura.[2]

We gather, then, that at this time the Bhojas had spread far and wide over India; they were found in the west, in the Madhyadeśa, and in the south, for King Bhīṣmaka, father of Rukmiṇī and father-in-law of Kṛṣṇa, is called a Bhoja. Thus Kṛṣṇa says, 'That mighty king of the Bhojas, Bhīṣmaka . . . who governs a fourth part of the world, who has conquered by his learning the Pāṇḍyas and Krathakauśikas . . . has (also) become a servitor to the king of Magadha (Jarāsandha). We are his relatives . . . yet he does not at all regard us. He is always doing us ill. Without knowing his own strength and the dignity of the race to which he belongs, Bhīṣmaka has placed himself under Jarāsandha's shelter, only seeing his blazing fame.'[3]

We have an indication of the position of this Bhoja king Bhīṣmaka in a later chapter of the *Sabhāparvan*, where we are told that Sahadeva, the youngest of the Pāṇḍava brothers, when on his expedition of conquest, proceeded towards Bhojakaṭa, the capital of the Bhojas under Bhīṣmaka, after conquering Avanti, i.e. Malwa in Central India.[4] Later in the same chapter[5] we read that after subjugating the king of Surāṣṭra or Kathiawar, Sahadeva sent ambassadors to Bhīṣmaka, the ruler of Bhoja-kaṭa, and also to his son Rukmin (who was probably associated with him in the government of the country); and we are told that Bhīṣmaka and his son respected the mandate of Sahadeva out of consideration for Kṛṣṇa.

The following story is told about the foundation of Bhojakaṭa. When Kṛṣṇa carried away Rukmin's sister by force from his father's capital, Kuṇḍinapura, Rukmin swore that he would not return home without defeating the abductor of his sister. As fate would have it, Rukmin was worsted in the fight that followed and true to his oath,

---

[1] *Sabhāparvan*, Chap. 14.
[2] *Ibid.*, Chap. 14, verses 32-3.
[3] *Ibid.*, Chap. 14, verses 21–4.
[4] *Ibid.*, Chap. 31, verses 10-11.
[5] *Ibid.*, Chap. 31, verses 62–4.

he never returned to Kuṇḍinapura, but built a new city of the Bhojas on the site of the battle-field, and called it Bhojakaṭa.[1]

Bhojakaṭa is interpreted by Vincent Smith as 'Castle of the Bhojas'. He says that the name 'implies that the province was named after a castle formerly held by the Bhojas . . .'[2] It is alluded to in the Chammak grant of the Vākāṭaka King Pravarasena II, which 'makes it clear that the Bhojakaṭa territory included the Ilichpur district in Berar or Vidarbha'.[3] Bhojakaṭa has been identified with Bhat-kuli in the Amraoti district of Berar. It is not improbable that the Bhojas had some relation with Bhojanagara, the capital of king Uśīnara of the Uśīnara country[4] near the Kankhal region where the Ganges issues from the hills. In any case we may conclude that the Bhojas and the Vidarbhas were closely related. Kālidāsa also calls the king of Vidarbha a Bhoja (*Raghuvaṃśa*, V, 39, 40).

It was said of the heroic Bhoja prince Rukmin that he was in the very front rank of the warriors of his time; the bow named *Vijaya* which he wielded was only equalled by the *Gāṇḍīva* of Arjuna and the *Śārṅgadhanu* of Kṛṣṇa. This prince is said to have been equally skilled with the bow and the sword and various other weapons, but to have been inordinately proud, and because of his boastfulness, his offer of aid was refused by both sides in turn before the Kurukṣetra War. On the eve of the war he came to the battle-field at the head of one complete Akṣauhiṇī of forces of every description.[5]

In the *Sabhāparvan*, we read that the whole confederacy of Anhakas, Yādavas and Bhojas abandoned Kaṃsa who was slain by Kṛṣṇa who had been appointed to do so (*niyogāt*).[6] It appears from this that Kṛṣṇa had at least the tacit approval of all the allied peoples who had been tyrannized over and ill-treated by Kaṃsa. Kaṃsa himself was a Bhoja, as we learn from what Kṛṣṇa said to the Kurus in their assembly on the eve of the battle.[7]

Another tribe with which the Bhojas are associated in the great Epic are the Kukuras who were evidently members of the Vṛṣṇi-cakra or confederacy of tribes[8]; for we are told in the *Udyogaparvan* of the Bhoja king joining the Kuru forces together with the Bhojas, Andhakas and Kukuras.[9] In another chapter of the *Udyogaparvan*

---

1 *Mahābhārata*, *Udyogaparvan*, Chap. 157; see also *ibid.*, Chap. 48, p. 74.
2 *Ind. Ant.*, 1923, 262-3.
3 Ray Chaudhuri, *P.H.A.I.*, 4th Edn., p. 77.
4 *Mahābhārata*, I, 85, 3533.
5 *Mbh.*, *Udyogaparvan*, Chap. 157.
6 *Mbh.*, *Sabhāparvan*, Chap. 62, p. 8.
7 *Mbh.*, *Udyogaparvan*, Chap. 128, p. 37.
8 *Mauṣalaparvan*, Chap. I, 7.
9 *Mbh.*, *Udyogaparvan*, Chap. 19.

also we find the Bhojas in company with the Andhakas, Vṛṣṇis, Kukuras, Sriñjayas and Cedis.[1] Again, when all the people in this confederacy of tribes were engaged in a deadly conflict among themselves, we find the Kukuras fighting with and exterminating their allies and friends, the Bhojas and Andhakas.[2] The Kukuras, Andhakas, and all the tribes in the Union rushed at each other like maniacs run amuck, and brought about the destruction of their closest friends.[3]

We have already seen that the kings among the Sātvatas or Sātvats were called Bhojas: Bhoja was the designation of the royal family of the Sātvatas in the days of the *Aitareya Brāhmaṇa*, and afterwards the name Bhoja must have been extended to the whole Sātvat tribe. In the *Mahābhārata* we find the names Bhoja and Sātvata used indiscriminately to designate the same individual, e.g. in the case of Kṛtavarman, the Hārdikya or son of Hṛdika. He was one of the greatest of the Bhojas, and was in the very front rank of the warriors of that warlike age. He led a complete Akṣauhinī or division of forces to the great Kurukṣetra war [4] (on the Kuru side), and appears to have been the leader of the allied army of the Bhoja-Andhaka-Kukura-Vṛṣṇi confederacy, as we learn from the *Udyogaparvan*.[5] Kṛtavarman appears to have been the official commander of the allied forces even before they came to the field of battle.[6] He seems to have belonged to the city of Mṛttikāvatī, as we may gather from the *Droṇaparvan*. When the young son of Subhadrā was making terrible slaughter in the Kuru army, and the Kuru heroes could not match him fighting singly according to the laws of honourable warfare, six of the leaders, Kṛtavarman amongst them, simultaneously made an onslaught against him.[7] Abhimanyu aimed a number of arrows at Bhoja Mārttikāvata, that is, the Bhoja from Mṛttikāvatī, who must have been Kṛtavarman.[8]

In various passages of the *Mahābhārata*,[9] Kṛtavarman is called either a Bhoja or a Sātvata, the two terms being used interchangeably. From a passage of the *Karṇaparvan* (*Mahābhārata*, VIII, 7, 8) Kṛtavarman's capital Mṛttikāvatī appears to have been

---

[1] *Mbh.*, *Udyogaparvan*, V, 28.

[2] *Mausalaparvan*, Chap. 5, verse 2.

[3] *Ibid.*, Chap. 3, pp. 40–3.

[4] *Rukmin* is mentioned as leader of the Bhojas.

[5] *Mbh.*, *Udyogaparvan*, Chap. 19, pp. 17-18, 25.

[6] *Ibid.*, Chap. 7.

[7] *Mbh.*, *Droṇaparvan*, Chap. 46, p. 4.

[8] *Ibid.*, 47, 8.

[9] For example, Kṛtavarman is mentioned as a Bhoja at *Mbh.*, *Udyogaparvan*, Chap. 57, p. 21; Chap. 165; *Karṇaparvan*, Chap. 2, etc.; and as a Sātvata in Chap. 143 (*Udyogaparvan*); *Bhīṣmaparvan*, Chaps. 16, 51, 56, 81, 86, 95; *Karṇaparvan*, Chap. 9, p. 80.

situated in the Ānarta country, for he is called a resident of Ānarta. Towards the end of the battle, when Droṇa was killed, Kṛtavarman was elected leader by the remnant of the Bhojas, Kaliṅgas and Vāhlīkas.[1] Kṛtavarman, the Bhoja, was one of the three heroes who attended Duryodhana when the latter took refuge in the Dvaipāyana lake.[2] We read of Kṛtavarman the Sātvata addressing the defeated Kuru monarch, and calling upon him to come out of his hiding place in the lake.[3] Kṛtavarman took part in the slaying of the Pañcālas and the sons of Draupadī, and then he and two other heroes went to give the dying king Duryodhana this welcome news.[4] Finally, he returned to his own country,[5] and was later slain by Sātyaki in the mutually destructive encounter of the confederacy of tribes, his son then being placed on the throne of Mṛttikāvatī by Kṛṣṇa.[6]

It is stated in the Purāṇas[7] that the Sātvats and the Bhojas were branches of the Yadu family who dwelt at Mathurā on the banks of the Yamunā; and the *Mahābhārata* tells us that Kṛṣṇa removed the Yādava headquarters from Mathurā to Dvārakā through fear of King Jarāsandha of Magadha. In the *Viṣṇupurāṇa*[8] we read that Sātvata was born in the family of Krosthu, son of Yadu. The descendants of Sātvata, son of Mahābhoja, were known as Bhojas.[9] According to the *Matsyapurāṇa*,[10] the Bhojas were pious, learned, truthful, valiant and charitable, and were performers of religious rites; but in another passage of this *Purāṇa* (34, 30) as well as in the *Mahābhārata* (I, 85, 3533), the Bhojas are relegated to the Mleccha caste. Pargiter thinks,[11] however, that this tradition is 'unintelligible compared with all other traditions, and is probably late, and certainly very doubtful'. As we learn from the Purāṇas,[12] the Bhojas were related to the Haihayas who were a branch of the Yādavas. The Haihayas are said to have comprised five families, the Vītihotras, Śāryātas, Bhojas, Avantis and Tuṇḍikeras. As we have seen, the Bhojas were closely related with the Vidarbhas; and they probably also held sway over Daṇḍaka, the region around Nasik. This is

---

1 *Mahābhārata*, VII, 193.
2 *Ibid.*, IX, 29, 53-4.
3 *Ibid.*, IX, 30, 9–13. See also *ibid.*, X, 1, X, 4, 6, etc.
4 *Ibid.*, X, 8; X, 9, 6.
5 *Ibid.*, XI, 11; XI, 66.
6 *Ibid.*, XVI, 3; XVI, 7.
7 *Matsyapurāṇa*, 43, 48; Chap. 44, pp. 46–8; *Vāyupurāṇa*, Chap. 94, p. 52; Chap. 95, p. 48; Chap. 96, pp. 1-2.
8 IV, 3.
9 Cf. *Bhāgavatapurāṇa*, Chap. 9, p. 24; *Kūrmapurāṇa*, Chap. 24, śl. 40; *Harivaṃśa*, Chap. 37.
10 Chap. 44, śl. 69.
11 *A.I.H.T.*, p. 260, f.n. 1.
12 *Agnipurāṇa*, Chap. 275, śloka 10; *Vāyupurāṇa*, Chap. 94, pp. 3–54; *Matsyapurāṇa*, Chap. 43, pp. 7–49, etc.

implied by a passage in Kauṭilya's *Arthaśāstra*[1] according to which a Bhoja named Dāṇḍakya, or king of Daṇḍaka, tried to seduce a Brāhmaṇa girl, as a result of which he perished with his relations and his kingdom.

The Jaina sacred books speak of the Bhojas as Kṣatriyas and descendants from those whom Ṛṣabha acknowledged as persons deserving of honour.[2] The *Jaina Sūtras* also tell us of a Bhoja princess, Rājimatī who showed extraordinary religious zeal and strength of mind in overcoming all temptations.[3]

In the Pāli Buddhist literature also we find references to Bhoja. In the *Saṃyutta Nikāya*[4] there is a mention of a Ṛṣi named Rohitassa Bhojaputta, i.e. one belonging to the Bhoja family or tribe. One of the Jātaka stories[5] tells that the Bodhisattva was born once as a Nāga king named Saṅkhapāla. He always used to give in charities and observe the religious precepts. On a certain sabbath day, while observing the precepts, he resolved to give away his own body in charity, and he became an iguana. Sixteen Bhojaputtas saw this iguana, made it weak by beating it, and carrying it off when they were seen by a merchant of Mithilā who caused Saṅkhapāla to be released.

The Bhojas, along with the Andhras, Pulindas and Rāṣṭrikas, were among the vassal tribes of Aśoka.[6] Scholars hold that the Bhojas and the Rāṣṭrikas were evidently ancestors of the Mahābhojas and Mahārathis of the Sātavāhana period.[7]

The next important mention of the Bhojas in the historical period is made in the Hāthigumphā Inscription of the Cheta king Khāravela (first century B.C.), which points out that Khāravela, the Mahārājā of Kaliṅga, defeated the Rāṭhikas and Bhojakas in the fourth year of his reign and compelled them to do homage to him. The Rāṭhikas and Bhojakas are evidently the Rāṣṭrikas and Bhojas of Aśoka's Rock Edict.

The Khālimpur grant of the Emperor Dharmapāladeva of Gauḍa (*c.* 800 A.D.) speaks of the king of Bhoja along with kings of Matsya, Kuru, Yadu and Yavana as having uttered benedictions at the coronation ceremony of the king of Kānyakubja.[8] R. D. Banerjee holds that the king of Bhoja was defeated by Dharmapāla, and compelled to accept Cakrāyudha instead of Indrarāja as lord

---

[1] 1919 Edn., p. 11.
[2] *Jaina Sūtras*, S.B.E., Pt. II, p. 71, n. 2.
[3] Pt. II, pp. 115–8.
[4] P.T.S. Ed., Pt. I, pp. 61-62.
[5] Vol. V, 164ff.
[6] *Rock Edicts*, V and XIII.
[7] Cf. Ray Chaudhuri, *P.H.A.I.*, 4th Ed., p. 259.
[8] *Gauḍalekhamālā*, p. 14.

of Kānyakubja. In Banerjee's view, Bhoja is to be identified with part of present Rajputana.[1]

The Arulala-Perumal Inscription and the Raṅganātha Inscription of Ravivarman refer to a Bhoja king of that name who belonged to the Yadu family of the Kerala country in S. India.[2] This king Ravivarman is declared in the inscription to have been wise, liberal and a protector of the good.

[1] *Vāṅgālār Itihāsa*, B.S. 1321, pp. 167-8.

[2] *Epigraphia Indica*, Vol. IV, Pt. IV, June 1896, p. 146.

CHAPTER LXXII

# THE MEKALAS

The Mekalas were a small tribe inhabiting the tract of country comprising the modern Amarkaṇṭak (Amarakaṇṭaka) hills and the surrounding region. In ancient times, the Amarkaṇṭak range was known as Mekala, whence the name of the tribe is derived; and as the river Narmadā (mod. Narbadā) has its source in these hills, she was known as Mekalasutā [1] or Mekalakanyā,[2] i.e. 'daughter of Mekala', or Mekalā.[3] The Mekala mountain (mod. Amarkaṇṭak) is a part of the Vindhyas; and in the *Purāṇas*, the Mekalas are referred to as a Vindhyan tribe. This is also supported by the *Vāmanapurāṇa* (Chap. 13)[4] which locates the Mekalas along with the Kārūṣas, Bhojas, Daśārṇas, Niṣadhas and others, just below the Vindhyan range. The identification of the locality is confirmed by mythological allusions as well; for Mekala is said to have been a Ṛṣi, the father of the river Narmadā,—a mythological interpretation of the well-known geographical fact. The mountain where the river rises is also known as Mekalādri (*Haimakośa*, IV, 149). According to the Bengal recension of the *Rāmāyaṇa*, Mount Mekala is referred to as the source of the river Son (*Kiṣkindhyā Kāṇḍa*, XL, 20).

According to the Epic tradition as contained in the *Droṇaparvan* (IV, 8) of the *Mahābhārata*, Karṇa is said to have conquered the Mekalas along with the Utkalas, Pauṇḍras, Kaliṅgas, Andhras, Niṣadas, Trigarttas and Vāhlīkas. In the *Rāmāyaṇa* also, the Mekala country is associated with the Utkala and Daśārṇa countries. The army of monkeys which was despatched in search of Sītā was asked to visit Mekala, Utkala, and Daśārṇa, among other countries of the south (Canto XLII).

The *Mārkaṇḍeya Purāṇa* probably associates the Mekalas with the Ambaṣṭhas (LVIII, 14): the reference is to Mekhalāmuṣṭa, which appears to be a corruption of Mekala and Ambaṣṭha. If this is the case, it doubtless refers to the time when the Ambaṣṭhas or a section of them had migrated from their original habitat in the Punjab to south-eastern India, near the Mekala hill in the upper regions of the Narmadā.

There is another reference to Mekala in the *Viṣṇupurāṇa* (IV, Chap. 24, 17), where ten kings are said to have had Mekala as their land of birth.

---

[1] S. Konow, *Karpūramañjarī*, p. 182.

[2] *Amarakoṣa*, I, 2, 3, 32, etc.

[3] *Abhidhānaratnamālā*, III, 52.

[4] Among the tribes mentioned in this list are the Kośalas who were definitely not located anywhere near the Vindhyas, but in the N.E. Accordingly, this list is not to be taken as accurate.

## CHAPTER LXXIII

# THE DAŚĀRṆAS

The Daśārṇas are mentioned in the Epics and Purāṇas, and also in Kālidāsa's *Meghadūta*. They appear to have had more than one settlement during the Epic period. The *Mahābhārata* seems to refer to two Daśārṇas, one in the west, which was conquered by Nakula (*Sabhāparvan*, Chap. 32), and another in the east (or south-east), which was subjugated by Bhīmasena (*Sabhāparvan*, Chap. 30). The *Rāmāyaṇa* and the Purāṇas point to a Daśārṇa country grouped with those of the Mālavas, Kārūṣas, Utkalas and Mekalas, who are all said to have lived in the Vindhyan tract.[1] This Daśārṇa is probably the same as the one conquered by Bhīmasena.

The Daśārṇa country in the west seems to have been more important than the other localities in the east or south-east. According to the *Meghadūta* (verses 24-5), the capital of this Daśārṇa country was Vidisa (mod. Bhilsā) on the Vetravatī (= mod. Betwā). The Daśārṇas thus occupied a site on the Daśārṇa river (which can still be traced in the modern Dashān river that flows through Bundelkhand, rising in Bhopal and emptying into the Betwa). According to Wilson,[2] a Daśārṇa river is said in the Purāṇas to rise in a mountain called Citrakūṭa (= Kāmptānāth-gir in Bundelkhand). This is doubtless identical with the modern Dashān river. The *Meghadūta* further mentions a hill called Nīcaḥ as situated in the Daśārṇa country (*loc. cit.*).

As we have seen, the Purāṇas associate the Daśārṇas with the Vindhyan tribes,—Mālavas, Kārūṣas, Mekalas, Utkalas, and Niṣadhas. In the *Rāmāyaṇa*, also their country is connected with those of the Mekalas and Utkalas, whither Sugrīva sends his monkey army in quest of Sītā (*Kiṣkindhyā K., loc. cit.*). The Daśārṇa country of the *Rāmāyaṇa* and the Purāṇas is thus different from the Daśārṇa of the *Meghadūta*; it is probably identical with Dosarene of the *Periplus of the Erythraean Sea*. According to Wilson,[3] eastern or south-eastern Daśārṇa formed a part of the Chattisgarh

[1] *Rāmāyaṇa*; *Kiṣkindhyā K.*, 41, 8–10; *Brahmāṇḍa P.*, Chap. 49; *Vāyu P.*, Chap. 45; *Matsya P.*, Chap. 114; *Mārkaṇḍeya P.*, Chap. 57; *Vāmana P.*, Chap. 13; etc.—'*Vindhya-pṛṣtha-nivāsinaḥ*'.

[2] *Essays Analytical*, etc., Vol. II, p. 336, f.n. 1.

[3] Wilson's *Viṣṇu P.*, Hall's Ed., Vol. II, p. 160, f.n. 3.

District in the Central Provinces, including the native State of Patna.[1] The territory was probably situated on the river Dosaron which is mentioned by Ptolemy, and which has been identified with the river Brāhmaṇī that flows through modern Cuttack and empties itself into the Bay of Bengal. As Ptolemy did not write from personal knowledge, he could not probably give the indigenous name of the river, but named it after the people inhabiting the region. Thus 'the Dosaron is the river of the region inhabited by the Daśārṇas, a people mentioned in the *Viṣṇupurāṇa* as belonging to the south-east of Madhyadeśa'.[2]

The Daśārṇas figure in the *Mahābhārata* as one of the tribes who fought for the Pāṇḍavas in the great Kurukṣetra war.[3] The Daśārṇa king at that time was Kṣatradeva, a mighty hero, who fought valiantly on elephant-back. He attacked the enemy-generals,[4] and the king of Prāgjyotiṣa or Kāmarūpa.[5] The warriors of the Daśārṇa king were all mighty heroes and could fight best on elephants.[6] According to Kauṭilya's *Arthaśāstra* (Book II, Chap. II), the elephants of Aṅga and Kaliṅga belonged to the best of their species, while those of Karūṣa, Daśārṇa and Aparānta ranked second, those of the Saurāṣṭras and allied tribes (Saurāṣṭrikāḥ pañcajanāḥ) being the worst.

We read elsewhere in the *Mahābhārata* of another Daśārṇa king, named Hiraṇyavarman who appears also as Hemavarman and Kāñcanavarman (both Hema and Kāñcana being synonyms of Hiraṇya, 'gold').[7] Pargiter thinks[8] that during the period of the Kurukṣetra war, Daśārṇa was a Yādava kingdom.[9]

Erakaccha, a town in the Dasaṇṇa (= Daśārṇa) country, is referred to in Pāli literature. We read in the *Petavatthu* and *Commentary* of a certain merchant of Erakaccha, and of the miseries which he suffered through lack of faith in the Buddha.[10] We are told[11] that the Therī Isidāsī was once reborn at Erakaccha as a wealthy

1 *J.A.S.B.*, 1905, pp. 7, 14.
2 McCrindle's *Ptolemy*, Mazumder's Ed., p. 71.
3 *Karṇaparvan*, Chap. 22, 3; *Bhīṣmaparvan*, Chaps. 95, 41, 43; *Droṇaparvan*, Chap. 25, 35.
4 *Bhīṣmaparvan*, Chap. 95, 41, 43.
5 *Droṇaparvan*, Chap. 25, 35.
6 *Karṇaparvan*, Chap. 22, 3.
7 *Mbh.*, V, 190, 7419; 193, 7493, 7506, 7511 and 7518.
8 *A.I.H.T.*, p. 280.
9 *Mbh.*, V, 190, 7417ff.; *Harivaṃśa*, Chap. 91, 4967.
10 *Petavatthu*, 20; *Commentary*, pp. 99–105.
11 *Therīgāthā*, 435; see also *Buddhist India*, p. 40.

craftsman, a worker in gold. Dasaṇṇa was apparently a·centre of the art of sword-making.[1] It is mentioned in the *Mahāvastu*[2] as one of the sixteen *Mahājanapadas*. We also read in the *Mahāvastu* that the Buddha distributed knowledge among the Daśārṇas who built a vihāra for him.[3]

[1] *Jātaka* (Fausböll), III, 338: '*Dasaṇṇakaṃ tikhiṇadhāraṃ asim*'.
[2] I, 34. (Senart's edition).
[3] Law: *A Study of the Mahāvastu*, p. 9.

## CHAPTER LXXIV

# THE PĀRIYĀTRAS

It is doubtful whether Pāriyātras, or Pāripātras as they were also called,[1] can ethnologically be classed as a tribe or people, to be distinguished from the Vindhyas with whom they lived contiguously, or from other peoples who had their habitat in and around the same locality. The Purāṇas, however, always enumerate them as a distinct people, associated with the Pāripātra mountains, from which they evidently took their name.

As already noticed, there are two variant forms of the mountainous region inhabited by this people, as given in the Purāṇas: Pāriyātra and Pāripātra; Pāripātra seems to be the more usual reading, though Pāriyātra occurs not infrequently. In the topographical list of the Purāṇas, the Pāriyātra or Pāripātra hills are mentioned as one of the seven hill ranges together forming the *Kulācalas* or *Kulaparvatas*, 'family mountains', i.e. mountain ranges or systems. These are the Mahendra, Malaya, Sahya, Śuktimat, Ṛkṣa, Vindhya and Pāripātra.[2] The *Bhāgavata*, *Vāyu*, *Mārkaṇḍeya* and *Padma Purāṇas* and the *Bhīṣmaparvan* of the *Mahābhārata* add a list of inferior mountains to these seven.[3] The seven principal hill ranges are similarly enumerated by all the Puranic authorities, and their situation is easily determined by the rivers which are listed as flowing from them.

Pāripātra in particular is always associated with the Vindhyas. Vindhya, as is well known, is the general name of the chain of hills that stretches across Central India, dividing India into its well-defined and natural north and south divisions; but it is evident from the Puranic list and the situations of the hills mentioned in it that in the Purāṇas the name Vindhya is generally restricted to the eastern division of the long range of hills. According to the *Vāyupurāṇa*, however, it is the part south of the river Narmadā, or the Sātpurā range of hills. Pāripātra constitutes the northern and

[1] *Mārkaṇḍeya Purāṇa*, 58, 8.

[2] E.g., *Viṣṇupurāṇa*, Wilson's Ed., Bk. II, Chap. III, pp. 127-8; also *Mārkaṇḍeya Purāṇa*, 57, 10; *Mahābhārata*, VI, 9, 11.

[3] *Bhāgavatapurāṇa*, V, 19, 16ff; *Mārkaṇḍeya P.*, LVII, 12ff.; *Mbh.*, *Bhīṣmaparvan*, śl. 317–378. 'As subordinate portions of them are thousands of mountains; some unheard of, though lofty, extensive and abrupt; and others, better known, though of lesser elevation, and inhabited by people of low stature.'

western portion of the Vindhyas, and may be said to include the range of hills now known as the Aravalli.

The *Viṣṇupurāṇa*, for example, mentions Pāriyātra or Pāripātra as situated on the west, associated with the semi-mythical mount Meru. 'Niṣadha and Pāriyātra are the limitative mountains on the west (of Meru), stretching, like those on the east, between the Nīla and Niṣadha ranges.' [1]

The list of the seven *Kulācalas* seems to have been known in some form or other to Ptolemy as early as the first half of the second century A.D.; for he also specifies seven ranges of hills, although his list does not correspond with the Puranic list, with the exception of the Ouindion, identical with the Vindhyas, and the Ouxenton, identical with the Ṛkṣa (Vant).[2] Wilson thought that Adeisathron might be identified with the Pāriyātra[3]; but this has been found to be untenable, and modern research tends to connect the range with the Western Ghāṭs, or, more properly, 'that section of the Western Ghāṭs which is immediately to the north of the Coimbatore gap, as it is there the Kāverī rises'.[4]

According to Rājaśekhara, all seven *Kulaparvatas* were comprised within the Kumārī-dvīpa whose southernmost limit, according to the *Skandapurāṇa* was the Pāriyātra.[5] In the period of the Brahmanical and Buddhist Sūtras too, Pāriyātra was the southernmost limit of contemporary Āryāvarta, while the eastern and western boundaries were formed by Kālakavana (probably near Allahabad) and Adarśana and Thūna (on the Sarasvatī) respectively.[6]

The Purāṇas refer to a number of rivers issuing from the Pāriyātra, e.g. the Mahī, the Varṇāśā or Parṇāśā, the Śiprā, the Carmaṇvatī, the Sindhu and the Vetravatī. The Mahī is well known; Varṇāśā or Parṇāśā has been identified by Pargiter with the modern Banās, a tributary of the Carmaṇvatī (Chambal). Sindhu is Kāli Sindhu, a tributary of the Carmaṇvatī, and Vetravatī is modern Betwa. Śiprā is the famous river immortalised in Sanskrit classical poetry. The *Viṣṇupurāṇa* mentions yet another river issuing from the Pāripātra mountains, namely, the Vedasmṛti[7] (or Vedasmṛta according to the *Mahābhārata*).[8]

1 *Viṣṇupurāṇa*, 2, II, Wilson's Ed., p. 123.
2 *Ptolemy's Ancient India*, by McCrindle, S. N. Majumdar's Ed., pp. 75-81.
3 *Viṣṇu Purāṇa*, Wilson's Ed., 2, III, p. 128.
4 McCrindle, *Ptolemy's Ancient India*, p. 80.
5 *Skandapurāṇa*, Kumārika-khaṇḍa, Chap. 39, 113: '*Pāriyātrasya caivārvāk khaṇḍaṃ Kaumārikaṃ smṛtam*'.
6 *Dharma-sūtra* of Bodhāyana, I, 1, 25. '*Prāgadarśanāt pratyak Kālakavanād dakṣiṇena Himavantam udak Pāriyātram etad Āryāvartam*'.
7 Wilson's Ed., p. 130 (2, III).
8 *Bhīṣmaparvan*.

The *Vāyupurāṇa* mentions the Kārūṣas and the Mālavas as dwelling along the Pāripātra mountains.[1] The Nasik Praśasti of Gautamīputra Śātakarṇi seems to associate the Kukuras also with the Pāriyātra.[2] This is probably the earliest epigraphic mention of the mountains. A more elaborate mention is made in the Mandasor Inscription of Yaśodharman and Viṣṇuvardhana,[3] where a large tract of land is described as 'containing many countries, which lie between the Vindhya (mountains), from the slopes of the summits of which there flows the pale mass of the water of (the river) Revā, and the mountain Pāriyātra, on which trees are bent down in (their) frolicsome leaps by the long-tailed monkeys (and which stretches) up to the ocean'.

[1] Wilson's Ed., p. 133 (2, III). Mālukas and Mārukas are variant readings for Kārūṣas. See also *Kūrma P.*, Pūrva Chap. 7, which seems to include the countries of Aparānta, Saurāṣṭra, Śūdra, Malapa (Mālava), Mālaka and others within the Pāriyātra area.

[2] *Bṛhatsaṃhitā*, XIV, 4.

[3] *C.I.I.*, Vol. III, p. 154.

# CHAPTER LXXV

## MISCELLANEOUS TRIBES

**PEṬENIKAS — GO-LĀṄGULAS — SAILUṢAS — KUSUMAS — NĀMAVĀSAKAS—ĀDHAKYAS—DAṆḌAKAS—PAURIKAS—ATHARVAS AND ARKALIṄGAS—MAULIKAS—MŪṢIKAS OR MŪṢAKAS—CULIKAS AND ŚŪLIKAS — KAṄKANAS — TOSALAS — VAIDIŚAS — TUṢTIKĀRAS — MĀHIṢAKAS OR MĀHIṢĪKAS—KĪKAṬAS—PRAVAṄGAS—RAṄGEYAS —MĀNADAS—UGRAS—TAṄGANAS—MUDAKARAS—ANTARGIRYAS —BAHIRGIRAS — ANŪPAS — KUKURAS — SURYĀRAKAS — VṚKAS — HĀRABHŪṢIKAS — MĀṬHARAS — JĀGUḌAS — BRAHMOTTARAS — BHṚGUKACCHAS—MĀHEYAS—BHOJAS—APARĀNTAS—HAIHAYAS —BHOGAVARDHANAS—SARAJAS—VĪRAHOTRAS—VINDHYAMAULEYAS — JĀṄGALAS — BHADRAKARAS — KSHUDRAKAS —PUṢKALAS—CĪNAS—TUKHĀRAS—SĀRASVATAS—AŚVAKŪṬAS—KULYAS — MALAKAS — BODHAS — DAŚAMĀLIKAS — HARṢAVARDHANAS—KUŚERUKAS—HAṂSAMĀRGAS—KUHAKAS—ŚATAPATHA —CARMAKHAṆḌIKAS—GABALAS—ŚATADRUJAS—URṆAS—DARVAS —BAHU-BHADRAS—TRAIPURAS—GAJĀHVAYAS—PARṆA-ŚAVARAS —ARBUDAS—KHASAS**

**Peṭenikas**

The Peṭenikas of Aśokan inscriptions have been plausibly identified with the Paiṭhānikas or inhabitants of Paiṭhān on the Godāvarī[1] in North-Western Hyderabad. Paiṭhān is the present name of ancient Pratiṣṭhāna which was a flourishing city during the rule of the Sātavāhana kings. Pratiṣṭhāna, the modern Paiṭhān on the north bank of the Godāvarī in the Aurangabad District of Hyderabad, is famous in literature as the capital of King Śātakarṇi (Sātavāhana or Sālivāhana) and his son Śakti-kumāra who are generally identified with the king Śātakarṇi and the prince Śakti-Śrī of the Nānāghāt inscriptions.[2] According to Dr. D. R. Bhandarkar the word 'Pitinika' of Aśokan inscriptions, as mentioned in Rock Edicts V and XIII, should not be treated as a separate word and is to be regarded as an adjective qualifying Rāṣṭrika (mentioned in Edict V) and Bhoja (mentioned in Edict XIII) which are mentioned along with it. In this connection Dr. Bhandarkar points to certain

[1] *Cambridge History of India*, Vol. I, p. 603.
[2] *Ibid.*, Vol. I, p. 531.

passages in the *Aṅguttara Nikāya* [1] where the term Pettanika occurs in the sense of one who enjoys property given by father.[2] Other scholars, however, identify the Pitinikas with the Paiṭhānakas or natives of Paiṭhān and some go so far as to suggest that they are the ancestors of the Sātavāhana rulers of Paiṭhān.[3] Both the author of the *Periplus* and Ptolemy mention Paiṭhāna or Baiṭhāna. Paiṭhān is placed by the author of the *Periplus* at a distance of twenty days' journey to the south of Barugaza (identified generally with Bharukaccha or modern Broach), and is spoken of as the greatest city in Dakhinabades or Dakṣiṇāpatha and Tagara (identified by some with Devagiri, by others with Junnar and by R. G. Bhandarkar with Dharur in Nizam's territory), ten days' east of Paiṭhān.

**Go-Lāṅgulas**

No people of the name Go-Lāṅgulas are known. The *Matsyapurāṇa* reads Cōḷas and Kulyas (CXIII, 46) and the *Vāyu* Caulyas and Kulyas instead (XLV, 124). The Cōḷas (Caulyas) were a well-known people and were famous from very early times, being one of the four tribes of the far south. The Kulyas are not met with anywhere; but undoubtedly they are the same people as the Kolas mentioned more than once in the *Mahābhārata*.[4] But the people cannot satisfactorily be identified.

**Sailuṣas**

The *Vāyu* (XLV, 125) and the *Matsya* (CXIII, 47) *Purāṇas* read Setūkas instead; but none of the names can be identified. Pargiter's suggestion that they might mean the people who lived near the Setu of Rāma is ingenious and may not altogether be improbable, for they are mentioned in connection with the people of the far south.

**Kusumas**

The Kusumas are also known as Kumanas[5] and Kupathas.[6] Pargiter suggests an identification with the Kurubas or Kurunbas, who were the same as the Pahlavas, an important tribe of Southern India.

**Nāma-Vāsakas**

The *Vāyupurāṇa* reads (XLV, 125) Vanavāsikas and the *Bhīṣmaparvan* list Vanavāsakās (IX, 366) which is the correct reading. Doubtless they refer to the people of the kingdom of Vanavāsī, a well-known region of the south in North Kanara in historical times, and not unknown to the author of the *Harivaṃśa* (XCV, 5213 and 5231–3). The *Matsyapurāṇa* reads Vāji-Vāsikas (CXIII, 47) which is apparently incorrect. It is ancient Vaijayantipura, also known as Jayantipura, capital of the

[1] III, 70 and 300.
[2] *Ind. Ant.*, 1919, p. 80.
[3] Cf. Woolner, *Aśoka*, p. 113; *J.R.A.S.*, 1923, 92.
[4] *Sabhāparvan*, XXX, 1171; *Aśvamedhaparvan*, LXXXIII, 2476-7.
[5] *Vāyupurāṇa*, XLV, 125.
[6] *Matsyapurāṇa*, CXIII, 47.

Kadambas and the Vejayantī of epigraphic records. It is held to be the same as the Buzantion of the *Periplus*.

**Ādhakyas**

The *Vāyu* and *Matsya Purāṇas* (XLV, 126 and CXIII, 48) read Āṭavyas which is no doubt the correct reading. Āṭavī as a city of the Deccan is mentioned in the *Mahābhārata*.[1] The Āṭavyas were certainly the same as the Āṭavikas of the Allahabad Pillar Inscription of Samudragupta, who were perhaps aboriginal tribes dwelling in the jungle tracts of Central India.

**Daṇḍakas**

The Daṇḍakas are undoubtedly the people dwelling in the Daṇḍaka forest celebrated in the *Rāmāyaṇa* in connection with the story of Rāma's exile. According to the description in the *Rāmāyaṇa*, the forest seems to have covered almost the whole of Central India from the Bundelkhand region to the Godāvarī,[2] but the *Mahābhārata* seems to limit the Daṇḍaka forest to the source of the Godāvarī.[3]

**Paurikas**

For Paurikas the *Vāyupurāṇa* reads Paunikas instead (XLV, 127) perhaps wrongly. According to the *Harivaṃśa*, Purikā was a city in the Māhiṣmatī kingdom (XCV, 5220–28). It is not improbable that Purikā was the city of the Paurikas.

**Atharvas and Arkaliṅgas**

These two names are evidently misreadings and it is difficult to find out what is the correct form. The *Vāyupurāṇa* reads *atha pārśve talaṅgāśca* while the *Matsya* gives *Atharvāśca Kaliṅgāśca*. All these readings are improbable. Tilaṅgas are well known as a southern people who are mentioned in connection with the southern peoples in the *Mārkaṇḍeya Purāṇa* (Chap. 58, verse 28). They are identical with the Trikaliṅgas. Avantas and Kaliṅgas though otherwise well known are nowhere located in the Madhyadeśa. The *Mārkaṇḍeya Purāṇa* speaks of the Avantas as a Vindhyan tribe (Chap. 57, verses 52 and 55). In the same Purāṇa, the Kaliṅgas are once spoken of as a northern tribe (*ibid.*, verse 37) and then again as a southern tribe (*ibid.*, v. 46). The reference to the Kaliṅgas as a northern tribe is undoubtedly wrong.

**Maulikas**

The *Vāyupurāṇa* reads Maunikas (XLV, 127) instead. The *Sabhāparvan* of the *Mahābhārata* refers to a people named Mauleyas. The Maulikas were evidently the people of Mūlaka mentioned in the Pārāyaṇavagga of the *Suttanipāta*.

1 *Sabhāparvan*, XXX, 1176.
2 *J.R.A.S.*, 1894, p. 241; cf. *Jātaka*, Fausböll, Vol. V, p. 29.
3 *Sabhāparvan*, XXX, 1169; *Vanaparvan*, LXXXV, 8183-4.

**The Mūṣikas or Mūṣakas**

The *Mahābhārata*[1] and the *Mārkaṇḍeya Purāṇa* mention a people called the Mūṣikas as dwelling in the south; the same people evidently were also called Mūṣakas who are mentioned twice in the *Mahābhārata*.[2] The *Mārkaṇḍeya Purāṇa* in another context refers to a people called Mriṣikas[3] as dwelling in the south-east and still another called Riṣikas[4] in the south. The Mriṣikas were apparently the same as the Mūṣikas or the Musakas. The Riṣikas were also a well-known people; they are referred to as dwelling in the north in the *Mahābhārata*,[5] in the *Rāmāyaṇa*[6] as well as in the *Matsyapurāṇa*.[7] Another section of the same people seems to have their location in the south.[8] It is difficult to say whether the Riṣikas were the same as the Mriṣikas or the Mūṣikas = Mūṣakas.

Pargiter suggests[9] that the Mūṣikas = Mūṣakas were probably settled on the banks of the river Musi on which stands modern Hyderabad. Dr. Ray Chaudhuri suggests[10] that it is not altogether improbable that the Mūchipa or Mūvīpa of the *Sāṅkhyāyana Śrauta Sūtra* are the same people as the Mūṣikas. It is also reasonable to suggest that the Mūṣikas = Mūṣakas were a southern offshoot of the Punjab tribe known to Alexander's historians as the Mousikenos.[11] Patañjali mentions a people called Mauṣikāra[12] which appears to have some connection with the Mūṣikas. A Musikanagara is referred to in the Hāthigumphā Inscription of King Khāravela of Kaliṅga who in the second year of his reign is said to have struck terror into the heart of the people of that place.[13]

**The Culikas and Śūlikas**

The Culikas and the Śūlikas are mentioned in *Mārkaṇḍeya* list[14] as two different peoples, but both in the north. For Culikas, the *Vāyupurāṇa* reads Pīḍikas[15] and the *Matsyapurāṇa* Sainikas instead.[16] The *Mārkaṇḍeya Purāṇa* in another context[17] places the Culikas in the Tortoise's tail at the westernmost part of India. For Śūlikas, the *Vāyupurāṇa* reads Culikas in the same context, and the *Matsyapurāṇa* says that they were a people through whose country flowed the river Cakṣu, one of the three large rivers which rising from the mid-Himalayan

---

1 *Bhīṣmaparvan*, IX, 366.
2 *Ibid.*, IX, 366 and 371.
3 LVIII, 16.
4 LVIII, 27.
5 *Sabhāparvan*, XXVI, 1033–6.
6 *Kiṣkindhyā Kāṇḍa*, XLIV, 13.
7 CXX, 53.
8 *Rāmāyaṇa*, *Kiskindhyā Kāṇḍa*, XLI, 16; *Harivaṃśa*, CXIX, 6724–6.
9 *Mārkaṇḍeya Purāṇa*, p. 366.
10 *P.H.A.I.*, 4th Ed., p. 80.
11 Cf. *Cambridge History of India*, Vol. I, p. 377.
12 IV, i, 4.
13 *Epigraphia Indica*, XX, 79, 87; Barua reads Aśvaka or Risika instead in his *Old Brāhmī Inscriptions*, p. 176; Thomas also finds no reference in the passage to any Musika city, *J.R.A.S.*, 1922, 83.
14 LVII, 40, 41.
15 XLV, 119.
16 CXIII, 43.
17 LVIII, 37.

region flows westward.[1] Pargiter suggests that Cakṣu may perhaps be meant for Vakṣu (= Vaṃkṣu) which is the Oxus, and says that in that case the Śūlikas would be a people on the Oxus in Turkistan.[2] He also points to the resemblance of the name Śūlikas with that of the Śūlakaras mentioned in the same canto of the *Mārkaṇḍeya Purāṇa*.[3]

But the Śūlikas are mentioned in the Harāhā Inscription of Īśānavarman Maukhari in a different context; there they are mentioned along with the Andhras and Gauḍas, all of whom appear to have been defeated by Īśānavarman. Dr. Ray Chaudhuri[4] suggests that the Śūlikas should be identified with the Cālukyas who are mentioned in the Mahākūṭa Pillar Inscription as Calikya, names so near to Culika of the Purāṇas. The Śūlikas may further be identified with the Solaki and Solaṅki of the Gujrat records. The Culikas and Śūlikas may thus be the same people.

The Śūlikas or the Śaulikas are further mentioned in the *Bṛhatsaṃhitā*[5] along with the Aparāntas, Vanavāsīs and the Vidarbhas. Elsewhere the *Bṛhatsaṃhitā* connects the same people[6] with the Gandhāras and Vokkāras (occupying modern Wakhan). This suggests that a section of the people must have once been dwelling in the north or north-west, and another in the western or Aparānta region. The kingdom of Śulik according to Tārānātha was located beyond Togara = Tegara = modern Ter[7] in the Deccan.

**The Kaṅkanas**

The Kaṅkanas as a tribe are referred to in the *Mārkaṇḍeya Purāṇa*[8] and the *Harivaṃśa*.[9] According to the latter source, they were defeated and degraded by King Sagara. They must have been the people dwelling along the low strip of land between the Western Ghats and the sea called in historical times Kaṅkan or Koṅkan. Their mention along with the Bhṛgukacchas in the *Mārkaṇḍeya Purāṇa* makes this identification more significant.

**The Tosalas**

The Tosalas are referred to in the *Mārkaṇḍeya Purāṇa* along with the Karūṣas, Keralas, Utkalas, Daśārṇas, Kośalas, Avantis, etc., all of whom dwelt on the slopes of Vindhya mountains. The *Matsyapurāṇa* reads Stosalas (CXIII, 53) erroneously, for Tosalas is the correct reading meaning the people of Tosali or Tosala and the adjoining region. Tosali or Tosala was the name of a country as well as of a city. The city of Tosali was the seat of the provincial government of Kaliṅga in the

---

1 CXX, 45, 46.
2 *Mārkaṇḍeya Purāṇa*, p. 342, note.
3 LVII, 40.
4 *P.H.A.I.*, 4th Ed., 509.
5 IX, 15; XIV, 8.
6 IX, 21; XVI, 35.
7 *Ind. Ant.*, IV, 364.
8 VIII, 22.
9 XIV, 784.

days of Aśoka. The country or janapada of 'Amita-Tosala' is referred to in the *Gauḍavyaha* along with its city Tosala.[1] In Pauranic literature, Tosala is always associated with Dakṣiṇa Kośala and distinguished from Kaliṅga. Tosala in medieval times seems to have been divided into two parts: Dakṣiṇa Tosala and Uttara Tosala.[2] The city of Tosala seems to have been the same as Tosalei of Ptolemy.

**Vaidiśas**

The Vaidiśas are undoubtedly the people of Vidiśā, a famous city of early times, the capital of the Daśārṇa country, immortalised by Kālidāsa in his *Meghadūtam*. Vidiśā is probably the modern Besnagar, close to Bhilsa. It was situated on the river Vetravatī, modern Betwa.

**Tuṣtikāras**

The name Tuṣtikāras seems to be a misreading. The *Vāyupurāṇa* reads Tuṇḍikeras (XLV, 134) which is supported by the *Mahābhārata*[3] and the *Harivaṃśa* (XXXIV, 1895). According to the *Harivaṃśa* they belonged to the Haihaya race (*ibid.*). The tribe seems to have left their trace in the little town of Tendukhera, a little to the north of the source of the Narmadā.[4] Sauṇḍikeras, which is the reading of the *Matsyapurāṇa*, is incorrect.

**The Māhiṣakas or Māhiṣikas**

The Māhiṣakas or Māhisīkas are referred to in the Purāṇas[5] as a people of the south. They are mentioned in the same context in the *Sabhāparvan* list[6] of the *Mahābhārata*. Undoubtedly they are the same people as the Māhismakas of the *Aśvamedhaparvan*[7] of the *Mahābhārata*, and were the inhabitants of the ancient region Māhismatī mentioned also in the *Mahābhārata*.[8] Māhiṣmatī seems to have been situated on the river Narmadā between the Vindhya and the Rikṣa and can safely be identified with the modern Mandhātā region, where there was a river called Māhiṣiki mentioned in the *Rāmāyaṇa*.[9] According to one passage in the *Harivaṃśa*,[10] the founder of Māhiṣmatī seems to have been Mucukunda, according to another[11] Māhismat. According to the Purāṇas,[12] Māhiṣmatī was founded by a prince of the Yadu lineage. Bhandarkar says that Avanti Dakṣiṇāpatha had its capital at Māhiṣmatī or Pāli Māhissati. The Purāṇas style the first dynasty of Māhiṣmatī as Haihaya,[13] whereas the *Mahāgovinda*

---

1 Cf. Levi, *Pre-Aryan et Pre-Dravidian L'Inde, J.A.*, July–Sept., 1923.
2 *Ep. Ind.*, IX, 286; XV, 3.
3 *Droṇaparvan*, XVII, 691; *Karṇaparvan*, V, 138.
4 Pargiter, *Mārkaṇḍeya Purāṇa*, p. 344, note.
5 *Mārkaṇḍeya Purāṇa*, LVII, 46; *Matsyapurāṇa*, CXIII, 47.
6 IX, 366.
7 LXXXIII, 2475.
8 *Sabhāparvan*, XXX, 1125–63.
9 *Kiṣkindhyā Kāṇḍa*, XLI, 16.
10 XCV, 5218ff.
11 XXXIII, 1846-7.
12 *Matsyapurāṇa*, XLIII, 10–29; XLIV, 36; *Vāyupurāṇa*, 94, 26; 95, 35.
13 *Ibid.*, 43, 8–29; *Vāyu*, 94, 5–26.

*Suttanta* mentions Māhissati as the capital of the Avantis, and refers to their king Vessabhu. But the *Mahābhārata* distinguishes between Avanti and Māhiṣmatī.[1]

**Kīkaṭas** The Kīkaṭas or Kīkaṭa tribe are mentioned in the *Ṛgveda* (III, 53, 14) as being under the rule of a king named Pramaganda. Yāska in his *Nirukta* (VI, 32) says that Kīkaṭa was a non-Aryan country (*anārya-nivāsa*). The author of the *Bṛhaddharma Purāṇa* echoes this feeling of Yāska when he says that the Kīkaṭa country was *pāpa-bhūmi* or impure country (*Kīkaṭe ca mṛto'pyeṣa pāpabhūmau na saṃśayaḥ*, XXVI, 47). The Gayā District was probably included in the Kīkaṭa country as is evident from the following passage of the *Bṛhaddharma Purāṇa* (XXV, 20, 22):

> 'Kīkaṭe nāma deśe' sti Kāka-karṇākhyo nṛpaḥ ।
> Prajānāṃ hitakṛnnityam Brahmadveṣakaras tathā ॥
> Tatra deśe Gayā nāma puṇyadeśo'sti viśrutaḥ ।
> Nadī ca Karṇadā nāma pitṛṇāṃ svargadāyinī ॥'

Similar statements are also found in the *Vāyu* and the *Bhāgavata Purāṇas* as well as in the commentary of Śrīdhara. E.g.: 'Kīkaṭeṣu Gayā puṇyā puṇyam Rājagṛham vanam ། Cyāvanasyāśramaṃ puṇyaṃ nadī puṇyā punaḥpunaḥ' (*Vāyu*, 108, 73). 'Buddho nāmnāñjanasutaḥ Kīkaṭeṣu bhaviṣyati' (*Bhāgavata*, 1, 3, 24). 'Kīkaṭeṣu madhye Gayāpradeśe' (Śrīdhara). Kīkaṭa thus was an impure country but later Brahmanical sources seem to have regarded some of its localities at least as holy, e.g. Gayā, Rājagṛha and the hermitage of the sage Cyavana. Later authorities seem to hold the Kīkaṭa country identical with Magadha. Thus in Hemacandra's *Abhidhānacintāmaṇi* we find: 'Kīkaṭā-Magadhāhvayāḥ'. According to Prof. A. B. Keith[2] if the Kīkaṭas of the *Ṛgveda* were, as has been suggested, really located in Magadha, the dislike of the country goes back to the *Ṛgveda* itself. The causes most probably have been the imperfect Brāhmanisation of the land and the predominance of aboriginal blood, which later in history rendered Magadha the headquarters of Buddhism.

**Pravaṅgas** The Pravaṅgas probably stand for those people who dwelt just in front of the Vaṅgas (Pravaṅga). It is not unlikely that they may be the same people as the Aṅgas.

**Raṅgeyas** This is evidently a copyist's mistake for Vaṅgeyas which is the reading of the *Vāyupurāṇa* (XLV, 122). The *Matsyapurāṇa* simply reads Vaṅgas. They are undoubtedly the people of ancient Vaṅga or Bengal.

---

1 *Mahābhārata*, II, 31, 10.

2 *Cambridge History of India*, Vol. I, p. 123.

**Mānadas**

The *Vāyupurāṇa* reads Māladas (XLV, 122). Pargiter assumes that here we have a reference to the people of modern Maldah in which are situated the old cities of Gauḍ and Pāṇḍuyā. The Māladas are also mentioned as an eastern people in the *Mahābhārata*.[1]

**Ugras**

The Ugras seem to have been a very old and once a well-known tribe. They are mentioned in the *Bṛhadāraṇyaka Upaniṣad* (III, 8, 2) and also in the *Uvāsagadasāo*.[2] According to the *Aṅguttara Nikāya*, the Uggas or Ugras are associated with Vesālī or Vaiśālī.[3] They are also connected with Hatthigāma according to the same Nikāya. The *Dhammapada Commentary* refers to a city called Ugga or Ugra. A passage in the *Sūtrakṛtāṅga* seems to suggest that the Ugras along with the Aikṣvākas, Bhogas and Kauravas were associated with the Jñātṛs and Licchavis as subjects of the Vajji rulers and members of the Vajji clan.[4]

**Taṅganas**

The *Vāyupurāṇa* reads Taṅganas (XLV, 120) and more than once in the *Mahābhārata*[5] we find reference to Taṅganas and Para-taṅganas. The Epic description shows that they were allied with the Kirātas and Pulindas.[6] From the description given in the *Mahābhārata* it appears that they were a rude tribe, for their main fighting weapon was stone.[7]

**Mudakaras**

The name Mudakaras is found in the *Mārkaṇḍeya Purāṇa*.[8] The *Vāyupurāṇa* gives Sujarakas and the *Matsya* Madgurakas. None of these names is identifiable. One may, nevertheless, guess that here is a name which is a corrupt rendering of Mudgagiri or Modagiri, mentioned in literature and inscriptions, which is generally identified with the hills of Monghyr in Bihar. Monghyr was also known as Mudgala-puri, Mudgalāśrama and so on. The Mudgalas or the people of Monghyr are also referred to in the *Mahābhārata*.[9]

**Antargiryas**

The Antargiryas must be those people dwelling in the hilly stretch of the Rajmahal ranges of the Santhal Parganas. They are mentioned in the *Bhīṣmaparvan* list of the *Mahābhārata*.

**Bahirgiras**

The Bahirgiras may also be said to have been associated with the hilly tracts of Bihar and from their mention along with the Antargiryas it seems that the people meant were

---

1 *Sabhāparvan*, XXIX, 1081-2; *Droṇaparvan*, VII, 183.
2 Hoernle's Ed., II, p. 139, art. 210.
3 Cf. *Uggo gahapati Vesāliko*; *Aṅguttara Nikāya*, 1, 26.
4 S.B.E., XLV, 339.
5 *Sabhāparvan*, LI, 1859; *Bhīṣmaparvan*, IX, 372.
6 *Vanaparvan*, CXL, 10863-5; *Sabhāparvan*, LI, 1858-9.
7 *Droṇaparvan*, CXXI, 4835-47.
8 *Mārkaṇḍeya Purāṇa*, 57, 42.
9 *Droṇaparvan*, XI, 397.

dwellers on the outskirts of the hills of Bhagalpur and Monghyr regions.

**Anūpas**

The Anūpas are mentioned as a tribe in the *Vāyupurāṇa* (XIV, 134); the *Matsyapurāṇa* reads Anipa (CXIII, 54) while the *Mārkaṇḍeya Purāṇa* (LVII, 55) reads Annajas. Anūpa literally means any marshy tract or country lying not very far from the seas. In this sense the word '*sāgarānūpa*' is used in several places in the *Mahābhārata*. Thus we find tracts known as Anūpa in Bengal [1] in the far south [2] on the western coast [3] in or near about Kathiawar.[4] From the *Harivaṃśa* we learn that the country of the Anūpa tribe lay near Surāṣṭra and Ānartta. The *Harivaṃśa* further informs us that it was to the south of Surāṣṭra (XCIV, 5142–80). In the *Mahābhārata* king Kārtavīrya and Nala are styled 'lords of Anūpa'.[5] It seems likely, therefore, that the Anūpas occupied the tract of country south of Surāṣṭra, around Māhiṣmatī on the Narmadā. Epigraphic evidence also lends support to such a view. The Nāsik Cave Inscription of Queen Gautamī Balaśrī records that her son conquered Anūpa along with other countries, namely, Mahārāṣṭra, Mūlaka (country round Paiṭhān), Suratha (Surāṣṭra or Kathiawar), Kukura (country near the Pāriyātra or the Western Vindhyas), Aparānta (northern Konkan), Vidarbha (Berar) and Ākarāvanti (eastern and western Malwa). Most of these tracts seem to have been reconquered from Gautamīputra by Śaka Mahākṣatrapa Rudradāman whose Junāgaḍh Rock Inscription states that his sway extended over Pūrv-āpar-ākar-āvanti (east and west Malwa), Anūpanivrit or the Māhiṣmatī (Māndhātā ?) region, Ānartta (tract round Dwārkā according to some; district round Vaḍanagara according to others),[6] Surāṣṭra (district round Junāgaḍh), Svabhra (the country on the banks of the Sābarmatī), Maru (Marwar), Kaccha (Cutch), Sindhu-Sauvīra (the lower Indus valley), Kukura (part of Central India, probably near the Pāriyātra Mt. according to the *Bṛhatsaṃhitā*, XIV, 4), Aparānta (north Konkan), and Niṣāda (in the region of the Sarasvatī and the western Vindhyas).[7]

**Kukuras**

The Kukuras as a tribe find mention in the *Bhāgavatapurāṇa*. They seem to have occupied the Dwārakā region which is described as: '*Kukur-Āndhaka-Vṛṣṇibhiḥ Juptāḥ*'. The *Vāyupurāṇa* also seems to refer to the tribe when it represents Ugrasena, the king of the Yādavas as 'Kukurodbhava' or 'originated from Kukura'. The *Bṛhatsaṃhitā* seems to locate the

1 *Sabhāparvan*, XXV, 1002; XXIX, 1101; XXXIII, 1268-9.
2 *Udyogaparvan*, XVIII, 578.
3 *Ibid.*, III, 81.
4 *Harivaṃśa*, CXIII, 6361–9; CXIV, 6410-11.
5 *Bhīṣmaparvan*, XCV, 4210.
6 Cf. *Bomb. Gaz.*, I, i, 6.
7 Cf. *Niṣādarāṣṭra*, *Mbh.*, III, 130–4 and *Pāriyātracaraḥ*, *Mbh.*, XII, 135, 3–5.

tribe in western or central India (XIV, 4). According to the Nāsik Cave Inscription of Queen Gautamī Balaśrī, her son conquered the Kukuras, Suraṭhas, Mūlakas, Aparāntas, Anūpas, Vidarbhas and others. From the Junāgaḍh Rock Inscription of Mahākṣatrapa Rudradāman we learn that most of these peoples along with the Kukuras were again conquered by him. These provinces were in all probability wrested from the hands of the contemporary Sātavāhana ruler of Deccan. According to Sir R. G. Bhandarkar, the Śātakarṇi lord of Dakṣiṇāpatha from whom Rudradāman conquered these provinces was Gautamīputra Śātakarṇi.[1] According to Rapson the Sātavāhana ruler of Deccan, whom Rudradāman defeated, was Pulumāyi.

**Suryārakas**

The name Suryārakas is a misreading for Sūrpārakas. The Sūrpāraka country was known from very early times, and is celebrated in the *Mahābhārata* in connection with the legend of Rāma Jāmadagnya.[2] There it is located in the western region, but some passages seem to locate it in the south as well.[3] This does not mean that there were two Sūrpārakas. The reason for this anomaly seems to be clear, for the country was near the southern sea in the western region. According to the same Epic,[4] it was situated on the sea near Prabhāsa, that is, modern Somnath in Kathiawar. The city of Sūrpāraka, identical with the modern town of Sopārā near Bassein, is said to have been founded by Rāma Jāmadagnya.[5]

**Vṛkas**

In the *Mahābhārata*[6] we find reference to the Vṛkas. The *Matsyapurāṇa* reads Andhakas instead. The Andhakas are intimately associated with the Yādavas and are often referred to in the *Mahābhārata*[7] but they are known to have been located in Western India or Aparānta. A more correct or better reading seems to be Vṛṣṇikas.

**Hārabhūṣikas**

The variant readings are Hārapūrikas[8] and Hāramurtikas.[9] None of these names is identifiable. Pargiter suggests Hāra-hūṇakas who are mentioned in the *Mahābhārata* as a people outside India on the west.[10]

**Māṭharas**

This reading is evidently wrong. The *Matsyapurāṇa* (CXIII, 43) reads Rāmaṭhas instead. The *Mahābhārata* makes mention of them and locates them in the

---

1 *Early History of the Dekkan*, 23.
2 *Vanaparvan*, LXXXV, 8185.
3 *Sabhāparvan*, XXX, 1169; *Vanaparvan*, LXXXVIII, 8337.
4 *Vanaparvan*, CXVIII, 10221–27.
5 *Harivaṃśa*, XCVI, 5300.
6 *Bhīsmaparvan*, LI, 2106.
7 *Udyogaparvan*, LXXXV, 304; *Harivaṃśa*, XXXV, 1907-8; *Ibid.*, XXXIX, 2041.
8 *Vāyu*, XLV, 116.
9 *Matsya*, CXIII, 41.
10 *Sabhāparvan*, XXXI, 1194; L, 1844; *Vanaparvan*, LI, 1991.

west.[1] The name of the people is also given as Ramaṭas or Ramaṭhas in the *Vāyupurāṇa* (XLV, 117) and also in the *Mahābhārata*. There is, however, no clue to their identification.

**Jāguḍas**

The *Vāyupurāṇa* reads Juguḍas, the *Matsya* Jīṅgalas. In another place the *Matsyapurāṇa* mentions the Jaguḍas as a people through whose country the Indus flows (CXX, 46–48).[2] But this indication is too vague to admit of any definite identification. The *Mahābhārata*[3] also mentions the Jāguḍas.

**Brahmottaras**

Pargiter suggests the reading Suhmotkalas[4] which is neither intended nor necessary, for evidently a better suggestion is that of the *Matsya* which reads Suhmottaras meaning the people who dwelt north of the Suhma country.

**Bhṛgukacchas**

In the Kūrmaniveśa section[5] of the *Mārkaṇḍeya Purāṇa* the Bhṛgukacchas are located in the south. Evidently this is the correct Sanskrit form of the name which we find in a corrupt form, Bhiru-kacchas, in another section of the same *Mārkaṇḍeya Purāṇa*,[6] whereas the *Matsyapurāṇa* reads Bharukacchas (CXIII, 50), who are the same people, namely, the Bhṛgukacchas of Sanskrit literature. Bhṛgukaccha, Bharukaccha, Bhirukaccha are all identical with the modern Broach or Bharuch which is the Barygaza of early Greek geographers. All these names survive in the modern Broach, on the mouth of the Narmadā. In early Buddhist literature as well as in the early centuries of the Christian era, the town was reputed to be an important seat of sea-going trade and commerce.

Along with the Bhṛgukacchas, the *Vāyu* (XLV, 131) and the *Matsya Purāṇas* (CXIII, 51) mention a people called the Kacchikas. These were undoubtedly the people of what is now known as Kutch or Cutch.

**Māheyas**

The Māheyas must have been the people dwelling on the banks of the Māhi. They are the same as the Māhikas of the *Bhīṣmaparvan* list of the *Mahābhārata* (IX, 354).

**Bhojas**

The *Vāyu* (XLV, 132) and *Matsya Purānas* (CXIII, 52) read Bhojas which is undoubtedly a more probable reading. The Bhojas were a Yādava tribe who dwelt in north-eastern Gujrat.

**Aparāntas**

The *Vāyupurāṇa* reads Aparitas and Matsya Purandharas instead; both are evidently erroneous. The *Bhīṣmaparvan* list of the *Mahābhārata* agrees with that of the

---

[1] *Sabhāparvan*, XXXI, 1195; *Vanaparvan*, LI, 1991; *Śāntiparvan*, LXV, 2430.

[2] Cf. Pargiter, *Mārkaṇḍeya Purāṇa*, p. 322, note.

[3] *Vanaparvan*, LI, 1991.

[4] *Mārkaṇḍeya Purāṇa*, p. 327, note.

[5] LVIII, 22.

[6] LVII, 51.

*Mārkaṇḍeya Purāṇa.* Mention is often made of this tribe in the *Mahābhārata* as Aparānta or Aparāntas.[1] Generally the term is applied to all the tribes living in the western region of India. But the *Mārkaṇḍeya* and *Bhīṣmaparvan* list must also be taken to signify a particular tribe. According to the astronomical list of the *Mārkaṇḍeya* (Chap. 58) the tribe seems to have been located north of the Sindhu-Sauvīra country. The word Aparānta in the narrowest sense or connotation of the term, that is, the kingdom of Aparānta is identified with northern Konkan with its capital at Śūrpāraka (modern Sopara). It lay to the west of Mahārāṣṭra. It is mentioned in the inscriptions of Aśoka where we find that his empire included all the Aparāntas (Śūrpāraka, Nāsik, etc., according to the *Mārkaṇḍeya Purāṇa* (57, 49–52)). The author of the *Periplus* mentions King Mambarus (identified by some with Nahapāna) whose capital was Minnagara in Ariake. According to D. R. Bhandarkar Minnagara is Mandasor and Ariake is Aparāntika. Ushavadāta's inscriptions show that Nahapāna's political influence extended from Poona and Śūrpāraka (N. Konkan) to Mandasor and Puṣkara (Ajmīr). From the Nāsik record of Queen Gautamī Balaśrī we learn that her son extended his sway over Aparānta as well as over other western countries. Later on Aparānta was reconquered by the Śaka Satrap Rudradāman of Western India, as we find from his Junāgaḍh Rock Inscription of the year 72, that is, 150 A.D.

**Haihayas**

The Purāṇas style the first dynasty of Māhiṣmatī as Haihaya.[2] This family is referred to in Kauṭilya's *Arthaśāstra* (p. 11). The Haihayas are said to have overthrown the Nāgas whose habitat was probably somewhere in the Narmadā region (cf. Nagpur). Five branches of the Haihayas are mentioned in the *Matsyapurāṇa*, namely, Vītihotras, Bhojas, Avantis, Kuṇḍikeras or Tuṇḍikeras and the Tālajaṅghas (43, 48-9). In the fourth century B.C. Avanti formed an integral part of the Magadhan empire. Thus Mahāpadma Nanda, the first Nanda king, is described in the *Vāyu, Matsya* and *Brahmāṇḍa Purāṇas* as '*ekarāṭ*', or sole and undisputed monarch of the earth and '*sarva Kṣatrāntaka*', that is, the destroyer of all kṣatriya families who ruled over the different parts of India along with the Saiśunāgas, viz. the Ikṣvākus, Kurus, Pañcālas, Kāśīs, Maithilas, Vītihotras, Haihayas, Kaliṅgas, Aśmakas, Śūrasenas and so on.[3] It appears, therefore, that the Haihayas were one of the ruling Kṣatriya dynasties of ancient India. In the *Mahābhārata* (XIII, 30) Pratardana, king of Kāśī, is said

---

[1] *Bhīsmaparvan*, IX, 355; *Vanaparvan*, CCXVII, 7885-6; *Śāntiparvan*, XLIX, 1780–82.

[2] *Matsya*, 43, 8–29; *Vāyu*, 94, 5–26.

[3] Ray Chaudhuri, *Political History of Ancient India*, 4th Ed., p. 141.

to have crushed the power of Vītahavyas or Haihayas. According to E. J. Rapson,[1] the Haihayas, Aśmakas and Vītihotras, like the Sūrasenas, belonged to the great family of the descendants of Yadu who occupied the countries of the river Chambal in the north and the river Narbadā in the south, though it is difficult to identify with precision the kingdoms indicated by these different names. Haihaya is often used as a synonym of Yādava to denote the whole group of peoples and the Vītihotras are said to be a branch of the Haihayas. The Vītihotras and the Aśmakas are closely associated in literature with the Avantis of Western Mālwā, whose capital was Ujjain (Ujjayinī) on the river Siprā, a tributory of the Chambal (Charmanvatī). In the Puranic list of ruling dynasties the rulers of Ujjain are not mentioned. The obvious explanation for this, as Rapson points out, is that they are probably styled Haihayas in the Purānas.[2]

**Bhogavardhanas**

The tribe cannot satisfactorily be identified. Bhogavadham occurs in the Barhut Inscriptions.[3]

**Sarajas**

The *Vāyu* and *Matsya Purāṇas* read Mālavas[4] which is no doubt the correct reading. The Mālavas had settlements in different parts of India. The tribe referred to here may probably mean that branch of the Mālavas which settled in and around that portion of Malwa which borders on the Vindhyas.

**Vīrahotras**

The *Vāyu* and *Matsya Purāṇas* read Vītihotras,[5] which seems to be the correct reading. They were descended from king Vītihotra and were a branch of the Haihaya race.[6] A variant of their name is given in the *Droṇaparvan* of the *Mahābhārata*.[7] The name Vīrahotra or Varahotra is met with in the Sāñci Inscriptions of the second century B.C.

**Vindhya-Mauleyas**

The *Matsyapurāṇa* erroneously reads Vindhya-puṣikas (CXIII, 48), but the *Vāyu* reads Vindhyamūlikas (XLV, 126). No particular people of the name are known, but the name may mean the 'people who live at the foot of the Vindhyas'.

**Jāṅgalas**

Pargiter rightly suggests that the Jāṅgalas are the same as the people of Kurujāṅgalas. Kuru-jāṅgala, that is, the waste land of the Kurus, was the eastern part of their territory and appears to have comprised the tract between the Ganges and North Pañcāla.[8] The Jāṅgalas are mentioned with the

[1] *Cambridge History of India*, Vol. I, p. 316.
[2] *Ibid.*, p. 316.
[3] Vide Barua and Sinha, *Barhut Inscriptions*, p. 15.
[4] XLV, 132 and CXIII, 52, respectively.
[5] XLV, 134; CXIII, 54.
[6] *Harivaṁśa*, XXXIV, 1895.
[7] LXX, 2436.
[8] *Rāmāyaṇa, Ayodhyā Kāṇḍa*, LXXII; *Mahābhārata, Sabhāparvan*, XIX, pp. 793-4.

Kurus and contiguous tribes. So Pargiter's assumption seems to be correct, for we do not hear of any other people of this name mentioned in ancient literature or inscription.

**Bhadrakaras**

It is very difficult to locate the Bhadrakaras or determine their identity. They are no doubt the same people as the Bhadrakāras[1] and the Bhadras[2] of the *Mahābhārata*. It is not unlikely that their habitat was near about the Kurus, the Matsyas and the Śūrasenas. It is not improbable that the Uttamabhadras known in historical times as a republican tribe were a section of the Epic and Pauranic Bhadrakas or Bhadras.

**Kshudrakas**

The Sudracae or Oxydrakai of the Punjab are generally held to be the same as Kshudrakas. They were settled between the Hydraotes (Rāvi) and the Hyphasis (Beas) during the age of Alexander as we learn from classical historians. According to Ray Chaudhuri[3] they were probably settled in the territory included within the present Montgomery District of the Punjab. They were one of the most numerous and warlike of all the Indian tribes in the Punjab. Arrian in one passage refers to the 'leading men of their cities and their provincial governors', besides other eminent men. Megasthenes,[4] as quoted by Strabo, records that the Persians got mercenary troops from India, namely, the Hydrakes, i.e. the Oxydrakai or Kshudrakas in the Punjab. The Malloi (Mālavas) and the Oxydrakai formed a grand alliance against the army of Alexander whom they opposed tooth and nail at first but finding it an impossible task they are said to have tendered their submission to the Macedonian conqueror by sending a thousand of their troops as hostages. They are alleged to have said that love of independence alone prompted them to oppose the invader.[5] In the *Mahābhārata*[6] we find mention of the Kshudrakas.

**Puṣkalas**

The Puṣkalas probably were the people from whom the name Puṣkalāvatī or Puṣkarāvatī,[7] the old capital of Gandhāra, derived its name. The *Vāyu* and *Matsya Purāṇas* read Prasthalas. The Prasthalas were evidently people of Prasthala,[8] closely connected with Trigarta and therefore located probably in the Punjab. Puṣkarāvatī or Puṣkalāvatī (Prākrit Pukkalaoti, whence the Peukelaotis of Arrian) is represented by the

[1] *Sabhāparvan*, XIII, 590. [2] *Vanaparvan*, CCLIII, 15256.
[3] *Political History of Ancient India*, 4th Ed., p. 205.
[4] *Cambridge History of India*, Vol. I, p. 331 f.n.
[5] *Ibid.*, Vol. I, pp. 375-6. [6] II, 52, 15; VII, 68, 9.
[7] *Rāmāyana Kiskindhyā Kāṇḍa*, XL, III, 23.
[8] *Mbh.*, *Virāṭaparvan*, XXX, 971; *Bhīṣmaparvan*, LXXV, 3296; *Droṇaparvan*, XVII, 691.

modern Prang and Chārsadda, 17 miles north-east of Peshawar on the Swat river.[1]

Peukelaotis represents Sanskrit Puṣkarāvatī which is mentioned in the *Bodhisattvāvadāna Kalpalatā* (32nd, p. 40). Puṣkalāvatī formed the western part of the old kingdom of Gandhāra. It lay on the road from Kabul to the Indus when Alexander invaded India. Arrian tells us that the Kabul falls into the Indus in the land called Peukelaotis. The people of the surrounding region are referred to sometimes as the 'Astakenoi' by classical historians. The reigning king at the time of Alexander's invasion was Astes (Hasti or Ashṭaka?) who was defeated and killed by Hephaestion, a general of Alexander. During the days of Aśoka, Puṣkarāvatī was the capital of Trans-Vindhyan Gandhāra. At a later age Indo-Greek kings of the house of Eukratides ruled for some time over Takṣaśilā, Puṣkarāvatī, Kāpiśa and Bactria.[2] Bhandarkar[3] draws our attention to an interesting coin on which the term *nagara-devatā* occurs, indicating that it is a civic coin bearing the image or the symbol of the tutelary or presiding deity of the city. On the obverse is a goddess with the Kharoṣṭhi legend *[Pa]Khalavadi-devada,* which has been taken to mean the tutelary divinity of Puṣkalāvatī. Puṣkalāvatī was a Hindu city and yet we find that the goddess on this coin wears Greek dress and a mural crown which is the emblem of a Greek civic deity. Bhandarkar holds that we cannot regard it as a Greek deity because a Hindu divinity may appear in a Greek or Hellenic garb on Indo-Bactrian coins.

**Cīnas**

In *Mārkaṇḍeya Purāṇa*[4] the Cīnas are mentioned. In the *Mahābhārata* we find them taking part in the Bhārata war as allies of the Kurus along with the king of Prāgjyotiṣa and the Kirātas of North-Eastern India. But the reference here is probably to those Chinese people who had settled somewhere from the north-west to the east along the Indian side of the Himalayas. Thus in one place in the *Mahābhārata*[5] they are associated with the Kāmbojas which shows that they were settled in the north-west, while in another[6] they are mentioned among the soldiers who followed Bhagadatta, king of Prāgjyotiṣa, i.e. roughly modern Assam. Other references in the *Mahābhārata*[7] seem to indicate that they were settled not very far from the sources of the Ganges. They appear as a well-known and highly respectable

1 Schoff, *The Periplus of the Erythraean Sea*, pp. 183-4.
2 *Political History of Ancient India*, 4th Ed., p. 352.
3 *Carmichael Lectures*, 1921, p. 34.
4 Chap. 57, 39.
5 *Bhīṣmaparvan*, IX, p. 373.
6 *Udyogaparvan*, XVIII, pp. 584-5.
7 *Vanaparvan*, CLXXVII, 12350; *Śāntiparvan*, CCCXXVII, 12226–9.

people.[1] Their country was famous for a particular breed of horses.[2] The *Mārkaṇḍeya Purāṇa* [3] mentions the Cīnas. A people called the Apara-Cīnas (Western Cīnas) is mentioned in the *Rāmāyaṇa*.[4]

The Pāli Buddhist literature refers to the kingdom of the Cīnas [5] which is situated far from the Andhakas, Muṇḍakas, Kolakas, etc. and to the China garment.[6] According to the *Milinda-Pañho*, Cīna was as old as Ujjenī, Bharukaccha, Kośala, Magadha, Sāketa, Suraṭṭha, etc.[7] The same text further points out that a king of China who when he wanted to charm the great ocean performed an act of truth at an interval of four months and then he entered into the great ocean on his chariot drawn by lions (*sīharathena*). In front of his chariot the mighty waves rolled back and flowed once more over the spot as soon as he left it (p. 121). The *Mahāvastu* [8] refers to the assembly of the Cīnas who were bound by its decision.

**Tukhāras**

The Tukhāras are mentioned in the *Mārkaṇḍeya Purāṇa* (LVII, 39) along with the Kāmbojas, Daradas, Barbaras and Cīnas, all of whom are described as 'races of men outside' (*vāhyato narāḥ*). The *Vāyupurāṇa* (XIV, 118) reads Tuṣāras instead, meaning of course the same people. They are mentioned in the *Mahābhārata* both as Tukhāras [9] as well as Tuṣāras.[10] The Tukhāras are also mentioned in the *Rāmāyaṇa*.[11] From the *Vanaparvan* of the *Mahābhārata* the Tukhāras seem to have been an outside northern race bordering on the Himalayas. The *Harivaṃśa* groups them along with the Śakas, Pahlavas, Daradas and others who are all branded as Mlecchas and Dasyus. Strabo (XI, 515) says: 'The best known of the nomad tribes are those who drove the Greeks out of Bactria,—the Asii, the Pasiani, the Tochari, and the Sacarauli, who came from the country on the other side of the Jaxartes, over against the Sacae and Sogdiani, which country was also in occupation of the Sacae.' Lassen identifies the Tukhāras with this Tochari tribe and locates them on the north of the Hindu Kush.[12] The geographer Ptolemy mentions the Tokeroi, who are doubtless identical with the Tukhāras as an important element of the Bactrian population. The *Periplus of the Erythraean Sea* seems to point to the same people when it speaks of 'the warlike nations of the Bactrians'. The Tukhāras continued as a tribe till

1 *Udyogaparvan*, XVIII, pp. 584-5.
2 *Ibid.*, LXXXV, 3049.
3 Chap. 57, 39.
4 *Kiṣkindhyā Kāṇḍa*, XLIV, p. 15.
5 *Cīnaraṭṭhā*, *Apadāna*, II, p. 359.
6 *Cīnāpaṭṭuṇṇā*, *Apadāna*, I, p. 2.
7 Trenckner Ed., pp. 327-8, 331.
8 Vol. I, p. 171.
9 *Sabhāparvan*, L, 1850.
10 *Vanaparvan*, LI, 1991; *Śāntiparvan*, LXV, 2429.
11 *Kiṣkindhyā Kāṇḍa*, XLIV, 15.
12 *Ind. Alt. Map.*

the ninth and tenth centuries of the Christian era when they seem to have played an important part in the history of Kashmir.

**Sārasvatas** The *Vāyupurāṇa* reads Sahasas and Sāśvatas instead (XLV, 130); but these names are not identifiable. The Sārasvatas are of course the people dwelling along the Sarasvatī, the river that flows into the sea past Prabhāsa, i.e. modern Somnath.[1]

**Aśvakūṭas** The Aśvakūṭas, as it is given in the *Mārkaṇḍeya Purāṇa* (p. 57, 32), is obviously a misreading, for the *Vāyupurāṇa* reads Kisaṣṇas, Kisaṣṭas or Kisadyas instead (XLV, 110), while the *Matsya* (CXIII, 35) reads Kirātas. We have, however, no other evidence to show that the Kirātas were in the Madhyadeśa. Epic and Pauranic tradition places them in the eastern region.

**Kulyas** Particulars of the tribe called Kulyas are not known. It may be possible that they were the same people as the Kulutas, a republican community, who are mentioned in inscriptions of about the first century A.D. The Kulutas dwelt in the Punjab with such tribes as the Mālavas, Yaudheyas, Ārjunāyanas, Udumbaras, Kunindas and others.

**Malakas** The *Vāyupurāṇa* reads Magadhas and the *Matsya* reads Mūkas. Both are evidently misreadings, for the Magadhas are mentioned as an eastern people in the *Mārkaṇḍeya Purāṇa* (Chap. 57, verse 44). Pargiter[2] suggests that the reading should be Malajas. The Malajas are mentioned in the *Mahābhārata*[3] and in the *Rāmāyaṇa*.[4] The course of the journey taken by Viśvāmitra and Rāma, as described in the *Rāmāyaṇa*, seems to show that they were neighbours of the Kārūṣas and occupied the district of Shahabad, west of the Sone.[5]

**Bodhas** The Bodhas are mentioned in the *Mahābhārata*[6] and perhaps also in the *Rāmāyaṇa*[7] as Bodhis. These people were probably located somewhere in the eastern districts of the Punjab.

The reading Bāhyas of the *Matsyapurāṇa* seems to be wrong, for this name is not found elsewhere unless we take them as identical with the Bāhīkas.

**Daśamālikas** The *Vāyupurāṇa* reads Daśamāṇikas (XLV, 117) while the *Matsya* reads Daśanāmakas (CXIII, 42). The *Bhīṣmaparvan* list, however, agrees with the

---

1 *Vanaparvan*, LXXXII, 5002–4; *Śalyaparvan*, XXXVI, 2048–51.
2 *Mārkaṇḍeya Purāṇa*, p. 309.
3 *Bhīṣmaparvan*, IX, 357.
4 *Ādi Kāṇḍa*, XXVII, 16–23.
5 *Ibid.*, pp. 8–16.
6 *Sabhāparvan*, XIII, 590 and *Bhīṣmaparvan*, IX, 347.
7 *Ayodhyā Kāṇḍa*, LXX, 15.

*Mārkaṇḍeya Purāṇa* in giving the above reading. We cannot, however, identify or locate the people.

**Harṣavardhanas**

The *Mārkaṇḍeya Purāṇa* gives a list of peoples (*Vāhyatonarāḥ*) who evidently dwelt on the borders of India. Among these mention is made of the Kāmbojas, Daradas, Barbaras, Harṣavardhanas, Cīnas and Tukhāras. Instead of Harṣavardhanas, the *Vāyupurāṇa* reads Priya-laukikas. But there is no clue whatsoever to the identification of these names.

**Kuśerukas**

The *Vāyupurāṇa* reads Kaśerukas and *Matsya* Daserakas instead. But none of them can be identified satisfactorily. Daserakas are, however, mentioned in the *Mahābhārata* [1] as taking part in the Kurukṣetra war.

**Haṃsamārgas**

The Haṃsamārgas are mentioned in the *Mārkaṇḍeya Purāṇa* as also in the *Bhīṣmaparvan* list of the *Mahābhārata*. According to the *Matsyapurāṇa*, the river Paosni flowed through the countries inhabited by Tamaras and Haṃsamārgas. The description of the *Matsyapurāṇa* seems to locate the two tribes in the region east of Tibet.

**Kuhakas**

The *Vāyupurāṇa* reads Ahukas or Āhūkas instead. They may be the same as the Kurus of the *Matsyapurāṇa* who are said to have dwelt on the Indus (CXX, 46–8).

**Śatapatha**

The name Śatapatha is unintelligible and obviously erroneous. Paṭaccara is indeed a better reading, for a people of this name is found in the *Mahābhārata*.[2]

**Carmakhaṇḍikas**

The *Matsyapurāṇa* reads Ātta-khaṇḍikas or Cātta-khaṇḍikas and the *Bhīṣmaparvan* list of the *Mahābhārata* (IX, 355) Carmamaṇḍalas instead. These names are not identifiable. Pargiter's suggestion of its identification with Samarkand is interesting.

**Gabalas**

For Gabalas, the *Vāyu* and *Matsya Purāṇas* read Yavanas, which undoubtedly is the correct reading (for details see *Yonas* or *Yavanas*).

**Śatadrujas**

The Śatadrujas are the people who dwelt along the river Sutlej. The *Vāyupurāṇa* reads Śakas and Hradas (XLV, 116), the *Matsya* reads Śakas and Druhyas instead. The Śakas were a well-known people who left their traces on Indian history. They were at first a northern or north-western people but later on they extended their dominions to the south, east and west. They are known to have established royal families as far east as Mathurā (Muttra) and as far south and west as Ujjain and Surāṣṭra

---

1 *Bhīṣmaparvan*, L, 2080; CXVIII, 5483; *Droṇaparvan*, XI, 397; XX, 798.
2 *Sabhāparvan*, XIII, 590-91; XXX, 1108; *Virāṭaparvan*, I, 11-2.

(Kathiawar). The Hradas cannot be identified. The Druhyas were undoubtedly an ancient people being mentioned as Druhyus in the *Ṛgveda* along with the Anus.

**Urṇas**

For the Urṇas, the *Vāyupurāṇa* reads Purāṇas. None of these names can, however, be identified with any amount of precision unless we find in the Urṇas a people inhabiting the Urṇadeśa which Lassen places on the Sutlej near Garhwal (*Ind. Alt. Map*).

**Darvas**

The *Mahābhārata* associates the Darvas with the Trigarttas, the Daradas and other northern tribes to the north of the Punjab.[1]

**Bahu-bhadras**

The name Bahu-bhadra is differently given as Bāhu-bādhas [2] and Bālabhadras [3] in the *Mahābhārata.* The *Matsyapurāṇa* reads Kaṇṭakāras while the *Vāyupurāṇa* reads Raddha Kaṭakas.[4]

**Traipuras**

The Traipuras are the people of Tripurī or Tripura which was both a city and a country. The city of Tripurī was the capital of the Cedi kingdom. It was a well-known city that derived its name from three cities or *tri-pura* once in possession of the asuras.[5] In the time of the Guptas, Tripuri-viṣaya was formed into a province under a Viceroy. It roughly corresponded to the modern Jubbulpur region which was the ancient Cedi country.

**Gajāhvayas**

The Gajāhvayas, according to the Kurmaniveśa section of the *Mārkaṇḍeya Purāṇa*, are located in the 'middle of the tortoise', along with the Udumbaras, etc.

Pargiter very ingenuously guessed that the Gajāhvayas were none other than the people of Hastināpura, the capital of the Kurus. By a play on the meaning of the word 'hastin', 'elephant', the city was also called Hastināpura, Gajapura, Gajāhvaya,[6] Gajasāhvaya,[7] Nāgapura,[8] Nāgāhva, Nāgasāhvaya,[9] etc.

**Parṇaśavaras**

The Parṇa-śavaras, located in the right foot of the tortoise, in the Kurmaniveśa section of the *Mārkaṇḍeya Purāṇa*,[10] were undoubtedly a tribe of the Śavaras. Presumably this particular section of the Śavaras used leaves of trees as their wearing apparel. A girdle of leaves serves as clothing of many aboriginal peoples of today and we have representations of such individuals in ancient Indian sculptures and paintings. The Parṇa-

---

1 Pargiter, *Mārkaṇḍeya Purāṇa*, p. 324 notes.
2 *Bhīṣmaparvan*, IX, 362.
3 *Karṇaparvan*, VI, 153.
4 Cf. *Vāyupurāṇa*, XLV, 117; *Matsyapurāṇa*, CXIII, 42.
5 *Sabhāparvan*, XXX, 1164; *Vanaparvan*, CCLIII, 15246; *Karṇaparvan*, XXXIII and XXXIV.
6 *Udyogaparvan*, p. clxxvi, 6071.
7 *Ādiparvan*, p. cxiii, 4441 and 4460.
8 *Ibid.*, 4461-2.
9 *Ibid.*, p. cxxxi, 5146.
10 LVIII, 19.

śavaras are incidentally mentioned in the early Bengali Caryāpadas and evidently these were the people from whom was derived the conception of the goddess Parṇa-śavarī in Vajrayāna-Buddhism.

**Arbudas**

The Arbudas must have been the people dwelling on and around the Arbuda mountain which is generally identified with modern Mt. Abu which is the southern end of the Aravalli hills.

**Khasas**

The Khasas are described in one place of the *Mārkaṇḍeya Purāṇa* (LVII, 56) as '*parvatāśrayiṇaḥ*' or dwelling along the mountains, and in another place as located in the middle of the tortoise along with the Śālvas, Nīpas, Śakas, Śūrasenas, etc. (LVIII, 6). Epic tradition as contained in the *Mahābhārata* brands them as a rude half-civilised tribe along with the Śakas, Daradas, etc. (*Sabhāparvan*, LI, 1859), while the *Harivaṃśa* records the reason why they were considered as such. It says that the people were once defeated and degraded by King Sagara (XIV, 784) and were hence regarded as Mlecchas (XCV, 6440-1). Manu also says that they were originally Kṣatriyas, but were later on degraded by the lapse of sacred rites and the absence of Brāhmaṇas in their midst (X, 43-4). The *Sabhāparvan* of the *Mahābhārata* places the people near the river Śailoda between the Meru and Mandāra mountains (LI, 1858-9). If the river Śailoda is the same as Śailodaka of the *Matsyapurāṇa* (CXX, 19-23), then the Khasas seem to have originally settled somewhere in Tibet or further north-west. Much later, in historical times, the Khasas are mentioned with some other tribes in the inscriptions of the Pālas and Senas of Bengal in such a way as to suggest that they enlisted themselves as mercenary troops in the army of the kings of those dynasties.

# INDEX

## ERRATA

| | | | | | | |
|---|---|---|---|---|---|---|
| Page | 10 | *Read* | Lamghan | *instead* | *of* | Laghmân |
| ,, | 93 | ,, | ,, | ,, | ,, | ,, |
| ,, | 160 | ,, | Gangaridai | *instead* | *of* | Gangridai |
| ,, | 213 | ,, | Paramabhaṭṭāraka | *instead* | *of* | Paramabhaṭṭakāra |
| ,, | 270 | , | of | *instead* | *of* | or |
| ,, | 348 | ,, | kingdoms | *instead* | *of* | kingdom |
| ,, | ,, | ,, | constitute | ,, | ,, | constitutes |
| ,, | 349 | ,, | Satrapy | ,, | ,, | Satrapa |
| ,, | 350 | ,, | Pahlavas | ,, | ,, | Pallavas |
| ,, | 382 | ,, | Pallavas | ,, | ,, | Pahlavas |

*Read* the *before the titles of* Chapters XLIII—XLV.